Marketing Classics

Marketing Classics

A Selection of Influential Articles

EIGHTH EDITION

25th Anniversary Edition

Ben M. Enis
University of Southern Califomia

Keith K. Cox
University of Houston

Michael P. Mokwa
Arizona State University

Prentice Hall International, Inc.

Printed in the United States of America

10 9 8 7 6 5 4 3 2 1

ISBN   0-13-207309-9

Prentice-Hall International (UK) Limited, London
Prentice-hall of Australia Pty. Limited, Sydney
Prentice-Hall Canada Inc., Toronto
Prentice-Hall Hispanoamericana, S. A., Mexico
Prentice-Hall of Japan, Inc., Tokyo
Simon & Schuster Asia Pte. Ltd., Singapore
Editora Prentice-Hall do Brasil, Ltda., Rio de Janeiro
Prentice-Hall, Inc., Upper Saddle River, New Jersey

CONTRIBUTORS

Derek F. Abell
Wroe Alderson
Paul F. Anderson
Richard P. Bagozzi
Russell W. Belk
Leonard L. Berry
Neil H. Borden
Louis P. Bucklin
Robert D. Buzzell
C. Samuel Craig
George S. Day
Susan P. Douglas
Gary L. Frazier
Bradley T. Gale
Hubert Gatignon
William Gregor
Russell I. Haley
Elizabeth C. Hirschman
Morris B. Holbrook
John A. Howard
Bernard J. Jaworski
George Katona
Ajay K. Kohli
Philip Kotler
Gene R. Laczniak
Mary Lambkin
Robert J. Lavidge

Theodore Levitt
Sidney J. Levy
David B. Montgomery
Charles R. O'Neal
A. Parasuraman
Michael E. Porter
Torger Reve
Al Ries
Thomas S. Robertson
Everett M. Rogers
William Rogers
Adrian B. Ryans
Jagdish N. Sheth
Allan D. Shocker
John E. Smallwood
Robert E. Spekman
Rajendra K. Srivastava
Gary A. Steiner
Louis W. Stern
Ralph G. M. Sultan
Gerard J. Tellis
Jack Trout
Frederick E. Webster, Jr.
Charles B. Weinberg
Yoram Wind
Valarie A. Zeithaml

CONTENTS

PREFACE

When *Marketing Classics* was conceived twenty-five years ago, we commented in the Preface:

> Marketing is that phase of human activity that produces economic want-satisfaction by matching consumers' needs and the resources of business firms. From the firm's point of view, consumer satisfaction is the result of its marketing strategy. Strategy is based on marketing philosophy and is derived from the analysis of consumers and their functional interrelationships with such market forces as economic conditions, competitors' actions, institutional change, and other environmental factors. This volume is a compilation of articles that provide broad insight into the field of marketing.
>
> The authors consider these works to be among the classics of marketing literature. These articles are generally recognized by marketing scholars as being of enduring significance to marketing thought. They are widely quoted, have led to new directions in marketing research, and reflect the views of influential scholars. Consequently, these are works with which serious marketing students should be familiar and to which they should have ready access. We believe the book will be a useful supplement to advanced undergraduate courses in marketing management and marketing strategy and to graduate courses in marketing fundamentals and marketing theory. The practitioner

might also enjoy having these familiar works in his [or her] library.

> The articles in this volume were chosen on the basis of extensive research in marketing literature, and the authors were fortunate to obtain the suggestions of a number of colleagues. Nevertheless, it would be presumptuous to imply that we have compiled the classic works of marketing. Marketing is too rich, too complex, too diverse a discipline to be subsumed in one volume. Our selections reflect our own perceptions of and biases about marketing.

This 25th Anniversary edition of *Marketing Classics* reflects our continuing attempt to match this concept to the needs of marketing students. This edition includes eleven new selections in such topical areas as marketing ethics, global strategy, and technology diffusion, but deletes a few genuine classics that our research indicates, for various reasons, are no longer frequently assigned to students.

Responses to questionnaires sent to many of the adopters of previous editions revealed that this anthology is used in a variety of courses, ranging from introductory marketing to doctoral-level seminars, in the United States, Canada, Europe, South America, Africa, and the Pacific Rim countries. Quite a few practitioners have also enjoyed these articles via seminars and individual reading. We are proud that the marketplace of ideas has accepted this anthology since 1969.

A new partner joins our editorial team for *Marketing Classics*, eighth edition: Michael P. Mokwa, our former student, now Professor and Chairman, Marketing Department, Arizona State University. We are as proud of him as we are of the book and welcome him as a full partner in this venture.

We are most grateful to the authors and publishers who granted permission to reprint their work. This literally is their book.

We appreciate comment and criticism on our selections. Many readers have returned questionnaires to us over the years, and/or have communicated with us in person, telephone, facsimile, and mail. We hope you will continue to do so. We particularly thank this time Professors Michael D. Hutt of Arizona State University, Gene R. Laczniak of Marquette University, and Patrick E. Murphy of the University of Notre Dame.

Marketing Classics, eighth edition, was prepared at Arizona State University. For all their decidedly unglamorous but absolutely essential work, we thank Charles Noble, Sandy Van Engelenhoven, Steven Evans, and Christopher Berger.

The people at Allyn and Bacon, especially our editor Suzy Spivey, have been most cooperative and helpful through the years. In spite of all this assistance, errors of omission and/or commission are likely, and differences of opinion as to the nature of marketing classics are inevitable. We are, of course, responsible and ask for your feedback and input into future editions.

B. M. E.
K. K. C.
M. P. M.

PART ONE

Marketing Philosophy

Any discipline or area of human inquiry is guided by a philosophy, a set of perspectives and principles that provide the grounding and rationale for its existence. In Part One, a cross-section of articles expresses the philosophy of marketing.

Levitt's article, "Marketing Myopia," is perhaps the discipline's most quoted and reprinted article. Vividly, it demonstrates the need for a broad interpretation of the marketing function and affirms the importance of marketing for an organization's survival. Levitt's thoughts on the continuing relevance of the article are also included. Alderson, in his trenchant style, provides his perspective of marketing. He views the discipline as being based in the economics of imperfect competition, composed of problem-solving activities of consumers and firms and illuminated by concepts from the social sciences.

In the late 1960s and early 1970s, marketing was acknowledged to be a pervasive social activity, and the management of human exchange became a focus in the discipline. Bagozzi's work rigorously explores the exchange perspective of marketing. His article describes the nature and dynamics of marketing exchanges. Kotler and Levy, pioneers of a broadened view of marketing, advocate that marketing activities are not confined to business but are applicable in all organizations. At the time their article was written, their perspective was very provocative. Today it is widely accepted.

The scope of marketing thought continues to expand. In the past decade, marketing was recognized as a global endeavor. Levitt was among the first to acknowledge the "Globalization of Markets" and to encourage firms to adapt their marketing activities to global realities.

Given that marketing is a social and managerial process, ethical issues abound. Laczniak presents some provocative scenarios to probe ethical sensitivity in marketing. He then discusses a variety of frameworks that encourage ethical analysis and decision making.

The nature and role of marketing have evolved in the contemporary organization. Anderson articulates and evaluates conventional "theories of the firm." He concludes that strategy is formulated through a bargaining process among multiple organizational constituencies. As such, marketing perspectives compete with other perspectives in the process of strategy formulation. Marketers must become strong and skillful advocates for their views.

Webster closes Part One with his latest in a continuing stream of intellectual contributions exploring "The Changing Role of Marketing in the Corporation." He observes that new forms of organization, including strategic partnerships and networks, are replacing traditional forms. He proposes a redefinition of marketing's role, focusing on the management of relationships that deliver superior value to customers.

Marketing Myopia

Theodore Levitt

Every major industry was once a growth industry. But some that are now riding a wave of growth enthusiasm are very much in the shadow of decline. Others which are thought of as seasoned growth industries have stopped growing. In every case the reason growth is threatened, slowed, or stopped is *not* because the market is saturated. It is because there has been a failure of management.

FATEFUL PURPOSES

The failure is at the top. The executives responsible for it, in the last analysis, are those who deal with broad aims and policies. Thus:

The railroads did not stop growing because the need for passenger and freight transportation

declined. That grew. The railroads are in trouble today not because the need was filled by others (cars, trucks, airplanes, even telephones), but because it was *not* filled by the railroads themselves. They let others take customers away from them because they assumed themselves to be in the railroad business rather than in the transportation business. The reason they defined their industry wrong was because they were railroad-oriented instead of transportation-oriented; they were product-oriented instead of customer-oriented.

Hollywood barely escaped being totally ravished by television. Actually, all the established film companies went through drastic reorganizations. Some simply disappeared. All of them got into trouble not because of TV's inroads but because of their own myopia. As with the railroads, Hollywood defined its business incorrectly. It thought it was in the movie business when it was actually in the entertainment business. "Movies" implied a specific, limited product. This produced a fatuous contentment which from the beginning led producers to view TV as a threat. Hollywood scorned and rejected TV when it should have welcomed it as an opportunity—an opportunity to expand the entertainment business.

Today TV is a bigger business than the old narrowly defined movie business ever was. Had Hollywood been customer-oriented (providing entertainment), rather than product-oriented (making movies), would it have gone through the fiscal purgatory that it did? I doubt it. What ultimately saved Hollywood and accounted for its recent resurgence was the wave of new young writers, producers, and directors whose previous success in television had decimated the old movie companies and toppled the big movie moguls.

There are other less obvious examples of industries that have been and are now endangering their futures by improperly defining their purposes. I shall discuss some in detail later and analyze the kind of policies that lead to trouble. Right now it may help to show what a thoroughly customer-oriented management *can* do to keep a growth industry growing, even after the obvious opportunities have been exhausted; and here there are two examples that have been around for a long time. They are nylon and glass—specifically, E.I. duPont de Nemours & Company and Corning Glass Works:

> Both companies have great technical competence. Their product orientation is unquestioned. But this alone does not explain their success. After all, who was more pridefully product-oriented and product-conscious than the erstwhile New England Textile companies that have been so thoroughly massacred? The duPonts and the Cornings have succeeded not primarily because of their product or research orientation but because they have been thoroughly customer-oriented also. It is constant watchfulness for opportunities to apply their technical know-how to the creation of customer-satisfying uses which accounts for their prodigious output of successful new products. Without a very sophisticated eye on the customer, most of their new products might have been wrong, their sales methods useless.

Aluminum has also continued to be a growth industry, thanks to the efforts of two wartime-created companies which deliberately set about creating new customer-satisfying uses. Without Kaiser Aluminum & Chemical Corporation and Reynolds Metals Company, the total demand for aluminum today would be vastly less than it is.

Error of Analysis

Some may argue that it is foolish to set the railroads off against aluminum or the movies off against glass. Are not aluminum and glass naturally so versatile that the industries are bound to have more growth opportunities than the railroads and movies? This view commits precisely the error I have been talking about. It defines an industry, or a product, or a cluster of know-how so narrowly as to guarantee its premature senescence. When we mention "railroads," we should make sure we mean "transportation." As transporters, the railroads still have a good chance for very considerable growth. They are not limited to the railroad business as such (though in my opinion rail transportation is potentially a much stronger transportation medium than is generally believed).

What the railroads lack is not opportunity, but some of the same managerial imaginativeness and audacity that made them great. Even an amateur like Jacques Barzun can see what is lacking when he says:

> I grieve to see the most advanced physical and social organization of the last century go down in shabby disgrace for lack of the same comprehensive imagination that built it up. What is lacking is the will of the companies to survive and to satisfy the public by inventiveness and skill.[1]

SHADOW OF OBSOLESCENCE

It is impossible to mention a single major industry that did not at one time qualify for the magic appellation of "growth industry." In each case its assumed strength lay in the apparently unchallenged superiority of its product. There appeared to be no effective substitute for it. It was itself a runaway substitute for the product it so triumphantly replaced. Yet one after another of these celebrated industries has come under a shadow. Let us look briefly at a few more of them, this time taking examples that have so far received a little less attention:

Dry Cleaning   This was once a growth industry with lavish prospects. In an age of wool garments, imagine being finally able to get them safely and easily clean. The boom was on.

Yet here we are 30 years after the boom started and the industry is in trouble. Where has the competition come from? From a better way of cleaning? No. It has come from synthetic fibers and chemical additives that have cut the need for dry cleaning. But this is only the beginning. Lurking in the wings and ready to make chemical dry cleaning totally obsolescent is that powerful magician, ultrasonics.

Electric Utilities   This is another one of those supposedly "no-substitute" products that has been enthroned on a pedestal of invincible growth. When the incandescent lamp came along, kerosene lights were finished. Later the water wheel and the steam engine were cut to ribbons by the flexibility, reliability, simplicity, and just plain easy availability of electric motors. The prosperity of electric utilities continues to wax extravagant as the home is converted into a museum of electric gadgetry. How can anybody miss by investing in utilities, with no competition, nothing but growth ahead?

But a second look is not quite so comforting. A score of nonutility companies are well advanced toward developing a powerful chemical fuel cell which could sit in some hidden closet of every home silently ticking off electric power. The electric lines that vulgarize so many neighborhoods will be eliminated. So will the endless demolition of streets and service interruptions during storms. Also on the horizon is solar energy, again pioneered by nonutility companies.

Who says that the utilities have no competition? They may be natural monopolies now, but tomorrow they may be natural deaths. To avoid this prospect, they too will have to develop fuel cells, solar energy, and other power sources. To survive, they themselves will have to plot the obsolescence of what now produces their livelihood.

Grocery Stores   Many people find it hard to realize that there ever was a thriving establishment known as the "corner grocery store." The supermarket has taken over with a powerful effectiveness. Yet the big food chains of the 1930's narrowly escaped being completely wiped out by the aggressive expansion of independent supermarkets. The first genuine supermarket was opened in 1930, in Jamaica, Long Island. By 1933 supermarkets were thriving in California, Ohio, Pennsylvania, and elsewhere. Yet the established chains pompously ignored them. When they chose to notice them, it was with such derisive descriptions as "cheapy," "horse-and-buggy," "cracker-barrel storekeeping," and "unethical opportunities."

The executive of one big chain announced at the time that he found it "hard to believe that people will drive for miles to shop for foods and sacrifice the personal service chains have perfected and to which Mrs. Consumer is accustomed."[2] As late as 1936, the National Wholesale Grocers convention and the New Jersey Retail Grocers Association said there was nothing to fear. They said that the supers' narrow appeal to the price buyer limited the size of their market. They had to draw from miles around. When imitators came, there would be wholesale liquidations as volume fell. The current high sales of the supers was said to be partly due to their novelty. Basically people wanted convenient neighborhood grocers. If the neighborhood stores "cooperate with their suppliers, pay attention to their costs, and improve their services," they would be able to weather the competition until it blew over.[3]

It never blew over. The chains discovered that survival required going into the supermarket business. This meant the wholesale destruction of their huge investments in corner store sites and in established distribution and merchandising methods. The companies with "the courage of their convictions" resolutely stuck to the corner store philosophy. They kept their pride but lost their shirts.

Self-Deceiving Cycle

But memories are short. For example, it is hard for people who today confidently hail the twin messiahs of electronics and chemicals to see how things could possibly go wrong with these galloping industries. They probably also cannot see how a reasonably sensible businessman could have been as myopic as the famous Boston millionaire who 50 years ago unintentionally sentenced his heirs to poverty by stipulating that his entire estate be forever invested exclusively in electric streetcar securities. His posthumous declaration, "There will always be a big demand for efficient urban transportation," is no consolation to his heirs who sustain life by pumping gasoline at automobile filling stations.

Yet, in a casual survey I recently took among a group of intelligent business executives, nearly half agreed that it would be hard to hurt their heirs by tying their estates forever to the electronics industry. When I then confronted them with the Boston street car example, they chorused unanimously, "That's different!" But is it? Is not the basic situation identical?

In truth, *there is no such thing* as a growth industry, I believe. There are only companies organized and operated to create and capitalize on growth opportunities. Industries that assume themselves to be riding some automatic growth escalator invariably descend into stagnation. The history of every dead and dying "growth" industry shows a self-deceiving cycle of bountiful expansion and undetected decay. There are four conditions which usually guarantee this cycle:

1. The belief that growth is assured by an expanding and more affluent population.
2. The belief that there is no competitive substitution for the industry's major product.
3. Too much faith in mass production and in the advantages of rapidly declining unit costs as output rises.
4. Preoccupation with a product that lends itself to carefully controlled scientific experimentation, improvement, and manufacturing cost reduction.

I should like now to begin examining each of these conditions in some detail. To build my case as boldly as possible, I shall illustrate the points with reference to three industries—petroleum, automobiles, and electronics—particularly petroleum, because it spans more years and more vicissitudes. Not only do these three have excellent reputations with the general public and also enjoy the confidence of sophisticated investors, but their managements have become known for progressive thinking in areas like financial control, product research, and management training. If obsolescence can cripple even these industries, it can happen anywhere.

POPULATION MYTH

The belief that profits are assured by an expanding and more affluent population is dear to the heart of every industry. It takes the edge off the apprehensions everybody understandably feels about the future. If consumers are multiplying and also buying more of your product or service, you can face the future with considerably more comfort than if the market is shrinking. An expanding market keeps the manufacturer from having to think very hard or imaginatively. If thinking is an intellectual response to a problem, then the absence of a problem leads to the absence of thinking. If your product has an automatically expanding market, then you will not give much thought to how to expand it.

One of the most interesting examples of this is provided by the petroleum industry. Probably our oldest growth industry, it has an enviable record. While there are some current apprehensions about its growth rate, the industry itself tends to be optimistic. But I believe it can be demonstrated that it is undergoing a fundamental yet typical change. It is not only ceasing to be a growth industry, but may actually be a declining one, relative to other business. Although there is widespread awareness of it, I believe that within 25 years the oil industry may find itself in much the same position of retrospective glory that the railroads are now in. Despite its pioneering work in developing and applying the present-value method of investment evaluation, in employee relations, and in working with backward countries, the petroleum business is a distressing example of how complacency and wrong-headedness can stubbornly convert opportunity into near disaster.

One of the characteristics of this and other industries that have believed very strongly in the beneficial consequences of an expanding population, while at the same time being industries with a generic product for which there has appeared to be no competitive substitute, is that the individual companies have sought to outdo their competitors by improving on what they are already doing.

This makes sense, of course, if one assumes that sales are tied to the country's population strings, because the customer can compare products only on a feature-by-feature basis. I believe it is significant, for example, that not since John D. Rockefeller sent free kerosene lamps to China has the oil industry done anything really outstanding to create a demand for its product. Not even in product improvement has it showered itself with eminence. The greatest single improvement, namely, the development of tetraethyl lead, came from outside the industry, specifically from General Motors and duPont. The big contributions made by the industry itself are confined to the technology of oil exploration, production, and refining.

Asking for Trouble

In other words, the industry's efforts have focused on improving the *efficiency* of getting and making its product, not really on improving the generic product or its marketing. Moreover, its chief product has continuously been defined in the narrowest possible terms, namely, gasoline, not energy, fuel, or transportation. This attitude has helped assure that:

> Major improvements in gasoline quality tend not to originate in the oil industry. Also, the development of superior alternative fuels comes from outside the oil industry, as will be shown later.
>
> Major innovations in automobile fuel marketing are originated by small new oil companies that are not primarily preoccupied with production or refining. These are the companies that have been responsible for the rapidly expanding multipump gasoline stations, with their successful emphasis on large and clean layouts, rapid and efficient driveway service, and quality gasoline at low prices.

Thus, the oil industry is asking for trouble from outsiders. Sooner or later, in this land of hungry inventors and entrepreneurs, a threat is sure to come. The possibilities of this will become more apparent when we turn to the next dangerous belief of many managements. For the sake of continuity, because this second belief is tied closely to the first, I shall continue with the same example.

Idea of Indispensability

The petroleum industry is pretty much persuaded that there is no competitive substitute for its major product, gasoline—or if there is, that it will continue to be a derivative of crude oil, such as diesel fuel or kerosene jet fuel.

There is a lot of automatic wishful thinking in this assumption. The trouble is that most refining companies own huge amounts of crude oil reserves. These have value only if there is a market for products into which oil can be converted—hence the tenacious belief in the continuing competitive superiority of automobile fuels made from crude oil.

This idea persists despite all historic evidence against it. The evidence not only shows that oil has never been a superior product for any purpose for very long, but it also shows that the oil industry has never really been a growth industry. It has been a succession of different businesses that have gone through the usual historic cycles of growth, maturity, and decay. Its over-all survival is owed to a series of miraculous escapes from total obsolescence, of last minute and unexpected reprieves from total disaster reminiscent of the Perils of Pauline.

Perils of Petroleum

I shall sketch in only the main episodes:

First, crude oil was largely a patent medicine. But even before that fad ran out, demand was greatly expanded by the use of oil in kerosene lamps. The prospect of lighting the world's lamps gave rise to an extravagant promise of growth. The prospects were similar to those

the industry now holds for gasoline in other parts of the world. It can hardly wait for the underdeveloped nations to get a car in every garage.

In the days of the kerosene lamp, the oil companies competed with each other and against gaslight by trying to improve the illuminating characteristics of kerosene. Then suddenly the impossible happened. Edison invented a light which was totally nondependent on crude oil. Had it not been for the growing use of kerosene in space heaters, the incandescent lamp would have completely finished oil as a growth industry at that time. Oil would have been good for little else than axle grease.

Then disaster and reprieve struck again. Two great innovations occurred, neither originating in the oil industry. The successful development of coal-burning domestic central-heating systems made the space heater obsolescent. While the industry reeled along came its most magnificent boost yet—the internal combustion engine, also invented by outsiders. Then when the prodigious expansion for gasoline finally began to level off in the 1920's, along came the miraculous escape of a central oil heater. Once again, the escape was provided by an outsider's invention and development. And when that market weakened, wartime demand for aviation fuel came to the rescue. After the war the expansion of civilian aviation, the dieselization of railroads, and the explosive demand for cars and trucks kept the industry's growth in high gear.

Meanwhile centralized oil heating—whose boom potential had only recently been proclaimed—ran into severe competition from natural gas. While the oil companies themselves owned the gas that now competed with their oil, the industry did not originate the natural gas revolution, nor has it to this day greatly profited from its gas ownership. The gas revolution was made by newly formed transmission companies that marketed the product with an aggressive ardor. They started a magnificent new industry, first against the advice and then against the resistance of the oil companies.

By all the logic of the situation, the oil companies themselves should have made the gas revolution. They not only owned the gas; they also were the only people experienced in handling, scrubbing, and using it, the only people experienced in pipeline technology and transmission, and they understood heating problems. But, partly because they knew that natural gas would compete with their own sale of heating oil, the oil companies pooh-poohed the potentials of gas.

The revolution was finally started by oil pipeline executives who, unable to persuade their own companies to go into gas, quit and organized the spectacularly successful gas transmission companies. Even after their success became painfully evident to the oil companies, the latter did not go into gas transmission. The multibillion dollar business which should have been theirs went to others. As in the past, the industry was blinded by its narrow preoccupation with a specific product and the value of its reserves. It paid little or no attention to its customers' basic needs and preferences.

The postwar years have not witnessed any change. Immediately after World War II the oil industry was greatly encouraged about its future by the rapid expansion of demand for its traditional line of products. In 1950 most companies projected annual rates of domestic expansion around 6% through at least 1975. Though the ratio of crude oil reserves to demand in the Free World was about 20 to 1, with 10 to 1 being usually considered a reasonable working ratio in the United States, booming demand sent oil men searching for more without sufficient regard to what the future really promised. In 1952 they "hit" in the Middle East; the ratio skyrocketed to 42 to 1. If gross additions to reserves continue at the average rate of the past five years (37 billion barrels annually), then by 1970 the reserve ratio will be up to 45 to 1. This abundance of oil has weakened crude and product prices all over the world.

Uncertain Future

Management cannot find much consolation today in the rapidly expanding petrochemical industry, another oil-using idea that did not originate in the leading firms. The total United States production of petrochemicals is equivalent to about 2% (by volume) of the demand for all petroleum products. Although the petrochemical industry is now expected to grow by about 10% per year, this will not offset other drains on the growth of crude oil consumption. Furthermore, while petrochemical products are many and growing, it is well to remember that there are nonpetroleum sources of the basic raw material, such as coal. Besides, a lot of plastics can be produced with relatively little oil. A 50,000-barrel-per-day oil refinery is not considered the absolute minimum size for efficiency. But a 50,000-barrel-per-day chemical plant is a giant operation.

Oil has never been a continuously strong growth industry. It has grown by fits and starts, always miraculously saved by innovations and developments not of its own making. The reason it has not grown in a smooth progression is that each time it thought it had a superior product safe from the possibility of competitive substitutes, the product turned out to be inferior and notoriously subject to obsolescence. Until now, gasoline (for motor fuel, anyhow) has escaped this fate. But, as we shall see later, it too may be on its last legs.

The point of all this is that there is no guarantee against product obsolescence. If a company's own research does not make it obsolete, another's will. Unless an industry is especially lucky, as oil has been until now, it can easily go down in a sea of red figures—just as the railroads have, as the buggy whip manufacturers have, as the corner grocery chains have, as most of the big movie companies have, and indeed as many other industries have.

The best way for a firm to be lucky is to make its own luck. That requires knowing what makes a business successful. One of the greatest enemies of this knowledge is mass production.

PRODUCTION PRESSURES

Mass-production industries are impelled by a great drive to produce all they can. The prospect of steeply declining unit costs as output rises is more than most companies can usually resist. The profit possibilities look spectacular. All effort focuses on production. The result is that marketing gets neglected.

John Kenneth Galbraith contends that just the opposite occurs.[4] Output is so prodigious that all effort concentrates on trying to get rid of it. He says this accounts for singing commercials, desecration of the countryside with advertising signs, and other wasteful and vulgar practices. Galbraith has a finger on something real, but he misses the strategic point. Mass production does indeed generate great pressure to "move" the product. But what usually gets emphasized is selling, not marketing. Marketing, being a more sophisticated and complex process, gets ignored.

The difference between marketing and selling is more than semantic. Selling focuses on the needs of the seller, marketing on the needs of the buyer. Selling is preoccupied with the seller's need to convert his product into cash; marketing with the idea of satisfying the needs of the customer by means of the product and the whole cluster of things associated with creating, delivering, and finally consuming it.

In some industries the enticements of full mass production have been so powerful that for many years top management in effect had told the sales departments, "You get rid of it; we'll worry about profits." By contrast, a truly marketing-minded firm tries to create value-satisfying goods and services that consumers will want to buy. What it offers for sale includes not only the generic product or service, but also how it is made available to the customer, in what form, when, under what conditions, and at what terms of trade. Most important, what it offers for sale is determined not by the seller but by the buyer. The

seller takes his cues from the buyer in such a way that the product becomes a consequence of the marketing effort, not vice versa.

Lag in Detroit

This may sound like an elementary rule of business, but that does not keep it from being violated wholesale. It is certainly more violated than honored. Take the automobile industry:

Here mass production is most famous, most honored, and has the greatest impact on the entire society. The industry has hitched its fortune to the relentless requirements of the annual model change, a policy that makes customer orientation an especially urgent necessity. Consequently the auto companies annually spend millions of dollars on consumer research. But the fact that the new compact cars are selling so well in their first year indicates that Detroit's vast researchers have for a long time failed to reveal what the customer really wanted. Detroit was not persuaded that he wanted anything different from what he had been getting until it lost millions of customers to other small car manufacturers.

How could this unbelievable lag behind consumer wants have been perpetuated so long? Why did not research reveal consumer preferences before consumers' buying decisions themselves revealed the facts? Is that not what consumer research is for—to find out before the fact what is going to happen? The answer is that Detroit never really researched the customer's wants. It only researched his preferences between the kinds of things which it had already decided to offer him. For Detroit is mainly product-oriented, not customer-oriented. To the extent that the customer is recognized as having needs that the manufacturer should try to satisfy, Detroit usually acts as if the job can be done entirely by product changes. Occasionally attention gets paid to financing, too, but that is done more in order to sell than to enable the customer to buy.

As for taking care of other customer needs, there is not enough being done to write about. The areas of the greatest unsatisfied needs are ignored, or at best get stepchild attention. These are at the point of sale and on the matter of automotive repair and maintenance. Detroit views these problem areas as being of secondary importance. That is underscored by the fact that the retailing and servicing ends of this industry are neither owned and operated nor controlled by the manufacturers. Once the car is produced, things are pretty much in the dealer's inadequate hands. Illustrative of Detroit's arm's-length attitude is the fact that, while servicing holds enormous sales-stimulating, profit-building opportunities, only 57 of Chevrolet's 7,000 dealers provide night maintenance service.

Motorists repeatedly express their dissatisfaction with servicing and their apprehensions about buying cars under the present selling setup. The anxieties and problems they encounter during the auto buying and maintenance processes are probably more intense and widespread today than 30 years ago. Yet the automobile companies do not *seem* to listen to or take their cues from the anguished consumer. If they do listen, it must be through the filter of their own preoccupation with production. The marketing effort is still viewed as a necessary consequence of the product, not vice versa, as it should be. That is the legacy of mass production, with its parochial view that profit resides essentially in low-cost full production.

What Ford Put First

The profit lure of mass production obviously has a place in the plans and strategy of business management, but it must always follow hard thinking about the customer. This is one of the most important lessons that we can learn from the contradictory behavior of Henry Ford. In a sense Ford was both the most brilliant and the most senseless marketer in American history. He was senseless because he refused to give the customer anything but a black car. He was brilliant because he fashioned a production system designed to fit market needs. We habitually celebrate him for the wrong reason, his production genius. His real genius was marketing. We think he was able to cut his selling price and therefore sell

millions of $500 cars because his invention of the assembly line had reduced the costs. Actually he invented the assembly line because he had concluded that at $500 he could sell millions of cars. Mass production was the *result* not the cause of his low prices.

Ford repeatedly emphasized this point, but a nation of production-oriented business managers refuses to hear the great lesson he taught. Here is his operating philosophy as he expressed it succinctly:

> Our policy is to reduce the price, extend the operations, and improve the article. You will notice that the reduction of price comes first. We have never considered any costs as fixed. Therefore we first reduce the price to the point where we believe more sales will result. Then we go ahead and try to make the prices. We do not bother about the costs. The new price forces the costs down. The more usual way is to take the costs and then determine the price, and although that method may be scientific in the narrow sense; it is not scientific in the broad sense, because what earthly use is it to know the cost if it tells you that you cannot manufacture at a price at which the article can be sold? But more to the point is the fact that, although one may calculate what a cost is, and of course all of our costs are carefully calculated, no one knows what a cost ought to be. One of the ways of discovering . . . is to name a price so low as to force everybody in the place to the highest point of efficiency. The low price makes everybody dig for profits. We make more discoveries concerning manufacturing and selling under this forced method than by any method of leisurely investigation.[5]

Product Provincialism

The tantalizing profit possibilities of low unit production costs may be the most seriously self-deceiving attitude that can afflict a company, particularly a "growth" company where an apparently assured expansion of demand already tends to undermine a proper concern for the importance of marketing and the customer.

The usual result of this narrow preoccupation with so-called concrete matters is that instead of growing, the industry declines. It usually means that the product fails to adapt to the constantly changing patterns of consumer needs and tastes, to new and modified marketing institutions and practices, or to product developments in competing or complementary industries. The industry has its eyes so firmly on its own specific product that it does not see how it is being made obsolete.

The classical example of this is the buggy whip industry. No amount of product improvement could stave off its death sentence. But had the industry defined itself as being in the transportation business rather than the buggy whip business, it might have survived. It would have done what survival always entails, that is, changing. Even if it had only defined its business as providing a stimulant or catalyst to an energy source, it might have survived by becoming a manufacturer of, say, fanbelts or air cleaners.

What may some day be a still more classical example is again, the oil industry. Having let others steal marvelous opportunities from it (e.g., natural gas, as already mentioned, missile fuels, and jet engine lubricants), one would expect it to have taken steps never to let that happen again. But this is not the case. We are now getting extraordinary new developments in fuel systems specifically designed to power automobiles. Not only are these developments concentrated in firms outside the petroleum industry, but petroleum is almost systematically ignoring them, securely content in its wedded bliss to oil. It is the story of the kerosene lamp versus the incandescent lamp all over again. Oil is trying to improve hydrocarbon fuels rather than to develop *any* fuels best suited to the needs of their users, whether or not made in different ways and with different raw materials from oil.

Here are some of the things which non-petroleum companies are working on:

Over a dozen such firms now have advanced working models of energy systems which, when perfected, will replace the internal combustion engine and eliminate the demand for gasoline. The superior merit of each of these systems is their elimination of frequent, time-consuming, and irritating refueling stops. Most of these systems are fuel cells designed to create electrical energy directly from chemicals without combustion. Most of them use chemicals that are not derived from oil, generally hydrogen and oxygen.

Several other companies have advanced models of electric storage batteries designed to power automobiles. One of these is an aircraft producer that is working jointly with several electric utility companies. The latter hope to use off-peak generating capacity to supply overnight plug-in battery regeneration. Another company, also using the battery approach, is a medium-size electronics firm with extensive small-battery experience that it developed in connection with its work on hearing aids. It is collaborating with an automobile manufacturer. Recent improvements arising from the need for high-powered miniature power storage plants in rockets have put us within reach of a relatively small battery capable of withstanding great overloads or surges of power. Germanium diode applications and batteries using sintered-plate and nickel-cadmium techniques promise to make a revolution in our energy sources.

Solar energy conversion systems are also getting increasing attention. One usually cautious Detroit auto executive recently ventured that solar-powered cars might be common by 1980.

As for the oil companies, they are more or less "watching developments," as one research director put it to me. A few are doing a bit of research on fuel cells, but almost always confined to developing cells powered by hydrocarbon chemicals. None of them are enthusiastically researching fuel cells, batteries, or solar power plants. None of them are spending a fraction as much on research in these profoundly important areas as they are on the usual run-of-the-mill things like reducing combustion chamber deposit in gasoline engines. One major integrated petroleum company recently took a tentative look at the fuel cell and concluded that although "the companies actively working on it indicate a belief in ultimate success . . . the timing and magnitude of its impact are too remote to warrant recognition in our forecasts."

One might, of course, ask: Why should the oil companies do anything different? Would not chemical fuel cells, batteries, or solar energy kill the present product lines? The answer is that they would indeed, and that is precisely the reason for the oil firms having to develop these power units before their competitors, so they will not be companies without an industry.

Management might be more likely to do what is needed for its own preservation if it thought of itself as being in the energy business. But even that would not be enough if it persists in imprisoning itself in the narrow grip of its tight product orientation. It has to think of itself as taking care of customer needs, not finding, refining, or even selling oil. Once it genuinely thinks of its business as taking care of people's transportation needs, nothing can stop it from creating its own extravagantly profitable growth.

Creative Destruction

Since words are cheap and deeds are dear, it may be appropriate to indicate what this kind of thinking involves and leads to. Let us start at the beginning—the customer. It can be shown that motorists strongly dislike the bother, delay, and experience of buying gasoline. People actually do not buy gasoline. They cannot see it, taste it, feel it, appreciate it, or really test it. What they buy is the right to continue driving their cars. The gas station

is like a tax collector to whom people are compelled to pay a periodic toll as the price of using their cars. This makes the gas station a basically unpopular institution. It can never be made popular or pleasant, only less unpopular, less unpleasant.

To reduce its unpopularity completely means eliminating it. Nobody likes a tax collector, not even a pleasant cheerful one. Nobody likes to interrupt a trip to buy a phantom product, not even from a handsome Adonis or a seductive Venus. Hence, companies that are working on exotic fuel substitutes which will eliminate the need for frequent refueling are heading directly into the outstretched arms of the irritated motorists. They are riding a wave of inevitability, not because they are creating something which is technologically superior or more sophisticated, but because they are satisfying a powerful customer need. They are also eliminating noxious odors and air pollution.

Once the petroleum companies recognize the customer-satisfying logic of what another power system can do, they will see that they have no more choice about working on an efficient, long-lasting fuel (or some way of delivering present fuels without bothering the motorist) than the big food chains had a choice about going into the supermarket business, or the vacuum tube companies had a choice about making semiconductors. For their own good the oil firms will have to destroy their own highly profitable assets. No amount of wishful thinking can save them from the necessity of engaging in this form of "creative destruction."

I phrase the need as strongly as this because I think management must make quite an effort to break itself loose from conventional ways. It is all too easy in this day and age for a company or industry to let its sense of purpose become dominated by the economies of full production and to develop a dangerously lopsided product orientation. In short, if management lets itself drift, it invariably drifts in the direction of thinking of itself as producing goods and services, not customer satisfactions. While it probably will not descend to the depths of telling its salesmen, "You get rid of it; we'll worry about profits," it can, without knowing it, be practicing precisely that formula for withering decay. The historic fate of one growth industry after another has been its suicidal product provincialism.

DANGERS OF R&D

Another big danger to a firm's continued growth arises when top management is wholly transfixed by the profit possibilities of technical research and development. To illustrate I shall turn first to a new industry—electronics—and then return once more to the oil companies. By comparing a fresh example with a familiar one, I hope to emphasize the prevalence and insidiousness of a hazardous way of thinking.

Marketing Shortchanged

In the case of electronics, the greatest danger which faces the glamorous new companies in this field is not that they do not pay enough attention to research and development, but that they pay *too much* attention to it. And the fact that the fastest growing electronics firms owe their eminence to their heavy emphasis on technical research is completely beside the point. They have vaulted to affluence on a sudden crest of unusually strong general receptiveness to new technical ideas. Also, their success has been shaped in the virtually guaranteed market of military subsidies and by military orders that in many cases actually preceded the existence of facilities to make the products. Their expansion has, in other words, been almost totally devoid of marketing effort.

Thus, they are growing up under conditions that come dangerously close to creating the illusion that a superior product will sell itself. Having created a successful company by making a superior product, it is not surprising that management continues to be oriented toward the product rather than the people who consume it. It develops the philosophy that continued growth is a matter of continued product innovation and improvement.

A number of other factors tend to strengthen and sustain this belief:

1. Because electronic products are highly complex and sophisticated, managements become top-heavy with engineers and scientists. This creates a selective bias in favor of research and production at the expense of marketing. The organization tends to view itself as making things rather than satisfying customer needs. Marketing gets treated as a residual activity, "something else" that must be done once the vital job of product creation and production is completed.

2. To this bias in favor of product research, development, and production is added the bias in favor of dealing with controllable variables. Engineers and scientists are at home in the world of concrete things like machines, test tubes, production lines, and even balance sheets. The abstractions to which they feel kindly are those which are testable or manipulatable in the laboratory, or, if not testable, then functional, such as Euclid's axioms. In short, the managements of the new glamour-growth companies tend to favor those business activities which lend themselves to careful study, experimentation, and control—the hard, practical, realities of the lab, the shop, the books.

What gets shortchanged are the realities of the *market*. Consumers are unpredictable, varied, fickle, stupid, shortsighted, stubborn, and generally bothersome. This is not what the engineer-managers say, but deep down in their consciousnesses is what they believe. And this accounts for their concentrating on what they know and what they can control, namely, product research, engineering, and production. The emphasis on production becomes particularly attractive when the product can be made at declining unit costs. There is no more inviting way of making money than by running the plant full blast.

Today the top-heavy science-engineering-production orientation of so many electronics companies works reasonably well because they are pushing into new frontiers in which the armed services have pioneered virtually assured markets. The companies are in the felicitous position of having to fill, not find markets; of not having to discover what the customer needs and wants, but of having the customer voluntarily come forward with specific new product demands. If a team of consultants had been assigned specifically to design a business situation calculated to prevent the emergence and development of a customer-oriented marketing viewpoint, it could not have produced anything better than the conditions just described.

Stepchild Treatment

The oil industry is a stunning example of how science, technology, and mass production can divert an entire group of companies from their main task. To the extent the consumer is studied at all (which is not much), the focus is forever on getting information which is designed to help the oil companies improve what they are now doing. They try to discover more convincing advertising themes, more effective sales promotional drives, what the market shares of the various companies are, what people like or dislike about service station dealers and oil companies, and so forth. Nobody seems as interested in probing deeply into the basic human needs that the industry might be trying to satisfy as in probing into the basic properties of the raw material that the companies work with in trying to deliver customer satisfaction.

Basic questions about customers and markets seldom get asked. The latter occupy a stepchild status. They are recognized as existing, as having to be taken care of, but not worth very much real thought or dedicated attention. Nobody gets as excited about the customers in his own backyard as about the oil in the Sahara Desert. Nothing illustrates better the neglect of marketing than its treatment in the industry press:

The centennial issue of the *American Petroleum Institute Quarterly,* published in 1959 to celebrate the discovery of oil in Titusville, Pennsylvania, contained 21 feature articles proclaiming the industry's greatness. Only one of these talked about its achievements in marketing, and that was only a pictorial record of how service station architecture has changed. The issue also contained a special section on "New Horizons," which was devoted to showing the magnificent role oil would play in America's future. Every reference was ebulliently optimistic, never implying once that oil might have some hard competition. Even the reference to atomic energy was a cheerful catalogue of how oil would help make atomic energy a success. There was not a single apprehension that the oil industry's affluence might be threatened or a suggestion that one "new horizon" might include new and better ways of serving oil's present customers.

But the most revealing example of the stepchild treatment that marketing gets was still another special series of short articles on "The Revolutionary Potential of Electronics." Under that heading this list of articles appeared in the table of contents:

"In the Search for Oil"
"In Production Operations"
"In Refinery Processes"

Significantly, every one of the industry's major functional areas is listed, *except* marketing. Why? Either it is believed that electronics holds no revolutionary potential for petrolem marketing (which is palpably wrong), or the editors forgot to discuss marketing (which is more likely, and illustrates its stepchild status).

The order in which the four functional areas are listed also betrays the alienation of the oil industry from the consumer. The industry is implicitly defined as beginning with the search for oil and ending with its distribution from the refinery. But the truth is, it seems to me, that the industry begins with the needs of the customer for its products. From that primal position its definition moves steadily backstream to areas of progressively lesser importance, until it finally comes to rest at the "search for oil."

Beginning & End

The view that an industry is a customer-satisfying process, not a goods-producing process, is vital for all businessmen to understand. An industry begins with the customer and his needs, not with a patent, a raw material, or a selling skill. Given the customer's needs, the industry develops backwards, first concerning itself with the physical *delivery* of customer satisfactions. Then it moves back further to *creating* the things by which these satisfactions are in part achieved. How these materials are created is a matter of indifference to the customer, hence the particular form of manufacturing, processing, or what-have-you cannot be considered as a vital aspect of the industry. Finally, the industry

moves back still further to *finding* the raw materials necessary for making its products.

The irony of some industries oriented toward technical research and development is that the scientists who occupy the high executive positions are totally unscientific when it comes to defining their companies' over-all needs and purposes. They violate the first two rules of the scientific method—being aware of and defining their companies' problems, and then developing testable hypotheses about solving them. They are scientific only about the convenient things, such as laboratory and product experiments. The reason that the customer (and the satisfaction of his deepest needs) is not considered as being "the problem" is not because there is any certain belief that no such problem exists, but because an organizational lifetime has conditioned management to look in the opposite direction. Marketing is a stepchild.

I do not mean that selling is ignored. Far from it. But selling, again, is not marketing. As already pointed out, selling concerns itself with the tricks and techniques of getting people to exchange their cash for your product. It is not concerned with the values that the exchange is all about. And it does not, as marketing invariably does, view the entire business process as consisting of a tightly integrated effort to discover, create, arouse, and satisfy customer needs. The customer is somebody "out there" who, with proper cunning, can be separated from his loose change.

Actually, not even selling gets much attention in some technologically minded firms. Because there is a virtually guaranteed market for the abundant flow of their new products, they do not actually know what a real market is. It is as if they lived in a planned economy, moving their products routinely from factory to retail outlet. Their successful concentration on products tends to convince them of the soundness of what they have been doing, and they fail to see the gathering clouds over the market.

CONCLUSION

Less than 75 years ago American railroads enjoyed a fierce loyalty among astute Wall Streeters. European monarchs invested in them heavily. Eternal wealth was thought to be the benediction for anybody who could scrape a few thousand dollars together to put into rail stocks. No other form of transportation could compete with the railroads in speed, flexibility, durability, economy, and growth potentials. As Jacques Barzun put it, "By the turn of the century it was an institution, an image of man, a tradition, a code of honor, a source of poetry, a nursery of boyhood desires, a sublimest of toys, and the most solemn machine—next to the funeral hearse—that marks the epochs in man's life."[6]

Even after the advent of automobiles, trucks, and airplanes, the railroad tycoons remained imperturbably self-confident. If you had told them 60 years ago that in 30 years they would be flat on their backs, broke, and pleading for government subsidies, they would have thought you totally demented. Such a future was simply not considered possible. It was not even a discussable subject, or an askable question, or a matter which any sane person would consider worth speculating about. The very thought was insane. Yet a lot of insane notions now have matter-of-fact acceptance—for example, the idea of 100-ton tubes of metal moving smoothly through the air 20,000 feet above the earth, loaded with 100 sane and solid citizens casually drinking martinis—and they have dealt cruel blows to the railroads.

What specifically must other companies do to avoid this fate? What does customer orientation involve? These questions have in part been answered by the preceding examples and analysis. It would take another article to show in detail what is required for specific industries. In any case, it should be obvious that building an effective customer-oriented company involves far more than good intentions or promotional tricks; it involves profound matters of human organization and leadership. For the present, let me merely suggest what appear to be some general requirements.

Visceral Feel of Greatness

Obviously the company has to do what survival demands. It has to adapt to the requirements of the market, and it has to do it sooner rather than later. But mere survival is a so-so aspiration. Anybody can survive in some way or other, even the skid-row bum. The trick is to survive gallantly, to feel the surging impulse of commercial mastery; not just to experience the sweet smell of success, but to have the visceral feel of entrepreneurial greatness.

No organization can achieve greatness without a vigorous leader who is driven onward by his own pulsing *will to succeed*. He has to have a vision of grandeur, a vision that can produce eager followers in vast numbers. In business, the followers are the customers. To produce these customers, the entire corporation must be viewed as a customer-creating and customer-satisfying organism. Management must think of itself not as producing products but as providing customer-creating value satisfactions. It must push this idea (and everything it means and requires) into every nook and cranny of the organization. It has to do this continuously and with the kind of flair that excites and stimulates the people in it. Otherwise, the company will be merely a series of pigeonholed parts, with no consolidating sense of purpose or direction.

In short, the organization must learn to think of itself not as producing goods or services but as *buying customers,* as doing the things that will make people *want* to do business with it. And the chief executive himself has the inescapable responsibility for creating this environment, this viewpoint, this attitude, this aspiration. He himself must set the company's style, its direction, and its goals. This means he has to know precisely where he himself wants to go, and to make sure the whole organization is enthusiastically aware of where that is. This is a first requisite of leadership, for *unless he knows where he is going, any road will take him there.*

If any road is okay, the chief executive might as well pack his attaché case and go fishing. If an organization does not know or care where it is going, it does not need to advertise that fact with a ceremonial figurehead. Everybody will notice it soon enough.

1975: RETROSPECTIVE COMMENTARY

Amazed, finally, by his literary success, Isaac Bashevis Singer reconciled an attendant problem: "I think the moment you have published a book, it's not any more your private property. . . . If it has value, everybody can find in it what he finds, and I cannot tell the man I did not intend it to be so." Over the past 15 years, "Marketing Myopia" has become a case in point. Remarkably, the article spawned a legion of loyal partisans, not to mention a host of unlikely bedfellows.

Its most common and, I believe, most influential consequence is the way certain companies for the first time gave serious thought to the question of what business they are really in.

The strategic consequences of this have in many cases been dramatic. The best-known case, of course, is the shift in thinking of one-self as being, in the "oil business" to being in the "energy business." In some instances the payoff has been spectacular (getting into coal, for example), and in others dreadful (in terms of the time and money spent so far on fuel cell research). Another successful example is a company with a large chain of retail shoe stores that redefined itself as a retailer of moderately priced, frequently purchased, widely assorted consumer specialty products. The result was a dramatic growth in volume, earnings, and return on assets.

Some companies, again for the first time, asked themselves whether they wished to be masters of certain technologies for which they would seek markets, or be masters of markets for which they would seek customer-satisfying products and services.

Choosing the former, one company has declared, in effect, "We are experts in glass technology. We intend to improve and expand that expertise with the object of creating products that will attract customers." This decision has forced the company into a much more systematic and customer-sensitive look at possible markets and users, even though its stated strategic object has been to capitalize on glass technology.

Deciding to concentrate on markets, another company has determined that "we want to help people (primarily women) enhance their beauty and sense of youthfulness." This company has expanded its line of cosmetic products, but has also entered the fields of proprietary drugs and vitamin supplements.

All these examples illustrate the "policy" results of "Marketing Myopia." On the operating level, there has been, I think, an extraordinary heightening of sensitivity to customers and consumers. R&D departments have cultivated a greater "external" orientation toward uses, users, and markets—balancing thereby the previously one-sided "internal" focus on materials and methods; upper management has realized that marketing and sales departments should be somewhat more willingly accommodated than before; finance departments have become more receptive to the legitimacy of budgets for market research and experimentation in marketing; and salesmen have been better trained to listen to and understand customer needs and problems, rather than merely to "push" the product.

A Mirror, Not a Window

My impression is that the article has had more impact in industrial-products companies than in consumer-products companies—perhaps because the former had lagged most in customer orientation. There are at least two reasons for this lag: (1) industrial-products companies tend to be more capital intensive, and (2) in the past, at least, they have had to rely heavily on communicating face-to-face the technical character of what they made and sold. These points are worth explaining.

Capital-intensive businesses are understandably preoccupied with magnitudes, especially where the capital, once invested, cannot be easily moved, manipulated, or modified for the production of a variety of products—e.g., chemical plants, steel mills, airlines, and railroads. Understandably, they seek big volumes and operating efficiencies to pay off the equipment and meet the carrying costs.

At least one problem results: corporate power becomes disproportionately lodged with operating or financial executives. If you read the charter of one of the nation's largest companies, you will see that the chairman of the finance committee, not the chief executive officer, is the "chief." Executives with such backgrounds have an almost trained incapac-

ity to see that getting "volume" may require understanding and serving many discrete and sometimes small market segments rather than going after a perhaps mythical batch of big or homogeneous customers.

These executives also often fail to appreciate the competitive changes going on around them. They observe the changes, all right, but devalue their significance or underestimate their ability to nibble away at the company's markets.

Once dramatically alerted to the concept of segments, sectors, and customers, though, managers of capital-intensive businesses have become more responsive to the necessity of balancing their inescapable preoccupation with "paying the bills" or breaking even with the fact that the best way to accomplish this may be to pay more attention to segments, or sectors, and customers.

The second reason industrial-products companies have probably been more influenced by the article is that, in the case of the more technical industrial products or services, the necessity of clearly communicating product and service characteristics to prospects results in a lot of face-to-face "selling" effort. But precisely because the product is so complex, the situation produces salesmen who know the product more than they know the customer, who are more adept at explaining what they have and what it can do than learning what the customer's needs and problems are. The result has been a narrow product orientation rather than a liberating customer orientation, and "service" often suffered. To be sure, sellers said, "We have to provide service," but they tended to define service by looking into the mirror rather than out the window. They *thought* they were looking out the window at the customer, but it was actually a mirror—a reflection of their own product-oriented biases rather than a reflection of their customers' situations.

A Manifesto, Not a Prescription

Not everything has been rosy. A lot of bizarre things have happened as a result of the article:

- Some companies have developed what I call "marketing mania"—they've become obsessively responsive to every fleeting whim of the customer. Mass production operations have been converted to approximations of job shops, with cost and price consequences far exceeding the willingness of customers to buy the product.
- Management has expanded product lines and added new lines of business without first establishing adequate control systems to run more complex operations.
- Marketing staffs have suddenly and rapidly expanded themselves and their research budgets without either getting sufficient prior organizational support or, thereafter, producing sufficient results.
- Companies that are functionally organized have converted to product, brand, or market-based organizations with the expectation of instant and miraculous results. The outcome has been ambiguity, frustration, confusion, corporate infighting, losses, and finally a reversion to functional arrangements that only worsened the situation.
- Companies have attempted to "serve" customers by creating complex and beautifully efficient products or services that buyers are either too risk-averse to adopt or incapable of learning how to employ—in effect, there are now steam shovels for people who haven't yet learned to use spades. This problem has happened repeatedly in the so-called service industries (financial services, insurance, computer-based services) and with American companies selling in less-developed economies.

"Marketing Myopia" was not intended as analysis or even prescription; it was intended as manifesto. It did not pretend to take a balanced position. Nor was it a new idea—Peter F. Drucker, J.B. McKitterick, Wroe Alderson, John Howard, and Neil Borden had each done more original and balanced work on "the marketing concept." My scheme, however, tied marketing more closely to the inner orbit of business policy. Drucker—especially in *The Concept of the Corporation* and *The Practice of Management*—originally provided me with a great deal of insight.

My contribution, therefore, appears merely to have been a simple, brief, and useful way of communicating an existing way of thinking. I tried to do it in a very direct, but responsible, fashion, knowing that few readers (customers), especially managers and leaders, could stand much equivocation or hesitation. I also knew that the colorful and lightly documented affirmation works better than the tortuously reasoned explanation.

But why the enormous popularity of what was actually such a simple preexisting idea? Why its appeal throughout the world to resolutely restrained scholars, implacably temperate managers, and high government officials, all accustomed to balanced and thoughtful calculation? Is it that concrete examples, joined to illustrate a simple idea and presented with some attention to literacy, communicate better than massive analytical reasoning that reads as though it were translated from the German? Is it that provocative assertions are more memorable and persuasive than restrained and balanced explanations, no matter who the audience? Is it that the character of the message is as much the message as its content? Or was mine not simply a different tune, but a new symphony? I don't know.

Of course, I'd do it again and in the same way, given my purposes, even with what more I now know—the good and the bad, the power of facts and the limits of rhetoric. If your mission is the moon, you don't use a car. Don Marquis's cockroach, Archy, provides some final consolation: "An idea is not responsible for who believes in it."

NOTES

1. Jacques Barzun, "Trains and the Mind of Man," *Holiday* (February 1960), p. 21.
2. For more details see M. M. Zimmerman, *The Super Market: A Revolution in Distribution* (New York, McGraw-Hill Book Company, Inc., 1955), p. 48.
3. Ibid., pp 45–47.
4. *The Affluent Society* (Boston, Houghton-Mifflin Company, 1958), pp. 152–160.
5. Henry Ford, *My Life and Work* (New York, Doubleday, Page & Company, 1923), pp. 146–147.
6. Op. cit., p. 20.

◆

The Analytical Framework for Marketing

Wroe Alderson

My assignment is to discuss the analytical framework for marketing. Since our general purpose here is to consider the improvement of the marketing curriculum, I assume that the paper I have been asked to present might serve two functions. The first is to present a perspective of marketing which might be the basis of a marketing course at either elementary or advanced levels. The other is to provide some clue as to the foundations in the social sciences upon which an analytical framework for marketing may be built.

Economics has some legitimate claim to being the original science of markets. Received economic theory provides a framework for the analysis of marketing functions which certainly merits the attention of marketing teachers and practitioners. It is of little importance whether the point of view I am about to present is a version of economics, a hybrid of economics and sociology, or the application of a new emergent general science of human behavior to marketing problems. The

Reprinted from Delbert Duncan (ed.), *Proceedings: Conference of Marketing Teachers from Far Western States* (Berkeley: University of California, 1958), pp. 15–28.

analytical framework which I find congenial at least reflects some general knowledge of the social sciences as well as long experience in marketing analysis. In the time available I can do no more than present this view in outline or skeleton form and leave you to determine how to classify it or whether you can use it.

An advantageous place to start for the analytical treatment of marketing is with the radical heterogeneity of markets. Heterogeneity is inherent on both the demand and the supply sides. The homogeneity which the economist assumes for certain purposes is not an antecedent condition for marketing. Insofar as it is ever realized, it emerges out of the marketing process itself.

The materials which are useful to man occur in nature in heterogeneous mixtures which might be called conglomerations since these mixtures have only a random relationship to human needs and activities. The collection of goods in the possessions of a household or an individual also constitutes a heterogeneous supply, but it might be called an assortment since it is related to anticipated patterns of future behavior. The whole economic process may be described as a series of transformations from meaningless to meaningful heterogeneity. Marketing produces as much homogeneity as may be needed to facilitate some of the intermediate economic processes but homogeneity has limited significance or utility for consumer behavior or expectations.

The marketing process matches materials found in nature or goods fabricated from these materials against the needs of households or individuals. Since the consuming unit has a complex pattern of needs, the matching of these needs creates an assortment of goods in the hands of the ultimate consumer. Actually the marketing process builds up assortments at many stages along the way, each appropriate to the activities taking place at that point. Materials or goods are associated in one way for manufacturing, in another way for wholesale distribution, and in still another way for retail display and selling. In between the various types of heterogeneous collections relatively homogeneous supplies are accumulated through the process of grading, refining, chemical reduction and fabrication.

Marketing brings about the necessary transformations in heterogeneous supplies through a multiphase process of sorting. Matching of every individual need would be impossible if the consumer had to search out each item required or the producer had to find the users of a product one by one. It is only the ingenious use of intermediate sorts which make it possible for a vast array of diversified products to enter into the ultimate consumer assortments as needed. Marketing makes mass production possible first by providing the assortment of supplies needed in manufacturing and then taking over the successive transformations which ultimately produce the assortment in the hands of consuming units.

To some who have heard this doctrine expounded, the concept of sorting seems

empty, lacking in specific behavioral content, and hence unsatisfactory as a root idea for marketing. One answer is that sorting is a more general and embracing concept than allocation, which many economists regard as the root idea of their science. Allocation is only one of the four basic types of sorting, all of which are involved in marketing. Among these four, allocation is certainly no more significant than assorting, one being the breaking down of a homogeneous supply and the other the building up of a heterogeneous supply. Assorting, in fact, gives more direct expression to the final aim of marketing but allocation performs a major function along the way.

There are several basic advantages in taking sorting as a central concept. It leads directly to a fundamental explanation of the contribution of marketing to the overall economy of human effort in producing and distributing goods. It provides a key to the unending search for efficiency in the marketing function itself. Finally, sorting as the root idea of marketing is consistent with the assumption that heterogeneity is radically and inherently present on both sides of the market and that the aim of marketing is to cope with the heterogeneity of both needs and resources.

At this stage of the discussion it is the relative emphasis on assorting as contrasted with allocation which distinguishes marketing theory from at least some versions of economic theory. This emphasis arises naturally from the preoccupation of the market analyst with consumer behavior. One of the most fruitful approaches to understanding what the consumer is doing is the idea that she is engaged in building an assortment, in replenishing or extending an inventory of goods for use by herself and her family. As evidence that this paper is not an attempt to set up a theory in opposition to economics it is acknowledged that the germ of the conception of consumer behavior was first presented some eighty years ago by the Austrian economist Böhm-Bawerk.

The present view is distinguished from that of Böhm-Bawerk in its greater emphasis on the probabilistic approach to the study of market behavior. In considering items for inclusion in her assortment the consumer must make judgments concerning the relative probabilities of future occasions for use. A product in the assortment is intended to provide for some aspect of future behavior. Each such occasion for use carries a rating which is a product of two factors, one a judgment as to the probability of its incidence and the other a measure of the urgency of the need in case it should arise. Consumer goods vary with respect to both measures. One extreme might be illustrated by cigarettes with a probability of use approaching certainty but with relatively small urgency or penalty for deprivation on the particular occasion for use. At the other end of the scale would be a home fire extinguisher with low probability but high urgency attaching to the expected occasion of use.

All of this means that the consumer buyer enters the market as a problem-solver. Solving a problem, either on behalf of a household or on behalf of a marketing organization means reaching a decision in the face of uncertainty. The consumer buyer and the marketing executive are opposite numbers in the double search which pervades marketing; one looking for the goods required to complete an assortment, the other looking for the buyers who are uniquely qualified to use his goods. This is not to say that the behavior of either consumers or executives can be completely characterized as rational problem-solvers. The intention rather is to assert that problem-solving on either side of the market involves a probabilistic approach to heterogeneity on the other side. In order to solve his own problems arising from the heterogeneous demand, the marketing executive should understand the processes of consumer decisions in coping with heterogeneous supplies.

The viewpoint adopted here with respect to the competition among sellers is essentially that which is associated in economics with such names as Schumpeter, Chamberlin, and J. M. Clark and with the emphasis on innovative competition, product differentiation and differential advantage. The basic assumption is that every firm occupies a position which is in some respects unique, being differentiated from all others by characteristics of its products, its services, its geographic location or its specific combination of these features. The survival of a firm requires that for some group of buyers it should enjoy a differential advantage over all other suppliers. The sales of any active marketing organization come from a core market made up of buyers with a preference for this source and a fringe market which finds the source acceptable, at least for occasional purchases.

In the case of the supplier of relatively undifferentiated products or services such as the wheat farmer, differential advantage may pertain more to the producing region than to the individual producer. This more diffused type of differential advantage often becomes effective in the market through such agencies as the marketing cooperative. Even the individual producer of raw materials, however, occupies a position in the sense that one market or buyer provides the customary outlet for his product rather than another. The essential point for the present argument is that buyer and seller are not paired at random even in the marketing of relatively homogeneous products but are related to some scale of preference or priority.

Competition for differential advantage implies goals of survival and growth for the marketing organization. The firm is perennially seeking a favorable place to stand and not merely immediate profits from its operations. Differential advantage is subject to change and neutralization by competitors. In dynamic markets differential advantage can only be preserved through continuous innovation. Thus competition presents an analogy to a succession of military campaigns rather than to the pressures and attrition of a single battle. A competitor may gain ground through a successful campaign based on new product features or merchandising ideas. It may lose ground or be forced to fall back on its core position because of the successful campaigns of others. The existence of the core position helps to explain the paradox of survival in the face of the destructive onslaughts of innovative competition.

Buyers and sellers meet in market transactions, each side having tentatively identified the other as an answer to its problem. The market transaction consumes much of the time and effort of all buyers and sellers. The market which operates through a network of costless transactions is only a convenient fiction which economists adopt for certain analytical purposes. Potentially the cost of transactions is so high that controlling or reducing this cost is a major objective in market analysis and executive action. Among economists John R. Commons has given the greatest attention to the transaction as the unit of collective action. He drew a basic distinction between strategic and routine transactions which for present purposes may best be paraphrased as fully negotiated and routine transactions.

The fully negotiated transaction is the prototype of all exchange transactions. It represents a matching of supply and demand after canvassing all of the factors which might affect the decision on either side. The routine transaction proceeds under a set of rules and assumptions established by previous negotiation or as a result of techniques of pre-selling which take the place of negotiation. Transactions on commodity and stock exchanges are carried out at high speed and low cost but only because of carefully established rules governing all aspects of trading. The economical routines of self-service in a supermarket are possible because the individual items on display have been presold. The routine transaction is the end-result of previous marketing effort and ingenious organization of institutions and processes. Negotiation is implicit in all routine transactions. Good routines induce both parties to save time and cost by foregoing explicit negotiations.

The negotiated transaction is the indicated point of departure for the study of exchange values in heterogeneous markets. Many considerations enter into the decision to trade or not to trade on either side of the market. Price is the final balancing or integrating factor which permits the deal to be made. The seller may accept a lower price if relieved from onerous requirements. The buyer may pay a higher price if provided with specified services. The integrating price is one that assures an orderly flow of goods so long as the balance of other considerations remains essentially unchanged. Some economists are uneasy about the role of the negotiated transaction in value determination since bargaining power may be controlling within wide bargaining limits. These limits as analyzed by Commons are set by reference to the best alternatives available to either partner rather than by the automatic control of atomistic competition. This analysis overlooks a major constraint on bargaining in modern markets. Each side has a major stake in a deal that the other side can live with. Only in this way can a stable supply relationship be established so as to achieve the economics of transactional routines. Negotiation is not a zero sum game since the effort to get the best of the other party transaction by transaction may result in a loss to both sides in terms of mounting transactional cost.

In heterogeneous markets price plays an important role in matching a segment of supply with the appropriate segment of demand. The seller frequently has the option of producing a stream-lined product at a low price, a deluxe product at a high price or selecting a price-quality combination somewhere in between. There are considerations which exert a strong influence on the seller toward choosing the price line or lines which will yield the greatest dollar volume of sales. Assuming the various classes of consumers having conflicting claims on the productive capacity of the supplier, it might be argued that the price-quality combination which maximized gross revenue represented the most constructive compromise among these claims. There are parallel considerations with respect to the claims of various participants in the firm's activities on its operating revenue. These claimants include labor, management, suppliers of raw materials and stockholders. Assuming a perfectly fluid situation with respect to bargaining among these claimants, the best chance for a satisfactory solution is at the level of maximum gross revenue. The argument becomes more complicated when the claims of stockholders are given priority, but the goal would still be maximum gross revenue as suggested in a recent paper by William J. Baumol. My own intuition and experience lead me to believe that the maximization of gross revenue is a valid goal of marketing management in heterogeneous markets and adherence to this norm appears to be widely prevalent in actual practice.

What has been said so far is doubtless within the scope of economics or perhaps constitutes a sketch of how some aspects of economic theory might be reconstructed on the assumption of heterogeneity rather than homogeneity as the normal and prevailing condition of the market. But there are issues raised by such notions as enterprise survival, expectations, and consumer behavior, which in my opinion cannot be resolved within the present boundaries of economic science. Here marketing must not hesitate to draw upon the concepts and techniques of the social sciences for the enrichment of its perspectives and for the advancement of marketing as an empirical science.

The general economist has his own justifications for regarding the exchange process as a smoothly functioning mechanism which operates in actual markets or which should be taken as the norm and standard to be enforced by government regulation. For the marketing man, whether teacher or practitioner, this Olympian view is untenable. Marketing is concerned with those who are obliged to enter the market to solve their problems, imperfect as the market may be. The persistent and rational action of these participants is the main hope for eliminating or moderating some of these imperfections so that the operation of the market mechanism may approximate that of the theoretical model.

To understand market behavior the marketing man takes a closer look at the nature of the participants. Thus he is obliged, in my opinion, to come to grips with the organized behavior system. Market behavior is primarily group behavior. Individual action in the market is most characteristically action on behalf of some group in which the individual holds membership. The organized behavior system is related to the going concern of John R. Commons but with a deeper interest in what keeps it going. The organized behavior system is also a much broader concept including the more tightly organized groups acting in the market such as business firms and households and loosely connected systems such as the trade center and the marketing channel.

The marketing man needs some rationale for group behavior, some general explanation for the formation and persistence of organized behavior systems. He finds this explanation in the concept of expectations. Insofar as conscious choice is involved, individuals operate in groups because of their expectations of incremental satisfactions as compared to what they could obtain operating alone. The expected satisfactions are of many kinds, direct or indirect. In a group that is productive activity is held together because of an expected surplus over individual output. Other groups such as households and purely social organizations expect direct satisfactions from group association and activities. They also expect satisfactions from future activities facilitated by the assortment of goods held in common. Whatever the character of the system, its vitality arises from the expectations of the individual members and the vigor of their efforts to achieve them through group action. While the existence of the group is entirely derivative, it is capable of operating as if it had a life of its own and was pursuing goals of survival and growth.

✗ Every organized behavior system exhibits a structure related to the functions it performs. Even in the simplest behavior system there must be some mechanism for decision and coordination of effort if the system is to provide incremental satisfaction. Leadership emerges at an early stage to perform such functions as directing the defense of the group. Also quite early is the recognition of the rationing function by which the leader allocates the available goods or satisfactions among the members of the group.

As groups grow in size and their functions become more complex functional specialization increases. The collection of individuals forming a group with their diversified skills and capabilities is a meaningful heterogeneous ensemble vaguely analogous to the assortment of goods which facilitates the activities of the group. The group, however, is held together directly by the generalized expectations of its members. The assortment is held together by a relatively weak or derivative bond. An item "belongs" to the assortment only so long as it has some

probability of satisfying the expectations of those who possess it.

This outline began with an attempt to live within the framework of economics or at least within an economic framework amplified to give fuller recognition to heterogeneity on both sides of the market. We have now plunged into sociology in order to deal more effectively with the organized behavior systems. Meanwhile we attempt to preserve the line of communication to our origins by basing the explanations of group behavior on the quasi-economic concept of expectations.

The initial plunge into sociology is only the beginning since the marketing man must go considerably further in examining the functions and structure of organized behavior systems. An operating group has a power structure, a communication structure and an operating structure. At each stage an effort should be made to employ the intellectual strategy which has already been suggested. That is, to relate sociological notions to the groundwork of marketing economics through the medium of such concepts as expectations and the processes of matching and sorting.

All members of an organized behavior system occupy some position or status within its power structure. There is a valid analogy between the status of an individual or operating unit within the system and the market position of the firm as an entity. The individual struggles for status within the system having first attained the goal of membership. For most individuals in an industrial society, status in some operating system is a prerequisite for satisfying his expectations. Given the minimal share in the power of the organization inherent in membership, vigorous individuals may aspire to the more ample share of power enjoyed by leadership. Power in the generalized sense referred to here is an underlying objective on which the attainment of all other objectives depends. This aspect of organized behavior has been formulated as the power principle, namely, "The rational individual will act in such a way to promote the power to act." The word *promote* deliberately glosses over an ambivalent attitude toward power, some individuals striving for enhancement and others being content to preserve the power they have.

Any discussion which embraces power as a fundamental concept creates uneasiness for some students on both analytical and ethical ground. My own answer to the analytical problem is to define it as control over expectations. In these terms it is theoretically possible to measure and evaluate power, perhaps even to set a price on it. Certainly it enters into the network of implications in a business enterprise. Management allocates or rations status and recognition as well as or in lieu of material rewards. As for the ethical problem, it does not arise unless the power principle is substituted for ethics as with Machiavelli. Admitting that the power principle is the essence of expediency, the ethical choice of values and objectives is a different issue. Whatever his specific objectives, the rational individual will wish to serve them expediently.

If any of this discussion of power seems remote from marketing let it be remembered that the major preoccupation of the marketing executive, as pointed out by Oswald Knauth, is with the creation or the activation of organized behavior systems such as marketing channels and sales organizations. No one can be effective in building or using such systems if he ignores the fundamental nature of the power structure.

The communication structure serves the group in various ways. It promotes the survival of the system by reinforcing the individual's sense of belonging. It transmits instructions and operating commands or signals to facilitate coordinated effort. It is related to expectations through the communication of explicit or implied commitments. Negotiations between suppliers and customers and much

that goes on in the internal management of a marketing organization can best be understood as a two-way exchange of commitments. A division sales manager, for example, may commit himself to produce a specified volume of sales. His superior in turn may commit certain company resources to support his efforts and make further commitments as to added rewards as an incentive to outstanding performance.

For some purposes it is useful to regard marketing processes as a flow of goods and a parallel flow of informative and persuasive messages. In these terms the design of communication facilities and channels becomes a major aspect of the creation of marketing system. Marketing has yet to digest and apply the insights of the rapidly developing field of communication theory which in turn has drawn freely from both engineering and biological and social sciences. One stimulating idea expounded by Norbert Wiener and others is that of the feedback of information in a control system. Marketing and advertising research are only well started on the task of installing adequate feedback circuits for controlling the deployment of marketing effort.

Social psychology is concerned with some problems of communication which are often encountered in marketing systems. For example, there are the characteristic difficulties of vertical communication which might be compared to the transmission of telephone messages along a power line. Subordinates often hesitate to report bad news to their superiors fearing to take the brunt of emotional reactions. Superiors learn to be cautious in any discussion of the subordinate's status for fear that casual comment will be interpreted as a commitment. There is often a question as to when a subordinate should act and report and when he should refer a matter for decision upstream. Progress in efficiency, which is a major goal in marketing, depends in substantial part on technological improvement in communication facilities and organizational skill in using them.

The third aspect of structure involved in the study of marketing systems is operating structure. Effective specialization within an organization requires that activities which are functionally similar be placed together but properly coordinated with other activities. Billing by wholesaler grocers, for example, has long been routinized in a separate billing department. In more recent years the advances in mechanical equipment have made it possible to coordinate inventory control with billing, using the same set of punch cards for both functions. Designing an operating structure is a special application of sorting. As in the sorting of goods to facilitate handling, there are generally several alternative schemes for classifying activities presenting problems of choice to the market planner.

Functional specialization and the design of appropriate operating structures is a constant problem in the effective use of marketing channels. Some functions can be performed at either of two or more stages. One stage may be the best choice in terms of economy or effectiveness. Decisions on the placement of a function may have to be reviewed periodically since channels do not remain static. Similar considerations arise in the choice of channels. Some types of distributors or dealers may be equipped to perform a desired service while others may not. Often two or more channels with somewhat specialized roles are required to move a product to the consumer. The product sponsor can maintain perspective in balancing out these various facilities by thinking in terms of a total operating system including his own sales organization and the marketing channels employed.

The dynamics of market organization pose basic problems for the marketing student and the marketing executive in a free enterprise economy. Reference has already been made to the competitive pursuit of dif-

ferential advantage. One way in which a firm can gain differential advantage is by organizing the market in a way that is favorable to its own operations. This is something else than the attainment of a monopolistic position in relation to current or potential competitors. It means creating a pattern for dealing with customers or suppliers which persists because there are advantages on both sides. Offering guarantees against price declines on floor stocks is one example of market organization by the seller. Attempts to systematize the flow of orders may range from various services offered to customers or suppliers all the way to complete vertical integration. Another dynamic factor affecting the structure of market may be generalized under the term "closure." It frequently happens that some marketing system is incomplete or out of balance in some direction. The act of supplying the missing element constitutes closure, enabling the system to handle a greater output or to operate at a new level of efficiency. The incomplete system in effect cries out for closure. To observe this need is to recognize a form of market opportunity. This is one of the primary ways in which new enterprises develop, since there may be good reasons why the missing service cannot be performed by the existing organizations which need the service. A food broker, for example, can cover a market for several accounts of moderate size in a way that the individual manufacturer would not be able to cover it for himself.

There is a certain compensating effect between closure as performed by new or supplementary marketing enterprises and changes in market organization brought about by the initiative of existing firms in the pursuit of differential advantage. The pursuit of a given form of advantage, in fact, may carry the total marketing economy out of balance in a given direction creating the need and opportunity for closure. Such an economy could never be expected to reach a state of equilibrium, although the tendency toward structural balance is one of the factors in its dynamics. Trade regulation may be embraced within this dynamic pattern as an attempt of certain groups to organize the market to their own advantage through political means. Entering into this political struggle to determine the structure of markets are some political leaders and some administrative officials who regard themselves as representing the consumer's interests. It seems reasonable to believe that the increasing sophistication and buying skill of consumers is one of the primary forces offsetting the tendency of the free market economy to turn into something else through the working out of its inherent dynamic forces. This was the destiny foreseen for the capitalistic system by Schumpeter, even though he was one of its staunchest advocates.

The household as an organized behavior system must be given special attention in creating an analytical framework for marketing. The household is an operating entity with an assortment of goods and assets and with economic functions to perform. Once a primary production unit, the household has lost a large part of these activities to manufacturing and service enterprises. Today its economic operations are chiefly expressed through earning and spending. In the typical household there is some specialization between the husband as primary earner and the wife as chief purchasing agent for the household. It may be assumed that she becomes increasingly competent in buying as she surrenders her production activities such as canning, baking and dressmaking, and devotes more of her time and attention to shopping. She is a rational problem solver as she samples what the market has to offer in her effort to maintain a balanced inventory or assortment of goods to meet expected occasions of use. This is not an attempt to substitute Economic Woman for the discredited fiction of Economic Man. It is only intended to assert

that the decision structure of consumer buying is similar to that for industrial buying. Both business executive and housewife enter the market as rational problem solvers, even though there are other aspects of personality in either case.

An adequate perspective on the household for marketing purposes must recognize several facets of its activities. It is an organized behavior system with its aspects of power, communication, and operating structure. It is the locus of forms of behavior other than instrumental or goal-seeking activities. A convenient three-way division, derived from the social sciences, recognizes instrumental, congenial, and symptomatic behavior. Congenial behavior is that kind of activity engaged in for its own sake and presumably yielding direct satisfactions. It is exemplified by the act of consumption as compared to all of the instrumental activities which prepare the way for consumption. Symptomatic behavior reflects maladjustment and is neither pleasure-giving in itself nor an efficient pursuit of goals. Symptomatic behavior is functional only to the extent that it serves as a signal to others that the individual needs help.

Some studies of consumer motivation have given increasing attention to symptomatic behavior or to the projection of symptoms of personality adjustment which might affect consumer buying. The present view is that the effort to classify individuals by personality type is less urgent for marketing than the classification of families. Four family types with characteristically different buying behavior have been suggested growing out of the distinction between the instrumental and congenial aspects of normal behavior. Even individuals who are fairly well adjusted in themselves will form a less than perfect family if not fully adapted to each other.

On the instrumental side of household behavior it would seem to be desirable that the members be well coordinated as in any other operating system. If not, they will not deliver the maximum impact in pursuit of family goals. On the congenial side it would appear desirable for the members of a household to be compatible. That means enjoying the same things, cherishing the same goals, preferring joint activities to solitary pursuits or the company of others. These two distinctions yield an obvious four-way classification. The ideal is the family that is coordinated in its instrumental activities and compatible in its congenial activities. A rather joyless household which might nevertheless be well managed and prosperous in material terms is the coordinated but incompatible household. The compatible but uncoordinated family would tend to be happy-go-lucky and irresponsible with obvious consequences for buying behavior. The household which was both uncoordinated and incompatible would usually be tottering on the brink of dissolution. It might be held together formally by scruples against divorce, by concern for children, or by the dominant power of one member over the others. This symptomology of families does not exclude an interest in the readjustment of individuals exhibiting symptomatic behavior. Such remedial action lies in the sphere of the psychiatrist and the social worker, whereas the marketer is chiefly engaged in supplying goods to families which are still functioning as operating units.

All of the discussion of consumers so far limits itself to the activities of the household purchasing agent. Actually the term *consumption* as it appears in marketing and economic literature nearly always means consumer buying. Some day marketing may need to look beyond the act of purchasing to a study of consumption proper. The occasion for such studies will arise out of the problems of inducing consumers to accept innovations or the further proliferation of products to be included in the household assortment. Mar-

keting studies at this depth will not only borrow from the social sciences but move into the realm of esthetic and ethical values. What is the use of a plethora of goods unless the buyer derives genuine satisfaction from them? What is the justification of surfeit if the acquisition of goods serves as a distraction from activities which are essential to the preservation of our culture and of the integrity of our personalities?

It has been suggested that a study of consumption might begin with the problem of choice in the presence of abundance. The scarce element then is the time or capacity for enjoyment. The bookworm confronted with the thousands of volumes available in a great library must choose in the face of this type of limitation.

The name *hedonomics* would appear to be appropriate for this field of study suggesting the management of the capacity to enjoy. Among the problems for hedonomics is the pleasure derived from the repetition of a familiar experience as compared with the enjoyment of a novel experience or an old experience with some novel element. Another is the problem of direct experience versus symbolic experience, with the advantages of intensity on the one hand and on the other the possibility of embracing a greater range of possible ideas and sensations by relying on symbolic representations. Extensive basic research will probably be necessary before hedonomics can be put to work in marketing or for the enrichment of human life through other channels.

This paper barely suffices to sketch the analytical framework for marketing. It leaves out much of the area of executive decision-making in marketing on such matters as the weighing of uncertainties and the acceptance of risk in the commitment of resources. It leaves out market planning which is rapidly becoming a systematic discipline centering in the possibilities for economizing time and space as well as resources. It leaves out all but the most casual references to advertising and demand formation. Advertising is certainly one of the most difficult of marketing functions to embrace within a single analytical framework. It largely ignores the developing technology of physical distribution. Hopefully what it does accomplish is to show how the essentially economic problems of marketing may yield to a more comprehensive approach drawing on the basic social sciences for techniques and enriched perspective.

Marketing as Exchange

Richard P. Bagozzi

The exchange paradigm has emerged as a framework useful for conceptualizing marketing behavior. Indeed, most contemporary definitions of marketing explicitly include exchange in their formulations.[1] Moreover, the current debate on "broadening" centers on the very notion of exchange: on its nature, scope, and efficacy in marketing.

This article analyzes a number of dimensions of the exchange paradigm that have not been dealt with in the marketing literature. First, it attempts to show that what marketers have considered as exchange is a special case of exchange theory that focuses primarily on direct transfers of tangible entities between two parties. In reality, marketing exchanges often are indirect, they may involve intangible and symbolic aspects, and more than two parties may participate. Second, the media and meaning of exchange are discussed in order to provide a foundation for specifying underlying mechanisms in marketing exchanges. Finally, global marketing is analyzed in light of the broadened concept of exchange.

The following discussion proceeds from the assumptions embodied in the generic concept of marketing as formulated by Kotler, Levy, and others.[2] In particular, it is assumed that marketing theory is concerned with two questions: (1) Why do people and organizations engage in exchange relationships? and (2) How are exchanges created, resolved, or avoided? The domain for the subject matter of marketing is assumed to be quite broad, encompassing all activities involving "exchange" and the cause and effect of phenomena associated with it. As in the social and natural sciences, marketing owes its definition to the outcome of debate and competition between divergent views in an evolutionary process that Kuhn terms a "scientific revolution."[3] Although the debate is far from settled, there appears to be a growing consensus that exchange forms the core phenomenon for study in marketing. Whether

"Marketing as Exchange," Richard P. Bagozzi, Vol. 39 (October 1975), pp. 32–39. Reprinted from *Journal of Marketing*, published by the American Marketing Association.

the specific instances of exchange are to be limited to economic institutions and consumers in the traditional sense or expanded to all organizations in the broadened sense deserves further attention by marketing scholars and practitioners. Significantly, the following principles apply to exchanges in both senses.

THE TYPES OF EXCHANGE

In general, there are three types of exchange: restricted, generalized, and complex.[4] Each of these is described below.

Restricted Exchange

Restricted exchange refers to two-party reciprocal relationships which may be represented diagrammatically as A ↔ B, where "↔" signifies "gives to and receives from" and A and B represent social actors such as consumers, retailers, salesmen, organizations, or collectivities.[5] Most treatments of, and references to, exchanges in the marketing literature have implicitly dealt with restricted exchanges; that is, they have dealt with customer-salesman, wholesaler-retailer, or other such dyadic exchanges.

      Restricted exchanges exhibit two characteristics:

> First, there is a great deal of attempt to maintain equality. This is especially the case with repeatable social exchange acts. Attempts to gain advantage at the expense of the other is [sic] minimized. Negatively, the breach of the rule of equality quickly leads to emotional reactions. . . . Secondly, there is a *quid pro quo* mentality in restricted exchange activities. Time intervals in mutual reciprocities are cut short and there is an attempt to balance activities and exchange items as part of the mutual reciprocal relations.[6]

The "attempt to maintain equality" is quite evident in restricted marketing exchanges.

Retailers, for example, know that they will not obtain repeat purchases if the consumer is taken advantage of and deceived. The "breach" in this rule of equality—which is a central tenet of the marketing concept—has led to picketing, boycotts, and even rioting. Finally, the fact that restricted marketing exchanges must involve a *quid pro quo* notion (something of value in exchange for something of value) has been at the heart of Luck's criticism of broadening the concept of marketing.[7] However, as will be developed below, there are important exceptions to the *quid pro quo* requirement in many marketing exchanges.

Generalized Exchange

Generalized exchange denotes univocal, reciprocal relationships among at least three actors in the exchange situation. Univocal reciprocity occurs "if the reciprocations involve at least three actors and if the actors do not benefit each other directly but only indirectly."[8] Given three social actors, for instance, generalized exchange may be represented as A → B → C → A, where "→" signifies "gives to." In generalized exchange, the social actors form a system in which each actor gives to another but receives from someone other than to whom he gave. For example, suppose a public bus company (B) asks a local department store chain (A) to donate or give a number of benches to the bus company. Suppose further that, after the department store chain (A) gives the benches to the bus company (B), the company (B) then places the benches at bus stops for the convenience of its riders (C). Finally, suppose that a number of the riders (C) see the advertisements placed on the benches by the department store chain (A) and later patronize the store as a result of this exposure. This sequence of exchange, A → B → C → A, is known as generalized exchange; while it fails to conform to the usual notions of *quid pro quo*, it certainly constitutes a marketing exchange of interest.

Complex Exchange

Complex exchange refers to a system of mutual relationship between at least three parties. Each social actor is involved in at least one direct exchange, while the entire system is organized by an interconnecting web of relationships.

Perhaps the best example of complex exchange in marketing is the channel of distribution. Letting A represent a manufacturer, B a retailer, and C a consumer, it is possible to depict the channel as A ↔ B ↔ C. Such open-ended sequences of direct exchanges may be designated *complex chain exchanges*.

But many marketing exchanges involve relatively closed sequences of relationships. For example, consider the claim made by Kotler that a "transaction takes place . . . when a person decides to watch a television program."[9] Recently, Carman and Luck have criticized this assertion, maintaining that it may not exhibit an exchange.[10] The differences stem from: (1) a disagreement on whether exchange must consist of transfers of tangible (as opposed to intangible) things of value, and (2) a neglect of the possibility of systems of exchange. Figure 3-1 illustrates the exchange between a person and a television program and how it may be viewed as a link in a system termed *complex circular exchange*.[11] In this system of exchange, the person experiences a direct transfer of intangibles between himself and the program. That is, he gives his attention, support (for example, as measured by the Nielsen ratings), potential for purchase, and so on, and receives entertainment, enjoyment, product information, and other intangible entities. The person also experiences an indirect exchange with the television program via a sequence of direct, tangible exchanges. Thus, after being informed of the availability of a book through an exchange with the television program and its advertising, a person may purchase it for, say, $10.00. The book's publisher, in turn, may purchase the services of an advertiser, paying what amounts to a percentage of each sale, say, $1.00. Finally, the advertiser receives the opportunity to place a commercial on the air from the television network in exchange for what amounts to a percentage of each sale, say, $.80. In this particular example, the occurrence of the direct intangible exchange was a necessary prerequisite for the development of the series of indirect tangible exchanges. Thus, an exchange *can* occur between a person and a television program.

Complex chain and complex circular exchanges involve predominantly conscious systems of social and economic relationships. In this sense, there is an overt coordination of activities and expectations, which Alderson called an organized behavioral system and which he reserved for the household, the firm, and the channel of distribution.[12] However, it should be evident that the designation "organized" is a relative one and that other exchange systems, such as the one shown in Figure 3-1, also evidence aspects of overt coordination in an economic, social, and symbolic sense.

Generalized and complex exchanges are also present in relatively unconscious systems of social and economic relationships. Thus, a modern economy may experience a covert coordination of activities through exchanges that occur when many individuals, groups, and firms pursue their own self-interest. This is what Adam Smith meant by his reference to an "invisible hand."[13] Similarly, in his analysis of primitive societies and marketing systems, Frazer has shown that exchange and the pursuit of self-interest can be the foundation for the web of kinship, economic, and social institutions.[14] The recent exchange theories of Homans and Blau are also based

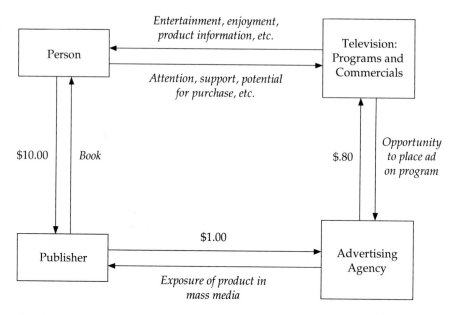

Figure 3-1
An Example of Complex Circular Exchange

on this individualistic assumption of self-interest.[15] It should be stressed, however, that the exchange tradition developed by Levi-Strauss is not an individualistic one but rather is built on social, collectivistic assumptions associated with generalized exchange.[16] These differences will become more apparent when social marketing is analyzed below.

THE MEDIA AND MEANING OF EXCHANGE

In order to satisfy human needs, people and organizations are compelled to engage in social and economic exchanges with other people and organizations. This is true for primitive as well as highly developed societies. Social actors obtain satisfaction of their needs by complying with, or influencing, the behavior of other actors. They do this by communicating and controlling the media of ex-

change which, in turn, comprise the links between one individual and another, between one organization and another. Significantly, marketing exchanges harbor meanings for individuals that go beyond the mere use of media for obtaining results in interactions.

The Media of Exchange

The media of exchange are the vehicles with which people communicate to, and influence, others in the satisfaction of their needs. These vehicles include money, persuasion, punishment, power (authority), inducement, and activation of normative or ethical commitments.[17] Products and services are also media of exchange. In consumer behavior research, marketers have extensively studied the effects of these vehicles on behavior. Moreover, it has been suggested that a number of these vehicles be used in conjunction with sociopsychological processes to explain the customer-salesman relationship.[18] It should be noted, however, that marketing is not solely concerned with influence processes, whether these involve manufacturers influencing consumers or consumers influencing manufacturers. Marketing is also concerned with meeting existing needs and anticipating future needs, and these activities do not necessarily entail attempts to influence or persuade.

To illustrate the multivariate nature of media in marketing exchanges, consider the example of the channel of distribution, a complex chain exchange. The firms in a channel of distribution are engaged in an intricate social system of behavioral relationships that go well beyond the visible exchange of products and money.[19] Typically, the traditional channel achieves its conscious coordination of effort through the mutual expectations of profit. In addition each firm in the channel may influence the degree of cooperation and compliance of its partners by offering inducements in the form of services, deals, or other benefits or by persuading each link in the channel that it is in its own best interest to cooperate. A firm may also affect the behavior of decisions of another firm through the use of the power it may possess. Wilkinson has studied five bases of power in the channel of distribution—reward, coercive, legitimate, referent, and expert power—and has tested aspects of these relationships between firms.[20] Finally, a firm may remind a delinquent member in the channel of its contractual obligations or even threaten the member with legal action for a breach of agreement. This influence medium is known as the activation of commitments.

The Meaning of Exchange

Human behavior is more than the outward responses or reactions of people to stimuli. Man not only reacts to events or the actions of others but he self-generates his own acts.[21] His behavior is purposeful, intentional. It is moti-

vated. Man is an information seeker and generator as well as an information processor. In short, human behavior is a conjunction of meaning with action and reaction.

Similarly, exchange is more than the mere transfer of a product or service for money. To be sure, most marketing exchanges are characterized by such a transfer. But the reasons behind the exchange—the explanation of its occurrence—lie in the social and psychological significance of the experiences, feelings, and meanings of the parties in the exchange. In general, marketing exchanges may exhibit one of three classes of meanings: utilitarian, symbolic, or mixed.

Utilitarian Exchange   A utilitarian exchange is an interaction whereby goods are given in return for money or other goods and the motivation behind the actions lies in the anticipated use or tangible characteristics commonly associated with the objects in the exchange. The utilitarian exchange is often referred to as an economic exchange, and most treatments of exchange in marketing implicitly rely on this usage. As Bartels notes with regard to the identity crisis in marketing:

> Marketing has initially and generally been associated exclusively with the distributive part of the *economic* institution and function. . . .
>
> The question, then, is whether marketing is identified by the *field* of economics in which the marketing techniques have been developed and generally applied, or by the so-called marketing *techniques*, wherever they may be applied.
>
> If marketing relates to the distributive function of the economy, providing goods and services, that *physical* function differentiates it from all other social institutions.[22]

Most marketers have traditionally conceptualized the subject matter of the discipline in these terms, and they have proceeded from the assumptions embodied in utilitarian exchange.

In general, utilitarian exchange theory is built on the foundation of *economic man.*[23] Thus, it is assumed that:

1. Men are rational in their behavior.
2. They attempt to maximize their satisfaction in exchanges.
3. They have complete information on alternatives available to them in exchanges.
4. These exchanges are relatively free from external influence.

Coleman has developed an elaborate mathematical framework for representing exchange behavior that assumes many of the features of economic man.[24] His model is based on the theory of purposive action, which posits that each "actor will choose that action which according to his estimate will lead to an expectation of the most beneficial consequences."[25] Among other things, the theory may be used to predict the outcomes and degree of control social actors have for a set of collective actions in an exchange system.

Symbolic Exchange   Symbolic exchange refers to the mutual transfer of psychological, social, or other intangible entities between two or more parties. Levy was one of the first marketers to recognize this aspect of behavior, which is common to many everyday marketing exchanges:

> . . . symbol is a general term for all instances where experience is mediated rather than direct; where an object, action, word, picture, or complex behavior is understood to mean not only itself but also some *other* ideas or feelings.
>
> The less concern there is with the concrete satisfactions of a survival level of existence, the more abstract human responses become. As behavior in the market place is increasingly elaborated, is also becomes increasingly symbolic. This idea needs some examination, because it means that sellers of goods are engaged, whether willfully or not, in selling

symbols, as well as practical merchandise. It means that marketing managers must attend to more than the relatively superficial acts with which they usually concern themselves when they do not think of their goods as having symbolic significance. . . . *People buy things not only for what they can do, but also for what they mean.*[26]

Mixed Exchange   Marketing exchanges involve both utilitarian and symbolic aspects, and it is often very difficult to separate the two. Yet, the very creation and resolution of marketing exchanges depend on the nature of the symbolic and utilitarian mix. It has only been within the past decade or so that marketers have investigated this deeper side of marketing behavior in their studies of psycho-graphics, motivation research, attitude and multiattribute models, and other aspects of buyer and consumer behavior. Out of this research tradition has emerged a picture of man in his true complexity as striving for both economic and symbolic rewards. Thus, we see the emergence of *marketing man*, perhaps based on the following assumptions:

1. Man is sometimes rational, sometimes irrational.
2. He is motivated by tangible as well as intangible rewards, by internal as well as external forces.[27]
3. He engages in utilitarian as well as symbolic exchanges involving psychological and social aspects.
4. Although faced with incomplete information, he proceeds the best he can and makes at least rudimentary and sometimes unconscious calculations of the costs and benefits associated with social and economic exchanges.
5. Although occasionally striving to maximize his profits, marketing man often settles for less than optimum gains in his exchanges.

6. Finally, exchanges do not occur in isolation but are subject to a host of individual and social constraints: legal, ethical, normative, coercive, and the like.

The important research question to answer is: *What are the forces and conditions creating and resolving marketing exchange relationships?* The processes involved in the creation and resolution of exchange relationships constitute the subject matter of marketing, and these processes depend on, and cannot be separated from, the fundamental character of human and organizational needs.

SOCIAL MARKETING

The marketing literature is replete with conflicting definitions of *social marketing*. Some have defined the term to signify the *use* of marketing skills in social causes,[28] while others have meant it to refer also to "the *study* of markets and marketing activities within a total social system."[29] Bartels recently muddied the waters with still a new definition that is vastly different from those previously suggested. For him, social marketing designates "the *application* of marketing techniques to *nonmarketing* fields."[30] Since these definitions cover virtually everything in marketing and even some things outside of marketing, it is no wonder that one author felt compelled to express his "personal confusion" and "uncomfortable" state of mind regarding the concept.[31]

But what is social marketing? Before answering this question, we must reject the previous definitions for a number of reasons. First, we must reject the notion that social marketing is merely the "use" or "application" of marketing techniques or skills to other areas. A science or discipline is something more than its technologies. "Social marketing" connotes what is social and what is

marketing, and to limit the definition to the tools of a discipline is to beg the question of the meaning of marketing. Second, social marketing is not solely the study of marketing within the frame of the total social system, and it is even more than the subject matter of the discipline. Rather, the meaning of social marketing—like that of marketing itself—is to be found in the unique *problems* that confront the discipline. Thus, as the philosopher of science, Popper, notes:

> The belief that there is such a thing as physics, or biology, or archaeology, and that these "studies" or "disciplines" are distinguishable by the subject matter which they investigate, appears to me to be a residue from the time when one believed that a theory had to proceed from a definition of its own subject matter. But subject matter, or kinds of things, do not, I hold, constitute a basis for distinguishing disciplines. Disciplines are distinguished partly for historical reasons and reasons of administrative convenience (such as the organization of teaching and of appointments), and partly because the theories which we construct to solve our problems have a tendency to grow into unified systems. But all this classification and distinction is a comparatively unimportant and superficial affair. *We are not students of some subject matter but students of problems.* And problems may cut right across the borders of any subject matter or discipline.[32]

Social marketing, then, addresses a particular type of problem which, in turn, is a subset of the generic concept of marketing. That is, social marketing is the answer to a particular question: Why and how are *exchanges* created and resolved in *social* relationships? Social relationships (as opposed to economic relationships) are those such as family planning agent—client, welfare agent—indigent, social worker—poor person, and so on.[33] Social marketing attempts to determine the dynamics and nature of the exchange behavior in these relationships.

But is there an exchange in a social relationship? Luck, for example, feels that "a person who receives a free service is not a buyer and has conducted no exchange of values with the provider of the service."[34] It is the contention in this article that there is most definitely an exchange in social marketing relationships, but the exchange is not the simple *quid pro quo* notion characteristic of most economic exchanges. Rather, social marketing relationships exhibit what may be called generalized or complex exchanges. They involve the symbolic transfer of both tangible and intangible entities, and they invoke various media to influence such exchanges.

Figure 3-2 illustrates a typical social marketing exchange. In this system, society authorizes government—through its votes and tax payments—to provide needed social services such as welfare. In return, the mem-

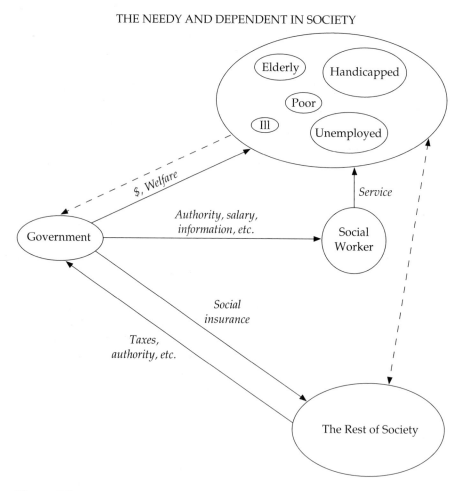

Figure 3-2
Social Marketing and Exchange

bers of society receive social insurance against common human maladies. Government, in turn, pays the salaries of social workers, gives them authority to provide social services, and so on. It also distributes welfare payments directly to the needy. These relatively contemporaneous transfers make this marketing system one of generalized exchange. In addition, a number of symbolic and delayed transfers occur that make the system also one of complex exchange. For example, as shown by dotted lines in the figure, in many cases the needy and dependent have given to the government in the past, since they may have paid taxes and voted. Moreover, members of society anticipate that they, or a number of their members, will become dependent and that social services represent an investment as well as an obligation. Hence, in one sense there is a mutual exchange between society and the needy separated, in part, by the passage of time. Finally, it should be noted that there are other tangential exchanges and forces occurring in this social marketing system that, depending on their balance, give it stability or promote change. The system achieves stability due, first, to the presence of the exchanges described above, which create mutual dependencies and univocal reciprocities; and, second, to symbolic exchanges, which reinforce the overt transfers. For example, the social worker gives to the needy but also receives back gratitude and feelings of accomplishment. The system undergoes change due to the dynamics of competing interests, as is exemplified in the efforts of lobbies and pressure groups to bring their needs to bear on the legislative process.

Thus, social marketing is really a subset of the generic concept of marketing in that it deals with the creation and resolution of exchanges in social relationships. Marketers can make contributions to other areas that contain social exchanges by providing theories and techniques for the understanding and control of such transactions. They do not usurp the authority of specialists in areas such as social work, but rather they aid and complement the efforts of these social scientists. It is not so much the fact that the subject matter of marketing overlaps with that of other disciplines as it is that the problems of marketing are universal. In answer to Bartels' query, "Is marketing a specific function with general applicability or a general function that is specifically applied?"[35]—one may state that it is neither. Rather, marketing is a general function of universal applicability. It is the discipline of exchange behavior, and it deals with problems related to this behavior.

CONCLUSIONS AND IMPLICATIONS

A number of broad research questions may be posed:

1. Why do marketing exchanges emerge? How do people and organizations satisfy their needs through exchange?
2. Why do some marketing exchanges persist in ongoing relationships while others fall apart?
3. What are the processes leading to changes in marketing exchange relationships? How do the social actors or third parties influence or control an exchange?
4. What are the consequences of imbalances in power, resources, knowledge, and so on, in a marketing exchange? What is an equitable exchange?
5. What are the relationships between conflict, cooperation, competition, and exchange?
6. At what level may marketing exchanges be analyzed? What are the consequences of viewing exchanges as single dyads or complex systems of relationships? What are the consequences of employing the individualistic reductionism of Homans versus the

collectivistic orientation of Levi-Strauss for understanding exchange behavior?

7. Is the exchange paradigm universal? Does it apply to the free-enterprise countries of the western world, the planned economies of the communist countries, and the primitive economies of the third world?

8. How well does the exchange paradigm meet the requirements for theory as specified by philosophy of science criteria?

Although marketing seems to defy simple definition and circumspection, it is essential that marketers locate the distinctive focus (or foci) of the discipline. Failure to do so impedes both the growth of the discipline and the character of its performance. Exchange is a central concept in marketing, and it may well serve as the foundation for that elusive "general theory of marketing." This article has attempted to explore some of the key concepts in the exchange paradigm. Future research and discussion must search for specific social and psychological processes that create and resolve marketing exchanges.

NOTES

1. See, for example, Marketing Staff of The Ohio State University, "A Statement of Marketing Philosophy," *Journal of Marketing*, Vol. 29 (January 1965), pp. 43–44; E. Jerome McCarthy, *Basic Marketing*, 5th ed. (Homewood, Ill.: Richard D. Irwin, 1975); Philip Kotler, *Marketing Management*, 2nd ed. (Englewood Cliffs, N. J.: Prentice-Hall, 1972), p. 12; and Ben M. Enis, *Marketing Principles* (Pacific Palisades, Calif.: Goodyear Publishing Co., 1974), p. 21.

2. Philip Kotler, "A Generic Concept of Marketing," *Journal of Marketing*, Vol. 36 (April 1972), pp. 46–54; and Philip Kotler and Sidney J. Levy, "Broadening the Concept of Marketing," *Journal of Marketing*, Vol. 33 (January 1969), pp. 10–15.

3. Thomas S. Kuhn, *The Structure of Scientific Revolutions*, 2nd ed. (Chicago: The University of Chicago Press, 1970).

4. The distinction between restricted and generalized exchange was first made by anthropologist Claude Levi-Strauss in *The Elementary Structure of Kinship* (Boston: Beacon Press, 1969). An extended critical analysis of restricted and generalized exchange may be found in Peter P. Ekeh, *Social Exchange Theory: The Two Traditions* (Cambridge, Mass.: Harvard University Press, 1974), Chap. 3.

5. Ekeh, same reference as footnote 4, p. 50.

6. Ekeh, same reference as footnote 4, pp. 51–52.

7. David J. Luck, "Broadening the Concept of Marketing—Too Far," *Journal of Marketing*, Vol. 33 (January 1969), pp. 10–15; and Luck, "Social Marketing: Confusion Compounded," *Journal of Marketing*, Vol. 38 (October 1974), pp. 70–72.

8. Ekeh, same reference as footnote 4, pp. 48, 50.

9. Kotler, same reference as footnote 2, p. 48.

10. James M. Carman, "On the Universality of Marketing," *Journal of Contemporary Business*, Vol. 2 (Autumn 1973), p. 5; and Luck, "Social Marketing," same reference as footnote 7, p. 72.

11. A form of circular exchange in primitive societies was first suggested by Bonislaw Malinowski in *Argonauts of the Western Pacific* (London: Routledge and Kegan Paul, 1922), p. 93; but in his concept the same physical items were transmitted to all parties, while in complex circular exchange as defined here different tangible or symbolic entities may be transferred.

12. Wroe Alderson, *Dynamic Marketing Behavior* (Homewood, Ill.: Richard D. Irwin, 1965), Chap. 1.

13. For a modern treatment of Adam Smith's contribution to exchange theory, see Walter Nord, "Adam Smith and Contemporary Social Exchange Theory," *The American Journal of Economics and Sociology*, Vol. 32 (October, 1974), pp. 421–436.

14. Sir James G. Frazer, *Folklore in the Old Testament*, Vol. 2 (London: Macmillan & Co., 1919).

15. George C. Homans, *Social Behavior: Its Elementary Forms*, rev. ed. (New York: Harcourt Brace Jovanovich, 1974); and Peter M. Blau, *Exchange and Power in Social Life* (New York: John Wiley & Sons, 1964).

16. Levi-Strauss, same reference as footnote 4. See also, Ekeh, same reference as footnote 4, Chaps. 3 and 4.

17. Talcott Parsons, "On the Concept of Influence," *Public Opinion Quarterly,* Vol. 27 (Spring 1963), pp. 37–62; and Parsons, "On the Concept of Political Power," *Proceedings of the American Philosophical Society,* Vol. 107 (June 1963), pp. 232–262. See also, Richard Emerson, "Power Dependence Relations," *American Sociological Review,* Vol. 27 (February 1962), pp. 31–40.

18. Richard P. Bagozzi, "Marketing as an Organized Behavioral System of Exchange," *Journal of Marketing,* Vol. 38 (October 1974), pp. 77–81.

19. See, for example, Louis W. Stern, *Distribution Channels: Behavioral Dimensions* (New York: Houghton Mifflin Co., 1969).

20. Ian Wilkinson, "Power in Distribution Channels," *Cranfield Research Papers in Marketing and Logistics,* Session 1973–1974 (Cranfield School of Management, Cranfield, Bedfordshire, England); and Wilkinson, "Researching the Distribution Channels for Consumer and Industrial Goods: The Power Dimension," *Journal of the Market Research Society,* Vol. 16 (No. 1, 1974), pp. 12–32.

21. This dynamic, as opposed to mechanistic, image of human behavior is described nicely in R. Harré and P. F. Secord, *The Explanation of Social Behavior* (Totawa, N.J.: Littlefield, Adams & Co., 1973).

22. Robert Bartels, "The Identity Crisis in Marketing," *Journal of Marketing,* Vol. 38 (October 1974), p. 75. Emphasis added.

23. For a modern treatment of economic man, see Harold K. Schneider, *Economic Man* (New York: The Free Press, 1974).

24. James S. Coleman, "Systems of Social Exchange," *Journal of Mathematical Sociology,* Vol. 2 (December 1972).

25. James S. Coleman, *The Mathematics of Collective Action* (Chicago: Aldine-Atherton, 1973).

26. Sidney J. Levy, "Symbols for Sale," *Harvard Business Review,* Vol. 37 (July–August 1959), pp. 117–119.

27. It should be stressed that man is motivated by the hope or anticipation of *future* rewards, and these may consist of classes of benefits not necessarily experienced in the past. See Homans's individualistic exchange theory, a learning perspective, same reference as footnote 15; Levi-Strauss's collectivistic, symbolic perspective, same reference as footnote 4; and Ekeh, same reference as footnote 4, pp. 118–124, 163.

28. Philip Kotler and Gerald Zaltman, "Social Marketing: An Approach to Planned Social Change," *Journal of Marketing,* Vol. 35 (July 1971), p. 5.

29. William Lazer and Eugene J. Kelley, eds., *Social Marketing: Perspective and Viewpoints* (Homewood, Ill.: Richard D. Irwin, 1973), p. 4. Emphasis added.

30. Same reference as footnote 22. Emphasis added.

31. Luck, "Social Marketing," same reference as footnote 7, p. 70.

32. Karl R. Popper, *Conjectures and Refutations* (New York: Harper & Row, 1963), p. 67.

33. For a conceptual framework comparing marketing and other social relationships, see Richard P. Bagozzi, "What Is a Marketing Relationship?" *Der Markt,* No. 51, 1974, pp. 64–69.

34. Luck, "Social Marketing," same reference as footnote 7, p. 71.

35. Same reference as footnote 22, p. 73.

Broadening the Concept of Marketing

Philip Kotler and Sidney J. Levy

The term *marketing* connotes to most people a function peculiar to business firms. Marketing is seen as the task of finding and stimulating buyers for the firm's output. It involves product development, pricing, distribution, and communication; and in the more progressive firms, continuous attention to the changing needs of customers and the development of new products, with product modifications and services to meet these needs. But whether marketing is viewed in the old sense of "pushing" products or in the new sense of "customer satisfaction engineering," it is almost always viewed and discussed as a business activity.

It is the authors' contention that marketing is a pervasive societal activity that goes considerably beyond the selling of toothpaste, soap, and steel. Political contests remind us that candidates are marketed as well as soap; student recruitment by colleges reminds us that higher education is marketed; and fund raising reminds us that "causes" are marketed. Yet these areas of marketing are typically ignored by the student of marketing. Or they are treated cursorily as public relations or publicity activities. No attempt is made to incorporate these phenomena in the body proper of marketing thought and theory. No attempt is made to redefine the meaning of product development, pricing, distribution, and communication in these newer contexts to see if they have a useful meaning. No attempt is made to examine whether the principles of "good" marketing in traditional product areas are transferable to the marketing of services, persons and ideas.

The authors see a great opportunity for marketing people to expand their thinking and to apply their skills to an increasingly interesting range of social activity. The challenge depends on the attention given to it; marketing will either take on a broader social meaning or remain a narrowly defined business activity.

"Broadening the Concept of Marketing," by Philip Kotler and Sidney J. Levy. Reprinted from *Journal of Marketing* (January 1969), pp. 10–15, published by the American Marketing Association. This article received the 1969 Alpha Kappa Psi award as outstanding article of the year.

THE RISE OF ORGANIZATIONAL MARKETING

One of the most striking trends in the United States is the increasing amount of society's work being performed by organizations other than business firms. As a society moves beyond the stage where shortages of food, clothing, and shelter are the major problems, it begins to organize to meet other social needs that formerly had been put aside. Business enterprises remain a dominant type of organization, but other types of organizations gain in conspicuousness and in influence. Many of these organizations become enormous and require the same rarefied management skills as traditional business organizations. Managing the United Auto Workers, Defense Department, Ford Foundation, World Bank, Catholic Church, and University of California has become every bit as challenging as managing Procter and Gamble, General Motors, and General Electric. These non-business organizations have an increasing range of influence, affect as many livelihoods, and occupy as much media prominence as major business firms.

All of these organizations perform the classic business functions. Every organization must perform a financial function insofar as money must be raised, managed, and budgeted according to sound business principles. Every organization must perform a production function in that it must conceive of the best way of arranging inputs to produce the outputs of the organization. Every organization must perform a personnel function in that people must be hired, trained, assigned, and promoted in the course of the organization's work. Every organization must perform a purchasing function in that it must acquire materials in an efficient way through comparing and selecting sources of supply.

When we come to the marketing function, it is also clear that every organization performs marketing-like activities whether or not they are recognized as such. Several examples can be given.

The police department of a major U.S. city, concerned with the poor image it has among an important segment of its population, developed a campaign to "win friends and influence people." One highlight of this campaign is a "visit your police station" day in which tours are conducted to show citizens the daily operations of the police department, including the crime laboratories, police lineups, and cells. The police department also sends officers to speak at public schools and carries out a number of other activities to improve its community relations.

Most museum directors interpret their primary responsibility as "the proper preservation of an artistic heritage for posterity."[1] As a result, for many people museums are cold marble mausoleums that house miles of relics that soon give way to yawns and tired feet. Although museum attendance in the United States advances each year, a large number of citizens are uninterested in museums. Is this indifference due to failure in the manner of presenting what museums have to offer? This nagging question led the new director of the Metropolitan Museum of Art to broaden the museum's appeal through sponsoring contemporary art shows and "happenings." His marketing philosophy of museum management led to substantial increases in the Met's attendance.

The public school system in Oklahoma City sorely needed more public support and funds to prevent a deterioration of facilities and exodus of teachers. It recently resorted to television programming to dramatize the work the public schools were doing to fight the high school dropout problem, to develop new teaching techniques, and to enrich the children. Although an expensive medium, television quickly reached large numbers of parents whose response and interest were tremendous.

Nations also resort to international marketing campaigns to get across important points about themselves to the citizens of other countries. The junta of Greek colonels who seized power in Greece in 1967 found the international publicity surrounding their cause to be extremely unfavorable and potentially disruptive of international recognition. They hired a major New York public relations firm and soon full-page newspaper ads appeared carrying the headline "Greece Was Saved From Communism," detailing in small print why the takeover was necessary for the stability of Greece and the world.[2]

An anti-cigarette group in Canada is trying to press the Canadian legislature to ban cigarettes on the grounds that they are harmful to health. There is widespread support for this cause but the organization's funds are limited, particularly measured against the huge advertising resources of the cigarette industry. The group's problem is to find effective ways to make a little money go a long way in persuading influential legislators of the need for discouraging cigarette consumption. This group has come up with several ideas for marketing anti-smoking to Canadians, including television spots, a paperback book featuring pictures of cancer and heart disease patients, and legal research on company liability for the smoker's loss of health.

What concepts are common to these and many other possible illustrations of organizational marketing? All of these organizations are concerned about their "product" in the eyes of certain "consumers" and are seeking to find "tools" for furthering their acceptance. Let us consider each of these concepts in general organizational terms.

Products

Every organization produces a "product" of at least one of the following types:

Physical Products   "Product" first brings to mind everyday items like soap, clothes, and food, and extends to cover millions of *tangible* items that have a market value and are available for purchase.

Services   Services are *intangible* goods that are subject to market transaction such as tours, insurance, consultation, hairdos, and banking.

Persons   Personal marketing is an endemic *human* activity, from the employee trying to impress his boss to the statesman trying to win the support of the public. With the advent of mass communications, the marketing of persons has been turned over to professionals. Hollywood stars have their press agents, political candidates their advertising agencies, and so on.

Organizations   Many organizations spend a great deal of time marketing themselves. The Republican Party has invested considerable thought and resources in trying to develop a modern look. The American Medical Association decided recently that it needed to launch a campaign to improve the image of the American doctor.[3] Many charitable organizations and universities see selling their *organization* as their primary responsibility.

Ideas   Many organizations are mainly in the business of selling *ideas* to the larger society. Population organizations are trying to sell the idea of birth control, and the Women's Christian Temperance Union is still trying to sell the idea of prohibition.

Thus the "product" can take many forms, and this is the first crucial point in the case for broadening the concept of marketing.

Consumers

The second crucial point is that organizations must deal with many groups that are interested in their products and can make a difference in its success. It is vitally important to the organization's success that it be sensitive to, serve, and satisfy these groups. One set of groups can be called the *suppliers*. *Suppliers* are those who provide the management group with the inputs necessary to perform its work and develop its product effectively. Suppliers include employees, vendors of the materials, banks, advertising agencies, and consultants.

The other set of groups are the *consumers* of the organization's product, of which four subgroups can be distinguished. The *clients* are those who are the immediate consumers of the organization's product. The clients of a business firm are its buyers and potential buyers; of a service organization those receiving the services, such as the needy (from the Salvation Army) or the sick (from County Hospital); and of a protective or a primary organization, the members themselves. The second group is the *trustees* or *directors*, those who are vested with the legal authority and responsibility for the organization, oversee the management, and enjoy a variety of benefits from the "product." The third group is the active *publics* that take a specific interest in the organization. For a business firm, the active publics include consumer rating groups, governmental agencies, and pressure groups of various kinds. For a university, the active publics include alumni and friends of the university, foundations, and city fathers. Finally, the fourth consumer group is the *general public*. These are all the people who might develop

attitudes toward the organization that might affect its conduct in some way. Organizational marketing concerns the programs designed by management to create satisfactions and favorable attitudes in the organization's four consuming groups: clients, trustees, active publics, and general public.

Marketing Tools

Students of business firms spend much time studying the various tools under the firm's control that affect product acceptance: product improvement, pricing, distribution, and communication. All of these tools have counterpart applications to nonbusiness organizational activity.

Nonbusiness organizations to various degrees engage in product improvement, especially when they recognize the competition they face from other organizations. Thus, over the years churches have added a host of nonreligious activities to their basic religious activities to satisfy members seeking other bases of human fellowship. Universities keep updating their curricula and adding new student services in an attempt to make the educational experience relevant to the students. Where they have failed to do this, students have sometimes organized their own courses and publications, or have expressed their dissatisfaction in organized protest. Government agencies such as license bureaus, police forces, and taxing bodies are often not responsive to the public because of monopoly status; but even here citizens have shown an increasing readiness to protest mediocre services, and more alert bureaucracies have shown a growing interest in reading a user's needs and developing the required product services.

All organizations face the problem of pricing their products and services so that they cover costs. Churches charge dues, universities charge tuition, governmental agencies charge fees, fund-raising organizations send out bills. Very often specific product charges are not sufficient to meet the organization's budget, and it must rely on gifts and surcharges to make up the difference. Opinions vary as to how much the users should be charged for the individual services and how much should be made up through general collection. If the university increases its tuition, it will have to face losing some students and putting more students on scholarship. If the hospital raises its charges to cover rising costs and additional services, it may provoke a reaction from the community. All organizations face complex pricing issues although not all of them understand good pricing practice.

Distribution is a central concern to the manufacturer seeking to make his goods conveniently accessible to buyers. Distribution also can be an important marketing decision area for nonbusiness organizations. A city's public library has to consider the best means of making its books available to the public. Should it establish one large library with an extensive collection of books, or several neighborhood branch libraries with duplication of books? Should it use bookmobiles that bring the books to the customers instead of relying exclusively on the customers coming to the books? Should it distribute through school libraries? Similarly the police department of a city must think through the problem of distributing its protective services efficiently through the community. It has to determine how much protective service to allocate to different neighborhoods; the respective merits of squad cars, motorcycles, and foot patrolmen; and the positioning of emergency phones.

Customer communication is an essential activity of all organizations although many nonmarketing organizations often fail to accord it the importance it deserves. Managements of many organizations think they have fully met their communication responsi-bilities by setting up advertising and/or public relations departments. They fail to realize that *everything about an organization talks*. Customers form impressions of an organization from its physical facilities, employees, officers, stationery, and a hundred other company surrogates. Only when this is appreciated do the members of the organization recognize that they all are in marketing, whatever else they do. With this understanding they can assess realistically the impact of their activities on the consumers.

CONCEPTS FOR EFFECTIVE MARKETING MANAGEMENT IN NONBUSINESS ORGANIZATIONS

Although all organizations have products, markets, and marketing tools, the art and science of effective marketing management have reached their highest state of development in the business type of organization. Business organizations depend on customer goodwill for survival and have generally learned how to sense and cater to their needs effectively. As other types of organizations recognize their marketing roles, they will turn increasingly to the body of marketing principles worked out by business organizations and adapt them to their own situations.

What are the main principles of effective marketing management as they appear in most forward-looking business organizations? Nine concepts stand out as crucial in guiding the marketing effort of a business organization.

Generic Product Definition

Business organizations have increasingly recognized the value of placing a broad definition on their products, one that emphasizes the basic customer need(s) being served. A modern soap company recognizes that its basic product is cleaning, not soap; a cosmetics company sees its basic product as beauty or hope, not lipsticks and makeup; a publishing company sees its basic product as information, not books.

The same need for a broader definition of its business is incumbent upon nonbusiness organizations if they are to survive and grow. Churches at one time tended to define their product narrowly as that of producing religious services for members. Recently, most churchmen have decided that their basic product is human fellowship. There was a time when educators said that their product was the three R's. Now most of them define their product as education for the whole man. They try to serve the social, emotional, and political needs of young people in addition to intellectual needs.

Target Groups Definition

A generic product definition usually results in defining a very wide market, and it is then necessary for the organization, because of limited resources, to limit its product offering to certain clearly defined groups within the market. Although the generic product of an automobile company is transportation, the company typically sticks to cars, trucks, and buses, and stays away from bicycles, airplanes, and steamships. Furthermore, the manufacturer does not produce every size and shape of car but concentrates on producing a few major types to satisfy certain substantial and specific parts of the market.

In the same way, nonbusiness organizations have to define their target groups carefully. For example, in Chicago the YMCA defines its target groups as men, women and children who want recreational opportunities and are willing to pay $20 or more a year for them. The Chicago Boys Club, on the other hand, defines its target group as poorer boys within the city boundaries who are in want of recreational facilities and can pay $1 a year.

Differentiated Marketing

When a business organization sets out to serve more than one target group, it will be maximally effective by differentiating its product offerings and communications. This is also true for nonbusiness organizations. Fund-raising organizations have recognized the advantage of treating clients, trustees, and various publics in different ways. These groups require differentiated appeals and frequency of solicitation. Labor unions find that they must address different messages to different parties rather than one message to all parties. To the company they may seem unyielding, to the conciliator they may appear willing to compromise, and to the public they seek to appear economically exploited.

Customer Behavior Analysis

Business organizations are increasingly recognizing that customer needs and behavior are not obvious without formal research and analysis; they cannot rely on impressionistic evidence. Soap companies spend hundreds of thousands of dollars each year researching how Mrs. Housewife feels about her laundry, how, when, and where she does her laundry, and what she desires of a detergent.

Fund raising illustrates how an industry has benefited by replacing stereotypes of donors with studies of why people contribute to causes. Fund raisers have learned that people give because they are getting something. Many give to community chests to relieve a sense of guilt because of their elevated state compared to the needy. Many give to medical charities to relieve a sense of fear that they may be struck by a disease whose cure has not yet been found. Some give to feel pride. Fund raisers have stressed the importance of identifying the motives operating in the marketplace of givers as a basis for planning drives.

Differential Advantages

In considering different ways of reaching target groups, an organization is advised to think in terms of seeking a differential advantage. It should consider what elements in its reputation or resources can be exploited to create a special value in the minds of its potential customers. In the same way Zenith has built a reputation for quality and International Harvester a reputation for service, a nonbusiness organization should base its case on some dramatic value that competitive organizations lack. The small island of Nassau can compete against Miami for the tourist trade by advertising the greater dependability of its weather; the Heart Association can compete for funds against the Cancer Society by advertising the amazing strides made in heart research.

Multiple Marketing Tools

The modern business firm relies on a multitude of tools to sell its product, including product improvement, consumer and dealer advertising, salesmen incentive programs, sales promotions, contests, multiple-size offerings, and so forth. Likewise nonbusiness organizations also can reach their audiences in a variety of ways. A church can sustain the interest of its members through discussion groups, newsletters, news releases, campaign drives, annual reports, and retreats. Its "salesmen" include the religious head, the board members, and the present members in terms of attracting potential members. Its advertising includes announcements of weddings, births and deaths, religious pronouncements, and newsworthy developments.

Integrated Marketing Planning

The multiplicity of available marketing tools suggests the desirability of overall coordina-

tion so that these tools do not work at cross purposes. Over time, the business firms have placed under a marketing vice-president activities that were previously managed in a semi-autonomous fashion, such as sales, advertising, and marketing research. Nonbusiness organizations typically have not integrated their marketing activities. Thus, no single officer in the typical university is given total responsibility for studying the needs and attitudes of clients, trustees, and publics, and undertaking the necessary product development and communication programs to serve these groups. The university administration instead includes a variety of "marketing" positions such as dean of students, director of alumni affairs, director of public relations, and director of development; coordination is often poor.

Continuous Marketing Feedback

Business organizations gather continuous information about changes in the environment and about their own performance. They use their salesmen, research department, specialized research services, and other means to check on the movement of goods, actions of competitors, and feelings of customers to make sure they are progressing along satisfactory lines. Nonbusiness organizations typically are more casual about collecting vital information on how they are doing and what is happening in the marketplace. Universities have been caught off guard by underestimating the magnitude of student grievance and unrest, and so have major cities underestimated the degree to which they were failing to meet the needs of important minority constituencies.

Marketing Audit

Change is a fact of life, although it may proceed almost invisibly on a day-to-day basis. Over a long stretch of time, it might be so fundamental as to threaten organizations that have not provided for periodic reexaminations of their purposes. Organizations can grow set in their ways and unresponsive to new opportunities or problems. Some great American companies are no longer with us because they did not change definitions of their businesses, and their products lost relevance in a changing world. Political parties become unresponsive after they enjoy power for a while and every so often experience a major upset. Many union leaders grow insensitive to new needs and problems until one day they find themselves out of office. For an organization to remain viable, its management must provide for periodic audits of its objectives, resources, and opportunities. It must reexamine its basic business, target groups, differential advantage, communication channels, and messages in the light of current trends and needs. It might recognize when change is needed and make it before it is too late.

IS ORGANIZATIONAL MARKETING A SOCIALLY USEFUL ACTIVITY?

Modern marketing has two different meanings in the minds of people who use the term. One meaning of marketing conjures up the terms selling, influencing, persuading. Marketing is seen as a huge and increasingly dangerous technology, making it possible to sell persons on buying things, propositions, and causes they either do not want or which are bad for them. This was the indictment in Vance Packard's *Hidden Persuaders* and numerous other social criticisms, with the net effect that a large number of persons think of marketing as immoral or entirely self-seeking in its fundamental premises. They can be counted on to resist the idea of organizational marketing as so much "Madison Avenue."

The other meaning of marketing unfortunately is weaker in the public mind; it is the concept of sensitively *serving and satisfying human needs*. This was the great contribution of the marketing concept that was promulgated in the 1950s, and that concept now counts many business firms as its practitioners. The marketing concept holds that the problem of all business firms in an age of abundance is to develop customer loyalties and satisfaction, and the key to this problem is to focus on the customer's needs.[4] Perhaps the short-run problem of business firms is to sell people on buying the existing products, but the long-run problem is clearly to create the products that people need. By this recognition that effective marketing requires a consumer orientation instead of a product orientation, marketing has taken a new lease on life and tied its economic activity to a higher social purpose.

It is this second side of marketing that provides a useful concept for all organizations. All organizations are formed to serve the interest of particular groups: hospitals serve the sick, schools serve the students, governments serve the citizens, and labor unions serve the members. In the course of evolving, many organizations lose sight of their original mandate, grow hard, and become self-serving. The bureaucratic mentality begins to dominate the original service mentality. Hospitals may become perfunctory in their handling of patients, schools treat their students as nuisances, city bureaucrats behave like petty tyrants toward the citizens, and labor unions try to run instead of serve their members. All of these actions tend to build frustration in the consuming groups. As a result some withdraw meekly from these organizations, accept frustration as part of their condition, and find their satisfactions elsewhere. This used to be the common reaction of ghetto Negroes and college students in the face of indifferent city and university bureaucracies. But new possibilities have arisen, and now the same consumers refuse to withdraw so readily. Organized dissent and protest are seen to be an answer, and many organizations thinking of themselves as responsible have been stunned into recognizing that they have lost touch with their constituencies. They had grown unresponsive.

Where does marketing fit into this picture? Marketing is that function of the organization that can keep in constant touch with the organization's consumers, read their needs, develop "products" that meet these needs, and build a program of communications to express the organization's purposes. Certainly selling and influencing will be large parts of organizational marketing; but, properly seen, selling follows rather than precedes the organization's drive to create products to satisfy its consumers.

CONCLUSION

It has been argued here that the modern marketing concept serves very naturally to describe an important facet of all organizational activity. All organizations must develop appropriate products to serve their sundry consuming groups and must use modern tools of communication to reach their consuming publics. The business heritage of marketing provides a useful set of concepts for guiding all organizations.

The choice facing those who manage nonbusiness organizations is not whether to market or not to market, for no organization can avoid marketing. The choice is whether to do it well or poorly, and on this necessity the case for organizational marketing is basically founded.

NOTES

1. This is the view of Sherman Lee, Director of the Cleveland Museum, quoted in *Newsweek*, Vol. 71 (April 1, 1968), p. 55.
2. "PR for Colonels," *Newsweek*, Vol. 71 (March 18, 1968), p. 70.
3. "Doctors Try an Image Transplant," *Business Week*, No. 2025 (June 22, 1968), p. 64.
4. Theodore Levitt, "Marketing Myopia," *Harvard Business Review*, Vol. 38 (July–August, 1960), pp. 45–56.

◆

The Globalization of Markets

Theodore Levitt

A powerful force drives the world toward a converging commonality, and that force is technology. It has proletarianized communication, transport, and travel. It has made isolated places and impoverished peoples eager for modernity's allurements. Almost everyone everywhere wants all the things they have heard about, seen, or experienced via the new technologies.

The result is a new commercial reality—the emergence of global markets for standardized consumer products on a previously unimagined scale of magnitude. Corporations geared to this new reality benefit from enormous economies of scale in production, distribution, marketing, and management. By translating these benefits into reduced world prices, they can decimate competitors that still live in the disabling grip of old assumptions about how the world works.

Gone are accustomed differences in national or regional preference. Gone are the days when a company could sell last year's models—or lesser versions of advanced products—in the less-developed world. And gone are the days when prices, margins, and profits abroad were generally higher than at home.

The globalization of markets is at hand. With that, the multinational commercial world nears its end, and so does the multinational corporation.

The multinational and the global corporation are not the same thing. The multinational corporation operates in a number of countries, and adjusts its products and practices in each—at high relative costs. The global corporation operates with resolute constancy—at low relative cost—as if the entire world (or major regions of it) were a single entity; it sells the same things in the same way everywhere.

Which strategy is better is not a matter of opinion but of necessity. Worldwide communications carry everywhere the constant drumbeat of modern possibilities to lighten and enhance work, raise living standards, divert, and entertain. The same countries that ask the world to recognize and respect the individuality of their cultures insist on the wholesale transfer to them of modern goods, services, and technologies. Modernity is not just a wish but also a widespread practice among those who cling, with unyielding passion or religious fervor, to ancient attitudes and heritages.

Who can forget the televised scenes during the 1979 Iranian uprisings of young men in fashionable French-cut trousers and silky body shirts thirsting with raised modern weapons for blood in the name of Islamic fundamentalism?

In Brazil, thousands swarm daily from pre-industrial Bahian darkness into exploding coastal cities, there quickly to install television sets in crowded corrugated huts and, next to battered Volkswagens, make sacrificial offerings of fruit and fresh-killed chickens to Macumban spirits by candlelight.

During Biafra's fratricidal war against the Ibos, daily televised reports showed soldiers carrying bloodstained swords and listening to transistor radios while drinking Coca-Cola.

In the isolated Siberian city of Krasnoyarsk, with no paved streets and censored news, occasional Western travelers are stealthily propositioned for cigarettes, digital watches, and even the clothes off their backs.

The organized smuggling of electronic equipment, used automobiles, western clothing, cosmetics, and pirated movies into primitive places exceeds even the thriving underground trade in modern weapons and their military mercenaries.

A thousand suggestive ways attest to the ubiquity of the desire for the most advanced things that the world makes and sells—goods of the best quality and reliability at the lowest price. The world's needs and desires have been irrevocably homogenized. This makes the multinational corporation obsolete and the global corporation absolute.

LIVING IN THE REPUBLIC OF TECHNOLOGY

Daniel J. Boorstin, author of the monumental trilogy *The Americans,* characterized our age as driven by "the Republic of Technology [whose] supreme law . . . is convergence, the tendency for everything to become more like everything else."

In business, this trend has pushed markets toward global commonality. Corporations sell standardized products in the same way everywhere—autos, steel, chemicals, petroleum, cement, agricultural commodities and equipment, industrial and commercial construction, banking and insurance services, computers, semiconductors, transport, electronic instruments, pharmaceuticals, and telecommunications, to mention some of the obvious.

Nor is the sweeping gale of globalization confined to these raw material or high-tech products, where the universal language of customers and users facilitates standardization. The transforming winds whipped up by the proletarianization of communication and travel enter every crevice of life.

Commercially, nothing confirms this as much as the success of McDonald's from the Champs Elysées to the Ginza, of Coca-Cola in Bahrain and Pepsi-Cola in Moscow, and of rock music, Greek salad, Hollywood movies, Revlon cosmetics, Sony televisions, and Levi jeans everywhere. "High-touch" products are as ubiquitous as high-tech.

Starting from opposing sides, the high-tech and the high-touch ends of the commercial spectrum gradually consume the undistributed middle in their cosmopolitan orbit. No one is exempt and nothing can stop the process. Everywhere everything gets more and more like everything else as the world's preference structure is relentlessly homogenized.

Consider the cases of Coca-Cola and Pepsi-Cola, which are globally standardized products sold everywhere and welcomed by everyone. Both successfully cross multitudes of national, regional, and ethnic taste buds trained to a variety of deeply ingrained local preferences of taste, flavor, consistency, effervescence, and aftertaste. Everywhere both sell well. Cigarettes, too, especially American-made, make year-to-year global inroads on territories previously held in the firm grip of other, mostly local, blends.

These are not exceptional examples. (Indeed their global reach would be even greater were it not for artificial trade barriers.) They exemplify a general drift toward the homogenization of the world and how companies distribute, finance, and price products.[1] Nothing is exempt. The products and methods of the industrialized world play a single tune for all the world, and all the world eagerly dances to it.

Ancient differences in national tastes or modes of doing business disappear. The commonality of preferences leads inescapably to the standardization of products, manufacturing, and the institutions of trade and commerce. Small nation-based markets transmogrify and expand. Success in world competition turns on efficiency in production, distribution, marketing, and management, and inevitably becomes focused on price.

The most effective world competitors incorporate superior quality and reliability into their cost structures. They sell in all national markets the same kind of products sold at home or in their largest export market. They compete on the basis of appropriate value—the best combinations of price, quality, reliability, and delivery for products that are globally identical with respect to design, function, and even fashion.

That, and little else, explains the surging success of Japanese companies dealing worldwide in a vast variety of products—both tangible products like steel, cars, motor-

cycles, hi-fi equipment, farm machinery, robots, microprocessors, carbon fibers, and now even textiles, and intangibles like banking, shipping, general contracting, and soon computer software. Nor are high-quality and low-cost operations incompatible, as a host of consulting organizations and data engineers argue with vigorous vacuity. The reported data are incomplete, wrongly analyzed, and contradictory. The truth is that low-cost operations are the hallmark of corporate cultures that require and produce quality in all that they do. High quality and low costs are not opposing postures. They are compatible, twin identities of superior practice.[2]

To say that Japan's companies are not global because they export cars with left-side drives to the United States and the European continent, while those in Japan have right-side drives, or because they sell office machines through distributors in the United States but directly at home, or speak Portuguese in Brazil is to mistake a difference for a distinction. The same is true of Safeway and Southland retail chains operating effectively in the Middle East, and to not only native but also imported populations from Korea, the Philippines, Pakistan, India, Thailand, Britain, and the United States. National rules of the road differ, and so do distribution channels and languages. Japan's distinction is its unrelenting push for economy and value enhancement. That translates into a drive for standardization at high quality levels.

Vindication of the Model T

If a company forces costs and prices down and pushes quality and reliability up—while maintaining reasonable concern for suitability—customers will prefer its world-standardized products. The theory holds, at this stage in the evolution of globalization, no matter what conventional market research and even common sense may suggest about different national and regional tastes, preferences, needs, and institutions. The Japanese have repeatedly vindicated this theory, as did Henry Ford with the Model T. Most important, so have their imitators, including companies from South Korea (television sets and heavy construction), Malaysia (personal calculators and microcomputers), Brazil (auto parts and tools), Colombia (apparel), Singapore (optical equipment), and yes, even from the United States (office copiers, computers, bicycles, castings), Western Europe (automatic washing machines), Rumania (housewares), Hungary (apparel), Yugoslavia (furniture), and Israel (pagination equipment).

Of course, large companies operating in a single nation or even a single city don't standardize everything they make, sell, or do. They have product lines instead of a single product version, and multiple distribution channels. There are neighborhood, local, regional, ethnic, and institutional differences, even within metropolitan areas. But although companies customize products for particular market segments, they know that success in a world with homogenized demand requires a search for sales opportunities in similar segments across the globe in order to achieve the economies of scale necessary to compete.

Such a search works because a market segment in one country is seldom unique; it has close cousins everywhere precisely because technology has homogenized the globe. Even small local segments have their global equivalents everywhere and become subject to global competition, especially on price.

The global competitor will seek constantly to standardize his offering everywhere. He will digress from this standardization only after exhausting all possibilities to retain it, and he will push for reinstatement of standardization whenever digression and divergence have occurred. He will never assume that the customer is a king who knows his own wishes.

Trouble increasingly stalks companies that lack clarified global focus and remain inattentive to the economics of simplicity and standardization. The most endangered companies in the rapidly evolving world tend to be those that dominate rather small domestic markets with high value-added products for which there are smaller markets elsewhere. With transportation costs proportionately low, distant competitors will enter the now-sheltered markets of those companies with goods produced more cheaply under scale-efficient conditions. Global competition spells the end of domestic territoriality, no matter how diminutive the territory may be.

When the global producer offers his lower costs internationally, his patronage expands exponentially. He not only reaches into distant markets, but also attracts customers who previously held to local preferences and now capitulate to the attractions of lesser prices. The strategy of standardization not only responds to worldwide homogenized markets but also expands those markets with aggressive low pricing. The new technological juggernaut taps an ancient motivation—to make one's money go as far as possible. This is universal—not simply a motivation but actually a need.

THE HEDGEHOG KNOWS

The difference between the hedgehog and the fox, wrote Sir Isaiah Berlin in distinguishing between Dostoevski and Tolstoy, is that the fox knows a lot about a great many things, but the hedgehog knows everything about one great thing. The multinational corporation knows a lot about a great many countries and congenially adapts to supposed differences. It willingly accepts vestigial national differences, not questioning the possibility of their transformation, not recognizing how the world is ready and eager for the benefit of modernity, especially when the price is right.

The multinational corporation's accommodating mode to visible national differences is medieval.

By contrast, the global corporation knows everything about one great thing. It knows about the absolute need to be competitive on a worldwide basis as well as nationally and seeks constantly to drive down prices by standardizing what it sells and how it operates. It treats the world as composed of few standardized markets rather than many customized markets. It actively seeks and vigorously works toward global convergence. Its mission is modernity and its mode, price competition, even when it sells top-of-the-line, high-end products. It knows about the one great thing all nations and people have in common: scarcity.

Nobody takes scarcity lying down; everyone wants more. This in part explains division of labor and specialization of production. They enable people and nations to optimize their conditions through trade. The median is usually money.

Experience teaches that money has three special qualities: scarcity, difficulty of acquisition, and transcience. People understandably treat it with respect. Everyone in the increasingly homogenized world market wants products and features that everybody else wants. If the price is low enough, they will take highly standardized world products, even if these aren't exactly what mother said was suitable, what immemorial custom decreed was right, or what market-research fabulists asserted was preferred.

The implacable truth of all modern production—whether of tangible or intangible goods—is that large-scale production of standardized items is generally cheaper within a wide range of volume than small-size production. Some argue that CAD/CAM will allow companies to manufacture customized products on a small scale—but cheaply. But the argument misses the point. (For a more detailed discussion, see the insert, "Economies of Scope.") If a company treats the world as one or two distinctive product markets, it can serve the world more economically than if it treats it as three, four, or five product markets.

ECONOMIES OF SCOPE

One argument that opposes globalization says that flexible factory automation will enable plants of massive size to change products and product features quickly, without stopping the manufacturing process. These factories of the future could thus produce broad lines of customized products without sacrificing the scale economies that come from long production runs of standardized items. Computer-aided design and manufacturing (CAD/CAM), combined with robotics, will create a new equipment and process technology (EPT) that will make small plants located close to their markets as efficient as large ones located distantly. Economies of scale will not dominate, but rather economies of scope—the ability of either large or small plants to produce great varieties of relatively customized products at remarkably low costs. If that happens, customers will have no need to abandon special preferences.

I will not deny the power of these possibilities. But possibilities do not make probabilities. There is no conceivable way in which flexible factory automation can achieve the scale economies of a modernized plant dedicated to mass production of standardized lines. The new digitized equipment and process technologies are available to all. Manufacturers with minimal customization and narrow product-line breadth will have costs far below those with more customization and wider lines.

Why Remaining Differences?

Different cultural preferences, national tastes and standards, and business institutions are vestiges of the past. Some inheritances die gradually; others prosper and expand into mainstream global preferences. So-called ethnic markets are a good example. Chinese food, pita bread, country and western music, pizza, and jazz are everywhere. They are market segments that exist in worldwide proportions. They don't deny or contradict global homogenization but confirm it.

Many of today's differences among nations as to products and their features actually reflect the respectful accommodation of multinational corporations to what they believe are fixed local preferences. They *believe* preferences are fixed, not because they are but because of rigid habits of thinking about what actually is. Most executives in multinational corporations are thoughtlessly accommodating. They falsely presume that marketing means giving the customer what he says he wants rather than trying to understand exactly what he'd like. So they persist with high-cost, customized multinational products and practices instead of pressing hard and pressing properly for global standardization.

I do not advocate the systematic disregard of local or national differences. But a company's sensitivity to such differences does not require that it ignore the possibilities of doing things differently or better.

There are, for example, enormous differences among Middle East countries. Some are socialist, some monarchies, some republics. Some take their legal heritage from the Napleonic Code, some from the Ottoman Empire, and some from the British common law; except for Israel, all are influenced by Islam. Doing business means personalizing the business relationship in an obsessively intimate fashion. During the month of Ramadan, business discussions can start only after 10 o'clock at night, when people are tired and full of food after a day of fasting. A company must almost certainly have a local partner; a local lawyer is required (as, say, in New York), and irrevocable letters of credit are essential. Yet, as Coca-Cola's Senior Vice President Sam Ayoub noted, "Arabs are much more capable of making distinctions between cultural and religious purposes on the one hand and economic realities on the other than is generally assumed. Islam is compatible with science and modern times."

Barriers to globalization are not confined to the Middle East. The free transfer of technology and data across the boundaries of the European Common Market countries are hampered by legal and financial impediments. And there is resistance to radio and television interference ("pollution") among neighboring European countries.

But the past is a good guide to the future. With persistence and appropriate means, barriers against superior technologies and economics have always fallen. There is no recorded exception where reasonable effort has been made to overcome them. It is very much a matter of time and effort.

A FAILURE IN GLOBAL IMAGINATION

Many companies have tried to standardize world practice by exporting domestic products and processes without accommodation or change—and have failed miserably. Their deficiencies have been seized on as evidence of bovine stupidity in the face of abject impossibility. Advocates of global standardization see them as examples of failures in execution.

In fact, poor execution is often an important cause. More important, however, is failure of nerve—failure of imagination.

Consider the case for the introduction of fully automatic home laundry equipment in Western Europe at a time when few homes had even semiautomatic machines. Hoover, Ltd., whose parent company was headquartered in North Canton, Ohio, had a prominent presence in Britain as a producer of vacuum cleaners and washing machines. Due to insufficient demand in the home market and low exports to the European continent, the large washing machine plant in England operated far below capacity. The company needed to sell more of its semiautomatic or automatic machines.

Because it had a "proper" marketing orientation, Hoover conducted consumer preference studies in Britain and each major continental country. The results showed feature preferences clearly enough among several countries (see Table 5-1).

The incremental unit variable costs (in pounds sterling) of customizing to meet just a few of the national preferences were:

	£	s	d
Stainless steel vs. enamel drum	1	0	0
Porthole window		10	0
Spin speed of 800 rpm vs. 700 rpm		15	0
Water heater	2	15	0
6 vs. 5 kilos capacity	1	10	0
	£6	10 s	0 d

$18.20 at the exchange rate of that time.

Table 5-1
Consumer Preferences as to Automatic Washing Machine Features in the 1960s

Features	Great Britain	Italy	West Germany	France	Sweden
Shell dimensions*	34" and narrow	Low and narrow	34" and wide	34" and narrow	34" and wide
Drum material	Enamel	Enamel	Stainless steel	Enamel	Stainless steel
Loading	Top	Front	Front	Front	Front
Front porthole	Yes/no	Yes	Yes	Yes	Yes
Capacity	5 kilos	4 kilos	6 kilos	5 kilos	6 kilos
Spin speed	700 rpm	400 rpm	850 rpm	600 rpm	800 rpm
Water-heating system	No[†]	Yes	Yes[††]	Yes	No[†]
Washing action	Agitator	Tumble	Tumble	Agitator	Tumble
Styling features	Inconspicuous appearance	Brightly colored	Indestructible appearance	Elegant appearance	Strong appearance

*34" height was (in the process of being adopted as) a standard work-surface height in Europe.
[†]Most British and Swedish homes had centrally heated hot water.
[††]West Germans preferred to launder at temperatures higher than generally provided centrally.

Considerable plant investment was needed to meet other preferences.

The lowest retail prices (in pounds sterling) of leading locally produced brands in the various countries were approximately:

U.K	£110
France	114
West Germany	113
Sweden	134
Italy	57

Product customization in each country would have put Hoover in a poor competitive position on the basis of price, mostly due to the higher manufacturing costs incurred by short production runs for separate features. Because Common Market tariff reduction programs were then incomplete, Hoover also paid tariff duties in each continental country.

How to Make a Creative Analysis

In the Hoover case, an imaginative analysis of automatic washing machine sales in each country would have revealed that:

1. Italian automatics, small in capacity and size, low-powered, without built-in heaters, with porcelain enamel tubs, were priced aggressively low and were gaining large market shares in all countries, including West Germany.
2. The best-selling automatics in West Germany were heavily advertised (three times more than the next most promoted brand), were ideally suited to national tastes, and were also by far the highest priced machines available in that country.
3. Italy, with the lowest penetration of washing machines of any kind (manual, semiautomatic, or automatic) was rapidly going directly to automatics, skipping the pattern of first buying hand-wringer,

manually assisted machines and then semiautomatics.
4. Detergent manufacturers were just beginning to promote the technique of cold-water and tepid-water laundering then used in the United States.

The growing success of small, low-powered, low-speed, low-capacity, low-priced Italian machines, even against the preferred but highly priced and highly promoted brand in West Germany, was significant. It contained a powerful message that was lost on managers confidently wedded to a distorted version of the marketing concept according to which you give the customer what he says he wants. In fact the customers *said* they wanted certain features, but their behavior demonstrated they'd take other features provided the price and the promotion were right.

In this case it was obvious that, under prevailing conditions, people preferred a low-priced automatic over any kind of manual or semiautomatic machine and certainly over higher priced automatics, even though the low-priced automatics failed to fulfill all their expressed preferences. The supposedly meticulous and demanding German consumers violated all expectations by buying the simple, low-priced Italian machines.

It was equally clear that people were profoundly influenced by promotions of automatic washers; in West Germany, the most heavily promoted ideal machine also had the largest market share despite its high price. Two things clearly influenced customers to buy: low price regardless of feature preferences and heavy promotion regardless of price. Both factors helped homemakers get what they most wanted—the superior benefits bestowed by fully automatic machines.

Hoover should have aggressively sold a simple, standardized high-quality machine at a low price (afforded by the 17% variable cost reduction that the elimination of £6-10-0 worth of extra features made possible). The suggested retail prices could have been somewhat less than £100. The extra funds "saved" by avoiding unnecessary plant modifications would have supported an extended service network and aggressive media promotions.

Hoover's media message should have been: *this* is the machine that you, the homemaker, *deserve* to have to reduce the repetitive heavy daily household burdens, so that *you* may have more constructive time to spend with your children and your husband. The promotion should also have targeted the husband to give him, preferably in the presence of his wife, a sense of obligation to provide an automatic washer for her even before he bought an automobile for himself. An aggressively low price, combined with heavy promotion of this kind, would have overcome previously expressed preferences for particular features.

The Hoover case illustrates how the perverse practice of the marketing concept and the absence of any kind of marketing imagination let multinational attitudes survive when customers actually want the benefits of global standardization. The whole project got off on the wrong foot. It asked people what features they wanted in a washing machine rather than what they wanted out of life. Selling a line of products individually tailored to each nation is thoughtless. Managers who took pride in practicing the marketing concept to the fullest did not, in fact, practice it at all. Hoover asked the wrong questions, then applied neither thought nor imagination to the answers. Such companies are like the ethnocentricists in the Middle Ages who saw with everyday clarity the sun revolving around the earth and offered it as Truth. With no additional data but a more searching mind, Copernicus, like the hedgehog, interpreted a more compelling and accurate reality. Data do not yield information except with the intervention of the mind. In-

formation does not yield meaning except with the intervention of imagination.

ACCEPTING THE INEVITABLE

The global corporation accepts for better or for worse that technology drives consumers relentlessly toward the same common goals—alleviation of life's burdens and the expansion of discretionary time and spending power. Its role is profoundly different from what it has been for the ordinary corporation during its brief, turbulent, and remarkably protean history. It orchestrates the twin vectors of technology and globalization for the world's benefit. Neither fate, nor nature, nor God but rather the necessity of commerce created this role.

In the United States two industries became global long before they were consciously aware of it. After over a generation of persistent and acrimonious labor shutdowns, the United Steelworkers of America have not called an industrywide strike since 1959; the United Auto Workers have not shut down General Motors since 1970. Both unions realize that they have become global—shutting down all or most of U.S. manufacturing would not shut out U.S. customers. Overseas suppliers are there to supply the market.

Cracking the Code of Western Markets

Since the theory of the marketing concept emerged a quarter of a century ago, the more managerially advanced corporations have been eager to offer what customers clearly wanted rather than what was merely convenient. They have created marketing departments supported by professional market researchers of awesome and often costly proportions. And they have proliferated extraordinary numbers of operations and product lines—highly tailored product and delivery systems for many different markets, market segments, and nations.

Significantly, Japanese companies operate almost entirely without marketing departments or market research of the kind so prevalent in the West. Yet, in the colorful words of General Electric's chairman John F. Welch, Jr., the Japanese, coming from a small cluster of resource-poor islands, with an entirely alien culture and an almost impenetrably complex language, have cracked the code of Western markets. They have done it not by looking with mechanistic thoroughness at the way markets are different but rather by searching for meaning with a deeper wisdom. They have discovered the one great thing all markets have in common—an overwhelming desire for dependable, world-standard modernity in all things, at aggressively low prices. In response, they deliver irresistible value everywhere, attracting people with products that market-research technocrats described with superficial certainty as being unsuitable and uncompetitive.

The wider a company's global reach, the greater the number of regional and national preferences it will encounter for certain product features, distribution systems, or promotional media. There will always need to be some accommodation to differences. But the widely prevailing and often unthinking belief in the immutability of these differences is generally mistaken. Evidence of business failure because of lack of accommodation is often evidence of other shortcomings.

Take the case of Revlon in Japan. The company unnecessarily alienated retailers and confused customers by selling world-standardized cosmetics only in elite outlets; then it tried to recover with low-priced world-standardized products in broader distribution, followed by a change in the company president and cutbacks in distribution as costs rose faster than sales. The problem was not that Revlon didn't understand the Japanese market; it didn't do the job right, wavered in its programs, and was impatient to boot.

By contrast, the Outboard Marine Corporation, with imagination, push, and persistence, collapsed long-established three-tiered distribution channels in Europe into a more focused and controllable two-step system—and did so despite the vociferous warnings of local trade groups. It also reduced the number and types of retail outlets. The result was greater improvement in credit and product-installation service to customers, major cost reductions, and sales advances.

In its highly successful introduction of Contac 600 (the timed-release decongestant) into Japan, SmithKline Corporation used 35 wholesalers instead of the 1,000-plus that established practice required. Daily contacts with the wholesalers and key retailers, also in violation of established practice, supplemented the plan, and it worked.

Denied access to established distribution institutions in the United States, Komatsu, the Japanese manufacturer of light-weight farm machinery, entered the market through over-the-road construction equipment dealers in rural areas of the Sunbelt, where farms are smaller, the soil sandier and easier to work. Here inexperienced distributors were able to attract customers on the basis of Komatsu's product and price appropriateness.

In cases of successful challenge to prevailing institutions and practices, a combination of product reliability and quality, strong and sustained support systems, aggressively low prices, and sales-compensation packages, as well as audacity and implacability, circumvented, shattered, and transformed very different distribution systems. Instead of resentment, there was admiration.

Still, some differences between nations are unyielding, even in a world of microprocessors. In the United States almost all manufacturers of microprocessors check them for reliability through a so-called parallel system of testing. Japan prefers the totally different sequential testing system. So Teradyne Corporation, the world's largest producer of microprocessor test equipment, makes one line for the United States and one for Japan. That's easy.

What's not so easy for Teradyne is to know how best to organize and manage, in this instance, its marketing effort. Companies can organize by product, region, function, or by using some combination of these. A company can have separate marketing organizations for Japan and for the United States, or it can have separate product groups, one working largely in Japan and the other in the United States. A single manufacturing facility or marketing operation might service both markets, or a company might use separate marketing operations for each.

Questions arise if the company organizes by product. In the case of Teradyne, should the group handling the parallel system, whose major market is the United States, sell in Japan and compete with the group focused on the Japanese market? If the company organizes regionally, how do regional groups divide their efforts between promoting the parallel vs. the sequential system? If the company organizes in terms of function, how does it get commitment in marketing, for example, for one line instead of the other?

There is no one reliably right answer—no one formula by which to get it. There isn't even a satisfactory contingent answer.[3] What works well for one company or one place may fail for another in precisely the same place, depending on the capabilities, histories, reputations, resources, and even the cultures of both.

THE EARTH IS FLAT

The differences that persist throughout the world despite its globalization affirm an ancient dictum of economics—that things are driven by what happens at the margin, not at the core. Thus, in ordinary competitive analysis, what's important is not the average price but the marginal price; what happens not in the usual case but at the interface of newly erupting conditions. What counts in commercial affairs is what happens at the cutting edge. What is most striking today is the underlying similarities of what is happening now to national preferences at the margin. These similarities at the cutting edge cumulatively form an overwhelming, predominant commonality everywhere.

To refer to the persistence of economic nationalism (protective and subsidized trade practices, special tax aids, or restrictions for home market producers) as a barrier to the globalization of markets is to make a valid point. Economic nationalism does have a powerful persistence. But, as with the present almost totally smooth internationalization of investment capital, the past alone does not shape or predict the future. (For reflections on the internationalization of capital, see the insert, "The Shortening of Japanese Horizons.")

Reality is not a fixed paradigm, dominated by immemorial customs and derived attitudes, heedless of powerful and abundant new forms. The world is becoming increasingly informed about the liberating and enhancing possibilities of modernity. The persistence of the inherited varieties of national preferences rests uneasily on increasing evidence of, and restlessness regarding, their inefficiency, costliness, and confinement. The historic past, and the national differences respecting commerce and industry it spawned and fostered everywhere, is now subject to relatively easy transformation.

Cosmopolitanism is no longer the monopoly of the intellectual and leisure classes; it is becoming the established property and defining characteristic of all sectors everywhere in the world. Gradually and irresistibly it breaks down the walls of economic insular-

THE SHORTENING OF JAPANESE HORIZONS

One of the most powerful yet least celebrated forces driving commerce toward global standardization is the monetary system, along with the international investment process.

Today money is simply electronic impulses. With the speed of light it moves effortlessly between distant centers (and even lesser places). A change of ten basis points in the price of a bond causes an instant and massive shift of money from London to Tokyo. The system has profound impact on the way companies operate throughout the world.

Take Japan, where high debt-to-equity balance sheets are "guaranteed" by various societal presumptions about the virtue of "a long view," or by government policy in other ways. Even here, upward shifts in interest rates in other parts of the world attract capital out of the country in powerful proportions. In recent years more and more Japanese global corporations have gone to the world's equity markets for funds. Debt is too remunerative in high-yielding countries to keep capital at home to feed the Japanese need. As interest rates rise, equity becomes a more attractive option for the issuer.

The long-term impact on Japanese enterprise will be transforming. As the equity proportion of Japanese corporate capitalization rises, companies will respond to the shorter-term investment horizons of the equity markets. Thus the much-vaunted Japanese corporate practice of taking the long view will gradually disappear.

ity, nationalism, and chauvinism. What we see today as escalating commercial nationalism is simply the last violent death rattle of an obsolete institution.

Companies that adapt to and capitalize on economic convergence can still make distinctions and adjustments in different markets. Persistent differences in the world are consistent with fundamental underlying commonalities; they often complement rather than oppose each other—in business as they do in physics. There is, in physics, simultaneously matter and anti-matter working in symbiotic harmony.

The earth is round, but for most purposes it's sensible to treat it as flat. Space is curved, but not much for everyday life here on earth.

Divergence from established practice happens all the time. But the multinational mind, warped into circumspection and timidity by years of stumbles and transnational troubles, now rarely challenges existing overseas practices. More often it considers any departure from inherited domestic routines as mindless, disrespectful, or impossible. It is the mind of a bygone day.

The successful global corporation does not abjure customization or differentiation for the requirements of markets that differ in product preferences, spending patterns, shopping preferences, and institutional or legal arrangements. But the global corporation accepts and adjusts to these differences only reluctantly, only after relentlessly testing their immutability, after trying in various ways to circumvent and reshape them as we saw in the cases of Outboard Marine in Europe, SmithKline in Japan, and Komatsu in the United States.

There is only one significant respect in which a company's activities around the world are important, and this is in what it produces and how it sells. Everything else derives from, and is subsidiary to, these activities.

The purpose of business is to get and keep a customer. Or, to use Peter Drucker's more refined construction, to *create* and keep a customer. A company must be wedded to the ideal of innovation—offering better or more preferred products in such combinations of ways, means, places, and at such prices that prospects *prefer* doing business with the company rather than with others.

Preferences are constantly shaped and reshaped. Within our global commonality enormous variety constantly asserts itself and thrives, as can be seen within the world's single largest domestic market, the United States. But in the process of world homogenization, modern markets expand to reach cost-reducing global proportions. With better and cheaper communication and transport, even small local market segments hitherto protected from distant competitors now feel the pressure of their presence. Nobody is safe from global reach and the irresistible economies of scale.

Two vectors shape the world—technology and globalization. The first helps determine human preferences; the second, economic realities. Regardless of how much preferences evolve and diverge, they also gradually converge and form markets where economies of scale lead to reduction of costs and prices.

The modern global corporation contrasts powerfully with the aging multinational corporation. Instead of adapting to superficial and even entrenched differences within and between nations, it will seek sensibly to force suitably standardized products and practices on the entire globe. They are exactly what the world will take, if they come also with low prices, high quality, and blessed reliability. The global company will operate, in this regard, precisely as Henry Kissinger wrote in *Years of Upheaval* about the continuing Japanese economic success—"voracious in its collection of information, impervious to pressure, and implacable in execution."

Given what is everywhere the purpose of commerce, the global company will shape the vectors of technology and globalization into its great strategic fecundity. It will systematically push these vectors toward their own convergence, offering everyone simultaneously high-quality, more or less standardized products at optimally low prices, thereby achieving for itself vastly expanded markets and profits. Companies that do not adapt to the new global realities will become victims of those that do.

NOTES

1. In a landmark article, Robert D. Buzzell pointed out the rapidity with which barriers to standardization were falling. In all cases they succumbed to more and cheaper advanced ways of doing things. See "Can You Standardize Multination Marketing?" *HBR* November–December 1968, p. 102.
2. There is powerful new evidence for this, even though the opposite has been urged by analysis of PIMS data for nearly a decade. See "Product Quality Cost Production and Business Performance—A Test of Some Key Hypotheses" by Lynn W. Phillips, Dae Chang, and Robert D. Buzzell, Harvard Business School Working Paper No. 83–13.
3. For a discussion of multinational reorganization, see Christopher A. Bartlett, "MNCs Get off the Reorganization Merry-Go-Round," *HBR* March–April 1983, p. 138.

◆

Framework for Analyzing Marketing Ethics

Gene R. Laczniak

The issue of ethics in marketing continues to be a concern for marketing practitioners, educators, and researchers. Virtually every business manager would agree that ethical implications are often inherent in marketing decisions. Particularly perplexing are some of the "tough question" situations which can occur where the degree of moral culpability in a specific case is subject to debate. Capsuled below are a few illustrations of such situations, which will be analyzed later. The situations described in these scenarios deal with the areas of distribution/retailing, promotion, product management, pricing, and nonbusiness marketing. Thus, almost every area of marketing strategy can pose serious ethical questions.

Over the years, marketing writers have tried to address some of the ethical concerns stemming from the practice of mar-

keting. A recent literature review on the topic of marketing ethics (Murphy and Laczniak 1981) identified and discussed nearly 100 articles, papers and books which include commentary related to specific ethical dimensions of marketing. Unfortunately, while the various writings contained many provocative suggestions, as well as some interesting insights, they were seldom based upon an underlying theory or framework of marketing ethics. Most often, the writings pointed out existing ethical abuses (e.g., Rudelius and Bucholz 1979), reported managerial perceptions of ethical behavior (e.g., Sturdivant and Cocanougher 1973; Ferrell and Weaver 1978) or provided some rudimentary suggestions for improving ethics (Kelley 1969; Kizelbach et al. 1979). A few marketing academics have tried to take a more global approach to the ethics issue (see Table 6-1 for a summary), but even these writings, taken as a whole, have lacked sophisticated theoretical foundations. Normally, references to ethical theories or decision rules have been limited to the citation of simple ethical maxims. Typical

Reprinted from the *Journal of Macromarketing*, Vol. 3 (1) (Spring, 1983), pp. 7–18. Published with permission by the Business Research Division, Graduate School of Business Admin, Univ. of Colorado.

Table 6-1
A Summary of Theoretical Commentaries on Marketing Ethics

Author/Year	Source[a]	Theme[b]
Walton (1961)	AMA Educator's Proceedings	Ethical standards of marketers are below par; however, society *in general* suffers from low moral standards.
Alderson (1964)	Report on Ethics to the AMA	Personal morality is constrained by organizational and ecological factors.
Patterson (1966)	*Journal of Marketing*	Operational guidelines are lacking for the ethical prescriptions postulated by organizations; more "checks and balances" needed.
McMahon (1967)	*Atlanta Economic Review*	A condemnation of "situational" ethics.
Farmer (1967)	*Journal of Marketing*	The public perceives the field of marketing as hucksterism.
Bartels (1967)	*Journal of Marketing*	Various external factors upon ethical behavior, such as culture and the given economic environment, are identified.
Westing (1967)	AMA Educator's Proceedings	Personal morality is the dominant factor in most ethical decisions; ethics exist above the law which regulates the lowest common denominator of expected behavior.
Colihan (1967)	AMA Educator's Proceedings	Consumer pressure will dictate marketing's ethics in years to come.
Pruden (1971)	*Marketing and Social Issues* (anthology)	Personal, organizational, and professional ethics interact to influence decision-making; sometimes they can conflict.
Steiner (1976)	*Journal of Marketing*	Marketers are perceived as unethical because of an inability of the public to perceive the value of the time, place, and possession utility provided by marketing.
Farmer (1977)	*Journal of Marketing*	Marketing will never be perceived as ethical because fundamentally it is persuasion.
Murphy, Laczniak, and Lusch (1978)	*Journal of the Academy of Marketing Science*	Organizational adjustments to insure ethical marketing are discussed.
Robin (1980)	AMA Theory Proceedings	The acceptance of relativist philosophy can alleviate ethical conflicts in marketing.

[a] For a full bibliographic citation, see References.
[b] For a more detailed discussion, see Murphy and Laczniak, 1981.

of these thumbnail ethical maxims are the following:

- *The golden rule:* Act in the way you would expect others to act toward you.
- *The utilitarian principle:* Act in a way that results in the greatest good for the greatest number.
- *Kant's categorical imperative:* Act in such a way that the action taken under the circumstances could be a universal law or rule of behavior.
- *The professional ethic:* Take only actions which would be viewed as proper by a disinterested panel of professional colleagues.
- *The TV test:* A manager should always ask: "Would I feel comfortable explaining to a national TV audience why I took this action?"

While not without value, these limited ethical frameworks have hampered the ethical analysis of marketing managers. They have also caused marketing educators some discomfort when discussing ethical issues in the classroom. In short, many marketing educators have shied away from lecturing on the topic of marketing ethics because of the perception that existing frameworks for analyzing marketing ethics are simplistic and lack theoretical rigor. The net result is that the seeming absence of theoretical frameworks for ethical decision-making has retarded the teaching, practice, and research of marketing ethics.

The purpose of this article is to present some existing ethical frameworks, which go beyond ethical maxims in their detail. These frameworks will likely be useful in (a) stimulating marketing ethics research, (b) establishing a background for discussion of ethical issues in the classroom, and (c) perhaps providing guidance for ethical decision-making by marketing managers. The frameworks discussed below hold within themselves no magical monopoly on moral propriety. Rather,

they are presented with the hope that they might engender additional ethical sensitivity among marketing academics, students, researchers, and managers.

FRAMEWORKS VS. THEORIES

Some readers will undoubtedly be concerned whether the viewpoints reflecting ethics to be described below should properly be designated as theories, frameworks, propositions, or some other metaphysical specification. Rawls (1971), whose perspective will be examined, characterizes his own work as a theory and it is accepted as such by most moral philosophers. In contrast, if one uses the definition of theory utilized by Hunt (1976, p. 104), the work of Rawls might not qualify as a theory because of its normative nature and the fact that it is derived from an idealization which is not reflective of the real world.

Others, such as Fisk (1982, p. 5), view a framework as being broader than a theory and therefore more akin to a general paradigm which can accommodate several consistent or contrasting theories. For example, the life cycle *framework* has spawned a variety of life cycle inspired theories. On this basis, deeming the ethical viewpoints described below as frameworks would be incorrect because they are somewhat narrower in scope.

Since all marketers would fail to agree that the opinions expressed below about ethics are either frameworks or theories, the author is in a dilemma. Clearly the viewpoints below are at minimum "skeletal structures designed to support a perspective"—in this case, a perspective about ethics. Since this conforms to the dictionary definition of framework, I will use that terminology and offer my apologies in advance to those philosophers of science who subscribe to a lexicon more linguistically precise than my own.

MARKETING SCENARIOS WHICH RAISE ETHICAL QUESTIONS[a]

SCENARIO 1

The Thrifty Supermarket Chain has 12 stores in the city of Gotham, U.S.A. The company's policy is to maintain the same prices for all items at all stores. However, the distribution manager knowingly sends the poorest cuts of meat and the lowest quality produce to the store located in the low-income section of town. He justifies this action based on the fact that this store has the highest overhead due to factors such as employee turnover, pilferage, and vandalism. *Is the distribution manager's economic rationale sufficient justification for his allocation method?*

SCENARIO 2

The Independent Chevy Dealers of Metropolis, U.S.A. have undertaken an advertising campaign headlined by the slogan: "Is your family's life worth 45 MPG?" The ads admit that while Chevy subcompacts are not as fuel efficient as foreign imports and cost more to maintain, they are safer according to government-sponsored crash tests. The ads implicitly ask if responsible parents, when purchasing a car, should trade off fuel efficiency for safety? *Is it ethical for the dealers association to use a fear appeal to offset an economic disadvantage?*

SCENARIO 3

A few recent studies have linked the presence of the artificial sweetener, subsugural, to cancer in laboratory rats. while the validity of these findings has been hotly debated by medical experts, the Food and Drug Administration has ordered products containing the ingredient banned from sale in the U.S. The Jones Company sends all of its sugar-free J. C. Cola (which contains subsugural) to European supermarkets because the sweetener has not been banned there. *Is it acceptable for the Jones Company to send an arguably unsafe product to another market without waiting for further evidence?*

SCENARIO 4

The Acme Company sells industrial supplies through its own sales force, which calls on company purchasing agents. Acme has found that providing the purchasing agent with small gifts helps cement a cordial relationship and creates goodwill. Acme follows the policy that the bigger the order, the bigger the gift to the purchasing agent. The gifts range from a pair of tickets to a sporting event to outboard motors and snowmobiles. Acme does not give gifts to personnel at companies which they know have an explicit policy prohibiting the acceptance of such gifts. *Assuming no laws are violated, is Acme's policy of providing gifts to purchasing agents morally proper?*

SCENARIO 5

The Buy American Electronics Company has been selling its highly rated System X Color TV sets (21″, 19″, 12″) for $700, $500 and $300 respectively. These prices have been relatively uncompetitive in the market. After some study, Buy American substitutes several cheaper components (which engineering says may reduce the quality of performance slightly) and passes on the savings to the consumer in the form of a $100 price reduction on each model. Buy American institutes a price-oriented promotional campaign which neglects to mention that the second generation System X sets are different from the first. *Is the company's competitive strategy ethical?*

SCENARIO 6

The Smith and Smith Advertising Agency has been struggling financially. Mr. Smith is approached by the representative of a small South American country which is on good terms with the U.S. Department of State. He wants S and S to create a multimillion dollar advertising and public relations campaign which will bolster the image of the country and increase the likelihood that it will receive U.S. foreign aid assistance and attract investment capital. Smith knows the country is a dictatorship which has been accused of numerous human rights violations. *Is it ethical for the Smith and Smith Agency to undertake the proposed campaign?*

[a]Adapted from Patrick E. Murphy and Gene R. Laczniak, 1981, p. 251.

RATIONALE FOR THE FRAMEWORKS

In the following pages, ethical frameworks developed by William David Ross, Thomas Garrett, and John Rawls are presented. Their paradigms have been selected because they are multidimensional, nonutilitarian in nature, and significant in some important fashion.

Multidimensional   One of the impediments that has limited the study of marketing ethics in the classroom is the perception by too many business educators that existing guidelines for ethical behavior are simplistic. This viewpoint has considerable validity. For example, what precisely is the value of the "golden rule" in assessing whether a firm should pay some bribe money in order to retain a lucrative foreign contract? Clearly, the usefulness of such a maxim is limited. One value of the three frameworks selected for presentation is that they illustrate that ethical frameworks do exist which go well beyond the frailty of a maxim in their sophistication. That is, there are ethical theories which attempt to specify multidimensional factors for consideration.

Nonutilitarian in Nature   In the main, much of the theoretical thinking about marketing ethics which has occurred has been implicitly based on utilitarian theory. Utilitarianism holds that actions should be judged primarily upon whether they produce "the greatest good for the greatest number." Utilitarianism, of course, is based historically on the well-known writings of Jeremy Bentham and John Stuart Mill. Many of the ethical defenses for the efficiency of the free market have also been rooted in utilitarianism. Typically, the argument revolves around showing how the unrestricted market allocates resources in a more beneficial manner to society than does a tightly controlled or regulated marketplace. In other words, free market capitalism benefits a greater number of persons than do controlled systems. There are many articulate, modern day spokesmen for utilitarianism (Sartorius 1975; Singer 1976). However, generally speaking, utilitarian analysis has been subjected to a large amount of criticism in recent years (Beauchamp and Bowie 1979). The crux of the objection to utilitarianism lies in the fact that a desirable *end* may come about because of an unjust *means*. Thus, in recent years, many moral philosophers have turned their attention to nonutilitarian theories which emphasize the *process* of arriving at outcomes as well as the *outcome* itself. Because of the relative familiarity of business managers with utilitarian thinking *and* the currency of examining other alternatives, the three frameworks highlighted below are nonutilitarian.

Significant   Each of the frameworks selected for explication is theoretically important for some reason. Ross was one of the first philosophers to try to specify a list of the major ethical responsibilities facing any person. In addition, Ross tried to create a paradigm which would be a supplement to rather than a replacement of utilitarian thinking. Garrett, in contrast, tried to take various streams of ethical thought and blend them in a fashion which would be useful to the practicing business manager. Thus, the major contribution of the Garrett work is its pragmatic orientation. Finally, the Rawls' theory is the most talked-about work on ethics in recent years. Rawls' writings have had an enormous influence on moral philosophy in the past decade and this impact is reflected in current writings on the topic of ethics.

With this general preface, attention is directed to the perspectives developed below.

THE PRIMA FACIE
DUTIES FRAMEWORK

In his theory of moral philosophy, English-man William David Ross tried to combine the underpinnings of utilitarianism with certain aspects of Kantian philosophical theory. The bulwark of the Ross (1930) model is the notion that there are several *prima facie* (at first sight) *duties* which, under most circumstances, constitute moral obligations. Ross contends that these prima facie duties are self-evident (1930, p. 29) in the sense that persons of sufficient mental maturity will recognize that there are certain acts they *ought to do*. Ross postulated six categories of prima facie duties:

a. Duties of fidelity—*these stem from previous actions which have been taken*. Generally, this would include (to name a few) the duty to remain faithful to contracts, to keep promises, to tell the truth and to redress wrongful acts. In a marketing context, this might include conducting all the quality and safety testing which has been promised consumers, maintaining a rigorous warrantee/servicing program and refraining from deceptive or misleading promotional campaigns. For example, in Scenario 2, the dealers association may decide that the heavy handed fear appeal is in bad taste because of the implicit duty of fidelity they have to potential auto buyers.

b. Duties of gratitude—*these are rooted in acts other persons have taken toward the person or organization under focus*. Generally, this means that a special obligation exists between relatives, friends, partners, cohorts, etc. In a marketing context, this might mean retaining an ad agency a while longer because it had rendered meritorious service for several years or extending extra credit to a historically "special customer" experiencing a cash flow problem.

In Scenario 4, Acme management may conclude that the duty of gratitude would allow the provision of a small gift if such a practice is not explicitly forbidden by the client organization.

c. Duties of justice—*these are based on the obligation to distribute rewards based upon merit*. The *justice* referred to here is justice beyond the letter of the law. For example, an organization using sealed-bid purchasing to secure services should award the contract according to procedure rather than allow the second or third lowest bidder to re-bid. Or in Scenario 1, the distribution manager might reason that the managerial problems caused by a few shoplifting or troublemaking customers is not a sufficient reason to discriminate against all of a store's buyers.

d. Duties of beneficence—*these rest on the notion that actions taken can improve the intelligence, virtue or happiness of others*. Basically, this is the obligation to do good, if a person has the opportunity. In Scenario 6, this might mean that the Smith and Smith Agency turns down the public relations contract, albeit financially attractive, because of the duty to support the human rights of others.

e. Duties of self-improvement—*these reside in the concept that actions should be taken which improve our own virtue, intelligence or happiness*. This seems to represent a modified restatement of *moral egoism*—act in a way that will promote one's own self interest. In a marketing context, this might justify a manager attempting to maximize the ROI of his "profit center" because such performance may lead to pay increases and organizational promotion. In Scenario 6, this might mean that Smith and Smith undertakes the PR contract in order to survive; after all, the charges against the client country have not been proven and the country's government is officially recognized by the U.S. Department of State.

f. Duties of nonmaleficence (noninjury)—
    these consist of duties not to injure others. In a marketing context, this might involve doing the utmost to insure product safety; providing adequate information to enable consumers to properly use the products they purchase; refraining from coercive tactics when managing a channel of distribution. For example, in Scenario 3, Jones Co. may decide against exporting the controversial soft drinks in order to maximize consumer safety, even though it believes the government's data to be invalid. (p. 21)

Several additional comments about these duties are now in order. First, Ross did not intend his duties to constitute a comprehensive code of ethics. Rather, Ross believed that the list represented several moral obligations which persons incurred above and beyond the law. Thus, *if* a person recognized a prima facie duty, a moral obligation existed which might mandate specific ethical action.

But how does one recognize when a prima facie duty is present? Ross argues that the action required in many situations will be self-evident or obvious. Ross did not mean obvious in the sense of ingrained natural instinct, but rather self-evident in a way that reasonable men would acknowledge the probability that a moral duty is present. For example, in Scenario 1, the distribution manager might inherently accept the argument that the *duty of justice* compels a more equitable distribution of products to the "low income" store, regardless of its managerial complications.

How does a person handle situations where there is a conflict among duties? For example, in Scenario 2, the Chevy dealer's highly emotional, fear-laden advertising may violate the implicit *duty of fidelity* the dealers have with consumers to refrain from manipulative promotion. On the other hand, if the crash test data is accurate, the dealers may feel that the *duty of self improvement* justifies implementing the campaign. How can such conflicts be resolved? Ross is clear, if not completely satisfying, on this point: "It may again be objected that . . . there are these various and often conflicting types of prima facie duty that leave us with no principle upon which to discern what is our actual duty in particular circumstances . . . for when we have to choose . . . the 'ideal utilitarian' theory can only fall back on an opinion . . . that one of the two duties is more urgent" (p. 23). Thus, conflicts among duties are resolved by our own opinion of how the general duties apply after carefully assessing the situation.

The discussion above may lead one to conclude that the Ross framework is rather arbitrary and incomplete. Certainly these are valid criticisms. However, the Ross framework interjects several important insights critical to the practice of ethical marketing. First, the Ross theory encourages managers to determine what their prima facie duties might be and to discharge them unless other such obligations take precedence. Thus, if a marketer knowingly misrepresents product quality to buyers, a *duty of fidelity* has been violated; if sales representatives are let go when their sales fall below quota, a *duty of gratitude* may be violated, and so on. Second, the Ross framework shifts attention in ethically sensitive situations away from *outcomes* (or ends) and toward a priori obligations. Put another way, the model emphasizes the constant moral obligations which *always* exist. It de-emphasizes the approach of attempting to predict results in morally sensitive situations. Such outcome-oriented approaches frequently are used to rationalize potentially unethical behavior. For instance (again alluding to the scenarios), if Jones Co. exports the subsugural laden soft drinks, they may speculate that consumers will not be hurt because the test data are invalid; *or* if Thrifty Supermarket continues its distribution policy, they may decide it is doubtful outsiders will ever know it. Thus, concern with outcomes may prohibit the examination of impending moral duties on the premise that no harm will probably occur.

THE PROPORTIONALITY FRAMEWORK

Another multidimensional model of business ethics has been articulated by Garrett (1966). The framework is distinctive because it was specifically developed with the practicing business manager in mind. In addition, it attempts to combine the appealing utilitarian concern for outcomes ("the greatest good . . .") with the Kantian preoccupation with process or means. Garrett contends that ethical decisions consist of three components: intention, means, and end.

Intention has to do with the motivation behind a person's actions. Garrett believes that what is intended by a particular act is an important component of morality. For example, the organization that formulates a code of marketing ethics motivated solely by the belief that such a code will help sell its products to religious or sectarian organizations, has *not* acted ethically. Thus, purity of intention is a factor in evaluating the ethics of a specific situation.

Means refers to the process or method used to effect intention and bring about specific ends. For example, suppose a sales representative whose family has recently incurred some substantial medical expenses, begins to overstock his customers and pad his expense account. His intention, to relieve the financial distress of his family, is good; however, the means chosen to accomplish this goal is unethical.

Ends deal with outcomes, results, or consequences of actions. Utilitarian theory is based on the precept that the correctness of an action is determined by calculating the end "goodness" resulting from that action compared with the "goodness" produced by alternative actions that could have been taken. Garrett's view is that ends are properly evaluated by analyzing the intrinsic nature of the acts themselves rather than the consequences which these acts produce. Or, put another way, it will not allow permitting the end to justify the means. For example, suppose a brewing company announces that all the revenues from beer sales at a new hotel will be donated to charity. However, suppose the distribution rights at the hotel had been obtained by bribery. In this instance, the ends (a charitable contribution) do not justify the means (bribery).

The above three elements—combining concern for intent (or will), means, and ends—have been synthesized by Garrett (1966) into his *principle of proportionality* which states:

> I am responsible for whatever I will as a means or an end. If both the means and end I am willing are good, in and of themselves, I may ethically permit or risk the foreseen but unwilled side effects if, and only if, I have a proportionate reason for doing so. To put it another way: I am not responsible for unwilled side effects if I have sufficient reason for risking or permitting them, granted always that what I do will, as a means or an end, is good. (p. 8)

This principle raises a number of issues which require clarification. Most important, what is the nature of the side effects which are permitted? Garrett elaborates upon these issues with several amplifications.

1. It is unethical to will, whether as a means or an end, a major evil to another. (p. 12)

By *major evil*, Garrett means the loss of a significant capacity that an entity (i.e., person, organization, etc.) needs to function. For example, in Scenario 3, suppose the substance subsugural had been linked to birth defects when consumed by pregnant women. Jones Co.'s strategy of exporting the product in order to avoid writing off a major financial loss (the end goal) would *not* be ethical because consumption of the Cola would have a reasonable probability of causing a major evil: a significant birth defect in a newborn.

2. It is unethical to risk or permit a major evil to another without a proportional reason. (p. 14)

The concept of "proportionate reason" is the focus here. The principle of proportionality specifies that the risk of an unpleasant side effect is permitted if there is a satisfactory reason for allowing the risk. Or, put another way, a proportionate reason exists when the good willed as means or end equals or outweighs the harmful side effects which are *not* willed as either a means or end. For example, let's again examine the Scenario 3 situation. Suppose Jones Co. researchers knew for a fact that the government studies were invalid and that subsugural would soon be declared benign by the FDA. This would constitute a proportionate reason for going ahead with the soft drink export.

3. It is unethical to will, risk or permit a minor evil without a proportionate reason. (p. 14)

By *minor evil*, Garrett means a harm to physical goods or to some means that are useful but not necessary for an entity's operation. For instance, in Scenario 5, suppose the potential reduction of quality in the Buy American TV sets is such that, even if it occurred, the video and audio difference in the TVs could not be perceived by consumers. In this case, the mi-

nor evil (an unstated quality difference) would be justified by a proportionate reason (higher market share for Buy American and lower prices for consumers).

The above constitutes the essence of the proportionality framework. It must be acknowledged that certain dimensions of the model remain vague or at least subjective. For example, where does one draw the line between a major evil and a minor evil? Attempting to influence a purchasing agent with a pair of $10 sports tickets (Scenario 4) is probably a minor evil. However, if the company receives the contract because of the gift and the competing bidder goes bankrupt, does it become a major evil? Similarly, what constitutes a proportional reason? In Scenario 6, is it a proportionate reason for the financially ailing Smith and Smith agency to take the PR contract knowing that a demur will simply result in another reputable agency doing the work?

Despite these difficulties, the Garrett framework has much to recommend its use. Basically, it provides the marketing manager with a three-phase rough and ready battery of questions which can be used to analyze the ethics of a given situation:

Phase 1: Given the situation, what is willed as means and end? If a major evil is willed, the action is unethical and should not be taken.
Phase 2: Given the situation, what are the foreseen but unwilled side effects? If there is no proportionate reason for risking or allowing a major evil *or* willing a minor evil, the action is unethical and should not be taken.
Phase 3: Given the situation, what are the alternative actions? Is there an alternative to the end which would provide more good consequences and less evil consequences? Not to select this alternative would be unethical.

Notice that the three elements of any ethical decision—intent (will), means, and end—are incorporated into the framework. Moreover, the approach is consistent with the type of analysis many managers already conduct in their planning and forecasting efforts. That is, it involves attempting to predict outcomes of strategies and compare them with alternative options. This lends a dimension of familiarity to the model for planning-oriented managers. Finally, the principle of proportionality provides a flexible model of ethical decision-making; that is, it does not postulate specific trespasses. Rather, it provides general, universal, and applicable guidelines which can be applied to a wide variety of managerial situations.

THE SOCIAL JUSTICE FRAMEWORK

In intellectual circles, one of the most influential books of recent years has been John Rawls' *A Theory of Justice* (1971). Rawls, a Harvard University moral philosopher, proposed a detailed system of social ethics which attempted to maximize rewards to those most disadvantaged in a given social system. Rawls used deductive reasoning to arrive at his conception of social justice.

Central to the Rawls' thesis is the construction of an imaginary state of affairs called the "original position." This hypothetical situation would be somewhat analogous to the time frame *preceding* a game of chance. No participant knows in advance what the game of chance might hold—i.e., if they will be winners or losers. So, too, in the original position, no person knows what their place in society will be once the "game" of life begins. They do not know their social status, educational opportunities, class position, physical or intellectual abilities, etc. They might be king or pauper.

Why is the original position and the "veil of ignorance" it imposes so important? Rawls believes that hypothesizing such a state is the only way to reason to a "pure" system of justice. That is, one which is unblemished by the knowledge of the current state of affairs. For example, if a person knows that he has wealth in the society, that person will likely consider a system which heavily taxes the rich in order to provide for the poor, as unjust. Or, if a person is poor, he will probably feel the opposite. Therefore, what Rawls seeks to obtain from the original position is a vehicle which can be used to deduce an ideal system of justice—one which rational men would choose *if* they knew nothing of what their own station in life might be.

Rawls' entire treatise is devoted to specifying the conclusions or consequences that persons would arrive at for assigning rights and duties in a social system, given the original position. Rawls' arguments defy easy explanation, but basically he concludes that rational men (not knowing what their fortune will be) would utilize a *minimax* method of decision-making. That is, they would choose a system which minimizes the maximum loss which they could incur. In other words, they would opt for a system which seeks to avoid harsh losses (slavery? starvation? indigence?) for those at the bottom of the scale, because conceivably this could be their position.

Rawls concludes that two principles of justice would be arrived at: the *liberty principle* and the *difference principle*.

> The liberty principle states that: *each person is to have an equal right to the most basic liberty compatible with a similar liberty for others.*
>
> The difference principle states that: *social and economic inequalities are to be arranged so that they are both* (a) *to the greatest benefit of the least disadvantaged, and* (b) *attached to positions and offices open to all.* (p. 60)

These principles require some elaboration. The liberty principle guarantees equal opportunity as well as basic liberties such as the freedom of speech, the right to vote, the right to due process of the law, ownership of property, etc. In addition, the principle explicitly states that greater liberty should always be preferred to lesser liberty provided it can be attained without major social dysfunctions. For example, suppose a law specified that airline pilots should be between 40 and 60 years of age, but data showed that this job could be done with the proper training by anyone between 25 and 70; it would be a violation of the principle of liberty to accept the more restricted scheme. Holding that airline pilots must be between 40 and 60 would be unethical to those outside this age bracket who could perform the job. Similarly, an industry code which mandated that all bicycles should be built to withstand crashes with automobiles up to 55 MPH, would also likely violate the principle.

The difference principle specifies the conditions which must exist in order to properly act contrary to the liberty principle. In essence, inequality of economic goods or social position (i.e., the lessening of liberty) can be tolerated only when the practice which generates the inequality works to the advantage of every individual affected *or* to the advantage of those members of the system who are least well off. However, the basic liberties (e.g., the right to vote) can never be traded for economic goods or temporary social position. In this fashion, Rawls' system is a bold contrast to that of classical utilitarianism. Why? Utilitarians would permit some individuals to become worse off so long as a greater number of others become better off. The Rawls' framework claims to prohibit this. It is highly egalitarian in the sense that actions are never permitted which disadvantage the least well off; the tendency instead is a "drive to equality" (pp. 100–108) which over time should benefit those worse off in a particular system more than those better off.

What are the ramifications of the social justice theory upon marketing ethics? In all fairness, it should be emphasized that Rawls did not conceive his theory would be readily transferred to marketing or for that matter business ethics generally. However, the two guiding principles alone seem to suggest some enormous implications. The principle of liberty emphasizes the inherent right of individual persons to determine their own destiny and to always be treated equitably by others. This maximization of personal liberty, subject, of course, to the claims of others, would seem to underscore the consumer's right to safety, information, choice, and redress. Applied to a specific situation, for example Scenario 5, the liberty principle would seem to demand that Buy American Company inform consumers of the change in components and the possible reduction in quality of the second generation System X sets. Not to take this course of action would unfairly restrict the liberty of choice consumers have in this situation.

The difference principle holds an even more striking implication. It emphasizes the fact that it would be unethical to exploit one group for the benefit of others. A particularly severe violation of the principle would occur if a group that was relatively worse off were victimized in order to benefit a better-situated group. For example, in Scenario 6, the difference principle would probably suggest that the Smith and Smith Agency forego the public relations contract because its acceptance could add legitimacy to the ruling foreign government and further jeopardize the position of a worse-off group—the citizens of the totalitarian country. On a more general plane, Rawls' principles would seem to affirm the ethical validity of the marketing concept which formally incorporates the rights of a less powerful group (consumers) into the planning and goal setting of a more powerful group (business).

THE VALUE OF THE FRAMEWORKS

The potential contribution of these frameworks should be clearly stated. First, the purpose of the above perspectives is *not* to provide precise answers to specific ethical dilemmas. In fact, an attempt to apply more than one framework to a particular situation could lead to a conflicting conclusion. For example, in Scenario 1, the Rawlsian would undoubtedly conclude that Thrifty Supermarkets must cease and desist its practice of sending its lower-quality products to the economically inefficient retail store because this allocation scheme further discriminates against the already disadvantaged, lowincome shopper. In contrast, one could argue using the Ross' *duty of gratitude* as a rationale, that Thrifty Supermarkets owes its loyal, upscale customers a special status when it comes to the selection of their meats and produce.

If these frameworks do not answer "tough questions" dealing with marketing ethics, what is their value? Their major purpose is to be used as a pedagogical tool to sensitize managers to the factors that are important in coming to grips with ethical issues. There are few irrefutably "right" answers to these questions. But the fact that management has systematically considered the options along with their ethical ramifications is of ultimate importance. Thus, the contribution of such devices is to provide marketing managers with a philosophical mnemonic which serves to remind them of their ethical responsibilities. The perspectives provided by writers such as Ross, Garrett, and Rawls em-

phasize that the factors involved in reaching an ethical judgment are deeper than the jingoism of ethical maxims of the "Thou shalt be good" caliber.

TOWARD A THEORY
OF MARKETING ETHICS

As noted earlier, there is nothing supernatural about the above frameworks. Their adoption will not automatically generate ethical behavior in marketing, nor do these models explain or predict the incidence of unethical behavior which can occur in marketing. However, taken together, they introduce certain advantages to marketing educators, practitioners, and researchers.

For educators, the frameworks provide perspectives which go beyond the proverbial ethical maxim. The frameworks represent quasi-models of intermediate sophistication that suggest a rationale for why particular moral choices might be made. In this sense, the introduction of this material establishes a useful background for the classroom analysis of marketing cases having ethical implications. Explaining the models to students provides the educator with the opportunity to inject ethical considerations into the discussion of mainstream marketing strategy.

For practitioners, the frameworks suggest a list of possible factors which might be utilized to decide "tough question" situations regarding ethics. Some speculation about the possible application of these frameworks to real-world situations was discussed above. The following is a series of questions designed to determine, in general terms, whether action A constitutes an ethical or an unethical response in a given situation. If the answer to any of the following questions is yes, then action A is most probably unethical, and should be reconsidered; if every question

truly can be answered negatively, then action
A is probably ethical.

Does action A violate the law?
Does action A violate any general moral obligations:
   duties of fidelity?
   duties of gratitude?
   duties of justice?
   duties of beneficence?
   duties of self-improvement?
   duties of nonmaleficence?
Does action A violate any special obligations
stemming from the type of marketing organization in question (e.g., the special duty
of pharmaceutical firms to provide safe
products)?
Is the intent of action A evil?
Are any major evils likely to result from or
because of action A?
Is a satisfactory alternative B, which produces
equal or more good with less evil than A,
being knowingly rejected?
Does action A infringe on the inalienable
rights of the consumer?
Does action A leave another person or group
less well off? Is this person or group already
relatively underprivileged?

The questions need not be pursued in any
lockstep fashion, but rather can be discussed
in an order dictated by the situation.

For researchers, the frameworks may
suggest some of the components necessary for
the construction of a model describing ethical
behavior in marketing. To be sure, such a
model should: (a) specify appropriate standards of ethical action, (b) demarcate the factors, both internal and external, which
influence the likelihood of ethical behavior,
and (c) provide a listing of the organizational
variables which might be adjusted to enhance
the probability of ethical action. In this vein,
the Ross framework identifies some fundamental duties or obligations which are incum-

bent upon managers and thereby would constitute several potential ethical standards. The
Garrett framework, on the other hand, specifies three variables—intention, process (or
means), and outcomes—which the researcher
would have to analyze in order to have a relatively accurate picture of the ethics inherent in
a particular action. It may very well be that
different internal and external variables influence different dimensions of the ethical action. For example, the *attitude of top
management* (an internal factor) may be a major influence upon the process or means a
manager selects to handle an ethical question;
in contrast, *professional standards* (an external
variable) may be a major determinant of a
manager's intent in a given situation. Thus,
Garrett provides insight into the necessary
requisites for empirically measuring the ethics
of a given action. Finally, the Rawls' framework suggests some special considerations
which could be introduced into an ethical
evaluation. Namely, Rawls provides a justification for giving special ethical consideration
to parties which are relatively worse off (i.e.,
socially disadvantaged). Rawls, in effect,
sketches the moral equivalent of "affirmative
action" ethics for marketing managers.

Assuming the frameworks of Ross,
Garrett and Rawls could be integrated into
one grand theory, it is still doubtful that the
theory would constitute a satisfactory model
of marketing ethics. Nevertheless, given the
relevance of ethical questions in marketing, it
is important that marketing academics continue to strive to develop a theory of marketing ethics.

On a more pragmatic level, the frameworks stimulate several suggestions concerning marketing ethics which could have a
beneficial influence at the macro level. First,
Garrett's concern with *major* and *minor* evils
suggests that researchers should attempt to
rank in terms of "severity," the various ethical
abuses that regularly occur in the field of mar-

keting. Since it is naive to believe that significant unethical conduct in marketing can be eliminated overnight, the resulting ranking could constitute a makeshift "hit list" which would then single out particular areas for concern and remedial action. For example, the recent passage of the Foreign Corrupt Practices Act forced most corporations operating overseas to reexamine the propriety of their selling practices. In publicizing areas of acute ethical concern, the marketing discipline could hopefully short circuit the necessity of legislation in order to engender ethical reform.

Second, Ross' compilation of prima facie duties, a listing formulated at the most general level, should motivate textbook writers in marketing to propose a listing of what they consider to be the minimum ethical responsibilities incumbent upon practicing marketing managers. While such specifications will undoubtedly cause some controversy and debate, the subsequent sifting and winnowing will spotlight the topic of ethics and should raise the moral sensitivities of students.

Third, Rawl's concern with the multifaceted impact of business policies upon various groups in society (especially the most disadvantaged) ideally should stimulate casewriters to incorporate ethical problems and analysis into the cases they author. The reason for this is that the case method is the best pedagogical tool for getting the student to visualize the influence of an organizational decision upon sundry stakeholders. Surely an inference which can be drawn from Rawls is that it is the duty of every discipline (including marketing) to foster mechanisms which will generate ethical introspection. The reputation of marketers may depend on it.

REFERENCES

Alderson, Wroe (1964), "Ethics, Ideologies and Sanctions," in *Report of the Committee on Ethical Standards and Professional Practices*, Chicago: American Marketing Association.

Bartels, Robert (1967), "A Model for Ethics in Marketing," *Journal of Marketing*, 31 (January), 20–26.

Beauchamp, Tom L., and Norman E. Bowie (1979), *Ethical Theory and Business*, Englewood Cliffs, NJ: Prentice-Hall.

Colihan, William J., Jr. (1967), "Ethics in Today's Marketing," in *Changing Marketing Systems*, Reed Moyers, ed., Chicago: American Marketing Association, 164–166.

Farmer, Richard N. (1967), "Would You Want Your Daughter to Marry a Marketing Man?" *Journal of Marketing*, 31 (January), 1–3.

——— (1977), "Would You Want Your Son to Marry a Marketing Lady?" *Journal of Marketing*, 41 (January), 15–18.

Ferrell, O. C., and K. Mark Weaver (1978), "Ethical Beliefs of Marketing Managers," *Journal of Marketing*, 42 (July), 69–73.

Fisk, George (1982), "Contributor's Guide for Choice of Topics for Papers," *Journal of Macromarketing*, 2 (Spring), 5–6.

Garrett, Thomas (1966), *Business Ethics*, Englewood Cliffs, NJ: Prentice-Hall.

Hunt, Shelby D. (1976), *Marketing Theory: Conceptual Foundations of Research in Marketing*, Columbus, OH: Grid.

Kelley, Eugene J. (1969), "Ethical Considerations for a Scientifically Oriented Marketing Management," in *Science in Marketing Management*, M. S. Mayer, ed., Toronto, Ontario: York University, 69–87.

Kizelbach, A. H., *et al.* (1979), "Social Auditing for Marketing Managers," *Industrial Marketing Management*, 8, 1–6.

McMahon, Thomas V. (1967), "A Look at Marketing Ethics," *Atlanta Economic Review*, 17 (March).

Murphy, Patrick E., and Gene R. Laczniak (1981), "Marketing Ethics: A Review with Implications for Managers, Educators and Researchers," in *Review of Marketing 1981*, B. Enis and K. Roering, eds., Chicago: American Marketing Association, 251–266.

———, ———, and Robert F. Lusch (1978), "Ethical Guidelines for Business and Social Marketing," *Journal of the Academy of Marketing Science*, 6 (Summer), 197–205.

Patterson, James M. (1966) "What Are the Social and Ethical Responsibilities of Marketing Executives?" *Journal of Marketing*, 30 (July), 12–15.

Pruden, Henry (1971), "Which Ethics for Marketers?" in *Marketing and Social Issues*, John R. Wish and Stephen H. Gamble, eds., New York: John Wiley and Sons, 98–104.

Rawls, John (1971), *A Theory of Justice*, Cambridge: Harvard University Press.

Robin, Donald P. (1980), "Values Issues in Marketing," in *Theoretical Developments in Marketing*, C. W. Lamb and P. M. Dunne, eds., Chicago: American Marketing Association, 142–145.

Ross, William David (1930), *The Right and the Good*, Oxford: Clarendon Press.

Rudelius, William, and Rogene A. Bucholz (1979) "Ethical Problems of Purchasing Managers," *Harvard Business Review*, 55 (March–April), 8, 12, 14.

Sartorius, Rolf E. (1975), *Individual Conduct and Social Norms: A Utilitarian Account of Social Union and Rule of Law*, Belmont, CA: Dickenson Publishing.

Singer, Peter (1976), "Freedoms and Utility in the Distribution of Health Care," in *Ethics and Health Policy*, R. Veatch and R. Branson, eds., Cambridge: Bellinger Publishing.

Steiner, John F. (1976), "The Prospect of Ethical Advisors for Business Corporation," *Business and Society* (Spring), 5–10.

Sturdivant, Frederick D., and A. Benton Cocanougher (1973), "What Are Ethical Marketing Practices?" *Harvard Business Review*, 51 (November–December), 10–12.

Walton, Clarence C. (1961), "Ethical Theory, Societal Expectations and Marketing Practices," in *The Social Responsibilities of Marketing*, William D. Stevens, ed., Chicago: American Marketing Association, 8–24.

Westing, J. Howard (1967), "Some Thoughts on the Nature of Ethics in Marketing," in *Changing Marketing Systems*, Reed Moyer, ed., Chicago: American Marketing Association, 161–163.

◆

Marketing, Strategic Planning and the Theory of the Firm

Paul F. Anderson

Would you tell me, please, which way I ought to go from here? asked Alice.

That depends a good deal on where you want to get to, said the Cat.

I don't much care where, said Alice.

Then it doesn't matter which way you go, said the Cat.

Lewis Carroll —*Alice's Adventures in Wonderland*

The obvious wisdom of the Cheshire's statement reveals an important fact concerning strategic planning: without a clear set of objectives, the planning process is meaningless. Two authorities on the subject refer to strategy as "the major link between the goals and objectives the organization wants to achieve and the various functional area policies and operating plans it uses to guide its day-to-day activities" (Hofer and Schendel 1978, p. 13). Other strategy experts generally agree that the process of goal formulation must operate prior to, but also be interactive

Paul F. Anderson, "Marketing, Strategic Planning and the Theory of the Firm," Vol. 46 (Spring 1982), pp. 15–26. Reprinted from *Journal of Marketing*, published by the American Marketing Association.

with, the process of strategy formulation (Ackoff 1970, Ansoff 1965, Glueck 1976, Newman and Logan 1971). Given the growing interest of marketers in the concept of strategic planning, it would appear fruitful to assess the current state of knowledge concerning goals and the goal formulation process.

Over the years, this general area of inquiry has fallen under the rubric of the "theory of the firm." One objective of this paper is to review some of the major theories of the firm to be found in the literature. The extant theories have emerged in the disciplines of economics, finance and management. To date, marketing has not developed its own comprehensive theory of the firm. Generally, marketers have been content to borrow their concepts of goals and goal formulation from these other disciplines. Indeed, marketing has shown a strange ambivalence toward the concept of corporate goals. The recent marketing literature pays scant attention to the actual content of corporate goal hierarchies. Even less attention is focused on the normative issue of what firm goals and objectives ought to be. Moreover, contemporary marketing texts devote little space to the subject. Typically, an author's perspective on corporate goals is revealed in his/her definition of the marketing concept, but one is hard pressed to find further development of the topic. There is rarely any discussion of how these goals come about or how marketing may participate in the goal formulation process.

This is not to say that received doctrine in marketing has been developed without regard for corporate objectives. The normative decision rules and procedures that have emerged always seek to attain one or more objectives. Thus it could be said that these marketing models implicitly assume a theory of the firm. However, the particular theory that serves as the underpinning of the model is rarely made explicit. More importantly, marketing theorists have devoted little attention to an exploration of the nature and implications of these theories. For example, the product portfolio (Boston Consulting Group 1970, Cordoza and Wind 1980), and PIMS (Buzzell, Gale and Sultan 1975) approaches that are so much in vogue today implicitly assume that the primary objective of the firm is the maximization of return on investment (ROI). This objective seems to have been accepted uncritically by many marketers despite its well-documented deficiencies (e.g., its inability to deal with timing, duration and risk differences among returns and its tendency to create behavioral problems when used as a control device; Hopwood 1976, Van Horne 1980). However, the concern expressed in this paper is not so much that marketers have adopted the wrong objectives, but that the discipline has failed to appreciate fully the nature and implications of the objectives that it has adopted.

As a result, in the last sections of the paper the outline of a new theory of the firm will be presented. It will be argued that the theories of the firm developed within economics, finance and management are inadequate in varying degrees as conceptual underpinnings for marketing. It is asserted that the primary role of a theory of the firm is to act as a kind of conceptual backdrop that functions heuristically to guide further theory development within a particular discipline. As such, the proposed model is less of a theory and more a Kuhnian-style paradigm (Kuhn 1970). Moreover, for a theory of the firm to be fruitful in this respect it must be congruent with the established research tradition of the field (Laudan 1977). It will be demonstrated, for example, that the theories emerging from economics and finance are inconsistent with the philosophical methodology and ontological framework of marketing. However, the proposed model is not only fully consonant with marketing's research tradition, but, unlike existing theories, it explicitly considers marketing's role in corporate goal formulation and strategic planning. Thus it is hoped that the theory will be able to provide a structure to guide future research efforts in these areas.

ECONOMIC THEORIES OF THE FIRM

In this section three theories of the firm are reviewed. The first, the neoclassical model, provides the basic foundation of contemporary microeconomic theory. The second, the market value model, performs a similar function with financial economics. Finally, the agency costs model represents a modification of the market value model to allow a divergence of interests between the owners and managers of the firm. In this sense, it operates as a transitional model between the economically oriented theories of this section and the behavioral theories of the section to follow. However, all three may be classified as economic models since they share the methodological orientation and conceptual framework of economic theory. Note that each postulates an economic objective for the firm and then derives the consequences for firm behavior under different assumption sets.

The Neoclassical Model

The neoclassical theory of the firm can be found in any standard textbook in economics. In its most basic form the theory posits a single product firm operating in a purely competitive environment. Decision making is vested in an owner-entrepreneur whose sole objective is to maximize the dollar amount of the firm's single period profits. Given the standard assumptions of diminishing returns in the short run and diseconomies of scale in the long run, the firm's average cost function will have its characteristic U-shape. The owner's unambiguous decision rule will be to set output at the point where marginal costs equal marginal revenues. The introduction of imperfections in the product market (such as those posited by the monopolistically competitive model) represent mere elaborations on the basic approach. The objective of the firm remains single period profit maximization.

The neoclassical model is well known to marketers. Indeed, it will be argued below that the profit maximization assumption of neoclassical economics underlies much of the normative literature in marketing management. It will be shown that this is true despite the fact that neoclassical theory is inconsistent with the basic research tradition of marketing. Moreover, the neoclassical model suffers from a number of limitations.

For example, the field of finance has challenged the profit maximization assumption because it fails to provide the business decision maker with an operationally feasible criterion for making investment decisions (Solomon 1963). In this regard, it suffers from an inability to consider risk differences among investment alternatives. When risk levels vary across projects, decision criteria that fo-cus only on profitability will lead to suboptimal decisions (Copeland and Weston 1979, Fama and Miller 1972, Van Horne 1980). As a result of these and other problems, financial economists have generally abandoned the neoclassical model in favor of a more comprehensive theory of the firm known as the market value model.

The Market Value Model

Given the assumptions that human wants are insatiable and that capital markets are perfectly competitive, Fama and Miller (1972) show that the objective of the firm should be to maximize its present market value. For a corporation this is equivalent to maximizing the price of the firm's stock. In contrast to the profit maximization objective, the market value rule allows for the consideration of risk differences among alternative investment opportunities. Moreover, the model is applicable to owner-operated firms as well as corporations in which there is likely to be a separation of ownership and control.

The existence of a perfectly competitive capital market allows the firm's management to pursue a single unambiguous objective despite the fact that shareholders are likely to have heterogeneous preferences for current versus future income. If, for example, some stockholders wish more income than the firm is currently paying in dividends, they can sell some of their shares to make up the difference. However, if other shareholders prefer less current income in favor of more future income, they can lend their dividends in the capital markets at interest. In either case shareholder utility will be maximized by a policy that maximizes the value of the firm's stock.

The value maximization objective is implemented within the firm by assessing all multiperiod decision alternatives on the basis of their risk-adjusted net present values

(Copeland and Weston 1979, Fama and Miller 1972, Van Horne 1980):

$$NPV_j = \sum_{i=1}^{n} \frac{A_i}{(1 + k_j)^i} \qquad (1)$$

where NPV_j equals the net present value of alternative j, A_i equals the net after-tax cash flows in year i, n is the expected life of the project in years, and k_i is the risk-adjusted, after-tax required rate of return on j. In the absence of capital rationing, the firm should undertake all projects whose net present values are greater than or equal to zero. Assuming an accurate determination of k_j, this will ensure maximization of the firm's stock price. The discount rate k_j should represent the return required by the market to compensate for the risk of the project. This is usually estimated using a parameter preference model such as the capital asset pricing model or (potentially) the arbitrage model (Anderson 1981). However, it should be noted that there are serious theoretical and practical difficulties associated with the use of these approaches (Anderson 1981; Meyers and Turnbull 1977; Roll 1977; Ross 1976, 1978).

From a marketing perspective this approach requires that all major decisions be treated as investments. Thus the decision to introduce a new product, to expand into new territories, or to adopt a new channel of distribution should be evaluated on the basis of its risk-adjusted net present value. While similar approaches have been suggested in marketing (Cravens, Hills and Woodruff 1980; Dean 1966; Howard 1965; Kotler 1971; Pessemier 1966), it has generally not been recognized that this implies the adoption of shareholder wealth maximization as the goal of the firm. Moreover, these approaches are often offered in piecemeal fashion for the evaluation of selected decisions (e.g., new products), and are not integrated into a consistent and coherent theory of the firm.

Despite the deductive logic of the market value model, there are those who question whether corporate managers are motivated to pursue value maximization. An essential assumption of the market value theory is that stockholders can employ control, motivation and monitoring devices to ensure that managers maximize firm value. However, in the development of their agency theory of the firm, Jensen and Meckling (1976) note that such activities by shareholders are not without cost. As a result, it may not be possible to compel managers to maximize shareholder wealth.

The Agency Costs Model

The separation of ownership and control in modern corporations gives rise to an agency relationship between the stockholders and managers of the firm. An agency relationship may be defined as "a contract under which one or more persons (the principal(s)) engage another person (the agent) to perform some service on their behalf which involves delegating some decision making authority to the agent" (Jensen and Meckling 1976, p. 308). In any relationship of this sort, there is a potential for the agent to expend some of the principal's resources on private pursuits. As such, it will pay the principal to provide the agent with incentives and to incur monitoring costs to encourage a convergence of interests between the objectives of the principal and those of the agent. Despite expenditures of this type, it will generally be impossible to ensure that all of the agent's decisions will be designed to maximize the principal's welfare. The dollar value of the reduction in welfare experienced by the principal along with the expenditures on monitoring activities are costs of the agency relationship. For corporate stockholders these agency costs include the reduction in firm value resulting from management's consumption of nonpecuniary benefits (perquisites) and the costs of hiring outside auditing agents.

The tendency of managers of widely held corporations to behave in this fashion will require the stockholders to incur monitoring costs in an effort to enforce the value maximization objective. Unfortunately, perfect monitoring systems are very expensive. Thus the stockholders face a cost-benefit trade-off in deciding how much to spend on monitoring activities. Since it is unlikely that it will pay the shareholders to implement a "perfect" monitoring system, we will observe corporations suboptimizing on value maximization even in the presence of auditing activities. This leads to implications for managerial behavior that are quite different from those predicted by the market value model. For example, the Fama-Miller model predicts that managers will invest in all projects that will maximize the present value of the firm. However, the agency costs model suggests that management may actually invest in suboptimal projects and may even forego new profitable investments (Barnea, Haugen and Senbet 1981).

The recognition that a firm might not pursue maximization strategies is a relatively new concept to the literature of financial economics. However, in the middle 1950s and early 1960s, various economists and management specialists began to question the neoclassical assumption of single objective maximization on the basis of their observations of managerial behavior. This led directly to the development of the behavioral theory of the firm.

BEHAVIORAL THEORIES OF THE FIRM

In this section two behaviorally oriented theories of the firm will be reviewed. While other approaches could also be included (Bower 1968, Mintzberg 1979), these models will lay the foundation for the development of a constituency-based theory in the last sections of the paper. The first approach is the behavioral model of the firm that emerged at the Carnegie Institute of Technology. The behavioral model can best be understood as a reaction against the neoclassical model of economic theory. The second approach is the resource dependence model of Pfeffer and Salancik (1978). The resource dependence perspective builds on a number of ideas contained in the behavioral model. For example, both approaches stress the coalitional nature of organizations. Moreover, both models emphasize the role of behavioral rather than economic factors in explaining the activities of firms.

The Behavioral Model

The behavioral theory of the firm can be found in the writings of Simon (1955, 1959, 1964), March and Simon (1958), and especially in Cyert and March (1963). The behavioral theory views the business firm as a coalition of individuals who are, in turn, members of subcoalitions. The coalition members include "managers, workers, stockholders, suppliers, customers, lawyers, tax collectors, regulatory agencies, etc." (Cyert and March 1963, p. 27).

The goals of the organization are determined by this coalition through a process of quasi-resolution of conflict. Different coalition members wish the organization to pursue different goals. The resultant goal conflict is not resolved by reducing all goals to a common dimension or by making them internally consistent. Rather, goals are viewed as "a series of independent aspiration-level constraints imposed on the organization by the members of the organizational coalition" (Cyert and March 1963, p. 117).

As Simon (1964) points out, in real world decision making situations acceptable alternatives must satisfy a whole range of requirements or constraints. In his view, singling out one constraint and referring to it as the goal of the activity is essentially arbitrary. This is because in many cases, the set of requirements selected as constraints will have much more to do with the decision outcome than the requirement selected as the goal. Thus he believes that it is more meaningful to refer to the entire set of constraints as the (complex) goal of the organization.

Moreover, these constraints are set at aspiration levels rather than maximization levels. Maximization is not possible in complex organizations because of the existence of imperfect information and because of the computational limitations faced by organizations in coordinating the various decisions made by decentralized departments and divisions. As a result, firm behavior concerning goals may be described as sacrificing rather than maximizing (Simon 1959, 1964).

Cyert and March (1963) see decentralization of decision making leading to a kind of local rationality within subunits of the organization. Since these subunits deal only with a small set of problems and a limited number of goals, local optimization may be possible, but it is unlikely that this will lead to overall optimization. In this regard, the firm not only faces information processing and coordination problems but is also hampered by the fact that it must deal with problems in a sequential fashion. Thus organizational subunits typically attend to different problems at different times, and there is no guarantee that consistent objectives will be pursued in solving these problems. Indeed, Cyert and March agree that the time buffer between decision situations provides the firm with a convenient mechanism for avoiding the explicit resolution of goal conflict.

Thus in the behavioral theory of the firm, goals emerge as "independent constraints imposed on the organization through a process of bargaining among potential coalition members" (Cyert and March 1963, p. 43). These objectives are unlikely to be internally consistent and are subject to change over time as changes take place in the coalition structure. This coalitional perspective has had a significant impact on the development of management thought. Both Mintzberg (1979) and Pfeffer and Salancik (1978) have developed theories of the firm that take its coalitional nature as given. In the following section the resource dependence approach of Pfeffer and Salancik is outlined.

The Resource Dependence Model

Pfeffer and Salancik (1978) view organizations as coalitions of interest which alter their purposes and direction as changes take place in the coalitional structure. Like Mintzberg (1979) they draw a distinction between internal and external coalitions, although they do not use these terms. Internal coalitions may be viewed as groups functioning within the organization (e.g., departments and functional areas). External coalitions include such stakeholder groups as labor, stockholders, creditors, suppliers, government and various interested publics. Pfeffer and Salancik place their primary emphasis on the role of environmental (i.e., external) coalitions in affecting the behavior of organizations. They believe that "to describe adequately the behavior of organizations requires attending to the coalitional nature of organizations and the manner in which organizations respond to pressures from the environment" (Pfeffer and Salancik 1978, p. 24).

The reason for the environmental focus of the model is that the survival of the organization ultimately depends on its ability to obtain resources and support from its external coalitions. Pfeffer and Salancik implicitly assume that survival is the ultimate goal of the organization and that to achieve this objective, the organization must maintain a coalition of parties willing to "legitimize" its existence (Dowling and Pfeffer 1975, Parsons 1960). To do this, the organization offers various inducements in exchange for contributions of resources and support (Barnard 1938, March and Simon 1958, Simon 1964).

However, the contributions of the various interests are not equally valued by the organization. As such, coalitions that provide "behaviors, resources and capabilities that are most needed or desired by other organizational participants come to have more influence and control over the organization" (Pfeffer and Salancik 1978, p. 27). Similarly, organizational subunits (departments, functional areas, etc.) which are best able to deal with critical contingencies related to coalitional contributions are able to enhance their influence in the organization.

A common problem in this regard is that the various coalitions make conflicting demands on the organization. Since the satisfaction of some demands limits the satisfaction of others, this leads to the possibility that the necessary coalition of support cannot be maintained. Thus organizational activities can be seen as a response to the constraints imposed by the competing demands of various coalitions.

In attempting to maintain the support of its external coalitions, the organization must negotiate exchanges that ensure the continued supply of critical resources. At the same time, however, it must remain flexible enough to respond to environmental contingencies. Often these objectives are in conflict, since the desire to ensure the stability and certainty of resource flows frequently leads to activities limiting flexibility and autonomy.

For example, backward integration via merger or acquisition is one way of coping with the uncertainty of resource dependence. At the same time, however, this method of stabilizing resource exchanges limits the ability of the firm to adapt as readily to environmental contingencies. Pfeffer and Salancik suggest that many other activities of organizations can be explained by the desire for stable resource exchanges, on the one hand, and the need for flexibility and autonomy on the other. They present data to support their position that joint ventures, interlocking directorates, organizational growth, political involvement and executive succession can all be interpreted in this light. Other activities such as secrecy, multiple sourcing and diversification can also be interpreted from a resource dependence perspective.

Thus the resource dependence model views organizations as "structures of coordinated behaviors" whose ultimate aim is to garner the necessary environmental support for survival (Pfeffer and Salancik 1978, p. 32). As in the behavioral model, it is recognized that goals and objectives will emerge as constraints imposed by the various coalitions of interests. However, the resource dependence model interprets these constraints as demands by the coalitions that must be met in order to maintain the existence of the organization.

RESEARCH TRADITIONS AND THE THEORY OF THE FIRM

In reflecting on the various theories of the firm presented herein, it is important to recognize that one of their primary roles is to function as a part of what Laudan calls a "research tradition" (Laudan 1977). A research tradition consists of a set of assumptions shared by researchers in a particular domain. Its main purpose is to provide a set of guidelines for theory development. In so doing it provides the researcher with both an ontological framework and a philosophical methodology.

The ontology of the research tradition defines the kinds of entities that exist within the domain of inquiry. For example, in the neoclassical model such concepts as middle management, coalitions, bureaucracy and reward systems do not exist. They fall outside the ontology of neoclassical economics. Similarly, the concepts of the entrepreneur, diminishing returns and average cost curves do not exist (or at least are not used) in the resource dependence model. The ontology of the research tradition defines the basic conceptual building blocks of its constituent theories.

The philosophical methodology, on the other hand, specifies the procedure by which concepts will be used to construct a theory. Moreover, it determines the way in which the concepts will be viewed by theorists working within the research tradition. For example, the neoclassical, market value and agency costs models have been developed in accordance with a methodology that could be characterized as deductive instrumentalism. The models are deductive in that each posits a set of assumptions or axioms (including assumptions about firm goals) from which implications for firm behavior are deduced as logical consequences (Hempel 1965, p. 336). The models are also instrumentalist in that their component concepts are not necessarily assumed to have real world referents. Instrumentalism views theories merely as calculating devices that generate useful predictions (Feyerabend 1964, Morgenbesser 1969, Popper 1963). The reality of a theory's assumptions or its concepts is irrelevant from an instrumentalist point of view.

It is essentially this aspect of economic instrumentalism that has drawn the most criticism from both economists and noneconomists. Over 30 years ago concerns for the va-

lidity of theory among economists emerged as the famous "marginalism controversy" which raged in the pages of the *American Economic Review* (Lester 1946, 1947; Machlup 1946, 1947; Stigler 1946, 1947). More recently, much of the criticism has come from proponents of the behavioral theory of the firm (Cyert and March 1963, Cyert and Pottinger 1979). Perhaps the most commonly heard criticism of the neoclassical model is that the assumption of a rational profit-maximizing decision maker who has access to perfect information is at considerable variance with the real world of business management (Cyert and March 1963, Simon 1955). Moreover, these critics fault the "marginalists" for concocting a firm with "no complex organization, no problems of control, no standard operating procedures, no budget, no controller [and] no aspiring middle management" (Cyert and March 1963, p. 8). In short, the business firm assumed into existence by neoclassical theory bears little resemblance to the modern corporate structure.

Concerns with the realism of assumptions in neoclassical theory have been challenged by Friedman (1953) and Machlup (1967). In Friedman's classic statement of the "positivist" viewpoint, he takes the position that the ultimate test of a theory is the correspondence of its predictions with reality. From Friedman's perspective the lack of realism in a theory's assumptions is unrelated to the question of its validity.

Machlup, in a closely related argument, notes that much of the criticism of neoclassical theory arises because of a confusion concerning the purposes of the theory (1967). He points out that the "firm" in neoclassical analysis is nothing more than a theoretical construct that is useful in predicting the impact of changes in economic variables on the behavior of firms in the aggregate. For example, the neoclassical model performs well in predicting the *direction* of price changes in an industry that experiences an increase in wage rates or the imposition of a tax. It does less well, however, in explaining the complex process by which a particular firm decides to implement a price change. Of course, this is to be expected since the theory of the firm was never intended to predict the real world behavior of individual firms.

Thus the question of whether corporations really seek to maximize profits is of no concern to the economic instrumentalist. Following Friedman, the only consideration is whether such assumptions lead to "sufficiently accurate predictions" of real world phenomena (1953, p. 15). Similarly, the financial economist is unmoved by criticism related to the lack of reality in the market value and agency cost models. The ultimate justification of the theory from an instrumental viewpoint comes from the accuracy of its predictions.

In contrast to the instrumentalism of the first three theories of the firm, the behavioral and resource dependence models have been developed from the perspective of realism. The realist believes that theoretical constructs should have real world analogs and that theories should describe "what the world is really like" (Chalmers 1978, p. 114). Thus, it is not unexpected that these models are essentially inductive in nature. Indeed, in describing their methodological approach Cyert and March state that they "propose to make detailed observations of the procedures by which firms make decisions and to use these observations as a basis for a theory of decision making within business organizations" (1963, p. 1).

Thus it can be seen that the theories of the firm that have been developed in economics and financial economics emerged from a very different research tradition than the behaviorally oriented theories developed in management. This fact becomes particularly significant in considering their adequacy as a framework for marketing theory development. For example, the discipline of market-

ing appears to be committed to a research tradition dominated by the methodology of inductive realism, yet it frequently employs the profit maximization paradigm of neoclassical economic theory. Despite the recent trend toward the incorporation of social objectives in the firm's goal hierarchy, and the recognition by many authors that firms pursue multiple objectives, profit or profit maximization figures prominently as the major corporate objective in leading marketing texts (Boone and Kurtz 1980, p. 12; Markin 1979, p. 34; McCarthy 1978, p. 29; Stanton 1978, p. 13). More significantly perhaps, profit maximization is the implicit or explicit objective of much of the normative literature in marketing management. While the terms may vary from return on investment to contribution margin, cash flow or cumulative compounded profits, they are all essentially profit maximization criteria. Thus such widely known and accepted approaches as product portfolio analysis (Boston Consulting Group 1970), segmental analysis (Mossman, Fischer and Crissy 1974), competitive bidding models (Simon and Freimer 1970), Bayesian pricing procedures (Green 1963), and many others all adhere to the profit maximization paradigm. It may seem curious that a discipline that drifted away from the research tradition of economics largely because of a concern for greater "realism" (Hutchinson 1952, Vaile 1950) should continue to employ one of its most "unrealistic" assumptions. In effect, marketing has rejected much of the philosophical methodology of economics while retaining a significant portion of its ontology.

It would seem that what is required is the development of a theory of the firm that is consistent with the existing research tradition of marketing. Such a theory should deal explicitly with the role of marketing in the firm and should attempt to explicate its relationship with the other functional areas (Wind 1981) and specify its contribution to the formation of corporate "goal structures" (Richards 1978). In this way it would provide a framework within which marketing theory development can proceed. This is particularly important for the development of theory within the area of strategic planning. It is likely that greater progress could be made in this area if research is conducted within the context of a theory of the firm whose methodological and ontological framework is consistent with that of marketing.

TOWARD A CONSTITUENCY-BASED THEORY OF THE FIRM

The theory of the firm to be outlined in this section focuses explicitly on the roles performed by the various functional areas found in the modern corporation. There are basically two reasons for this. First, theory development in business administration typically proceeds within the various academic disciplines corresponding (roughly) to the functional areas of the firm. It is felt that a theory explicating the role of the functional areas will be of greater heuristic value in providing a framework for research within these disciplines (and within marketing in particular).

Second, a theory of the firm that does not give explicit recognition to the activities of these functional subunits fails to appreciate their obvious importance in explaining firm behavior. As highly formalized internal coalitions operating at both the corporate and divisional levels, they often share a common frame of reference and a relatively consistent set of goals and objectives. These facts make the functional areas an obvious unit of analysis in attempting to explain the emergence of goals in corporations.

The proposed theory adopts the coalitional perspectives of the various behaviorally oriented theories of the firm and relies especially on the resource dependence model. As a matter of analytical convenience, the theory divides an organization into both internal and external coalitions. From a resource dependence perspective, the task of the organization is to maintain itself by negotiating resource exchanges with external interests. Over time the internal coalitions within corporate organizations have adapted themselves to enhance the efficiency and effectiveness with which they perform these negotiating functions. One approach that has been taken to accomplish this is specialization. Thus certain coalitions within the firm may be viewed as specialists in negotiating exchanges with certain external coalitions. By and large these internal coalitions correspond to the major functional areas of the modern corporate structure.

For example, industrial relations and personnel specialize in negotiating resource exchanges with labor coalitions; finance, and to a lesser extent, accounting specialize in negotiating with stockholder and creditor groups; materials management and purchasing specialize in supplier group exchanges; and, of course, marketing specializes in negotiating customer exchanges. In addition, public relations, legal, tax and accounting specialize to a greater or lesser extent in negotiating the continued support and sanction of both government and public coalitions. In most large corporations the production area no longer interacts directly with the environment. With the waning of the production orientation earlier in this century, production gradually lost its negotiating functions to specialists such as purchasing and industrial relations on the input side and sales or marketing on the output side.

The major resources that the firm requires for survival include cash, labor and material. The major sources of cash are customers, stockholders and lenders. It is, therefore, the responsibility of marketing and finance to ensure the required level of cash flow in the firm. Similarly, it is the primary responsibility of industrial relations to supply the labor, and materials management and purchasing to supply the material necessary for the maintenance, growth and survival of the organization.

As Pfeffer and Salancik point out, external coalitions that control vital resources have greater control and influence over organizational activities (1978, p. 27). By extension, functional areas that negotiate vital resource exchanges will come to have greater power within the corporation as well. Thus, the dominance of production and finance in the early decades of this century may be attributed to the fact that nearly all vital resource exchanges were negotiated by these areas. The ascendence, in turn, of such subunits as industrial relations and personnel (Meyer 1980), marketing (Keith 1960), purchasing and materials management (Keith 1960), purchasing and materials management (*Business Week* 1975) and public relations (Kotler and Mindak 1978) can be explained in part by environmental changes which increased the importance of effective and efficient resource exchanges with the relevant external coalitions. For example, the growth of unionism during the 1930s did much to enhance the role and influence of industrial relations departments in large corporations. Similarly, the improved status of sales and marketing departments during this same period may be linked to environmental changes including the depressed state of the economy, the rebirth of consumerism, and a shift in demand away from standardized "Model-T type products" (Ansoff 1979, p. 32). More recently, the OPEC oil embargo, the institutionalization of consumerism, and the expansion of government regulation into new areas (OSHA, Foreign Corrupt Practices Act, Affirmative Action, etc.) have had a similar impact on such areas as purchasing, public relations and legal.

Thus the constituency-based model views the major functional areas as specialists in providing particular resources for the firm. The primary objective of each area is to ensure an uninterrupted flow of resources from the appropriate external coalition. As functional areas tend to become specialized in dealing with particular coalitions, they tend to view these groups as constituencies both to be served and managed. From this perspective, the chief responsibility of the marketing area is to satisfy the long-term needs of its customer coalition. In short, it must strive to implement the marketing concept (Keith 1960, Levitt 1960, McKitterick 1957).

Of course, in seeking to achieve its own objectives, each functional area is constrained by the objectives of the other departments. In attempting to assure maximal consumer satisfaction as a means of maintaining the support of its customer coalition, marketing will be constrained by financial, technical and legal considerations imposed by the other functional areas. For example, expenditures on new product development, market research and advertising cut into the financial resources necessary to maintain the support of labor, supplier, creditor and investor coalitions. When these constraints are embodied in the formal performance measurement system, they exert a significant influence on the behavior of the functional areas.

In this model, firm objectives emerge as a series of Simonian constraints that are negotiated among the various functions. Those areas that specialize in the provision of crucial resources are likely to have greater power in the negotiation process. In this regard, the marketing area's desire to promote the marketing concept as a philosophy of the entire firm may be interpreted by the other functional areas as a means of gaining bargaining leverage by attempting to impress them with the survival value of customer support. The general failure of the other areas to embrace this philosophy may well reflect their belief in the importance of their own constituencies.

Recently, the marketing concept has also been called into question for contributing to the alleged malaise of American business. Hayes and Abernathy (1980) charge that excessive emphasis on marketing, research and short-term financial control measures has led to the decline of U.S. firms in world markets. They argue that American businesses are losing more and more of their markets to European and Japanese firms because of a failure to remain technologically competitive. They believe that the reliance of American firms on consumer surveys and ROI control encourages a low-risk, short run investment philosophy, and point out that market research typically identifies consumers' current desires but is often incapable of determining their future wants and needs. Moreover, the short run focus of ROI measures and the analytical detachment inherent in product portfolio procedures tends to encourage investment in fast payback alternatives. Thus Hayes and Abernathy believe that American firms are reluctant to make the higher risk, longer-term investments in new technologies necessary for effective competition in world markets. They feel that the willingness of foreign firms to make such investments can be attributed to their need to look beyond their relatively small domestic markets for success. This has encouraged a reliance on technically superior products and a longer-term payoff perspective.

From a resource dependence viewpoint the Hayes and Abernathy argument seems to suggest that the external coalitions of U.S. firms are rather myopic. If the survival of the firm is truly dependent on the adoption of a longer-term perspective, one would expect this to be forced on the firm by its external coalitions. Indeed, there is ample evidence from stock market studies that investor coali-

tions react sharply to events affecting the longer run fortunes of firms (Lev 1974, Lorie and Hamilton 1973). Moreover, recent concessions by government, labor and supplier coalitions to Chrysler Corporation suggest a similar perspective among these groups.

However, the real problem is not a failure by internal and external coalitions in recognizing the importance of a long run investment perspective. The real difficulty lies in designing an internal performance measurement and reward system that balances the need for short run profitability against long-term survival. A number of factors combine to bias these reward and measurement systems in favor of the short run. These include:

- Requirements for quarterly and annual reports of financial performance.
- The need to appraise and reward managers on an annual basis.
- The practical difficulties of measuring and rewarding the long-term performance of highly mobile management personnel.
- Uncertainty as to the relative survival value of emphasis on short run versus long run payoffs.

As a result of these difficulties, we find that in many U.S. firms the reward system focuses on short run criteria (Ouchi 1981). This naturally leads to the use of short-term financial control measures and an emphasis on market surveys designed to measure consumer reaction to immediate (and often minor) product improvements. In some cases the marketing area has adopted this approach in the name of the marketing concept.

However, as Levitt (1960) noted more than two decades ago, the real lesson of the marketing concept is that successful firms are able to recognize the fundamental and enduring nature of the customer needs they are attempting to satisfy. As numerous case studies point out, it is the *technology* of want satisfaction that is transitory. The long-run investment perspective demanded by Hayes and Abernathy is essential for a firm that focuses its attention on transportation rather than trains, entertainment rather than motion pictures, or energy rather than oil. The real marketing concept divorces strategic thinking from an emphasis on contemporary technology and encourages investments in research and development with long-term payoffs. Thus, the "market-driven" firms that are criticized by Hayes and Abernathy have not really embraced the marketing concept. These firms have simply deluded themselves into believing that consumer survey techniques and product portfolio procedures automatically confer a marketing orientation on their adopters. However, the fundamental insight of the marketing concept has little to do with the use of particular analytical techniques. The marketing concept is essentially a state of mind or world view that recognizes that firms survive to the extent that they meet the real needs of their customer coalitions. As argued below, one of the marketing area's chief functions in the strategic planning process is to communicate this perspective to top management and the other functional areas.

IMPLICATIONS FOR STRATEGIC PLANNING

From a strategic planning perspective, the ultimate objective of the firm may be seen as an attempt to position itself for long run survival (Wind 1979). This, in turn, is accomplished as each functional area attempts to determine the position that will ensure a continuing supply of vital resources. Thus the domestic auto industry's belated downsizing of its product may be viewed as an attempt to ensure the support of its customer coalition in the 1980s and 1990s (just as its grudging acceptance of the UAW in the late 1930s and early 1940s

reflected a need to ensure a continuing supply of labor).

Of course, a firm's functional areas may not be able to occupy all of the favored long run positions simultaneously. Strategic conflicts will arise as functional areas (acting as units at the corporate level or as subunits at the divisional level) vie for the financial resources necessary to occupy their optimal long-term positions. Corporate management as the final arbiter of these disputes may occasionally favor one area over another, with deleterious results. Thus, John De Lorean, former group executive at General Motors, believes that the firm's desire for the short run profits available from larger cars was a major factor in its reluctance to downsize in the 1970s (Wright 1979). He suggests that an overwhelming financial orientation among GM's top executives consistently led them to favor short run financial gain over longer-term marketing considerations. Similarly, Hayes and Abernathy (1980) believe that the growing dominance of financial and legal specialists within the top managements of large U.S. corporations has contributed to the slighting of technological considerations in product development.

Against this backdrop marketing must realize that its role in strategic planning is not preordained. Indeed, it is possible that marketing considerations may not have a significant impact on strategic plans unless marketers adopt a strong advocacy position within the firm (Mason and Mitroff 1981). On this view, strategic plans are seen as the outcome of a bargaining process among functional areas. Each area attempts to move the corporation toward what it views as the preferred position for long run survival, subject to the constraints imposed by the positioning strategies of the other functional units.

This is not to suggest, however, that formal-analytical procedures have no role to play in strategic planning. Indeed, as Quinn's

(1981) research demonstrates, the actual process of strategy formulation in large firms is best described as a combination of the formal-analytical and power-behavioral approaches. He found that the formal planning system often provides a kind of infrastructure that assists in the strategy development and implementation process, although the formal system itself rarely generates new or innovative strategies. Moreover, the study shows that strategies tend to emerge incrementally over relatively long periods of time. One reason for this is the need for top management to obtain the support and commitment of the firm's various coalitions through constant negotiation and implied bargaining (Quinn 1981, p. 61).

Thus, from a constituency-based perspective, marketing's role in strategic planning reduces to three major activities. First, at both the corporate and divisional levels it must identify the optimal long-term position or positions that will assure customer satisfaction and support. An optimal position would reflect marketing's perception of what its customers' wants and needs are likely to be over the firm's strategic time horizon. Since this will necessarily involve long run considerations, positioning options must be couched in somewhat abstract terms. Thus the trend toward smaller cars by the domestic auto industry represents a very broad response to changing environmental, social and political forces and will likely affect the industry well into the 1990s. Other examples include the diversification into alternate energy sources by the petroleum industry, the movement toward "narrowcasting" by the major networks, and the down-sizing of the single family home by the construction industry. The length of the time horizons involved suggests that optimal positions will be determined largely by fundamental changes in demographic, economic, social and political factors. Thus strategic positioning is more likely to be guided by long-term demographic and socioeconomic research (Lazer 1977) than by surveys of consumer attitudes.

Marketing's second major strategic planning activity involves the development of strategies designed to capture its preferred positions. This will necessarily involve attempts to gain a competitive advantage over firms pursuing similar positioning strategies. Moreover, the entire process is likely to operate incrementally. Specific strategies will focus on somewhat shorter time horizons and will be designed to move the firm toward a particular position without creating major dislocations within the firm or the marketplace (Quinn 1981). Research on consumers' current preferences must be combined with demographic and socioeconomic research to produce viable intermediate strategies. For example, Detroit's strategy of redesigning all of its subcompact lines has been combined with improved fuel efficiency in its larger cars (*Business Week* 1980).

Finally, marketing must negotiate with top management and the other functional areas to implement its strategies. The coalition perspective suggests that marketing must take an active role in promoting its strategic options by demonstrating the survival value of a consumer orientation to the other internal coalitions.

Marketing's objective, therefore, remains long run customer support through consumer satisfaction. Paradoxically, perhaps, this approach requires marketers to have an even greater grasp of the technologies, perspectives and limitations of the other functional areas. Only in this way can marketing effectively negotiate the implementation of its strategies. As noted previously, the other functional areas are likely to view appeals to the marketing concept merely as a bargaining ploy. It is the responsibility of the marketing area to communicate the true long run focus and survival orientation of this concept to the other interests in the firm. However, this cannot be accomplished if the marketing function itself does not understand the unique orientations and decision methodologies employed by other departments.

For example, the long run investment perspective implicit in the marketing concept can be made more comprehensive to the financial coalition if it is couched in the familiar terms of capital budgeting analysis. Moreover, the marketing area becomes a more credible advocate for this position if it eschews the use of short-term ROI measures as its sole criterion for internal decision analysis. At the same time, an appreciation for the inherent limitations of contemporary capital investment procedures will give the marketing area substantial leverage in the negotiation process (Anderson 1981).

In the final analysis, the constituency model of the firm suggests that marketing's role in strategic planning must be that of a strong advocate for the marketing concept. Moreover, its advocacy will be enhanced to the extent that it effectively communicates the true meaning of the marketing concept in terms that are comprehensible to other coalitions in the firm. This requires an intimate knowledge of the interests, viewpoints and decision processes of these groups. At the same time, a better understanding of the true nature of the constraints imposed by these interests will allow the marketing organization to make the informed strategic compromises necessary for firm survival.

REFERENCES

Ackoff, Russell (1970), *A Concept of Corporate Planning*, New York: John Wiley & Sons.

Anderson, Paul F. (1981), "Marketing Investment Analysis," in *Research in Marketing*, 4, Jagdish N. Sheth, ed., Greenwich, CT: JAI Press, 1–37.

Ansoff, Igor H. (1965), *Corporate Strategy*, New York: McGraw-Hill.

———— (1979), "The Changing Shape of the Strategic Problem," in *Strategic Management: A View of Business Policy and Planning*, Dan E. Schendel and Charles W. Hofer, eds., Boston: Little, Brown and Company, 30–44.

Barnard, Chester I. (1938), *The Functions of the Executive*, London: Oxford University Press.

Barnea, Amir, Robert A. Haugen and Lemma W. Senbet (1981), "Market Imperfections, Agency Problems and Capital Structure: A Review," *Financial Management*, 10 (Summer), 7–22.

Boone, Louis E. and David L. Kurtz (1980), *Foundations of Marketing*, 3rd ed., Hinsdale, IL: Dryden Press.

Boston Consulting Group (1970), *The Product Portfolio*, Boston: The Boston Consulting Group.

Bower, Joseph L. (1968), "Descriptive Decision Theory from the 'Administrative' Viewpoint," in *The Study of Policy Formation*, Raymond A. Bauer and Kenneth J. Gergen, eds., New York: Collier-Macmillan, 103–148.

Business Week (1975), "The Purchasing Agent Gains More Clout," (January 13), 62–63.

———— (1980), "Detroit's New Sales Pitch," (September 22), 78–83.

Buzzell, Robert D., Bradley T. Gale and Ralph G. M. Sultan (1975), "Market Share: A Key to Profitability," *Harvard Business Review*, 53 (January–February), 97–106.

Cardozo, Richard and Yoram Wind (1980), "Portfolio Analysis for Strategic Product—Market Planning," working paper, The Wharton School, University of Pennsylvania.

Chalmers, A. F. (1978), *What Is This Thing Called Science?* St. Lucia, Australia: University of Queensland Press.

Copeland, Thomas E. and J. Fred Weston (1979), *Financial Theory and Corporate Policy*, Reading, MA: Addison-Wesley Publishing Company.

Cravens, David W., Gerald E. Hills and Robert B. Woodruff (1980), *Marketing Decision Making*, rev. ed., Homewood, IL: Richard D. Irwin.

Cyert, Richard M. and James G. March (1963), *A Behavioral Theory of the Firm*, Englewood Cliffs, NJ: Prentice-Hall.

———— and Garrel Pottinger (1979), "Towards a Better Microeconomic Theory," *Philosophy of Science*, 46 (June), 204–222.

Dean, Joel (1966), "Does Advertising Belong in the Capital Budget?" *Journal of Marketing*, 30 (October), 15–21.

Dowling, John and Jeffrey Pfeffer (1975), "Organizational Legitimacy," *Pacific Sociological Review,* 18 (January), 122–36.

Fama, Eugene and Merton H. Miller (1972), *The Theory of Finance,* Hinsdale, IL: Dryden Press.

Feyerabend, Paul K. (1964), "Realism and Instrumentalism: Comments on the Logic of Factual Support," in *The Critical Approach to Science and Philosophy,* Mario Bunge, ed., London: The Free Press of Glencoe, 280–308.

Friedman, Milton (1953), "The Methodology of Positive Economics," in *Essays in Positive Economics,* Chicago: University of Chicago Press.

Glueck, William (1970), *Policy, Strategy Formation and Management Action,* New York: McGraw-Hill.

Green, Paul E. (1963), "Bayesian Decision Theory in Pricing Strategy," *Journal of Marketing,* 27 (January), 5–14.

Hayes, Robert H. and William J. Abernathy (1980), "Managing Our Way to Economic Decline," *Harvard Business Review,* 58 (July–August), 67–77.

Hempel, Carl G. (1965), *Aspects of Scientific Explanation,* New York: Macmillan Publishing Co.

Hofer, Charles W. and Dan Schendel (1978), *Strategy Formulation: Analytical Concepts,* St. Paul, MN: West Publishing Company.

Hopwood, Anthony (1976), *Accounting and Human Behavior,* Englewood Cliffs, NJ: Prentice-Hall.

Howard, John A. (1965), *Marketing Theory,* Boston: Allyn and Bacon.

Hutchinson, Kenneth D. (1952), "Marketing as a Science: An Appraisal," *Journal of Marketing,* 16 (January), 286–93.

Jensen, Michael C. and William H. Meckling (1976), "Theory of the Firm: Managerial Behavior, Agency Costs and Ownership Structure," *Journal of Financial Economics,* 3 (October), 305–60.

Keith, Robert J. (1960), "The Marketing Revolution," *Journal of Marketing,* 24 (January), 35–38.

Kotler, Philip (1971), *Marketing Decision Making,* New York: Holt, Rinehart and Winston.

_____ and William Mindak (1978), "Marketing and Public Relations," *Journal of Marketing,* 42 (October), 13–20.

Kuhn, Thomas S. (1970), *The Structure of Scientific Revolutions,* 2nd ed., Chicago: University of Chicago Press.

Laudan, Larry (1977), *Progress and Its Problems,* Berkeley, CA: University of California Press.

Lazer, William (1977), "The 1980's and Beyond: A Perspective," *MSU Business Topics,* 25 (Spring), 21–35.

Lester, R. A. (1946), "Shortcomings of Marginal Analysis for Wage-Employment Problems," *American Economic Review,* 36 (March) 63–82.

_____ (1947), "Marginalism, Minimum Wages, and Labor Markets," *American Economic Review,* 37 (March), 135–48.

Lev, Baruch (1974), *Financial Statement Analysis: A New Approach,* Englewood Cliffs, NJ: Prentice-Hall.

Levitt, Theodore (1960), "Marketing Myopia," *Harvard Business Review,* 38 (July–August), 24–47.

Lorie, James H. and Mary T. Hamilton (1973), *The Stock Market: Theories and Evidence,* Homewood, IL: Richard D. Irwin.

Machlup, Fritz (1946), "Marginal Analysis and Empirical Research," *American Economic Review,* 36 (September), 519–54.

_____ (1947), "Rejoinder to an Antimarginalist," *American Economic Review,* 37 (March), 148–54.

_____ (1967), "Theories of the Firm: Marginalist, Behavioral, Managerial," *American Economic Review,* 57 (March), 1–33.

March, James G. and Herbert A. Simon (1958), *Organizations,* New York: John Wiley & Sons.

Markin, Rom (1979), *Marketing,* New York: John Wiley & Sons.

Mason, Richard O. and Ian I. Mitroff (1981), "Policy Analysis as Argument," working paper, University of Southern California.

McCarthy, E. Jerome (1978), *Basic Marketing,* 6th ed., Homewood, IL: Richard D. Irwin.

McKitterick, J. B. (1957), "What Is the Marketing Management Concept?" in *Readings in Marketing 75/76,* Guilford, CT: Dushkin Publishing Group, 23–26.

Meyer, Herbert E. (1980), "Personnel Directors Are the New Corporate Heros," in *Current Issues in Personnel Management,* Kendrith M. Rowland et al., eds., Boston: Allyn and Bacon, 2–8.

Meyers, Stewart C. and Stuart M. Turnbull (1977), "Capital Budgeting and the Capital Asset Pricing Model: Good News and Bad News," *Journal of Finance,* 32 (May), 321–336.

Mintzberg, Henry (1979), "Organizational Power and Goals: A Skeletal Theory," in *Strategic Management,* Dan E. Schendel and Charles W. Hofer, eds., Boston: Little, Brown and Company.

Morgenbesser, Sidney (1969), "The RealistInstrumentalist Controversy," in *Philosophy, Science and Method*, New York: St. Martin's Press, 200–18.

Mossman, Frank H., Paul M. Fischer and W. J. E. Crissy (1974), "New Approaches to Analyzing Marketing Profitability," *Journal of Marketing*, 38 (April), 43–48.

Newman, William H. and James P. Logan (1971), *Strategy, Policy and Central Management*, Cincinnati: South-Western Publishing Company.

Ouchi, William G. (1981), *Theory Z*, Reading, MA: Addison-Wesley.

Parsons, Talcott (1960), *Structure and Process in Modern Societies*, New York: Free Press.

Pessemier, Edgar A. (1966), *New-Product Decisions: An Analytical Approach*, New York: McGraw-Hill.

Pfeffer, Jeffrey and Gerald R. Salancik (1978), *The External Control of Organizations*, New York: Harper and Row.

Popper, Karl R. (1963), *Conjectures and Refutations*, New York: Harper & Row.

Quinn, James Brian (1981), "Formulating Strategy One Step at a Time," *Journal of Business Strategy*, 1 (Winter), 42–63.

Richards, Max D. (1978), *Organizational Goal Structures*, St. Paul: West Publishing Company.

Roll, Richard (1977), "A Critique of the Asset Pricing Theory's Tests: Part I," *Journal of Financial Economics*, 4 (March), 129–76.

Ross, Stephen A. (1976), "The Arbitrage Theory of Capital Asset Pricing," *Journal of Economic Theory*, 13 (December), 341–60.

—— (1978), "The Current Status of the Capital Asset Pricing Model (CAPM)," *Journal of Finance*, 33 (June), 885–901.

Simon, Herbert A. (1955), "A Behavioral Model of Rational Choice," *Quarterly Journal of Economics*, 69 (February), 99–118.

—— (1959), "Theories of Decision Making in Economics and Behavioral Science," *American Economic Review*, 49 (June), 253–83.

—— (1964), "On the Concept of Organizational Goal," *Administrative Science Quarterly*, 9 (June), 1–22.

Simon, Leonard S. and Marshall Freimer (1970), *Analytical Marketing*, New York: Harcourt, Brace & World.

Solomon, Ezra (1963), *The Theory of Financial Management*, New York: Columbia University Press.

Stanton, William J. (1978), *Fundamentals of Marketing*, 5th ed., New York: McGraw-Hill.

Stigler, G. J. (1946), "The Economics of Minimum Wage Legislation," *American Economic Review*, 36 (June), 358–65.

—— (1947), "Professor Lester and the Marginalists," *American Economic Review*, 37 (March), 154–57.

Vaile, Roland S. (1950), "Economic Theory and Marketing," in *Theory in Marketing*, Reavis Cox and Wroe Alderson, eds., Chicago: Richard D. Irwin.

Van Horne, James C. (1980), *Financial Management and Policy*, 5th ed., Englewood Cliffs, NJ: Prentice-Hall.

Wind, Yoram (1979), "Product Positioning and Market Segmentation: Marketing and Corporate Perspectives," working paper, The Wharton School, University of Pennsylvania.

—— (1981), "Marketing and the Other Business Functions," in *Research in Marketing*, 5, Jagdish N. Sheth, ed., Greenwich, CT: JAI Press, 237–64.

Wright, Patrick J. (1979), *On a Clear Day You Can See General Motors*, Grosse Pointe, MI: Wright Enterprises.

The Changing Role of Marketing in the Corporation

Frederick E. Webster, Jr.

For the past two decades, some subtle changes in the concept and practice of marketing have been fundamentally reshaping the field. Many of these changes have been initiated by industry, in the form of new organizational types, without explicit concern for their underlying theoretical explanation or justification. On the academic side, prophetic voices have been speaking (Arndt 1979, 1981, 1983; Thorelli 1986; Van de Ven 1976; Williamson 1975) but seldom heard because, representing several different disciplines, they did not sing as a chorus. More basically, perhaps, few listeners were ready to hear the message or to do the intellectual work necessary to pull the several themes together. Like the Peruvian Indians who thought the sails of the Spanish invaders on the horizon were some phenomenon of the weather and did nothing to prepare themselves for attack (Handy 1990), marketers may ignore some important information in their environment simply because it is not consistent with their past experience.

Frederick E. Webster, Jr., "The Changing Role of Marketing in the Corporation," Vol. 56 (Oct. '92), pp. 1–17. Reprinted from the *Journal of Marketing*, published by the American Marketing Association.

The purpose of this article is to outline both the intellectual and the pragmatic roots of changes that are occurring in marketing, especially marketing *management*, as a body of knowledge, theory, and practice and to suggest the need for a new paradigm of the marketing function within the firm. First, the origins of the marketing management framework, the generally accepted paradigm of the marketing discipline for the past three decades, are considered. Then shifting managerial practice is examined, especially the dissolution of hierarchical bureaucratic structures in favor of networks of buyer-seller relationships and strategic alliances. Within those new forms of organization, the changing role of marketing is discussed and a reconceptualization of marketing as a field of study and practice is outlined.

MARKETING AS A SOCIAL AND ECONOMIC PROCESS

It is sobering to recall that the study of marketing did not always have a managerial focus. The early roots of marketing as an area of academic study can be found, beginning around 1910, in midwestern American land-grant universities, where a strong involvement with the farm sector created a concern for agricultural markets and the processes by which products were brought to market and prices determined. The analysis was centered around commodities and the institutions involved in moving them from farm, forest, sea, mine, and factory to industrial processors, users, and consumers. Within this tradition, three separate schools evolved that focused on the *commodities* themselves, on the marketing *institutions* through which products were brought to market, especially brokers, wholesalers, and retailers in their many forms and variations (Breyer 1934; Duddy and Revzan 1953), and finally on the *functions* performed by these institutions (McGarry 1950; Weld 1917). All of these approaches tended to be descriptive rather than normative, with the functional being the most analytical and leading to the development of a conceptual framework for the marketing discipline (Bartels 1962; Rathmell 1965).

These early approaches to the study of marketing are interesting because of the relative absence of a *managerial* orientation. Marketing was seen as a set of social and economic processes rather than as a set of managerial activities and responsibilities. The institutional and functional emphasis began to change in 1948, when the American Marketing Association (1948, p. 210) defined marketing as:

> The performance of business activities directed toward, and incident to, the flow of goods and services from producer to consumer or user.

This definition, modified only very slightly in 1960, represented an important shift of emphasis. Though it grew out of the functional view, it defined marketing functions as business activities rather than as social or economic processes. The managerial approach brought relevance and realism to the study of marketing, with an emphasis on problem solving, planning, implementation, and control in a competitive marketplace.

MARKETING MANAGEMENT

The *managerial* approach to the study of marketing evolved in the 1950s and 1960s. Several textbooks using a marketing management perspective appeared during this period (Alderson 1957; Davis 1961; Howard 1957; Kotler 1967; McCarthy 1960). These early managerial authors defined marketing management as a decision-making or problem-solving process and relied on analytical frameworks from economics, psychology, sociology, and statistics. The first marketing casebook, incorporating a managerial framework by definition, had emerged from of the Harvard Business School very early (Copeland 1920), but without any descriptive material or analytical framework to accompany the cases. Marketing management became a widely accepted business function, growing out of a more traditional sales management approach, with an emphasis on product planning and development, pricing, promotion, and distribution. Marketing research gained prominence in management practice as a vehicle for aligning the firm's productive capabilities with the needs of the marketplace. The articulation of the *marketing concept* in the mid to late 1950s posited that marketing was *the* principal function of the firm (along with innovation) because the main purpose of any business was to create a satisfied customer (Drucker 1954; Levitt 1960; McKitterick 1957). Profit was not the objective; it was the reward for creating a satisfied customer.

The managerial focus was *not* readily accepted by everyone in academic circles, nor was the marketing concept completely adopted by industry (McNamara 1972; McGee and Spiro 1988; Webster 1988). In academia, the functionalists and institutionalists held their ground well into the 1960s, stressing the value of understanding marketing institutions and functions and viewing marketing from a broader economic and societal perspective. Over the previous 50 years, a substantial body of theory and empirical knowledge had been developed and mature marketing scholars felt compelled to defend and protect it. The argument *against* the managerial point of view centered on its inability to consider the broader social and economic functions and issues associated with marketing, beyond the level of the firm. For example, the Beckman and Davidson (1962) text, built around a functionalist perspective, and the most widely used text in the field at the time, was promoted as follows: "Balanced treatment of the development and the present status of our marketing system; Conveys a broad understanding of the complete marketing process, its essential economic functions, and the institutions performing them; Strengthens the social and economic coverage of marketing in all its significant implications; Proper emphasis accorded to the managerial viewpoint" (advertisement, *Journal of Marketing*, April 1962, p. 130). It is the last phrase, "proper emphasis," that implies the criticism that the managerial approach, by itself, is incomplete.

The analytical frameworks of the new managerial approach were drawn from economics, behavioral science, and quantitative methods. The incorporation of the behavioral and quantitative sciences gave important legitimacy to marketing as a separate academic discipline. Such frameworks were consistent with the very strong thrust of the 1960s toward more rigorous approaches in management education, encouraged by two very influential foundation studies (Gordon and Howell 1959; Pierson 1959). These studies advocated education based on a rigorous, analytical approach to decision making as opposed to a descriptive, institutional approach which, it was argued, should be held to "an irreducible minimum" (Gordon and Howell 1959, p. 187). The managerial perspective became the dominant point of view in marketing texts and journals, supported by management science and the behavioral sciences.

MARKETING AS AN OPTIMIZATION PROBLEM

Scholars on the leading edge of marketing responded with enthusiasm to the call for greater analytical rigor. At the root of most of the new managerial texts and the evolving research literature of marketing science was the basic microeconomic paradigm, with its emphasis on profit maximization (Anderson 1982). The basic units of analysis were transactions in a competitive market and fully integrated firms controlling virtually all of the factors of production (Arndt 1979; Thorelli 1986). Market transactions connected the firm with its customers and with other firms (Johnston and Lawrence 1988).

Analysis for marketing management focused on demand (revenues), costs, and profitability and the use of traditional economic analysis to find the point at which marginal cost equals marginal revenue and profit is maximized. Behavioral science models were used primarily to structure problem definition, helping the market researcher to define the questions that are worth asking and to identify important variables and the relationships among them (Massy and Webster 1964). Statistical analysis was used to manipulate the data to test the strength of the hypothesized relationships or to look for relationships in the data that had not been hypothesized directly.

The application of formal, rigorous analytical techniques to marketing problems required specialists of various kinds. Marketing departments typically included functional specialists in sales, advertising and promotion, distribution, and marketing research, and perhaps managers of customer service, marketing personnel, and pricing. Early organizational pioneers of professional marketing departments included the consumer packaged goods companies with brand management systems, such as Procter & Gamble, Colgate-Palmolive, General Foods, General Mills, and Gillette. In other companies, the marketing professionals were concentrated at the corporate staff level in departments of market research and operations research or management science. Examples of the latter include General Electric, IBM, and RCA. Large, full-service advertising agencies built strong research departments to support their national advertiser account relationships. Other large firms, such as Anheuser-Busch and General Electric, also entered into research partnerships with university-based consulting organizations.

Such specialized and sophisticated professional marketing expertise fit well into the strategy, structure, and culture of large, divisionalized, hierarchical organizations.

THE LARGE, BUREAUCRATIC, HIERARCHICAL ORGANIZATION

When we think of marketing management, we think of large, divisionalized, functional organizations—the kind depicted by the boxes and lines of an organizational chart. The large, bureaucratic, hierarchical organization, almost always a corporation in legal terms, was the engine of economic activity in this country for more than a century (Miles and Snow 1984). It was characterized by multiple layers of management, functional specialization, integrated operations, and clear distinctions between line and staff responsi-

bilities. It had a pyramid shape with increasingly fewer and more highly paid people from the bottom to the top.

The larger the firm, the more activities it could undertake by itself and the fewer it needed to obtain by contracting with firms and individuals outside the organization. The logic of economies of scale equated efficiency with size. The epitome of the fully integrated firm was the Ford Motor Company, and most notably its River Rouge plant, which produced a single, standardized product, the Model A. Ford-owned lake steamships docked at one end of the plant with coal and iron ore (from Ford's own mines) and complete automobiles and tractors came out at the other end. Molten iron from the blast furnaces was carried by ladles directly to molds for parts, bypassing the costly pig iron step. Waste gases from the blast furnaces became fuel for the powerful plant boilers, as did the sawdust and shavings from the body plant. Gases from the cooking ovens provided process heat for heat-treatment and paint ovens (Ford 1922, p. 151–153). Elsewhere, Ford owned sheep farms for producing wool, a rubber plantation in Brazil, and its own railroad to connect its facilities in the Detroit region (Womack, Jones, and Roos 1991, p. 39). Integration required large size. Large size begat low cost.

Large, hierarchical, integrated corporate structures were the dominant organization form as the managerial approach to marketing developed in the 1950s and 1960s, and firms created marketing departments, often as extensions of the old sales department. Such large organizations moved deliberately, which is to say slowly, and only after careful analysis of all available data and options for action. The standard microeconomic profit maximization paradigm of marketing management fit well in this analytical culture. Responsible marketing management called for careful problem definition, followed by the development and evaluation of multiple decision alternatives, from which a course of action would ultimately be chosen that had the highest probability, based on the analysis, of maximizing profitability.

When the world was changing more slowly than it is today, such caution was wise in terms of preserving valuable assets that had been committed to clearly defined tasks, especially when those assets were huge production facilities designed for maximum economies of scale in the manufacture of highly standardized products. The task of the marketing function was first to develop a thorough understanding of the marketplace to ensure that the firm was producing goods and services required and desired by the consumer. With an optimal product mix in place, the marketing function (through its sales, advertising, promotion, and distribution subfunctions) was responsible for generating demand for these standardized products, for creating consumer preference through mass and personal communications, and for managing the channel of distribution through which products flowed to the consumer. Sound marketing research and analysis provided support for conducting these activities most efficiently and effectively, for testing alternative courses of action in each and every area.

Marketing as a management function tended to be centralized at the corporate level well into the 1970s. Marketing organizations were often multitiered, with more experienced senior managers reviewing and coordinating the work of junior staff and relating marketing to other functions of the business, especially through the budgeting and financial reporting process. Corporate centralization allowed the development of specialized expertise and afforded economies of scale in the purchase of marketing services such as market research, advertising, and sales pro-

motion. It also permitted tighter control of marketing efforts for individual brands and of sales efforts across the entire national market. This arrangement began to change in the late 1970s and into the 1980s as the concept of the strategic business unit (SBU) gained widespread favor and corporate managements pushed operating decisions, and profit and loss responsibility, out to the operating business units. Though marketing became a more decentralized function in many large companies, it is not clear that the result was always heightened marketing effectiveness.

The larger the organization, the larger the number of managers, analysts, and planners who were not directly involved in making or selling products. The burden of administrative costs, mostly in the form of salaries for these middle layers of management, became an increasing handicap in the competitive races that shaped up in the global marketplace of the 1970s and 1980s. More and more organizations found it necessary to downsize and delayer, some through their own initiative and many through threatened or actual acquisition and restructuring by new owners whose vision was not clouded by the continuity of experience. Global competition resulted in increasingly better product performance at lower cost to the customer. Rapid advances in telecommunications, transportation, and information processing broadened the choice set of both industrial buyers and consumers to the point that a product's country of origin was relatively unimportant and geographic distance was seldom a barrier, especially in areas where non-American producers had superior reputations for quality, service, and value. In most American industries, companies had little choice but to reduce costs through reorganization and restructuring of assets, as well as through technological improvements in products and manufacturing processes.

THE ORGANIZATIONAL RESPONSE

During the 1980s, new forms of business organization became prominent features of the economic landscape. Even before the forces of global competition became clearly visible, there was a trend toward more flexible organization forms, forms that are difficult to capture with a traditional organization chart (Miles and Snow 1984, 1986; Powell 1990; Thorelli 1986). The new organizations emphasized partnerships between firms; multiple types of ownership and partnering within the organization (divisions, wholly owned subsidiaries, licensees, franchisees, joint ventures, etc.); teamwork among members of the organization, often with team members from two or more cooperating firms; sharing of responsibility for developing converging and overlapping technologies; and often less emphasis on formal contracting and managerial reporting, evaluation, and control systems. The best visual image of these organizations may be a wheel instead of a pyramid, where the spokes are "knowledge links" between a core organization at the hub and strategic partners around the rim (Badaracco 1991). These forms were pioneered in such industries as heavy construction, fashion, weapon systems contracting, and computers, where markets often span geographic boundaries, technology is complex, products change quickly, and doing everything yourself is impossible. Such organizations today are found in businesses as diverse as glass, chemicals, hospital supplies, book publishing, and tourism.

These confederations of specialists are called by many names including "networks" (Miles and Snow 1986; Thorelli 1968), "value-adding partnerships" (Johnston and Lawrence 1988), "alliances" (Ohmae 1989), and "shamrocks" (Handy 1990). All are characterized by flexibility, specialization, and an emphasis on relationship management in-

stead of market transactions. They depend on administrative processes but they are not hierarchies (Thorelli 1986); they engage in transactions within ongoing relationships and they depend on negotiation, rather than market-based processes, as a principal basis for conducting business and determining prices, though market forces almost always influence and shape negotiation. The purpose of these new organization forms is to respond quickly and flexibly to accelerating change in technology, competition, and customer preferences.

TYPES OF RELATIONSHIPS AND ALLIANCES

There is no strong consensus at the present time about the terminology and typology for describing the new organization forms. However, some important distinctions among types of relationships and alliances are necessary before we can consider the role of marketing within them. We can think of a continuum from pure transactions at one end to fully integrated hierarchical firms at the other end (Figure 8-1). As we move along this continuum, we see that firms use more administrative and bureaucratic control and less market control in the pursuit of economic efficiency. One step away from pure transactions is repeated transactions between buyer and seller. The next step is a long-term relationship that is still adversarial and depends heavily on market control. Then comes a real partnership, in which each partner approaches total dependence on the other in a particular area of activity and mutual trust replaces the adversarial assumptions. Prices are now determined by negotiation, subject to some market pressures, rather than by the market itself. The next step is strategic alliances, which are defined by the formation of a new entity such as a product development

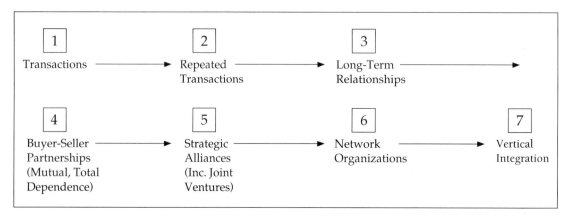

Figure 8-1
The Range of Marketing Relationships

team, a research project, or a manufacturing facility, to which both parties commit resources and which serves clear strategic purposes for both. Joint ventures, resulting in the formation of a new firm, are the epitome of strategic alliances. Like their parents, joint ventures are fully integrated firms with their own capital structures, something that other forms of strategic alliance lack. Network organizations are the corporate structures that result from multiple relationships, partnerships, and strategic alliances.

We can now consider how the role of the marketing function changes in the focal firm as we move along the continuum from transactions to network organizations.

Markets and Transactions

The starting point of this analysis is a *transaction* between two economic actors in the competitive marketplace. In a pure *market* form of economic organization, all activity is conducted as a set of discrete, market-based transactions and virtually all necessary information is contained in the price of the product that is exchanged. The marketing job is simply to find buyers.

In the traditional microeconomic profit-maximization paradigm, the firm engages in market transactions as necessary to secure the resources (labor, capital, raw materials, etc.) it requires for the production of the goods and services it sells in the competitive marketplace. Each transaction is essentially independent of all other transactions, guided solely by the price mechanism of the free, competitive market as the firm seeks to buy at the lowest available price.

In addition to the costs associated with the price paid, however, there are costs associated with the transaction itself, what Coase (1937, p. 390) called the "cost of using the price mechanism." These costs include the costs of discovering what the relevant prices are, of negotiating and contracting, and of monitoring supplier performance, including quality and quantity of goods delivered. For Coase, the problem was to explain why, given these "marketing costs" (as he called them, p. 394, *not* "transactions costs," the phrase we use today), the firm did not internalize virtually all exchanges of value rather than depending on the competitive market. Coase proposed that the reason is that costs are also associated with internal performance of value-creation activities, including decreasing returns to the entrepreneurial function and misallocation of resources to activities in which the firm is incapable of creating value to the same extent as a specialist. It is worth noting that this suggestion, stated in an article published in 1937, is very similar to the notion of "distinctive competency" that appeared in the strategy literature more than 50 years later (Prahalad and Hamel 1990).

Pure transactions are rare, though they mark the beginning of the continuum for thinking about types of relationships and alliances and provide a useful starting point for theoretical analysis. In fact, throughout the 1970s, the marketing literature emphasized transactions as a central construct and the basic unit of analysis for the marketing discipline (Bagozzi 1975). Some authors even advocated a definition of a transaction that included *any* exchange of value between two parties, thus broadening the concept of marketing to include virtually all human interaction (Kotler and Levy 1969). A pure transaction is a one-time exchange of value between two parties with no prior or subsequent interaction. Price, established in the competitive marketplace, contains all of the information necessary for both parties to conclude the exchange. In a pure transaction, there is no brand name, no recognition of the customer by the seller, no credit extension, no preference, no loyalty, and no differentiation of one producer's output from that of another.

Most transactions in fact take place in the context of ongoing relationships between marketers and customers. Nonetheless, there has been a long-standing and clear tendency for marketing practice and theory to focus on the sale, the single event of a transaction, as the objective of marketing activity and the dependent variable for analysis. This emphasis on single transactions fits well with the profit-maximization paradigm and the related analytical techniques of optimization. There is no need to consider people or social processes when the units of analysis are products, prices, costs, firms, and transactions.

Repeated Transactions— The Precursors of a Relationship

One step along the continuum from a pure transaction is the repeated, frequent purchase of branded consumer packaged goods and some industrial components, maintenance, and operating supplies. In the marketing of such products, advertising and sales promotion are key activities and each brand spends aggressively to try to win the customer's preference, loyalty, and repeat purchase. Marketing's role is to guide product differentiation and to create preference and loyalty that will earn higher prices and profits. Direct contact between customers and the marketer is unlikely. The sale is the end result of the marketing process and, though repeat purchases are important to the economics of advertising and sales promotion activity, there is no meaningful, ongoing relationship between company and customer. Even here, however, the presence of brand loyalty and repeat purchase means we have moved beyond a pure transaction. The rudiments of trust and credibility are present, which can be the foundations of a relationship. Consumers simply find it easier and more convenient to shop in the same store and to buy a familiar brand, thus minimizing the time and effort needed to obtain and process information about different alternatives. Consumers can negotiate more favorable terms of sale from a vendor who is attracted to the possibility of future transactions with them. Relationships make transactions more cost efficient.

The importance of *relationships* in marketing is more clearly seen in industrial markets, though it is now also better understood in consumer markets as resellers have gained increased power and as information technology has put individual consumers in more direct contact with resellers and manufacturers. Interactive databases are making relational marketing a reality for consumer goods. For products such as consumer durable goods, whose benefits are derived over a long period of time rather than being consumed in a single use and for which after-sale service is often required, there is an ongoing relationship with the customer, though responsibility for the relationship is often an issue and a source of conflict between customer, reseller, and manufacturer.

As an historical footnote, Henry Ford never had any doubt on this question. He wrote, "When one of my cars breaks down I know I am to blame" (Ford 1922, p. 67) and "A manufacturer is not through with his customer when a sale is completed. He has then only started with his customer. In the case of an automobile the sale of the machine is only something in the nature of an introduction" (p. 41). Likewise, L. L. Bean's original promise to his customers 80 years ago, what he called his Golden Rule, is now held up as a standard for others to follow:

> Everything we sell is backed by a 100% guarantee. We do not want you to have anything from L. L. Bean that is not completely satisfactory. Return anything you buy from us at any time for any reason if it proves otherwise.

These quotations help to underscore the fact that relationship marketing is not new in management thinking. However, there appears to have been a fairly long period of time when it was not a top priority for most companies, and it was not part of the basic conceptual structure of the field as an academic discipline.

Long-Term Relationships

In industrial markets, buyer-seller relationships have typically involved relatively long-term contractual commitments, but even here the relationship was often arm's-length and adversarial, pitting the customer against the vendor in a battle focused on low price. It was common practice for a buyer to maintain a list of qualified vendors who would be invited to submit bids for a particular procurement on a product with specifications drawn in a way to attract maximum competition (Corey 1978; Spekman 1988).

The importance of managing these buyer-seller relationships as strategic assets began to be recognized in the marketing literature of the 1980s (Jackson 1985; Webster 1984). Jackson proposed that industrial marketers characterize firms as either transaction or relationship customers and scale the commitment of resources accordingly. In these longer term buyer-seller relationships, prices are an outcome of a negotiation process based on mutual dependence, not determined solely by market forces, and quality, delivery, and technical support become more important. Competitive forces in the global marketplace of the 1980s forced many firms to move significantly along the continuum from arm's-length relationships with vendors and customers to much stronger partnerships characterized by much greater interdependence. In traditional manufacturing businesses such as those in the automobile industry, the world was changing so fast that the standard ways of doing business were passé.

In the 1980s, the automobile industry became the bellwether for new forms of relationship with industrial suppliers (Womack, Jones, and Roos 1991), and it is instructive to look briefly at the auto business specifically. Ford's River Rouge plant was an exception to the way the industry organized production. Ford got into trouble soon after the plant was opened as Alfred Sloan's General Motors began to offer consumers a much wider range of models, colors, and features, and the Model A fell from favor with customers. GM depended heavily on other vendors, including its own wholly owned but independent subsidiaries such as Harrison Radiator, AC Spark Plug, and Saginaw Steering (Womack, Jones, and Roos 1991, p. 138–139), for almost 70% of the value of production. The automobile manufacturers for decades had depended on thousands of vendors, with many vendors for each item, in a system that was fundamentally and intentionally adversarial. Relationships were short-term. Suppliers were adversaries for their customers, competing for an "unfair" share of the economic value created by the use of their products in the customer's manufacturing process. They fought over price. Competition among vendors, through systems of competitive bidding around extremely tight product specifications, was the method by which vendor greed and opportunism were controlled. The largest share of the business usually went to the vendor with the lowest price, though several others were given smaller shares to keep them involved, to keep pressure on the low price supplier, and to provide alternative sources of supply in the event of delivery or quality problems. Incoming inspection was the key step in quality control and reject rates tended to be high.

Mutual, Total-Dependence Buyer-Seller Partnerships

Global competitors saw an opportunity in all of this. The Japanese manufacturers, in particular, striving to compete in the North American market thousands of miles from home, had learned a valuable lesson: quality does not just sell better, *it also costs less*. Designing products for manufacturability as well as performance and doing it right the first time costs less than detecting and removing defects later. Quality and low cost depend heavily on a system of strategic partnerships with a small number of vendors that are incorporated in the early stages of product development, a pattern of cooperation virtually

unknown in the adversarial sourcing systems of the U.S. manufacturers (Womack, Jones, and Roos 1991). Japanese *kanban* or *just-in-time* systems provided a new model for American manufacturers: reliance on one or a few vendors for a particular part who promise to deliver 100% usable product, usually in quantities just sufficient for one eight-hour production shift, on an incredibly tight schedule whereby trucks must arrive within a very few minutes of the programmed time. Higher quality and lower inventory costs and other related costs resulted from total reliance on a network of sole-source vendors in a system of total interdependence (Frazier, Spekman, and O'Neal 1988).

Firms in the American automobile industry studied their Japanese competitors and attempted to incorporate the lessons learned in their management of procurement and relationships with vendors. The rest of America began to learn from what was happening in the automobile industry, as well as in telecommunications, computers, office equipment, and other fields. American marketers began to see the necessity of moving away from a focus on the individual sale, the transaction as a conquest, and toward an understanding of the need to develop long-term, mutually supportive relationships with their customers. Many of America's premier industrial firms such as GE, IBM, DuPont, Monsanto, and Honeywell restructured themselves around the fundamental concept of strategic customer partnerships with customers such as American Airlines, Ford, Milliken, Procter & Gamble, and the federal government.

Another Japanese institution, the *keiretsu*, provides yet another model that is shaping the new American organizational landscape (Gerlach 1987). *Kanban* systems depend on the close relationship of suppliers and subcontractors within the *keiretsu*. In many respects, the *keiretsu* are the predecessors of the networks and alliances now emerging in the Western world (not to mention the obvious fact that many alliance partners are, in fact, Japanese firms). The *keiretsu* are complex groupings of firms with interlinked ownership and trading relationships. They are neither formal organizations with clearly defined hierarchical structures nor impersonal, decentralized markets. They are bound together in long-term relationships based on reciprocity. The trading partners may hold small ownership positions in one another, but primarily to symbolize the long-term commitment of the relationship rather than strictly for financial gain. A key outcome of this arrangement is great stability in these long-term relationships. Such stability contributes to a sharing of information among the companies and promotes aggressive, long-term growth policies (Gerlach 1987). The experience of Japanese managers with *keiretsu* and similar forms of interfirm cooperation is a major reason for their greater skill and comfort level in the management of strategic alliances in comparison with American managers (Montgomery and Weiss 1991).

Strategic Alliances

In some cases, the partnership between a supplier and its customer takes the form of an entirely new venture, a true strategic alliance. One of the essential features of a true strategic alliance is that it is intended to move each of the partners toward the achievement of some long-term, *strategic,* goal. This strategic objective is one distinguishing feature that separates strategic alliances from previous forms of interfirm cooperation. According to Devlin and Bleakley (1988, p. 18), "Strategic alliances take place in the context of a company's long-term strategic plan and seek to improve or dramatically change a company's competitive position." This definition of strategic alliances, with its emphasis on improving a firm's competitive position, supports the no-

tion that they are an important *marketing* phenomenon. Another important characteristic of strategic alliances is shared objectives and a commitment of resources by both parties.

There are multiple types of strategic alliances; virtually all are within the theoretical domain of marketing as they involve partnerships with customers or resellers or with real or potential competitors for the development of new technology, new products, and new markets. Some are new ventures formed between vendors and customers to ensure a smooth flow of raw materials, components, or services into the customers' manufacturing operations. Others are formed between potential competitors in order to cooperate in the development of related or convergent technologies, in the development of a new product or class of products, or in the development of a new market. Some alliances are formed between manufacturers and resellers. All strategic alliances are collaborations among partners involving the commitment of capital and management resources with the objective of enhancing the partners' competitive positions. Strategic alliances are much closer to the *hierarchy* end of the transactions (market)–hierarchy continuum, but they stop short of internalizing the functions within the firm itself. Instead, they create a separate entity to be managed by bureaucratic and administrative controls.

Joint Ventures

Joint ventures, as the term is used here, are only one kind of strategic alliance, though the terms are often used interchangeably. The unique feature of a joint venture is that a new firm is created, with its own capital structure, as well as the sharing of other resources. Joint ventures are typically established to exist in perpetuity, though the founding partners may subsequently change their ownership participation. Other types of strategic alliances, such as product development projects, have a finite life by definition. In fact, this finiteness with its inherent flexibility is one of the advantages of strategic alliances in comparison with more traditional organization forms. Interestingly, the joint venture soon faces all of the problems of its parent firms in terms of creating multiple partnerships and alliances and determining its core competence and its unique positioning in the value chain between vendors and customers.

Networks

Networks are the complex, multifaceted organization structures that result from multiple strategic alliances, usually combined with other forms of organization including divisions, subsidiaries, and value-added resellers. (Some authors have mistakenly used the terms "strategic alliances" and "networks" interchangeably.) The alliances are the individual agreements and collaborations between partners, such as Ford and Mazda in the creation of the new Escort and Explorer automobiles or General Motors and Toyota in the formation of the NUMMI joint venture. General Motors, though still a classic example of a traditional, hierarchical, bureaucratic, multidivisional organization and currently in the throes of a major downsizing (Taylor 1992), is evolving toward a network organization with multiple joint-venture partners including global competitors Toyota, Daewoo, Volvo, Suzuki, and Isuzu, as well as a host of strategic partnerships with vendors. Ford likewise has a large number of partnerships and alliances and is evolving into a network organization.

The basic characteristic of a network organization is *confederation,* a loose and flexible coalition guided from a hub where the key functions include development and management of the alliances themselves, coordination of financial resources and technology,

definition and management of core competence and strategy, developing relationships with customers, and managing information resources that bind the network. In the context of the network organization, marketing is the function responsible for keeping all of the partners focused on the customer and informed about competitor product offerings and changing customer needs and expectations.

James Houghton, Chairman of Corning, Incorporated, for example, describes his company as a network with alliances as a key part of its structure (Houghton 1989). At the hub of the wheel (Figure 8-2) is a set of functional specialties such as contract negotiation, legal services, and financial coordination that provide the linkages that bind together technology, shared values, and shared resources. The center is also responsible for establishing priorities and managing the linkages that define the network; information management is a central strategic function and information technology has been a key facilitator of these new organizational forms. Another key responsibility of the center is to define, develop, and maintain the core competencies that are at the heart of the firm's ability to compete successfully in the global marketplace (Prahalad and Hamel 1990). In fact, one of the key core competencies of a network organization may be the ability to design, manage, and control strategic partnerships with customers, vendors, distributors, and others.

There is an interesting paradox here: in the move toward strategic alliances, even the largest firms become more focused and specialized in their core activities. They realize that there is an increasingly smaller set of activities that represent true distinctive competence on their part. The trick is to avoid trying to do everything, especially the things they cannot do well, and to find other firms that also need a partner that *can* do the things the large firm does best. Strategic alliances be-

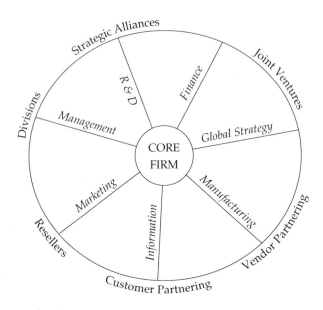

Figure 8-2
Network Organizations

come a primary tool in developing the firm's core competence and competitive advantage.

Instead of vertical integration being the preferred model, the network paradigm is built around the assumption that small is better, that each part or process or function should be the responsibility of a specialized, independent entity, efficiently organized and managed, that has world class competence. Across the board—for all factors of production including parts and subassemblies, services such as transportation and maintenance, and professional marketing services such as marketing research, some selling functions, and most distribution functions—the bias has shifted from "make" to "buy," from ownership to partnership, from fixed cost to variable cost, but in the context of stable, long-term relationships. A firm must define ever more narrowly those core competencies to which it will devote scarce resources in order to develop new knowledge and skills. For all other areas, it must depend on strategic partners who have placed their own focused bets in the game of becoming world class competitors.

IBM is another example of a firm that is reinventing itself as a network organization. As one of the first steps in this direction, the personal computer was designed over a long weekend by an IBM management taskforce gathered informally at a Florida retreat. Actual manufacturing relied on a network of hardware and software suppliers for all components. Besides the design work, IBM's own contribution to the manufacturing process was an assembly plant and several minutes of assembly and testing time per machine. Gradually, some of the vendor partnerships and alliances were terminated as IBM brought some manufacturing activities back into the firm. Subsequently, IBM committed itself to "open architecture," making IBM's technology widely available to all software writers who wanted to develop applications programs, in recognition of the fact that not even IBM had the resources necessary to do the job of writing software for thousands of distinct applications segments. (Some observers have argued that open architecture and reliance on outside vendors meant that IBM itself no longer had any distinctive competitive advantage of its own.) Most recently, IBM has announced a major strategic alliance with Apple Computer and a substantial downsizing and restructuring into a set of more autonomous, independent businesses (Carey and Coy 1991). A key strategic issue for IBM management is to define the set of skills and resources that represent the distinctive competencies of IBM *per se* and a set of technical and strategic challenges and opportunities that require the scope and scale of an IBM.

To sum up, there is a clear evolution away from arm's-length transactions and traditional hierarchical, bureaucratic forms of organization toward more flexible types of partnerships, alliances, and networks. Within these new types of organizations, traditional ways of organizing the marketing activity must be reexamined, with focus on long-term customer relationships, partnerships, and strategic alliances.

REDEFINING MARKETING'S ROLE

From an academic or theoretical perspective, the relatively narrow conceptualization of marketing as a profit-maximization problem, focused on market transactions or a series of transactions, seems increasingly out of touch with an emphasis on long-term customer relationships and the formation and management of strategic alliances. The intellectual core of marketing management needs to be expanded beyond the conceptual framework of microeconomics in order to address more fully the set of organizational and strategic issues inherent in relationships and alliances. In focusing on relationships—though we are still talking about buying and selling, the fundamental activities of interest to marketing— we are now considering phenomena that have traditionally been the subject of study by psychologists, organizational behaviorists, political economists, and sociologists. The focus shifts from products and firms as units of analysis to people, organizations, and the social processes that bind actors together in ongoing relationships.

In the following sections, the changing role of marketing within the organization is examined more closely. Then suggestions are made for how the conceptual base of marketing must be expanded. Finally, some implications for management action are discussed and suggestions are made for the research areas that should be given highest priority if marketing's knowledge and theory base is to address the most important issues facing managers and organizations.

In the new organization environment, the marketing function as we know it is undergoing radical transformation and, in some cases, has disappeared altogether as a distinct management function at the corporate level. Just as the distinction between the firm and its market environment (both suppliers and customers) becomes blurred in network organizations built around long-term strategic partnerships, so do traditional functional boundaries within the firm become less distinct.

To consider the new role of marketing within the evolving corporation, we must recognize that marketing really operates at three distinct levels, reflecting three levels of strategy. These can be defined as the corporate, business or SBU, and functional or operating levels (Boyd and Walker 1990; Hofer and Schendel 1978). Much of the confusion over the years about a definition of marketing and an understanding of the marketing concept can be traced to a failure to make these distinctions (Houston 1986; McGee and Spiro 1988; McNamara 1972; Shapiro 1988). One of the results of the movement toward new organizational forms will be to make these distinct roles more explicit.

In addition to the three levels of strategy, we can identify three distinct dimensions of marketing—marketing as *culture*, marketing as *strategy*, and marketing as *tactics*. Though each marketing dimension is found at each level of strategy, the emphasis accorded the separate dimensions of marketing varies with the level of strategy and the level within the hierarchy of the organization.

Marketing as culture, a basic set of values and beliefs about the central importance of the customer that guide the organization (as articulated by the marketing concept), is primarily the responsibility of the corporate and SBU-level managers. Marketing as strategy is the emphasis at the SBU level, where the focus is on market segmentation, targeting, and positioning in defining how the firm is to compete in its chosen businesses. At the operating level, marketing managers must focus on marketing tactics, the "4Ps" of product, price, promotion, and place/distribution, the elements of the marketing mix. Each level of strategy, and each dimension of marketing, must be developed in the context of the preceding level. As we move down the levels of strategy, we move from strategy formulation to strategy implementation.

At the Corporate Level: Market Structure Analysis, Customer Orientation and Advocacy, and Positioning the Firm in the Value Chain

At the corporate level, the strategic problem is to define what business the company is in and to determine the mission, scope, shape, and structure of the firm. Increasingly, firms are paying specific attention to the question of firm scope and shape, as seen in the decision to enter into strategic alliances. In other words, the question of whether to depend on markets,

long-term relationships, strategic alliances, or integrated multifunctional hierarchy is seen to require specific management analysis and judgment. The first order of business in the strategic puzzle, then, is to determine the firm's position in the value chain: What will it buy? What will it make? What will it sell? These decisions require careful assessment of the firm's distinctive competencies (Prahalad and Hamel 1990) and a decision to focus on the things the firm does best. As mentioned previously, this is the question raised theoretically in 1937 by Ronald Coase, whose work received the Nobel Prize in Economics in 1991: When should the firm depend on outside suppliers and when should it perform activities and functions internally? Today's analysis permits consideration of a much more flexible set of organization forms—relationships and alliances of various kinds.

At this level of strategy, the role of marketing is threefold: (1) to assess market attractiveness by analyzing customer needs and requirements and competitive offerings in the markets potentially available to the firm, and to assess its potential competitive effectiveness, (2) to promote customer orientation by being a strong advocate for the customer's point of view versus that of other constituencies in management decision making, as called for by the marketing concept (Anderson 1982), and (3) to develop the firm's overall value proposition (as a reflection of its distinctive competence, in terms reflecting customer needs and wants) and to articulate it to the marketplace and throughout the organization. A major function of the statement of mission, distinctive competence, and overall value proposition is to make clear what the firm will *not* do, as well as what it will do as stated by corporate objectives and goals. At the corporate level, marketing managers have a critical role to play as advocates, for the customer and for a set of values and beliefs that put the customer first in the firm's decision making, and to communicate the value proposition as part of that culture throughout the organization both internally and in its multiple relationships and alliances.

In network organizations, the marketing function has a unique role that is different from its role in traditional hierarchical structures—to help design and negotiate the strategic partnerships with vendors and technology partners through which the firm deploys its distinctive competence to serve particular market opportunities. Thus, marketing may be involved in relationships with vendors at least as much as, if not more than, relationships with customers as part of the process of delivering superior value to customers. Negotiating skills traditionally associated with managing major customer accounts may be equally valuable in managing vendor relationships. Some firms are already moving managers between sales/marketing and procurement responsibilities, recognizing the transferability of these skills.

At the Business (SBU) Level: Market Segmentation and Targeting, Positioning the Product, and Deciding When and How to Partner

At the business unit or SBU level, the key strategy question is *how* to compete in the firm's chosen businesses. This level of competitive strategy is developed by managers in the individual business units. Business strategy is based on a more detailed and careful analysis of customers and competitors and of the firm's resources and skills for competing in specific market segments (Day and Wensley 1988). The key outcomes of this planing process are market segmentation, market targeting, and positioning in the target segments. A trend of the last decade was to delegate more of the strategic planning process from corporate headquarters out to the individual business units, helping to clarify the distinction between corporate and business-level strategy. These planning activities were historically associated with marketing strategy at the corporate level in hierarchical organizations. Clearly, in network organizations, these responsibilities devolve to the business unit level. In fact, at the SBU level, the distinction between marketing and strategic planning can become blurred; in some firms these functions are likely to be performed by the same people.

In network organizations, marketing managers at the business unit level also have a new responsibility for deciding which marketing functions and activities are to be purchased in the market, which are to be performed by strategic partners, and which are to be performed internally. This responsibility applies to the whole range of professional services (marketing research, telemarketing, advertising, sales promotion, package design, etc.) as well as to suppliers of raw materials, components, and subassemblies and to resellers. When is a vendor merely a vendor and when is it a strategic partner committed to a mutually dependent long-term relationship in delivering solutions to customer problems? Similar questions must be asked about channel members. In a customer-oriented company, committed to the marketing concept at the corporate level, marketing management at the business unit level has a critical role in guiding the analysis that leads to answers to these questions. In all cases, the answer will be that which enables the business to deliver superior value to customers in comparison with its competitors. It is the unique characteristic of network organizations that these questions are asked and that the organization form—transaction versus relationships versus hierarchy—remains flexible, depending on what the market requires. In this sense, network organizations are by definition "market-driven" and represent a maturation of the marketing concept.

At the Operating Level: The Marketing Mix and Managing Customer and Reseller Relationships

At the operating or tactical level, we are back on the more familiar ground of the marketing mix—decisions about products, pricing, promotion, and distribution that implement the business strategy. This is the level of strategy normally called "functional strategy," and in our case "*marketing* strategy," as distinct from corporate and business strategies. It, too, is the responsibility of business-level managers, but at the operating level it is delegated to functional specialists, the marketing managers. This is where the tools of management science and the optimization paradigm apply, as the business attempts to allocate its financial, human, and production resources to markets, customers, and products in the most productive fashion. But even here, marketing is taking on a new form, in both consumer goods and industrial products and services companies, as market forces compel companies to do a more thorough job of responding to customer needs and developing long-term customer relationships.

Regis McKenna, a popular marketing consultant and writer, has described well the new requirements for the marketing function (at both the SBU and operating levels) in a recent *Harvard Business Review* article (McKenna 1991, p. 148):

> The marketer must be the integrator, both internally—synthesizing technological capability with market needs—and externally—bringing the customer into the company as a participant in the development and adaptation of goods and services. It is a fundamental shift in the role and purpose of marketing: from manipulation of the customer to genuine customer involvement; from telling and selling to communicating and sharing knowledge; from last-in-line function to corporate-credibility champion. . . .
>
> The relationships are the key, the basis of customer choice and company adaptation. After

all, what is a successful brand but a special relationship? And who better than a company's marketing people to create, sustain, and interpret the relationship between the company, its suppliers, and its customers?

For firms like Corning and IBM that are redefining themselves as networks of strategic alliances, the key activities in the core organization have to do with strategy, coordination, and relationship management. These activities are essentially knowledge-based and involve the management of information. CEOs manage "the central cores of worldwide webs of product and knowledge links" (Badaracco 1991, p. 148).

To summarize, there is a clear evolution toward entirely new forms of organization for conducting business affairs in the global marketplace and it requires reconceptualization of the role of the marketing function within the organization. In the traditional view, the firm was a distinct entity whose borders were defined by an organization chart, which clearly delineated the boundary between the firm and the external environment. The external environment consisted of markets, in which firms engaged in transactions with vendors for the resources needed to conduct their affairs and with customers who purchased their products and services. The fundamental difference in the new economic order is that *this clear distinction between firms and markets, between the company and its external environment, has disappeared* (Badaracco 1991). It is highly significant, for example, that the management of General Electric Company, the sixth largest American firm in terms of sales and assets, and the country's leading exporter after Boeing, has articulated a vision of GE as "a boundary-less company" for the 1990s. According to the 1990 GE Annual Report:

> In a boundary-less company, suppliers aren't "outsiders." They are drawn closer and become

trusted partners in the total business process. Customers are seen for what they are—the life-blood of a company. Customers' vision of their needs and the company's view become identical, and every effort of every man and woman in the company is focused on satisfying those needs.

In a boundary-less company, internal functions begin to blur. Engineering doesn't design a product and then "hand it off" to manufacturing. They form a team, along with marketing and sales, finance, and the rest. Customer service? It's not somebody's job. It's everybody's job.

Clearly, evolving organization forms, emphasizing flexibility in responding to changing customer needs, create new definitions of marketing's role and responsibilities. We have examined how these new responsibilities differ at the corporate, business, and operating levels. In each instance, the new emphasis on long-term relationships and ongoing assessment of which functions and activities to purchase, to perform internally, or to engage in with a strategic partner creates new dimensions to the marketing task. These new responsibilities and tasks cannot be well understood by using only the traditional profit-maximizing optimization framework that has been the core of marketing theory for the past four decades.

THE NEED FOR AN EXPANDED CONCEPTUAL FRAMEWORK

The marketer must manage three sets of relationships—with customers, with suppliers, and with resellers. In both industrial buyer-seller relationships and in manufacturer-reseller relationships, we are talking about *interorganizational* relationships. In the microeconomic paradigm, the units of analysis are products, prices, firms, and transactions. In the new world of marketing management, we must also look at people, processes, and organizations.

Marketing scholars face two mandates for the 1990s. The first is to develop an expanded view of the marketing function within the firm, one that specifically addresses the role of marketing in firms that go to market through multiple partnerships and that is sensitive to the multiple levels of strategy within the organization. The second is to develop a base of empirical research that broadens our understanding of the forces leading to the development of long-term customer relationships, strategic partnerships with vendors, alliances for the codevelopment of technologies, and the issues involved in creating, managing, and dissolving these partnerships over time. Whereas the historical marketing management model has depended most heavily on economics, statistics, mathematics, psychology, and social psychology, the broadened view of the marketing function calls for work that spans the disciplines of political economy, organizational psychology, legal analysis, political science (government), and cultural anthropology.

In contrast to the microeconomic paradigm and its emphasis on prices, the political economy paradigm is better suited to understanding these firm-to-firm relationships. This is the argument first presented by Johan Arndt in articles published in 1979, 1981, and 1983. The political economy paradigm looks at marketing organizations as social systems—"dynamic, adapting, and internally differentiated. Important dimensions of marketing behavior are authority and control patterns, distributions of power, conflict and conflict management, and external and internal determinants of institutional change" (Arndt 1983, p. 52). Political economy has obvious potential to help us understand the role of marketing in managing relationships with other organizations and in developing support within the firm for activities necessary to respond to the changing marketplace. The political economy model has recently been applied most aggressively in the study of channel conflict (Dwyer, Schurr, and Oh 1987; Frazier 1983), but it offers solid potential for better understanding of all types of relationships and alliances in marketing (Day and Klein 1987). It is cited here as evidence of the availability of alternative conceptualizations of the functions of marketing to move the field beyond its historically narrow focus on transactions and prices based on the traditional microeconomic paradigm.

The field of organizational behavior also offers many opportunities for productive partnerships for marketing scholars who want to address such areas as negotiation, coalitions, team-building, conflict resolution, and group processes related to such activities as new product development that are part of managing marketing partnerships. At the intersection of the organizational behavior, economics, and strategic management disciplines, there is an effort to develop a resource-based theory of the firm, one that moves beyond traditional emphases of the microeconomic paradigm. This integrative approach has potential to address the issues of developing distinctive competence and defining the firm's position in the value chain, finding those sources of competitive advantage that are knowledge-based and "costly to copy" and therefore the *raison d'être* of the firm (Conner 1991; Grant 1991). Customer knowledge and a culture of customer orientation are two important examples of such resources.

The focus of the political economy and organizational behavior models seems to be more appropriate for a *strategic* view of the marketing function as distinct from the *sales* or demand stimulation function, for which the microeconomic paradigm is still more fitting. Whereas the microeconomic model centers on consumers and transactions, the political economy and organizational behavior models are more useful in analyzing relationships with industrial customers, suppliers, joint venture partners, resellers, and other stakeholders (Anderson 1982). It should help us to understand better the changing role of marketing in the corporation. The conceptual foundations of marketing must be enriched, blending economics, political science, and organizational behavior as well as appropriate frameworks from legal analysis, sociology, anthropology, and social psychology to enhance our understanding of the processes of negotiation, coordination, and cooperation that define marketing relationships. Just as we know that most marketing transactions take place in the context of longer term relationships, so we need models that focus on the relationships themselves, not just on the market exchanges that are the subject of the microeconomic paradigm.

Theory development must be accompanied by aggressive programs of empirical research for understanding strategic marketing relationships more completely. Programs of clinical and survey research should be guided by strong theoretical frameworks from allied social science disciplines. Top priority should be given to analysis of the forces and factors that cause firms to move along the continuum from transactions to long-term relationships to strategic alliances and, perhaps, back again.

Some studies have shown modest success rates for strategic alliances, especially those that involve partners of different nationalities and cultures (Bleeke and Ernst 1991; Harrigan 1986). Marketers in collaboration with scholars in the field of cultural anthropology could productively turn their attention to analyzing the differences in values, beliefs, decision making, information processing, and teamwork, among other variables, that must be managed to achieve success in transnational partnerships (Montgomery 1991; Montgomery and Weiss 1991; Webster and Deshpandé 1990).

More careful analysis is needed of the forces reshaping the marketing function at both the corporate and the SBU levels. In collaboration with organizational behavior researchers, marketers need to get into companies and examine the multiple new forms marketing is taking. What is the relationship between marketing and the strategic planning function? How do marketing and purchasing work together in designing and managing strategic vendor partnerships? What issues arise in blending these functions?

In consumer goods marketing, research is needed to understand the factors that lead consumers to seek out and value ongoing relationships with brands, manufacturers, and resellers of various kinds. What are the factors that consumers find attractive in dealing with direct marketers? How can marketers develop and manage these long-term relationships, given the power of databases and interactive marketing? What is the marketing potential inherent in such new developments as the Prodigy network and other extensions of information technology into the household? How will customer expectations about their relationships with marketers be shaped by these new capabilities?

A successful program of research will develop and refine models of the marketing function, incorporating concepts and propositions from multiple behavioral and organizational science disciplines. The net result will be a much richer understanding of those activities we call marketing and have defined as a distinct field of inquiry. Marketing is more than an economic optimization problem; it is a central component of the guidance system of the firm and we need to understand its functioning in much richer detail, especially within the complicated structures of network organizations.

CONCLUSIONS

Marketing is responsible for more than the sale, and its responsibilities differ depending on the level of organization and strategy. It is the management function responsible for making sure that every aspect of the business is focused on delivering superior value to customers in the competitive marketplace. The business is increasingly likely to be a network of strategic partnerships among designers, technology providers, manufacturers, distributors, and information specialists. The business will be defined by its customers, not its products or factories or offices. This is a critical point: in network organizations, it is the ongoing relationship with a set of customers that represents the most important business asset. Marketing as a distinct management function will be responsible for being expert on the customer and keeping the rest of the network organization informed about the customer. At the corporate and business unit levels, marketing may merge with strategic planning or, more generally, the strategy development function, with shared responsibility for information management, environmental scanning, and coordination of the network activities.

There has been a shift from a transactions to a relationship focus. Customers become partners and the firm must make long-term commitments to maintaining those relationships with quality, service, and innovation (Anderson and Narus 1991). Given the increased importance of long-term, strategic relationships with both customers and vendors, organizations must place increased emphasis on relationship management skills. As these skills reside in people, rather than organization structures or roles or tasks, key marketing personnel who have these skills will become increasingly valuable as business assets (Thorelli 1986). These skills may define the core competence of some organizations as links between their vendors and customers in the value chain. This common focus on customer value and relationship management may result in much stronger coordination of the procurement, sales, and marketing functions in a manner analogous to the merchandising function in retailing firms. Such coordination would be consistent with the two major trends of elimination of boundaries between management functions within organizations and a blurring of the boundaries between the firm and its market environment. In a world of strategic partnerships, it is not uncommon for a partner to be simultaneously customer, competitor, and vendor, as well as partner. Consequently, it is difficult to keep the traditional management functions distinct in dealing with strategic partners.

Marketing can no longer be the sole responsibility of a few specialists. Rather, everyone in the firm must be charged with responsibility for understanding customers and contributing to developing and delivering value for them (Webster 1988). It must be part of everyone's job description and part of the organization culture. Organization culture, focused on the customer, will be increasingly seen as a key strategic resource defining the network organization's uniqueness and coordinating its several parts toward common mission and objectives (Conner 1991; Fiol 1991).

Firms that are unable to achieve this focus on the customer will either disappear or become highly specialized players, taking strategic direction from others, in a network organization. Customer focus may require increasingly large investments in information and information technology, giving some advantage to firms large enough to make preemptive investments in these areas.

Impersonal, mass communications, especially media advertising, are becoming less effective, whereas personal, targeted, special purpose communications have become more important. This change is reflected in the decline of the traditional advertising business—independent advertising agencies developing ads and placing them in broadcast and print media. In their place have emerged global communication companies, international networks of specialists and integrated marketing communications mega-agencies working with their multinational clients on specific projects.

Distributors must be treated as strategic partners (Anderson and Narus 1990), linked to the manufacturing firm with sophisticated telecommunications and data-processing systems that afford seamless integration of manufacturing, distribution, and marketing activities throughout the network. Consumer marketers continue to shift resources toward the trade and away from the consumer *per se*, and traditional selling functions for the field sales organization are evolving toward a broader definition of responsibilities for relationship management, assisted by interactive information management capability.

The implementation of market-driven strategy will require skills in designing, developing, managing, and controlling strategic alliances with partners of all kinds, and keeping them all focused on the ever-changing customer in the global marketplace. The core firm will be defined by its end-use markets and its knowledge base, as well as its technical competence, not by its factories and its office buildings. Customer focus, market segmentation, targeting, and positioning, assisted by information technology, will be the flexible bonds that hold the whole thing together.

REFERENCES

Alderson, W. (1957), *Marketing Behavior and Executive Action*. Homewood, IL: Richard D. Irwin, Inc.

American Marketing Association (1948), "Report of the Definitions Committee," R. S. Alexander, Chairman, *Journal of Marketing*, 13 (October), 202–10.

Anderson, James C., and James A. Narus (1990), "A Model of Distributor Firm and Manufacturer Firm Working Partnerships," *Journal of Marketing*, 54 (January), 42–58.

____ and ____ (1991), "Partnering as a Focused Market Strategy," *California Management Review*, 33 (Spring), 95–113.

Anderson, Paul F. (1982), "Marketing, Strategic Planning and the Theory of the Firm," *Journal of Marketing*, 46 (Spring), 15–26.

Arndt, Johan (1979), "Toward a Concept of Domesticated Markets," *Journal of Marketing*, 43 (Fall), 69–75.

____ (1981), "The Political Economy of Marketing Systems: Reviving the Institutional Approach," *Journal of Macromarketing*, 1 (Fall), 36–47.

____ (1983), "The Political Economy Paradigm: Foundation for Theory Building in Marketing," *Journal of Marketing*, 47 (Fall), 44–54.

Badaracco, Joseph L. (1991), *The Knowledge Link: How Firms Compete through Strategic Alliances*. Boston: Harvard Business School Press.

Bagozzi, Richard (1975), "Marketing as Exchange," *Journal of Marketing*, 39 (October), 32–9.

Bartels, Robert (1962), *The Development of Marketing Thought*. Homewood, IL: Richard D. Irwin, Inc.

Beckman, Theodore N., and William R. Davidson (1962), *Marketing*. 7th ed. New York: The Ronald Press Co. (The original edition of this book was published in 1927 as *Principles of Marketing*, by Maynard, Weilder, and Davidson.)

Bleeke, Joel, and David Ernst (1991), "The Way to Win in Cross Border Alliances," *Harvard Business Review*, 69 (November–December), 127–35.

Boyd, Harper W., Jr., and Orville C. Walker, Jr. (1990), *Marketing Management: A Strategic Approach*. Homewood, IL: Richard D. Irwin, Inc.

Breyer, Ralph (1934), *The Marketing Institution*. New York: McGraw-Hill Book Company, Inc.

Carey, John, and Peter Coy (1991), "The New IBM," *Business Week*, 3244 (December 16), 112–18.

Coase, Ronald H. (1937), "The Nature of the Firm," *Economica*, 4, 386–405.

Conner, Kathleen R. (1991), "A Historical Comparison of Resource-Based Theory and Five Schools of Thought within Industrial Organization Economics: Do We Have a New Theory of the Firm?" *Journal of Management*, 17 (1), 121–54.

Copeland, M. T. (1920), *Marketing Problems*. New York: A. W. Shaw.

Corey E. Raymond (1978), *Procurement Management: Strategy, Organization, and Decision-Making*. Boston: CBI Publishing Co., Inc.

Davis, K. R. (1961), *Marketing Management*. New York: The Ronald Press Co.

Day, George S., and Saul Klein (1987), "Cooperative Behavior in Vertical Markets: The Influence of Transaction Costs and Competitive Strategies," in *Review of Marketing*, Michael J. Houston, ed. Chicago: American Marketing Association, 39–66.

____ and Robin Wensley (1988), "Assessing Advantage: A Framework for Diagnosing Competitive Superiority," *Journal of Marketing*, 52 (April), 1–20.

Devlin, Geoffrey, and Mark Bleakley (1988), "Strategic Alliances—Guidelines for Success," *Long-Range Planning*, 21 (5), 18–23.

Drucker, Peter F. (1954). *The Practice of Management*. New York: Harper & Row Publishers, Inc.

Duddy, E. A., and Revzan, D. A. (1953), *Marketing: An Institutional Approach*. 2nd ed. New York: McGraw-Hill Book Company.

Dwyer, F. Robert, Paul H. Schurr, and Sejo Oh (1987), "Developing Buyer-Seller Relationships," *Journal of Marketing*, 51 (April), 11–27.

Fiol, C. Marlene (1991), "Managing Culture as a Competitive Resource: An Identity-Based View of Sustainable Competitive Advantage," *Journal of Management*, 17 (1), 191–211.

Ford, Henry (1922), *My Life and Work*. New York: Doubleday, Page & Company. (Reprinted by Ayer Company, Publishers, Salem, NH, 1987.)

Frazier, Gary L. (1983), "Interorganizational Exchange Behavior in Marketing Channels: A Broadened Perspective," *Journal of Marketing*, 47 (Fall), 68–78.

____, Robert E. Spekman, and Charles R. O'Neal (1988), "Just-in-Time Exchange Relationships in Industrial Markets," *Journal of Marketing*, 52 (October), 52–67.

General Electric Company (1991), *1990 Annual Report* (March).

Gerlach, Michael (1987), "Business Alliances and the Strategy of the Japanese Firm," *California Management Review*, 30 (Fall), 126–42.

Gordon, R. A., and J. E. Howell (1959), *Higher Education for Business*. New York: Columbia University Press. (This study was sponsored by the Ford Foundation.)

Grant, Robert M. (1991), "The Resource-Based Theory of Competitive Advantage: Implications for Strategy Formulation," *California Management Review*, 33 (Spring), 114–35.

Handy, Charles (1990), *The Age of Unreason*. Boston: Harvard Business School Press.

Harrigan, Kathryn R. (1986), *Managing for Joint Venture Success*. Lexington, MA: Lexington Books.

Hofer, Charles W., and Dan Schendel (1978), *Strategy Formulation: Analytical Concepts*. St. Paul: West Publishing Company.

Houghton, James R. (1989), "The Age of the Hierarchy Is Over," *The New York Times* (Sunday, September 24), Sec. 3, 3.

Houston, Franklin S. (1986), "That Marketing Concept: What It Is and What It Is Not," *Journal of Marketing*, 50 (April), 81–7.

Howard, J. A. (1957), *Marketing Management: Analysis and Planning*. Homewood, IL: Richard D. Irwin, Inc.

Jackson, Barbara B. (1985), "Build Customer Relationships That Last," *Harvard Business Review*, 63 (November–December), 120–8.

Johnston, Russell, and Paul R. Lawrence (1988), "Beyond Vertical Integration—The Rise of the Value-Adding Partnership," *Harvard Business Review*, 66 (July–August), 94–101.

Kotler, Philip (1967), *Marketing Management: Analysis, Planning, and Control*. Englewood Cliffs, NJ: Prentice-Hall, Inc.

_____ and Sidney J. Levy (1969), "Broadening the Concept of Marketing," *Journal of Marketing*, 33 (January), 10–15.

Levitt, Theodore (1960), "Marketing Myopia," *Harvard Business Review*, 38 (July–August), 24–47.

Massy, William F., and Frederick E. Webster, Jr. (1964), "Model-Building in Marketing Research," *Journal of Marketing Research*, 1 (May), 9–13.

McCarthy, E. J. (1960), *Basic Marketing: A Managerial Approach*. Homewood, IL: Richard D. Irwin, Inc.

McGarry, Edmund D. (1950), "Some Functions of Marketing Reconsidered," in *Theory in Marketing*, Reavis Cox and Wroe Alderson, eds. Homewood, IL: Richard D. Irwin, Inc., 268.

McGee, Lynn W., and Rosann Spiro (1988), "The Marketing Concept in Perspective," *Business Horizons*, 31 (May–June), 40–5.

McKenna, Regis (1991), "Marketing Is Everything," *Harvard Business Review*, 69 (January–February), 65–79.

McKitterick, J. B. (1957), "What Is the Marketing Management Concept?" in *The Frontiers of Marketing Thought*, Frank M. Bass, ed. Chicago: American Marketing Association, 71–82.

McNamara, Carlton P. (1972), "The Present Status of the Marketing Concept," *Journal of Marketing*, 36 (January), 50–7.

Miles, Raymond, and Charles Snow (1984), "Fit, Failure, and the Hall of Fame," *California Management Review*, 26 (Spring), 10–28.

_____ and _____ (1986), "Network Organizations: New Concepts for New Forms," *California Management Review*, 28 (Spring), 62–73.

Montgomery, David B. (1991), "Understanding the Japanese as Customers, Competitors, and Collaborators," *Japan and the World Economy*, 3 (1), 61–91.

_____ and Allan M. Weiss (1991), "Managerial Preferences for Strategic Alliance Attributes," Research Paper #1134 (August), Graduate School of Business, Stanford University.

Ohmae, Kenichi (1989), "The Global Logic of Strategic Alliances," *Harvard Business Review*, 67 (March–April), 143–54.

Pfeffer, Jeffrey, and Gerald R. Salancik (1978), *The External Control of Organizations*. New York: Harper & Row Publishers, Inc.

Pierson, F. C. (1959), *The Education of American Businessmen*. New York: McGraw-Hill Book Company. (This study was sponsored by the Carnegie Foundation.)

Powell, Walter W. (1990), "Neither Market nor Hierarchy: Network Forms of Organization," *Research in Organizational Behavior*, 12, 295–336.

Prahalad, C. K., and Gary Hamel (1990), "The Core Competence of the Corporation," *Harvard Business Review*, 68 (May–June), 79–91.

Rathmell, John M. (1965), "The Marketing Function," Chapter 1 in *Marketing Handbook*, 2nd ed., Albert Wesley Frey, ed. New York: The Ronald Press Co. 1–33.

Shapiro, Benson P. (1988), "What the Hell Is Market Oriented?" *Harvard Business Review*, 65 (November–December), 119–25.

Spekman, Robert E. (1988), "Strategic Supplier Selection: Understanding Long-Term Buyer Relationships," *Business Horizons*, 31 (July–August), 75–81.

Taylor, Alex, III (1992), "Can GM Remodel Itself?" *Fortune*, 124 (January 13), 26–34.

Thorelli, Hans (1986), "Networks: Between Markets and Hierarchies," *Strategic Management Journal*, 7 (1986), 37–51.

Vaile, R. S., E. T. Grether, and R. Cox (1952), *Marketing in the American Economy*. New York: The Ronald Press Co.

Van de Ven, Andrew (1976), "On the Nature, Formation, and Maintenance of Relations among Organizations," *Academy of Management Review*, 1 (October), 24–36.

Webster, Frederick E., Jr. (1984), *Industrial Marketing Strategy*, 2nd ed. New York: John Wiley & Sons, Inc.

_____ (1988), "The Rediscovery of the Marketing Concept," *Business Horizons*, 31 (May–June), 29–39.

_____ and Rohit Deshpandé (1990), *Analyzing Corporate Cultures in Approaching the Global Marketplace*, Report No. 90–111 (June). Cambridge, MA: Marketing Science Institute.

Weld, L. D. H. (1917), "Marketing Functions and Mercantile Organization," *American Economic Review* (June), 306–18.

Williamson, Oliver (1975), *Markets and Hierarchies*. Glencoe, IL: The Free Press.

Womack, James P., Daniel T. Jones, and Daniel Roos (1991), *The Machine That Changed the World*. Harper Perennial Edition. New York: Harper Collins Publishers.

Buyer and Market Behavior

The marketing objectives of any organization imply an understanding of human behavior, especially the behavior of buyers and markets. The articles in Part Two represent some of marketing's most interesting and enduring attempts to analyze and understand buyer and market behaviors.

The traditional, normative framework for understanding the buyer, as Alderson points out in Part One, is provided by economic theory. However, marketing scholars have never been satisfied with the sterility of economics. Katona led a movement to integrate economic theory and the behavioral sciences. His paper is an enduring overview of what has come to be known as "the new theory of consumer economics."

A number of comprehensive frameworks have been proposed to facilitate the study and understanding of buyer behavior. Two of the most significant are included here. "The Theory of Buyer Behavior," by Howard and Sheth, presents the most widely acknowledged general model of consumer behavior. It has been extensively debated and subjected to numerous empirical tests. Webster and Wind also offer a general framework, but they focus on the behavior of the organizational buyer. They describe an interplay among organizational, social, and personal factors that influence the decision process.

Belk extends our understanding of the buying and consumption processes, demonstrating that situational variables, such as physical and social surroundings, individual moods, and the timing of purchase or consumption, can have a powerful influence on consumer behavior. Holbrook and Hirschman argue that purchase and consumption are not all business. Rather, consumer behavior is an experiential process through which consumers have fun and express their feelings while pursuing enjoyment and pleasure. Holbrook and Hirschman present a general model to elaborate their perspective and contrast it with the conventional "information processing" perspective.

Rogers has devoted his professional life to studying the diffusion of innovations, focusing his attention on the dynamics of communication and behavioral change. He provides a thoughtful overview and critical review of diffusion research. Robertson and Gatignon extend diffusion research into the organizational context. Specifically, they propose a model to study and manage technological diffusion among organizations. Competitive market factors play a significant role in this process.

Strategically, it is important to analyze market and buyer behavior in order to identify different groups of buyers, and then to tailor marketing efforts for the different groups better than competitors can. These are the processes of market segmentation, target marketing, and positioning. Haley was an early proponent of market segmentation. He advocated and demonstrated a useful approach, called "benefit segmentation," in which different consumer value systems could be linked to products and marketing efforts. He believed that benefit segmentation never fails to provide fresh insights into markets or to uncover market opportunities.

Trout and Ries dig into the consumer's mind in their pioneering conceptualization of product positioning. Using many classic vignettes and the context of advertising, they show that markets are highly competitive and that firms must be aggressive and analytical in the creation and execution of their strategies. The positioning concept has evolved considerably since its introduction and remains focal to strategy formulation in marketing and advertising.

◆

Rational Behavior and Economic Behavior

George Katona

While attempts to penetrate the boundary lines between psychology and sociology have been rather frequent during the last few decades, psychologists have paid little attention to the problems with which another sister discipline, economics, is concerned. One purpose of this paper is to arouse interest among psychologists in studies of economic behavior. For that purpose it will be shown that psychological principles may be of great value in clarifying basic questions of economics and that the psychology of habit formation, of motivation, and of group belonging may profit from studies of economic behavior.

A variety of significant problems, such as those of the business cycle or inflation, of consumer saving or business investment, could be chosen for the purpose of such demonstration. This paper, however, will be concerned with the most fundamental assumption of economics, the principle of rationality. In order to clarify the problems involved in this principle, which have been neglected by contemporary psychologists, it will be necessary to contrast the most common forms of methodology used in economics with those employed in psychology and to discuss the role of empirical research in the social sciences.

THEORY AND HYPOTHESES

Economic theory represents one of the oldest and most elaborate theoretical structures in the social sciences. However, dissatisfaction with the achievements and uses of economic theory has grown considerably during the past few decades on the part of economists who are interested in what actually goes on in economic life. And yet leading sociologists and psychologists have recently declared, "Economics is today, in a theoretical sense, probably the most highly elaborated, sophisticated, and refined of the disciplines dealing with action."[1]

To understand the scientific approach of economic theorists, we may divide them

Reprinted from *Psychological Review* (September, 1953), pp. 307–318. Copyright 1953 by the American Psychological Association.

into two groups. Some develop an a priori system from which they deduce propositions about how people *should* act under certain assumptions. Assuming that the sole aim of businessmen is profit maximization, these theorists deduce propositions about marginal revenues and marginal costs, for example, that are not meant to be suited for testing. In developing formal logics of economic action, one of the main considerations is elegance of the deductive system, based on the law of parsimony. A wide gap separates these theorists from economic research of an empirical-statistical type which registers what they call aberrations or deviations, due to human frailty, from the norm set by theory.

A second group of economic theorists adheres to the proposition that it is the main purpose of theory to provide hypotheses that can be tested. This group acknowledges that prediction of future events represents the most stringent test of theory. They argue, however, that reality is so complex that it is necessary to begin with simplified propositions and models which are known to be unreal and not testable.[2] Basic among these propositions are the following three which traditionally have served to characterize the economic man or the rational man:

1. The principle of complete information and foresight. Economic conditions—demand, supply, prices, etc.—are not only given but also known to the rational man. This applies as well to future conditions about which there exists no uncertainty, so that rational choice can always be made. (In place of the assumption of certainty of future developments, we find nowadays more frequently the assumption that risks prevail but the probability of occurrence of different alternatives is known; this does not constitute a basic difference.)
2. The principle of complete mobility. There are no institutional or psychological fac-

tors which make it impossible, or expensive, or slow, to translate the rational choice into action.
3. The principle of pure competition. Individual action has no great influence on prices because each man's choice is independent from any other person's choice and because there are no "large" sellers or buyers. Action is the result of individual choice and is not group-determined.

Economic theory is developed first under these assumptions. The theorists then introduce changes in the assumptions so that the theory may approach reality. One such step consists, for instance, of introducing large-scale producers, monopolists, and oligopolists, another of introducing time lags, and still another of introducing uncertainty about the probability distribution of future events. The question raised in each case is this: Which of the original propositions needs to be changed, and in what way, in view of the new assumptions?

The fact that up to now the procedure of gradual approximation to reality has not been completely successful does not invalidate the method. It must be acknowledged that propositions were frequently derived from unrealistic economic models which were susceptible to testing and stimulated empirical research. In this paper, we shall point to a great drawback of this method of starting out with a simplified a priori system and making it gradually more complex and more real—by proceeding in this way one tends to lose sight of important problems and to disregard them.

The methods most commonly used in psychology may appear at first sight to be quite similar to the methods of economics which have just been described. Psychologists often start with casual observations, derive from them hypotheses, test those through more systematic observations, reformulate and revise their hypotheses accordingly, and test them again. The process of hypotheses-observations-hypotheses-observations often goes on with no end in sight. Differences from the approach of economic theory may be found in the absence in psychological research of detailed systematic elaboration prior to any observation. Also, in psychological research, findings and generalizations in one field of behavior are often considered as hypotheses in another field of behavior. Accordingly, in analyzing economic behavior[3] and trying to understand rationality, psychologists can draw on (a) the theory of learning and thinking, (b) the theory of group belonging, and (c) the theory of motivation. This will be done in this paper.

HABITUAL BEHAVIOR AND GENUINE DECISION MAKING

In trying to give noneconomic examples of "rational calculus," economic theorists have often referred to gambling. From some textbooks one might conclude that the most rational place in the world is the Casino in Monte Carlo where odds and probabilities can be calculated exactly. In contrast, some mathematicians and psychologists have considered scientific discovery and the thought processes of scientists as the best examples of rational or intelligent behavior.[4] An inquiry about the possible contributions of psychology to the analysis of rationality may then begin with a formulation of the differences between (a) associative learning and habit formation and (b) problem solving and thinking.

The basic principle of the first form of behavior is repetition. Here the argument of Guthrie holds: "The most certain and dependable information concerning what a man will do in any situation is information concerning what he did in that situation on its last occurrence."[5] This form of behavior depends upon the frequency of repetition as well as on its

recency and on the success of past performances. The origins of habit formation have been demonstrated by experiments about learning nonsense syllables, lists of words, mazes, and conditioned responses. Habits thus formed are to some extent automatic and inflexible.

In contrast, problem-solving behavior has been characterized by the arousal of a problem or question, by deliberation that involves reorganization and "direction," by understanding of the requirements of the situation, by weighing of alternatives and taking their consequences into consideration and, finally, by choosing among alternative courses of action.[6] Scientific discovery is not the only example of such procedures; they have been demonstrated in the psychological laboratory as well as in a variety of real-life situations. Problem solving results in action which is new rather than repetitive; the actor may have never behaved in the same way before and may not have learned of any others having behaved in the same way.

Some of the above terms, defined and analyzed by psychologists, are also being used by economists in their discussion of rational behavior. In discussing, for example, a manufacturer's choice between erecting or not erecting a new factory, or raising or not raising his prices or output, reference is usually made to deliberation and to taking the consequences of alternative choices into consideration. Nevertheless, it is not justified to identify problem-solving behavior with rational behavior. From the point of view of an outside observer, habitual behavior may prove to be fully rational or the most appropriate way of action under certain circumstances. All that is claimed here is that the analysis of two forms of behavior—habitual versus genuine decision making—may serve to clarify problems of rationality. We shall proceed therefore by deriving six propositions from the psychological principles. To some extent, or in certain fields of behavior, these are findings or empirical generalizations to some extent, or in other fields of behavior, they are hypotheses.

1. Problem-solving behavior is a relatively rare occurrence. It would be incorrect to assume that everyday behavior consistently manifests such features as arousal of a problem, deliberation, or taking consequences of the action into consideration. Behavior which does not manifest these characteristics predominates in everyday life and in economic activities as well.

2. The main alternative to problem-solving behavior is not whimsical or impulsive behavior (which was considered the major example of "irrational" behavior by nineteenth-century philosophers). When genuine decision making does not take place, habitual behavior is the most usual occurrence: people act as they have acted before under similar circumstances, without deliberating and choosing.

3. Problem-solving behavior is recognized most commonly as a deviation from habitual behavior. Observance of the established routine is abandoned when in driving home from my office, for example, I learn that there is a parade in town and choose a different route, instead of automatically taking the usual one. Or, to mention an example of economic behavior: Many businessmen have rules of thumb concerning the timing for reorder of merchandise; yet sometimes they decide to place new orders even though their inventories have not reached the usual level of depletion (for instance, because they anticipate price increases), or not to order merchandise even though that level has been reached (because they expect a slump in sales).

4. Strong motivational forces—stronger than those which elicit habitual behavior—must be present to call forth problem-solving behavior. Being in a "crossroad situation," facing "choice points," or perceiving that something new has occurred are typical instances in which we are motivated to deliberate and choose. Pearl Harbor and the Korean aggression are extreme examples of "new" events; economic behavior of the problem-solving type was found to have prevailed widely after these events.

5. Group belonging and group reinforcement play a substantial role in changes of behavior due to problem solving. Many people become aware of the same events at the same time; our mass media provide the same information and often the same interpretation of events to groups of people (to businessmen, trade union members, sometimes to all Americans). Changes in behavior resulting from new events may therefore occur among very many people at the same time. Some economists[7] argued that consumer optimism and pessimism are unimportant because usually they will cancel out; in the light of sociopsychological principles, however, it is probable, and has been confirmed by recent surveys, that a change from optimistic to pessimistic attitudes, or vice versa, sometimes occurs among millions of people at the same time.

6. Changes in behavior due to genuine decision making will tend to be substantial and abrupt, rather than small and gradual. Typical examples of action that results from genuine decisions are cessation of purchases or buying waves, the shutting down of plants or the building of new plants, rather than an increase or decrease of production by 5 or 10 percent.[8]

Because of the preponderance of individual psychological assumptions in classical economics and the emphasis placed on group behavior in this discussion, the change in underlying conditions which has occurred during the last century may be illustrated by a further example. It is related—the author does not know whether the story is true or fictitious—that the banking house of the Rothschilds, still in its infancy at that time, was one of the suppliers of the armies of Lord Wellington in 1815. Nathan Mayer Rothschild accompanied the armies and was present at the Battle of Waterloo. When he became convinced that Napoleon was decisively defeated, he released carrier pigeons so as to transmit the news to his associates in London and reverse the commodity position of his bank. The carrier pigeons arrived in London before the news of the victory became public knowledge. The profits thus reaped laid, according to the story, the foundation to the outstanding position of the House of Rothschild in the following decades.

The decision to embark on a new course of action because of new events was then made by one individual for his own profit. At present, news of a battle, or of change of government, or of rearmament programs, is transmitted in short order by press and radio to the public at large. Businessmen—the manufacturers or retailers of steel or clothing, for instance—usually receive the same news about changes in the price of raw materials or in demand, and often consult with each other. Belonging to the same group means being subject to similar stimuli and reinforcing one another in making decisions. Acting in the same way as other members of one's group or of a reference group have acted under similar circumstances may also occur without deliberation and choice. New action by a few manufacturers will, then, frequently or even usually not be compensated by reverse action on the part of others. Rather the direction in which the economy of an entire country moves—and often the world economy as well—will tend to be subject to the same influences.

After having indicated some of the contributions which the application of certain psychological principles to economic behavior may make, we turn to contrasting that approach with the traditional theory of rationality. Instead of referring to the formulations of nineteenth-century economists, we shall quote from a modern version of the classical trend of thought. The title of a section in a recent article by Kenneth J. Arrow is "The Principle of Rationality." He describes one of the criteria of rationality as follows: "We can imagine the individual as listing, once and for all, all conceivable consequences of his actions in order of his preference for them."[9] We are first concerned with the expression "all conceivable consequences." This expression seems to contradict the principle of selectivity of human behavior. Yet habitual behavior is highly selective since it is based on (repeated) past experience, and problem-solving behavior likewise is highly selective since reorganization is subject to a certain direction instead of consisting of trial (and error) regarding all possible avenues of action.

Secondly, Arrow appears to identify rationality with consistency in the sense of repetition of the same choice. It is part and parcel of rational behavior, according to Arrow, that an individual "makes the same choice each time he is confronted with the same set of alternatives."[10] Proceeding in the same way on successive occasions appears, however, a characteristic of habitual behavior. Problem-solving behavior, on the other hand, is flexible. Rationality may be said to reflect adaptability and ability to act in a new way when circumstances demand it, rather than to consist of rigid or repetitive behavior.

Thirdly, it is important to realize the differences between the concepts, action, decision, and choice. It is an essential feature of the approach derived from considering problem-solving behavior that there is action without deliberate decision and choice. It then becomes one of the most important problems of research to determine under what conditions genuine decision and choice occur prior to an action. The three concepts are, however, used without differentiation in the classical theory of rationality and also, most recently, by Parsons and Shils. According to the theory of these authors, there are "five discrete choices (explicit or implicit) which every actor makes before he can act;" before there is action "a decision must always be made (explicitly or implicitly, consciously or unconsciously)."[11]

There exists, no doubt, a difference in terminology, which may be clarified by mentioning a simple case: Suppose my telephone rings: I lift the receiver with my left hand and say, "Hello." Should we then argue that I made several choices, for instance, that I decided not to lift the receiver with my right hand and not to say, "Mr. Katona speaking"? According to our use of the terms *decision* and *choice*, my action was habitual and did not involve "taking consequences into consideration."[12] Parsons and Shils use the terms *decision* and *choice* in a different sense, and Arrow may use the terms *all conceivable consequences* and *same set of alternatives* in a different sense from the one employed in this paper. But the difference between the two approaches appears to be more far-reaching. By using the terminology of the authors quoted, and by constructing a theory of rational action on the basis of this terminology, fundamental problems are disregarded. If every action by definition presupposes decision making, and if the malleability of human behavior is not taken into consideration, a one-sided theory of rationality is developed and empirical research is confined to testing a theory which covers only some of the aspects of rationality.

This was the case recently in experiments devised by Mosteller and Nogee. These authors attempt to test basic assumptions of economic theory, such as the rational choice among alternatives, by placing their subjects in a gambling situation (a variation of poker dice) and compelling them to make a decision, namely, to play or not to play against the experimenter. Through their experiments the authors prove that "it is feasible to measure utility experimentally,"[13] but they do not shed light on the conditions under which rational behavior occurs or on the inherent features of rational behavior. Experiments in which making a choice among known alternatives is prescribed do not test the realism of economic theory.

MAXIMIZATION

Up to now we have discussed only one central aspect of rationality—means rather than ends. The end of rational behavior, according to economic theory, is maximization of profits in the case of business firms and maximization of utility in the case of people in general.

A few words, first, on maximizing profits. This is usually considered the simpler case because it is widely held (*a*) that business firms are in business to make profits and (*b*) that profits, more so than utility, are a quantitative, measurable concept.

When empirical research, most commonly in the form of case studies, showed that businessmen frequently strove for many things in addition to profits or in place of profits, most theorists were content with small changes in their systems. They redefined profits so as to include long-range profits and what has been called nonpecuniary or psychic profits. Striving for security or for power was identified with striving for profits in the more distant future; purchasing goods from a high bidder who was a member of the same fraternity as the purchaser, rather than from the lowest bidder—to cite an example often used in textbooks—was thought to be maximizing of nonpecuniary profits. Dissatisfaction with this type of theory construction is rather widespread. For example, a leading theorist wrote recently:

> If *whatever* a business man does is explained by the principle of profit maximization—because he does what he likes to do, and he likes to do what maximizes the sum of his pecuniary and nonpecuniary profits—the analysis acquires the character of a system of definitions and tautologies, and loses much of its value as an explanation of reality.[14]

The same problem is encountered regarding maximization of utility. Arrow defines rational behavior as follows: " . . . among all the combinations of commodities an individual can afford, he chooses that combination which maximizes his utility or satisfaction"[15] and speaks of the "traditional identification of rationality with maximization of some sort."[16] An economic theorist has recently characterized this type of definition as follows:

> The statement that a person seeks to maximize utility is (in many versions) a tautology: it is impossible to conceive of an observational phenomenon that contradicts it. . . . What if the theorem is contradicted by observation: Samuelson says it would not matter much in the case of utility theory; I would say that it would not make the slightest difference. For there is a free variable in his system: the tastes of consumers. . . . Any contradiction of a theorem derived from utility theory can always be attributed to a change of tastes, rather than to an error in the postulates or logic of the theory.[17]

What is the way out of this difficulty? Can psychology, and specifically the psychology of motivation, help? We may begin by characterizing the prevailing economic theory as a single-motive theory and contrast it with a theory of multiple motives. Even in case of a single decision of one individual, multiplicity of motives (or of vectors or forces in the field), some reinforcing one another and some conflicting with one another, is the rule rather than the exception. The motivational patterns prevailing among different individuals making the same decision need not be the same; the motives of the same individual who is in the same external situation at different times may likewise differ. This approach opens the way (*a*) for a study of the relation of different motives to different forms of behavior and (*b*) for an investigation of changes in motives. Both problems are disregarded by postulating a single-motive theory and by restricting empirical studies to attempts to confirm or contradict that theory.

The fruitfulness of the psychological approach may be illustrated first by a brief reference to business motivation. We may rank the diverse motivational patterns of businessmen by placing the striving for high immediate profits (maximization of short-run profits, to use economic terminology; charging whatever the market can bear, to use a popular expression) at one extreme of the scale. At the other extreme we place the striving for prestige or power. In between we discern striving for security, for larger business volume, or for profits in the more distant future. Under what kinds of business conditions will motivational patterns tend to conform with the one or the other end of the scale? Preliminary studies would seem to indicate that the worse the business situation is, the more frequent is striving for high immediate profits, and the better the business situation is, the more frequent is striving for nonpecuniary goals.[18]

Next we shall refer to one of the most important problems of consumer economics as well as of business-cycle studies, the deliberate choice between saving and spending. Suppose a college professor receives a raise in his salary or makes a few hundred extra dollars through a publication. Suppose, furthermore, that he suggests thereupon to his wife that they should buy a television set while the wife argues that the money should be put in the bank as a reserve against a "rainy day." Whatever the final decision may be, traditional economic theory would hold that the action which gives the greater satisfaction was chosen. This way of theorizing is of little value. Under what conditions will one type of behavior (spending) and under what conditions will another type of behavior (saving) be more frequent? Psychological hypotheses according to which the strength of vectors is related to the immediacy of needs have been put to a test through nationwide surveys over the past six years.[19] On the basis of survey findings the following tentative generalization was established: Pessimism, insecurity, expectation of income declines or bad times in the near future promote saving (putting the extra money in the bank), while optimism, feeling of security, expectation of income increases, or good times promote spending (buying the television set, for instance).

Psychological hypotheses, based on a theory of motivational patterns which change with circumstances and influence behavior, thus stimulated empirical studies. These studies, in turn, yielded a better understanding of past developments and also, we may add, better predictions of forthcoming trends than did studies based on the classical theory. On the other hand, when conclusions about utility or rationality were made on an a priori basis, researchers lost sight of important problems.[20]

DIMINISHING UTILITY, SATURATION, AND ASPIRATION

Among the problems to which the identification of maximizing utility with rationality gave rise, the measurability of utility has been prominent. At present the position of most economists appears to be that while interpersonal comparison of several consumers' utilities is not possible, and while cardinal measures cannot be attached to the utilities of one particular consumer, ordinal ranking of the utilities of each individual can be made. It is asserted that I can always say either that I prefer A to B, or that I am indifferent to having A or B, or that I prefer B to A. The theory of indifference curves is based on this assumption.

In elaborating the theory further, it is asserted that rational behavior consists not only of preferring more of the same goods to less (\$2 real wages to \$1, or two packages of cigarettes to one package, for the same service performed) but also of deriving diminishing increments of satisfaction from successive units of a commodity.[21] In terms of an old textbook example, one drink of water has tremendous value to a thirsty traveler in a desert; a second, third, or fourth drink may still have some value but less and less so; an nth drink (which he is unable to carry along) has no value at all. A generalization derived from this principle is that the more of a commodity or the more money a person has, the smaller are his needs for that commodity or for money, and the smaller his incentives to add to what he has.

In addition to using this principle of saturation to describe the behavior of the rational man, modern economists applied it to one of the most pressing problems of contemporary American economy. Prior to World War II the American people (not counting business firms) owned about 45 billion dollars in liquid assets (currency, bank deposits, government bonds) and these funds were highly concentrated among relatively few families; most individual families held no liquid assets at all (except for small amounts of currency). By the end of the year 1945, however, the personal liquid-asset holdings had risen to about 140 billion dollars and four out of every five families owned some bank deposits or war bonds. What is the effect of this great change on spending and saving? This question has been answered by several leading economists in terms of the saturation principle presented above. "The rate of saving is . . . a diminishing function of the wealth the individual holds"[22] because "the availability of liquid assets raises consumption generally by reducing the impulse to save."[23] More specifically: a person who owns nothing or very little will exert himself greatly to acquire some reserve funds, while a person who owns much will have much smaller incentives to save. Similarly, incentives to increase one's income are said to weaken with the amount of income. In other words, the strength of motivation is inversely correlated with the level of achievement.

In view of the lack of contact between economists and psychologists, it is hardly surprising that economists failed to see the relevance for their postulates of the extensive experimental work performed by psychologists on the problem of levels of aspiration. It is not necessary in this paper to describe these studies in detail. It may suffice to formulate three generalizations as established in numerous studies of goal-striving behavior:[24]

1. Aspirations are not static, they are not established once for all time.
2. Aspirations tend to grow with achievement and decline with failure.
3. Aspirations are influenced by the performance of other members of the group to which one belongs and by that of reference groups.

From these generalizations hypotheses were derived about the influence of assets on saving which differed from the postulates of the saturation theory. This is not the place to describe the extensive empirical work undertaken to test the hypotheses. But it may be reported that the saturation theory was not confirmed; the level-of-aspiration theory likewise did not suffice to explain the findings. In addition to the variable "size of liquid-asset holdings," the studies had to consider such variables as income level, income change, and saving habits. (Holders of large liquid assets are primarily people who have saved a high proportion of their income in the past!)[25]

The necessity of studying the interaction of a great number of variables and the change of choices over time leads to doubts regarding the universal validity of a one-dimensional ordering of all alternatives. The theory of measurement of utilities remains an empty frame unless people's established preferences of *A* over *B* and of *B* over *C* provide indications about their probable future behavior. Under what conditions do people's preferences give us such clues and under what conditions do they not? If at different times *A* and *B* are seen in different contexts—because of changed external conditions or the acquisition of new experiences—we may have to distinguish among several dimensions.

The problem may be illustrated by an analogy. Classic economic theory postulates a one-dimensional ordering of all alternatives; Gallup asserts that answers to questions of choice can always be ordered on a yes-uncertain (don't know)-no continuum; are both arguments subject to the same reservations? Specifically, if two persons give the same answer to a poll question (e.g., both say "Yes, I am for sending American troops to Europe" or "Yes, I am for the Taft-Hartley Act") may they mean different things so that their identical answers do not permit any conclusions about the similarity of their other attitudes and their behavior? Methodologically it follows from the last argument that yes-no questions need to be supplemented by open-ended questions to discern differences in people's level of information and motivation. It also follows that attitudes and preferences should be ascertained through a multi-question approach (or scaling) which serves to determine whether one or several dimensions prevail.

ON THEORY CONSTRUCTION

In attempting to summarize our conclusions about the respective merits of different scientific approaches, we might quote the conclusions of Arrow which he formulated for social science in general rather than for economics:

> To the extent that formal theoretical structures in the social sciences have not been based on the hypothesis of rational behavior, their postulates have been developed in a manner which we may term *ad hoc*. Such propositions . . . depend, of course, on the investigator's intuition and common sense.[26]

The last sentence seems strange indeed. One may argue the other way around and point out that such propositions as "the purpose of business is to make profits" or "the best businessman is the one who maximizes profits" are based on intuition or supposed common sense, rather than on controlled observation. The main problem raised by the quotation concerns the function of empirical research. There exists an alternative to developing an axiomatic system into a full-fledged theoretical model in advance of testing the theory through observations. Controlled observations should be based on hypotheses, and the formulation of an integrated theory need not be delayed until all observations are completed. Yet theory construction is part of the process of hypothesis-observation-revised hypothesis and prediction-observation, and systematization should rely on some empirical research. The proximate aim of scientific research is a body of empirically validated generalizations and not a theory that is valid under any and all circumstances.

The dictum that "theoretical structures in the social sciences must be based upon the hypothesis of rational behavior" presupposes that it is established what rational behavior is. Yet, instead of establishing the characteristics

of rational behavior a priori, we must first determine the conditions a^1, b^1, c^1 under which behavior of the type x^1, y^1, z^1, and the conditions a^2, b^2, c^2 under which behavior of the type x^2, y^2, z^2 is likely to occur. Then, if we wish, we may designate one of the forms of behavior as rational. The contributions of psychology to this process are not solely methodological; findings and principles about noneconomic behavior provide hypotheses for the study of economic behavior. Likewise, psychology can profit from the study of economic behavior because many aspects of behavior, and among them the problems of rationality, may be studied most fruitfully in the economic field.

This paper was meant to indicate some promising leads for a study of rationality, not to carry such study to its completion. Among the problems that were not considered adequately were the philosophical ones (rationality viewed as a value concept), the psychoanalytic ones (the relationships between rational and conscious, and between rational and unconscious), and those relating to personality theory and the roots of rationality. The emphasis was placed here on the possibility and fruitfulness of studying forms of rational behavior, rather than the characteristics of *the* rational man. Motives and goals that change with and are adapted to circumstances, and the relatively rare but highly significant cases of our becoming aware of problems and attempting to solve them, were found to be related to behavior that may be called truly rational.

NOTES

1. T. Parsons and E. A. Shils, (Editors), *Toward a General Theory of Action* (Cambridge, Mass.: Harvard University Press, 1951).
2. A variety of methods used in economic research differ, of course, from those employed by the two groups of economic theorists. Some research is motivated by dissatisfaction

with the traditional economic theory; some is grounded in a systematization greatly different from traditional theory (the most important example of such systematization is national income accounting); some research is not clearly based on any theory; finally, some research has great affinity with psychological and sociological studies.

3. The expression "economic behavior" is used in this paper to mean behavior concerning economic matters (spending, saving, investing, pricing, etc.). Some economic theorists use the expression to mean the behavior of the "economic man," that is, the behavior postulated in their theory of rationality.

4. Reference should be made first of all to Max Wertheimer who in his book *Productive Thinking* uses the terms "sensible" and "intelligent" rather than "rational." Since we are mainly interested here in deriving conclusions from the psychology of thinking, the discussion of psychological principles will be kept extremely brief. See M. Wertheimer, *Productive Thinking* (New York: Harper, 1945); G. Katona, *Organizing and Memorizing* (New York: Columbia University Press, 1940); and G. Katona, *Psychological Analysis of Economic Behavior* (New York: McGraw-Hill, 1951), especially Chapters 3 and 4.

5. E. R. Guthrie, *Psychology of Learning* (New York: Harper, 1935), p. 228.

6. Cf. the following statement by a leading psychoanalyst: "Rational behavior is behavior that is effectively guided by an understanding of the situation to which one is reacting." French adds two steps that follow the choice between alternative goals, namely, commitment to a goal and commitment to a plan to reach a goal. See T. M. French, *The Integration of Behavior* (Chicago: University of Chicago Press, 1952).

7. J. M. Keynes, *The General Theory of Employment, Interest and Money* (New York: Harcourt, Brace, 1936), p. 95.

8. Some empirical evidence supporting these six propositions in the area of economic behavior has been assembled by the Survey Research Center of the University of Michigan. See G. Katona, "Psychological Analysis of Business Decisions and Expectations," *American Economic Review* (1946), pp. 44–63.

9. K. J. Arrow, "Mathematical Models in the Social Sciences," in D. Lemer and H. D. Lasswell (Editors), *The Policy Sciences* (Stanford: Stanford University Press, 1951), p. 135.

10. In his recent book Arrow adds after stating that the economic man "will make the same decision each time he is faced with the same range of alternatives": "The ability to make consistent decisions is one of the symptoms of an integrated personality." See K. J. Arrow, *Social Choice and Individual Values* (New York: Wiley, 1951), p. 2.

11. T. Parsons and E. A. Shils, *op. cit.*

12. If I have reason not to make known that I am at home, I may react to the ringing of the telephone by fright, indecision, and deliberation (should I lift the receiver or let the telephone ring?) instead of reacting in the habitual way. This is an example of problem-solving behavior characterized as deviating from habitual behavior. The only example of action mentioned by Parsons and Shils, "a man driving his automobile to a lake to go fishing," may be habitual or may be an instance of genuine decision making.

13. F. Mosteller and P. Nogee, "An Experimental Measurement of Utility," *Journal of Political Economy* (1951), pp. 371–405.

14. F. Machlup, "The Marginal Analysis and Empirical Research," *American Economic Review* (1946), p. 526.

15. K. J. Arrow, *op cit.*

16. K. J. Arrow, *Social Choice and Individual Values* (New York: Wiley, 1951). The quotation refers specifically to Samuelson's definition but also applies to that of Arrow.

17. G. J. Stigler, "Review of P. A. Samuelson's Foundations of Economic Analysis," *Journal of American Statistical Association* (1984), p. 603.

18. G. Katona, *Psychological Analysis of Economic Behavior* (New York: McGraw-Hill, 1951), pp. 193–213.

19. In the Surveys of Consumer Finances, conducted annually since 1946 by the Survey Research Center of the University of Michigan for the Federal Reserve Board and reported in the *Federal Reserve Bulletin*. See a forthcoming pub-

lication of the Survey Research Center on consumer buying and inflation during 1950–52.

20. It should not be implied that the concepts of utility and maximization are of no value for empirical research. Comparison between maximum utility as determined from the vantage point of an observer with the pattern of goals actually chosen (the "subjective maximum"), which is based on insufficient information, may be useful. Similar considerations apply to such newer concepts as "minimizing regrets" and the "minimax."

21. This principle of diminishing utility was called a "fundamental tendency of human nature" by the great nineteenth century economist, Alfred Marshall.

22. G. Haberler, *Prosperity and Depression*, 3rd ed. (Geneva: League of Nations, 1941), p. 199.

23. The last quotation is from the publication of the U.S. Department of Commerce, *Survey of Current Business*, May 1950, p. 10.

24. K. Lewin et al., "Level of Aspiration," in J. Hunt (Editor), *Personality and the Behavior Disorders* (New York: Ronald, 1944).

25. The empirical work was part of the economic behavior program of the Survey Research Center under the direction of the author.

26. K. J. Arrow, "Mathematical Models in the Social Sciences," in D. Lerner and H. D. Lasswell (Editors), *The Policy Sciences* (Stanford: Stanford University Press, 1951), p. 137.

◆

A Theory of Buyer Behavior

John A. Howard and Jagdish N. Sheth

In the last fifteen years, considerable research on consumer behavior both at the
conceptual and empirical levels has accumulated. This can be gauged by reviews of the
research.[1] As a consequence we believe that
sufficient research exists in both the behavioral sciences and consumer behavior to
attempt a comprehensive theory of buyer behavior. Furthermore, broadly speaking, there
are two major reasons at the basic research
level which seem to have created the need to
take advantage of this opportunity. The first
reason is that a great variety exists in today's
effort to understand the consumer, and unfortunately there is no integration of this variety.
The situation resembles the seven blind men
touching different parts of the elephant and
making inferences about the animal which
differ, and occasionally contradict one another. A comprehensive theory of buyer behavior would hopefully not only provide a
framework for integrating the existing variety

but also would prepare the researcher to
adopt appropriate research designs which
would control sources of influences other
than those he is immediately interested in.
The difficulty of replicating a study and the
possibility of getting contradictory findings
will be minimized accordingly.

The second major basic research reason
for a comprehensive theory is the potential
application of research in buying behavior to
human behavior in general. In asserting the
need to validate psychological propositions in
a real world context Sherif has repeatedly and
eloquently argued for applied research.[2] Also,
McGuire argues that social psychology is
moving toward theory-oriented research in
settings because a number of forces are encouraging the movement away from laboratory research, and he cites the current work in
buyer behavior as one of these forces.[3]

Again, one way that we can contribute
to "pure" areas of behavioral science is by
attempting a comprehensive theory which
would help to identify and to iron out our
own inconsistencies and contradictions. Such
an attempt looks ambitious on the surface, but

Reprinted from Reed Moyer (ed.), *Changing Marketing Systems . . .
Consumer, Corporate and Government Interfaces: Proceedings of the
1967 Winter Conference of the American Marketing Association*, 1967,
published by the American Marketing Association.

after several years of work and drawing upon earlier work,[4] we are confident that it can be achieved.

A BRIEF SUMMARY OF THE THEORY

Before we describe each component of the theory in detail, it will be helpful to discuss briefly the essentials of our view of the consumer choice process.

Much of buying behavior is more or less repetitive brand choice decisions. During his life cycle, the buyer establishes purchase cycles for various products which determine how often he will buy a given product. For some products, this cycle is very lengthy, as for example in buying durable appliances, and, therefore, he buys the product quite infrequently. For many other products, however, the purchase cycle is short and he buys the product frequently as is the case for many grocery and personal care items. Since there is usually the element of repeat buying, we must present a theory which incorporates the dynamics of purchase behavior over a period of time if we wish to capture the central elements of the empirical process.

In the face of repetitive brand choice decisions, the consumer simplifies his decision process by storing relevant information and routinizing his decision process. What is crucial, therefore, is to identify the elements of decision making, to observe the structural or substantive changes that occur in them over time due to the repetitive nature, and show how a combination of the decision elements affect search processes and the incorporation of information from the buyer's commercial and social environment.

The buyer, having been motivated to buy a product class, is faced with a brand choice decision. The elements of his decision are: (1) a set of motives, (2) several courses of action, and (3) decision mediators by which the motives are matched with the alternatives. Motives are specific to a product class, and they reflect the underlying needs of the buyer. The alternative courses of actions are the purchase of one of the various brands with their potential to satisfy the buyer's motives. There are two important notions involved in the definition of alternatives as brands. First, the brands which are alternatives of the buyer's choice decision at any given time are generally a small number, collectively called his "evoked set." The size of the evoked set is only two or three, a fraction of the brands he is aware of and still smaller fraction of the total number of brands actually available in the market. Second, any two consumers may have quite different alternatives in their evoked sets.

The decision mediators are a set of rules that the buyer employs to match his motives and his means of satisfying those motives. They serve the function of ordering and structuring the buyer's motives and then ordering and structuring the various brands based on their potential to satisfy these ordered motives. The decision mediators develop by the process of learning about the buying situation. They are, therefore, influenced by information from the buyer's environment and even more importantly by the actual experience of purchasing and consuming the brand.

When the buyer is just beginning to purchase a product class such as when a purchase is precipitated by a change in his life cycle, he lacks experience. In order, therefore, to develop the decision mediators, he *actively seeks information* from his commercial and social environments. The information that he either actively seeks or accidentally receives is subject to perceptual processes which not only limit the intake of information (magnitude of information is affected) but modify it to suit his own frame of reference (quality of information is affected). These modifications are significant since they distort the neat "marketing stimulus-customer response" relation.

Along with active search for information, the buyer may, to some extent, generalize from past similar experiences. Such generalization can be due to physical similarity of the new product class to the old product class. For example, in the initial purchases of Scotch whiskey, the buyer may generalize his experiences in buying of gin. Generalization can also occur even when the two product classes are physically dissimilar but have a common meaning such as deriving from a company-wide brand name. For example, the buyer could generalize his experiences in buying a refrigerator or range to his first purchase of a dishwasher of the same brand.

Whatever the source, the buyer develops sufficient decision mediators to enable him to choose a brand which seems to have the best potential for satisfying his motives. If the brand proves satisfactory, the potential of that brand to satisfy his motives is increased. The result is that the probability of buying that brand is likewise increased. With repeated satisfactory purchases of one or more brands, the buyer is likely to manifest a routinized decision process whereby the sequential steps in buying are well structured so that some event which triggers the process may actually complete the choice decision. Routinized purchasing implies that his decision mediators are well established and that the buyer has strong brand preferences.

The phase of repetitive decision making, in which the buyer reduces the complexity of a buying situation with the help of information and experience, is called the *psychology of simplification*. Decision making can be divided into three stages and used to illustrate the psychology of simplification: Extensive Problem Solving, Limited Problem Solving and Routinized Response Behavior. The further he is along in simplifying his environment, the less is the tendency toward active search behavior. The environmental stimuli related to the purchase situation become more meaningful and less ambiguous. Furthermore, the buyer establishes more cognitive consistency among the brands as he moves toward routinization and the incoming information is then screened both with regard to its magnitude and quality. He becomes less attentive to stimuli which do not fit his cognitive structure and he distorts those stimuli which are forced upon him.

A surprising phenomenon, we believe, occurs in many instances of frequently purchased products such as in grocery and personal care items. The buyer, after attaining routinization of his decision process, may find himself in too simple a situation. He is likely to feel the monotony or boredom associated with such repetitive decision making. It is also very likely that he is dissatisfied with even the most preferred brand. In both cases, he may feel that all existing alternatives including the preferred brand are unacceptable. He therefore feels a need to *complicate* his buying situation by considering new brands, and this process can be called the *psychology of complication*. The new situation causes him to identify a new brand, and so he begins again to simplify in the manner described earlier. Thus with a frequently purchased item buying is a continuing process with its ups and downs in terms of information seeking analogous to the familiar cyclical fluctuations in economic activity.

ELEMENTS OF THEORY

Any theory of human behavior needs some means for explaining individual differences. The marketing manager also is interested in differentiated masses of buyers. He wants to understand and separate individual differences so that he can classify or segment the total market based upon individual differences. By understanding the psychology of the individual buyer we may achieve this classification. Depending on the internal state of the buyer, a given stimulus may result in a given response. For example, one buyer who urgently needs a product may respond to the ad of a brand in that product class by buying it whereas another buyer who does not need the product may simply notice the ad and store the information or ignore the ad. A construct such as "level of motivation" will then explain the divergent reactions to the same stimulus. Alternatively, two buyers may both urgently need a product, but they buy two different brands. This can be explained by another construct: predisposition toward a brand.

Figure 10-1 represents the theory of buyer behavior. The central rectangular box isolates the various internal state variables and processes which combined together show the state of the buyer. The inputs to the rectangular box are the stimuli from the marketing and social environments. The outputs are a variety of responses that the buyer is likely to manifest based on the interaction between the stimuli and his internal state. Besides the inputs and outputs, there are a set of seven influences which affect the variables in the rectangular box.[5] These variables appear at the top of the diagram and are labelled "exogenous variables." Their function is to provide a means of adjusting for the interpersonal differences discussed above. The variables within the rectangular box serve the role of endogenous variables in the sense that changes in them are explained but they are something less than endogenous variables. They are not well defined and hence are not measurable. They are hypothetical constructs. Their values are inferred from relations among the output intervening variables. Several of the exogenous variables such as personality, social class and culture have traditionally been treated as part of the endo-

genous variables. We believe that they affect more specific variables, and by conceptualizing their effect as via the hypothetical constructs, we can better understand their role.

Thus it will be seen that the theory of buyer behavior has four major components; the stimulus variables, the response variable, the hypothetical constructs and the exogenous variables. We will elaborate on each of the components below both in terms of their substance and their interrelationships.

Stimulus Variables

At any point in time, the hypothetical constructs which reflect the buyer's internal state are affected by numerous stimuli from the environment. The environment is classified as Commercial or Social. The commercial environment is the marketing activities of various firms by which they attempt to communicate to the buyer. From the buyer's point of view, these communications basically come either via the physical brands themselves or some linguistic or pictorial representations of the attributes of the brands. If the elements of the brands such as price, quality, service, distinctiveness or availability are communicated through the physical brands (significates) then the stimuli are defined and classified as significative stimuli. If, on the other hand, the attributes are communicated in linguistic or pictorial symbols such as in mass media, billboards, catalogs, salesmen, etc., then the stimuli from commercial stores are classified as symbolic stimuli. We view the marketing mix as the optimum allocation of funds between the two major channels of communication—significative or symbolic—to the buyer.

Each commercial input variable is hypothesized to be multivariate. Probably the five major dimensions of a brand—price, quality, distinctiveness, availability and service—summarize the various attributes. The same dimensions are present in both signifi-

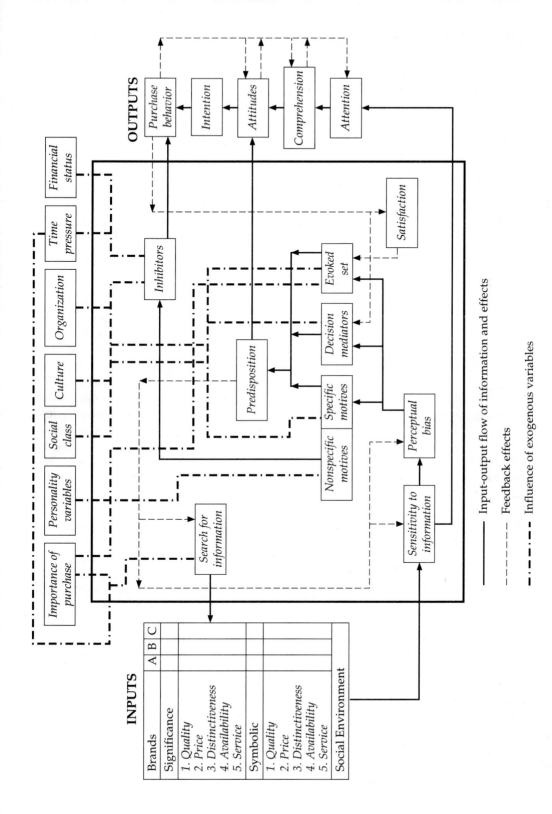

INPUTS

Brands	A	B	C
Significance			
1. Quality			
2. Price			
3. Distinctiveness			
4. Availability			
5. Service			
Symbolic			
1. Quality			
2. Price			
3. Distinctiveness			
4. Availability			
5. Service			
Social Environment			

OUTPUTS

——— Input-output flow of information and effects

------ Feedback effects

–·–·– Influence of exogenous variables

Figure 10-1
A Theory of Buyer Behavior

cative or symbolic communication which become the input stimuli for the buyer. However, certain dimensions may be more appropriately conveyed by significative rather than symbolic communication and vice versa. For example, price is easily communicated by both channels; shape may best be communicated by two-dimensional pictures rather than verbal communication. Finally, size may not be easily communicated by any symbolic representation: the physical product (significate) may be necessary.

The third stimulus input variable is social stimuli. It refers to the information that the buyer's social environment provides regarding a purchase decision. The most obvious is word of mouth communication.

The inputs to the buyer's mental state from the three major sources are then processed and stored by their interaction with a series of hypothetical constructs, and the buyer may react immediately or later.

Hypothetical Constructs

The hypothetical constructs and their interrelationships are the result of an integration of Hull's learning theory,[6] Osgood's cognitive theory,[7] and Berlyne's theory of exploratory behavior[8] along with other ideas.

We may classify the constructs into two classes: (i) those that have to do with perception, and (ii) those having to do with learning. Perceptual constructs serve the function of information processing while the learning constructs serve the function of concept formation. It is interesting that, after years of experience in advertising, Reeves has a very similar classification:[9] his "penetration" is analogous to perceptual variables and his "unique selling propositions" is analogous to learning variables. We will at first describe the learning constructs since they are the motor components of decision making; the perceptual constructs which serve the important role

of obtaining and processing information are more complex and will be described later.

Learning Constructs   The learning constructs are labeled as: (1) Motives—Specific and Nonspecific, (2) Brand Potential of Evoked Set, (3) Decision Mediators, (4) Predisposition toward the brands, (5) Inhibitors, and (6) Satisfaction with the purchase of the brand.

Motive is the impetus to action. Motives or goals may be thought of as constituting a means-end chain and hence, as being general or specific depending upon their position in the chain. Motives can refer to the buyer's specific goals in purchasing a product class. The buyer is motivated by the expectation or anticipation due to past learning of outcome from the purchase of each of the brands in his evoked set.

The specific motives—lower level motives in the means-end chain—are very closely anchored to the attributes of a product class and in this way they become purchase criteria. Examples of specific motives for buying a dietary product such as Metrecal or Sego are low calories, nutrition, taste, and value.

Very often, several specific motives are nothing more than indicators of some underlying more general motive, that is, some motive that is higher in the means-end chain. In the above example, the specific motives of nutrition and low calories might be merely indicators of the common motive of good health.

Motives also serve the important function of raising the buyer's general motivational state or arousal and thereby tuning up the buyer, causing him to pay attention to environmental stimuli. Examples of nonspecific motives are probably anxiety, fear, many of the personality variables such as authoritarianism, exhibitionism, aggressiveness, etc., and social motives of power, status, prestige, etc. Although they are nonspecific, they are not innate, but rather learned, mostly due to acculturation. The nonspecific motives also possess a hierarchy within themselves. For example, anxiety is considered to be the source of another motive, that of the need of money.[10]

Brand Potential of Evoked Set is the second learning construct. A buyer who is familiar with a product class has an evoked set of alternatives to satisfy his motives. The elements of his evoked set are some of the brands that make up the product class. The concept is important because for this buyer the brands in his evoked set constitute competition for the seller.

A brand is, of course, a class concept like many other objects or things. The buyer attaches a *word* to this concept—a label—which is the brand name such as "Campbell's Tomato Soup." Whenever he sees a can of Campbell's Tomato Soup or hears the phrase, the image conveys to him certain satisfactions, procedures for preparation, etc. In short, it conveys certain meaning including its potential to satisfy his motives.

Various brands in the buyer's evoked set will generally satisfy the goal structure differently. One brand may possess potential to the extent that it is an ideal brand for the buyer. Another brand, on the other hand, may satisfy motives just enough to be part of his evoked set. By the process of learning the buyer obtains and stores knowledge regarding each brand's potential and then rank orders them in terms of their want-satisfying potential. The evoked set, in short, is a set of alternatives with each alternative's payoff. Predisposition mentioned below enables the buyer to choose one among them.

Decision-Mediator is the third learning construct and it brings together motives and alternatives. The brand potential of each of the brands in his evoked set are the decision alternatives with their payoffs. Decision mediators are the buyer's mental rules for matching the alternatives with his motives, for rank-ordering them in terms of their want-satisfying capacity. As mental rules, they exhibit reasons wherein the cognitive elements related to the alternatives and the motives are structured. The words that he uses to describe these attributes are also the words that he thinks with and that he finds are easy to remember. The criterial attributes are important to the manufacturer because if he knows them he can deliberately build into his brand and promotion those characteristics which will differentiate his brand from competing brands.

The decision mediators thus represent enduring cognitive rules established by the process of learning, and their function is to obtain meaningful and congruent relations among brands so that the buyer can manifest goal-directed behavior. The aim of the theory of buyer behavior is not just the identification of motives and the respective brands but to show their structure as well. It is the decision mediators which provide this structure.

In view of the fact that decision mediators are learned, principles of learning become crucial in their development and change over time. There are two broad sources of learning: (1) actual experiences, and (2) information. Actual experiences can be either with the *same* buying situation in the past or with a *similar* buying situation. The latter is generally labelled as generalization as discussed earlier. Similarly, information as a source of learning can be from: (1) the buyer's commercial environment, or (2) his social environment. Later, we will elaborate on each of the sources of learning.

Predisposition, the fourth construct, is the summary effect of the previous three constructs. It refers to the buyer's preference toward brands in his evoked set. It is, in fact, an aggregate index which is reflected in attitude which, in turn, is measured by attitude scales. It might be visualized as the "place" where brands in Evoked Set are compared with Mediator's choice criteria to yield a judgment on the relative contribution of the brands to the buyer's motives. This judgment includes not only an estimate of the value of the brand to him but also an estimate of the confidence with which he holds that position. This uncertainty aspect of Predisposition can be called "brand ambiguity," in that, the more confident he holds it, the less ambiguous is the connotative meaning of the brand to the buyer and the more likely he is to buy it.[11]

Inhibitors, the fifth learning construct, are forces in the environment which create important disruptive influences in the actual purchase of a brand even when the buyer has reasoned out that that brand will best satisfy his motives. In other words, when the buyer is both predisposed to buy a brand and has the motivation to buy some brand in the product class, he may not buy it because several environmental forces inhibit its purchase and prevent him from satisfying his preferences.

We postulate at least four types of inhibitors. They are: (1) high price of the brand, (2) lack of availability of the brand, (3) time pressure on the buyer, and (4) the buyer's financial status. The first two are part of the environmental stimuli, and therefore, they are part of the input system. The last two come from the two exogenous variables of the same name. It should be pointed out that social constraints emanating from other exogenous variables may also create temporary barriers to the purchase of a brand.

An essential feature of all inhibitors is that they are *not internalized* by the buyer because their occurrence is random and strictly situational. However, some of the inhibitors may persist systematically over time as they concern a given buyer. If they persist long enough, the buyer is likely to incorporate them as part of his decision mediators and thus to internalize them. The consequence is that they may affect even the structure of alternatives and motives.

Satisfaction, the last of the learning constructs, refers to the degree of congruence between the actual consequences from purchase and consumption of a brand and what was expected from it by the buyer at the time of purchase. If the actual outcome is adjudged by the buyer as *at least* equal to the expected, the buyer will feel satisfied. If, on the other hand, the actual outcome is adjudged as less than what he expected, the buyer will feel dissatisfied and his attitude will be less favorable. Satisfaction or dissatisfaction with a brand can exist with respect to any one of the different attributes. If the brand proves more satisfactory than he expected, the buyer has a tendency to enhance the attractiveness of the brand. Satisfaction will, therefore, affect the reordering of the brands in the evoked set for the next buying decision.

Relations among Learning Constructs   Underlying Predisposition toward the brands and related variables, several important notions are present. The simplest way to describe them is to state that we may classify a decision process as either Extensive Problem Solving, Limited Problem Solving or Routinized Response Behavior depending on the strength of Predisposition toward the brands. In the early phases of buying, the buyer has not yet developed decision mediators well enough; specifically his product class concept is not well formed and predisposition is low. As he acquires information and gains experience in buying and consuming the brand, Decision Mediators become firm and Predisposition toward a brand is generally high.

In Extensive Problem Solving, Predisposition toward the brands is low. None of the brands is discriminated enough based on their criterial attributes for the buyer to show greater brand preference toward any one brand. At this state of decision making, brand ambiguity is high with the result that the buyer actively seeks information from his environment. Due to greater search for information, there exists a greater *latency of re-*

sponse—the time interval from the initiation of a decision to its completion. Similarly, deliberation or reasoning will be high since he lacks a well-defined product class concept which is the denotative aspect of mediator. He is also likely to consider many brands as part of Evoked Set, and stimuli coming from the commercial environment are less likely to trigger any immediate purchase reaction.

When Predisposition toward the brands is moderate, the buyer's decision process can be called Limited Problem Solving. There still exists brand ambiguity since the buyer is not able to discriminate and compare brands so that he may prefer one brand over others. He is likely to seek information but not to the extent that he seeks it in Extensive Problem Solving. More importantly, he seeks information more on a relative basis to compare and discriminate various brands rather than to compare them absolutely on each of the brands. His deliberation or thinking is much less since Decision Mediators are tentatively well defined. Evoked Set will consist of a small number of brands, each having about the same degree of preference.

In Routinized Response Behavior, the buyer will have a high level of Predisposition toward brands in his evoked set. Furthermore, he has now accumulated sufficient experience and information to have little brand ambiguity. He will in fact discriminate among brands enough to show a strong preference toward one or two brands in the evoked set. He is unlikely to actively seek any information from his environment since such information is not needed. Also, whatever information he passively or accidentally receives, he will subject it to selective perceptual processes so that only congruent information is allowed. Very often, the congruent information will act as "triggering cues" to motivate him to manifest purchase behavior. Much of impulse purchase, we believe, is really the outcome of a strong predisposition and such a

facilitating commercial stimulus as store display. The buyer's evoked set will consist of a few brands toward which he is highly predisposed. However, he will have greater preference toward one or two brands in his evoked set and less toward others.

As mentioned earlier, Predisposition is an aggregate index of decision components. Thus, any changes in the components due to learning from experience or information imply some change in Predisposition. The greater the learning, the more the predisposition toward the brands in the evoked set. The exact nature of learning will be described later when we discuss the dynamics of buying behavior.

Perceptual Constructs   Another set of constructs serves the function of information procurement and processing relevant to a purchase decision. As mentioned earlier, information can come from any one of the three stimulus inputs—significative commercial stimuli, symbolic commercial stimuli, and social stimuli. Once again we will here only describe the constructs; their utilization by the buyer will be explained when we discuss the dynamics of buying behavior. The perceptual constructs in Figure 10-1 are: (a) Sensitivity to Information, (b) Perceptual Bias, and (c) Search for Information.

A perceptual phenomenon implies either ignoring a physical event which could be a stimulus, seeing it attentively or sometimes imagining what is not present in reality. All perceptual phenomena essentially create some change in quantity or quality of objective information.

Sensitivity to Information refers to the opening and closing of sensory receptors which control the intake of information. The manifestation of this phenomenon is generally called perceptual vigilance (paying attention) or perceptual defense (ignoring the information). Sensitivity to Information, therefore, primarily serves as a gatekeeper to information entering into the buyer's mental state. It thus controls the quantity of information input.

Sensitivity to Information, according to Berlyne,[12] is a function of the degree of ambiguity of the stimuli to which the buyer is exposed. If the stimulus is very familiar or too simple, the ambiguity is low and the buyer will not pay attention unless he is predisposed to such information from past learning. Furthermore, if ambiguity of the stimulus continues to be low, the buyer feels a sense of monotony and actually seeks other information, and this act can be said to *complicate* his environment. If the stimulus is very complex and ambiguous, the buyer finds it hard to comprehend and, therefore, he ignores it by resorting to perceptual defense. Only if the stimulus is in the moderate range of ambiguity is the buyer motivated to pay attention and to freely absorb the objective information.

In a single communication, the buyer may at first find the communication complex and ambiguous and so he will resort to perceptual defense and tend to ignore it. As some information enters, however, he finds that it is really at the medium level of ambiguity and so pays attention. On the other hand, it might be that the more he pays attention to it, the more he finds the communication too simple and, therefore, ignores it as the process of communication progresses.

A second variable which governs Sensitivity to Information is the buyer's predisposition toward the brand about which the information is concerned. The more interesting the information, the more likely the buyer is to open up his receptors and therefore to pay attention to the information. Hess has recently measured this by obtaining the strength of pupil dilation.

Perceptual Bias is the second perceptual construct. The buyer not only selectively attends to information, but he may actually distort it once it enters his mental state. In other words, quality of information can be altered by the buyer. This aspect of the perceptual process is summarized in Perceptual Bias. The buyer may distort the cognitive elements contained in information to make them congruent with his own frame of reference as determined by the amount of information he already has stored. A series of cognitive consistency theories have been recently developed to explain how this congruency is established and what the consequences are in terms of the distortion of information we might expect.[13] Most of the qualitative change in information arises because of feedback from various decision components such as Motives, Evoked Set and Decision Mediators. These relations are too complex, however, to describe in the summary.

The perceptual phenomena described above are likely to be less operative if the information is received from the buyer's social environment. This is because: (i) the source of social information, such as a friend, is likely to be favorably regarded by the buyer and therefore proper, undistorted reception of information will occur, and (ii) the information itself is modified by the social environment (the friend) so that it conforms to the needs of the buyer and, therefore, further modification is less essential.

Search for Information is the third perceptual construct. During the total buying phase which extends over time and involves several repeat purchases of a product class, there are stages when the buyer *actively* seeks information. It is very important to distinguish the times when he passively receives information from the situations where he actively seeks it. We believe that perceptual distortion is less operative in the latter instances and that a commercial communication, therefore, at that stage has a high probability of influencing the buyer.

The active seeking of information occurs when the buyer senses ambiguity of the brands in his evoked set. As we saw earlier, this happens in the Extensive Problem Solving and Limited Problem Solving phases of the decision process. The ambiguity of brand exists because the buyer is not certain of the outcomes from each brand. In other words, he has not yet learned enough about the alternatives to establish an expectancy of potential of the brands to satisfy his motives. This type of brand ambiguity is essentially confined to initial buyer behavior which we have called Extensive Problem Solving. However, ambiguity may still exist despite knowledge of the potential of alternative brands. This ambiguity is with respect to his inability to discriminate because his motives are not well structured: he does not know how to order them. He may then seek information which will resolve the conflict among goals, a resolution that is implied in his learning of the appropriate product class aspect of decision mediators that we discussed earlier.

There is yet another stage of total buying behavior in which the buyer is likely to seek information. It is when the buyer has not only routinized his decision process but he is so familiar and satiated with repeat buying that he feels bored. Then, all the existing alternatives in his evoked set including the most preferred brand become unacceptable to him. He seeks change or variety in that buying situation. In order to obtain this change, he actively searches for information on other alternatives (brands) that he never considered before. At this stage, he is particularly receptive to any information about new brands. Incidentally, here is an explanation for advertising in a highly stable industry. This phenomenon has long baffled both the critics and defenders of the institution of advertising. Newcomers to the market and forgetting do not provide a plausible explanation.

We have so far described the stimulus input variables and the hypothetical constructs. Now we proceed to describe the output of the system—the responses of the buyer.

Response Variables

The complexity of buyer behavior does not stop with hypothetical constructs. Just as there is a variety of inputs, there exists a variety of buyer responses which become relevant for different areas of marketing strategy. This variety of consumer responses can be easily appreciated from the diversity of measures to evaluate advertising effectiveness. We have attempted to classify and order this diversity of buyer responses in the output variables. Most of the output variables are directly related to some and not other constructs. Each output variable serves different purposes both in marketing practice and fundamental research. Let us at first describe each variable and then provide a rationale for their interrelationships.

Attention   Attention is related to Sensitivity to Information. It is a response of the buyer which indicates the magnitude of his information intake. Attention is measured continuously during the time interval when the buyer receives information. There are several psychophysical methods of quantifying the degree of attention that the buyer pays to a message. The pupil dilation is one.

Comprehension   Comprehension refers to the store of knowledge about the brand that the buyer possesses at any point in time. This knowledge could vary from his simply being aware of a single brand's existence to a complete description of the attributes of the product class of which the brand is an element. It reflects the denotative meaning of the brand and in that sense it is strictly in the cognitive realm. It lacks the motivational aspects of behavior. Some of the standard measures of advertising effectiveness such as awareness, aided or unaided recall, and recognition may capture different aspects of the buyer's comprehension of the brand.

Attitude toward a Brand   Attitude toward a brand is the buyer's evaluation of the brand's potential to satisfy his motives. It, therefore, includes the connotative aspects of the brand concept: it contains those aspects of the brand which are relevant to the buyer's goals. Attitude is directly related to Predisposition and so it consists of both the evaluation of a brand in terms of the criteria of choice from Mediator and the confidence with which that evaluation is held.

Intention to Buy   Intention to buy is the buyer's forecast of his brand choice some time in the future. Like any forecast, it involves assumptions about future events including the likelihood of any perceived inhibitors creating barriers over the buyer's planning horizon. Intention to buy has been extensively used in the purchases of durable goods with some recent refinements in terms of the buyer's confidence in his own forecast; these studies are in terms of broadly defined product classes.[14] We may summarize this response of the buyer as something short of actual purchase behavior.

Purchase Behavior   Purchase Behavior refers to the overt act of purchasing a brand. What becomes a part of a company's sales or what the consumer records in a diary as a panel member, however, is only the terminal act in the sequence of shopping and buying. Very often, it is useful to observe the complete movement of the buyer from his home to the store and his purchase in the store. Yoell, for example, shows several case histories where a time and motion study of consumers' purchase behavior has useful marketing implications.[15] We think that at times it may be helpful to go so far as to incorporate the act of consumption into the definition of Purchase Behavior. We have, for example, developed and used the technique of sequential decision making where the buyer verbally describes the sequential pattern of his purchase behavior in a given buying situation. Out of this description a "flow chart" of decision making is obtained which reveals the number and the structure of the decision rules that the buyer employs.

Purchase Behavior is the overt manifestation of the buyer's Predisposition in conjunction with any Inhibitors that may be present. It differs from Attitude to the extent that Inhibitors are taken into consideration. It differs from Intention to the extent that it is the actual manifestation of behavior which the buyer only forecasted in his intention.

Several characteristics of Purchase Behavior become useful if we observe the buyer in a repetitive buying situation. These include the incidence of buying a brand, the quantity bought, and the purchase cycle. Several stochastic models of brand loyalty, for example, have been developed in recent years.[16] Similarly, we could take the magnitude purchased and compare light buyers with heavy buyers to determine if heavy buyers are more loyal buyers.

Interrelationship of Response Variables   In Figure 10-1, it will be seen that we have ordered the five response variables to create a hierarchy. The hierarchy is similar to the variety of hierarchies used in practice such as AIDA (Attention, Interest, Desire and Action), to the Lavidge and Steiner hierarchy of advertising effectiveness,[17] as well as to the different mental states that a person is alleged by the anthropologists and sociologists to pass through when he adopts an innovation.[18] There are, however, some important differences which we believe will clarify certain conceptual and methodological issues raised by Palda and others.[19]

First, we have added a response variation called Attention which is crucial since it reflects whether a communication is received by the buyer. Secondly, several different aspects of the cognitive realm of behavior such as awareness, recall, recognition, etc., are lumped into one category called Comprehension to suggest that they all are varying indicators of the buyer's storage of information about a brand which can be extended to *product class,* and in this way we obtain leverage toward understanding buyer innovation. Third, we have defined Attitude to include both affective and conative aspects since anyone who wants to establish causal relations between attitude and behavior must bring the motivational aspects into attitude. Furthermore, we separate the perceptual and the preference maps of the buyer into Comprehension and Attitude respectively. Fourth, we add another variable, Intention to Buy, because there are several product classes in both durable and semi-durable goods where properly defined and measured intentions have already proved useful. To the extent that Intention incorporates the buyer's forecast of his inhibitors, it might serve the useful function of informing the firm how to remove the inhibitors before the actual purchase behavior is manifested.

Finally, and most importantly, we have incorporated several feedback effects which were described when we discussed the hypothetical constructs. We will now show the relations as direct connections among response variables but the reader should bear in mind that these "outside" relations are merely the reflection of relations among the hypothetical constructs. For example, Purchase Behavior via Satisfaction entails some consequences which affect Decision Mediators and brand potential in Evoked Set; any change in them can produce change in Predisposition. Attitude is related to Predisposition and, therefore, it can also be changed in the period from prepurchase to post-purchase. In incorporating this feedback, we are opening the way to resolving the controversy whether Attitude causes Purchase Behavior or Purchase Behavior causes Attitude. Over a period of time, the relation is interdependent, each affecting the other. Similarly, we have a feedback from Attitude to Comprehension and Attention, the rationale for which was given when we described the perceptual constructs.

DYNAMICS OF BUYING BEHAVIOR

Let us now explain the changes in the hypothetical constructs which occur due to learning.

The learning constructs are, of course, directly involved in the change that we label "learning." Since some of the learning constructs indirectly govern the perceptual constructs by way of feedbacks, there is also an indirect effect back upon the learning constructs themselves. As mentioned earlier, learning of Decision Mediators which structure Motives and Evoked Set of Brands which contain brand potentials can occur from two broad sources: (i) past experience and (ii) information. Experience can be further classified as having been derived from buying a specified product or buying some similar product. Similarly, information can come from the buyer's commercial environment or his social environment, and if commercial, it can be significative or symbolic.

We will look at the development and change in learning constructs as due to: (i) generalization from similar buying situations, (ii) repeat buying of the same product class, and (iii) information.

Generalization from Similar Purchase Situations

Some decision mediators are common across several product classes because many motives are common to a wide variety of purchasing activity. For example, a buyer may satisfy his health motive from many product classes by looking for nutrition. Similarly, many product classes are all bought at the same place which very often leads to spatial or contiguous generalization. The capacity to generalize provides the buyer with a truly enormous range of flexibility in adapting his purchase behavior to the myriad of varying market conditions he faces.

Generalization refers to the transfer of responses and of the relevance of stimuli from past situations to new situations which are similar. It saves the buyer time and effort in seeking information in the face of uncertainty that is inevitable in a new situation. Generalization can occur at any one of the several levels of purchase activity, but we are primarily interested in generalization of those decision mediators which only involve brand choice behavior in contrast to store choice or choice of shopping time and day. In other words, we are concerned with brand generalization.

Repeat Purchase Experiences

Another source of change in the learning constructs is the repeated purchase of the same product class over a period of time.

In Figure 10-1 the purchase of a brand entails two types of feedbacks, one affecting the decision mediators and the other affecting the brand potential of the evoked set. First, the experience of buying with all its cognitive aspects of memory, reasoning, etc., has a learning effect on the decision mediators. This occurs irrespective of which specific brand the buyer chooses in any one purchase decision because the decision mediators like the motives are product-specific and not limited to any one brand. Hence every purchase has an incremental effect in firmly establishing the decision mediators. This is easy to visualize if we remember that buying behavior is a series

of mental and motor steps while the actual choice is only its terminal act.

Purchase of a brand creates certain satisfactions for the buyer which the consumer compares with his expectations of the brand's potential and this expectation is the basis on which he made his decision in the first place. This comparison of expected and actual consequences causes him to be satisfied or dissatisfied with his purchase of the brand. Hence, the second feedback from Purchase Behavior to Satisfaction changes the attractiveness of the brand purchased. If the buyer is satisfied with his consumption, he enhances the potential of the brand and this is likely to result in greater probability of its repeat purchase. If he is dissatisfied, the potential of the brand is diminished, and its probability of repeat purchase is also similarly reduced.

If there are no inhibitory forces which influence him, the buyer will continue to buy a brand which proves satisfactory. In the initial stages of decision making he may show some tendency to oscillate between brands in order to formulate his decision mediators. In other words, he may learn by trial-and-error at first and then settle on a brand and therefore he may buy the brand with such regularity to suggest that he is brand loyal. Unless a product is of very high risk, however, there is a limit as to how long this brand loyalty will continue: he may become bored with his preferred brand and look for something new.

Information as a Source of Learning

The third major source by which the learning constructs are changed is information from the buyer's (i) commercial environment consisting of advertising, promotion, salesmanship and retail shelf display of the competing companies, and (ii) his social environment consisting of his family, friends, reference group and social class.

We will describe the influence of information at first as if the perceptual constructs were absent. In other words, we assume that the buyer receives information with perfect fidelity as it exists in the environment. Also, we will discuss separately the information from the commercial and social environments.

Commercial Environment   The company communicates about its offerings to the buyers either by the physical brand (significates) or by symbols (pictorial or linguistic) which represent the brand. In other words, significative and symbolic communication are the two major ways of interaction between the sellers and the buyers.

In Figure 10-1, the influence of information is shown on Motives, Decision Mediators, Evoked Set, and Inhibitors. We believe that the influence of commercial information on motives (specific and nonspecific) is limited. The main effect is primarily to *intensify* whatever motives the buyer has rather than to create new ones. For example, physical display of the brand may intensify his motives above the threshold levels which combined with strong predisposition can result in impulse (unplanned) purchase. A similar reaction is possible when an ad creates sufficient intensity of motives to provide an impetus for the buyer to go to the store. A second way to influence motives is to show the *perceived instrumentality* of the brand and thereby make it a part of the buyer's defined set of alternatives. Finally, to a very limited extent, marketing stimuli may change the *content of the motives*. The general conception both among marketing men and laymen is that marketing stimuli change the buyer's motives. However, on a closer examination it would appear that what is changed is the *intensity* of buyer's motives already provided by the social environment. Many dormant or latent motives may become stimulated. The secret of success very

often lies in identifying the change in motives created by social change and intensifying them as seems to be the case in the recent projection of youthfulness in many buying situations.

Marketing stimuli are also important in determining and changing the buyer's evoked set. Commercial information tells him of the existence of the brands (awareness), their identifying characteristics (Comprehension plus brand name) and their relevance to the satisfaction of the buyer's needs (Attitude).

Marketing stimuli are also important in creating and changing the buyer's decision mediators. They become important sources for learning decision mediators when the buyer has no prior experience to rely upon. In other words, when he is in the extensive problem-solving (EPS) stage, it is marketing and social stimuli which are the important sources of learning. Similarly, when the buyer actively seeks information because all the existing alternatives are unacceptable to him, marketing stimuli become important in *changing* his decision mediators.

Finally, marketing stimuli can unwittingly create inhibitors. For example, a company feels the need to emphasize price-quality association, but it may result in high-price inhibition in the mind of the buyer. Similarly, in emphasizing the details of usage and consumption of a product, the communication may create the inhibition related to time pressure.

Social Environment   The social environment of the buyer—family, friends, reference groups—is another major source of information in his buying behavior. Most of the inputs are likely to be symbolic (linguistic) although at times the physical product may be shown to the buyer.

Information from his social environment also affects the four learning constructs:

Motives, Decision Mediators, Evoked Set and Inhibitors. However, the effect on these constructs is different from that of the commercial environment. First, the information about the brands will be considerably modified by the social environment before it reaches the buyer. Most of the modifications are likely to be in the nature of adding connotative meanings to brand descriptions, and of the biasing effects of the communication's perceptual variables like Sensitivity to Information and Perceptual Bias. Second, the buyer's social environment will probably have a very strong influence on the content of his motives and their ordering to establish a goal structure. Several research studies have concentrated on such influences.[20] Third, the social environment may also affect his evoked set. This will be particularly true when the buyer lacks experience. Furthermore, if the product class is important to the buyer and he is technically incompetent or uncertain in evaluating the consequences of the brand for his needs, he may rely more on the social than on the marketing environment for information. This is well documented by several studies using the perceived risk hypothesis.[21]

Exogenous Variables

Earlier we mentioned that there are several influences operating on the buyer's decisions which we treat as exogenous, that is, we do not explain their formation and change. Many of these influences come from the buyer's social environment and we wish to separate the effects of his environment which have occurred in the past and are not related to a specific decision from those which are current and directly affect the decisions that occur during the period the buyer is being observed. The inputs during the observation period provide information to the buyer to help his current decision making. The past influences are already imbedded in the values of

the perceptual and learning constructs. Strictly speaking, therefore, there is no need for some of the exogenous variables which have influenced the buyer in the past. We bring them out explicitly, however, for the sake of research design where the research may control or take into account individual differences among buyers due to such past influences. Incorporating the effects of these exogenous variables will reduce the size of the unexplained variance or error in estimation which it is particularly essential to control under field conditions. Figure 10-1 presents a set of exogenous variables which we believe provide the control essential to obtaining satisfactory predictive relations between the inputs and the outputs of the system. Let us briefly discuss each of the exogenous variables.

Importance of Purchase refers to differential degrees of ego-involvement or commitment in different product classes. It, therefore, provides a mechanism which must be carefully examined in interproduct studies. Importance of Purchase will influence the size of the Evoked Set and the magnitude of Search for Information. The more important the product class, the larger the Evoked Set.

Time Pressure is a current exogenous variable and, therefore, specific to a decision situation. It refers to the situation when a buyer feels pressed for time due to any of several environmental influences and so must allocate his time among alternative uses. In this process a re-allocation unfavorable to the purchasing activity can occur. Time pressure will create inhibition as mentioned earlier. It will also unfavorably affect Search for Information.

Financial Status refers to the constraint the buyer may feel because of lack of financial resources. This affects his purchase behavior to the extent that it creates a barrier to purchasing the most preferred brand. For example, a buyer may want to purchase a Mercedes-Benz but lacks sufficient financial resources and, therefore, he will settle for some low-priced American automobile such as a Ford or Chevrolet. Its effect is via Inhibitor.

Personality Traits take into consideration many of the variables such as self-confidence, self-esteem, authoritarianism and anxiety which have been researched to identify individual differences. It will be noted that these individual differences are "topic free" and, therefore, are supposed to exert their effect across product classes. We believe their effect is felt on: (i) nonspecific Motives and (ii) Evoked Set. For example, the more anxious a person, the greater the motivational arousal; dominant personalities are more likely by a small margin to buy a Ford instead of a Chevrolet; the more authoritarian a person, the narrower the category width of his evoked set.

Social and Organizational Setting (Organization) takes us to the group, to a higher level of social organization than the individual. It includes both the informal social organization such as family and reference groups which are relevant for *consumer behavior* and the formal organization which constitutes much of the environment for *industrial purchasing*. Organizational variables are those of small group interaction such as power, status and authority. We believe that the underlying process of intergroup conflicts in both industrial and consumer buying behavior are in principle very similar and that the differences are largely due to the formalization of industrial activity. Organization, both formal and social, is a crucial variable because it influences all the learning constructs.

Social Class refers to a still higher level of social organization, the social aggregate. Several indices are available to classify people into various classes. The most common perhaps is the Warner classification of people into upper-upper, lower-upper, upper-middle, lower-middle, upper-lower, and lower-classes. Social class mediates the relation between the input and the output by influencing: (i) specific Motives, (ii) Decision Mediators, (iii) Evoked Set, and (iv) Inhibitors. The latter influence is more important particularly in the adoption of innovations.

Culture provides an even more comprehensive social framework than social class. Culture consists of patterns of behavior, symbols, ideas and their attached values. Culture will influence Motives, Decision Mediators, and Inhibitors.

CONCLUSIONS

In the preceding pages we have summarized a theory of buyer brand choice. It is complex. We strongly believe that complexity is essential to adequately describe buying behavior, from the point of view of both marketing practice and public policy.

We hope that the theory can provide new insights into past empirical data and guide future research so as to instill with coherence and unity current research which now tends to be atomistic and unrelated. We are vigorously pursuing a large research program aimed at testing the validity of the theory. The research was designed in terms of the variables specified by the theory and our most preliminary results cause us to believe that it was fruitful to use the theory in this way. Because it specifies a number of relationships, it has clearly been useful in interpreting the preliminary findings. Above all, it is an aid in communication among the researchers and with the companies involved.

Finally, a number of new ideas are set forth in the theory, but we would like to call attention to three in particular. The concept of evoked set provides a means of reducing the noise in many analyses of buying behavior. The product class concept offers a new dimension for incorporating many of the complexities of innovations and especially for integrating systematically the idea of innovation into a framework of psychological constructs. Anthropologists and sociologists have been pretty much content to deal with peripheral variables in their investigations of innovation. The habit-perception cycle in which perception and habit respond inversely offers hope for explaining a large proportion of the phenomenon that has long baffled both the critics and defenders of advertising: large advertising expenditures in a stable market where, on the surface, it would seem that people are already sated with information.

NOTES

1. Jagdish N. Sheth, "A Review of Buyer Behavior," *Management Science,* Vol. 13 (August 1967), pp. B718–B756; John A. Howard, *Marketing Theory* (Boston, Mass.: Allyn and Bacon, 1965).
2. Musafer Sherif and Carolyn Sherif, "Interdisciplinary Coordination as a Validity Check: Retrospect and Prospects," in M. Sherif (ed.), *Problems of Interdisciplinary Relationships in the Social Sciences* (Chicago: Aldine Publishing Company, 1968).
3. William J. McGuire, "Some Impending Reorientations in Social Psychology," *Journal of Experimental Social Psychology,* Vol. 3 (1967), pp. 124–139.
4. Patrick Suppes, *Information Processing and Choice Behavior* (Technical Paper No. 9: Institute for Mathematical Studies in the Social Sciences, Stanford University, January 31, 1966), p. 27; John A. Howard, *op. cit.*
5. Terminology in a problem area that cuts across both economics and psychology is different because each discipline has often defined its terms differently from the other. We find the economists definitions of exogenous versus endogenous, and theory versus model more useful than those of the psychologist. The psychologist's distinction of hypothetical constructs and intervening variables, however, provides a helpful breakdown of endogenous variables. Finally, for the sake of exposition we have often here not clearly distinguished between the theory and its empirical counterparts. Although this practice encourages certain ambiguities, and we lay ourselves open to the charge of reifying our theory, we believe that for most readers it will simplify the task of comprehending the material.
6. Clark C. Hull, *Principles of Behavior* (New York: Appleton-Century-Crofts, Inc., (1943); Clark C. Hill, *A Behavior System* (New Haven: Yale University Press, 1952).
7. Charles E. Osgood, "A Behavioristic Analysis of Perception and Meaning as Cognitive Phenomena," *Symposium on Cognition, University of Colorado,* 1955 (Cambridge, Harvard University Press, 1957), pp. 75–119; Charles E. Osgood, "Motivational Dynamics of Language Behavior," in J. R. Jones (ed.), *Nebraska Symposium on Motivation,* 1957 (Lincoln: University of Nebraska Press, 1957), pp. 348–423.
8. D. E. Berlyne, "Motivational Problems Raised by Exploratory and Epistemic Behavior," in Sigmund Koch (ed.), *Psychology: A Study of a Science,* Vol. 5 (New York: McGraw-Hill Book Company, 1963).
9. Rosser Reeves, *Reality in Advertising* (New York: Alfred A. Knopf, Inc., 1961).
10. J. S. Brown, *The Motivation of Behavior* (New York: McGraw-Hill Book Company, 1961).
11. George S. Day, "Buyer Attitudes and Brand Choice Behavior," Unpublished Ph.D. Dissertation, Graduate School of Business, Columbia University, 1967.
12. Berlyne, *op. cit.*
13. S. Feldman (ed.), *Cognitive Consistency: Motivational Antecedents and Behavioral Consequents* (Academic Press, 1966); Martin Fishbein (ed.), *Readings in Attitude Theory and Measurement* (New York: John Wiley & Sons, 1967).
14. Thomas F. Juster, *Anticipations and Purchases: An Analysis of Consumer Behavior* (Princeton University Press, 1964).
15. William Yoell, *A Science of Advertising through Behaviorism.* Unpublished manuscript, December, 1965.
16. Sheth, *op. cit.*

17. R. J. Lavidge and G. A. Steiner, "A Model for Predictive Measurements of Advertising Effectiveness," *Journal of Marketing* (October, 1961), pp. 50–68.

18. Everett M. Rogers, *The Diffusion of Innovations* (New York: Free Press, 1962).

19. Kristian S. Palda, "The Hypothesis of a Hierarchy of Effects: A Partial Evaluation," *Journal of Marketing Research* (February, 1966), pp. 13–24.

20. Sheth, *op. cit.*

21. Donald F. Cox, *Risk Taking and Information Handling in Consumer Behavior* (Boston, Mass.: Graduate School of Business Administration, Harvard University, 1967).

◆

A General Model for Understanding Organizational Buying Behavior

Frederick E. Webster, Jr., and Yoram Wind

Industrial and institutional marketers have often been urged to base their strategies on careful appraisal of buying behavior within key accounts and in principal market segments. When they search the available literature on buyer behavior, however, they find virtually exclusive emphasis on consumers, not industrial buyers. Research findings and theoretical discussions about consumer behavior often have little relevance for the industrial marketer. This is due to several important differences between the two purchase processes. Industrial buying takes place in the context of a formal organization influenced by budget, cost, and profit considerations. Furthermore, organizational (i.e., industrial and institutional) buying usually involves many people in the decision process with complex interactions among people and among individual and organizational goals.

Similar to his consumer goods counterpart, the industrial marketer could find a model of buyer behavior useful in identifying those key factors influencing response to marketing effort. A buyer behavior model can help the marketer to analyze available information about the market and to identify the need for additional information. It can help to specify targets for marketing effort, the kinds of information needed by various purchasing decision makers, and the criteria that they will use to make these decisions. A framework for analyzing organizational buying behavior could aid in the design of marketing strategy.

The model to be presented here is a *general* model. It can be applied to all organizational buying and suffers all the weaknesses of general models. It does not describe a specific buying situation in the richness of detail required to make a model operational, and it cannot be quantified. However, generality offers a compensating set of benefits. The model presents a comprehensive view of organizational buying that enables one to evaluate the relevance of specific variables and thereby permits greater insight into the basic processes of industrial buying behavior. It identifies the *classes* of variables that must be

"A General Model for Understanding Organizational Buying Behavior," Frederick E. Webster, Jr., and Yoram Wind, Vol. 36 (April 1972), pp. 12–19. Reprinted from *Journal of Marketing*, published by the American Marketing Association.

examined by any student of organizational buying, practitioner, or academician. Although major scientific progress in the study of organizational buying will come only from a careful study of specific relationships among a few variables within a given class, this general model can help to identify those variables that should be studied. It can be useful in generating hypotheses and provides a framework for careful interpretation of research results that makes the researcher more sensitive to the complexities of the processes he is studying.

TRADITIONAL VIEWS

Traditional views of organizational buying have lacked comprehensiveness. The literature of economics, purchasing, and, to a limited degree, marketing has emphasized variables related to the buying task itself and has emphasized "rational," economic factors. In these economic views, the objective of purchasing is to obtain the minimum price or the lowest total cost-in-use (as in the materials management model[1]). Some of the models focussing on the buying task have emphasized factors that are not strictly economic such as reciprocal buying agreements[2] and other constraints on the buyer such as source loyalty.[3]

Other traditional views of organizational buying err in the opposite direction, emphasizing variables such as emotion, personal goals, and internal politics that are involved in the buying decision process but not related to the goals of the buying task. This "nontask" emphasis is seen in models which emphasize the purchasing agent's interest in obtaining personal favors,[4] in enhancing his own ego,[5] or in reducing perceived risk.[6] Other nontask models have emphasized buyer-salesman interpersonal interaction[7] and the multiple relationships among indi-

viduals involved in the buying process over time.[8] The ways in which purchasing agents attempt to expand their influence over the buying decision have also received careful study.[9] These views have contributed to an understanding of the buying process, but none of them is complete. To the extent that these models leave out task or nontask variables they offer incomplete guidelines for the industrial market strategist and researcher. The tendency in interpreting research results based on these simple models is to overemphasize the importance of some variables and to understate or ignore the importance of others.

AN OVERVIEW OF A GENERAL MODEL

The fundamental assertion of the more comprehensive model to be presented here is that organizational buying is a decision-making process carried out by individuals, in interaction with other people, in the context of a formal organization.[10] The organization, in turn, is influenced by a variety of forces in the environment. Thus, the four classes of variables determining organizational buying behavior are *individual, social, organizational* and *environmental*. Within each class, there are two broad categories of variables: Those directly related to the buying program, called *task* variables; and those that extend beyond the buying problem, called *nontask* variables. This classification of variables is summarized and illustrated in Table 11-1.

The distinction between task and nontask variables applies to all of the classes of variables, and subclasses, to be discussed below. It is seldom possible to identify a given set of variables as exclusively task or nontask; rather, any given set of variables will have both task and nontask dimensions although one dimension may be predominant. For example, motives will inevitably have both di-

Table 11-1
Classification and Examples of Variables Influencing Organizational Buying Decisions

	Task	Nontask
Individual	Desire to obtain lowest price	Personal values and needs
Social	Meetings to set specifications	Informal, off-the-job interactions
Organizational	Policy regarding local supplier preference	Methods of personnel evaluation
Environmental	Anticipated changes in prices	Political climate in an election year

mensions—those relating directly to the buying problem to be solved and those primarily concerned with personal goals. These motives overlap in many important respects and need not conflict; a strong sense of personal involvement can create more effective buying decisions from an organizational standpoint.

Organizational buying behavior is a complex *process* (rather than a single, instantaneous act) and involves many persons, multiple goals, and potentially conflicting decision criteria. It often takes place over an extended period of time, requires information from many sources, and encompasses many interorganizational relationships.

The organizational buying process is a form of problem-solving, and a *buying situation* is created when someone in the organization perceives a problem—a discrepancy between a desired outcome and the present situation—that can potentially be solved through some buying action. Organizational buying behavior includes all activities of organizational members as they define a buying situation and identify, evaluate, and choose among alternative brands and suppliers. The *buying center* includes all members of the organization who are involved in that process. The roles involved are those of user, influencer, decider, buyer, and gatekeeper (who controls the flow of information into the buying center). Members of the buying center are motivated by a complex interaction of individual and organizational goals. Their relationships with one another involve all the complexities of interpersonal interactions. The formal organization exerts its influence on the buying center through the subsystems of tasks, structure (communication, authority, status, rewards, and work flow), technology, and people. Finally, the entire organization is embedded in a set of environmental influences including economic, technological, physical, political, legal, and cultural forces. An overview of the model and a diagrammatic presentation of the relationships among these variables are given in Figure 11-1.

ENVIRONMENTAL INFLUENCES

Environmental influences are subtle and pervasive as well as difficult to identify and to measure. They influence the buying process by providing information as well as constraints and opportunities. Environmental influences include physical (geographic, climate, or ecological), technological, economic, political, legal, and cultural factors. These influences are exerted through a variety of institutions including business firms (suppliers, competitors, and customers), governments, trade unions, political parties, educational and medical institutions, trade associations,

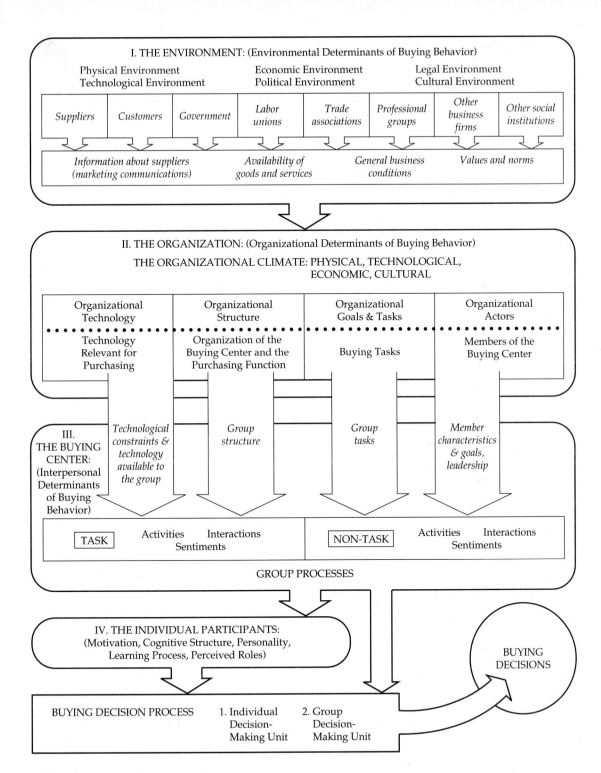

Figure 11-1
A Model of Organizational Buying Behavior

and professional groups. The nature of these institutional forms will vary significantly from one country to another, and such differences are critical to the planning of multinational marketing strategies.

As Figure 11-1 illustrates, environmental influences have their impact in four distinct ways. First, they define the availability of goods and services. This function reflects especially the influence of physical, technological, and economic factors. Second, they define the general conditions facing the buying organization including the rate of economic growth, the level of national income, interest rates, and unemployment. Economic and political forces are the dominant influences on general business conditions. Some of these forces, such as economic factors, are predominantly (but not exclusively) task variables whereas others such as political variables may be more heavily nontask in nature. Third, environmental factors determine the values and norms guiding interorganizational and interpersonal relationships between buyers and sellers as well as among competitors, and between buying organizations and other institutions such as governments and trade associations. Such values and norms may be codified into laws, or they may be implicit. Cultural, social, legal, and political forces are the dominant sources of values and norms. Finally, environmental forces influence the information flow into the buying organization. Most important here is the flow of marketing communications from potential suppliers, through the mass media and through other personal and impersonal channels. Information flows reflect a variety of physical, technological, economic, and cultural factors.

The marketing strategist, whose customers are organizations, must carefully appraise each set of environmental factors and identify and analyze the institutions that exert those influences in each of the market segments served. This kind of analysis is especially important in entering new markets. For example, economic factors as revealed in measures of general business conditions must be continually assessed where market prices fluctuate and buyers make decisions to build or reduce inventories based on price expectations. Similarly, the impact of technological change in markets served must be considered as the basis for strategic decisions in the areas of product policy and promotion. The necessity of analyzing institutional forms is most readily apparent when markets are multinational in scope and require specific consideration of government policies and trade union influences. Environmental factors are important determinants of organizational buying behavior, but they can be so basic and pervasive that it is easy, and dangerous, to overlook them in analyzing the market.

ORGANIZATIONAL INFLUENCES

Organizational factors cause individual decision makers to act differently than they would if they were functioning alone or in a different organization. Organizational buying behavior is motivated and directed by the organization's goals and is constrained by its financial, technological, and human resources. This class of variables is primarily task-related. For understanding the influence of the formal organization on the buying process, Leavitt's classification of variables is most helpful.[11] According to Leavitt's scheme, organizations are multivariate systems composed of four sets of interacting variables:

Tasks—the work to be performed in accomplishing the objectives of the organization.
Structure—subsystems of communication, authority, status, rewards, and work flow.

Technology—problem-solving inventions used by the firm including plant and equipment and programs for organizing and managing work.

People—the actors in the system.

Each of these subsystems interacts with, and is dependent upon, the others for its functioning. Together, these four interacting sets of factors define the information, expectations, goals, attitudes, and assumptions used by each of the individual actors in their decision making. This general model defines four distinct but interrelated sets of variables that must be carefully considered in the development of marketing strategies designed to influence that process: buying tasks, organization structure, buying technology, and the buying center.

Buying Tasks

Buying tasks are a subset of organizational tasks and goals that evolves from the definition of a buying situation. These are pure task variables by definition. The specific tasks that must be performed to solve the buying problem can be defined as five stages in the buying decision process. (1) Identification of need; (2) establishment of specifications; (3) identification of alternatives; (4) evaluation of alternatives; and (5) selection of suppliers.[12] Buying tasks can be further defined according to four dimensions:

1. The *organizational purpose* served—e.g., whether the reason for buying is to facilitate production, or for resale, or to be consumed in the performance of other organizational functions.

2. The *nature of demand,* especially whether demand for the product is generated within the buying organization or by forces outside of the organization (i.e.,

"derived" demand) as well as other characteristics of the demand pattern such as seasonal and cyclical fluctuations.

3. The *extent of programming,* i.e., the degree of routinization at the five stages of the decision process.

4. The *degree of decentralization* and the extent to which buying authority has been delegated to operating levels in the organization.

Each of these four dimensions influences the nature of the organizational buying process and must be considered in appraising market opportunities. At each of the five stages of the decision process, different members of the buying center may be involved, different decision criteria are employed, and different information sources may become more or less relevant. Marketing strategies must be adjusted accordingly. There are rich research opportunities in defining the influence of different members of the buying center at various stages of the buying process.[13]

Organizational Structure

The formal organizational structure consists of subsystems of communication, authority, status, rewards, and work flow, all of which have important task and nontask dimensions. Each of these subsystems deserves careful study by researchers interested in organizational buying. The marketing literature does not include studies in this area. A beginning might be several rigorous observational or case studies.

The *communication* subsystem performs four essential functions: (1) information; (2) command and instruction; (3) influence and persuasion; and (4) integration.[14] The marketer must understand how the communication system in customer organizations *informs* the members of the buying center about buying problems, evaluation criteria (both task and nontask related), and alternative sources of supply. He must appraise how *commands* and *instructions* (mostly task-related) flow through the hierarchy defining the discretion and latitude of individual actors. The pattern of *influence* and *persuasion* (heavily nontask in nature) defines the nature of interpersonal interactions within the buying center. Organizational members may differ in the extent to which they prefer either commands and instructions or more subtle influence and persuasion to guide the actions of subordinates. The *integrative* functions of communication become critical in coordinating the functioning of the buying center and may be one of the primary roles of the purchasing manager.

The *authority* subsystem defines the power of organizational actors to judge, command, or otherwise act to influence the behavior of others along both task and nontask dimensions. No factor is more critical in understanding the organizational buying process because the authority structure determines who sets goals and who evaluates (and therefore determines rewards for) organizational performance. The authority structure interacts with the communication structure to determine the degree of decentralization in the decision process.

The *status* system is reflected in the organization chart and defines the hierarchical structure of the formal organization. It also expresses itself in an informal structure. Both the formal and the informal organization define each individual's position in a hierarchy with respect to other individuals. Job descriptions define positions within the organization and the associated dimensions of responsibility and authority. Knowing the responsibility, authority, and the position in the internal status hierarchy of each member of the buying center is a necessary basis for developing an account strategy for the organizational cus-

tomer. A complete theory of organizational buying will permit accurate predictions of an organizational actor's influence based upon his position and role.

The *rewards* system defines the payoffs to the individual decision maker. It is intimately related to the authority system which determines the responsibilities of organizational actors for evaluating other individuals. Here is the mechanism for relating organizational task accomplishment to individual nontask objectives. Persons join organizations in anticipation of the rewards given by the organization and agree to work toward organizational objectives in return for those rewards. A careful analysis of the formal and social reward structure of the organization as it affects and is perceived by the members of the buying center can be most helpful in predicting their response to marketing effort. The key fact is that people work for organizations in order to earn rewards related to personal goals, both economic and noneconomic.[15]

Every buying organization develops task-related procedures for managing the *work flow* of paperwork, samples, and other items involved in the buying decision process. The flow of paperwork also has nontask aspects which reflect the composition of the buying center as well as the authority and communication subsystems of an organizational structure. Needless to say, marketers must understand the mechanical details of buying procedures. Such procedures also provide documentation of the buying process that can provide useful data for the academic researcher.

Buying Technology

Technology influences both what is bought and the nature of the organizational buying process itself. In the latter aspect, technology defines the management and information systems that are involved in the buying decision process, such as computers and management science approaches to such aspects of buying as "make or buy" analysis. More obviously, technology defines the plant and equipment of the organization, and these, in turn, place significant constraints upon the alternative buying actions available to the organization. It is a common failing of industrial marketing strategy, especially for new product introductions, to underestimate the demands that will be placed upon existing technology in customer organizations.[16] A material, for example, may require new dies and mixing equipment, new skills of production personnel, and substantial changes in methods of production.

Buying Center

The buying center is a subset of the organizational actors, the last of the four sets of variables in the Leavitt scheme. The buying center was earlier defined as consisting of five roles: users, influencers, deciders, buyers, and gatekeepers. Since people operate as part of the total organization, the behavior of members of the buying center reflects the influence of others as well as the effect of the buying task, the organizational structure, and technology.

This interaction leads to unique buying behavior in each customer organization. The marketing strategist who wishes to influence the organizational buying process must, therefore, define and understand the operation of these four sets of organizational variables—tasks, structure, technology, and actors—in each organization he is trying to influence. The foregoing comments provide only the skeleton of an analytical structure for considering each of these factors and its implications for marketing action in a specific buying situation. The marketer's problem is to define the locus of buying responsibility within the customer organization, to define the composition of the buying center, and to understand the structure of roles and authority within the buying center.

SOCIAL (INTERPERSONAL) INFLUENCES

The framework for understanding the buying decision process must identify and relate three classes of variables involved in group functioning in the buying center. First, the various roles in the buying center must be identified. Second, the variables relating to interpersonal (dyadic) interaction between persons in the buying center and between members of the buying center and "outsiders" such as vendors' salesmen must be identified. Third, the dimensions of the functioning of the group as a whole must be considered. Each of these three sets of factors is discussed briefly in the following paragraphs.

Within the organization as a whole only a subset of organizational actors is actually involved in a buying situation. The buying center includes five roles:

Users—those members of the organization who use the purchased products and services.

Buyers—those with formal responsibility and authority for contracting with suppliers.

Influencers—those who influence the decision process directly or indirectly by providing information and criteria for evaluating alternative buying actions.

Deciders—those with authority to choose among alternative buying actions.

Gatekeepers—those who control the flow of information (and materials) into the buying center.

Several individuals may occupy the same role; e.g., there may be several influencers. Also, one individual may occupy more than one role; e.g., the purchasing agent is often both buyer and gatekeeper.

To understand interpersonal interaction within the buying center, it is useful to consider three aspects of role performance: (1) Role *expectations* (prescriptions and prohibitions for the behavior of the person occupying the role and for the behavior of other persons toward a given role); (2) role *behavior* (actual behavior in the role); and (3) role *relationships* (the multiple and reciprocal relationships among members of the group). Together, these three variables define the individual's *role set.* An awareness of each of these dimensions is necessary for the salesman responsible for contacting the various members of the buying center. It is especially important to understand how each member expects the salesman to behave toward him and the important ongoing relationships among roles in the buying center.

As illustrated in Figure 11-1, the nature of group functioning is influenced by five classes of variables—the individual members' goals and personal characters, the nature of leadership within the group, the structure of the group, the tasks performed by the group, and external (organizational and environmental) influences. Group processes involve not only activities but also interactions and sentiments among members, which have both task and nontask dimensions. Finally, the output of the group is not only a task-oriented problem solution (a buying action) but also nontask satisfaction and growth for the group and its members.

In analyzing the functioning of the buying center, it helps to focus attention on the buyer role, primarily because a member of the purchasing department is most often the marketer's primary contact point with the organization. Buyers often have authority for managing the contacts of suppliers with other organizational actors, and thus also perform the "gatekeeper" function. While the buyer's

authority for selection of suppliers may be seriously constrained by decisions at earlier stages of the decision process (especially the development of specifications), he has responsibility for the terminal stages of the process. In other words, the buyer (or purchasing agent) is in most cases the final decision maker and the target of influence attempts by other members of the buying center.

In performing their task, purchasing agents use a variety of tactics to enhance their power which vary with the specific problems, the conditions of the organization, and the purchasing agent's personality. The tactics used by purchasing agents to influence their relationships with other departments can be viewed as a special case of the more general phenomenon of "lateral" relationships in formal organizations—those among members of approximately equal status in the formal organizational hierarchy.[17] These include *rule-oriented* tactics (e.g., appealing to the boss for the enforcement of organizational policy; appealing to rules and formal statements of authority); *rule-evading* tactics (e.g., compliance with requests from users that violate organizational policies); *personal-political* tactics (e.g., reliance on informal relationships and friendships to get decisions made and an exchange of favors with other members of the buying center); *educational* tactics (e.g., persuading other members of the organization to think in purchasing terms and to recognize the importance and potential contribution of the purchasing function); and finally, *organizational-interactional* tactics (e.g., change the formal organizational structure and the pattern of reporting relationships and information flows).

Buyers who are ambitious and wish to extend the scope of their influence will adopt certain tactics and engage in bargaining activities in an attempt to become more influential at earlier stages of the buying process. These tactics or bargaining strategies define the nature of the buyer's relationships with others of equal organizational status and structure the social situation that the potential supplier must face in dealing with the buying organization. An understanding of the nature of interpersonal relationships in the buying organization is an important basis for the development of marketing strategy.

THE INFLUENCE OF THE INDIVIDUAL

In the final analysis, all organizational buying behavior is individual behavior. Only the individual as an individual or a member of a group can define and analyze buying situations, decide, and act. In this behavior, the individual is motivated by a complex combination of personal and organizational objectives, constrained by policies and information filtered through the formal organization, and influenced by other members of the buying center. The individual is at the center of the buying process, operating within the buying center that is in turn bounded by the formal organization which is likewise embedded in the influences of the broader environment. It is the specific individual who is the target for marketing effort, not the abstract organization.

The organizational buyer's personality, perceived role set, motivation, cognition, and learning are the basic psychological processes which affect his response to the buying situation and marketing stimuli provided by potential vendors. Similar to consumer markets, it is important to understand the organizational buyer's psychological characteristics and especially his predispositions, preference structure, and decision model as the basis for marketing strategy decisions. Some initial attempts to develop categories of buying decision makers according to characteristic decision styles ("normative" and "conservative") have been reported.[18] Cultural, organizational, and social factors are important

influences on the individual and are reflected in his previous experiences, awareness of, attitudes and preference toward particular vendors and products and his particular buying decision models.

The organizational buyer can, therefore, be viewed as a constrained decision maker. Although the basic mental processes of motivation, cognition, and learning as well as the buyer's personality, perceived role set, preference structure, and decision model are uniquely individual; they are influenced by the context of interpersonal and organizational influences within which the individual is embedded. The organizational buyer is motivated by a complex combination of individual and organizational objectives and is dependent upon others for the satisfaction of these needs in several ways. These other people define the role expectations for the individual, they determine the payoffs he is to receive for his performance, they influence the definition of the goals to be pursued in the buying decision, and they provide information with which the individual attempts to evaluate risks and come to a decision.

Task and Nontask Motives

Only rarely can the organizational buyer let purely personal considerations influence his buying decisions: In a situation where "all other things are equal," the individual may be able to apply strictly personal (nontask) criteria when making his final decision. In the unlikely event that two or more potential vendors offer products of comparable quality and service at a comparable price, then the organizational buyer may be motivated by purely personal, nontask variables such as his personal preferences for dealing with a particular salesman, or some special favor or gift available from the supplier.

The organizational buyer's motivation has both task and nontask dimensions. Task-related motives relate to the specific buying problem to be solved and involve the general criteria of buying "the right quality in the right quantity at the right price for delivery at the right time from the right source." Of course, what is "right" is a difficult question, especially to the extent that important buying influencers have conflicting needs and criteria for evaluating the buyer's performance.

Nontask-related motives may often be more important, although there is frequently a rather direct relationship between task and nontask motives. For example, the buyer's desire for promotion (a nontask motive) can significantly influence his task performance. In other words, there is no necessary conflict between task and nontask motives and, in fact, the pursuit of nontask objectives can enhance the attainment of task objectives.

Broadly speaking, nontask motives can be placed into two categories: achievement motives and risk-reduction motives. Achievement motives are those related to personal advancement and recognition. Risk-reduction motives are related, but somewhat less obvious, and provide a critical link between the individual and the organizational decision-making process. This is also a key component of the behavior theory of the firm[19] where uncertainty avoidance is a key motivator of organizational actors.

The individual's perception of risk in a decision situation is a function of uncertainty (in the sense of a probabilistic assessment) and of the value of various outcomes. Three kinds of uncertainty are significant: Uncertainty about available alternatives; uncertainty about the outcomes associated with various alternatives; and uncertainty about the way relevant other persons will react to various outcomes.[20] This uncertainty about the reaction of other persons may be due to incomplete information about their goals or about how an outcome will be evaluated and rewarded.

Information gathering is the most obvious tactic for reducing uncertainty, while decision avoidance and lowering of goals are means of reducing the value of outcomes. A preference for the status quo is perhaps the most common mode of risk reduction, since it removes uncertainty and minimizes the possibility of negative outcomes. This is one explanation for the large amount of source loyalty found in organizational buying and is consistent with the "satisficing" postulate of the behavioral theory of the firm.

The individual determinants of organizational buyer behavior and the tactics which buyers are likely to use in their dealing with potential vendors must be clearly understood by those who want to affect their behavior.

SUMMARY

This article has suggested the major dimensions and mechanisms involved in the complex organizational buying process. The framework presented here is reasonably complete although the details clearly are lacking. It is hoped that these comments have been sufficient to suggest a general model of the organizational buying process with important implications for the development of effective marketing and selling strategies as well as some implicit suggestions for scholarly research. The model is offered as a skeleton identifying the major variables that must be appraised in developing the information required for planning strategies. Hopefully, the model has also suggested some new insights into an important area of buying behavior presently receiving inadequate attention in the marketing literature.

NOTES

1. Dean S. Ammer, *Materials Management* (Homewood, Illinois: Richard D. Irwin, Inc., 1962), pp. 12 and 15.

2. Dean S. Ammer, "Realistic Reciprocity," *Harvard Business Review*, Vol. 40 (January–February, 1962), pp. 116–124.

3. Yoram Wind, "Industrial Source Loyalty," *Journal of Marketing Research*, Vol. 7 (November, 1970), pp. 450–457.

4. For a statement of this view, see J. B. Matthews, Jr., R. D. Buzzell, T. Levitt, and R. Frank, *Marketing: An Introductory Analysis* (New York: McGraw-Hill Book Company, Inc., 1964), p. 149.

5. For an example, see William J. Stanton, *Fundamentals of Marketing*, Second Ed. (New York: McGraw-Hill Book Company, Inc., 1967), p. 150.

6. Theodore Levitt, *Industrial Purchasing Behavior: A Study of Communications Effects* (Boston: Division of Research, Graduate School of Business Administration, Harvard University, 1965).

7. Henry L. Tosi, "The Effects of Expectation Levels and Role Consensus on the Buyer-Seller Dyad," *Journal of Business*, Vol. 39 (October, 1966), pp. 516–529.

8. Robert E. Weigand, "Why Studying the Purchasing Agent Is Not Enough," *Journal of Marketing*, Vol. 32, (January, 1968), pp. 41–45.

9. George Strauss, "Tactics of Lateral Relationship," *Administrative Science Quarterly*, Vol. 7 (September, 1962), pp. 161–186.

10. The complete model is presented and discussed in detail in Frederick E. Webster, Jr. and Yoram Wind, *Organizational Buying Behavior* (Englewood Cliffs, New Jersey: Prentice-Hall, Inc., in press).

11. Harold J. Leavitt, "Applied Organization Change in Industry: Structural, Technical, and Human Approaches," in *New Perspectives in Organizational Research*, W. W. Cooper, H. J. Leavitt, and M. W. Shelly, II, eds. (New York: John Wiley and Sons, Inc., 1964), pp. 55–71.

12. A modified version of this model is presented in P. J. Robinson, C. W. Faris, and Y. Wind, *Industrial Buying and Creative Marketing* (Boston: Allyn & Bacon, Inc., 1967), p. 14.

13. For research on the influence of organizational actors and information sources at various stages of the decision process, see Urban B. Ozanne and Gilbert A. Churchill, "Adoption Research: Information Sources in the Industrial Purchasing Decision," in *Marketing and the New Science of Planning*, Robert L. King, ed. (Chicago, Ill.: American Marketing Association, Fall, 1968), pp. 352–359; and Frederick E. Webster, Jr., "Informal Communication in Industrial Markets," *Journal of Marketing Research*, Vol. 7 (May, 1970), pp. 186–189.

14. Lee Thayer, *Communication and Communication Systems* (Homewood, Ill.: Richard D. Irwin, Inc., 1968), pp. 187–250.

15. Yoram Wind, "A Reward-Balance Model of Buying Behavior in Organizations," in *New Essays in Marketing Theory*, G. Fisk ed. (Boston: Allyn & Bacon, 1971).

16. Frederick E. Webster, Jr., "New Product Adoption in Industrial Markets: A Framework for Analysis," *Journal of Marketing*, Vol. 33 (July, 1969), pp. 35–39.

17. Same reference as footnote 9.

18. David T. Wilson, H. Lee Mathews, and Timothy W. Sweeney, "Industrial Buyer Segmentation: A Psychographic Approach," paper presented at the Fall, 1971 Conference of the American Marketing Association. See also Richard N. Cardozo, "Segmenting the Industrial Market," in *Marketing and the New Science of Planning*, Robert L. King ed. (Chicago: American Marketing Association, 1969), pp. 433–440.

19. Richard M. Cyert and James G. March, *A Behavioral Theory of the Firm* (Englewood Cliffs, N.J.: Prentice-Hall, 1963).

20. Donald F. Cox, ed., *Risk Taking and Information Handling in Consumer Behavior* (Boston: Division of Research, Graduate School of Business Administration, Harvard University, 1967).

◆

Situational Variables
and Consumer Behavior

Russell W. Belk

Growing recognition of limitations in the ability of individual consumer characteristics to explain variation in buyer behavior has prompted a number of appeals to examine situational influences on behavior. Ward and Robertson argued that "situational variables may account for considerably more variance than actor-related variables" (1973, p. 26). Lavidge (1966) cautioned that many buyer behaviors may be enacted only under specific conditions and necessitate situational investigations of intra-individual variability. Engel, Kollat, and Blackwell (1969) urged that *both* individual and situational factors must be considered in order to explain consumer choices. Nevertheless, those and other suggestions to include situational variables in research on consumer behavior have gone largely unheeded. The primary obstacle has been the absence of an adequate conception of the variables which comprise a situation. It is the purpose of the following discussion to explore such concepts and to suggest directions

for the study of situational influence in consumer behavior.

CONSUMER SITUATIONS AND RELATED CONCEPTS

Situations, Behavioral Settings, and Environments

As a starting point for a definition, most theoreticians would agree that a situation comprises a point in time and space (Belk, 1975). For students of human behavior, a discrete time and place occupied by one or more persons identifies a situation of potential interest. A somewhat larger alternative unit of analysis would be Barker's (1968) "behavioral setting." A behavioral setting is not only bounded in time and space, but also by a complete sequence of behavior or an "action pattern." For example, a basketball game or a piano lesson is a behavioral setting because each involves an interval in time and space in which certain behaviors can be expected regardless of the particular persons present. But

Reprinted by permission from *Journal of Consumer Research* (December 1975), pp. 157–164.

such patterns of behavior require stretching the time and place dimensions to broader and more continuous units than those defining a situation. While a behavioral setting might be a store which is open from 8:00 AM to 6:00 PM (Barker, 1968, p. 19), the current perspective would recognize a number of discrete situations which may occur within this setting.

The concept of an "environment" extends the time, place, and behavioral dimensions still further. Although there is less agreement as to what bounds and defines an environment,[1] it is clear that situations and behavioral settings are subunits within an environment. In one of his early formulations Lewin pointed out that an environment may be thought of as the chief characteristics of a more or less permanent "situation" (Lewin, 1933). In this sense situations represent momentary encounters with those elements of the total environment which are available to the individual at a particular time. Environment is also broader in terms of the geographic area over which it applies. For example, while the "legal environment" may be described to consist of laws, legal institutions, and interpretive tendencies within a governmental territory, and the behavioral setting may refer to a certain courtroom, the specific experience of individual *A* being cross-examined by attorney *G* during trial *M* in city *R* at 4:00 on day *X*, can only be described from a narrower situational perspective. It is this latter view of the conditions for experiences and the effect of these conditions on specific behavioral outcomes which the current perspective seeks to develop.

Situational Versus Non-Situational Determinants of Consumer Behavior

A second group of concepts from which situations must be distinguished are the nonsituational determinants of a particular consumer behavior. Figure 12-1 shows a familiar stimulus-

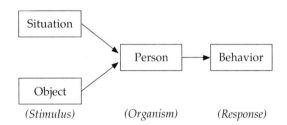

Figure 12-1
A Revised S–O–R Paradigm

organism-response paradigm which has been modified to divide the stimulus into an object and its situation. This split is analogous to the perceptual distinctions between figure and ground or focal and contextual cues (Helson, 1964). That is, because behavior with respect to a product or service object is of primary significance in consumer behavior, the object to which the consumer is directly responding will be regarded as a unique source of behavioral influence. In not including personal and object characteristics within the concept of the situation there is also a purposeful departure from Lewin's (1935) formulation of the life space. The rationale for this more limited view of situation is the greater possibility of operationalizing a construct which has an existence apart from the individual's total consciousness. For there to be hope of really adding to the ability to explain consumer behavior, this separate existence is essential.[2]

It might seem that a clear distinction may be made between persons, objects, and situations as separate sources of influence on behavior, but some potential for confusion exists in attempting to separate the characteristics of each determinant. R. L. Thorndike's (1947) concept of "lasting and general characteristics of the individual" is a useful device in distinguishing personal and situational characteristics. These individual features, including personality, intellect, sex, and race, are stable over times and places of observation and may therefore be attributed consistently to the individual. Where the feature is more transitory, such as having a headache, it must be considered to be at least partly a function of the situation. It is necessary to impose similar constraints on the conception of object characteristics in order to categorize a description such as a brand of soda being 10¢ less than competing brands. In cases where the characteristic tends to be a lasting and general feature of the brand it may be attributed to the object. Where the characteristic is specific to a time and place (e.g., a special sale) it should be regarded as a characteristic of the situation.

Characteristics of Consumer Situations

Consistent with the previous distinctions, a consumer situation may be viewed as comprising "... all those factors particular to a time and place of observation which do not follow from a knowledge of personal (intraindividual) and stimulus (choice alternative) attributes and which have a demonstrable and systemic effect on current behavior" (Belk, 1974a). The greatest problem in operationalizing this view lies in defining "all those factors." Several attempts have been made to develop comprehensive taxonomies of situational characteristics. Using general guidelines suggested by Sherif and Sherif (1956), Sells (1963) constructed a subjective classification of over 200 situational variables including gravity, temperature, group structure, role requirements, and novelty of the situation in relation to prior experiences. Unfortunately, from the point of view of the current conception of situation, Sells' classification also includes some characteristics of the individual (e.g., age, sex, race) and environment (e.g., sources of food, erosion, language), and excludes certain descriptors of the physical locale (e.g., noises, colors, room or area size).

Classification attempts by Bellows (1963), Wolf (1966), and Moos (1973), are less complete and suffer from similar drawbacks. Although also incomplete and parochial in its focus, a limited taxonomy by Allen (1965) of the situational factors found to affect conformity highlights several important social dimensions (e.g., public/private, interdependence of participants) and task dimensions (e.g., difficulty, importance) of the situation. These features contrast sharply with the taxonomy of 66 bipolar adjectival scales constructed by Kasmar (1970) to measure situations. From an initial list of 300 characteristics generated through room description protocols obtained from architecture students, scales were developed to describe 13 aspects of the situation; size, volume, scale, mood, color, texture, function, illumination, esthetic quality, climate, color, acoustical quality, and miscellaneous. Such characteristics provide a comprehensive description of the design features of the situation, but they completely neglect the social and task attributes which Allen's review (1965) emphasized. Furthermore a higher order factor analysis of data from Kasmar's scales has shown them to be highly redundant in terms of an underlying affective dimension (Mehrabian and Russell, 1974). Mehrabian and Russell's own (1974) attempt to develop three comprehensive situational descriptors (pleasure, arousal, and dominance) is also not very satisfying to depict the array of possible situational dimensions. However, by selectively combining features suggested in the various taxonomies cited, a skeletal notion of what is meant by "all those factors" comprising a situation may be offered. The following five groups of situational characteristics represent the general features from these taxonomies which are consistent with the current definition of situation.

1. *Physical surroundings* are the most readily apparent features of a situation. These fea-

tures include geographical and institutional location, decor, sounds, aromas, lighting, weather, and visible configurations of merchandise or other material surrounding the stimulus object.

2. *Social Surroundings* provide additional depth to a description of a situation. Other persons present, their characteristics, their apparent roles, and interpersonal interactions occurring are potentially relevant examples.

3. *Temporal Perspective* is a dimension of situations which may be specified in units ranging from time of day to season of the year. Time may also be measured relative to some past or future event for the situational participant. This allows conceptions such as time since last purchase, time since or until meals or payday, and time constraints imposed by prior or standing commitments.

4. *Task Definition* features of a situation include an intent or requirement to select, shop for, or obtain information about a general or specific purchase. In addition, task may reflect different buyer and user roles anticipated by the individual. For instance, a person shopping for a small appliance as a wedding gift for a friend is in a different situation than he would be in shopping for a small appliance for personal use.

5. *Antecedent States* make up a final group of features which characterize a situation. These are momentary moods (such as acute anxiety, pleasantness, hostility, and excitation) or momentary conditions (such as cash on hand, fatigue, and illness) rather than chronic individual traits. These conditions are further stipulated to be immediately antecedent to the current situation in order to distinguish states which the individual brings to the situation from states of the individual which result from the situation. For instance, a person may select a

certain motion picture because he feels depressed (an antecedent state and a part of the choice situation), but the fact that the movie causes him to feel happier is a response to the consumption situation.[3] This altered state may then become antecedent for behavior in the next choice situation encountered, such as passing a street vendor on the way out of the theater.

Given a conception of the dimensions characterizing a situation, the final element of the definition of a situation requiring clarification is the requirement that these features have a "demonstrable and systematic effect on current behavior." To a greater extent than the problem of situational dimensions, this is an empirical question which has been the subject of some research. The following section reviews this research and examines the extent to which situational knowledge can be expected to add to our ability to explain consumer behavior.

ASSESSMENTS OF SITUATIONAL EFFECTS ON CONSUMER BEHAVIOR

Inventory Evidence

In the past six or seven years a small but growing number of empirical tests of situational influence in consumer behavior have been conducted using inventories of situational scenarios and choice alternatives. These inventories ask subjects to rate the likelihood that they would choose each of several alternative products or services under each of several sets of situational conditions. Summary descriptions of seven of these inventories are provided in the Appendix. It may well be argued that the situations investigated in these studies do not constitute random samples of possible situations and do not always reflect the full range of situational dimensions just outlined. Despite the fact that most of the inventories have relied on pretests to generate familiar situations, the argument is undoubtedly valid. Even so, any demonstration that behavior differs widely between the situations specified is evidence that there are important situational determinants for the class of choices considered.

Results comparing the relative influence from persons, products (responses), situations, and their interactions are presented in Table 12-1 for the six product categories that have been examined.[4] For all inventories the effects explaining the smallest proportions of variance are those which reflect superfluous response styles. For instance, a sizable interaction term for persons by situations would only indicate that some subjects view using

any of the products in certain situations as more likely than do other subjects. Similarly, sizable main effects for persons or situations would have little meaning since they do not involve preference differences by product. A more dominant influence is the responses by situations interaction, especially for the meat and beverage inventories. This is the variance component which directly reflects the influence of systemic situational differences in product preferences. Furthermore, the lower contributions from the responses main effect in all inventories except motion pictures, suggest that general product popularity is a substantially less important determinant of consumer preferences than are situational conditions. For the meat and beverage inventories the small interaction terms for persons

Table 12-1
Analysis of Consumer Behavior Variance[a] (percents of total variance)

	Response Category[b]					
Source	Beverage Products	Meat Products	Snack Products A	Fast Foods[c]	Leisure Activities[d]	Motion Pictures
Persons (P)	0.5%	4.6%	6.7%	8.1%	4.5%	0.9%
Situations (S)	2.7%	5.2%	0.4%	2.2%	2.0%	0.5%
Products (Responses: R)	14.6%	15.0%	6.7%	13.4%	8.8%	16.6%
R × S	39.8%	26.2%	18.7%	15.3%	13.4%	7.0%
P × S	2.7%	2.9%	6.1%	2.2%	4.0%	1.9%
P × R	11.8%	9.7%	22.4%	20.1%	21.2%	33.7%
P × S × R	—[e]	—[e]	3.4%	—[e]	—[e]	—[e]
Residual	27.8%[f]	36.4%	35.6%	38.7%	46.1%	39.4%
Total	100.0%	100.0%	100.0%	100.0%	100.0%	100.0%

[a] Components of variance analyses for mixed effects model with subjects random. For computational details, see Gleser, Cronbach and Rajaratnam (1965) and Endler and Hunt (1966).
[b] Inventories are described in Appendix.
[c] Variance components from this inventory have not previously been presented.
[d] Means of four samples.
[e] Not obtained due to single presentations of each situation-response combination.
[f] Incorrectly reported as entirely P × S × R.

by responses reveal that in these categories situational influence also outstrips *individual* product preferences. For other inventories, again excepting motion pictures, the effects of situational and individual influences are jointly dominant. Motion pictures is the only category examined in which situational effects appear to be minimal. In this case individual preferences appear to be the consistent choice determinant with the general popularity of the movies following in importance.

A recent challenge to the validity of these inventory-based findings has been presented by Lutz and Kakkar (1975). They argued that the experimental procedure of having subjects rate the same choice alternatives under all situational conditions may have spuriously inflated the situations by products interaction term. In order to test this possibility they replicated Belk's (1974a) snack product inventory, but exposed each subject to only one level of the situation factor (see Appendix for a description of their experiment). Their analysis obtained a contribution of less than 6 percent for the situations by products interaction, with a residual term which accounted for over 86 percent of the variance.[5] Unfortunately, their analysis assumed an inappropriate completely randomized factorial design rather than the split plot factorial design which was actually employed (Winter, 1971, pp. 366–371, Kirk, 1968, pp. 245–318). This problem renders their analysis meaningless and leaves the question of artifactual situational influence open. By altering the numbers of situations or responses by a factor of one half, Belk (1974b) has shown the variance component estimates of this inventory to be relatively stable across the resulting formats. Comparable results have been found by Endler and Hunt (1969) for a similar anxiety inventory. However, since these examinations do not reduce the

number of situations to one per subject, the possibility that situational influence has been overestimated by these inventories still exists.

Other Evidence

Evidence of the importance of consumer situations has been found using other approaches which lend additional credence to a conclusion that situational influence is a pervasive factor in consumer behavior. Using multidimensional scaling Green and Rao (1972) found that consumer perceptions of and preferences for various bread and pastry items changed markedly over differing meal and menu situations. In a series of experimental choice simulations Hansen (1972) found that selection of a hairdryer as a gift depended upon characteristics of the supposed recipient, and that information seeking and choices from a fixed menu varied according to the description of the restaurant. Grønhaug (1972) found that buyers of tableware utilized different types and sources of information depending upon whether the purchase was for personal use or for a gift. By having subjects reconstruct word of mouth incidents, Belk (1971) found that one-third of the conversations about a new freeze dried coffee took place where the prior conversation concerned food, and that another third of the conversations began while drinking coffee. Sandell (1968b) was able to condition choice of specific cigarette brands to either stressful or boring situations and to consumption of a specific brand of beer.

Anecdotal evidence of situational influences abounds as well. For example, in retail settings the mere presence of children (Wells and LoSciuto, 1966), friends (Bell, 1967), and sales personnel (Albaum, 1967) have been observed to alter purchase outcomes; as time since last meal increased so did the total food bill of non-obese supermarket shoppers in a study by Nisbett and Kanouse (1968); Pennington (1965) found appliance sales were most frequent when customer and salesman were similar in their propensity to bargain; and greater risk was found to be perceived in buying the same good by mail than at a retail store (Spence, Engel and Blackwell, 1970).

From the variety of methods employed in these studies it appears that situational effects can be demonstrated both descriptively and experimentally. Although the amount of research specifically focused on situational influence is still quite small, a number of instances have been found in which situations can be shown to affect consumer behavior systematically. There is further encouragement for situational research from the refreshing fact that analyses of the behavioral inventories specifying situations have been able to explain the majority of variance encountered.

SITUATIONAL RESEARCH
IN CONSUMER BEHAVIOR

Despite the substantial promise and appeal of research which employs situational variables to explain consumer choice behavior, several basic issues require resolution before this potential can be fully realized. Foremost among the issues which this research must address is the question of the most appropriate means of measuring situations. Two alternative perspectives proposed have been labeled "psychological" (Lutz and Kakkar, 1975) and "objective" (Belk, 1975) measurements. Psychological measurements of situations rely on the subjects' perceptions of the situation and are an extension of sociological inquiry into the "situation as defined" (Thomas, 1927). The premise for such measurements is that the way an individual construes a situation

should be more important to behavior than the inherent features of that situation. Objective measurements of situations restrict themselves to features of the situation as it exists before subjects' interpretations. The primary rationale for this perspective is that it removes the idiosyncrasies of perception which may otherwise limit aggregation and manipulation of consumer situations. The possibility has also been raised that some situational influences, such as subtle cueing effects, may operate without the subject's perceptual awareness. Without some sort of hybrid measurement which merges these perspectives, it appears that situational research must utilize both types of measurements.

A related issue concerns the most appropriate means of manipulating situations in experimental research. Both psychologically and objectively defined situations may be manipulated by assigning subjects to different times, places, and conditions, although successful manipulations of psychologically defined situations may need to be more clever or elaborate. However, this sort of research is costly and is best limited to the investigation of one or two situational dimensions at a time. Alternatively, and more commonly, the projective use of situational scenarios may continue to be used. Typically these scenarios have ranged from a one phrase to one paragraph written description of situational conditions. Photographs, motion pictures, and video tapes are possible refinements of stimulus input in this procedure, but these methods favor visual cues and may unnaturally focus attention and control the *rate* of experience. Perhaps the best means of manipulation, short of actually modifying situational conditions, is to couple written descriptions of features such as temporal perspective, task definition, and antecedent states, with visual and auditory input of physical and social surroundings. Comparisons of results using each alternative means of manipulation will be needed to assess their relative adequacy.

Whether the existence of a particular situational effect has been determined under simulated or actual conditions, interpretation of the importance of this effect requires knowledge of the frequency of occurrence of these conditions. Because consumers can selectively seek or avoid many of the situations they encounter and because all unanticipated situations are not equally common, descriptive evidence of the frequency of situational occurrences is needed. A number of time budget studies based on consumer diaries (e.g., Szali, 1973) are available which provide general records of the times and places of consumer activities. But even the most detailed consumer accounts (e.g., Muse, 1946) seldom go beyond "shopping" in their descriptions of purchase situations. Nevertheless activity diaries appear to be a useful approach to gathering relevant data on situational occurrences. In addition to providing data on relevant situational variables, this approach may simultaneously measure individual characteristics and behavioral outcomes which can be cross tabulated with situations to obtain a picture of individual differences in situational exposure and susceptibility to situational influence.

The ultimate problem for all future situational research is the lack of a comprehensive taxonomy of situational characteristics and normal combinations of these characteristics. Hopefully this discussion has made some headway in establishing a general conceptualization of consumer situations, but obviously greater detail is necessary. It is a false hope at this point to expect that we can systematically investigate a complete list of situational characteristics, because no such list exists. Only by continuing to conceptualize and research situational characteristics under a guiding understanding of the scope and criteria for situations can such a summary ever be achieved.

APPENDIX: SUMMARY DETAILS FOR SEVEN SITUATIONAL INVENTORIES

1. *Beverages.* Sandell (1968a) presented 31 student subjects with ten beverages (e.g., coffee, water, beer) which they rated in seven situations (e.g., when alone, feeling sleepy in the afternoon, reading the paper in the morning) using a seven-point scale from "extremely unwilling" to "extremely willing" (to try). Situations and beverages tested were apparently chosen subjectively, although five subjects who did not appear to view the products as alternatives were eliminated.

2. *Leisure Activities.* Bishop and Witt (1970) investigated the effect of ten situations (e.g., returning from studying at a noisy library, relaxing Friday afternoon following a busy week, waking up fresh and rested on a Saturday morning) on the likelihood of engaging in each of 13 leisure activities (e.g., go shopping for clothes, watch television, visit a friend) using a five-point scale from "almost certainly" to "I would not feel like" (doing this). Situations were selected based on five alternative theories of leisure behavior, and leisure activities were based on their frequency of occurrence in previous community surveys. Subjects were male and female students at two colleges and totalled 141.

3. *Meat Products.* Belk (1974a) examined choices of 11 different meat products (e.g., hamburger, steak, chicken) in nine different situations (e.g., party for friends, meal on a weekday evening, at a nice restaurant with friends) using five-point scales from "extremely likely" to "not at all likely," administered to 100 members of a community. Situations and meat products were chosen from protocols and familiarity pretests.

4. *Motion Pictures.* Belk (1974b) had 100 students rate 12 hypothetical motion pictures

(e.g., The Motorcycle Freaks, Summer of Dreams, Only Fools are Sad) described in mock advertisements, in nine situations (e.g., on a weeknight with friends of the same sex, just for something to do, together with spouse or date at their request) on a five-point scale. Situations were selected via protocols and pretests based on familiarity, and motion pictures were structured to parallel currently popular themes.

5. *Snack Products A.* Belk (1974b) varied ten different situations (e.g., while watching television with family, going on a long automobile trip, an urge for a between meal snack) and had 100 student subjects rate the likelihood of choosing each of ten snack products (e.g., potato chips, pastries, ice cream) on two occasions (two weeks apart) using five-point scales. Situations and products were chosen as in the meat inventory.

6. *Snack Products B.* Lutz and Kakkar (1975) replicated Belk's snack product inventory except that subjects in each of ten groups of from 24 to 36 students responded within only one of the situations and on only one occasion. Each group rated products in a different situation and a total of 306 subjects were employed.

7. *Fast Foods.* Using data collected by Leo Burnett U.S.A., Belk (1975) analyzed the effect of ten different situations (e.g., too tired to cook dinner, unexpected dinner guests, having a few friends over for a casual get-together) on responses to a six-point likelihood scale for each of ten (confidential) fast food outlets and related meal choices. Subjects were 98 housewives in a single community.

NOTES

1. A great deal of the effort in the emerging discipline of environmental or ecological psychology has been spent in debating boundaries. See for example Barker (1963), Craik (1970), Proshansky, Ittelson, and Rivlin (1970), Ittelsoti (1973), and Rivlin (1973).

2. This point is elaborated by Belk (1975). Mausner (1963) captured the argument in stating that "if one specifies the stimulus in terms of the nature of the receiver, lawfulness becomes impossible."

3. Hansen (1972) distinguishes between purchase, consumption, and communication situations. Comments in this paper concentrate primarily on consumer purchase choices.

4. The research reported generally employed a situations by products by persons repeated measures experimental design. While nearly all main effects and two way interactions yielded significant F-ratios, proportions of variance accounted for by each effect are more revealing (Belk, 1974a).

5. Hays' Omega squared statistic (Hays, 1964) was employed to derive these estimates. Since this statistic assumed a completely fixed effects model, results are not strictly comparable to those of the mixed effects components of variance method employed in the other studies reported.

REFERENCES

Albaum, G. "Exploring Interaction in a Marketing Situation," *Journal of Marketing Research,* 4 (May, 1967), 168–72.

Allen, B. L. "Situational Factors in Conformity," in Leonard Berkowitz, *Advances in Experimental Social Psychology,* Vol. 2, New York: Academic Press, 1965.

Barker, R. G. *The Stream of Behavior.* New York: Appleton-Century-Crofts, 1963.

———. *Ecological Psychology: Concepts and Methods for Studying the Environment of Human Behavior,* Stanford University Press, 1968.

Belk, R. W. "Occurrence of Word of Mouth Buyer Behavior as a Function of Situation and Advertising Stimuli," *Proceedings,* American Marketing Association Fall Conference, 1971, 419–22.

———. "An Exploratory Assessment of Situational Effects in Buyer Behavior," *Journal of Marketing Research,* 11 (May, 1974a), 156–163.

_____. "Application and Analysis of the Behavior Differential Inventory for Assessing Situational Effects in Consumer Behavior," in Scott Ward and Peter Wright (eds.), *Advances in Consumer Research*, Vol. 1. Urbana: Association for Consumer Research, 1974b.

_____. "The Objective Situation as a Determinant of Consumer Behavior," in Mary Jane Schlinger (ed.) *Advances in Consumer Research*, Vol. 2. Chicago: Association for Consumer Research, 1975.

Bell, G. D. "Self-Confidence and Persuasion in Car Buying," *Journal of Marketing Research*, 4 (February, 1967), 46–52.

Bellows, R. "Towards a Taxonomy of Social Situations," in Stephen B. Sells (ed.), *Stimulus Determinants of Behavior*, New York: Ronald, 1963.

Bishop, D. W. and P. A. Witt, "Sources of Behavioral Variance During Leisure Time," *Journal of Personality and Social Psychology*, 16 (October, 1970), 352–60.

Craik, K. H. "Environmental Psychology," in Kenneth H. Craik, et al. *New Directions in Psychology*, Vol. 4, New York: Holt, Rinehart and Winston, 1970.

Endler, N. S. and J. McV. Hunt. "Sources of Behavioral Variance as Measured by the S–R Inventory of Anxiousness," *Psychological Bulletin*, 65 (1966), 336–46.

Engel, J. F., D. T. Kollat, and R. D. Blackwell. "Personality Measures and Market Segmentation," *Business Horizons*, 12 (June, 1969), 61–70.

Gleser, G. L., L. J. Cronbach and N. Rajaratnam. "Generalizability of Scores Influenced by Multiple Sources of Variance," *Psychometricka*, 30 (1965), 395–418.

Green, P. E. and V. R. Rao, "Configural Synthesis in Multidimensional Scaling," *Journal of Marketing Research*, 9 (February, 1972), 65–68.

Grønhaug, K. "Buying Situation and Buyer's Information Behavior," *European Marketing Research Review*, 7 (September, 1972), 33–48.

Hansen, F. *Consumer Choice Behavior*. New York: The Free Press, 1972.

Hays, W. L. *Statistics for Psychologists*. New York: Rinehart and Winston, 1964.

Helson, H. "Current Trends and Issues in Adaptation-Level Theory," *American Psychologist*, 19 (1964), 26–38.

Ittelson, W. H. *Environment and Cognition*. New York: Seminar Press, 1973.

Kasmar, J. V. "The Development of a Usable Lexicon of Environmental Descriptors," *Environment and Behavior*, 2 (1970), 133–169.

Kirk, R. E. *Experimental Design: Procedures for the Behavior Sciences*, Belmont, California: Wadsworth Publishing, 1968.

Lavidge, R. J. "The Cotton Candy Concept: IntraIndividual Variability," in Lee Adler and Irving Crespi, *Attitude Research at Sea*, Chicago: American Marketing Association, 1966, 39–50.

Lewin, K. "Environmental Forces in Child Behavior and Development," in Carl C. Murchison, *Handbook of Child Psychology*, second edition, revised. Worcester, Massachusetts: Clark University Press, 1933, 94–127.

Lewin, K. *A Dynamic Theory of Personality*. New York: McGraw-Hill, 1935.

Lutz, R. J. and P. K. Kakkar. "The Psychological Situation as a Determinant of Consumer Behavior," in Mary Jane Schlinger (ed.), *Advances in Consumer Research*, Vol. 2. Chicago: Association for Consumer Research, 1975.

Mausner, B. M. "The Specification of the Stimulus Situation in a Social Interaction," in Stephen B. Sells, *Stimulus Determinants of Behavior*. New York: Ronald, 1963.

Mehrabian, A. and J. A. Russell. *An Approach to Environmental Psychology*. Cambridge: M.I.T. Press, 1974.

Moos, R. H. "Conceptualizations of Human Environments," *American Psychologist*, 28 (1973), 652–663.

Muse, M. "Time Expenditures in Homemaking Activities in 183 Vermont Farm Homes," *Vermont Agricultural Experimental Station Bulletin*, No. 530, 1946.

Nisbett, R. E. and D. E. Kanouse, "Obesity, Food Deprivation and Supermarket Shopping Behavior," *Journal of Personality and Social Psychology*, 12 (August, 1969), 289–94.

Pennington, A. L. "Customer-Salesman Bargaining Behavior in Retail Transactions," *Journal of Marketing Research*, 5 (August, 1965), 255–62.

Proshansky, H. M., W. H. Ittelson, and L. G. Rivlin. (eds.) *Environmental Psychology*, New York: Holt, Rinehart and Winston, 1970.

Sandell, R. G. "Effects of Attitudinal and Situational Factors on Reported Choice Behavior," *Journal of Marketing Research*, 4 (August, 1968a), 405–08.

———. "The Effects of Attitude Influence and Representational Conditioning on Choice Behavior," Stockholm: The Economic Research Institute, Stockholm School of Economics, 1968b.

Sells, S. B. "Dimensions of Stimulus Situations Which Accounts for Behavioral Variance," in Stephen B. Sells (ed.), *Stimulus Determinants of Behavior*, New York: Ronald, 1963.

Sherif, M. and C. W. Sherif. *An Outline of Social Psychology*, Rev. Ed. New York: Harper and Row, 1956.

Spence, H. E., J. R. Engel, and Roger D. Blackwell. "Perceived Risk in Mail-Order and Retail Store Buying," *Journal of Marketing Research*, 7 (August, 1970), 364–69.

Szali, A. et al. (eds) *The Use of Time*. The Hague: Mouten, 1973.

Thomas, W. L. "The Behavior Pattern and the Situation," *Proceedings*, Twenty-second Annual Meeting, American Sociological Society, 22 (1927), 1–13.

Thorndike, R. L. *Research Problems and Techniques*. Washington: U.S. Government Printing Office, Report No. 3 AAF Aviation Psychology Program, 1947.

Ward, S. and T. S. Robertson. "Consumer Behavior Research: Promise and Prospects," in Scott Ward and Thomas S. Robertson, *Consumer Behavior: Theoretical Sources*. Englewood Cliffs: Prentice-Hall, 1973, 3–42.

Wells, W. D. and A. LoSciuto. "A Direct Observation of Purchasing Behavior," *Journal of Marketing Research*, (August, 1966), 227–33.

Winer, B. J. *Statistical Principles in Experimental Design*, Second Edition. New York: McGraw-Hill, 1971.

Wolf, R. "The Measurement of Environments," in Anne Anastasi (ed.), *Testing Problems in Perspective*, Washington, D.C.: American Council on Education, 1966, 491–503.

◆

The Experiential Aspects of Consumption: Consumer Fantasies, Feelings, and Fun

Morris B. Holbrook and Elizabeth C. Hirschman

In its brief history, the study of consumer behavior has evolved from an early emphasis on rational choice (microeconomics and classical decision theory) to a focus on apparently irrational buying needs (some motivation research) to the use of logical flow models of bounded rationality (e.g., Howard and Sheth 1969). The latter approach has deepened into what is often called the "information processing model" (Bettman 1979). The information processing model regards the consumer as a logical thinker who solves problems to make purchasing decisions. The information processing perspective has become so ubiquitous in consumer research that, like fish in water, many researchers may be relatively unaware of its pervasiveness.

Recently, however, researchers have begun to question the hegemony of the information processing perspective on the grounds that it may neglect important con-

"The Experiential Aspects of Consumption: Consumer Fantasies, Feelings, and Fun," Holbrook, Morris B. and Elizabeth C. Hirschman, Vol. 9 (Sept. '82), pp. 132–140. Reprinted from *Journal of Consumer Research*, published by The University of Chicago Press.

sumption phenomena (e.g., Olshavsky and Granbois 1979; Sheth 1979). Ignored phenomena include various playful leisure activities, sensory pleasures, daydreams, esthetic enjoyment, and emotional responses. Consumption has begun to be seen as involving a steady flow of fantasies, feelings, and fun encompassed by what we call the "experiential view." This experiential perspective is phenomenological in spirit and regards consumption as a primarily subjective state of consciousness with a variety of symbolic meanings, hedonic responses, and esthetic criteria. Recognition of these important aspects of consumption is strengthened by contrasting the information processing and experiential views.[1]

CONTRASTING VIEWS OF CONSUMER BEHAVIOR

Our bases for contrasting the information processing and experiential views appear in Figure 13-1. This diagram is not all-inclusive. It simply represents some key variables typi-

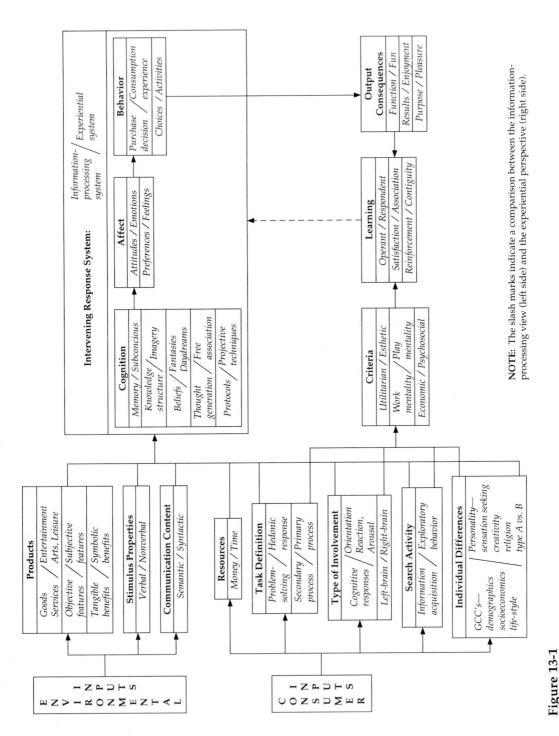

Figure 13-1
Contrasts between the Information-Processing and Experiential Views of Consumer Behavior

NOTE: The slash marks indicate a comparison between the information-processing view (left side) and the experiential perspective (right side).

cally considered in logical flow models of consumer behavior. In brief, various environmental and consumer inputs (products, resources) are processed by an intervening response system (cognition-affect-behavior) that generates output consequences which, when appraised against criteria, result in a learning feedback loop. Individual differences, search activity, type of involvement, and task definition affect the criteria by which output consequences are evaluated.

Though Figure 13-1 neglects some variables that have interested consumer researchers,[2] it reflects the general viewpoint embodied by most popular consumer behavior models. Moreover, the diagram facilitates the intended comparison between approaches by distinguishing between the phenomena of primary interest to the information processing perspective (left side of slash marks) and those of central concern to the experiential view (right side of slash marks). In the following sections, we discuss these distinctions as they pertain to (1) environmental inputs, (2) consumer inputs, (3) intervening responses, and (4) output consequences, criteria, and learning effects.

ENVIRONMENTAL INPUTS

Products

Much consumer research has focused on the tangible benefits of conventional goods and services (soft drinks, toothpaste, automobiles) that perform utilitarian functions based on relatively objective features (calories, fluoride, miles per gallon). By contrast, the experiential perspective explores the symbolic meanings of more subjective characteristics (cheerfulness, sociability, elegance).

All products—no matter how mundane—may carry a symbolic meaning (Levy 1959, 1980). In some cases, the symbolic role is especially rich and salient: for example, enter-tainment, the arts, and leisure activities encompass symbolic aspects of consumption behavior that make them particularly fertile ground for research. These areas have recently received increased attention from consumer researchers concerned with products like musical recordings, singers, fashion designs, architectural styles, paintings, museum exhibitions, novels, concerts, performing arts series, and associated patterns of leisure activity (Hirschman and Holbrook 1981). The growth of research on leisure, entertainment, and the arts reflects a shift of attention toward the experimental side of the distinctions shown in Figure 13-1.

Methodologically, the shift promotes certain advantages. One benefit stems from the tendency for leisure, entertainment, and arts products to prompt high levels of interest and involvement among their target markets. The growing body of work in these areas suggests that respondents can typically provide meaningful data on perceptions and preferences across a broad array of relevant objects or activities. Hence, applications of multivariate methods may be more valid with this type of product than with some low-involvement consumer nondurables, such as detergents or canned peas, for which consumers may be unable to make valid perceptual or affective distinctions among more than a few different brands. For this reason, many of our available statistical procedures—especially those directed toward intraindividual analysis across brands—may actually be more appropriate within the context of experiential consumption than for the frequently purchased nondurables to which they have typically been applied.

Stimulus Properties

Traditional consumer research paradigms have concentrated on product attributes that lend themselves to verbal descriptions. Both conjoint analysis and multiattribute models, for example, have relied heavily on designs that make use of verbal stimuli. However, many products project important nonverbal cues that must be seen, heard, tasted, felt, or smelled to be appreciated properly. Indeed, in many consumption situations (viewing a movie, eating at a restaurant, playing tennis), several sensory channels operate simultaneously. Yet scant research on nonverbal multisensory properties has been reported in the literature. Accordingly, the experiential perspective supports a more energetic investigation of multisensory psychophysical relationships in consumer behavior.

Turning one's attention from primarily verbal to nonverbal sensory cues requires a very different mode of presenting experimental stimulus objects. While verbal descriptions have often sufficed in conventional research on consumer preferences, an experiential outlook must involve subjects in consumption-like experiences based on real—or at least realistic—product samples.

Communication Content

Content analyses of communication in consumer research have more often focused on drawing inferences about the source of a message than on explaining its effects (Kassarjian 1977). When the latter perspective has been considered, it has generally involved the information processing orientation toward the study of consumer responses to the semantic aspects of communication content (Shimp and Preston 1981). Focusing on effects attributable to the syntactic aspects of message content— that is, their structure and style—is more germane to the experiential perspective.

In other disciplines, message syntax has often been found to exert a direct effect on hedonic response. This concept is central, for example, to the so-called "Wundt curve" and its relationship to collative stimulus properties such as uncertainty or complexity (Berlyne 1971). This information theoretic

perspective has been applied at length in analyses of emotional responses to music and other art forms by researchers exploring its relevance to the esthetic process (Platt 1970).

Work on syntactic structure in consumer research is less well developed. However, Taylor's (1953) "Cloze" technique has been used to measure subjective verbal uncertainty in English prose (Wallendorf, Zinkhan, and Zinkhan 1981) and advertising copy (Zinkhan and Martin 1981).

CONSUMER INPUTS

Resources

In examining the resources that a consumer brings to the exchange transaction, conventional research has generally focused on monetary income constraints and the effects of prices. In more recent economic analysis, this money-oriented focus has been expanded to acknowledge the fundamental role played by the consumer's allocation of time resources to the "household production function" (Becker 1976). In this view, households produce and consume "commodities" that combine inputs of goods and time to maximize overall utility, subject to resource constraints.

The investigation of subjective time resources may help to unravel the mysteries of the psychotemporal expenditures involved in experiential consumption. Studying the nature and allocation of discretionary time deserves high priority. Movement in this direction has appeared in several review articles, in special conference sessions, and in a recent issue of the *JCR* [*Journal of Consumer Research*] devoted to the subject of time in consumer behavior (March 1981).

Task Definition

In making assumptions concerning the consumer's task definition, the information processing and experiential perspectives envision different kinds of consumption behavior. The information processing view conjures up an image of the consumer as a problem solver engaged in the goal-directed activities of searching for information, retrieving memory cues, weighing evidence, and arriving at carefully considered judgmental evaluations. Freud called such mental activities "secondary process" thinking. It is "secondary" in the sense that it reflects the way our mental processes function as a result of socialization (Hilgard 1962).

By contrast, the experiential view emphasizes the importance of primary process thinking in accord with the pleasure principle. Primary process thinking involves a task definition oriented toward hedonic response and is "primary" in the sense that it hearkens back to the way a baby pursues immediate pleasure or gratification (Hilgard 1962). This type of consumption seeks fun, amusement, fantasy, arousal, sensory stimulation, and enjoyment. Indeed, the evidence suggests that consumers typically spend the majority of their lives eating, sleeping, chatting with friends, making love, and watching television (Robinson 1977, p. 35). Surely, any meaningful attempt to model such relatively pleasure-oriented consumption must pay attention to its hedonic components.

Regarding consumption as a primary process directed toward the hedonic pursuit of pleasure raises certain methodological issues. These include: (1) the need to develop better measures of hedonic response—especially valid and operational definitions of what constitutes "pleasure"; (2) the fact that hedonic responses are likely to be unusually susceptible to fluctuations across situations, thereby posing problems of reliability and validity; and (3) the difficulty of using available indices of chronic hedonic energy, such as sensation seeking, in the context of explaining acute, volatile, sensory-emotive phenomena. The experiential view performs a useful role

by insistently calling attention to these conceptual and methodological problems.

Type of Involvement

We focus here not on the degree of involvement (low versus high), but rather on its type (engagement of cognitive responses versus orientation reaction involving arousal). Krugman's (1965) early definition of involvement emphasized the tendency to make personal connections between one's own life and the stimulus, explicitly excluding components such as attention, interest, or excitement. This early view has proven most congenial to information processing proponents, who define involvement in terms of personal relevance or multiplicity of cognitive responses (Leavitt, Greenwald, and Obermiller 1981). Attention, interest, excitement, and so forth bear more directly on the experiential view by emphasizing degree of activation or arousal, with consequent implications for the availability of psychobiological indices (Kroeber-Riel 1979). Krugman's (1971) later work on brain-wave patterns has moved in this direction and thus appears to represent a shift toward the experiential model.

Further, any argument that involvement is primarily a left-brain phenomenon refers implicitly to cognitive responses associated with analytic, logical, problem-oriented cerebration (Hansen 1981). If one referred instead to "involvement" in the sense of the orientation reflex, its arousal component might be more closely associated with right-brain phenomena related to emotion.

The use of psychobiological indices of arousal and the interest in right-brain hemispheric specialization have prompted increased attention from consumer researchers. Numerous problems arise when interpreting the results of these physiological approaches. Ryan (1980) has challenged the construct validity of psychobiological measures. In this light, Olson, Reynolds, and Ray's (1982) findings on psychophysiological advertising effects raise almost as many questions as they answer. Similarly, Hansen and Lundsgaard (1981) have reported rather discouraging convergent validities among various indices of brain lateralization. Taken together, these difficulties point out that work on the physiological components of consumption remains in its infancy and needs further conceptual and methodological development in measures of arousal and hemispheric involvement.

Search Activity

The nature of the associated search activity is closely tied to involvement issues. Here, proponents of the information processing perspective adopt various strategies for the study of information acquisition. Those inclined toward laboratory methods have developed ingenious techniques to study how cues are acquired (Russo 1978). Meanwhile, survey researchers have investigated the general characteristics of information seekers at the cross-cultural level (Thorelli, Becker, and Engledow 1975).

By contrast, the experiential view of search activity might draw more heavily from the work by psychologists on exploratory behavior (Berlyne 1960). For example, Howard and Sheth (1969) consider stimulus ambiguity, working through arousal, as a determinant of specific exploration via what they call "overt search." More diversive exploration—such as that involved in exposure to entertainment media—has sometimes been explained as a form of play, as in the "ludic" theory of mass communication (Huizinga 1970; Stephenson 1967).

Diversive exploration via the entertainment and arts media appears to be a context well suited to the extension of Berlyne's (1960) work on exploratory behavior. Indeed, toward the end of his career, Berlyne (1971) devoted increased attention to the experimental

study of esthetics, focusing particularly on a proposed nonmonotonic relationship between stimulus complexity and hedonic value. Aspects of his approach may be usefully applied to an investigation of the consumption experience. However, in making such extensions, three methodological refinements appear critical: (1) esthetic stimuli should be designed to vary in complexity over a range broad enough to permit the full nonmonotonic relationship to appear; (2) the success of this experimental manipulation should be checked by obtaining a measure of subjective uncertainty analogous to the Cloze-based index described earlier; and (3) the subjective uncertainty measure should be treated as an intervening variable that mediates the effect of stimulus complexity on hedonic response.

Individual Differences

For some time, consumer researchers' interest in individual differences has focused on general customer characteristics such as demographics, socioeconomic status, and psychographics. The relatively poor performance of personality measures in predicting consumer behavior has encouraged their gradual abandonment in favor of the subcategory of psychographics known as life style variables. Recently, in a move toward the experiential view, the concept of life style has been generalized to include more explicit consideration of the use of time (Lee and Ferber 1977).

The investigation of experiential consumption appears to offer considerable scope for the revival of personality and allied variables, such as subculture, though the specific dimensions investigated will almost certainly differ from those of interest to the information processing view. Some experimentally relevant personality constructs include:

- *Sensation seeking* (Zuckerman 1979), a variable likely to affect a consumer's tendency to enjoy more complex entertainment, to be fashion conscious, to prefer spicy and crunchy foods, to play games, and to use drugs

- *Creativity* and related variables tied to variety-, novelty-, or arousal-seeking (Raju 1980)
- *Religious world view* (Hirschman 1982), a dimension that affects daydreaming as well as other forms of sensation and pleasure seeking
- *Type A versus Type B personality* (Friedman and Roseman 1974), a dimension closely linked with perceived time pressure and therefore likely to affect the way one allocates psychotemporal expenditures among work and leisure activities

Research on individual differences in experiential consumption has already found contrasts among religions and nationalities in the types of entertainment preferred, hedonic motives for engaging in leisure activities, and resulting levels of enthusiasm expressed. These ethnic differences appear to depend on intervening variables such as use of imagery, sensation seeking, and the desire to escape reality.

INTERVENING RESPONSE SYSTEM

Cognition

Due to its cognitively oriented perspective, the information processing approach has focused on memory and related phenomena: the consumer's cognitive apparatus is viewed as a complex knowledge structure embodying intricately interwoven subsystems of belief referred to as "memory schemas" or "semantic networks" (Olson 1980). Such knowledge structures include what Freudians call "manifest" content—those ideas that are accessible to introspection and therefore form the substance of conscious thought patterns.

By contrast, the experiential perspective focuses on cognitive processes that are more subconscious and private in nature. Interest centers on consumption-related flights of fancy involving pictorial imagery (Richardson 1969), fantasies (Klinger 1971), and daydreams (Singer 1966). Such material often masks embarrassing or socially sensitive ideas and perceptions. This "latent" content does not appear in overt verbal reports, either because it has been repressed or because its anxiety-provoking nature encourages disguise at a subconscious level.

In its treatment of cognitive phenomena, particularly material of a subconscious nature, the experiential view borders somewhat on motivation research (e.g., Dichter 1960). However, there are two methodological differences. First, we believe that much relevant fantasy life and many key symbolic meanings lie just below the threshold of consciousness—that is, that they are subconscious or preconscious as opposed to unconscious—and that they can be retrieved and reported if sufficiently indirect methods are used to overcome sensitivity barriers. Second, we advocate the use of structured projective techniques that employ quantifiable questionnaire items applicable to samples large enough to permit statistical hypothesis testing.

Affect

It might be argued that, in the area of affect, the conventional information processing approach has been studying experiential consumptions all along. After all, the traditional expectancy value models ($\Sigma E \cdot V$) conform in spirit to Bentham's felicific calculus. Fundamentally, however, the information processing perspective emphasizes only one aspect of hedonic response—namely, like or dislike of a particular brand (attitude) or its rank relative to other brands (preference). This attitudinal component represents only a tiny subset of the emotions and feelings of interest to the experiential view.

The full gamut of relevant emotions includes such diverse feelings as love, hate, fear, joy, boredom, anxiety, pride, anger, disgust, sadness, sympathy, lust, ecstasy, greed, guilt, elation, shame, and awe. This sphere of human experience has long been neglected by psychologists, who are just beginning to expand early work on arousal in order to develop systematic and coherent models of emotion (Plutchik 1980).

Such psychological conceptualizations of emotion are still in their seminal stages and, understandably, have not yet cross-pollinated the work of consumer researchers. Yet, it is clear that emotions form an important substrate of consumption and that their systematic investigation is a key requirement for the successful application of the experiential perspective.

Behavior

At the behavioral level, traditional consumer research has focused almost exclusively on the choice process that generates purchase decisions culminating in actual buying behavior. Thus, brand purchase is typically viewed as the most important behavioral outcome of the information processing model.

A quarter of a century ago, however, Alderson (1957) drew a sharp distinction between buying and consuming. This contrast was further elaborated in Boyd and Levy's (1963) discussion of the consumption system with its emphasis on brand-usage behavior. By focusing on the configuration of activities involved in consumption, this viewpoint calls attention to the experiences with a product that one gains by actually consuming it.

Few consumer researchers have followed this lead, although the study of product usage and related activities is clearly a requisite cornerstone to the development of the ex-

periential model. The importance of such study is reinforced by the emphasis on entertainment-, arts-, and leisure-related offerings, which often depend more on the allocation of time than of money. Given the operation of the pleasure principle in multisensory gratification, exciting fantasies, and cathected emotions, one's purchase decision is obviously only a small component in the constellation of events involved in the overall consumption experience.

In exploring the nature of that overall experience, the approach envisioned here departs from the traditional positivist focus on directly observable buying behavior and devotes increased attention to the mental events surrounding the act of consumption. The investigation of these mental events requires a willingness to deal with the purely subjective aspects of consciousness. This exploration of consumption as conscious experiences must be rigorous and scientific, but the methodology should include introspective reports, rather than relying exclusively on overt behavioral measures. The necessary methodological shift thus leads toward a more phenomenological approach—i.e., "a free commentary on whatever cognitive material the subject is aware of" (Hilgard 1980).[3]

A recent state-of-the-art review of theory, method, and application in the study of conscious experience has been provided by Singer (1981/1982). Comparable approaches in conventional consumer research would include problem-solving protocols, thought-generation techniques, and similar ideation-reporting procedures. It remains for the experiential perspective to extend this cognitively oriented work toward the investigation of *all* aspects of the consumption experience. In such a phenomenological approach, experience is "acknowledged as a part of the psychological universe and addressed as an object of study" (Koch 1964, p. 34):

The phenomenologist . . . accepts, as the subject-matter of his inquiry, all data of experiences. . . . Colors and sounds are data; so are impressions of distance and duration; so are feelings of attraction and repulsion; so are yearnings and fears, ecstasies and disillusionments; . . . . These are data, given in experience, to be accepted as such and wondered about. (MacLeod 1964, p. 51)

MacLeod's statement comes close to encapsulating our central theme—namely, that the conventional approach to consumer research addresses only a small fraction of the phenomenological data that compose the entire experience of consumption. Investigation of the remaining components of the consumption experience should serve as one key target of future methodological developments in consumer research.

One qualitative approach, advocated by Levy, "accepts introspection as data" and involves the use of personal narratives: "A protocol in which a consumer tells the story of how the product is consumed can be examined for how the consumer interprets the consumption experience" (1981, p. 50). Such relatively unstructured procedures may be usefully complemented by more structured quantitative methods.[4] Toward this end, Pekala and Levine argue for a "phenomenological or introspective approach" to investigate the "structure of conscious experience" (1981/1982, pp. 30–31) and present a Phenomenology of Consciousness Questionnaire (PCQ) consisting of 60 Likert-type items drawn from 15 different content areas. Factor analysis of the PCQ suggests the existence of nine important dimensions: altered experience, awareness, imagery, attention/memory, negative affect, alertness, positive affect, volition, and internal dialogue. This instrument has not (to our knowledge) been applied in consumer research, but future applications may help elucidate the experiential aspects of consumption.

OUTPUT CONSEQUENCES, CRITERIA, AND LEARNING

Output Consequences and Criteria

From the information processing perspective, the consequences of consumer choice typically are viewed in terms of the product's useful function. The criteria for evaluating the success of a purchasing decision are therefore primarily utilitarian in nature—as, when judging a "craft," one asks how well it serves its intended purpose or performs its proper function (Becker 1978). The operative logic behind this criterion reflects a work mentality in which objects attain value primarily by virtue of the economic benefits they provide.

By contrast, in the experiential view, the consequences of consumption appear in the fun that a consumer derives from a product—the enjoyment it offers and the resulting feeling of pleasure that it evokes (Klinger 1971, p. 18). In this generally neglected perspective, the criteria for successful consumption are essentially esthetic in nature and hinge on an appreciation of the product for its own sake, apart from any utilitarian function that it may or may not perform (McGregor 1974). This is analogous to the appreciation of a work of "art" (versus a "craft") as a thing in itself, without regard to its functional utility (Becker 1978). In making such appraisals, one conforms to a play mentality (Huizinga 1970) wherein perceived benefits are primarily psychosocial and "episodes designated as playful are assumed to be free from any immediate purpose" (Lancy 1980, p. 474): "Play is disinterested, self-sufficient, an interlude from work. It brings no material gain" (Stephenson 1967, pp. 192–193).[5]

As indicated in Figure 13-1, the relative salience of evaluative criteria is assumed to depend in part on the individual's task definition, type of involvement, search activity, and personality. For example, where the consumption task is defined as the pursuit of hedonic response, esthetic criteria would be likely to apply. A similar play mentality should prevail when involvement is primarily right cerebral hemisphere oriented, when diversive exploration is directed toward the alleviation of boredom, and when a sensation-seeking, creative, non-Protestant, or Type B personality is involved.

Consumer researchers have devoted little attention to the underlying determinants of fun and playful activities even though it appears that consumers spend many of their wakeful hours engaged in events that can be explained on no other grounds. It would be difficult, for example, to account for the popularity of a television program like *Dallas* on the basis of functional utility in providing solutions to life's many problems. Clearly, its success depends instead on conformity to some set of esthetic standards associated with the play mentality. Better understanding of such standards is a vital link in the further development of the experiential view.

Learning

Ever since Howard and others included a feedback loop via brand satisfaction in the early models of buyer behavior (Howard and Sheth 1969), it has been clear that learning effects exert a strong impact on future components of the intervening response system (shown by a dotted feedback line in Figure 13-1). The traditional view of learning in consumer behavior has been based on operant conditioning or instrumental learning, where satisfaction with the purchase serves to reinforce future behavioral responses in the form of repeat purchases.

But Howard and Sheth (1969) also recognized a second learning principle, contiguity, which depends on the frequency with which neutral events have been paired in experience. The resulting patterns of association, which Osgood (1957) called "associative hierarchies," exhibit a form of respondent conditioning. When extended to the experiential perspective, this contiguity principle suggests that sensations, imagery, feelings, pleasures, and other symbolic or hedonic components which are frequently paired together in experience tend to become mutually evocative, so that "fantasy, dreams, and certain forms of play can similarly be construed as respondent sequences" (Klinger 1971, p. 35). This argument implies that—though satisfaction certainly constitutes one important experiential component—the stream of associations that occur during consumptions (imagery, daydreams, emotions) may be equally important experiential aspects of consumer behavior.

CONCLUSION

Much buyer behavior can be explained usefully by the prevailing information processing perspective. Conventional research, however, has neglected an important portion of the consumption experience. Thus our understanding of leisure activities, consumer esthetics, symbolic meanings, variety seeking, hedonic response, psychotemporal resources, daydreaming, creativity, emotions, play, and artistic endeavors may benefit from a broadened view.

Abandoning the information processing approach is undesirable, but supplementing and enriching it with an admixture of the experiential perspective could be extremely fruitful. Such an expansion of consumer research will raise vital but previously neglected issues concerning (1) the role of esthetic products, (2) multisensory aspects of product enjoyment, (3) the syntactic dimensions of communication, (4) time budgeting in the pursuit of pleasure, (5) product-related fantasies and imagery, (6) feelings arising from consumption, and (7) the role of play in providing enjoyment and fun. This is the point of asking questions concerning the nature of experiential consumption—questions such as:

- "Which painting is the most beautiful?"
- "Which tastes better, chocolate or strawberry?"
- "What makes Beethoven great?"
- "How much do you watch television?"
- "What do you see when you turn out the lights?"
- "What makes you happy?"
- "How did you spend your vacation?"

In sum, the purpose of this paper has been neither to advocate a "new" theory of consumer behavior nor to reject the "old" approach, but rather to argue for an enlarged view that avoids any adherence to the "-isms" or "-ologies" that so often constrict scientific inquiry. One cannot reduce the explanation of human behavior to any narrowly circumscribed and simplistic model, whether that model be behavioristic or psychoanalytic, ethological or anthropomorphic, cognitive or motivational: the behavior of people in general and of consumers in particular is the fascinating and endlessly complex result of a multifaceted interaction between organism and environment. In this dynamic process, neither problem-directed nor experiential components can safely be ignored. By focusing single mindedly on the consumer as information processor, recent consumer research has tended to neglect the equally important experiential aspects of consumption, thereby limiting our understanding of consumer behavior. Future research should work toward redressing this imbalance by broadening our

area of study to include some consideration of consumer fantasies, feelings, and fun.

NOTES

1. Throughout the discussion, most arguments are supported by one or two key references. Much more extensive documentation appears in earlier versions of the paper that may be obtained from the authors.
2. For example, Figure 13-1 omits the effects of general economic conditions and related expectations, some elements of the marketing mix (e.g., channels of distribution), social influence through reference groups, perceived risk and other conflict-related phenomena, joint decision making in households, and considerations of economic externalities or social welfare.
3. The recently accumulating studies on the stream of consciousness serve also to introduce the new introspectionism. In this light, consider the avowed objective of the new journal entitled *Imagination, Cognition and Personality:* "An important purpose of this journal is to provide an interdisciplinary forum for those interested in the scientific study of the stream of consciousness, directly relevant to theory, research, and application" (Pope and Singer 1981/1982, p. 2).
4. Levy (1981) views his analysis as "structural." The distinction between "structured" and "unstructured" methods pursued here refers to the type of data-collection procedure.
5. Note that, in no sense, do we imply that the esthetic criteria involved in the play mentality are irrational or maladaptive. Indeed, as Becker's (1976) work has made clear, rational economic models can be built to account for playful activities—not to mention child bearing, marriage, and other forms of behavior generally viewed as psychosocial or nonpurposive in origin. We merely wish to indicate that, in our current state of knowledge, the psychodynamics of enjoyment and fun are perhaps less well understood than are the more technological and physiological relationships that underlie the conventional utili-

tarian approach to customer value (cf. Becker 1976, pp. 13–14).

REFERENCES

Alderson, Wroe (1957), *Marketing Behavior and Executive Action*, Homewood, IL: Richard D. Irwin.

Becker, Gary S. (1976), *The Economic Approach to Human Behavior*, Chicago: University of Chicago Press.

Becker, Howard S. (1978), "Arts and Crafts," *American Journal of Sociology*, 83 (4), 862–889.

Berlyne, Daniel E. (1960), *Conflict, Arousal, and Curiosity*, New York: McGraw-Hill.

———— (1971), *Aesthetics and Psychobiology*, New York: Appleton-Century-Crofts.

Bettman, James R. (1979), *An Information Processing Theory of Consumer Choice*, Reading, MA: Addison-Wesley.

Boyd, Harper W., Jr., and Sidney J. Levy (1963). "New Dimensions in Consumer Analysis," *Harvard Business Review*, 41 (November–December), 129–140.

Dichter, Ernest (1960), *The Strategy of Desire*, Garden City, NY: Doubleday.

Friedman, Meyer, and Ray H. Rosenman (1974), *Type A: Your Behavior and Your Heart*, New York: Knopf.

Hansen, Flemming (1981), "Hemispheric Lateralization: Implications for Understanding Consumer Behavior," *Journal of Consumer Research*, 8 (June), 23–36.

———— and Niels Erik Lundsgaard (1981), "Brain Lateralization and Individual Differences in People's Reaction to Mass Communication," working paper, Copenhagen School of Economics and Business Administration.

Hilgard, Ernest R. (1962), "Impulsive Versus Realistic Thinking: An Examination of the Distinction between Primary and Secondary Processes in Thought," *Psychological Bulletin*, 59 (6), 477–488.

———— (1980), "Consciousness in Contemporary Psychology," *Annual Review of Psychology*, 31, 1–26.

Hirschman, Elizabeth C. (1982), "Religious Affiliation and Consumption Processes: An Initial Paradigm," forthcoming in *Research in Marketing*.

———— and Morris B. Holbrook, eds. (1981), *Symbolic Consumer Behavior*, Ann Arbor, MI: Association for Consumer Research.

Howard, John A., and Jagdish N. Sheth (1969), *The Theory of Buyer Behavior*, New York: John Wiley.

Huizinga, Johan (1970), *Homo Ludens: A Study of the Play Element in Culture*, New York: Harper & Row.

Kassarjian, Harold H. (1977), "Content Analysis in Consumer Research," *Journal of Consumer Research*, 4 (June), 8–18.

Klinger, Eric (1971), *Structure and Functions of Fantasy*, New York: Wiley-Interscience.

Koch, Sigmund (1964), "Psychology and Emerging Conceptions of Knowledge as Unitary," in *Behaviorism and Phenomenology*, ed. T. W. Wann, Chicago: University of Chicago Press, 1–45.

Kroeber-Riel, Werner (1979), "Activation Research: Psychobiological Approaches in Consumer Research," *Journal of Consumer Research*, 5 (March), 240–250.

Krugman, Herbert E. (1965), "The Impact of Television Advertising: Learning without Involvement," *Public Opinion Quarterly*, 29 (Fall), 349–356.

———— (1971), "Brain Wave Measures of Media Involvement," *Journal of Advertising Research*, 11 (February), 3–10.

Lancy, David F. (1980), "Play in Species Adaptation," *Annual Review of Anthropology*, 9, 471–495.

Leavitt, Clark, Anthony G. Greenwald, and Carl Obermiller (1981), "What Is Low Involvement Low In?" in *Advances in Consumer Research*, Vol. 8, ed. Kent B. Monroe, Ann Arbor, MI: Association for Consumer Research, 15–19.

Lee, Lucy Chao, and Robert Ferber (1977), "Use of Time as a Determinant of Family Market Behavior," *Journal of Business Research*, 5 (March), 75–91.

Levy, Sidney J. (1959), "Symbols for Sale," *Harvard Business Review*, 37 (July–August), 117–124.

———— (1980), "The Symbolic Analysis of Companies, Brands, and Customers," Albert Wesley Frey Lecture, Graduate School of Business, University of Pittsburgh, PA.

———— (1981), "Interpreting Consumer Mythology: A Structural Approach to Consumer Behavior," *Journal of Marketing*, 45 (Summer), 49–61.

MacLeod, R. B. (1964), "Phenomenology: A Challenge to Experimental Psychology," in *Behaviorism and Phenomenology*, ed. T. W. Wann, Chicago, University of Chicago Press, 47–78.

McGregor, Robert (1974). "Art and the Aesthetic," *Journal of Aesthetics and Art Criticism*, 32 (Summer), 549–559.

Olshavsky, Richard W., and Donald H. Granbois (1979), "Consumer Decision Making—Fact or Fiction?" *Journal of Consumer Research,* 6 (September), 93–100.

Olson, Jerry C. (1980), "Encoding Processes: Levels of Processing and Existing Knowledge Structures," in *Advances in Consumer Research,* Vol. 7, ed. Jerry Olson, Ann Arbor, MI: Association for Consumer Research, 154–160.

———, Thomas Reynolds, and William J. Ray (1982), "Using Psychophysiological Measures in Advertising Effects Research," paper presented at the 1981 Convention of the Association for Consumer Research, October 22–25, St. Louis, MO.

Osgood, Charles E. (1957), "Motivational Dynamics of Language Behavior," in *Nebraska Symposium on Motivation,* ed. Marshall R. Jones, Lincoln: University of Nebraska Press, 348–424.

Pekala, Ronald J., and Ralph L. Levine (1981/1982), "Mapping Consciousness: Development of an Empirical-Phenomenological Approach," *Imagination, Cognition, and Personality,* 1(1), 29–47.

Platt, John (1970), *Perception and Change.* Ann Arbor: University of Michigan Press.

Plutchik, Robert (1980), *Emotion: A Psychoevolutionary Synthesis.* New York: Harper & Row.

Pope, Kenneth S., and Jerome L. Singer (1981/1982), "Imagination, Cognition, and Personality: Personal Experience, Scientific Research, and Clinical Application," *Imagination, Cognition and Personality,* 1(1), 1–4.

Raju, P. S. (1980), "Optimum Stimulation Level: Its Relationship to Personality, Demographics, and Exploratory Behavior," *Journal of Consumer Research,* 7 (December), 272–282.

Richardson, Alan (1969), *Mental Imagery,* New York: Springer.

Robinson, John P. (1977), *A Social-Psychological Analysis of Everyday Behavior,* New York: Praeger.

Russo, J. Edward (1978), "Eye Fixations Can Save the World: A Critical Evaluation and a Comparison between Eye Fixations and Other Information Processing Methodologies," in *Advances in Consumer Research,* Vol. 5, ed. H. Keith Hunt, Ann Arbor, MI: Associations for Consumer Research, 561–570.

Ryan, Michael J. (1980), "Psychobiology and Consumer Research: A Problem of Construct Validity," *Journal of Consumer Research,* 7 (June), 92–96.

Sheth, Jagdish N. (1979), "The Surpluses and Shortages in Consumer Behavior Theory and Research," *Journal of the Academy of Marketing Science,* 7(4), 414–427.

Shimp, Terence A., and Ivan L. Preston (1981), "Deceptive and Nondeceptive Consequences of Evaluative Advertising," *Journal of Marketing,* 45 (Winter), 22–32.

Singer, Jerome L. (1966), *Daydreaming: An Introduction to the Experimental Study of Inner Experience,* New York: Random House.

——— (1981/1982), "Towards the Scientific Study of Imagination," *Imagination, Cognition and Personality,* 1(1), 5–28.

Stephenson, William (1967), *The Play Theory of Mass Communication,* Chicago: University of Chicago Press.

Taylor, Wilson L. (1953), " 'Cloze Procedure:' A New Tool for Measuring Readability," *Journalism Quarterly,* 30 (Fall), 415–433.

Thorelli, Hans B., Helmut Becker, and Jack Engledow (1975), *The Information Seekers,* Cambridge, MA: Ballinger.

Wallendorf, Melanie, George Zinkhan, and Lydia Zinkhan (1981), "Cognitive Complexity and Aesthetic Preference," in *Symbolic Consumer Behavior,* ed. Elizabeth C. Hirschman and Morris B. Holbrook, Ann Arbor, MI: Association for Consumer Research, 52–59.

Zinkhan, George M., and Claude R. Martin, Jr. (1981), "Two Copy Testing Techniques: The Cloze Procedure and the Cognitive Complexity Test," working paper, Graduate School of Business, University of Michigan.

Zuckerman, Marvin (1979), *Sensation Seeking: Beyond the Optimal Level of Arousal,* Hillsdale, NJ: Lawrence Erlbaum.

◆

New Product Adoption and Diffusion

Everett M. Rogers

The studies of the diffusion of innovations, including the part played by mass communication, promise to provide an empirical and quantitative basis for developing more rigorous approaches to theories of social change.

Melvin L. De Fleur (1966, p. 138)

Diffusion of innovations has the status of a bastard child with respect to the parent interests in social and cultural change: too big to ignore but unlikely to be given full recognition.

Frederick C. Fliegel and Joseph F. Kivlin (1966, p. 235n)

Diffusion research is thus emerging as a single, integrated body of concepts and generalizations, even though the investigations are conducted by researchers in several scientific disciplines.

Everett M. Rogers (1971, p. 47)

The purposes of this paper are (1) to summarize what we have learned from research on the diffusion of innovations that contributes to our understanding of new product adoption and diffusion, (2) to discuss how the academic history and the intellectual structuring of the diffusion field have affected its contributions and its shortcomings, and (3) to indicate future research priorities on the diffusion of innovations.

Our focus here is especially on the last 10-year period and on the diffusion of a particular type of innovation (new products), but for historical and comparative purposes, we also must briefly deal with the origins of diffusion research.

Since about the mid-1960s, there has been considerable interest in diffusion research on the part of consumer researchers and a certain degree of integration of diffusion frameworks and research findings into the literature on consumer behavior. For example, the leading textbook on consumer behavior today features a chapter on the diffusion and adoption of innovations. Many marketing texts these days have a chapter on diffusion, or at least give considerable coverage to such topics as the innovation-decision process, adopter categories, opinion leadership, and the S-shaped diffusion curve.

Reprinted from Everett M. Rogers, "New Product Adoption and Diffusion," *Journal of Consumer Research*, Vol. 2 (March 1976), published by The Journal of Consumer Research, Inc.

Further, about 8 percent of the 1,800 publications dealing with empirical research on the diffusion of innovations, available to date, were authored by researchers associated with the field of marketing. These studies, mostly conducted since the mid-1960s, focus on new products as innovations. The present paper deals not only with these 8 percent of all diffusion publications but also with the other 92 percent, since I believe that the findings, methodologies, and theoretic frameworks from research on various types of innovations has applicability to consumers' adoption of new products. The adoption of most innovations entails the purchase of a new product, although this fact has often not been recognized by diffusion scholars.

THE RISE OF DIFFUSION RESEARCH AS AN INVISIBLE COLLEGE

From Revolutionary Paradigm to Classical Model

The origins of research on the diffusion of innovations trace from (1) the German-Austrian and the British schools of diffusionism in anthropology (whose members claimed that most changes in a society resulted from the introduction of innovations from other societies) and (2) the French sociologist Gabriel Tarde (1903), who pioneered the proposing the S-shaped diffusion curve and the role of opinion leaders in the process of "imitation." But the "revolutionary paradigm" for diffusion research occurred in the early 1940s when two sociologists, Bryce Ryan and Neal Gross (1943), published their seminal study of the diffusion of hybrid seed corn among Iowa farmers.

Any given field of scientific research begins with a major breakthrough or reconceptualization that provides a new way of looking at some phenomenon (Kuhn, 1962).

This revolutionary paradigm typically sets off a furious amount of intellectual effort as promising young scientists are attracted to the field, either to advance the new conceptualization with their research or to disprove certain of its aspects. Gradually, a scientific consensus about the field is developed, and perhaps after several generations of academic scholars, the "invisible college" (composed of researchers on a common topic who are linked by communication ties) declines in scientific interest as fewer findings of an exciting nature are turned up. These are the usual stages in the normal growth of science, Kuhn (1962) claims.

Research on the diffusion of innovations has followed these rise-and-fall stages rather closely, although the final stage of demise has not yet begun (Crane, 1972). The hybrid corn study set forth a new approach to the study of communication and change that was soon followed up by an increasing number of scholars in a wide variety of scientific fields. Within 10 years (by 1952), over 100 diffusion researches were completed; during the next decade (by 1962), another 450; and by the end of 1974, another 1,250. So today there are over 2,700 publications about the diffusion of innovations, including about 1,800 empirical research reports and 900 other writings (Figure 14-1).[1] The amount of scientific activity in investigating the diffusion of innovations has increased at an exponential rate (doubling almost every two years) since the revolutionary paradigm appeared 32 years ago, as Kuhn's (1962) theory of the growth of science would predict.

The main elements in the "classical model" of the diffusion of new ideas that emerged are (1) the *innovation*, defined as an idea, practice, or object perceived as new by an individual or other relevant unit of adoption, (2) which is *communicated* through certain *channels* (3) over *time* (4) among the members of a *social system*. The Ryan and

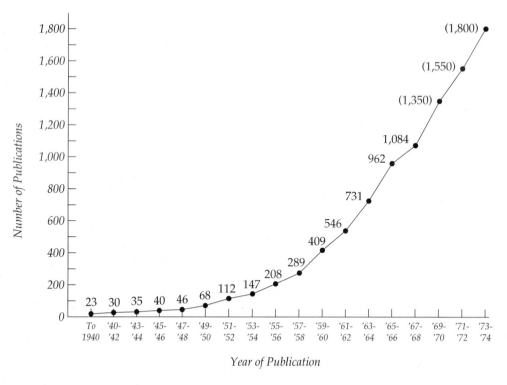

Figure 14-1
Cumulative Number of Empirical Diffusion Research Publications,
by Year of Publication

Gross (1943) study focused on hybrid corn, one of the most important innovations in Midwestern agriculture. Data were gathered by personal interviews with all the Iowa farmers in two communities. The rate of adoption of the agricultural innovation followed an S-shaped, normal curve when plotted on a cumulative basis over time. The first farmers to adopt (the innovators) were more cosmopolite (indicated by traveling more frequently to Des Moines) and of higher socioeconomic status than later adopters. The typical Iowa farmer first heard about the innovation from a seed corn salesman, but interpersonal communication with peers was the most frequent channel leading to persuasion. The innovation process from awareness/ knowledge to final adoption averaged about nine years, indicating that considerable time was required for adoption to occur.

Diffusion research is a particular type of communication research, but it began outside the academic field of communication. This was mostly a matter of timing, since the Ryan and Gross (1943) study preceded the first university centers or departments on communication by a good dozen years. Research of persuasion and attitude change, on nonverbal communication, and on most of the other important topics for communication research also began in psychology, anthropology, sociology, or other social sciences and then came to flower in the hands of communication scholars. The diffusion research approach was taken up in a variety of fields: education, anthropology, medical sociology, marketing, geography, and, most of all, rural sociology. Each of these disciplines pursued diffusion research in its specialized way and, for some time, without much interchange with the other diffusion research traditions.

The Intellectual Watershed of 1960

The year 1960 was in several respects a turning point for research on the diffusion of innovations. For one thing, the old disciplinary boundaries began to break down, and diffusion research began to emerge as "a single, integrated body of concepts and generalizations" (Rogers, 1971, p. 47). This emergence did not necessarily mean that all diffusion scholars completely agreed on definitions of concepts or on the most appropriate methods of inquiry, but at least the scholars generally recognized that they were investigating the same basic type of human behavior. Evidence of this recognition is shown in the works cited in their publications, as well as in the methods and models that they followed.

Second, researchers in the academic field of mass communication began to engage in diffusion research, at first by investigating the diffusion of major news events carried by the mass media: Alaskan statehood, the launching of Sputnik, and President Kennedy's assassination. The most noted news-event diffusion study, itself representing a "mini-revolutionary paradigm," was by Deutschmann and Danielson (1960). Today there are over 100 such news-event diffusion studies. Communication scholars soon began to study many types of other innovations, including technological innovations in agriculture, health, and family planning, especially in the developing nations of Latin America, Africa, and Asia.[2]

The early 1960s marked the beginning of a sharp takeoff in the number of diffusion studies in developing countries. Pioneering ventures in this direction by S. A. Rahim (1961) in Bangladesh and by Paul J. Deutschmann and Orlando Fals Borda (1962a, b) in Colombia suggested that new ideas spread among peasants in villages in a generally similar pattern to their diffusion in more media-saturated settings like the United States and Europe. The diffusion process, and the concepts and models utilized to analyze it, seemed to be cross-culturally valid, at least in the sense that comparable results were found in the new settings.

There were compelling reasons for the fast growth of diffusion studies in developing countries after 1960. Technology was assumed to be at the heart of development, at least in the dominant paradigm of development popular until very recent years.[3] In fact, innovativeness was thought to be the best single indicant of the multifaceted dimension called "modernization," the individual-level equivalent of development at the societal or system level (Rogers, 1969). Therefore, microlevel investigations of the diffusion of technological innovations among villagers were of direct relevance to development planners and other government officials in developing nations. These research results, and the general framework of diffusion, provided development agencies with both a kind of theoretical approach and an evaluation procedure.

The number of diffusion researches in developing nations totaled only about 54 in 1960 (13 percent of all diffusion studies), but rose steeply to over 800 or so by 1975, when about half of all diffusion studies were conducted in Latin America, Africa, and Asia. The major developing country of study is India, with over 450 of the 800 diffusion researches in developing countries.

An important boost to the internationalization of the diffusion field was the rise of KAP surveys in developing countries during the 1960s. KAP studies are sample surveys of knowledge (K), attitudes (A), and practice (P)—that is, adoption—of family planning innovations. K, A, and P are the logical dependent variables in evaluations of family planning communication campaigns, and, as national family planning programs arose after 1960 in many developing nations (especially in Asia) to cope with the population problem, KAP-type diffusion researches blossomed on all sides. Over 500 such KAP surveys were conducted in 72 nations by 1973 (Rogers, 1973, p. 377); India alone was the location for over half these investigations.

With the exception of the Taichung experiment in Taiwan (Freedman and Takeshita, 1969), the intellectual contribution of these KAP surveys "to scientific understanding of human behavior change has been dismal" (Rogers, 1973, p. 378). However, the KAP studies have provided a useful function by generally showing that most parents in developing countries want fewer children than they actually have, and that the majority desire a government family planning program. Even the harshest critic of KAP studies, Professor Philip M. Hauser (1967, p. 405), stated: "KAP survey results, erroneous or not, have helped to persuade prime ministers, parliaments, and the general population to move in a desirable direction and have provided family planning program administrators with 'justification' for budgets and programs."

Intellectually speaking, the family planning diffusion studies were generally disappointing, although several modifications in the "classical diffusion model" (such as the payment of incentives to promote diffusion and the use of nonprofessional change agent aides to help overcome the taboo nature of family planning communication) did emerge when family planning programs found the model wanting (Rogers, 1973). Also, the family planning diffusion studies gave a boost to field experimental research designs,[4] for over

a dozen such experiments in various nations followed the Taichung study (Rogers and Agarwala-Rogers, 1975).

The rise of these field experiments, in place of one-shot survey designs, helped to overcome some of the methodological difficulties of diffusion studies in coming to grips with the "over-time" aspects of the communication of new ideas.

MARKETING RESEARCH ON DIFFUSION

While many of the field experimental designs in the diffusion field were conducted in developing nations and were concerned with family planning innovations, a number of other field experiments were carried out in the United States by marketing researchers.

The marketing tradition of diffusion research has come on strong since the early 1960s. Marketing managers of firms have long been concerned with how to launch new products more efficiently. One reason for this interest is the high failure rate of new consumer products, estimated at 92 percent of the approximately 6,000 new consumer items introduced each year (Connor, 1964).

The adoption of most innovations involves sale of a new product, of course, and it was easy for commercial firms to conceive of their new products as innovations and to adapt the theoretical and methodological framework of diffusion research to marketing problems. University faculty members in graduate schools of business led the way into diffusion research (Zaltman, 1965), to be followed soon after by marketing researchers in the employ of commercial firms. Unfortunately, a large proportion of these research reports lie only in the secret files of the sponsoring companies because of competitive threat, and they are thus unavailable to attempts at academic synthesis and the progress of scientific understanding of the diffusion process.

Much of the diffusion research in the marketing field was conducted either by the commercial manufacturers of the new product or by university professors with the sponsorship, or at least the cooperation, of the manufacturers. One advantage of this close relationship was that the diffusion researchers in the field of marketing often had some degree of control over the diffusion strategies that were used to promote the new products. This is a particularly important ingredient in the conduct of field experiments on diffusion. In fields other than marketing, diffusion scholars have seldom been able to manipulate the "treatment" variables, and it has therefore been impossible to conduct field experiments.

Perhaps a somewhat typical illustration of the field experimental approach by marketing researchers is provided by Arndt's (1967) study of the diffusion of a new food product. A letter about this innovation, enclosing a coupon allowing its purchase at one-third price, was sent to 495 housewives living in a married-student apartment complex. Personal interviews were carried out with these consumers 16 days after the diffusion campaign was launched. Arndt found that interpersonal communication about the new product frequently led to its initial purchase. Housewives who perceived the innovation as risky were more likely to seek the advice of their neighborhood opinion leaders about it. Naturally, this type of field experiment allowed determination of the impact of the reduced-price sample offer; the measure of impact was the rate of adoption (that is, purchase) of the new food product.

The diffusion research tradition of marketing has displayed an especially strong bias toward producing research results of use to the innovation's source (that is, the manufacturer of the new product) rather than to the consumers. This pro-innovation and pro-source orientation is also characteristic of other branches of diffusion research (a point to which we shall return), but less so than in the field of marketing.

One cannot help but wonder how the research approach (and the understandings that were obtained) might have been different if the Ryan and Gross (1943) hybrid corn study had been sponsored by the Iowa Farm Bureau Federation rather than by the Iowa Agricultural Extension Service and if the Coleman, Katz, and Menzel (1966) investigation of a new medical drug had been conducted under the auspices of the American Medical Association rather than Pfizer Drug Company. Perhaps "diffusion" research would have been called something like "innovation-seeking" or the "evaluation of innovations" had the receivers been in control (Rogers, 1971, p. 79).

The source-bias in marketing research on diffusion is especially surprising since this scientific specialty is often called "*consumer research*" in graduate schools of marketing, and it is often inspired by the "marketing concept," an approach that puts the consumer in control of the marketing process, at least in principle (Kotler and Zaltman, 1971). In diffusion researches following the marketing concept, the customer has often been studied, but usually to the advantage of the seller of the new product or service.

Even though the studies were usually commissioned by the selling agencies, consumers have often benefited from the diffusion researches in which they were respondents if their needs were met by the new products that emerged from such diffusion researches. These investigations *can* put the consumer in the driver's seat regarding new products, especially through a variant of diffusion inquiry called "acceptability research," in which the consumers' desires are determined and then a new product is designed to meet these previously unmet needs.

Acceptability research began at the hands of marketing researchers and is now also followed in wider contexts. For example, the World Health Organization is currently involved in a research program in which the desired qualities of contraceptives are determined for the fertile audience in Latin America, Africa and Asia to guide WHO biomedical researchers in the invention and development of future methods of family planning. This acceptability approach puts the potential consuming couples in the position, via survey research, of helping design more acceptable contraceptives.

Nevertheless, certain basic consumer-oriented research questions have not been asked in diffusion research, such as, How can the consumer be protected against the influence of advertising (or other promotional) messages? What information does the consumer need to know in order to make intelligent innovation decisions?

LACK OF A PROCESS ORIENTATION

We shall now consider the first of three important conceptual/methodological biases in diffusion research, which also characterize other types of communication research:

1. Lack of a process orientation.
2. A pro-innovation bias (and an associated ignoring of causality).
3. A psychological orientation, leading to short-changing structure.

Every textbook definition of the concept of communication either states or directly implies that it is a *process*.[5] Thus, one might expect an overwhelming emphasis in research and theory on the conceptualization of communication as process. However, a recent analysis by Arundale (1971) shows that the research designs and measurements of com-

munication almost never allow analysis of the over-time aspects of communication that would be necessary to explore process adequately. Very little communication research includes data at more than one observation point, and almost none at more than two such points in time. Therefore, almost all communication research is unable to trace the change in a variable over time; it deals only with the present tense of behavior. Communication thus becomes, in the actuality of communication research, an artificially halted snapshot.

Why has communication research not dealt more adequately with the change-over-time aspects of process?

1. We lack concepts and propositions that reflect a process orientation.
2. Time-series data are expensive to gather, unless one depends on respondent recall, a procedure that is often less than satisfactory.
3. Data gathering repeated over time leads to problems of respondent sensitization (unless one uses unobtrusive and nonreactive measurement methods), since communication research itself is a communication process.
4. Communication researchers are often pressured by research sponsors, doctoral requirements, and other logistic forces to produce immediate results; this is a strong discouragement to over-time research designs.

Thus, unfortunately, we define communication as process, but then proceed in communication research to treat communication as a one-shot affair.

Diffusion research is only slightly "less bad" in this respect than other types of communication research. Because *time* is one of the four essential elements in the diffusion process, and thus receives more explicit attention than in other types of communication research, it should be stressed in the research designs utilized in diffusion research.

These designs consist mainly of correlational analyses of cross-sectional data gathered in one-shot surveys of the respondents, thus following exactly the method pioneered by Ryan and Gross (1943). By 1968 (the last time a tabulation was made of the methodologies used in diffusion studies), only 65 of the then 1,084 empirical diffusion publications (about 6 percent) reported results from field experiments, and most of these field experiments had been done since 1960 (our turning-point year in the diffusion field, as mentioned earlier). Even allowing for the 67 diffusion publications (another 6 percent) that reported longitudinal panel studies at two or more points in time, the vast majority (about 88 percent) of all diffusion researches are one-shot surveys permitting only cross-sectional data analysis. Such research designs cannot tell us very much about the *process* of diffusion over time other than what can be reconstructed from recall data.

Diffusion studies are particularly able to rely on "moving pictures" of behavior rather than on "snapshots" because of their unique capacity to trace the sequential flow of an innovation through a social system. However, diffusion researchers mainly have relied on their respondents' ability to recall their date of awareness or adoption of a new idea. Essentially, the respondent is asked to look back over his shoulder and mentally reconstruct his past history of innovation experiences. This hindsight ability is not very accurate and undoubtedly varies on the basis of (1) the innovations' salience to the respondents; (2) the length of time over which recall is requested; and (3) individual differences in education, mental ability, etc.

Future diffusion research ought to develop improved methods for tracer studies, in which alternative sources of data are used to provide validity checks on recall data over time.[6] Much greater use should be made of field experiments and longitudinal panel studies, which, by their research designs, are able to take "moving pictures" of the diffusion process.

THE PRO-INNOVATION BIAS AND CAUSALITY

The second important bias found in most diffusion research is an inherent pro-change bias, which assumes that the innovations studied are "good" and should be adopted by everyone. Undoubtedly hybrid corn was profitable for each of the Iowa farmers in the Ryan and Gross (1943) study, but most other innovations that have been studied do not have this high degree of relative advantage. Many individuals, for their own good, should *not* adopt then.

The pro-innovation bias, coupled with the unfortunate and overwhelming dependence on survey research designs, means that diffusion research has mostly studied "what is" instead of "what could be" about diffusion processes. Therefore, method has followed the assumption that innovation is good, that the present process of diffusion is satisfactory and needs only minor tune-up rather than a major overhauling. Röling, Ascroft, and Chege (1974) have heavily scored diffusion research on this count, arguing that it has often led to increased inequity; field experimental designs are needed to test alternatives to current practice instead of replicating more surveys of "what is."

The pro-innovation bias in diffusion research, and its overwhelming reliance on correlational analysis of survey data, often led in the past to avoiding or ignoring the issue of causality. We often speak of "independent" and "dependent" variables in diffusion research, having taken these terms from experimental designs and then used them rather loosely with correlational analysis. A dependent variable thus means little more than the main variable in which the investigator is interested. In about 60 percent of all diffusion researches, the dependent variable is *innovativeness,* defined as the degree to which a responding unit is relatively earlier in adopting an innovation than other units in the system. It is implied that the independent variables "lead to" innovativeness, although it is often unstated or uncertain whether this really means that an independent variable *causes* innovativeness.

In order for variable X to be the cause of variable Y, (1) X must precede Y in time order, (2) they must be related or covary, and (3) X must have a "forcing quality" on Y. Most diffusion researches have only determined that various independent variables covary with innovativeness; correlational analysis of one-shot survey data does not allow the determination of time order. Diffusion research has tarried too long at step 3 in Table 14-1 and should move on to step 4.

Correlational studies face a particular problem of time order that might be called "yesterday's innovativeness": In most diffusion surveys, innovativeness is measured "today" with recall data about past adoption behavior, while the independent variables are measured in the present tense. It is obviously impossible for an individual's attitudes, formed and measured now, to cause his adoption of an innovation three years previously (this would amount to X following Y in time order, thus making it impossible for X to cause Y).

So again we see the importance of research designs that allow us to learn the over-time aspects of diffusion. Field experiments are ideally suited to the purpose of assessing the effect of various independent variables (the treatments) on the dependent variable of innovativeness.

In order for X to cause Y, they must covary. If such covariance is very low, X is probably not a cause of Y. If their common variance is high, X *may* be a cause of Y. Diffusion research has specialized in determining the correlates of innovativeness.

Forcing quality, the way in which X acts on Y, is a theoretical rather than an empirical issue. The theoretical reasoning why certain variables might have a forcing quality on others needs to be given much greater attention in diffusion research. Theoretical approaches from other fields of communication study may have application to conceptualizing the forcing quality of certain independent variables on innovativeness and other dependent variables.

THE PSYCHOLOGICAL BIAS THAT SHORT-CHANGES STRUCTURE

The psychological bias in diffusion research stems from (1) its historical roots in academe and (2) the researchers' acceptance of how social problems are defined. Several early communication scholars came from psychological backgrounds, and it was only natural that their models of communication (and diffusion) largely ignored social-structural variables that affect communication. The transactional and relational nature of human communication tended to be overlooked, and this shortcoming was also characteristic of diffusion research, at least until fairly recently.

The Individual as the Unit of Analysis

The overwhelming focus on the *individual* as the unit of analysis in communication research (while largely ignoring the importance of communication *relationships* between sources and receivers) is often due to the assumption that the individual, as the unit of response, must consequently be the unit of analysis (Coleman, 1958–59). The monadic view of human behavior determined that "the kinds of substantive problems on which such

Table 14-1
A Classification of Stages in Social Science Research

Research Stages	Research Purpose	Research Method
1. Problem delineation	To define what we are looking for, and the extent to which it is a social problem	Qualitative analysis, such as case studies, observation, unstructured interviews, and literature review
2. Variable identification	To define variables which might be linked to the problem, and to describe possible interconnections between these variables	Exploratory case studies, and other qualitative methods that are low on structure
3. Determinations of relationships among the variables	To determine the clusters of relevant variables required for prediction, and to analyze their patterns of relationships	Cross-sectional, correlational analysis of quantitative survey data
4. Establishment of causality among the variables	To determine which factors are critical in promoting or inhibiting the problem	Longitudinal studies, and small-scale experiments with (1) over-time data, (2) in which at least one variable changes prior to the others, so as to determine time order
5. Manipulation of causal variables for policy-formation purposes	To determine the correspondence between a theoretical problem solution and the manipulative factors	Field experiments
6. Evaluation of alternative policies/ programs	To assess the expected, as well as the unanticipated consequences of various programs/ policies before and after they are applied on a large scale, and to determine the effectiveness of such programs in overall program solution	Controlled field comparisons, such as the interrupted time-series field experiment

Source: Based on Gordon, MacEachron, and Fisher, "A Contingency Model for the Design of Problem-Solving Research Problems," *Millbank Memorial Fund Quarterly,* Spring 1974, p. 193. Permission for use granted by the Millbank Memorial Fund.

research focused tended to be problems of 'aggregate psychology,' that is *within*-individual problems, and never problems concerned with relations between people" (Coleman, 1958–59, p. 28). The use of survey methods in

communications research has "destructured" behavior:

Using random sampling of individuals, the survey is a sociological meatgrinder, tearing the individual from his social context and guaranteeing that nobody in the study interacts with anyone else in it. It is a little like a biologist putting his experimental animals through a hamburger machine and looking at every hundredth cell through a microscope; anatomy and physiology get lost; structure and function disappear and one is left with cell biology. [Barton, 1968, p. 1]

The main focus in diffusion research on the individual as the unit of analysis has only recently shifted to the dyad, clique, network, or system of individuals, centering on the communication relationships between individuals rather than on the individuals themselves. Encouraging attempts to overcome the psychological bias in diffusion research are provided by network analysis and by the open-systems approach.

These conceptual/methodological approaches suggest that even when the individual is the unit of response, the communication relationship (even though *it* can't "speak") can be the unit of analysis via some type of sociometric measurement. Sampling and data analysis procedures for relational analysis are being worked out,[7] but we still lack relational concepts and theories linking these concepts. Until diffusion scholars begin to think in relational terms, there will not be much relational analysis.

Person-Blame

The second reason for the artificially "destructured" psychological bias in communication research is the acceptance of a *person-blame-causal-attribution* definition of the social problems that we study: Individual-blame is the tendency to hold an individual responsible for his problems. Obviously, what is done about a social problem, including research, depends on how it is defined. Since communication scientists seldom participate in the identification and definition of social problems, they borrow or accept these definitions from alarmists, government officials, and other scientists.

Many illustrations of individual-blame can be cited in behavioral research. Caplan and Nelson (1973) found a high degree of individual-blame in psychological research on such problems as highway safety and race relations. They asked, "Why do we constantly study the poor rather than the nonpoor in order to understand the origins of poverty?"

An example of individual-blame is the poster produced by a pharmaceutical manufacturer: "LEAD PAINT CAN KILL!" The poster blamed mothers for allowing their children to eat paint. In New Haven, Connecticut, with the highest reported rates of lead paint poisoning of children in the U.S., landlords are legally prohibited from using lead paint on the inside of residences (W. Ryan, 1971). But the poster blames the mother, not the paint manufacturers or the landlords. And this tendency toward stressing individual-blame rather than system-blame is very common in communication research.

Diffusion research was originally (and for many years) as guilty as other types of communication research in following an individual-blame approach:

We note an assumption in diffusion writings that the rate of adoption should be speeded up, that the innovation should be adopted by receivers, etc. [This is a consequence of the pro-innovation bias of diffusion research.] Seldom is it implied in diffusion documents that the source or the channels may be at fault for not providing more adequate information, for promoting inadequate or inappropriate innovations, etc. (Rogers, 1971, p. 79)

This psychological bias in diffusion research began with the hybrid seed corn study. Strangely, Ryan and Gross (1943) did not gather sociometric data about the interpersonal diffusion of the innovation within their two Iowa communities of study even though (1) they found that interpersonal communication from neighbors was essential in clinching adoption decisions and (2) their sampling design of a complete census of farmers in the two communities was ideal for gathering relational data for network-analysis purposes.

RESTORING SOCIAL STRUCTURE TO DIFFUSION RESEARCH

The refocusing of diffusion researches had to wait until later investigations, especially the drug study among medical doctors by Coleman et al. (1966). Then it became a common procedure for diffusion scholars to ask their respondents sociometric questions of the general form, "From whom in this system did you obtain information that led you to adopt this innovation?" The sociometric dyad represented by each answer to this question could consequently be punched on an IBM card (including data on the characteristics of the seeker *and* the sought), which then became the unit of analysis.

The relational data thus obtained were utilized to provide deeper insight into the role of opinion leaders in the two-step flow of communication, a conceptualization that was originated by Lazarsfeld, Berelson, and Gaudet (1944) prior to most diffusion research. Later research showed that the two-step flow hypothesis was mainly a gross oversimplification, since the flow of communication may actually have any number of steps, but the concept of opinion leadership has much theoretical and practical utility. Diffusion researches were able to advance understandings of opinion leadership because of their unique capacity to focus on the *flow* of innovations, new messages (to the receiver) that seem to leave deeper (and hence more recallable) scratches on men's minds. The

tracer quality of an innovation's diffusion pathways aids the investigation of the flow of communication messages, and especially the role of certain individuals such as opinion leaders in this flow. For instance, the complicated relationship of leadership and group norms, first raised theoretically by George Homans (1961, p. 339), has received rather definite empirical elucidation by diffusion scholars, resulting in the proposition: *"When the system's norms favor change, opinion leaders are more innovative, but when the norms are traditional, opinion leaders are not especially innovative"* (Rogers, 1971, p. 219).

Network Analysis of Diffusion

Most communication research has largely ignored the effect of social structure on communication behavior, as we pointed out earlier, and diffusion research to date has only partly realized its full potential in this regard. *Network analysis* is a method of research for identifying the communication structure of a system in which sociometric data about communication flows or patterns are analyzed by using interpersonal relationships as the units of analysis (Rogers and Agarwala-Rogers, 1976). This tool promises to capitalize on the unique ability of diffusion inquiry to reconstruct specific message flows in a system and then to overlay the social structure of the system on these flows. The innovation's diffusion brings life to the otherwise static nature of the structural variables; network analysis permits understanding the social structure as it channels the process of diffusion. About the only other place in communication research where network analysis has been used to restore social structure to the communication process is in a few recent investigations of organizational communication.

The first, and very partial, attempts toward network analysis of the diffusion process simply identified opinion leaders in a system and determined their mass media and interpersonal communication behavior. This approach was only a slight extension of the usual monadic analysis, moving toward a relation type of analysis.

Next, diffusion scholars began to plot sequential-over-time sociograms of the diffusion of an innovation among the members of a system. Tentative steps were taken toward using communication relationships (such as sociometric dyads) as the units of analysis. The advance allowed data analysis of a "who-to-whom" communication matrix and facilitated inquiry into the identification (1) of cliques within the total system[8] and how such structural subgroupings affected the diffusion of an innovation and (2) of specialized communication roles such as liaisons, bridges, and isolates,[9] thus allowing communication research to proceed far beyond the relatively simpler issue of studying just opinion leadership. Further, the measurement of various structural indexes (such as system connectedness and system openness[10]) for individuals, cliques, or entire systems (such as organizations or communities) now became possible. Generally, system innovativeness is positively related to connectedness and to system openness.

These network analyses necessitated a new kind of sampling, as well as a shift to relational units of analysis. Instead of random samples of scattered individuals in a large population, the network studies usually depended on gathering data from *all* the eligible respondents in a system (such as a village) or a sample of such systems (Table 14-2). Usually

Table 14-2
Comparison of Monadic and Relational Analysis in Research on the Diffusion of Innovations

Characteristics of the Research Approach	Type of Diffusion Research Approach	
	Monadic Analysis	*Relational Analysis*
1. Unit of analysis	The individual	The communication relationship between two (or more) individuals
2. Most frequent sample design	Random samples of scattered individuals in a large sample (in order to maximize the generalizability of the research results)	Complete census of all eligible respondents in a system (such as a village), or a sample of such intact systems
3. Type of data utilized	Personal and social characteristics of individuals, and their communication behavior	Same as for monadic analysis, plus sociometric data about communication relationships
4. Main type of data analysis methods	Correlational analysis of cross-sectional survey data	Various types of network analysis of cross-sectional survey data
5. Main purpose of research	To determine the variables (usually characteristics of individuals) related to innovativeness	To determine how social-structural variables affect diffusion flows in a system

these sample designs meant less emphasis on the ability to generalize the research results, which was traded off for a greater focus on understanding the role of social structures on diffusion flows. If such research were to study social structure, it had to sample intact social structures, or at least the relevant parts of them.

The Strength of Weak Ties

Out of the network analysis of interpersonal diffusion grew a research issue that came to be called "the strength of weak ties" (Granovetter, 1973; Liu and Duff, 1972).[11] The proposition summarizing this research is, *The informational strength of dyadic communication relationships is inversely related to the degree of homophily (and the strength of the attraction) between the source and the receiver.* Or, in other words, an innovation is diffused to a larger number of individuals and traverses a greater social distance when passed through weak ties rather than strong ones (Granovetter, 1973).

For any given topic, each individual operates in his/her particular communication environment consisting of a number of friends and acquaintances with whom the topic is discussed most frequently. These friends are usually highly homophilous (or similar) with the individual and with each other, and most of the individual's friends are friends of each other, thus constituting an "interlocking network" (Laumann, 1973; Rogers, 1973). This homophily and close attraction facilitate effective communication, but they act as a barrier preventing new ideas from entering the network. There is thus not much informational strength in the interlocking network; some heterophilous ties into the network are needed to give it more openness. These "weak ties" enable innovations to flow from clique to clique via liaisons and bridges. There is a cohesive power to the weak ties.

Laumann (1973) found important differences in political behavior, organizational participation, and consumer behavior between Detroit men with interlocking networks and those with radial networks. Thus the nature of these personal communication networks is perhaps one important way to distinguish consumers, at least in their receptivity to innovations. Innovators have more radial personal networks, and interlocking networks are more likely centered on later adopters.

Network analysis of the diffusion of the IUD in the Philippines demonstrated this strength of weak ties: The innovation spread most easily within interlocking cliques among housewives of very similar social status (Liu and Duff, 1972). But heterophilous flows were necessary to link these cliques; usually these "weak ties" connected two women who were not close friends and allowed the IUD to travel from a higher-status to a somewhat lower-status housewife. Therefore, at least occasional heterophilous dyadic communication in a network was a structural prerequisite for effective diffusion.

The case of network analysis on the strength of weak ties illustrates an important recent trend in diffusion research: The concepts used in this analysis are *relational* constructs. Perhaps we are seeing the real beginning of relational thinking in communication research.

CONCLUSIONS

Our quick tour of the past 12 years of diffusion research provides many examples of Thorstein Veblen's concept of "trained incapacity": By being taught to "see" innovativeness, opinion leadership, and other aspects of the classical model of diffusion, we failed to "see" much else. Acceptance of a revolutionary paradigm by scholars in a field enables them to cope with uncertainty and information overload through the simplification of reality that the paradigm represents. It also imposes and standardizes a set of assumptions and conceptual biases that, once begun, are difficult to recognize and overcome.

In my opinion the research designs, concepts, and measurement procedures of diffusion research have been very stereotyped. This similarity has facilitated the synthesis of diffusion findings, a task to which I have contributed: in fact, all diffusion studies look a good deal alike. But such standardization of research approaches has also greatly limited the contribution of diffusion research to more effective social programs and to furthering the scientific understanding of communication and human behavior change. Presumably this indictment is what one dean of a U.S. school of communication had in mind when he characterized the diffusion field as "a mile and an inch deep."

Nevertheless, I believe that *research on the diffusion of innovations has played an important role in helping put social structure back in the communication process.* Focus on structural variables has increasingly characterized diffusion research in the past decade, and the techniques of network analysis promise exciting further steps in this direction. Eventually this trend may help communication research shed its psychological bias and person-blame orientation.

For network analysis to fulfill its potential, however, I feel we must improve the methods of data gathering and measurement. Sociometric questions about communication behavior leave much to be desired; adequate evidence of their accuracy and stability over time are presently lacking. Unobtrusive, nonreactive measures are needed to provide validity checks on sociometry, leading to a multiple-measurement approach. At present, I believe our data-analysis techniques for rational analysis of communication behavior have far outrun the quality of our measurement.

Longitudinal panel designs for network analysis of diffusion processes are also

needed; along with field experiments, they help secure the necessary data to illuminate the over-time process aspects of diffusion (and communication) and to facilitate exploration of the causal relationships involved in communication behavior.

Time is an explicit element in all diffusion research. But the measurement of time is one of the most egregious methodological weaknesses of past diffusion inquiry through its overwhelming dependence on recall data.

Thus network analysis of over-time data and field experiments are robust tools offering promise for research on the diffusion of innovations in the years ahead.

Consumer researchers have already made important contributions to understanding the diffusion of innovations, and the diffusion model has extended the scope of investigations of the consumption of new products.

NOTES

1. All of these 1,800 empirical research publications, plus another 900 nonempirical, publications (bibliographies, theoretical works, etc.), are held in the Diffusion Documents Center in the Department of Population Planning at the University of Michigan. A bibliography of these 2,700 items (Rogers and Thomas, 1975) is available from the Department at no cost.

2. Detail on the convergence of diffusion research with communication research is provided by Katz (1960) and Rogers (1967).

3. In addition to assuming that capital-intensive technology was the vital ingredient in development, the dominant paradigm assumed that a nation had to pass through an industrial revolution en route to development, and that economic growth (guided by central planning agencies and quantified in aggregate terms like GNP) largely constituted the nature of development. After the paradigm shift, the newer conceptions of development stressed (1) the *equality* of distribution, (2) popular *participation* in decentralized development planning and execution, (3) *self-*

reliance and independence in development, and (4) *integration* of traditional with modern systems (Rogers, 1975a).

4. A *field experiment* is an active intervention by an experimenter who administers a treatment (in the form of a program, project, or activity) to randomly selected respondents arranged in groups that are equivalent in the way they are chosen, with at least one treatment group and one control group (who do not receive the treatment).

5. A common definition of *communication* is the process by which an idea is transferred from a source to a receiver with the intent to change his/her behavior.

6. For example, in a study of the diffusion of a new drug among medical doctors, the physicians' recall data were checked against pharmacists' sales records for each doctor (Coleman et al., 1966).

7. *Relational analysis* is a research approach in which the unit of analysis is a relationship between two or more individuals (Rogers and Bhowmik, 1970–71).

8. A *clique* is a subsystem whose elements interact with each other relatively more frequently than with other members of the communication system.

9. A *liaison* is an individual who interpersonally connects two or more cliques within a system, without belonging to any clique. A *bridge* is an individual who is a member of a communication clique and has a link to an individual who is a member of a different communication clique. An *isolate* is an individual who has few communication contacts with the rest of the system.

10. *System connectedness* is the degree to which the members of a system as a whole are linked with each other in communication flows. *System openness* is the degree to which a system exchanges information with its environment.

11. These two sets of authors independently discovered the diffusion strength of weak sociometric ties, and although approaching the issue in somewhat different ways, they published articles with virtually identical titles within a few months of each other in 1972–73. Professors Liu, Duff, and Granovetter were

well read in the diffusion literature but had not previously published on this topic, and their articles showed a relatively fresh approach to analyzing diffusion networks. Perhaps this relative newness in working with the classical diffusion model was one requisite for the originality of their contribution.

REFERENCES

Arndt, J. "Role of Product-Related Conversations in the Diffusion of a New Product," *Journal of Marketing Research*, 4 (August 1967), 291–95.

Arundale, R. B. *The Concept of Process in Human Communication Research.* Unpublished doctoral dissertation, Michigan State University, 1971.

Barton, A. H. "Bringing Society Back In: Survey Research and Macro-Methodology," *American Behavioral Scientist*, 12 (November–December 1968), 1–9.

Caplan, N. and S. D. Nelson. "On Being Useful: The Nature and Consequences of Psychological Research on Social Problems," *American Psychologist*, 28 (March 1973), 199–211.

Coleman, J. S. "Relational Analysis: The Study of Social Organization with Survey Methods," *Human Organization*, 17, (Winter 1958–59), 28–36.

Coleman, J. S., E. Katz, and H. Menzel, *Medical Innovation: A Diffusion Study.* Indianapolis: Bobbs-Merrill, 1966.

Connor, J. T. "Needed: New Economics for a New Era," *Printer's Ink*, 287 (May 29, 1964), 35–37.

Crane, D. *Invisible Colleges: Diffusion of Knowledge in Scientific Communities.* Chicago: University of Chicago Press, 1972.

De Fleur, M. L. *Theories of Mass Communication.* New York: McKay, 1966.

Deutschmann, P. J. and O. F. Borda. *Communication and Adoption Patterns in an Andean Village.* San José, Costa Rica: Programa Interamericano de Información Popular and Facultad de Sociologia, Universidad Nacional de Colombia, 1962a.

Deutschmann, P. J. and O. F. Borda. *La Comunicación de las Ideas entre-los-Campesinos Colombianos: Un Análisis Socio-Estadistico. Monografias Sociologicas* 14. Bogota: Universidad Nacional de Colombia, 1962b.

Deutschmann, P. J. and W. A. Danielson. "Diffusion of Knowledge of the Major News Story," *Journalism Quarterly*, 37 (Summer 1960), 345–55.

Fliegel, F. C. and J. E. Kivlin. "Attributes of Innovations as Factors in Diffusion," *American Journal of Sociology*, 72 (November 1966), 235–48.

Freedman, R. and J. Y. Takeshita. *Family Planning in Taiwan: An Experiment in Social Change.* Princeton: Princeton University Press, 1969.

Gordon, G., A. E. MacEachron, and G. L. Fisher. "A Contingency Model for the Design of Problem-Solving Research Problems: A Perspective on Diffusion Research," *Milbank Memorial Fund Quarterly/Health and Society*, 52 (Spring 1974) 185–220.

Granovetter, M. "The Strength of Weak Ties," *American Journal of Sociology*, 78 (May 1973), 1360–80.

Hauser, P. M. " 'Family Planning and Population Programs': A Book Review Article," *Demography*, 4 (no. 1, 1967), 397–414.

Homans, G. C. *Social Behavior: Its Elementary Forms.* New York: Harcourt, Brace and World, 1961.

Katz, E. "Communication Research and the Image of Society: Convergence of Two Traditions," *American Journal of Sociology*, 65 (March 1960), 435–40.

Kotler, P., and G. Zaltman, "Social Marketing: An Approach to Planned Social Change," *Journal of Marketing*, 35 (July 1971), 3–12.

Kuhn, T. K. *The Structure of Scientific Revolutions.* Chicago: University of Chicago Press, 1962.

Laumann, E. O. *Bonds of Pluralism: The Form and Substance of Urban Social Networks.* New York: Wiley, 1973.

Lazarsfeld, P. F., B. Berelson, and H. Gaudet. *The People's Choice.* New York: Duell, Sloan, and Pearce, 1944.

Liu, W. T. and R. W. Duff. "The Strength in Weak Ties," *Public Opinion Quarterly*, 36 (Fall 1972), 361–66.

Rahim, S. A. *Diffusion and Adoption of Agricultural Practices: A Study of Pattern of Communication, Diffusion and Adoption of Improved Agricultural Practice in a Village in East Pakistan.* Technical publication no. 7. Comilla, Pakistan: (Bangladesh) Academy for Village Development, 1961.

Robertson, T. S. *Innovative Behavior and Communication.* New York: Holt, Rinehart & Winston, 1971.

Rogers, E. M. "Mass Communication and the Diffusion of Innovations: Conceptual Convergence of Two Research Traditions." Paper presented at the Association for Education in Journalism, Boulder, Colorado, 1967.

_____. *Modernization among Peasants: The Impact of Communication.* New York: Holt, Rinehart & Winston, 1969.

_____. *Communication of Innovations: A Cross-Cultural Approach.* (2nd ed.) New York: Free Press, 1971.

_____. *Communication Strategies for Family Planning.* New York: Free Press, 1973.

_____. "The Anthropology of Modernization and the Modernization of Anthropology," *Reviews in Anthropology*, 2 (August 1975a), 345–58.

_____. "Where We Are in Understanding Innovation." Paper presented at the East-West Communication Institute Conference on Communication and Change: Ten Years After, Honolulu, January 12–17, 1975b.

Rogers, E. M. and R. Agarwala-Rogers, eds. *Evaluation Research on Family Planning Communication.* UNESCO Technical Report. Paris: UNESCO, 1975.

Rogers, E. M. and R. Agarwala-Rogers. *Communication in Organizations.* New York: Free Press, 1976.

Rogers, E. M. and D. K. Bhowmik. "Homophily-Heterophily: Relational Concepts for Communication Research," *Public Opinion Quarterly*, 34 (Winter 1970–71), 523–38.

Rogers, E. M. and P. C. Thomas, *Bibliography on the Diffusion of Innovations.* Ann Arbor: Department of Population Planning, University of Michigan, 1975.

Röling, N., J. Ascroft, and F. Chege. "Innovation and Equity in Rural Development." Paper presented at the World Congress of Sociology, Toronto, 1974.

Ryan, B. and N. C. Gross. "The Diffusion of Hybrid Seed Corn in Two Iowa Communities," *Rural Sociology*, 8 (March 1943), 15–24.

Ryan, W. *Blaming the Victim.* New York: Pantheon, 1971.

Tarde, G. *The Laws of Imitation.* Trans. by E. C. Parsons. New York: Holt, 1903.

Zaltman, G. *Marketing Contributions for the Behavioral Sciences.* New York: Harcourt, Brace and World, 1965.

◆

Competitive Effects on Technology Diffusion

Thomas S. Robertson and Hubert Gatignon

Diffusion research within marketing is nested primarily in the behavioral domain. Consumer behavior researchers have adopted the paradigm of Rogers (1983) without much qualification. Research on diffusion has tended to focus at the individual consumer level, and the number of research projects focusing on organizational adoption of innovations is reasonably limited (Baker and Parkinson 1977; Cooper 1979; Czepiel 1976; Robertson and Wind 1980; Webster 1989; Zaltman, Duncan, and Holbek 1973). Similarly, most research has been on reasonably low technology products, with the exception of such work as that of Czepiel (1974), Dickerson and Gentry (1983), Hirschman (1980), and Leonard-Barton (1985).

This article seeks to extend the extant conceptualization for research within marketing on the diffusion of innovations. The objective is to derive an enriched model for the study of *technological diffusion* at the *organiza-*

tional level. The theoretical base of the article will be on *competitive behavior* (Weitz 1985), and we will suggest a number of propositions as to how both the supply-side competitive environment and the adopter industry competitive environment affect the diffusion of innovations. Since most of the propositions are derived from other fields of inquiry—particularly economics and organizational behavior—the evidentiary base for consumer behavior is limited.

To the extent that competitive variables have been pursued in diffusion research within marketing, it has been almost exclusively within the *diffusion modeling* domain (Bass 1969; Mahajan and Muller 1979). For example, a number of recent models, which are empirically estimated, have included marketing mix variables, such as advertising, price and personal selling (Bass 1980; Horsky and Simon 1983; Lilien, Rao, and Kalish 1981; Simon and Sebastian 1982), and have demonstrated the impact of these factors on diffusion rates. In a sense, these are competitive variables since the levels are determined relative to the competitive levels, for example, pricing

Robertson, Thomas S. and Hubert Gatignon, "Competitive Effects on Technology Diffusion," Vol. 50 (July '86), pp. 1–12. Reprinted from *Journal of Marketing*, published by the American Marketing Association.

decisions or advertising-to-sales ratios. However, explicit consideration of competitive factors has only been included in analytical diffusion models (Mate 1982; Rao and Bass 1985; Teng and Thompson 1983; Thompson and Teng 1984). Empirical research on diffusion from a behavioral perspective has almost totally ignored competitive factors.

A COMPETITIVE BEHAVIOR PARADIGM

A diffusion paradigm stressing competitive factors is shown in Figure 15-1. The most important distinguishing characteristics of this paradigm, versus the Rogers (1983) paradigm, are twofold. First, *the competitive environment of suppliers* is explicitly linked to the adop-

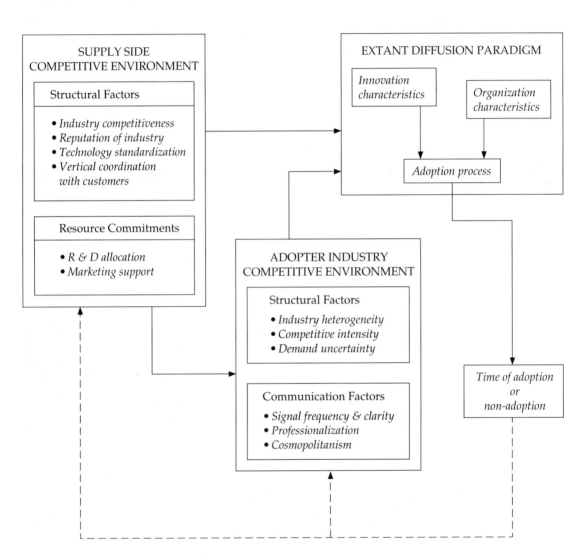

Figure 15-1
A Competitive Behavior Paradigm for Technology Diffusion among Organizations

tion/diffusion process. The structural characteristics of the industry and the resource commitments of supplier firms are shown as determinants of the rate of diffusion. Researchers familiar with diffusion theory within marketing will recognize that supply-side factors have not been pursued in diffusion research. Indeed, to a very large extent most research seems to assume that there is only one firm supplying the innovation—a condition which rarely holds.

Secondly, the *competitive environment among potential adopters* is important in determining receptivity to innovation. Adopter industry variables, such as industry competitiveness, heterogeneity, and return on investment, have been pursued in economics (Mansfield 1968; Stoneman 1981) and organizational behavior research (Kimberly and Evanisko 1981), but the level of conceptualization and research within marketing is meager. This may be due to the belief that competitive variables account for a smaller share of the variance than innovation characteristics and adopter category factors. The lack of research, however, may also be due to a bias among behavioral researchers toward studying only consumer characteristics and not competitive factors.

A description of the enhanced organizational diffusion model is as follows. Diffusion occurs within the boundaries of an industry. The diffusion pattern at the industry level is the outcome of the distribution of individual firm adoption decisions. These individual firm adoption decisions are influenced by the compatibility between the innovation's characteristics and those of the potential adopting unit. Adoption is further influenced and mediated by the supply-side competitive environment and the adopter industry competitive environment.

The objectives now will be to develop a set of propositions for research on organizational diffusion focused on the supply-side

and adopter industry variable and to propose some research considerations. First, however, we shall clarify our focus on technological innovations, since this is the thrust of our concern.

TECHNOLOGICAL INNOVATIONS

Many innovations utilize "technology." Our interest, however, is in new products, services, or systems which utilize technology and which are perceived to have significant consequences for existing production or consumption patterns. This type of innovation has often been referred to as a "discontinuous" innovation, that is, an innovation which alters existing patterns of production or consumption or creates new patterns of consumption (Robertson 1971). Examples are microcomputers, electronic mail, or video recording.

The key to defining innovations is the perception of the product among potential adopters. An innovation may be "high technology" from the supplier's vantage point, but if it is not perceived by customers as altering and improving their business functions—that is, a discontinuous innovation—then it is not of interest in the present context. Here, we shall use the term *technological innovations* as synonymous with discontinuous innovations. We are interested in these high technology products which, according to Shanklin and Ryans (1984), have the potential to "create or revolutionize markets and demand" (p. 166).

Technological innovations are generally complex products, possessing attributes with which the potential adopting unit may be unfamiliar. Because of the unfamiliarity, the adopting unit does not have a knowledge structure that can be used to evaluate and make judgments about the product. High technology innovations are typically costly in monetary terms and have high switching costs. The uncertainty about these consequences and about the innovation itself assumes a major importance in the organization's adoption decision process. The severity of the learning requirement for the potential adopting unit makes it difficult to forecast diffusion rates, since it may be necessary to educate potential customers about the new technology before they can evaluate it and render a judgment and a statement of intention to purchase (Wilton and Pessemier 1981).

The concern in the present case is with the adoption of technologies by business firms. These technologies may be designed to provide cost reductions in the production, distribution, or marketing processes. They may also provide a means for producing higher quality or innovative products that afford new benefits for the firm's consumers or allow the firm to reach new market segments. Flexible automation, for example, would seem to have the potential to offer more highly targeted innovations for specific subsegments of the market (Boston Consulting Group 1985).

Because of the emphasis on these technological innovations (process or products), adoption is not the only relevant concern of diffusion research. The *degree of use* of that technology is also an important variable that describes the extent of diffusion of that innovation. Rogers (1985) presents some evidence that a significant number of adopters of a communication technology use the innovation very little. Although throughout the following discussion the focus is on diffusion, we refer to *depth of usage* as well as *time of adoption* in characterizing diffusion.

SUPPLY-SIDE FACTORS AFFECTING DIFFUSION

The suppliers of a new technology affect the diffusion potential and speed of diffusion

based on their actions in determining the characteristics of the innovation and its pricing and in allocating resources in the innovation. This perspective is in many ways contrary to the prevalent focus of marketing research on diffusion of innovations, which has been conducted mainly by consumer behavior researchers utilizing the Rogers (1983) paradigm. Existing research tends to ignore how supply-side competitive actions change the diffusion process.

Diffusion theory is quite incomplete unless it recognizes the proactive nature of these actions. In fact, it is an anomaly that diffusion research in marketing has focused so much on competitive behavior. For the most part, research takes the innovation as a given and studies the innovation's compatibility with the consumer group leading to an adoption decision. A direct relationship seems to be assumed between customer characteristics and adoption decisions. As a result, the most common form of empirical research has been to study the characteristics of product category innovators.

Recent modeling of the diffusion process has seized the initiative and explicitly considered supply-side factors affecting diffusion levels. In particular, resource allocations to marketing have been modeled in order to forecast the shape of the diffusion process (Bass 1980; Dolan and Jeuland 1981; Horsky and Simon 1983; Robinson and Fornell 1985).

Supply-Side Structural Factors

The structural characteristics of the industry offering the innovation affect the speed of diffusion and the total market potential realized. The competitiveness of the supplier industry, the reputation of supplier firms, the competitive standardization of the technology, and the level of vertical coordination all affect the speed of diffusion. It might also be argued that the organizational culture of the industry and its participant firms affects innovativeness, but given the limited research base (Cherian and Deshpande 1985; Robertson and Wind 1980), this approach will not be developed here.

Competitiveness   Industry competitiveness is generally assessed by the number of competitors, the concentration ratios, and the mobility barriers which competitors are able to erect (Porter 1980). These measures of competitiveness are interrelated and, in turn, affect competitor resource allocations and pricing philosophies (Eliashberg and Chatterjee 1985; Gatignon 1984). It is our thesis that high levels of supplier competitive intensity lead to more rapid diffusion and the achievement of higher levels of market penetration for the innovation (Brown 1981).

Under high competitive intensity, greater resource allocations and more aggressive pricing policies are likely to materialize, thus encouraging more rapid diffusion. These competitive effects have been reported in the strategic literature (Abell and Hammond 1979). Highly competitive periods correspond to industry "shake-outs;" price wars are likely to occur when sales growth is at a peak. This phenomenon is formalized by Eliashberg and Jeuland (1986), where, through an analytic model, it is shown that prices go down after a new entry, and demand increases as a result of price sensitivity.

At a later stage of the product life cycle, competitive intensity remains high, but producers will be much more focused on secondary demand than on primary demand. Experience curve pricing will drive down industry price levels and bring more customers into the market at a faster pace (Bass 1980). By the same token, however, high competitive intensity is likely to limit the market penetration level for any individual supplier (Karnani 1983).

Proposition 1: The greater the competitive intensity of the supplier group, the more rapid the diffusion and the higher the diffusion level.

Reputation   Supplier reputation may be a somewhat elusive concept. However, particularly when a supplier group is in competition with another supplier group, reputation may be quite important. Given the availability of substitutes, as in paper versus plastic or synthetic versus natural fibers, the reputation of the supplier industry is important. By reputation is meant established relationships and confidence among potential adopters (Berger 1985).

The notion of reputation was developed by Nelson (1970, 1974) as a function of the nature of the product. Nelson makes a distinction between search and experience goods: the quality of search goods can be verified, which is not possible for experience goods. Satterthwaite (1979) reinforces this notion, arguing that even after purchase, quality is difficult to judge. This leads Shapiro (1983) to suggest that sellers might establish reputation upon entry by selling a high quality product, even below cost, and then enjoy the benefits of that reputation.

The thesis is that high reputation supplier groups will achieve faster initial diffusion, although the eventual shape of the diffusion curve and the market potential realized will ultimately depend on the technology and not on supplier reputation. It may also be that for high reputation firms, the source credibility that operates leads to greater source dependence and less operation of interorganizational influence. In particular, borrowing from communications theory, a high reputation supplier will generate a faster penetration rate when there are uncertainties about the new product's performance. Then, the credibility of the supplier mediates uncertainty by potential clients. However, if there is little uncertainty about the performance of the innovation, which would occur mostly for continuous innovations, then reputation might not be a competitive advantage.

Proposition 2: The more favorable the reputation of the supplier group, the more rapid the initial diffusion.

Technology Standardization   The speed of diffusion can be enhanced by reasonable standardization of a technology or retarded if competing standards prevail. This is Abernathy and Utterback's (1978) concept of *dominant design*. This factor is particularly important for high technology products, especially those dependent on software and auxiliary components, such as VCRs, computers, and automated tellers (ATMs).

Customer resistance may be a function of the perceived risk of buying a product that may turn out to be the wrong standard. Customer behavior, therefore, suggests that the sooner the industry attains standardization on a dominant design, the more rapid the diffusion process, since customers will be more receptive to the innovation as the perceived risk of buying the wrong standard declines.

There are also positive benefits of standardization, particularly if there is a "network externality" such that a consumer's value for a product increases when other consumers have compatible products—as in telephones or personal computer software (Farrell and Saloner 1985). Rogers (1985) illustrates this thesis with communication technologies. At the extreme, there is no value in being a single adopter, such as with a telephone: the technology is only useful if other adopters exist and if the technologies are standardized. Therefore, technology standardization is a condition for the diffusion of these innovations. In addition, diffusion is a function of the existing mass of current adopters.

Standardization should also have the effect of reducing price levels in the market, thus speeding diffusion. Standardization on a dominant design allows firms industrywide to take advantage of experience curve effects. A standard of technology also reduces product differentiation among suppliers, thus heightening price competition (Farrell and Saloner 1985) and, quite likely, the price levels of replacement parts. The disadvantage of standardization, according to Farrell and Saloner, may be that it can "trap" an industry if it adheres to an absolute or inferior standard when better standards may become available.

Proposition 3: The more standardized the technology, the more rapid the diffusion.

Vertical Coordination   In industries where suppliers and customers have a high degree of vertical dependence, such as airframe manufacturers and airlines, there may be a propensity to coordination and interlocking relationship (Palmer 1983; Schoorman, Bazerman, and Atkin 1981). It would be expected that a high degree of vertical coordination is positively associated with more rapid diffusion by increasing the flow of information. This relationship may be demonstrated in the medical equipment and drug industries where interlocks between suppliers and leading edge teaching hospitals advance the acceptance of medical innovations.

Vertical coordination provides access to external informational environments, which are focused and potentially valuable information sources. Such boundary spanning activities (Aiken and Hage 1972) have been found to be positively associated with organizational innovativeness (Kimberly 1978). There is also some preliminary evidence that vertical coordination is more likely to occur under environmental uncertainty. The logic is that as an organization's environment becomes more turbulent, vertical coordination will help an organization "to gather, analyze, and act on relevant information" (Galaskiewicz 1985, p. 288). However, transaction cost analysis argues that vertical coordination is the appropriate response to uncertainty *only* in the presence of transaction-specific assets to be acquired by the contractual partners (Anderson 1985; Williamson 1979).

A potentially useful extension of the vertical coordination concept is Von Hippel's (1984) notion of "lead users," which he defines as "individuals or firms who have needs which are not now prevalent among users of a given product, but which can be predicted to become general and to constitute a commercially interesting market in the future" (p. 8). These customers, "who face tomorrow's needs today," can be instrumental in identifying new product opportunities, testing new product prototypes, and providing opinion leadership for later adopters. If such lead users can be identified, they can be linked to a manufacturer as an extension of the R&D/marketing process in order to speed technological acceptance and diffusion.

Proposition 4: The greater the vertical coordination between suppliers and customers, the more rapid the diffusion.

Supply-Side Resource Commitments

The allocation of resources which a supplier industry makes to a new technology will have a major bearing on the speed of diffusion. Both resource commitments to (1) ongoing R&D and (2) marketing programs will positively affect diffusion potential.

R&D Resource Allocation   It has been documented that there is a positive relationship between research and development commitments and the invention/innovation process (Kamien and Schwartz 1982). Greater expenditures in R&D lead to enhanced technologies and, we assume, a more rapid rate of new product introductions by the industry. There is also some evidence that rivalry within an industry stimulates R&D output (Grabowski and Baxter 1973). Existing theory and research tend to suggest that R&D performance is maximized at a degree of industry concentration between pure monopoly and perfect competition (Hambrick and MacMillan 1985; Loury 1979).

Our interest is somewhat different—not in the rate of innovation but in the rate of diffusion. It is our thesis that greater expenditures in R&D by supplier firms will lead to enhanced technologies and a greater range of technological alternatives, which, in turn, will lead to more rapid diffusion and to broader diffusion (Mansfield 1982). McGuinness and Little (1981), for example, have found that intensity of technological effort exerted by an industry is associated with a greater proportion of its output that is exported to other countries, that is, a broader diffusion profile. This is compatible with the Vernon (1971) research stream which indicates that the strength of U.S. exports is in the development of differentiated laborsaving technologies of a price-inelastic nature.

In the domestic market, the enriched technological stream of products offered as a result of high R&D allocations should better meet the range of consumer needs by market segment. This should expand the market potential and lead to more rapid diffusion.

Proposition 5: The greater the allocation of R&D resources within an industry, the more rapid the diffusion process for new technologies and the higher the diffusion level.

Marketing Support   Resource allocations to marketing and the particular marketing actions of the supplier group will be pivotal in speeding the diffusion process and affecting the maximum market penetration level. The greater the levels of advertising, personal selling, promotional support, and distribution support, the faster the diffusion process. Recent modeling of the diffusion of innovations has sought to reflect how the actions of the firm marketing the innovation alter the expected shape of the diffusion process (Bass 1980; Dolan and Jeuland 1981; Horsky and Simon 1983; Kalish 1983; Roberts and Urban 1984; Simon and Sebastian 1982).

Allocations of funds to marketing research will be important in providing customer input to help guide R&D and in "positioning" the technology after it is designed to achieve a certain customer perception. Many new technologies, in fact, are customer-initiated, as Von Hoppel (1984) has demonstrated. A company's major source of ideas for new product opportunities may be its own customers, and marketing research may be instrumental in providing information in order to positively mediate perceived innovation characteristics.

Marketing expenditures in advertising, personal selling, and other forms of communication are important influences on the speed and pattern of diffusion. Generally, marketing actions are designed to achieve more rapid diffusion acceleration in order to foster a quicker return on investment, to erect barriers to entry, and to establish customer loyalty. Indeed, a few empirical studies, based on models of diffusion and extended to include marketing mix variables, have shown that marketing actions accelerate the diffusion process (Bass 1980; Horsky and Simon 1983; Lilien, Rao, and Kalish 1981; Simon and Sebastian 1982).

Marketing actions also have a major bearing on the organizational characteristics of those firms which will adopt, given explicit allocation of resources by *market segment*. Although it is interesting to study the characteristics of innovators or early adopter firms,

it is also worthy of note that these firms may have been targeted by marketing actions and that the firms with dissimilar characteristics may have been excluded.

Diffusion research almost totally ignores these intentions and resource allocations of the firms marketing the innovation. Even the research on new product diffusion conducted by marketing and consumer behavior researchers ignores the intention of supplier firms (Gatignon and Robertson 1985). Thus, research which discovers that innovators are, for example, large firms may only be confirming the market segment selection of the marketer.

Proposition 6: The greater the allocation of marketing resources, the more rapid the diffusion process and the higher the diffusion level.

ADOPTER INDUSTRY FACTORS AFFECTING DIFFUSION

The industry within which a potential adopting organization operates affects receptivity to innovation. In some industries there will be competitive pressure to consider new technologies and in others there may be a general lethargy. The willingness to innovate would seem to be a function of two broad sets of variables which we shall consider—structural and communication factors. The structural factors include industry homogeneity, competitive intensity, and demand uncertainty. The communication factors include signal frequency and clarity, level of professionalization, and the cosmopolitanism of the industry.

Adopter Industry Structural Factors

Industry Heterogeneity   Speed of diffusion will be maximized at an intermediate level of industry heterogeneity. The transmission of information within a highly homogeneous industry—homophilous communication—is likely to be lower in innovation content than information transmitted within a heterogeneous industry—heterophilous communication. Rogers (1983) notes that "heterophilous communication has a special informational potential, even though it may be realized only rarely" (p. 275).

The value of heterophilous influence was documented in research by Granovetter (1973), who discovered that "weak ties" were important in job searches, mainly because people with homophilous ties were unlikely to know anything more than the information recipients, since their contacts were similar. In the consumer behavior literature, Kaigler-Evans, Leavitt, and Dickey (1977) have used the notion of a "point of optimal heterophily." This is the balance point between personal contact that is so similar as to provide minimum new information versus personal contact that is so dissimilar that communication breaks down. In their research they provide preliminary evidence for the effectiveness of sources who are in this middle range of heterophily.

In drawing a parallel to organizational adoption of technology, it is proposed that intermediate industry heterogeneity is equivalent to the optimal point of heterophily. If the industry is highly homogeneous, informational potential regarding new technologies is reduced. If the industry is highly heterogeneous, communication breaks down due to lack of a common focus.

Proposition 7: Rapidity of technological diffusion will be maximized at an intermediate level of industry heterogeneity.

Competitive Intensity   The acceptance of innovation is positively associated with competitive intensity—to a point. Indeed, the relationship between competitive intensity

and innovation receptivity is probably curvilinear, much as the relationship between competitive intensity and R&D performance is curvilinear (Loury 1979). Reasonable levels of competitiveness encourage the acceptance of innovation, but beyond some point, the financial resources of the industry are depleted and the acceptance of innovation is stifled. Innovativeness is also stifled under monopolistic conditions whereby the incentive for change is expected to be low, although there is some debate about this in the economic literature (Salter 1960; Swan 1970).

The acceptance of technological innovation by industry participants may be particularly important in building or maintaining barriers to entry. Levin (1978) has shown how innovation preserves cost advantage and maintains market structure: "By financing R&D out of quasi-rents earned on their superior technology, existing firms generate further technical progress which continuously recreates their cost advantage over potential entrants" (p. 347). In fact, Abernathy and Utterback (1978) have suggested that as competition increases, the type of innovations adopted changes from major product innovations to process innovations.

Proposition 8: Rapidity of technological diffusion will be maximized at an intermediate level of competitive intensity.

Demand Uncertainty   In industries that are unable to forecast demand accurately, incumbent competitors cannot know the levels of marketing activity and the levels of output necessary to preempt new entrants (Dasgupta and Stiglitz 1980). Consequently, the higher the degree of uncertainty in predicting demand, the more intense competition will be among existing competitors and the more likely firms will be to adopt innovations. This does not hold when competition is stable, as in some regulated industries. In this case, environmental uncertainty decreases the likelihood of adoption of an innovation by an organization behaving rationally (Fidler and Johnson 1984).

This receptivity to innovation is most pronounced if the strategy for preempting new entry requires new technologies for cost reduction or for gaining new market segments. Therefore, the conditions for a positive effect of demand uncertainty on the rate of diffusion of innovations are: when existing competition uses cost as a barrier to entry and there is a potential for price reductions (or for a gain in marketing efficiency); and when the preempting strategy is to fill the gaps in satisfying the heterogeneous needs of the market, given that the new products or new segments require a technological innovation.

Related to demand uncertainty is the inaccuracy of predicting consumer needs (Eliashberg, Tapiero, and Wind 1985). This inaccuracy increases with the heterogeneity in population tastes and with normative changes (Feder and O'Mara 1982; Peterson and Mahajan 1978). Because of the variability in consumer demand, diverse products and services are required to satisfy these segments' needs and, consequently, more innovations are needed which are perceived by consumers as providing important benefits. This was verified empirically by Baldridge and Burnham (1975) in the noncommercial context of innovations adopted by schools.

A similar situation arises when a change in the environment causes changes in consumers' needs, or a technological gap (March and Simon 1958). Thus, the higher the environmental uncertainty, the higher the need for changing technologies and the higher the rate of adoption of innovations (Ettlie 1983). Other researchers have shown that environmental uncertainty stimulates a change in strategy or policy (Eliashberg and Chatterjee 1985b; Hambrick 1981) and, in particular, promotes an aggressive technology policy (Ettlie and Bridges 1982). In turn, aggressive technology policies generate a greater likelihood of adoption of innovations (Ettlie 1983).

Proposition 9: Demand uncertainty is generally positively related to the acceptance of innovations.

Adopter Industry Communication Factors

Signal Frequency and Clarity   An interesting dimension in analyzing an industry is the amount of signaling which occurs among competitors and the clarity of these signals. Signals may be announced intentions and explanations for such actions as new investments, production processes, pricing systems, or product introductions. In the present case we are interested in the amount of signaling about the adoption of new technologies by member firms and the clarity of these signals. Clarity would be judged by the extent to which a unique cause can be inferred, as well as the past truthfulness of signals from a particular competitor (Heil 1985).

Industries may be characterized as to openness in communication and lack of ambiguity in signaling. Alternatively, industries may be very closed in revealing information, or may send deliberately ambiguous or potentially misleading signals. The communication openness of an industry refers to the amount of potentially useful information that is communicated among competitors. Communication openness can be measured by such variables as the number of trade journals, number of trade associations, attendance at trade association and industry meetings, number of press briefings, informational content of annual reports, and the number of interfirm contacts which occur.

Research by Czepiel (1974) within the steel industry found a high level of communication openness, although we lack comparative research within other industries. According to Czepiel, "While there are available no outside criteria for comparison, . . . industry members have regular opinion/advice relationships with between two and three other firms in the industry . . . " (p. 175). He did find two distinct social networks—a "Big Steel" network and a "Mini-Mill" network. The major source of information about the new technology studied was industry friendship relationships, followed by colleagues and suppliers. Czepiel suggests that the communication openness of the steel industry may be a function of its maturity and commonality of technology and that such openness is less likely in other industries where "production technology may yield significant competitive advantage" (p. 178).

The expectation is that signal frequency and clarity are positively related to the rate of diffusion for new technologies. Communication openness and information sharing are likely to increase the available information about innovations and to ease the adoption decision process. Signal clarity is likely to enhance the information content, such that announcements will be believed by fellow competitors, thus speeding the diffusion process.

Proposition 10: Frequency of signaling and signal clarity are positively related to the speed and level of diffusion.

Professionalization   A key variable in most theories of diffusion and in diffusion models is the amount of social influence transmitted within an industry. Social influence would seem to be increased to the extent that the industry is professionalized, such that a firm's employees identify with their profession as well as with their firm. This would increase the likelihood of accessing extraorganizational information about innovations (Leonard-Barton 1985).

In line with Moch and Morse (1977), it is expected that organizations are more likely to adopt innovations when they have specialist professionals who define the innovation as compatible with their needs and interests. In a similar vein, Robertson and Wind (1983) have argued that professionals are more important than managers (in the hospital domain) in affecting receptivity to innovation. Fennell (1984), however, found that the presence of a professional medical component did not facilitate adoption of employee health programs among private sector firms. Among manufacturing firms (in the shoe industry), Bigoness and Perreault (1981) documented that firms possessing internal technical expertise are more innovative than firms without such expertise. On balance, the evidence supports the proposition that industry professionalization is positively associated with innovation receptivity.

Proposition 11: The greater the professionalization of an industry, the more rapid the diffusion.

Cosmopolitanism   Finally, the greater the cosmopolitanism of an industry, the more rapid the rate of diffusion. This refers to an external (rather than local) orientation. It has generally been found that cosmopolitanism or "external integration" is positively associated with innovativeness. This has been documented in agricultural research (Rogers 1983), consumer research (Gatignon and Robertson 1985), and in organizational behavior research (Kimberly 1978; Ozanne and Churchill 1971; Robertson and Wind 1983). Counte and Kimberly (1974), however, confirm that the role of cosmopolitanism depends on the innovation. In their research on a "locally-based" medical innovation, cosmopolitanism did not separate adopters from nonadopters: "Perhaps this was because receptive individuals perceived possible participation as resulting in status rewards in the local medical community, not in reference to some externally-based group, set, or institution" (p. 196).

Although cosmopolitanism has been studied mainly at the individual or organizational level, we believe that there is value in the notion of industry cosmopolitanism. This could be assessed by level of international sales, number of markets targeted, percentage of employees who have worked in other industries, etc. Just as for the individual organization, industry cosmopolitanism increases access to new information and encourages a more rapid diffusion process. Indeed, Gatignon, Eliashberg, and Robertson (1985) have recently extended the concept to a national level. In seeking to explain diffusion patterns of appliance innovations in a number of European countries, they found that national cosmopolitanism—as measured by levels of international mail, telephone, and travel—was a meaningful explanatory factor.

At an industry level, the value of cosmopolitanism has been studied by Mansfield (1968). He found that the most important source of technology in a number of mature industries was outside rather than within the industry. An industry's integration into external information environments may be an important source of new ideas and complementary technologies.

Proposition 12: The greater the cosmopolitanism of an industry, the more rapid the diffusion.

FUTURE RESEARCH

This article has stressed an alternative paradigm for research on diffusion of innovation focused on competitive factors. It has been argued that the prevalent research base has

been grounded in behavioral theory and has largely ignored the role of the supplier industry in affecting diffusion rates as well as the competitive environment among potential adopters.

Although this argument could be made for diffusion both at the organizational level and the ultimate consumer level, the focus here has been on organizational adoption of innovations. Similarly, although the argument could hold for both high and low technology products, we have linked our analysis to the realm of high technology, or discontinuous innovations.

A set of propositions has been offered as to how supply-side and adopter industry variables affect diffusion. These propositions have been derived by combining a number of different literature bases in marketing, economics, and organizational behavior. The combination of these vantage points provides a conceptualization for future research probing organizational acceptance of new technologies.

Although some of the propositions suggested have received empirical support in the disciplines from which they are derived, our intent is to provide a conceptual framework that will advance research within the marketing discipline. The framework illustrated in Figure 15-1 and the propositions to be tested encompass priority areas for systematic investigation. Indeed, many of the propositions have considerable relevance for the practice of new product marketing. An industry's product policy and distribution strategies, for example, should be affected by the relationships suggested as to how diffusion varies according to vertical coordination and technology standardization strategies, as well as how diffusion is affected by marketing resource commitments.

Most marketing research on diffusion theory considers the adoption of a single innovation by multiple adopters—usually individuals but sometimes organizations. Research generally addresses the issue of determining the characteristics of the adopter or the innovation characteristics that affect adoption. When the research objective concerns the properties of the innovation, the research is across products and the adoption unit characteristics are basically ignored. In the study of organizational adoption of innovations, some of our propositions can be researched with the same methodology, that is, a single innovation adopted by multiple organizations. However, organizations are nested within industries—a level at which certain propositions in this article are formulated. Therefore, future research must consider another dimension of the unit of analysis—the industry level.

Some propositions can be tested by analyzing the adoption of a single innovation by multiple organizations within an industry. Some require a single innovation adopted by multiple organizations in multiple industries. Other propositions can be tested with a cross section of innovations adopted by multiple organizations within an industry, and others necessitate multiple innovations, multiple organizations, and multiple industries. Clearly, the varying degree of complexity of such tests needs to be considered in the design of a research program. The supply-side propositions could be studied if multiple firms with various levels of reputation, or various levels of marketing support, for example, offered a similar innovation. On the other hand, the demand-side propositions all require the analysis of adoption by multiple industries.

Although almost all diffusion research has utilized survey methodologies, it would be desirable to extend the research base to experimental approaches. The mechanisms that explain the relationships posited are not easily traceable with surveys, and probing causal processes would be a desirable addition to our knowledge base. A new stream of research might utilize experimental designs in which respondents make adoption decisions facing different competitive environments as described in scenarios (Heil 1985; Robertson and Wind 1980). Although methodological problems arise in this type of experimental setting—particularly concerning external validity—it might be a viable route to test process-based hypotheses.

In conclusion, we have advocated a heightened focus on the diffusion of technological innovations across organizations. Particular stress has been given to how competitive factors affect diffusion patterns, both at the level of the supplier industry and within the potential adopter industry. A set of propositions has been suggested relating a set of variables to expected diffusion patterns. Research has been encouraged at the industry level of analysis as well as at the level of the individual firm. Experimental designs for diffusion research have also been suggested, in addition to the prototypical survey methodologies generally utilized.

REFERENCES

Abell, Derek F. and John S. Hammond (1979), *Strategic Market Planning*, Englewood Cliffs, NJ: Prentice-Hall.

Abernathy, William J. and James M. Utterback (1978), "Patterns of Industrial Innovations," *Technology Review*, 80 (June/July), 41–47.

Aiken, M. and Jerald Hage (1972), "Organizational Permeability, Boundary Spanners and Organizational Structure," paper presented at the 67th Annual Meeting of the American Sociological Association, New Orleans.

Anderson, Erin (1985), "The Salesperson as Outside Agent or Employee: A Transaction Cost Analysis," *Marketing Science*, 4 (Summer), 234–254.

Baker, Michael J. and Stephen T. Parkinson (1977), "Information Source Preference in the Industrial Adoption Decision," in *Proceedings of the American Marketing Association*, Barnett A. Greenberg and Danny N. Bellenger, eds., Chicago: American Marketing Association, 258–261.

Baldridge, J. Victor and Robert A. Burnham (1975), "Organizational Innovation: Individual, Organizational, and Environmental Impacts," *Administrative Science Quarterly*, 20 (June), 165–176.

Bass, Frank M. (1969), "A New Product Growth Model for Consumer Durables," *Management Science*, 15 (no. 5), 215–227.

———— (1980), "The Relationship between Diffusion Curves, Experience Curves, and Demand Elasticities for Consumer Durable Technological Innovations," *Journal of Business*, 53 (July), 551–557.

Berger, Lawrence (1985), "Word-of-Mouth Reputation in Auto Insurance Markets," Ph.D. dissertation, University of Pennsylvania.

Bigoness, William J. and William D. Perreault, Jr. (1981), "A Conceptual Paradigm and Approach for the Study of Innovators," *Academy of Management Journal*, 24 (March), 68–82.

Boston Consulting Group (1985), "Perspectives: Flexible Automation," unpublished working paper.

Brown, Lawrence A. (1981), *Innovation Diffusion: A New Perspective*, New York: Methuen.

Cherian, Joseph and Rohit Deshpandé (1985), "The Impact of Organizational Culture on the Adoption of Industrial Innovations," working paper, Department of Marketing, University of Texas, Austin.

Cooper, Robert G. (1979), "The Dimensions of Industrial New Product Success and Failure," *Journal of Marketing*, 43 (Summer), 93–103.

Counte, Michael A. and John R. Kimberly (1974), "Organizational Innovation in a Professionally Dominated System: Responses of Physicians to a New Program in Medical Education," *Journal of Health and Social Behavior*, 15 (September), 188–199.

Czepiel, John A. (1974), "Word-of-Mouth Processes in the Diffusion of a Major Technological Innovation," *Journal of Marketing Research*, 11 (May), 172–180.

———— (1976), "Decision Group and Firm Characteristics in an Industrial Adoption Decision," in *Marketing: 1776–1976 and Beyond*, Kenneth L. Berhnhardt, ed., Chicago: American Marketing Association, 340–343.

Dasgupta, P. and J. Stiglitz (1980), "Uncertainty, Industry Structure, and the Speed of R&D," *The Bell Journal of Economics*, 11 (Spring), 1–28.

Dickerson, Mary Dee and James W. Gentry (1983), "Characteristics of Adopters and Non-Adopters of Home Computers," *Journal of Consumer Research*, 10 (September), 225–235.

Dolan, Robert J. and Abel P. Jeuland (1981), "Experience Curves and Dynamic Demand Models: Implications for Optimal Pricing Strategies," *Journal of Marketing*, 45 (Winter), 52–62.

Eliashberg, Jehoshua and Abel P. Jeuland (1986), "The Impact of Competitive Entry in a Developing Market upon Dynamic Pricing Strategies," *Marketing Science*, in press.

———— and Rabikar Chatterjee (1985a), "Analytical Models of Competition with Implications for Marketing: Issues, Findings, and Outlook," *Journal of Marketing Research*, 22 (August), 283–296.

———— and ———— (1985b), "Stochastic Issues in Modeling the Innovation Diffusion Process," in *Innovation Diffusion Models of New Product Acceptance*, V. Mahajan and Y. Wind, eds., Cambridge, MA: Ballinger.

———— Charles C. Tapiero, and Yoram Wind (1985), "New Products Diffusion Models with Stochastic Parameters," working paper, University of Pennsylvania.

Ettlie, John E. (1983), "Organizational Policy and Innovation among Suppliers to the Food Processing Sector," *Academy of Management Journal*, 26 (no. 1), 27–44.

———— and W. P. Bridges (1982), "Environmental Uncertainty and Organizational Technology Policy," *IEEE Transactions on Engineering Management*, EM–29, 2–10.

Farrell, Joseph and Garth Saloner (1985), "Standardization, Compatibility, and Innovations," *Rand Journal of Economics*, 16 (Spring), 70–83.

Feder, Gershon and Gerald T. O'Mara (1982), "On Information and Innovation Diffusion: A Bayesian Approach," *American Agricultural Economics Association Proceedings*, (February), 145–147.

Fennell, Mary L. (1984), "Synergy, Influence, and Information in the Adoption of Administrative Innovations," *Academy of Management Journal*, 27 (March), 113–129.

Fidler, Lori A. and J. David Johnson (1984), "Communication and Innovation Implementation," *Academy of Management Journal*, 9 (no. 4), 704–711.

Galaskiewicz, Joseph (1985), "Interorganizational Relations," in *Annual Review of Sociology*, Ralph H. Turner and James F. Short, Jr., eds., Palo Alto, CA: Annual Reviews, Inc., 281–304.

Gatignon, Hubert (1984), "Competition as a Moderator of the Effect of Advertising on Sales," *Journal of Marketing Research*, 21 (4), 387–398.

———, Jehoshua Eliashberg, and Thomas S. Robertson (1985), "Determinants of Diffusion Patterns: A Cross-Country Analysis," working paper, The Wharton School, University of Pennsylvania.

——— and Thomas S. Robertson (1985), "A Propositional Inventory for New Diffusion Research," *Journal of Consumer Research*, 11 (March), 849–867.

Grabowski, H. G. and N. D. Baxter (1973), "Rivalry in Industrial Research and Development," *Journal of Industrial Economics*, 21 (July), 209–235.

Granovetter, Mark S. (1973), "The Strength of Weak Ties," *American Journal of Sociology*, 78 (no. 6), 1360–1380.

Hambrick, Donald C. (1981), "Specialization of Environmental Scanning Activities among Upper Level Mangers," *Journal of Management Studies*, 18 (July), 299–320.

——— and Ian C. MacMillan (1985), "Efficiency of Product R&D in Business Units: The Role of Strategic Context," *Academy of Management Journal*, 28 (September), 527–547.

Heil, Oliver (1985), "Signaling in Competitive Marketing Environments," working paper, The Wharton School, University of Pennsylvania.

Hirschman, Elizabeth C. (1980), "Innovativeness, Novelty Seeking, and Consumer Creativity," *Journal of Consumer Research*, 7 (December), 289–295.

Horsky, Dan and Leonard S. Simon (1983), "Advertising and the Diffusion of New Products," *Marketing Science*, 2 (Winter), 1–17.

Kaigler-Evans, Karen, Clark Leavitt, and Lois Dickey (1977), "Source Similarity and Fashion Newness as Determinants of Consumer Innovation," in *Advances in Consumer Research*, Vol. 5, H. Keith Hunt, ed., Ann Arbor: Association for Consumer Research, 738–742.

Kalish, Shlomo (1983), "Monopolistic Pricing with Dynamic Demand and Production Cost," *Marketing Science*, 2 (no. 2), 135–159.

Kamien, Morton I. and Nancy L. Schwartz (1982), *Marketing Structure and Innovation*, Cambridge: Cambridge University Press.

Karnani, Aneel (1983), "Minimum Market Share," *Marketing Science*, 2 (no. 1), 75–93.

Kimberly, John R. (1978), "Hospital Adoption of Innovation: The Role of Integration into External Informational Environments," *Journal of Health & Social Behavior*, 19 (December), 361–373.

——— and Michael J. Evanisko (1981), "Organizational Innovation: The Influence of Individual, Organizational, and Contextual Factors on Hospital Adoption of Technological and Administrative Innovations," *Academy of Management Journal*, 24 (December), 689–713.

Leonard-Barton, Dorothy (1985), "Experts as Negative Opinion Leaders in the Diffusion of a Technological Innovation," *Journal of Consumer Research*, 11 (March), 914–926.

Levin, Richard C. (1978), "Technical Change, Barriers to Entry, and Market Structure," *Economica*, 45 (November), 347–361.

Lilien, Gary L., Ambar G. Rao, and Shlomo Kalish (1981), "Bayesian Estimation and Control of Detailing Effort in a Repeat Purchase Diffusion Environment," *Management Science*, 27 (May), 493–506.

Loury, Glenn C. (1979), "Market Structure and Innovation," *Quarterly Journal of Economics*, 33 (August), 395–410.

Mahajan, Vijay and Eitan Muller (1979), "Innovation Diffusion and New Product Growth Models in Marketing," *Journal of Marketing*, 43 (Fall), 55–68.

Mansfield, Edwin (1968), *Industrial Research and Technological Innovation*, New York: Norton.

——— (1982), *Technology Transfer, Productivity, and Economic Policy*, New York: Norton.

March, James G. and Herbert A. Simon (1958), *Organizations*, New York: Wiley.

Mate, Karol V. (1982), "Optimal Advertising Strategies of Competing Firms Marketing New Products," working paper, Washington University, St. Louis.

McGuinness, Norman W. and Blair Little (1981), "The Influence of Product Characteristics on the Export Performance of New Industrial Products," *Journal of Marketing*, 45 (Spring), 110–112.

Moch, M. K. and E. V. Morse (1977), "Size, Centralization, and Organizational Adoption of Innovations," *American Sociological Review*, 42 (October), 716–725.

Nelson, Philip (1970), "Information and Consumer Behavior," *Journal of Political Economy*, 78 (March–April), 311–325.

_____ (1974), "Advertising as Information," *Journal of Political Economy*, 82 (July–August), 729–754.

Ozanne, Urban B. and Gilbert A. Churchill, Jr. (1971), "Five Dimensions of the Industrial Adoption Process," *Journal of Marketing Research*, 8 (August), 322–328.

Palmer, Donald (1983), "Broken Ties: Interlocking Directorates and Intercorporate Coordination," *Administrative Science Quarterly*, 28 (March), 40–55.

Peterson, Robert A. and Vijay Mahajan (1978), "Multi-Product Growth Models," in *Research in Marketing*, J. Sheth, ed., Greenwich, CT: JAI Press, 201–231.

Porter, Michael E. (1980), *Competitive Strategy*, New York: The Free Press.

Rao, Ram C. and Frank M. Bass (1985), "Competition, Strategy, and Price Dynamics: A Theoretical and Empirical Investigation," *Journal of Marketing Research*, 22 (August), 283–296.

Roberts, John H. and Glen L. Urban (1984), "New Consumer Durable Brand Choice: Modeling Multiattribute Utility, Risk, and Belief Dynamics," working paper, University of New South Wales.

Robertson, Thomas S. (1971), *Innovative Behavior and Communication*, New York: Holt.

_____ and Yoram Wind (1980), "Organizational Psychographics and Innovativeness," *Journal of Consumer Research*, 7 (June), 24–31.

_____ and _____ (1983), "Organizational Cosmopolitanism and Innovativeness," *Academy of Management Journal*, 26 (June), 332–338.

Robinson, William T. and Claes Fornell (1985), "Sources of Market Pioneer Advantages in Consumer Goods Industries," *Journal of Marketing Research*, 22 (August), 305–317.

Rogers, Everett M. (1983), *Diffusion of Innovations*, 3rd ed., New York: The Free Press.

_____ (1985), "Interdependencies among Users of a New Communication Technology," paper presented at the Association for Consumer Research Conference, Las Vegas (October).

Salter, W. E. G. (1960), *Productivity and Technical Change*, Cambridge: Cambridge University Press.

Satterthwaite, M. (1979), "Consumer Information: Equilibrium Industry Price and the Number of Sellers," *Bell Journal of Economics*, 10 (Autumn), 483–502.

Schoorman, F. David, Max H. Bazerman, and Robert S. Atkin (1981), "Interlocking Directorates: A Strategy for Reducing Environmental Uncertainty," *Academy of Management Review*, 6 (no. 2), 243–251.

Shanklin, William L. and John K. Ryans, Jr. (1984), "Organizing for High-Tech Marketing," *Harvard Business Review*, 84 (November–December), 164–171.

Shapiro, C. (1983), "Premiums for High Quality Products as Returns to Reputation," *Quarterly Journal of Economics*, 97 (no. 4), 659–679.

Simon, Hermann and Karl-Heinz Sebastian (1982), "Diffusion and Advertising: The German Telephone Campaign," working paper no. 0.9, Marketing Science Group of Germany.

Stoneman, P. (1981), "Intra-Firm Diffusion, Bayesian Learning, and Profitability," *The Economic Journal*, 91 (June), 375–388.

Swan, Peter L. (1970), "Market Structure and Technological Progress: The Influence of Monopoly on Product Innovation," *Quarterly Journal of Economics*, 84 (no. 4), 627–638.

Teng, Jinn-Tsair and Gerald L. Thompson (1983), "Oligopoly Models for Optimal Advertising When Production Costs Obey a Learning Curve," *Management Science*, 29 (September), 1087–1101.

Thompson, Gerald L. and Jinn-Tsair Teng (1984), "Optimal Pricing and Advertising Policies for New Product Oligopoly Models," *Marketing Science*, 3 (Spring), 148–168.

Vernon, Raymond (1971), *Sovereignty at Bay*, New York: Basic Books.

Von Hippel, Eric (1984), "Novel Product Concepts from Lead Users: Segmenting Users by Experience," working paper no. 84–109, Marketing Science Institute, Cambridge, MA.

Webster, Frederick E., Jr. (1969), "New Product Adoption in Industrial Markets: A Framework for Analysis," *Journal of Marketing*, 33 (July) 35–39.

Weitz, Barton A. (1985), "Introduction to Special Issue on Competition in Marketing," *Journal of Marketing Research*, 22 (August), 228–236.

Williamson, Oliver E. (1979), "Transaction-Cost Economics: The Governance of Contractual Relations," *Journal of Law and Economics*, 22 (October), 233–262.

Wilton, Peter C. and Edgar A. Pessemier (1981), "Forecasting the Ultimate Acceptance of an Innovation: The Effects of Information," *Journal of Consumer Research*, 8 (September), 162–171.

Zaltman, Gerald, Robert Duncan, and Jonny Holbek (1973), *Innovations and Organizations*, New York: Wiley.

◆

Benefit Segmentation: A Decision-Oriented Research Tool

Russell I. Haley

Market segmentation has been steadily moving toward center stage as a topic of discussion in marketing and research circles. Hardly a conference passes without at least one session devoted to it. Moreover, in March the American Management Association held a three-day conference entirely concerned with various aspects of the segmentation problem.

According to Wendell Smith, "segmentation is based upon developments on the demand side of the market and represents a rational and more precise adjustment of product and marketing effort to consumer or user requirements."[1] The idea that all markets can be profitably segmented has now received almost as widespread acceptance as the marketing concept itself. However, problems remain. In the extreme, a marketer can divide up his market in as many ways as he can describe his prospects. If he wishes, he can define a left-handed segment, or a blue-eyed segment, or a German-speaking segment. Consequently, current discussion revolves largely around which of the virtually limitless alternatives is likely to be more productive.

SEGMENTATION METHODS

Several varieties of market segmentation have been popular in the recent past. At least three kinds have achieved some degree of prominence. Historically, perhaps the first type to exist was geographic segmentation. Small manufacturers who wished to limit their investments, or whose distribution channels were not large enough to cover the entire country, segmented the U.S. market, in effect, by selling their products only in certain areas.

However, as more and more brands became national, the second major system of segmentation—demographic segmentation—became popular. Under this philosophy targets were defined as younger people, men, or families with children. Unfortunately, a number of recent studies have shown that demographic variables such as age, sex, income,

Reprinted from *Journal of Marketing,* published by the American Marketing Association. Russell I. Haley, "Benefit Segmentation: A Decision-Oriented Research Tool," *Journal of Marketing,* Vol. 32, pp. 30–35, July 1968.

occupation and race are, in general, poor predictors of behavior and consequently, less than optimum bases for segmentation strategies.[2]

More recently, a third type of segmentation has come into increasing favor—volume segmentation. The so-called "heavy half" theory, popularized by Dik Twedt of the Oscar Mayer Company,[3] points out that in most product categories one-half of the consumers account for around 80% of the consumption. If this is true, the argument goes, shouldn't knowledgeable marketers concentrate their efforts on these high-volume consumers? Certainly they are the most *valuable* consumers.

The trouble with this line of reasoning is that not all heavy consumers are usually available to the same brand—because they are not all seeking the same kinds of benefits from a product. For example, heavy coffee drinkers consist of two types of consumers—those who drink chain store brands and those who drink premium brands. The chain store customers feel that all coffees are basically alike and, because they drink so much coffee, they feel it is sensible to buy a relatively inexpensive brand. The premium brand buyers, on the other hand, feel that the few added pennies which coffees like Yuban, Martinson's, Chock Full O'Nuts, and Savarin cost are more than justified by their fuller taste. Obviously, these two groups of people, although they are both members of the "heavy half" segment, are not equally good prospects for any one brand, nor can they be expected to respond to the same advertising claims.

These three systems of segmentation have been used because they provide helpful guidance in the use of certain marketing tools. For example, geographic segmentation, because it describes the market in a discrete way, provides definite direction in media purchases. Spot TV, spot radio, and newspapers can be bought for a geographical segment selected for concentrated effort. Similarly, demographic segmentation allows media to be bought more efficiently since demographic data on readers, viewers, and listeners are readily available for most media vehicles. Also, in some product categories demographic variables are extremely helpful in differentiating users from nonusers, although they are typically less helpful in distinguishing between the users of various brands. The heavy-half philosophy is especially effective in directing dollars toward the most important parts of the market.

However, each of these three systems of segmentation is handicapped by an underlying disadvantage inherent in its nature. All are based on an ex post facto analysis of the kinds of people who make up various segments of a market. They rely on *descriptive* factors rather than *causal* factors. For this reason they are not efficient predictors of future buying behavior, and it is future buying behavior that is of central interest to marketers.

BENEFIT SEGMENTATION

An approach to market segmentation whereby it is possible to identify market segments by causal factors rather than descriptive factors, might be called "benefit segmentation." The belief underlying this segmentation strategy is that the benefits which people are seeking in consuming a given product are the basic reasons for the existence of true market segments. Experience with this approach has shown that benefits sought by consumers determine their behavior much more accurately than do demographic characteristics or volume of consumption.

This does not mean that the kinds of data gathered in more traditional types of segmentation are not useful. Once people have been classified into segments in accordance with the benefits they are seeking, each segment is contrasted with all of the other segments in terms of its demography, its volume of consumption, its brand perceptions, its media habits, its personality and life-style, and so forth. In this way, a reasonably deep understanding of the people who make up each segment can be obtained. And by capitalizing on this understanding, it is possible to reach them, to talk to them in their own terms, and to present a product in the most favorable light possible.

The benefit segmentation approach is not new. It has been employed by a number of America's largest corporations since it was introduced in 1961.[4] However, case histories have been notably absent from the literature because most studies have been contracted for privately, and have been treated confidentially.

The benefit segmentation approach is based upon being able to measure consumer value systems in detail, together with what the consumer thinks about various brands in the product category of interest. While this concept seems simple enough, operationally it is very complex. There is no simple straightforward way of handling the volumes of data that have to be generated. Computers and sophisticated multivariate attitude measurement techniques are a necessity.

Several alternative statistical approaches can be employed, among them the so-called "Q" technique of factor analysis, multi-dimensional scaling, and other distance measures.[5] All of these methods relate the ratings of each respondent to those of every other respondent and then seek clusters of individuals with similar rating patterns. If the items related are potential consumer benefits, the clusters that emerge will be groups of people who attach similar degrees of importance to the various benefits. Whatever the statistical approach selected, the end result of the analysis is likely to be between three and seven consumer segments, each representing a potentially productive focal point for marketing efforts.

Each segment is identified by the benefits it is seeking. However, it is the *total configuration* of the benefits sought which differentiates one segment from another, rather than the fact that one segment is seeking one particular benefit and another a quite different benefit. Individual benefits are likely to have appeal for several segments. In fact, the research that has been done thus far suggests that most people would like as many benefits as possible. However, the *relative* importance they attach to individual benefits can differ importantly and, accordingly, can be used as an effective lever in segmenting markets.

Of course, it is possible to determine benefit segments intuitively as well as with computers and sophisticated research methods. The kinds of brilliant insights which produced the Mustang and the first 100-millimeter cigarette have a good chance of succeeding whenever marketers are able to tap an existing benefit segment.

However, intuition can be very expensive when it is mistaken. Marketing history is replete with examples of products which someone felt could not miss. Over the longer term, systematic benefit segmentation research is likely to have a higher proportion of successes.

But is benefit segmentation practical? And is it truly operational? The answer to both of these questions is "yes." In effect, the crux of the problem of choosing the best segmentation system is to determine which has the greatest number of practical marketing implications. An example should show that benefit segmentation has a much wider range of implications than alternative forms of segmentation.

An Example of Benefit Segmentation

While the material presented here is purely illustrative to protect the competitive edge of companies who have invested in studies of this kind, it is based on actual segmentation studies. Consequently, it is quite typical of the kinds of things which are normally learned in the course of a benefit segmentation study.

The toothpaste market has been chosen as an example because it is one with which everyone is familiar. Let us assume that a benefit segmentation study has been done and four major segments have been identified—one particularly concerned with decay prevention, one with brightness of teeth, one with the flavor and appearance of the product, and one with price. A relatively large amount of supplementary information has also been gathered (Table 16-1) about the people in each of these segments.

The decay prevention segment, it has been found, contains a disproportionately large number of families with children. They are seriously concerned about the possibility of cavities and show a definite preference for fluoride toothpaste. This is reinforced by their

personalities. They tend to be a little hypochondriacal and, in their life-styles, they are less socially-oriented than some of the other groups. This segment has been named The Worriers.

The second segment, comprised of people who show concern for the brightness of their teeth, is quite different. It includes a relatively large group of young marrieds. They smoke more than average. This is where the swingers are. They are strongly social and their life-style patterns are very active. This is probably the group to which toothpastes such as Macleans or Plus White or Ultra Brite would appeal. This segment has been named the Sociables.

In the third segment, the one which is particularly concerned with the flavor and appearance of the product, a large portion of the brand deciders are children. Their use of spearmint toothpaste is well above average. Stripe has done relatively well in this seg-

Table 16-1
Toothpaste Market Segment Description

Segment Name:	The Sensory Segment	The Sociables	The Worriers	The Independent Segment
Principal benefit sought:	Flavor, product appearance	Brightness of teeth	Decay prevention	Price
Demographic strengths:	Children	Teens, young people	Large families	Men
Special behavioral characteristics:	Users of spearmint-flavored toothpaste	Smokers	Heavy users	Heavy users
Brands disproportionately favored:	Colgate, Stripe	Macleans, Plus White, Ultra Brite	Crest	Brands on sale
Personality characteristics:	High self-involvement	High sociability	High hypochondriasis	High autonomy
Life-style characteristics:	Hedonistic	Active	Conservative	Value-oriented

ment. They are more ego-centered than other segments, and their life-style is outgoing but not to the extent of the swingers. They will be called The Sensory Segment.

The fourth segment, the price-oriented segment, shows a predominance of men. It tends to be above average in terms of toothpaste usage. People in this segment see very few meaningful differences between brands. They switch more frequently than people in other segments and tend to buy a brand on sale. In terms of personality, they are cognitive and they are independent. They like to think for themselves and make brand choices on the basis of their judgment. They will be called The Independent Segment.

MARKETING IMPLICATIONS OF BENEFIT SEGMENTATION STUDIES

Both copy directions and media choices will show sharp differences depending upon which of these segments is chosen as the target—The Worriers, The Sociables, The Sensory Segment, or The Independent Segment. For example, the tonality of the copy will be light if The Sociable Segment or The Sensory Segment is to be addressed. It will be more serious if the copy is aimed at The Worriers. And if The independent Segment is selected, it will probably be desirable to use rational, two-sided arguments. Of course, to talk to this group at all it will be necessary to have either a price edge or some kind of demonstrable product superiority.

The depth-of-sell reflected by the copy will also vary, depending upon the segment which is of interest. It will be fairly intensive for The Worrier Segment and for The Independent Segment, but much more superficial and mood-oriented for The Sociable and Sensory Segments.

Likewise, the setting will vary. It will focus on the product for The Sensory Group,

on socially-oriented situations for The Sociable Group, and perhaps on demonstration or on competitive comparisons for The Independent Group.

Media environments will also be tailored to the segments chosen as targets. Those with serious environments will be used for The Worrier and Independent Segments, and those with youthful, modern and active environments for The Sociable and The Sensory Groups. For example, it might be logical to use a large proportion of television for The Sociable and Sensory Groups, while The Worriers and Independents might have heavier print schedules.

The depth-of-sell needed will also be reflected in the media choices. For The Worrier and Rational Segments longer commercials—perhaps 60-second commercials—would be indicated, while for the other two groups shorter commercials and higher frequency would be desirable.

Of course, in media selection the facts that have been gathered about the demographic characteristics of the segment chosen as the target would also be taken into consideration.

The information in Table 16-1 also has packaging implications. For example, it might be appropriate to have colorful packages for The Sensory Segment, perhaps aqua (to indicate fluoride) for The Worrier Group, and gleaming white for The Sociable segment because of their interest in bright white teeth.

It should be readily apparent that the kinds of information normally obtained in the course of a benefit segmentation study have a wide range of marketing implications. Sometimes they are useful in suggesting physical changes in a product. For example, one manufacturer discovered that his product was well suited to the needs of his chosen target with a single exception in the area of flavor. He was able to make a relatively inexpensive modification in his product and thereby strengthen his market position.

The new product implications of benefit segmentation studies are equally apparent. Once a marketer understands the kinds of segments that exist in his market, he is often able to see new product opportunities or particularly effective ways of positioning the products emerging from his research and development operation.

Similarly, benefit segmentation information has been found helpful in providing direction in the choice of compatible point-of-purchase materials and in the selection of the kinds of sales promotions which are most likely to be effective for any given market target.

Generalizations from Benefit Segmentation Studies

A number of generalizations are possible on the basis of the major benefit segmentation studies which have been conducted thus far. For example, the following general rules of thumb have become apparent:

- It is easier to take advantage of market segments that already exist than to attempt to create new ones. Some time ago the strategy of product differentiation was heavily emphasized in marketing textbooks. Under this philosophy it was believed that a manufacturer was more or less able to create new market segments at will by making his product somewhat different from those of his competitors. Now it is generally recognized that fewer costly errors will be made if money is first invested in consumer research aimed at determining the present contours of the market. Once this knowledge is available, it is usually most efficient to tailor marketing strategies to existing consumer-need patterns.
- No brand can expect to appeal to all consumers. The very act of attracting one seg-

ment may automatically alienate others. A corollary to this principle is that any marketer who wishes to cover a market fully must offer consumers more than a single brand. The flood of new brands which have recently appeared on the market is concrete recognition of this principle.

- A company's brands can sometimes cannibalize each other but need not necessarily do so. It depends on whether or not they are positioned against the same segment of the market. Ivory Snow sharply reduced Ivory Flakes' share of the market, and the Ford Falcon cut deeply into the sales of the standard size Ford because, in each case, the products were competing in the same segments. Later on, for the same companies, the Mustang was successfully introduced with comparatively little damage to Ford; and the success of Crest did not have a disproportionately adverse effect on Gleem's market position because, in these cases, the segments to which the products appealed were different.
- New and old products alike should be designed to fit *exactly* the needs of some segment of the market. In other words, they should be aimed at people seeking a specific combination of benefits. It is a marketing truism that you sell people one at a time—that you have to get *someone* to buy your product before you get *anyone* to buy it. A substantial group of people must be interested in your specific set of benefits before you can make progress in a market. Yet, many products attempt to aim at two or more segments simultaneously. As a result, they are not able to maximize their appeal to any segment of the market, and they run the risk of ending up with a dangerously fuzzy brand image.
- Marketers who adopt a benefit segmentation strategy have a distinct competitive edge. If a benefit segment can be located which is seeking exactly the kinds of satis-

factions that one marketer's brand can offer better than any other brand, the marketer can almost certainly dominate the purchases of that segment. Furthermore, if his competitors are looking at the market in terms of traditional types of segments, they may not even be aware of the existence of the benefit segment which he has chosen as his market target. If they are ignorant in this sense, they will be at a loss to explain the success of his brand. And it naturally follows that if they do not understand the reasons for his success, the kinds of people buying his brand, and the benefits they are obtaining from it, his competitors will find it very difficult to successfully attack the marketer's position.

- An understanding of the benefit segments which exist within a market can be used to advantage when competitors introduce new products. Once the way in which consumers are positioning the new product has been determined, the likelihood that it will make major inroads into segments of interest can be assessed, and a decision can be made on whether or not counteractions of any kind are required. If the new product appears to be assuming an ambiguous position, no money need be invested in defensive measures. However, if it appears that the new product is ideally suited to the needs of an important segment of the market, the manufacturer in question can introduce a new competitive product of his own, modify the physical properties of existing brands, change his advertising strategy, or take whatever steps appear appropriate.

Types of Segments Uncovered through Benefit Segmentation Studies

It is difficult to generalize about the types of segments which are apt to be discovered in the course of a benefit segmentation study. To a large extent, the segments which have been found have been unique to the product categories being analyzed. However, a few types of segments have appeared in two or more private studies. Among them are the following:

The Status Seeker a group which is very much concerned with the prestige of the brands purchased.

The Swinger a group which tries to be modern and up to date in all of its activities. Brand choices reflect this orientation.

The Conservative a group which prefers to stick to large successful companies and popular brands.

The Rational Man a group which looks for benefits such as economy, value, durability, etc.

The Inner-Directed Man a group which is especially concerned with self-concept. Members consider themselves to have a sense of humor, to be independent and/or honest.

The Hedonist a group which is concerned primarily with sensory benefits.

Some of these segments appear among the customers of almost all products and services. However, there is no guarantee that a majority of them or, for that matter, any of them exist in any given product category. Finding out whether they do and, if so, what should be done about them is the purpose of benefit segmentation research.

CONCLUSION

The benefit segmentation approach is of particular interest because it never fails to provide fresh insight into markets. As was indicated in the toothpaste example cited earlier, the marketing implications of this analytical research tool are limited only by the imagination of the person using the information a segmentation study provides. In effect, when segmentation studies are conducted, a number of smaller markets emerge instead of one large one. Moreover, each of these smaller markets can be subjected to the same kinds of thorough analyses to which total markets have been subjected in the past. The only difference—a crucial one—is that the total market was a heterogeneous conglomeration of subgroups. The so-called average consumer existed only in the minds of some marketing people. When benefit segmentation is used, a number of relatively homogeneous segments are uncovered. And, because they are homogeneous, descriptions of them in terms of averages are much more appropriate and meaningful as marketing guides.

NOTES

1. Wendell R. Smith, "Product Differentiation and Market Segmentation as Alternative Product Strategies," *Journal of Marketing*, Vol. XXI (July, 1956), pp. 3–8.
2. Ronald E. Frank, "Correlates of Buying Behavior for Grocery Products" *Journal of Marketing*, Vol. 31 (October, 1967), pp. 48–53; Ronald E. Frank, William Massey, and Harper W. Boyd, Jr., "Correlates of Grocery Product Consumption Rates," *Journal of Marketing Research*, Vol. 4 (May, 1968), pp. 184–190; and Clark Wilson, "Homemaker Living Patterns and Marketplace Behavior—A Psychometric Approach," in John S. Wright and Jac L. Goldstucker, Editors, *New Ideas for Successful Marketing*, Proceedings of 1966 World Congress (Chicago: American Marketing Association, June, 1966), pp. 305–331.
3. Dik Warren Twedt, "Some Practical Applications of the 'Heavy Half' Theory" (New York: Advertising Research Foundation 10th Annual Conference, October 6, 1964).
4. Russell I. Haley, "Experimental Research on Attitudes toward Shampoos," an unpublished paper (February, 1961).
5. Ronald E. Frank and Paul E. Green, "Numerical Taxonomy in Marketing Analysis: A Review Article," *Journal of Marketing Research*, Vol. V (February, 1968), pp. 83–98.

Positioning Cuts through Chaos in Marketplace

Jack Trout and Al Ries

As far as advertising is concerned, the good old days are gone forever.

As the president of a large consumer products company said recently, "Count on your fingers the number of successful new national brands introduced in the last two years. You won't get to your pinky."

Not that a lot of companies haven't tried. Every supermarket is filled with shelf after shelf of "half successful" brands. The manufacturers of these me-too products cling to the hope that they can develop a brilliant advertising campaign which will lift their off-spring into the winner's circle.

Meanwhile, they hang in there with coupons, deals, point of purchase displays. But profits are hard to come by and that "brilliant" advertising campaign, even if it comes, doesn't ever seem to turn the brand around.

No wonder management people turn skeptical when the subject of advertising comes up. And instead of looking for new ways to put the power of advertising to work, management invents schemes for reducing the cost of what they are currently doing. Witness the rise of the house agency, the media buying service, the barter deal.

ADS DON'T WORK LIKE THEY USED TO

The chaos in the marketplace is a reflection of the fact that advertising just doesn't work like it used to. But old traditional ways of doing things die hard. "There's no reason that advertising can't do the job" say the defenders of the status quo, "as long as the product is good, the plan is sound and the commercials are creative."

But they overlook one big, loud reason. The marketplace itself. The noise level today is far too high. Not only the volume of advertising, but also the volume of products and brands.

To cope with this assault on his or her mind, the average consumer has run out of brain power and mental ability. And with a rising standard of living the average consumer is less and less interested in making the "best" choice. For many of today's more afflu-ent customers, a "satisfactory" brand is good enough.

Advertising prepared in the old, tradi-tional ways has no hope of being successful in today's chaotic marketplace.

In the past, advertising was prepared in isolation. That is, you studied the product and its features and then you prepared advertis-ing which communicated to your customers and prospects the benefits of those features.

It didn't make much difference whether the competition offers those features or not. In the traditional approach, you ig-nored competition and made every claim seem like a preemptive claim. Mentioning a competitive product, for example, was con-sidered not only bad taste, but poor strategy as well.

In the positioning era, however, the rules are reversed. To establish a position, you must often not only name competitive names, but also ignore most of the old advertising rules as well.

In category after category, the prospect already knows the benefits of using the prod-uct. To climb on his product ladder, you must relate your brand to the brands already there.

AVIS TOOK 'AGAINST' POSITION

In today's marketplace, the competitor's im-age is just as important as your own. Some-times more important. An early success in the positioning era was the famous Avis cam-paign.

The Avis campaign will go down in marketing history as a classic example of es-tablishing the "against" position. In the case of Avis, this was a position against the leader.

"Avis is only Number 2 in rent-a-cars, so why go with us? We try harder."

For 13 straight years, Avis lost money. Then they admitted they were No. 2 and have

made money every year since. Avis was able to make substantial gains because they recog-nized the position of Hertz and didn't try to attack them head-on.

VW MADE "UGLY" POSITION WORK

A company can sometimes be successful by accepting a position that no one else wants. For example, virtually all automobile manu-facturers want the public to think they make cars that are good looking. As a result, Volks-wagen was able to establish a unique position for themselves. By default.

The strength of this position, of course, is that it communicates the idea of reliability in a powerful way. "The 1970 VW will stay ugly longer" was a powerful statement be-cause it is psychologically sound. When an advertiser admits a negative, the reader is in-clined to give them the position.

A similar principle is involved in Smucker's jams and jellies. "With a name like Smucker's," says the advertising, "you know it's got to be good."

BATTLE OF THE COLAS

The advantage of owning a position can be seen most clearly in the soft drink field. Three major cola brands compete in what is really not a contest. For every ten bottles of Coke, only four bottles of Pepsi and one bottle of Royal Crown are consumed.

While there may be room in the market for a No. 2 cola, the position of Royal Crown is weak. In 1970, for example, Coca-Cola's sales increase over the previous year (168,000,000 cases) was more than Royal Crown's entire volume (156,000,000 cases).

Obviously, Coke has a strong grip on the cola position. And there's not much room left for the other brands. But, strange as it might seem, there might be a spot for a reverse kind of product. One of the most interesting positioning ideas is the one currently being used by Seven-Up. It's the "Un-Cola" and it seems silly until you take a closer look.

"Wet and Wild" was a good campaign in the image era. But the "Un-Cola" is a great program in the positioning era. Sales jumped something like 10 percent the first year the product was positioned against the cola field. And the increases have continued.

The brilliance of this idea can only be appreciated when you comprehend the intense share of mind enjoyed by the cola category. Two out of three soft drinks consumed in the U.S. are cola drinks.

A somewhat similar positioning program is working in the media field. This is the "third newsweekly" concept being used by *Sports Illustrated* to get into the mind of the media buyer.

It obviously is an immensely successful program. But what may not be so obvious, is why it works. The "third newsweekly" certainly doesn't describe *Sports Illustrated*. (As the Un-Cola doesn't describe Seven-Up.)

What it does do, however, is to relate the magazine to a media category that is uppermost in the prospect's mind (as the Un-Cola relates to the soft drink category that is uppermost in the mind).

Both the Seven-Up and the *Sports Illustrated* programs are dramatic reminders that positioning is not something you do with the product. Positioning is something you do with the mind. That is, you position the product in the mind of the prospect.

YOU CAN REPOSITION COMPETITOR

In order to position your own brand, it's sometimes necessary to reposition the competitor.

In the case of Beck's beer, the repositioning is done at the expense of Lowenbrau: "You've tasted the German beer that's the most popular in America. Now taste the German beer that's the most popular in Germany."

This strategy works because the prospect had assumed something about Lowenbrau that wasn't true.

The current program for Raphael aperitif wine also illustrates this point. The ads show a bottle of "made in France" Raphael and a bottle of "made in U.S.A." Dubonnet. "For $1.00 a bottle less," says the headline, "you can enjoy the imported one." The shock, of course, is to find that Dubonnet is a product of the U.S.

PLIGHT OF AIRLINE X

In the positioning era, the name of a company or product is becoming more and more important. The name is the hook that allows the mind to hang the brand on its product ladder. Given a poor name, even the best brand in the world won't be able to hang on.

Take the airline industry. The big four domestic carriers are United, American, TWA and an airline we'll call Airline X.

Like all airlines, Airline X has had its ups and downs. Unfortunately, there have been more downs than ups. But unlike some of its more complacent competitors, Airline X has tried. A number of years ago, it brought in big league marketing people and pushed in the throttle.

Airline X was among the first to "paint the planes," "improve the food" and "dress up the stewardesses" in an effort to improve its reputation.

And Airline X hasn't been bashful when it comes to spending money. Year after year, it has one of the biggest advertising budgets in the industry. Even though it advertises itself as "the second largest passenger carrier of all the airlines in the free world," you may not have guessed that Airline X is Eastern. Right up there spending with the worldwide names.

For all that money, what do you think of Eastern? Where do you think they fly? Up and down the East Coast, to Boston, Washington, Miami, right? Well, Eastern also goes to St. Louis, New Orleans, Atlanta, San Francisco, Acapulco. But Eastern has a regional name and their competitors have broader names which tell the prospect they fly everywhere.

Look at the problem from just one of Eastern's cities, Indianapolis. From Indianapolis, Eastern flies *north* to Chicago, Milwaukee and Minneapolis. And *south* to Birmingham and Mobile. They just don't happen to fly *east*.

And then there is the lush San Juan run which Eastern has been serving for more than 25 years. Eastern used to get the lion's share of this market. Then early last year American Airlines took over Trans Caribbean. So today, who is number one to the San Juan sun? Why American, of course.

No matter how hard you try, you can't hang "The Wings of Man" on a regional name. When the prospect is given a choice, he or she is going to prefer the national airline, not the regional one.

B. F. GOODRICH HAS IDENTITY CRISIS

What does a company do when its name (Goodrich) is similar to the name of a much larger company in the same field (Goodyear)?

Goodrich has problems. They could reinvent the wheel and Goodyear would get most of the credit.

If you watched the Super Bowl last January, you saw both Goodrich and Goodyear advertise their "American-made radial-ply tires." But which company do you think got their money's worth at $200,000 a pop?

We haven't seen the research, but our bet would be on Goodyear, the company that owns the tire position.

BEWARE OF THE CO-NAME TRAP

But even bad names like Eastern and Goodrich are better than no name at all.

In *Fortune's* list of 500 largest industrials, there are now 16 corporate nonentities. That is, 16 major American companies have legally changed their names to meaningless initials.

How many of these companies can you recognize: ACF, AMF, AMP, ATO, CPC, ESB, FMC, GAF, NVF, NL, PPG, RCA, SCM, TRW, USM and VF?

These are not tiny companies either. The smallest of them, AMP, has more than 10,000 employees and sales of over $225,000,000 a year.

What companies like ACF, AMF, AMP and the others fail to realize is that their initials have to stand for something. A prospect must know your name first before he or she can remember your initials.

GE stands for General Electric. IBM stands for International Business Machines. And everyone knows it. But how many people knew that ACF stood for American Car & Foundry?

Furthermore, now that ACF has legally changed its name to initials, there's presumably no way to even expose the prospect to the original name.

An exception seems to be RCA. After all, everyone knows that RCA stands for, or rather used to stand for, Radio Corp. of America.

That may be true today. But what about tomorrow? What will people think 20 years from now when they see those strange initials. Roman Catholic Archdiocese?

And take Corn Products Co. Presumably it changed its name to CPC International because it makes products out of lots of things besides corn, but you can't remember "CPC" without bringing Corn Products Co. to mind. The tragedy is CPC made the change to "escape" the past. Yet the exact opposite occurred.

LINE EXTENSION CAN BE TRAP, TOO

Names are tricky. Consider the Protein 21/29 shampoo, hair spray, conditioner, concentrate mess.

Back in 1970, the Mennen Co. introduced a combination shampoo conditioner called "Protein 21." By moving rapidly with a $6,000,000 introductory campaign (followed by a $9,000,000 program the next year), Mennen rapidly carved out a 13 percent share of the $3,000,000 shampoo market.

Then Mennen hit the line extension lure. In rapid succession, the company introduced Protein 21 hair spray, Protein 29 hair spray (for men), Protein 21 conditioner (in two formulas), Protein 21 concentrate. To add to the confusion, the original Protein 21 was available in three different formulas (for dry, oily and regular hair).

Can you imagine how confused the prospect must be trying to figure out what to put on his or her head? No wonder Protein 21's share of the shampoo market has fallen from 13 percent to 11 percent. And the decline is bound to continue.

FREE RIDE CAN BE COSTLY

Another similar marketing pitfall recently befell, of all companies, Miles Laboratories.

You can see how it happens. A bunch of the boys are sitting around a conference table trying to name a new cold remedy.

"I have it," says Harry. "Let's call it Alka-Seltzer Plus. That way we can take advantage of the $20,000,000 we're already spending to promote the Alka-Seltzer name."

"Good thinking, Harry," and another money-saving idea is instantly accepted.

But lo and behold, instead of eating into the Dristan and Contac market, the new product turns around and eats into the Alka-Seltzer market.

And you know Miles must be worried. In every TV commercial, the "Alka-Seltzer" gets smaller and smaller and the "Plus" gets bigger and bigger.

Related to the free-ride trap, but not exactly the same, is another common error of judgment called the "well known name" trap.

Both General Electric and RCA thought they could take their strong positions against IBM in computers. But just because a company is well known in one field doesn't mean it can transfer that recognition to another.

In other words, your brand can be on top of one ladder and nowhere on another. And the further apart the products are conceptually, the greater the difficulty of making the jump.

In the past when there were fewer companies and fewer products, a well-known name was a much greater asset than it is today. Because of the noise level, a "well-known company" has tremendous difficulty trying to establish a position in a different field than the one in which it built its reputation.

YOU CAN'T APPEAL TO EVERYONE

A human emotion called "greed" often leads an advertiser into another error. American Motors' introduction of the Hornet is one of the best examples of the "everybody" trap.

You might remember the ads, "The little rich car. American Motors Hornet: $1,994 to $3,589."

A product that tries to appeal to everyone winds up appealing to no one. People who want to spend $3,500 for a car don't buy the Hornet because they don't want their friends to think they're driving a $1,900 car. People who want to spend $1,900 for a car don't buy the Hornet because they don't want a car with $1,600 worth of accessories taken off of it.

AVOID THE F.W.M.T.S. TRAP

If the current Avis advertising is any indication, the company has "forgotten what made them successful."

The original campaign not only related No. 2 Avis to No. 1 Hertz, but also exploited the love that people have for the underdog. The new campaign (Avis is going to be No. 1) not only is conventional "brag and boast" advertising, but also dares the prospect to make the prediction not come true.

Our prediction: Avis ain't going to be No. 1. Further prediction: Avis will lose ground to Hertz and National.

Another company that seems to have fallen into the forgotten what made them successful trap is Volkswagen.

"Think small" was perhaps the most famous advertisement of the sixties. Yet last year VW ran an ad that said, "Volkswagen introduces a new kind of Volkswagen. Big."

O.K., Volkswagen, should we think small or should we think big?

Confusion is the enemy of successful positioning. Prediction: Rapid erosion of the Beetle's position in the U.S. market.

The world seems to be turning faster.

Years ago, a successful product might live 50 years or more before fading away. Today, a product's life cycle is much shorter. Sometimes it can be measured in months instead of years.

New products, new services, new markets, even new media are constantly being born. They grow up into adulthood and then slide into oblivion. And a new cycle starts again.

Yesterday, beer and hard liquor were campus favorites. Today it's wine.

Yesterday, the well-groomed man had his hair cut every week. Today, it's every month or two.

Yesterday, the way to reach the masses was the mass magazines. Today, it's network TV. Tomorrow, it could be cable.

The only permanent thing in life today is change. And the successful companies of tomorrow will be those companies that have learned to cope with it.

The acceleration of "change" creates enormous pressures on companies to think in terms of tactics rather than strategy. As one respected advertising man commented, "The day seems to be past when long-range strategy can be a winning technique."

But is change the way to keep pace with change? The exact opposite appears to be true.

The landscape is littered with the debris of projects that companies rushed into in attempting to "keep pace." Singer trying to move into the boom in home appliances. RCA moving into the boom of computers. General Foods moving into the boom in fast-food outlets. Not to mention the hundreds of companies that threw away their corporate identities to chase the passing fad to initials.

While the programs of those who kept at what they did best and held their ground have been immensely successful. Maytag selling their reliable appliances. Walt Disney selling his world of fantasy and fun. Avon calling.

And take margarine. Thirty years ago the first successful margarine brands positioned themselves against butter. "Tastes like the high-priced spread," said a typical ad.

And what works today? Why the same strategy. "It isn't nice to fool Mother Nature," says the Chiffon commercial, and sales go up

25 percent. Chiffon is once again the best selling brand of soft margarine.

LONG-RANGE THINKING IMPORTANT

Change is a wave on the ocean of time. Short-term, the waves cause agitation and confusion, but long-term the underlying currents are much more significant.

To cope with change, it's important to take a long-range point of view. To determine your basic business. Positioning is a concept that is cumulative. Something that takes advantage of advertising's long-range nature.

In the seventies a company must think even more strategically than it did before. Changing the direction of a large company is like trying to turn an aircraft carrier. It takes a mile before anything happens. And if it was a wrong turn, getting back on course takes even longer.

To play the game successfully, you must make decisions on what your company will be doing not next month or next year, but in five years, ten years. In other words, instead of turning the wheel to meet each fresh wave, a company must point itself in the right direction.

You must have vision. There's no sense building a position based on a technology that's too narrow. Or a product that's becoming obsolete. Remember the famous *Harvard Business Review* article entitled "Marketing Myopia?" It still applies.

If a company has positioned itself in the right direction, it will be able to ride the currents of change, ready to take advantage of those opportunities that are right for it. But when an opportunity arrives, a company must be ready to move quickly.

Because of the enormous advantages that accrue to being the leader, most companies are not interested in learning how to *compete* with the leader. They want to be the leader. They want to be Hertz rather than Avis. *Time* rather than *Newsweek*. General Electric rather than Westinghouse.

Historically, however, product leadership is usually the result of an accident, rather than a preconceived plan.

The xerography process, for example, was offered to 32 different companies (including IBM and Kodak) before it wound up at the old Haloid Co. Renamed Haloid Xerox and then finally Xerox, the company has since dominated the copier market. Xerox now owns the copier position.

Were IBM and Kodak stupid to turn down xerography? Of course not. These companies reject thousands of ideas every year.

Perhaps a better description of the situation at the time was that Haloid, a small manufacturer of photographic supplies, was desperate, and the others weren't. As a result, it took a chance that more prudent companies couldn't be expected to take.

When you trace the history of how leadership positions were established, from Hershey in chocolate to Hertz in rent-a-cars, the common thread is not marketing skill or even product innovation. The common thread is seizing the initiative before the competitor has a chance to get established. In someone's oldtime military terms, the marketing leader "got there firstest with the mostest." The leader usually poured in the marketing money while the situation was still fluid.

IBM, for example, didn't invent the computer. Sperry Rand did. But IBM owns the computer position because they built their computer fortress before competition arrived.

And the position that Hershey established in chocolate was so strong they didn't need to advertise at all, a luxury that competitors like Nestle couldn't afford.

You can see that establishing a leadership position depends not only on luck and timing, but also upon a willingness to "pour it on" when others stand back and wait.

Yet all too often, the product leader makes the fatal mistake of attributing its success to marketing skill. As a result, it thinks it can transfer that skill to other products and other marketing situations.

Witness, for example, the sorry record of Xerox in computers. In May of 1969, Xerox exchanged nearly 10,000,000 shares of stock (worth nearly a billion dollars) for Scientific Data Systems Inc. Since the acquisition, the company (renamed Xerox Data Systems) has lost millions of dollars, and without Xerox's support would have probably gone bankrupt.

And the mecca of marketing knowledge, International Business Machines Corp., hasn't done much better. So far, the IBM plain-paper copier hasn't made much of a dent in Xerox's business. Touché.

The rules of positioning hold for all types of products. In the packaged goods area, for example, Bristol-Meyers tried to take on Crest toothpaste with Fact (killed after $5,000,000 was spent on promotion). Then they tried to go after Alka-Seltzer with Resolve (killed after $11,000,000 was spent). And according to a headline in the February 7 [1972] issue of *Advertising Age*, "Bristol-Meyers will test Dissolve aspirin in an attempt to unseat Bayer."

The suicidal bent of companies that go head-on against established competition is hard to understand. They know the score, yet they forge ahead anyway. In the marketing war, a "charge of the light brigade" happens every day. With the same predictable result.

ONE STRATEGY FOR LEADER

Successful marketing strategy usually consists of keeping your eyes open to possibilities and then striking before the product leader is firmly fixed.

As a matter of fact, the marketing leader is usually the one who moves the ladder into the mind with his or her brand nailed to the one and only rung. Once there, what can a company do to keep its top-dog position?

There are two basic strategies that should be used hand in hand. They seem contradictory, but aren't. One is to ignore competition, and the other is to cover all bets.

As long as a company owns the position, there's no point in running ads that scream "We're No. 1." Much better is to enhance the product category in the prospect's mind. Notice the current IBM campaign that ignores competition and sells the value of computers. All computers, not just the company's types.

Although the leader's advertising should ignore the competition, the leader shouldn't. The second rule is to cover all bets.

This means a leader should swallow his or her pride and adopt every new product development as soon as it shows signs of promise. Too often, however, the leader pooh-poohs the development, and doesn't wake up until it's too late.

ANOTHER STRATEGY FOR NON-LEADERS

Most companies are in the No. 2, 3, 4 or even worse category. What then?

Hope springs eternal in the human breast. Nine times out of ten, the also-ran sets out to attack the leader, à la RCA's assault on IBM. Result: Disaster.

Simply stated, the first rule of positioning is this: You can't compete head-on against a company that has a strong, established position. You can go around, under or over, but never head-to-head.

The leader owns the high ground. The No. 1 position in the prospect's mind. The top rung of the product leader.

The classic example of No. 2 strategy is Avis. But many marketing people misread the

Avis story. They assume the company was successful because it tried harder.

Not at all. Avis was successful because it related itself to the position of Hertz. Avis preempted the No. 2 position. (If trying harder were the secret of success, Harold Stassen would be president.)

Most marketplaces have room for a strong No. 2 company provided they position themselves clearly as an alternative to the leader. In the computer field, for example, Honeywell has used this strategy successfully.

"The other computer company vs. Mr. Big," says a typical Honeywell ad. Honeywell is doing what none of the other computer companies seems to be willing to do. Admit that IBM is, in fact, the leader in the computer business. Maybe that's why Honeywell and Mr. Big are the only large companies reported to be making money on computers.

SOME 'STRONG' POSITIONS AREN'T

Yet there are positions that can be taken. These are positions that look strong, but in reality are weak.

Take the position of Scott in paper products. Scott has about 40 percent of the $1.2 billion market for towels, napkins, toilet tissues and other consumer paper products. But Scott, like Mennen with Protein 21, fell into the line-extension trap.

ScotTowels, ScotTissue, Scotties, Scottkins, even BabyScott. All of these items undermined the Scott foundation. The more products hung on the Scott name, the less meaning the name had to the average consumer.

When Procter & Gamble attacked with Mr. Whipple and his tissue-squeezers, it was no contest. Charmin is now the No. 1 brand in the toilet-tissue market.

In Scott's case, a large "share of market" didn't mean they owned the position. More important is a large "share of mind."

The housewife could write "Charmin, Kleenex, Bounty and Pampers" on her shopping list and know exactly what products she was going to get. "Scott" on a shopping list has no meaning. The actual brand names aren't much help either. Which brand, for example, is engineered for the nose, Scotties or ScotTissue?

In positioning terms, the name "Scott" exists in limbo. It isn't firmly ensconced on any product ladder.

ELIMINATE EGOS FROM DECISION MAKING

To repeat, the name is the hook that hangs the brand on the product ladder in the prospect's mind. In the positioning era, the brand name to give a product is probably a company's single, most important marketing decision.

To be successful in the positioning era, advertising and marketing people must be brutally frank. They must try to eliminate all ego from the decision making process. It only clouds the issue.

One of the most critical aspects of "positioning" is being able to evaluate objectively products and how they are viewed by customer and prospects.

As a rule, when it comes to building strong programs, trust no one, especially managers who are all wrapped up in their products. The closer people get to products, the more they defend old decisions or old promises.

Successful companies get their information from the marketplace. That's the place where the program has to succeed, not in the product manager's office.

A company that keeps its eye on Tom, Dick and Harry is going to miss Pierre, Hans and Yoshio.

Marketing is rapidly becoming a worldwide ball game. A company that owns a position in one country now finds that it can use that position to wedge its way into another.

IBM has 62 percent of the German computer market. Is this fact surprising? It shouldn't be. IBM earns more than 50 percent of its profits outside the U.S.

As companies start to operate on a worldwide basis, they often discover they have a name problem.

A typical example is U.S. Rubber, a worldwide company that marketed many products not made of rubber. Changing the name to Uniroyal created a new corporate identity that could be used worldwide.

CREATIVITY TAKES BACK SEAT

In the seventies, creativity will have to take a back seat to strategy.

Advertising Age itself reflects this fact. Today you will find fewer stories about individual campaigns and more stories about what's happening in an entire industry. Creativity alone isn't a worthwhile objective in an era where a company can spend millions of dollars on great advertising and still fail miserably in the marketplace.

Consider what Harry McMahan calls the "Curse of Clio." In the past, the American Festival has made special awards to "Hall of Fame Classics." Of the 41 agencies that won these Clio awards, 31 have lost some or all of these particular accounts.

But the cult of creativity dies hard. One agency president said recently, "Oh, we do positioning all the time. But after we develop the position, we turn it over to the creative department." And too often, of course, the creativity does nothing but obscure the positioning.

In the positioning era, the key to success is to run the naked positioning statement unadorned by so-called creativity.

ASK YOURSELF THESE QUESTIONS

If these examples have moved you to want to apply positioning thinking to your own company's situation, here are some questions to ask yourself:

1. *What position, if any, do we already own in the prospect's mind?*

   Get the answer to this question from the marketplace, not the marketing manager. If this requires a few dollars for research, so be it. Spend the money. It's better to know exactly what you're up against now than to discover it later when nothing can be done about it.

2. *What position do we want to own?*

   Here is where you bring out your crystal ball and try to figure out the best position to own from a long-term point of view.

3. *What companies must be outgunned if we are to establish that position?*

   If your proposed position calls for a head-to-head approach against a marketing leader, forget it. It's better to go around an obstacle rather than over it. Back up. Try to select a position that no one else has a firm grip on.

4. *Do we have enough marketing money to occupy and hold the position?*

   A big obstacle to successful positioning is attempting to achieve the impossible. It takes money to build a share of mind. It takes money to establish a position. It takes money to hold a position once you've established it.

   The noise level today is fierce. There are just too many "me-too" products and too many "me-too" companies vying for the mind of the prospect. Getting noticed is getting tougher.

5. *Do we have the guts to stick with one consistent positioning concept?*

With the noise level out there, a company has to be bold enough and consistent enough to cut through.

The first step in a positioning program normally entails running fewer programs, but stronger ones. This sounds simple, but actually runs counter to what usually happens as corporations get larger. They normally run more programs, but weaker ones. It's this fragmentation that can make many large advertising budgets just about invisible in today's media storm.

6. *Does our creative approach match our positioning strategy?*

Creative people often resist positioning thinking because they believe it restricts their creativity. And it does. But creativity isn't the objective in the seventies. Even "communications" itself isn't the objective.

The name of the marketing game in the seventies is "positioning." And only the better players survive.

RETROSPECTIVE COMMENTARY

THE POSITIONING ERA:
A VIEW TEN YEARS LATER

If one word could be said to have marked the course of advertising in the decade of the '70s it is the word "positioning." Positioning has become the buzzword of advertising and marketing people, not only in this country, but around the world.

It was just 10 years ago that the word and the concept were introduced for the first time to the advertising community in the pages of *Industrial Marketing* and *Advertising Age.*

The article, written by Jack Trout, named names and made predictions, all based on the "rules" of a game Jack called positioning.

On positioning's 10th anniversary, it might be interesting to look back at that 1969 article and see what changes have taken place.

> Today's marketplace is no longer responsive to strategies that worked in the past. There are just too many products, too many companies and too much marketing noise. We have become an overcommunicated society. (1969)

The question most frequently asked us is "why"? Why do we need a new approach to advertising and marketing?

The answer today is the same as it was then. We have become an overcommunicated society. With only 5% of the world's population, America consumes 57% of the world's advertising output. The per capita consumption of advertising in the U.S. today is about $200 a year.

If you spend $1,000,000 a year on advertising, you are bombarding the average consumer with less than 1/2¢ of advertising, spread out over 365 days—a consumer who is already exposed to $200 worth of advertising from other companies.

In our overcommunicated society, to talk about the "impact" of advertising is to seriously overstate the potential effectiveness of your messages. It's an egocentric view that bears no relationship to the realities of the marketplace itself.

In the communication jungle out there, the hope to score big is to be selective, to concentrate on narrow targets, to practice segmentation. In a word, "positioning" is still the name of the game today.

> The mind, as a defense against the volume of today's communications, screens and rejects much of the information offered it. In general, the mind accepts only that which matches prior knowledge or experience. (1969)

Millions of dollars have been wasted trying to change minds with advertising. Once a mind is made up, it's almost impossible to change it. Certainly not with a weak force like advertising.

The average person can tolerate being told something about which he or she knows nothing. (This is why "news" is an effective advertising approach.) But the average person can't tolerate being told he or she is "wrong." Mind changing is the road to advertising disaster.

Back in 1969, Jack used the computer industry as an example of the folly of trying to change minds.

Company after company tried to tell people its computers were "better" than IBM's. Yet that doesn't "compute" in the prospect's mind. "If you're so smart," says the prospect, "how come you're not rich like IBM?"

The computer "position" in the minds of most people is filled with the name of a company called "IBM." For a competitive company manufacturer to obtain a favorable position in the prospect's mind, he or she must somehow relate the company to IBM's position.

In other words, don't try to change the prospect's mind at all. Accept what's up there and work around it. It's the only hope in today's overcommunicated society.

> Positioning is a game where the competitor's image is just as important as your own. Sometimes more important. (1969)

The classic example is the famous Avis campaign.

"Avis is only No. 2 in rent-a-cars. So why go with us? We try harder." This program was extremely successful for Avis until corporate egos got in the way. Then the company launched a campaign which said "Avis is going to be No. 1."

No way.

Be honest. In the last 15 years, Avis has run many different advertising campaigns. "The wizard of Avis." "You don't have to run through airports." Etc. But what is the single theme that leaps into your mind when someone mentions Avis?

Of course, "Avis is only No. 2., etc." Yet Avis in the last few years has consistently ignored this No. 2 concept.

We call this the "F.W.M.T.S." trap. (Forgot What Made Them Successful.)

If you want to be successful today, you can't ignore the competitor's position. Nor can you walk away from your own. In the immortal words of Woody Allen, "Play it where it lies."

Another advertiser that fell into the F.W.M.T.S. trap is Seven-Up. With the "Uncola" campaign, the company successfully positioned its 7UP drink as an alternative to Coke and Pepsi. (Almost two-thirds of all the soft drinks consumed in the U.S. are cola drinks.)

But the current campaign says, "America is turning 7UP." American is doing no such thing, Seven-Up is advertising its aspirations. No different conceptually than the "Avis is going to be No. 1" campaign. And no more effective.

> In the positioning era, the name of your company or product is becoming more and more important. (1969)

No aspect of positioning has proved as controversial as the "importance of the name."

Our 1969 example was Eastern Airlines. Among the four largest domestic airlines, Eastern consistently ranks at the bottom on passenger surveys.

Why? Eastern has a "regional" name that puts them in a different category than the big nationwide carriers (American, United, Trans World Airlines). The name Eastern puts the airline in the same category with Southern, North Central, Piedmont, Allegheny. The regional airline category.

After 10 years of effort, Eastern still ranks at the bottom of the big four.

You see what you expect to see. The passenger who has a bad experience on American or United says, "It just was one of those things." An exception to the good service he or she was expecting.

The passenger who has a bad experience on Eastern says, "It's that darn Eastern Airlines again." A continuation of the bad service he or she was expecting.

One prime objective of all advertising is to heighten expectations. To create the illusion that the product or service will perform the miracles you expect. And presto, it does.

Recently, Allegheny Airlines has seen the light. The new name: USAir. Now watch them take off.

Yes, but that's consumer advertising and the industrial customer buys on reason, not emotion. On logic and facts.

As IBM's competitors. Or Xerox's or General Electric's.

Especially for high technology, high visibility products like computers and copiers, the average industrial customer tends to be far more economical than your average Charmin-squeezing housewife. (Who, more often than not, is downright practical.)

Industrial customers are also cursed by a "play it safe" attitude.

You can't blame them. No housewife ever got fired for buying the wrong brand of coffee. But plenty of industrial buyers have been in deep trouble over a high-technology buy that went sour. (Babcock & Wilcox will have trouble pushing its nuclear power plants in the future no matter how "superior" its specs are.)

The trend in industrial products is toward more sophistication, more use of integrated circuits, fiber optics, lasers, etc. So you can expect the industrial buyer to buy more on feelings, hunches and especially reputation. And less on objective production comparisons.

Which is why "factual expository copy" is getting less important in industrial advertising and "positioning" more important.

> Your program has to go beyond just establishing a name. Too many programs start there and end there. To secure a worthwhile position for a corporate name, you need a thought to go with it. (1969)

Ten years ago, the Olin campaign was getting a lot of creative kudos. And the ads were beautifully done. But what is Olin? What is its position?

Even today, these questions have no clear-cut answer in the mind of the prospect.

Line Extension Trap

You can't hang a company on a name. You need an idea. Of all the positioning concepts suggested by the 1969 article, this one has proved to be the most useful. It led directly to what we call "the line extension trap."

When the marketing history of the '70s is written, the single most significant trend will have to be "line extension." Line extension has swept through the marketing community like Sherman through Georgia. And for some very sound reasons.

Logic is on the side of line extension. Arguments of economists. Trade acceptance. Customer acceptance. Lower advertising costs. Increased income. Reduced costs. The corporate image.

As we said, logic is on the side of line extension. Truth, unfortunately, is not. The paradox of marketing is that conventional wisdom is almost always wrong.

Xerox went out and bought a computer company with a perfectly good name. Scientific Data Systems.

And what was the first thing they did? They changed the name to Xerox Data Systems. Then they ran an ad that said. "This Xerox machine can't make a copy."

Any Xerox machine that couldn't make a copy was headed for trouble, believe us.

When Xerox folded their computer operations, it cost another $84,000,000 to sweep up the mess.

Singer went out and did the same thing with the old, respected Friden name. One of their introductory ads said, "Singer Business Machines introduces Touch & Know."

Get it? Touch and know, touch and sew.

This is the ultimate positioning mistake. To try to transfer a generic brand name to a different product sold to a different market. And then, to top it all off, to knock off your own sewing machine slogan.

Touch and Go would have been more appropriate. When they folded this operation, Singer set a record. They recorded one of the largest one quarter write-offs ever reported by any company anywhere in the world—$341,000,000.

If your corporate name is inappropriate for the new product you intend to market, create a new one. And a new position.

> One thing that's worse than a 'just a name' program is one without a name. That sounds like it could never happen, doesn't it? Well, it does when companies use initials instead of a name. (1969)

This idea was later developed into what we call "The no-name trap." Of all the positioning concepts outlined back in 1969, this one generated the most instant acceptance. The superiority of a name over a meaningless set of initials could generally be documented by market research.

The initialitus that struck American business in the late '60s and early '70s abated. Some companies even went back to their original names.

> A company has no hope to make progress head-on against the position that IBM has established. (1969)

This is perhaps the most quoted sentence from the original article—so true today as it was then.

IBM has an overwhelming position in the broad middle range of computers. So, how do you compete against IBM in computers? The 1969 article had a suggestion on how to do it.

> It's almost impossible to dislodge a strongly dug-in leader who owns the high ground. You're a lot better off to open up a new front or position—that is, unless you enjoy being shot-up. (1969)

A New Front

The big computer successes in the '70s were the companies that avoided going head-to-head with IBM—Digital Equipment Corp. and Data General, in particular, at the low end of the market.

Even Apple and Radio Shack have done profitable computer business, in the home market.

This "new front" idea has been developed in our marketing warfare seminars into a concept called "flanking warfare." You avoid the competitor's high-ground by out-flanking them.

> Another problem that occurs fairly often is represented by the one B. F. Goodrich faces. What do you do when your name (Goodrich) is similar to the name of a larger company in the same field [Goodyear]? (1969)
>
> Goodrich has problems. Our research indicates that they could reinvent the wheel and Goodyear would get the most of the credit. If ever a company could benefit from a name change, they're one. (1969)

In 1968, Goodyear had sales of $2,926,000,000 while B. F. Goodrich's sales were $1,340,000,000. A ratio of 2.2 to 1.

Ten years later, in 1978, Goodyear had sales of $7,489,000,000 while B. F. Goodrich had sales of $2,594,000,000. A ratio of 2.9 to 1.

So the rich get richer. Fair enough.

But what is odd is that the loser's advertising continues to get all the publicity. "We're the other guys" got a lot of favorable attention in the press. But not a lot of favorable attention from the tire-buying public.

The Real Reckoning

But what really rattled the cages of the Madison Ave. mavens was positioning's implied attack on "creativity."

Even though creativity was not mentioned in the 1969 article, we didn't hesitate to attack it later on. By 1972, we were saying, "Creativity is dead. The name of the advertising game in the '70s is positioning."

In truth, the decade of the '70s might well be characterized as a "return to reality." White knights and black eyepatches gave way to such positioning concepts as Lite Beer's "Everything you've always wanted in a great beer. And less."

Poetic? Yes. Artful? Yes. But also a straightforward, clearly defined explanation of the basic positioning premise.

On the occasion of positioning's 10th anniversary, it might be appropriate to ask, where do we go from here?

If creativity belonged to the '60s and positioning to the '70s, where will we be in the '80s?

Would you believe us if we told you in the next decade we will be burying the marketing concept?

Probably not, but we'll tell you anyway.

For at least 50 years now, astute advertising people have preached the marketing gospel. "The customer is king," said the marketing moguls. Over and over again, they used their wondrous presentations to warn top management that to be "production" oriented instead of "customer" oriented was to flirt with disaster.

But it's beginning to look like "King Customer" is dead. And that they're selling a corpse to their management.

Plenty of companies who have dutifully followed their marketing experts have seen millions of dollars disappear in valiant but disastrous customer-oriented efforts.

Who do you suppose masterminded those classic positioning mistakes? Not amateurs, but full-fledged marketing professionals with briefcases full of credentials.

General Electric in computers. Singer in business machines. Sara Lee in frozen dinners.

Of course, these marketing executives had excuses. "Product problems." "Not enough capital." Or the ever popular, "Not enough distribution" were often cited to explain these failures.

Can it be that marketing, itself, is the problem?

Many managers are beginning to realize that something is wrong—that the traditional definition of marketing (to be customer-oriented) is becoming an obsolete concept.

A New Perspective

To get a better perspective of the situation, you have to go back to the '20s, when industry started its dramatic march forward. It was then that business first became production oriented. This was the heyday of Henry Ford and his Model T.

You could have any color you wanted as long as it was black. Mr. Ford was more interested in keeping his production lines rolling (and his prices down) than in keeping his customers satisfied.

You might think that advertising was an unnecessary luxury in a production-oriented economy. Quite the contrary.

Advertising was an important ingredient in the scheme of things. Advertising's first commandment was "Mass advertising creates mass demand which makes mass production possible."

Neat. Except that General Motors tooled up its production lines to please its prospects rather than its production engineers and quickly grabbed the sales leadership from Ford.

Things haven't been the same since.

In the aftermath of World War II, business became customer-oriented with a vengeance.

The marketing man was in charge, no doubt about it, and his prime minister was marketing research.

But today, every company has become marketing oriented. Knowing what the customer wants isn't too helpful if a dozen other companies are already serving his or her wants.

American Motors' problem is not the customer. American Motors' problem is General Motors, Ford and Chrysler.

To be successful today, a company must be "competitor" oriented. It must look for weak points in the positions of its competitors and then launch marketing attacks against those weak points. For example, while others were losing millions in the computer business, DEC was making millions by exploiting IBM's weakness in small computers.

Similarly, Savin established a successful beachhead in small, inexpensive copiers. A weak point in the Xerox lineup.

And from out of nowhere came a product called Bubble Yum to take a big bite out of the bubble gum market. By exploiting the competitions' weakness of being hard to chew, they over-ran some strongly entrenched brands that had been around for years.

There are those who would say that competitors are always considered in a well-thought-out marketing plan. Indeed they are. Usually towards the back of the book under a heading entitled "Competitive Evaluation." Almost as an afterthought.

Upfront with prominence is the major part of the plan. The details of marketplace, the various demographic segments and a myriad of "customer" research statistics carefully gleaned from endless focus groups, test panels, concept and market tests.

The Battle Plan

The future marketing plan won't look like this. In fact, it won't be called a marketing plan at all. But a competitive plan, or a battle plan.

In the battle plan of the future, many more pages will be dedicated to the competition. The plan will carefully dissect each participant in the marketplace. It will develop a list of competitive strengths and weaknesses as well as a plan of action to either exploit or defend against them.

There might even come a day when this plan will contain a dossier on each of the competitors' key management people which will include their favorite tactics and style of operation. (Not unlike those Germans kept on the Allied commanders in World War II.)

And we're not talking about the distant future. Already the first signs of this trend are starting to appear in the professional journals.

In the August, 1978, issue of *Management Review,* is a report entitled, "Customer or competitor: Which guideline for marketing?" In the article, Alfred R. Oxenfeldt and William L. Moore spell out six "weaknesses" that can make a firm vulnerable to an attack from a competitor. The article's basic premise was that switching to a competitor orientation can provide a better payoff.

In the August, 1978, issue of *Business Horizons,* William S. Sachs and George Benson state the issue more directly: "Is it time to discard the marketing concept?"

These articles point out that a small, but growing, number of experts believe that the customer isn't what he or she used to be.

Confusion has set in. In many categories, customers no longer perceive any large differences in products. Thus brand choice will not be based on a rational search of all brands in the category but on a brand that was previously tried. Or the leader. Or the one positioned to the prospect's segment.

Once buying patterns are established, it has become more and more difficult to change them. The customer doesn't really want to accept any more information on a category that he or she has already cataloged in the mind. No matter how dramatically or how creatively this information is presented.

What does all this portend for the marketing people of the '80s? Or whatever they are going to be called.

In simple terms, it means that they have to be prepared to wage marketing warfare. Successful marketing campaigns will have to be planned like military campaigns.

Strategic planning will become more and more important. Companies will have to learn how to attack, defend and flank their competition. And when to resort to guerrilla warfare.

They will need better intelligence on how to anticipate competitive moves.

On the personal level, successful marketing people will have to exhibit many of the same virtues that make a great general—courage, boldness, loyalty and perseverance.

The winners in the marketing battles of the future will be those men and women who have best learned the lessons of military history—the marketing people who have learned to plan like Alexander the Great, maneuver like Napoleon Bonaparte and fight like George S. Patton.

They will also be the marketing people who know their competitors better than they know their own customers.

Marketing Strategy

A dominant trend in the marketing discipline during the past twenty years has been an increasing emphasis on strategic issues and perspectives. The articles in Part Three present some of the discipline's most relevant thinking about strategic marketing analysis and planning.

The marketing concept has been the cornerstone for strategic thought in the discipline since the 1950s. Many articles and most textbooks in marketing have advocated adoption of the concept as a fundamental business philosophy. Kohli and Jaworski carefully examine the meaning and relevance of the marketing concept. They use the term *market orientation* to describe the implementation of the marketing concept, and they present an integrating framework to facilitate research and managerial action.

Markets are dynamic and competitive. Organizations must continuously anticipate and respond to change. Abell introduces the notion of "strategic windows" as an organizing framework to manage strategic change in a timely manner. Porter believes that the essence of strategy formulation involves understanding and coping with competitive behaviors. He blends ideas from economics, strategic management, and marketing to create a useful, and often quoted, framework for thinking about competitors and formulating sustainable competitive positions. Montgomery and Weinberg argue that strategic plans are no better than the information on which they are based. They discuss the importance of strategic information systems and describe how to link an intelligence system to the competitive marketplace.

What is your market? Answering this question is fundamental and appears simple; but although it is fundamental, it is not simple. Day, Shocker, and Srivastava suggest that identifying product-market boundaries and dynamics is essential to the basic definition of a business. They describe and evaluate a variety of customer-oriented approaches to accomplish the task. Buzzell, Gale, and Sultan use the empirical PIMS database to demonstrate significant connections among marketing strategies, market share, and profitability. This classic work has been extended, refined, and criticized. Day creates an integrative approach for product planning, describing a variety of analytical methods that can guide strategic thinking and action. He includes discussions of the experience curve, the product life cycle, the Boston Consulting Group's growth-share matrix, and the relevance of market share information and prescriptions.

Marketing takes place in a variety of contexts, each somewhat distinctive. Douglas and Craig argue that issues of global marketing have become more complex. They imply that some early prescriptions, such as Levitt presents in Part One, warrant critical evaluation. They present a model of global marketing evolution and development to guide strategy formulation.

Marketing in nonprofit organizations and government agencies often requires social change. Sheth and Frazier develop a model of strategy mix choices for planned social change and demonstrate its applicability. The model is anchored in behavioral theories and can be used in business as well as by nonprofit organizations. Parasuraman, Zeithaml, and Berry investigate the nature of service quality. They suggest that service quality can be defined and measured as a comparison of expectations to performance, and they introduce their "gaps" model to help understand, measure, and manage service quality.

◆

Market Orientation: The Construct, Research Propositions, and Managerial Implications

Ajay K. Kohli and Bernard J. Jaworski

Though the marketing concept is a cornerstone of the marketing discipline, very little attention has been given to its implementation. The marketing concept is essentially a business *philosophy,* an ideal or a policy statement (cf. Barksdale and Darden 1971; McNamara 1972). The business philosophy can be contrasted with its *implementation* reflected in the activities and behaviors of an organization. In keeping with tradition (e.g., McCarthy and Perreault 1984, p. 36), we use the term "market orientation" to mean the implementation of the marketing concept. Hence, a market-oriented organization is one whose actions are consistent with the marketing concept.

In recent years, there has been a strong resurgence of academic as well as practitioner interest in the marketing concept and its implementation (e.g., Deshpande and Webster 1989; Houston 1986; Olson 1987; Webster 1988). We seek to further that interest by pro-

viding a foundation for the systematic development of a theory of market orientation. Given its widely acknowledged importance, one might expect the concept to have a clear meaning, a rich tradition of theory development, and a related body of empirical findings. On the contrary, a close examination of the literature reveals a lack of clear definition, little careful attention to measurement issues, and virtually no empirically based theory. Further, the literature pays little attention to the contextual factors that may make a market orientation either more or less appropriate for a particular business. The purpose of this article is to delineate the domain of the market orientation construct, provide an operational definition, develop a propositional inventory, and construct a comprehensive framework for directing future research.

We first describe our method. Essentially, we draw on the literature in marketing and related disciplines, and supplement it with findings from field interviews with managers in diverse functions, hierarchical levels, and organizations. Our discovery-oriented approach (cf. Deshpande 1983; Mahrer 1988)

Ajay K. Kohli and Bernard J. Jaworski, "Market Orientation: The Construct, Research Propositions, and Managerial Implications," Vol. 54 (April '90), pp. 1–18. Reprinted from the *Journal of Marketing,* published by the American Marketing Association.

is similar to the qualitative, practitioner-based approach used by Parasuraman, Zeithaml, and Berry (1985) and is designed to tap the "cause and effect" maps of managers (see Zaltman, LeMasters, and Heffring 1982).

We then compare and contrast the alternative conceptualizations in the literature with the view that emerges from the field interviews and provide a synthesis. Next we develop a series of research propositions in the spirit of propositional inventories developed in such diverse areas as sales management (cf. Walker, Churchill, and Ford 1977; Weitz 1981), organization of marketing activities (cf. Ruekert, Walker, and Roering 1985), diffusion of technology (cf. Robertson and Gatignon 1986), information processing (cf. Alba and Hutchinson 1987), and marketing control systems (cf. Jaworski 1988). These literature-based and field-based propositions are synthesized in an integrative framework that provides for a parsimonious conceptualization of the overarching factors of interest. Finally, we conclude with a discussion that alerts managers to important issues involved in modifying business orientations.

METHOD

Literature Review

A review of the literature of the last 35 years reveals relatively little attention to the marketing concept. The limited research primarily comprises (1) descriptive work on the extent to which organizations have adopted the concept (e.g., Barksdale and Darden 1971; Hise 1965; Lusch, Udell, and Laczniak 1976; McNamara 1972), (2) essays extolling the virtues of the business philosophy (e.g., *Business Week* 1950; McKitterick 1957; Viebranz 1967), (3) work on the limits of the concept (e.g., Houston 1986; Levitt 1969; Tauber 1974), and to a lesser extent (4) discussions of factors that

facilitate or hamper the implementation of the marketing concept (e.g., Felton 1959; Lear 1963; Webster 1988). We draw on these limited writings, especially the last category, and also on related literature in the management discipline.

Field Interviews

The field research consisted of in-depth interviews with 62 managers in four U.S. cities. Because the purpose of the study was theory construction (i.e., elicitation of constructs and propositions), it was important to tap a wide range of experiences and perspectives in the course of the data collection. Therefore, a purposive or "theoretical" sampling plan (Glaser and Strauss 1967) was used to ensure that the sample included marketing as well as non-marketing managers in industrial, consumer, and service industries. Care also was taken to sample large as well as small organizations.

Of the 62 individuals interviewed, 33 held marketing positions, 15 held nonmarketing positions, and 14 held senior management positions. A total of 47 organizations were included in the sample; multiple individuals were interviewed in certain organizations. The organizations of 18 interviewees marketed consumer products, those of 26 marketed industrial products, and those of 18 marketed services. In size, the organizations ranged from four employees to several tens of thousands. The sample thus reflects a diverse set of organizations, departments, and positions, and hence is well suited for obtaining a rich set of ideas and insights. In addition to managers, 10 business academicians at two large U.S. universities were interviewed. The purpose of these interviews was to tap insights that might not emerge from the literature review and the field interviews.

A standard format generally was followed for the interview. After a brief description of the research project, each interviewee was asked about four issues along the following lines.

1. What does the term "market/marketing orientation" mean to you? What kinds of things does a market/marketing-oriented company *do*?
2. What organizational factors foster or discourage this orientation?
3. What are the positive consequences of this orientation? What are the negative consequences?
4. Can you think of business situations in which this orientation may not be very important?

These questions provided a structure for each interview, but it was frequently necessary to explain and clarify some of the questions, as well as probe deeper with additional questions to elicit examples, illustrations, and other insights.

The personal interviews typically lasted about 45 minutes and were audiotaped unless the interviewee requested otherwise. The information obtained from these interviews affords novel insights into the meaning, causes, and consequences of a market orientation. Though a large number of new insights emerged from the study, we focus on the more "interesting" ones (see Zaltman, LeMasters, and Heffring 1982) and those with the greatest potential for stimulating future research.

MARKET ORIENTATION: THE CONSTRUCT

Comparing Literature and Field Perspectives

A review of the literature reveals diverse definitions of the marketing concept. Felton (1959, p. 55) defines the marketing concept as "a corporate state of mind that insists on the inte-
gration and coordination of all the marketing functions which, in turn, are melded with all other corporate functions, for the basic purpose of producing maximum long-range corporate profits." In contrast, McNamara (1972, p. 51) takes a broader view and defines the concept as "a philosophy of business management, based upon a companywide acceptance of the need for customer orientation, profit orientation, and recognition of the important role of marketing in communicating the needs of the market to all major corporate departments." Variants of these ideas are offered by Lavidge (1966), Levitt (1969), Konopa and Calabro (1971), Bell and Emory (1971), and Stampfl (1978).

Three core themes or "pillars" underlie these *ad hoc* definitions: (1) customer focus, (2) coordinated marketing, and (3) profitability (cf. Kotler 1988). Barksdale and Darden (1971, p. 36), point out, however, that these idealistic policy statements represented by the marketing concept are of severely limited practical value, and assert that "the major challenge is the development of *operational* definitions of the marketing concept..." (emphasis added). Hence, though the literature sheds some light on the philosophy represented by the marketing concept, it is unclear as to the specific activities that translate the philosophy into practice, thereby engendering a market orientation. Even so, it appears reasonable to conclude from the literature that a market-oriented organization is one in which the three pillars of the marketing concept (customer focus, coordinated marketing, profitability) are operationally manifest.

The view of market orientation that emerges from the field interviews is consistent with the "received view" in the literature, though certain differences are evident. Importantly, the field interviews provide a significantly clearer idea of the construct's domain and enable us to offer a more precise definition. This precision facilitates theory development, construct measurement, and eventually theory testing. In the following discussion, we first compare the field-based view of market orientation with the received view on the three commonly accepted pillars—customer focus, coordinated marketing, and profitability—and then elaborate on the elements of the field-based view of the construct.

Customer Focus   Without exception, the managers interviewed were consistent in the view that a customer focus is the central element of a market orientation. Though they agreed with the traditional view that a customer focus involves obtaining information from customers about their needs and preferences, several executives emphasized that it goes far beyond customer research. The comments suggest that being customer oriented involves taking actions based on market intelligence, not on verbalized customer opinions alone. Market intelligence is a broader concept in that it includes consideration of (1) exogenous market factors (e.g., competition, regulation) that affect customer needs and preferences and (2) current as well as *future* needs of customers. These extensions do not challenge the spirit of the first pillar (customer focus); rather, they reflect practitioners' broader, more strategic concerns related to customers.

Coordinated Marketing   Few interviewees explicitly mentioned coordinated marketing in the course of the discussions, but the majority emphasized that a market orientation is not solely the responsibility of a marketing department. Moreover, the executives interviewed emphasized that it is critical for a variety of departments to be cognizant of customer needs (i.e., aware of market intelligence) and to be responsive to those needs. Thus, the interviewees stressed the importance of concerted action by the various departments of an organization. Importantly, the

field findings limit the domain of the second pillar of market orientation to coordination *related to market intelligence*. This focused view of coordination is important because it facilitates operationalizing the construct by clearly specifying the type of coordination that is relevant.

Profitability   In sharp contrast to the received view, however, the idea that profitability is a component of market orientation is conspicuously absent in the field findings. Without exception, interviewees viewed profitability as a *consequence* of a market orientation rather than a part of it. This finding is consistent with Levitt's (1969, p. 236) strong objection to viewing profitability as a component of a market orientation, which he asserts is "like saying that the goal of human life is eating."

   Thus, the meaning of the market orientation construct that surfaced in the field is essentially a more precise and operational view of the first two pillars of the marketing concept—customer focus and coordination. The findings suggest that a market orientation entails (1) one or more departments engaging in activities geared toward developing and understanding of customers' current and future needs and the factors affecting them, (2) sharing of this understanding across departments, and (3) the various departments engaging in activities designed to meet select customer needs. In other words, a market orientation refers to the organizationwide generation, dissemination, and responsiveness to market intelligence.

   Further, though the term "marketing orientation" has been used in previous writings, the label "market orientation" appears to be preferable for three reasons. First, as Shapiro (1988) suggests, the latter label clarifies that the construct is not exclusively a concern of the marketing function; rather, a variety of departments participate in generating market intelligence, disseminating it, and taking actions in response to it. Hence labeling the construct as "marketing orientation" is both restrictive and misleading. Second, the label "market orientation" is less politically charged in that it does not inflate the importance of the marketing function in an organization. The label removes the construct from the province of the marketing department and makes it the responsibility of all departments in an organization. Consequently, the orientation is more likely to be embraced by nonmarketing departments. Third, the label focuses attention on *markets* (that include customers and forces affecting them), which is consistent with the broader "management of markets" orientation proposed by Park and Zaltman (1987, p. 7) for addressing limitations in currently embraced paradigms. We next discuss in more detail each of the three elements of a market orientation—intelligence generation, dissemination, and responsiveness.

Explicating the Market
Orientation Construct

Intelligence Generation   The starting point of a market orientation is market intelligence. Market intelligence is a broader concept than customers' verbalized needs and preferences in that it includes an analysis of exogenous factors that influence those needs and preferences. For example, several managers indicated that a market orientation includes monitoring factors such as government regulations and competition that influence the needs and preferences of their customers. Several interviewees who cater to organizational customers emphasized that a market orientation includes an analysis of changing conditions in *customers'* industries and their impact on the needs and wants of customers. Likewise, the importance of monitoring competitor actions and how they might affect

customer preferences emerged in the course of the interviews. (Day and Wensley 1983 also point out the limitations of focusing on customers to the exclusion of competitors.) Hence, though market intelligence pertains to customer needs and preferences, it includes an analysis of how they may be affected by exogenous factors such as government regulation, technology, competitors, and other environmental forces. Environmental scanning activities are subsumed under market intelligence generation.

An important idea expressed by several executives is that effective market intelligence pertains not just to current needs, but to future needs as well. This idea echoes Houston's (1986) assertion and reflects a departure from conventional views (e.g., "find a need and fill it") in that it urges organizations to *anticipate* needs of customers and initiate steps to meet them. The notion that market intelligence includes anticipated customer needs is important because it often takes years for an organization to develop a new product offering. As a senior vice president of a large industrial services company observed:

> [When] should [our company] enter the [certain services] area? Is there a market there yet? Probably not. But there's going to be one in 1990, '91, '92, '96. And you don't want to be too late because it's going to take you a couple of years getting up to speed, getting your reputation established. So you've really got to jump into it two years before you think [the market for it is going to develop].

Though assessment of customer needs is the cornerstone of a market orientation, defining customers may not be simple. In some cases, businesses may have consumers (i.e., end users of products and services) as well as clients (i.e., organizations that may dictate or influence the choices or end users). For example, executives of several packaged goods companies indicated that it is critical for their organizations to understand the needs and preferences of not just end customers but also retailers through whom their products are sold. This sentiment reflects the growing power of retailers over manufacturers owing to the consolidation of the former, retailers' access to scanner data, and increased competition among manufacturers due to proliferation of brands. As one executive indicated, keeping retailers satisfied was important to ensure that they carried and promoted his products, which in turn enabled him to cater to the needs of his end customers.

Interestingly, in the 1920s and 1930s, the term "customer" primarily referred to distributors who purchased goods and made payments (McKitterick 1957). Starting about the 1950s, the focus shifted from distributors to end consumers and their needs and wants. Today the appropriate focus appears to be the market, which includes end users and distributors as well as exogenous forces that affect their needs and preferences.

Identifying who an organization's customers are is even more complex when service is provided to one party, but payments are received from another. For example, the director of marketing for a health care organization recalled:

> In the past we asked patients what they wanted for services, how they wanted the service delivered. Now the patient is no longer making those decisions. [It is] more complicated. [We define] our customers today as those paying for the patient's care.

The generation of market intelligence relies not just on customer surveys, but on a host of complementary mechanisms. Intelligence may be generated through a variety of formal as well as informal means (e.g., informal discussion with trade partners) and may involve collecting primary data or consulting secondary sources. The mechanisms include meetings and discussions with customers and trade partners (e.g., distributors), analysis of sales reports, analysis of worldwide customer databases, and formal market research such as customer attitude surveys, sales response in test markets, and so on. The following quotation from the director of marketing in a high-tech industrial products company illustrates the information collection and analysis activity.

> We do a lot of visiting with customers, talking with customers on the phone, we read the trade press—it is full of good information about what our competitors are doing. We always want to position relative to competitors. A lot of marketing is information gathering.

Importantly, intelligence generation is not the exclusive responsibility of a marketing department. For example, R&D engineers may obtain information at scientific conferences, senior executives might uncover trends reported in trade journals, and so on. Managers in several industrial products companies indicated that it was routine for their R&D personnel to interact directly with customers to assess their needs and problems and develop new business targeted at satisfying those needs. One company we interviewed goes to extreme lengths to encourage exchange of information between nonmarketing employees and customers. For its annual "open house," invitations to customers are hand delivered by manufacturing—not marketing—personnel. Customers visit the plant and interact with shop floor personnel as well as white collar employees. This approach not only enables manufacturing personnel to understand better the purchase motivations of customers, but also helps customers to appreciate the limits and constraints of processes involved in manufacturing items they require. As the president of this company described it:

> [The "open house"] does two things for you. First, it impresses the customers that the people in manufacturing are interested in your

business, and the other thing is that it impresses on the people in manufacturing that there are people who buy the product—real, live-bodied, walking-around people. *Our* people learn, but our *customers* are educated at the same time.

To help it anticipate customer needs accurately, one blue chip industrial product company assigns certain individuals exclusively to the task of studying trends and forces in the industries to which major customer groups belong (see related discussion by Lenz and Engledow 1986). This company goes so far as to identify future needs of customers and plan future offerings jointly with customers. The important point is that generation of market intelligence does not stop at obtaining customer opinions, but also involves careful analysis and subsequent interpretation of the forces that impinge on customer needs and preferences. Equally important, the field findings suggest that the generation of market intelligence is not and probably cannot be the exclusive responsibility of a marketing department (see also Webster 1988). Rather, market intelligence is generated collectively by individuals and departments throughout an organization. Mechanisms therefore must be be in place for intelligence generated at one location to be disseminated effectively to other parts of an organization.

Intelligence Dissemination As the interviews progressed, it became increasingly clear that responding effectively to a market need requires the participation of virtually all departments in an organization—R&D to design and develop a new product, manufacturing to gear up and produce it, purchasing to develop vendors for new parts/materials, finance to fund activities, and so on. Several managers noted that for an organization to adapt to market needs, market intelligence must be communicated, disseminated, and perhaps

even sold to relevant departments and individuals in the organization. Marketing managers in two consumer products companies developed and circulated periodic newsletters to facilitate dissemination of market intelligence. These activities echo suggestions in the literature that organizational direction is a result of marketing managers educating and communicating with managers in other functional areas (Levitt 1969) and that marketers' most important role may be selling within the firm (Anderson 1982). As noted before, however, market intelligence need not always be disseminated by the marketing department to other departments. Intelligence may flow in the opposite direction, depending on where it is generated. Effective dissemination of market intelligence is important because it provides a shared basis for concerted actions by different departments. A vice president of an industrial products company recounted the intelligence dissemination process for a new product required by a customer:

> I get engineering involved. Engineering gets production involved. We have management lunches and informal forums. Call reports circulate. By the time you design, [you have] engineering, production, and purchasing involved early in the process.

A formal intelligence dissemination procedure is obviously important, but the discussions with managers indicated that informal "hall talk" is an extremely powerful tool for keeping employees tuned to customers and their needs. Despite sparse treatments of the effects of informal information dissemination in virtually any literature (for a rare exception, see Aguilar 1967), the importance of this factor is well recognized by managers and it is tapped extensively. For example, the vice president of a manufacturing firm indicated that customer information is disseminated in her organization by telling stories about customers, their needs, personality characteristics, and even their families. The idea is to have the secretaries, engineers, and production personnel "get to know" customers. Her description of informal intelligence dissemination follows.

> One goal when I took over was to know everything about customers, [whether] they liked cats, know [their] wives' names, favorite pet peeve about our products. Our sales reps need to know this . . . I do a lot of storytelling. Later, [I] developed software to computerize all this. Everyone in the organization has access to this database.

This emphasis on intelligence dissemination parallels recent acknowledgement of the important role of "horizontal communication" in service organizations (Zeithaml, Berry, and Parasuraman 1988). Horizontal communications is the lateral flow that occurs both within and between departments (Daft and Steers 1985) and serves to coordinate people and departments to facilitate the attainment of overall organizational goals. Horizontal communication of market intelligence is one form of intelligence dissemination within an organization.

Responsiveness   The third element of a market orientation is responsiveness to market intelligence. An organization can generate intelligence and disseminate it internally; however, unless it responds to market needs, very little is accomplished. Responsiveness is the action taken in response to intelligence that is generated and disseminated. The following statement by an account executive in a service organization describes this type of responsiveness.

> We are driven by what the customer wants. [We] try to gather data, do research, put together new products based on this research, and then promote them.

The field findings indicate that responsiveness to market intelligence takes the form

of selecting target markets, designing and offering products/services that cater to their current and anticipated needs, and producing, distributing, and promoting the products in a way that elicits favorable end-customer response. Virtually all departments—not just marketing—participate in responding to market trends in a market-oriented company.

Synthesis and Commentary

From the preceding discussion, we offer the following formal definition of market orientation.

> Market orientation is the organizationwide *generation* of market intelligence pertaining to current and future customer needs, *dissemination* of the intelligence across departments, and organizationwide *responsiveness* to it.

Defining market orientation as organizationwide generation, dissemination, and responsiveness to market intelligence addresses the concerns of Barksdale and Darden (1971) by focusing on specific *activities* rather than philosophical notions, thereby facilitating the operationalization of the marketing concept. Interestingly, it appears more appropriate to view a market orientation as a continuous rather than a dichotomous either-or construct. As the sales manager for Asia in an industrial products company put it:

> The first thing to recognize is that there is no absolute, that there are many shades of gray.

In other words, organizations differ in the extent to which they generate market intelligence, disseminate it internally, and take action based on the intelligence. It therefore is appropriate to conceptualize the market orientation of an organization as one of degree, on a continuum, rather than as being either present or absent. This conceptualization facilitates measurement by avoiding certain difficulties inherent in asking informants to indicate whether or not their organization is market oriented (e.g., it may be somewhat market oriented). The proposed definition suggests that a measure of market orientation need only assess the *degree* to which a company is market oriented, that is, generates intelligence, disseminates it, and takes actions based on it. Relatedly, the appropriate unit of analysis appears to be the strategic business unit rather than the corporation because different SBUs of a corporation are likely to be market oriented to different degrees.

We next discuss antecedents and consequences of a market orientation, and moderators of the linkage between market orientation and business performance. We draw on the marketing literature, management literature, and field interviews for developing propositions.

RESEARCH PROPOSITIONS

Figure 18-1 is a conceptual framework for the following discussion. Briefly, the framework comprises four sets of factors: (1) antecedent conditions that foster or discourage a market orientation, (2) the market orientation construct, (3) consequences of a market orientation, and (4) moderator variables that either strengthen or weaken the relationship between market orientation and business performance. We discuss each of the four factors and develop propositions based on the literature and the field interviews.

Antecedents to a Market Orientation

Antecedents to a market orientation are the organizational factors that enhance or impede the implementation of the business philoso-

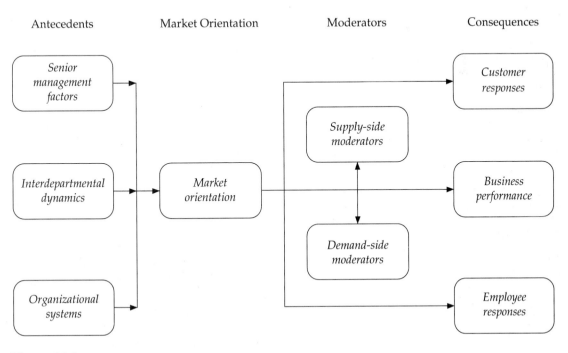

Figure 18-1
Antecedents and Consequences of a Market Orientation

phy represented by the marketing concept. Our examination of the literature and the insights from the field interviews reveal three hierarchically ordered categories of antecedents to a market orientation: individual, intergroup, and organizationwide factors. We label these as senior management factors, interdepartmental dynamics, and organizational systems, respectively.

Senior Management Factors   The role of senior management emerged as one of the most important factors in fostering a market

orientation (see Figure 18-2). Interviewees repeatedly emphasized the powerful impact of top managers on an organization. The following quotations are representative of the ideas that surfaced in the interviews.

> We'll do almost a $100 million [worth of sales] this year. We have a customer that bought [a mere] $10,000 worth of services. [He] calls the president [and launches into a long tirade of complaints]. [The president] writes down what he says and responds to him in writing. He investigates the difficulty. He gets back to him. In that process, if you are a junior engineer who

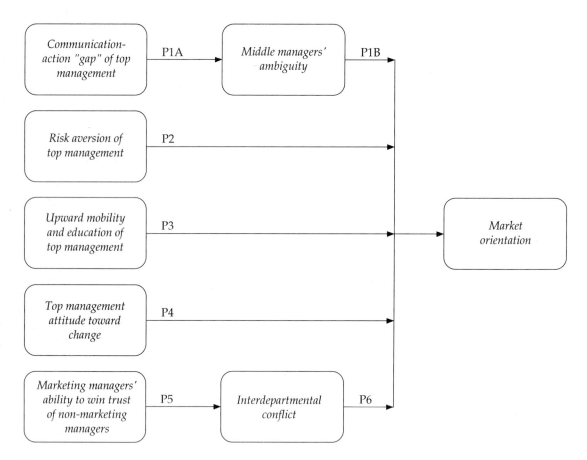

Figure 18-2
Senior Management Factors and Market Orientation

just worked on a $10,000 project and the *president* calls you up and says "let's talk about this and work out some kind of response to him," the word spreads throughout the base of the company [that] we're a customer-oriented company, we're marketplace oriented, we want to satisfy customer needs.

—Senior vice president,
industrial services company

The founder of this organization is a salesman. His shortcoming is that he does not know what marketing is. We reflect the leader.

—Marketing manager,
service organization

The critical role of top managers in fostering a market orientation is also reflected in the literature. For example, Webster (1988) asserts that a market orientation originates with top management and that "customer-oriented values and beliefs are uniquely the responsibility of top management" (p. 37). Likewise, Felton (1959) asserts that the most important ingredient of a market orientation is an appropriate state of mind, and that it is attainable only if "the board of directors, chief executive, and top-echelon executives appreciate the need to develop this marketing state of mind" (p. 55). In other words, the commitment of top managers is an essential prerequisite to a market orientation.

Additionally, Levitt (1969, p. 244) argues that one of the factors that facilitates the implementation of the marketing concept is the presence of "the right signals from the chief operating officer to the entire corporation regarding its continuing commitment to the marketing concept." In a similar vein, Webster (1988, p. 37) suggests that "CEOs must give clear signals and establish clear values and beliefs about serving the customer." Thus, these scholars assert that in addition to being committed to a market orientation, top managers must clearly *communicate* their commitment to all concerned in an organization.

Interestingly, the management literature goes a step further to provide novel insights. Argyris (1966) argues that a key factor affecting junior managers is the *gap* between what top managers say and what they do (e.g., they *say* "be market oriented," but cut back market research funds, discourage changes). Argyris examined 265 decision-making meetings with senior executives and concluded that the actual behavior of managers does not conform to their verbal espousals. One could argue, however, that if the gap is consistent over time, junior managers may to be able to infer what top managers truly desire. In contrast, if the size and/or direction of the gap is inconsistent over time, junior managers are unlikely to be able to infer top managers' actual preferences. Such variability is likely to lead to ambiguity about the amount of effort and resources junior managers should allocate to market-oriented tasks, thereby leading to lower market orientation. Hence:

P_{1a}: The greater the variability over time in the gap between top managers' communications and actions relating to a market orientation, the greater the junior managers' ambiguity about the organization's desire to be market oriented.

P_{1b}: The greater the junior managers' ambiguity about the organization's desire to be market oriented, the lower the market orientation of the organization.

A market orientation involves being responsive to market intelligence. Changing market needs call for the introduction of innovative products and services to match the evolving needs. The introduction of new/modified offerings and programs, however, is inherently risky because the new offerings may fail. As two executives noted:

Hospitals cannot survive unless they are innovative throughout the organization. It means taking risks, doing some real concrete things with customers.

—Marketing director, service organization

To be marketing oriented is not to be safe because you're running a risk. You have to invest in your ideas. To not be marketing oriented is to be safe. [It means doing] the same old [thing]. You're not investing in your business, not [taking] risks.

—President, industrial services company

In the course of the discussion with the latter executives, it became clear that top managers' response to innovative programs that do not succeed sends clear signals to junior employees in an organization. If top managers demonstrate a willingness to take risks and accept occasional failures as being natural, junior managers are more likely to propose and introduce new offerings in response to changes in customer needs. In contrast, if top managers are risk averse and intolerant of failures, subordinates are less likely to be responsive to changes in customer needs. Hence:

P_2: The greater the risk aversion of top managers, the lower the market orientation of the organization.

Because a market orientation involves being responsive to changing customer/client needs with innovative marketing programs and strategies, it can be viewed as a continuous innovative behavior. Hambrick and Mason (1984) suggest that organizations headed by top managers who are young, have extensive formal education, and are of low socioeconomic origin (and, by implication, have demonstrated upward social mobility) are more likely to pursue risky and innovative strategies. In the diffusion of innovations literature, formal education and upward mobility are reported as being related consistently to innovative behavior (see Rogers 1983, ch. 7). However, the age variable does not pro-

duce consistent findings across studies. Taken together, these findings suggest that the market orientation of an organization may be a function of the formal education of its senior managers and the extent to which they are upwardly mobile. More formally:

P_3: The greater the senior managers' (1) educational attainment and (2) upward mobility, the greater the market orientation of the organization.

A positive attitude toward change has been linked consistently to individual willingness to innovate. In a comprehensive review, Rogers (1983, p. 260) reports that 43 of 57 studies found a positive relationship between these two constructs. Willingness to adapt and change marketing programs on the basis of analyses of consumer and market trends is a hallmark of a market-oriented firm. Hence, top managers' openness to new ideas and acceptance of the view that change is a critical component to organizational success are likely to facilitate a market orientation. That is:

P_4: The more positive the senior managers' attitude toward change, the greater the market orientation of the organization.

Certain characteristics of department managers and the nature of interactions among them appear likely to affect an organization's market orientation through their impact on interdepartmental conflict (see Figure 18-2). Interdepartmental conflict is tension between two or more departments that arises from incompatibility of actual or desired responses (cf. Gaski 1984; Raven and Kruglanski 1970, p. 70). Felton (1959) and Levitt (1969) suggest that it is critical for a marketing vice president to be able to win the confidence and cooperation of his or her corporate peers to minimize conflict and engender a market orientation, though they do not elaborate on the factors that afford this ability. The implication is that:

P_5: The greater the ability of top marketing managers to win the confidence of senior nonmarketing managers, the lower the interdepartmental conflict.

Interdepartmental dynamics   Interdepartmental dynamics are the formal and informal interactions and relationships among an organization's departments. In P_5 we introduced the first interdepartmental construct, conflict. We begin our discussion in this section with the linkage between interdepartmental conflict and market orientation, then examine additional interdepartmental dynamics (see Figure 18-3).

Levitt (1969), Lusch, Udell, and Laczniak (1976), and Felton (1959) suggest that interdepartmental conflict may be detrimental to the implementation of the marketing concept. Interdepartmental conflict may stem from natural desires of individual departments to be more important or powerful, or may even be inherent in the charters of the various departments. For example, Levitt (1969) argues that the job of a manufacturing vice president is to run an efficient plant. Therefore it is only natural for that individual to oppose costly endeavors that might be called for by a market orientation. Recent research (e.g., Ruekert and Walker 1987) suggests that interdepartmental conflict inhibits communication across departments. Hence interdepartmental conflict appears likely to inhibit market intelligence dissemination, an integral component of a market orientation. Additionally, tension among departments is likely to inhibit concerted response by the departments to market needs, also a component of market orientation. We therefore expect that:

P_6: The greater the interdepartmental conflict, the lower the market orientation of the organization.

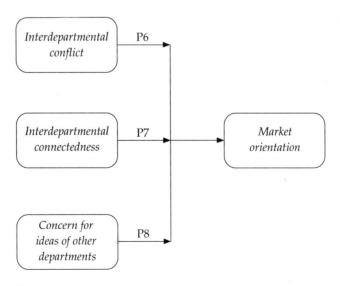

Figure 18-3
Interdepartmental Dynamics and Market Orientation

A second interdepartmental dynamic that emerged in several interviews as an antecedent of a market orientation is interdepartmental connectedness. This variable is the degree of formal and informal direct contact among employees across departments. For example, one executive noted that to improve its market orientation, her organization opened communication channels across departments—in marked contrast to the earlier practice of departments operating independently of one another and coordinated only by top management. One interviewee indicated that her organization *formally* required periodic meetings of employees from different departments, thereby facilitating the sharing of market intelligence.

The importance of interdepartmental connectedness in facilitating the dissemination of and responsiveness to market intelligence is supported by the evaluation literature (cf. Cronbach and Associates 1981) and the marketing literature (cf. Deshpande and Zaltman 1982). Indeed, the key predictors of research information utilization in program evaluation settings are the extent and quality of interaction between the evaluators and the program personnel (see Patton 1978). Hence:

P_7: The greater the interdepartmental connectedness, the greater the market orientation of the organization.

As Figure 18-3 illustrates, an additional construct pertaining to interdepartmental dynamics suggested by the literature on group dynamics is concern for others' ideas (Argyris 1965, 1966). Concern for others' ideas refers to openness and receptivity to the suggestions and proposals of other individuals or groups. In the previously noted study on decision making, Argyris (1966) observed that low levels of concern are related directly to restricted information flows, distrust, and antagonism, which result in ineffective group processes.

Therefore, low levels of concern for the ideas of individuals in other departments can be expected to impede the dissemination of market intelligence across departments as well as the responsiveness of individuals to intelligence generated in other departments. That is:

P_8: The greater the concern for ideas of employees in other departments, the greater the market orientation of the organization.

Organizational Systems   The third set of antecedents to a market orientation relate to organizationwide characteristics and therefore are labeled "organizational systems" (see Figure 18-4). A set of barriers to a market orientation briefly hinted at in the marketing literature is related to the structural form of organizations. Lundstrom (1976) and Levitt (1969) discuss departmentalization or specialization as a barrier to communication (and hence intelligence dissemination). Additionally, Stampfl (178) argues that greater formalization and centralization make organizations less adaptive to marketplace and environmental changes.

These references to organizational structure have their roots in the organizational sciences literature. Formalization is the degree to which rules define roles, authority relations, communications, norms and sanctions, and procedures (Hall, Haas, and Johnson 1967). Centralization is defined as the delegation of decision-making authority throughout an organization and the extent of participation by organizational members in decision making (Aiken and Hage 1968). Historically, both formalization and centralization have been found to be related inversely to information utilization (Deshpande and Zaltman 1982; Hage and Aiken 1970; Zaltman, Duncan, and Holbek 1973). In our context, information utilization corresponds to being responsive to market intelligence. Thus, the

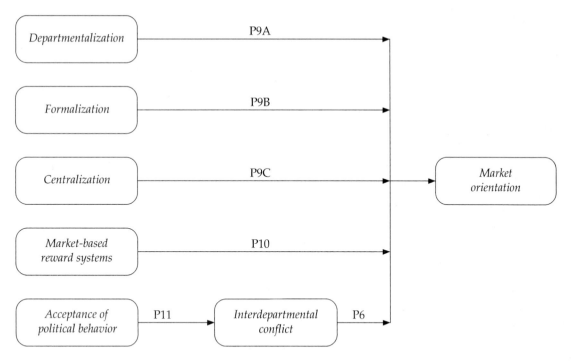

Figure 18-4
Organizational Systems and Market Orientation

literature suggests that structural characteristics of an organization can influence its market orientation.

Interestingly, there is reason to believe that organizational structure may not affect all three components of a market orientation in the same way. Because a market orientation essentially involves doing something new or different in response to market conditions, it can be viewed as a form of innovative behavior. Zaltman, Duncan, and Holbek (1973, p. 62) characterize innovative behavior as having two stages, (1) the initiation stage (i.e., awareness and decision-making stage) and (2) the implementation stage (i.e., carrying out the decision). In our context, the initiation stage corresponds to intelligence generation, dissemination, and the design of organizational response, whereas the implementation stage corresponds to the actual organizational response.

Zaltman, Duncan, and Holbek (1973) draw on numerous studies to argue that organizational dimensions such as departmentalization, formalization, and centralization may have opposite effects on the two stages of innovative behavior. In particular, they indicate that whereas these variables may hinder the initiation stage of innovative behavior, they may facilitate the implementation stage of innovative behavior. Hence departmentalization, formalization, and centralization may be related inversely to intelligence generation, dissemination, and response design, but positively to response implementation.

P_{9a}: The greater the departmentalization, (1) the lower the intelligence generation, dissemination, and response design and (2) the greater the response implementation.

P_{9b}: The greater the formalization, (1) the lower the intelligence generation, dissemination, and response design and (2) the greater the response implementation.

P_{9c}: The greater the centralization, (1) the lower the intelligence generation, dissemination, and response design and (2) the greater the response implementation.

The management literature reflects a rich history of work on measurement/reward systems and their effects on the attitudes and behavior of employees (see Hopwood 1974; Lawler and Rhode 1976 for reviews). Recent research in marketing builds on this work by emphasizing the importance of measurement and reward systems in shaping both desirable and undesirable behaviors (cf. Anderson and Chambers 1985; Jaworski 1988). Webster (1988, p. 38) argues that "the key to developing a market-driven, customer-oriented business lies in how managers are evaluated and rewarded." He observes that if managers are evaluated primarily on the basis of short-term profitability and sales, they are likely to focus on those criteria and neglect market factors such as customer satisfaction that ensure the long-term health of an organization.

Webster's observations are supported by the practices of several organizations included in our study. Though only one organization sampled appears to tie compensation to market-oriented performance, if rewards are construed more broadly to include appreciation, recognition, and approval, a larger number of organizations in the sample measure and reward market-based performance. For example, several organizations make it a point to single out and recognize employees who are identified by customers as being particularly helpful. Other organizations have instituted one or more variations of the "employee of the month" theme.

However, considerable variance is evident in the extent to which organizations measure and reward market-based performance. One marketing manager recounted a current situation in which employees are rewarded for short-term financial performance (i.e., units sold). She noted that this system works against a long-run market orientation and any long-run strategic orientation that the organization may decide to take. A sales manager in an industrial firm made a similar observation, noting that his sales reps may lead the company astray because their reward systems are based on sales in the short run. Currently, no system is in place to encourage them to think strategically. The preceding discussion suggests that:

P_{10}: The greater the reliance on market-based factors for evaluating and rewarding managers, the greater the market orientation of the organization.

All of the preceding organizationwide characteristics involve formal systems within organizations. Recent writings in the management literature reflect an increasing recognition of the important role of looser, less formal systems in shaping organizational activities (e.g., Feldman and March 1981; Ouchi 1979; Ouchi and Wilkens 1985; Pettigrew 1979; Smircich 1983). More recently, these informal characteristics have gained the attention of marketing academicians (cf. Deshpande and Webster 1989; Jaworski 1988). Though several different concepts can be identified, an informal organizational characteristic that appears to be particularly relevant as a determinant of a market orientation is political norm structure, a variable discussed in some detail by Porter, Allen, and Angel (1981).

Political behavior consists of individuals' attempts to promote self-interests and threaten others' interests (Porter, Allen, and Angel 1981). Political norm structure is an informal system that reflects the extent to which members of an organization view political behavior in the organization as being acceptable. A market orientation calls for a concerted response by the various departments of an organization to market intelligence. A highly politicized system, however, has the potential for engendering interdepartmental conflict (thereby inhibiting a market orientation). Hence,

P_{11}: The greater the acceptance of political behavior in an organization, the greater the interdepartmental conflict.

Linkages among the Market Orientation Components

Literature suggests that the three elements of a market orientation may be interrelated. For example, the literature on source credibility (cf. Petty and Cacioppo 1986; Zaltman and Moorman 1988) suggests that individuals in an organization are likely to be more responsive to intelligence generated by individual(s) who are regarded as having high expertise and trustworthiness. That is, responsiveness to market intelligence is likely to be a function of the characteristics of the source that generates the intelligence. Further, the literature on research utilization (cf. Deshpande and Zaltman 1982) suggests that responsiveness may be a function of such factors as the political acceptability of intelligence and the extent to which it challenges the status quo. Similarly, the extent to which intelligence is disseminated within an organization may depend on the political acceptability of intelligence and the challenge posed to the status quo. Hence the source of market intelligence and the very nature of intelligence may affect its dissemination and utilization (i.e., responsiveness). More formally:

P_{12a}: The greater the perceived expertise of the source generating market intelligence, the greater the responsiveness to it by the organization.

P_{12b}: The greater the perceived trustworthiness of the source generating market intelligence, the greater the responsiveness to it by the organization.

P_{12c}: The smaller the challenge to the status quo posed by market intelligence, the greater (1) its dissemination and (2) the responsiveness to it by the organization.

P_{12d}: The greater the political acceptability of market intelligence, the greater (1) its dissemination and (2) the responsiveness to it by the organization.

Consequences of a Market Orientation

Several insights obtained from the field interviews and the literature pertain to the consequences of a market orientation. The interviews uncovered an interesting consequence of a market orientation that is of major significance to large corporations. As the sales manager for Europe of an industrial products company indicated:

> [Market orientation leads to a] cohesive product focus, clear leadership, better coordination of sales activities, much better job of reviewing products from a worldwide basis, help in terms of differentiation.

In essence, the executive suggests that a market orientation facilitates clarity of focus and vision in an organization's strategy. This benefit corresponds to consistency, the first of Rumelt's (1981) four criteria—consistency, frame, competence, and workability—for evaluating strategies. Consistency is the extent to which a strategy reflects mutually consistent goals, objectives, and policies. Though strategies formulated by a single individual seldom have internal inconsistencies, the likelihood of inconsistencies increases when strategies emerge from interactions and negotiations among multiple individuals in different parts of an organization. A market orientation appears to provide a unifying focus for the efforts and projects of individuals and departments within the organization, thereby leading to superior performance.

Not surprisingly, virtually all of the executives interviewed noted that a market orientation enhances the performance of an organization. The typical response to our question about positive consequences was a "laundry list" of favorable business performance indicators such as ROI, profits, sales volume, market share, and sales growth. Preliminary support for some of these consequences is reported by Narver and Slater (1988). Hence:

P_{13}: The greater the market orientation of an organization, the higher its business performance.

The second set of consequences that emerged from the interviews relate to the effects of a market orientation on employees. These effects are not addressed in the extant literature. A large number of executives noted that a market orientation provides psychological and social benefits to employees. Several respondents noted that a market orientation leads to a sense of pride in belonging to an organization in which all departments and individuals work toward the common goal of serving customers. Accomplishing this objective results in employees sharing a feeling of worthwhile contribution, as well as higher levels of job satisfaction and commitment to the organization. The vice president of a consumer products company described some of these consequences as:

> . . . better esprit de corps. [You get the feeling] that what you are doing is satisfying. I think people feel the need to contribute, to help individuals, the society, to make a contribution.

The esprit de corps construct has received some attention in the management literature (e.g., Jones and James 1979) and is very similar to the teamwork construct identified by Zeithaml, Berry, and Parasuraman (1988) in a services marketing context. The latter authors suggest that this variable is instrumental in reducing the gap between service quality specifications and actual delivery, thereby improving consumers' perceptions of service quality. Interestingly, our findings suggest that the esprit de corps within an organization may itself be improved by a market orientation. Therefore we propose that:

P_{14}: The greater the market orientation, the greater the (1) esprit de corps, (2) job satisfaction, and (3) organizational commitment of employees.

The third set of consequences of a market orientation identified by the respondents involves customer attitudes and behavior. The thrust of the comments is that a market orientation leads to satisfied customers who spread the good word to other potential customers and keep coming back to the organization. The following quotations illustrate these ideas.

> . . . customer satisfaction, [positive] word of mouth, repeat business is enhanced. Customer retention is better for us, [it is] much less expensive.
>
> —Executive vice president, consumer products company

> . . . develops firm reputation, happy customers. Coming through when a customer is in a jam helps [our] reputation.
>
> —Vice president, industrial products company

These ideas also reflect Kotler's (1988) assertion that a market orientation is likely to lead to greater customer satisfaction and repeat business. Hence:

P_{15}: The greater the market orientation, (1) the greater the customer satisfaction and (2) the greater the repeat business from customers.

The literature reflects few *empirical* studies of the consequences of a market orientation. Most studies focus primarily on the extent to which the marketing concept has been adopted by organizations, rather than its specific consequences. One noteworthy exception is the Lawton and Parasuraman (1980) study. The authors found that the adoption of the marketing concept had no apparent effect on the sources of new product ideas, the use of marketing research in new product planning, and the innovativeness of new product offerings. In a sense, these findings run counter to the assertions of such authors as Bennett and Cooper (1981), Kaldor (1971), and Tauber (1974), who argue that the adoption of the marketing concept inhibits organizations from developing truly breakthrough innovations. Lawton and Parasuraman (1980) caution, however, that additional research using new measures is needed before firm conclusions can be drawn.

Environmental Moderators of the Market Orientation–Business Performance Linkage

With a few exceptions, writings in the literature tend to view the marketing concept as a universally relevant philosophy. In contrast, the field interviews elicited several environmental contingencies or conditions under which the impact of a market orientation on business performance is likely to be minimal. That is, the field findings suggest that certain contingencies moderate (i.e., increase or decrease) the strength of the relationship between market orientation and business performance. In the following discussion, we consider four such contingencies or moderator variables.

One moderator that surfaced in the course of the interviews is market turbulence—changes in the composition of customers and their preferences. This variable is more focused than the widely studied environmental turbulence construct. The role of market turbulence in influencing the desirability of a market orientation was highlighted by the experience of two consumer (food) products companies that marketed their products in a specific region in the United States. The population in this region had remained unchanged for years, and the preferences of the customers were known and stable. Neither company did much market research. Over the last few years, however, the region had received a tremendous influx of population from other parts of the country. Both companies were forced to initiate research to assess the needs and preferences of the new potential customers, and to develop new products to suit their particular preferences. These experiences suggest that when an organization caters to a fixed set of customers with stable preferences, a market orientation is likely to have little effect on performance because little adjustment to a marketing mix is necessary to cater effectively to stable preferences of a given set of customers. In contrast, if the customer sets or their preferences are less stable, there is a greater likelihood that the company's offerings will become mismatched with customers' needs over a period of time. An organization therefore must ascertain the changed preferences of customers and adjust its offerings to match them. That is:

P_{16}: The greater the market turbulence, the stronger the relationship between a market orientation and business performance.

Several authors (e.g., Bennett and Cooper 1981; Houston 1986; Kaldor 1971; Tauber 1974) point out that many generic product class innovations do not evolve from consumer research. Rather, these innovations are developed by R&D personnel who are often outside the industries into which the innovations eventually assimilate. Similar notions emerged in the interviews. As two of the managers interviewed indicated:

> [It is important to] recognize that new products do not always originate from the customer, [particularly] in high-tech industry. [An organization needs] to balance R&D [initiated] projects as well as customer/market driven products.
> —Sales manager, industrial products company

> Let me explain why we are not marketing oriented. We are a complex business, the industry is changing dramatically. Some of our products did not exist three years ago. The technology is changing. Everyone is getting wrapped up in production/operations.
> —Marketing manager, service organization

The basic idea expressed in the quotations is that in industries characterized by rapidly changing technology (note that firms in such industries often sell to other *firms*), a market orientation may not be as important as it is in technologically stable industries. "Technology" here refers to the entire process of transforming inputs to output and the delivery of those outputs to the end customer. The proposition is *not* that a market orientation is unimportant in technologically turbulent industries, but rather that it is *less* important. That is:

P_{17}: The greater the technological turbulence, the weaker the relationship between a market orientation and business performance.

Several executives noted that the degree of competition in an industry has a straightforward bearing on the importance of a market orientation. Strong competition leads to multiple choices for customers. Consequently, an organization must monitor and respond to customers' changing needs and preferences to ensure that customers select its offerings over competing alternatives. As two executives indicated:

> Historically, [we] were a technically driven company. In the early years it was a successful approach. If we had a better mousetrap, customers would search [us] out. However, as more companies came up with more solutions, we had to become more market oriented. Find out what solution [the] customer is looking for, and try to solve it. In the past little time was spent with customers. Now coordinate with customer, solution for him, try to utilize that development energy to provide solution for segment.
> —Sales manager, industrial product firm

> One thing is that marketing and advertising change so much. What worked last year may not work this year. A lot of it has to do with the competitive nature that you're in at the time because people's needs change. . . . If you don't have competition, you don't need it as much.
> —Marketing director, service organization

Thus, an organization with a monopoly in a market may perform well regardless of whether or not it modifies its offerings to suit changing customer preferences (see also Houston 1986, p. 84). As one service executive noted, "If one has a patent or lock on the product, it may not be efficient to allocate resources to marketing." In other words, the benefits afforded by a market orientation are greater for organizations in a competitive industry than for organizations operating in less competitive industries.

P_{18}: The greater the competition, the stronger the relationship between a market orientation and business performance.

Several executives indicated that in strong economies characterized by strong demand, an organization may be able to "get away with" a minimal amount of market orientation. In contrast, in a weak economy, customers are likely to be very value conscious and organizations must be more in tune with and responsive to customer needs in order to offer good value for money. Paradoxically, marketing seems to require more resources precisely at times when the organization is short of resources because of weak business conditions. As one academician noted:

> I think in weak economies, on the one hand [there is a] need to be more marketing oriented [because] consumers might need better inducements, their dollar has to go farther. On the other hand, to be marketing oriented requires greater amounts of money that they may not be able to provide at that point.

The preceding observations suggest the following proposition.

P$_{19}$: The weaker the general economy, the stronger the relationship between a market orientation and business performance.

Our 19 research propositions fit the broad framework depicted in Figure 18-1. Note that moderator variables discussed are labeled supply-side and demand-side moderators. The latter relate to the nature of demand in an industry (e.g., customer preferences, value consciousness) whereas the former refer to the nature of competition among suppliers and technology they employ. The framework in Figure 18-1 facilitates parsimonious conceptualization and, more importantly, offers the potential for extending research by identifying additional constructs that may fit into each of the broad categories (senior management factors, interdepartmental dynamics, etc.).

MANAGERIAL IMPLICATIONS

Our propositions have direct managerial implications. First, our research suggests that a market orientation may or may not be very desirable for a business, depending on the nature of its supply- and demand-side factors. Second, the research clearly delineates the factors that can be expected to foster or discourage a market orientation. These factors are largely controllable by managers and therefore can be altered by them to improve the market orientation of their organizations. Overall, our research gives managers a comprehensive view of what a market orientation is, ways to attain it, and its likely consequences.

To Be or Not to Be Market Oriented

Our study suggests that though a market orientation is likely to be related to business performance in general, under certain conditions it may not be critical. A market orientation requires the commitment of resources. The orientation is useful only if the benefits it affords exceed the cost of those resources. Hence, under conditions of limited competition, stable market preferences, technologically turbulent industries, and booming economies, a market orientation may not be related strongly to business performance. Managers of businesses operating under these conditions should pay close attention to the cost-benefit ratio of a market orientation.

Implementing a Market Orientation

Our research provides very specific suggestions about the factors that foster or discourage a market orientation in organizations. Because the factors identified are controllable by senior managers, deliberate engendering of a market orientation is possible.

For example, our findings suggest that senior managers must themselves be convinced of the value of a market orientation and *communicate* their commitment to junior employees. Though annual reports and public interviews proclaiming a market orientation are helpful, junior employees need to witness behaviors and resource allocations that reflect a commitment to a market orientation. Senior managers must develop positive attitudes toward change and a willingness to take calculated risks. A market orientation is almost certain to lead to a few projects or programs that do not succeed. However, supportive reaction to failures is critical for engendering a change-oriented philosophy represented by the marketing concept.

We also identify interdepartmental dynamics that can be managed through appropriate in-house efforts. Interdepartmental variables—conflict, connectedness—clearly have a key role in influencing the dissemination of the responsiveness to market intelligence. Some inexpensive ways to manage these two antecedents (conflict, connectedness) include (1) interdepartmental lunches, (2) sports leagues that require mixed-department teams, and (3) newsletters that "poke fun" at various interdepartmental relations. More advanced efforts include (1) exchange of employees across departments, (2) cross-department training programs, and (3) senior department managers spending a day with executives in other departments. Such efforts appear to foster an understanding of the personalities of managers in other departments, their culture, and their particular perspectives.

The third set of variables that senior managers might alter to foster a market orientation pertains to organizationwide systems. The impact of structural factors such as formalization and centralization is unclear because, though they appear to inhibit the generation and dissemination of market intelligence, these very factors are likely to help an organization implement its response to mar-

ket intelligence effectively. How an organization should structure itself appears to depend on the activity involved. Clearly, however, senior managers can help foster a market orientation by changing reward systems from being completely finance based (e.g., sales, profits) to being at least partly market based (e.g., customer satisfaction, intelligence obtained). Simultaneously, informal norms such as the acceptability of political behavior in the organization should be changed to facilitate concerted response by the departments to market developments.

The Pace and Dynamics of Change

The change in orientation takes place slowly. We were apprised of certain organizations that were actively involved in becoming more market oriented, but planned to complete the change process over a period of about four years. In describing a change to a market focus, an executive director noted that there is always a "pull and tug between a new idea and old ways of doing things." It appears especially difficult to "carry" employees who are concerned that a movement along the market orientation dimension might jeopardize their power in the organization or expose other inadequacies related to their jobs.

Further, the balance of power across departments must be managed carefully in any effort to become more market oriented. Though a market orientation involves the efforts of virtually all departments in an organization, the marketing department typically has a larger role by virtue of its contact with customers and the market. Individuals in marketing departments may try to relegate other departments to a secondary status. One health care administrator recounted that when the organization had begun to emphasize a market philosophy, it had started treating marketing personnel as the "blue-eyed boys" of the organization. Within a very short time, personnel in other departments began to resent this treatment and raised questions with the chief executive ("What are you doing for us?").

For any change to take place, an organization first must perceive a gap between its current and its preferred orientation. We were apprised of several instances in which members of an organization felt they were very customer oriented, but in fact were hardly so. An executive narrated the example of a service organization's employees who felt they were very responsive to customer needs. However, when the interactions of these employees with customers (hospital patients) were videotaped and played back to the employees, they were horrified at the callous manner in which they saw themselves treating customers. As Weick (1979) notes, it is the perceptions of situations that are the triggers of action.

The Quality of Market Orientation

Though in general organizations that develop market intelligence and respond to it are likely to perform better and have more satisfied customers and employees than ones that do not, simply engaging in market-oriented activities does not ensure the *quality* of those activities. The quality of market intelligence itself may be suspect or the quality of execution of marketing programs designed in response to the intelligence may be poor. In such instances, a market orientation may not produce the desired functional consequences. For example, to meet a customer's needs, one industrial products company went to extreme lengths to customize small batches of products for the customer, which resulted in poor financial performance. Similarly, one executive noted that a company's efforts may so raise customer expectations about product quality, response time, and other factors as to result in either uneconomical operations or

dissatisfied customers. This difficulty parallels the problem posed by overpromising in service settings discussed by Zeithaml, Berry, and Parasuraman (1988). Though we do not address the issue of variations in the quality of market intelligence, its dissemination, and organizational response, these variations clearly are important and warrant consideration by both managers and researchers.

CONCLUSION

We attempt to clarify the domain of the market orientation construct and provide a working definition and a foundation for developing a measure of the construct. Additionally, we identify three classes of factors affecting a market orientation and interrelationships among the elements of market orientation. We highlight the impact of a market orientation on an organization's strategy, employee dispositions, and customer attitudes and behavior. Finally, and in a significant departure from previous work, we introduce supply- and demand-side factors as potential moderators of the impact of market orientation on business performance.

Our propositional inventory and integrative framework represent efforts to build a foundation for the systematic development of a theory of market orientation. However, the objective of our research is theory construction rather than theory testing. Much work remains to be done in terms of developing a suitable measure of market orientation and empirically testing our propositions.

In recent years, considerable interest has focused on organizational resources and positions that represent sustainable competitive advances (e.g., Day and Wensley 1988). Much less attention has focused on organizational *processes,* such as market orientation, that represent a long-term advantage. Because a market orientation is not easily engendered, it may be considered an additional and distinct form of sustainable competitive advantage.

REFERENCES

Aguilar, Francis (1967), *Scanning Business Environments*. New York: MacMillan and Company.

Aiken, Michael and Jerald Hage (1968), "Organizational Independence and Intraorganizational Structure," *American Sociological Review*, 33, 912–30.

Alba, Joseph W. and J. Wesley Hutchinson (1987), "Dimensions of Consumer Expertise," *Journal of Consumer Research*, 12 (March), 411–54.

Anderson, Paul (1982), "Marketing, Strategic Planning, and the Theory of the Firm," *Journal of Marketing*, 46 (Spring), 15–26.

_____ and Terry Chambers (1985), "A Reward/Measurement Model of Organizational Buying Behavior," *Journal of Marketing*, 49 (Spring), 7–23.

Argyris, Chris (1965), *Organization and Innovation*. Homewood, IL: Richard D. Irwin, Inc.

_____ (1966), "Interpersonal Barriers to Decision Making," *Harvard Business Review*, 44 (March–April), 84–97.

Barksdale, Hiram C. and Bill Darden (1971), "Marketers' Attitude Toward the Marketing Concept," *Journal of Marketing*, 35 (October), 29–36.

Bell, Martin L. and C. William Emory (1971), "The Faltering Marketing Concept," *Business Horizons*, 22 (June), 76–83.

Bennett, Roger and Robert Cooper (1981), "Beyond the Marketing Concept," *Business Horizons*, 22 (June), 76–83.

Business Week (1950), "Marketing Men Take Over GE Units" (June 24).

Cronbach, Lee J. and Associates (1981), *Toward Reform in Program Evaluation*. San Francisco, CA: Jossey Bass Inc., Publishers.

Daft, Richard L. and Richard Steers (1985), *Organizations: A Micro/Macro Approach*. Glenview, IL: Scott, Foresman and Company.

Day, George S. and Robin Wensley (1983), "Marketing Theory with a Strategic Orientation," *Journal of Marketing*, 47 (Fall), 79–89.

_____ and _____ (1988), "Assessing Advantage: A Framework for Diagnosing Competitive Superiority," *Journal of Marketing*, 52 (April), 1–20.

Deshpande, Rohit (1983), " 'Paradigms Lost:' On Theory and Method in Research in Marketing," *Journal of Marketing*, 47 (Fall), 101–10.

_____ and Frederick E. Webster, Jr. (1989), "Organizational Culture and Marketing: Defining the Research Agenda," *Journal of Marketing*, 53 (January), 3–15.

_____ and Gerald Zaltman (1982), "Factors Affecting the Use of Market Research Information: A Path Analysis," *Journal of Marketing Research*, 19 (February), 14–31.

Feldman, Martha S. and James G. March (1981), "Information in Organizations as Symbols and Signals," *Administrative Science Quarterly*, 26 (June), 171–86.

Felton, Arthur P. (1959), "Making the Marketing Concept Work," *Harvard Business Review*, 37 (July–August), 55–65.

Gaski, John F. (1984), "The Theory of Power and Conflict in Channels of Distribution," *Journal of Marketing*, 48 (Summer), 9–29.

Glaser, Barney and Anselm Strauss (1967), *The Discovery of Grounded Theory*. Chicago: Aldine Publishing Company.

Hage, Jerald and Michael Aiken (1970), *Social Change in Complex Organizations*. New York: Random House, Inc.

Hall, Richard H., J. Eugene Haas, and Norman J. Johnson (1967), "Organizational Size, Complexity, and Formalization," *American Sociological Review*, 32 (December), 903–11.

Hambrick, Donald C. and Phyllis A. Mason (1984), "Upper Echelons: The Organization as a Reflection of Its Top Managers," *Academy of Management Review*, 9 (2), 193–206.

Hise, Richard T. (1965), "Have Manufacturing Firms Adopted the Marketing Concept?" *Journal of Marketing*, 29 (July), 9–12.

Hopwood, Anthony (1974), *Accounting and Human Behavior*. London: Haymarket Publishing Limited.

Houston, Franklin S. (1986), "The Marketing Concept: What It Is and What It Is Not," *Journal of Marketing*, 50 (April), 81–7.

Jaworski, Bernard J. (1988), "Toward a Theory of Marketing Control: Environmental Context, Control Types, and Consequences," *Journal of Marketing*, 52 (July), 23–39.

Jones, A. P. and L. R. James (1979), "Psychological Climate: Dimensions and Relationships of Individual and Aggregate Work Environment Perceptions," *Organization Behavior and Human Performance*, 23, 201–50.

Kaldor, A. G. (1971), "Imbricative Marketing," *Journal of Marketing*, 35 (April), 19–25.

Konopa, L. J. and P. J. Calabro (1971), "Adoption of the Marketing Concept by Large Northeastern Ohio Manufacturers," *Akron Business and Economic Review*, 2 (Spring), 9–13.

Kotler, Philip (1988), *Marketing Management*. Englewood Cliffs, NJ: Prentice-Hall, Inc.

Lavidge, R. J. (1966), "Marketing Concept Often Gets only Lip Service," *Advertising Age*, 37 (October), 52.

Lawler, Edward E. and John G. Rhode (1976), *Information and Control in Organizations*. Pacific Palisades, CA: Goodyear Publishing Company.

Lawton, Leigh and A. Parasuraman (1980), "The Impact of the Marketing Concept on New Product Planning," *Journal of Marketing*, 44 (Winter), 19–25.

Lear, Robert W. (1963), "No Easy Road to Market Orientation," *Harvard Business Review*, 41 (September–October), 53–60.

Lenz, R. T. and Jack L. Engledow (1986), "Environmental Analysis Units and Strategic Decision Making: A Field Study of Selected 'Leading Edge' Corporations," *Strategic Management Journal*, 7 (January–Feburary), 69–89.

Levitt, Theodore (1969), *The Marketing Mode*. New York: McGraw-Hill Book Company.

Lundstrom, William J. (1976), "The Marketing Concept: The Ultimate in Bait and Switch," *Marquette Business Review*, 20 (Fall), 214–30.

Lusch, Robert F., Jon G. Udell, and Gene R. Laczniak (1976), "The Practice of Business," *Business Horizons*, 19 (December), 65–74.

Mahrer, Alvin R. (1988), "Discovery-Oriented Psychotherapy Research," *American Psychologist*, 43 (September), 694–702.

McCarthy, E. Jerome and William D. Perreault, Jr. (1984), *Basic Marketing*, 8th ed. Homewood, IL: Richard D. Irwin, Inc.

McKitterick, J. B. (1957), "What Is the Marketing Management Concept?" in *The Frontiers of Marketing Thought and Science*, Frank M. Bass, ed. Chicago: American Marketing Association, 71–92.

McNamara, Carlton P. (1972), "The Present Status of the Marketing Concept," *Journal of Marketing*, 36 (January), 50–7.

Narver, John C. and Stanley F. Slater (1988), "Market Orientation: Construct Measurement and Analysis of Effects on Performance," presentation at Marketing Science Institute Conference (September), Boston.

Olson, David (1987), "When Consumer Firms Develop a Marketing Orientation," paper presented at Marketing Science Institute Miniconference on Developing a Marketing Orientation (April), Cambridge, MA.

Ouchi, William G. (1979), "A Conceptual Framework for the Design of Organizational Control Mechanisms," *Management Science*, 25 (September), 833–47.

_____ and Alan C. Wilkens (1985), "Organizational Culture," *Annual Review of Sociology*, 11, 457–83.

Parasuraman, A., Valerie A. Zeithaml, and Leonard L. Berry (1985), "A Conceptual Model of Service Quality and Its Implications for Future Research," *Journal of Marketing*, 49 (Fall), 41–50.

Park, C. Whan and Gerald Zaltman (1987), *Marketing Management*. Chicago: Dryden Press.

Patton, Michael Q. (1978), *Utilization Focused Evaluation*. Beverly Hills, CA: Sage Publications, Inc.

Pettigrew, Andrew M. (1979), "On Studying Organizational Cultures," *Administrative Science Quarterly*, 24 (December), 570–81.

Petty, Richard E. and John T. Cacioppo (1986), *Communication and Persuasion: Central and Peripheral Routes to Attitude Change*. New York: Springer-Verlag.

Porter, Lyman W., Robert W. Allen, and Harold Angel (1981), "The Politics of Upward Influence in Organizations," in *Research in Organizational Behavior*, Vol. 3, B. Staw and L. Cummings, eds. Greenwich, CT: JAI Press, Inc.

Raven, Bertram H. and Aric W. Kruglanski (1970), "Conflict and Power," in *The Structure of Conflict*, Paul Swingle, ed. New York: Academic Press, Inc., 69–109.

Robertson, Thomas S. and Hubert Gatignon (1986), "Competitive Effects on Technology Diffusion," *Journal of Marketing*, 50 (July), 1–12.

Rogers, Everett M. (1983), *Diffusion of Innovations*, 3rd ed. New York: The Free Press.

Ruekert, Robert and Orville C. Walker, Jr. (1987), "Marketing's Interaction with Other Functional Units: A Conceptual Framework and Empirical Evidence," *Journal of Marketing*, 51 (January), 1–19.

——, ——, and Kenneth J. Roering (1985), "The Organization of Marketing Activities: A Contingency Theory of Structure and Performance," *Journal of Marketing*, 49 (Winter), 13–25.

Rumelt, Richard P. (1981), "Evaluation of Strategy: Theory and Models," in *Strategic Management: A New View of Business Policy and Planning*, Dan E. Schendel and Charles W. Hofer, eds. Boston: Little, Brown, & Company, Inc., 196–212.

Shapiro, Benson P. (1988), "What the Hell Is 'Market Oriented'?" *Harvard Business Review*, 66 (November–December), 119–25.

Smircich, Linda (1983), "Concepts of Culture and Organizational Analysis," *Administrative Science Quarterly*, 28 (September), 339–58.

Stampfl, Ronald W. (1978), "Structural Constraints, Consumerism, and the Marketing Concept," *MSU Business Topics*, 26 (Spring), 5–16.

Tauber, Edward M. (1974), "How Marketing Discourages Major Innovation," *Business Horizons*, 17 (June), 22–6.

Viebranz, Alfred C. (1967), "Marketing's Role in Company Growth," *MSU Business Topics*, 15 (Autumn), 45–9.

Walker, Orville C., Jr., Gilbert A. Churchill, Jr., and Neil M. Ford (1977), "Motivation and Performance in Industrial Selling: Present Knowledge and Needed Research," *Journal of Marketing Research*, 14 (May), 156–68.

Webster, Frederick E., Jr. (1988), "Rediscovering the Marketing Concept," *Business Horizons*, 31 (May–June), 29–39.

Weick, Karl (1979), *The Social Psychology of Organizing*, 2nd ed. Reading, MA: Addison-Wesley Publishing Company.

Weitz, Barton A. (1981), "Effectiveness in Sales Interactions: A Contingency Framework," *Journal of Marketing*, 45 (Winter), 85–103.

Zaltman, Gerald, Robert Duncan, and Jonny Holbek (1973), *Innovations and Organizations*. New York: John Wiley & Sons, Inc.

——, Karen LeMasters, and Michael Heffring (1982), *Theory Construction in Marketing*. New York: John Wiley & Sons, Inc.

—— and Christine Moorman (1988), "The Importance of Personal Trust in the Use of Research," *Journal of Advertising Research*, 28 (October–November), 16–24.

Zeithaml, Valarie A., Leonard L. Berry, and A. Parasuraman (1988), "Communication and Control Processes in the Delivery of Service Quality," *Journal of Marketing*, 52 (April), 35–48.

◆

Strategic Windows

Derek F. Abell

Strategic Market Planning involves the management of any business unit in the dual tasks of *anticipating* and *responding* to changes which affect the marketplace for their products. This article discusses both of these tasks. Anticipation of change and its impact can be substantially improved if an organizing framework can be used to identify sources and directions of change in a systematic fashion. Appropriate responses to change require a clear understanding of the alternative strategic options available to management as a market evolves and change takes place.

DYNAMIC ANALYSIS

When changes in the market are only incremental, firms may successfully adapt themselves to the new situation by modifying current marketing or other functional programs. Frequently, however, market changes are so far-reaching that the competence of the

Derek F. Abell, "Strategic Windows," Vol. 42 (July 1978). Reprinted from *Journal of Marketing*, published by the American Marketing Association.

firm to continue to compete effectively is called into question. And it is in such situations that the concept of "strategic windows" is applicable.

The term "strategic window" is used here to focus attention on the fact that there are only limited periods during which the "fit" between the key requirements of a market and the particular competencies of a firm competing in that market is at an optimum. Investment in a product line or market area should be timed to coincide with periods in which such a strategic window is open. Conversely, disinvestment should be contemplated if what was once a good fit has been eroded—i.e., if changes in market requirements outstrip the firm's capability to adapt itself to them.

Among the most frequent questions which management has to deal with in this respect are:

Should funds be committed to a proposed new market entry? Now? Later? Or not at all? If a commitment is to be made, how large should it be?

Should expenditures of funds of plant and equipment or marketing to support existing product lines be expanded, continued at historical levels, or diminished?

When should a decision be made to quit and throw in the towel for an unprofitable product line or business area?

Resource allocation decisions of this nature all require a careful assessment of the future evolution of the market involved and an accurate appraisal of the firm's capability to successfully meet key market requirements. The strategic window concept encourages the analysis of these questions in a dynamic rather than a static framework, and forces marketing planners to be as specific as they can about these future patterns of market evolution and the firm's capacity to adapt to them.

It is unfortunate that the heightened interest in product portfolio analysis evident in the last decade has failed to adequately encompass these issues. Many managers routinely classify their various activities as "cows," "dogs," "stars," or "question marks" based on a *static* analysis of the *current* position of the firm and its market environment.

Of key interest, however, is the question not only of where the firm is today, but of how well equipped it is to deal with *tomorrow*. Such a *dynamic* analysis may foretell non-incremental changes in the market which work to disqualify market leaders, provide opportunities for currently low share competitors, and sometimes even usher in a completely new cast of competitors into the marketplace. Familiar contemporary examples of this latter phenomenon include such products as digital watches, women's pantyhose, calculators, charter air travel, office copiers, and scientific instrumentation.

In all these cases existing competitors have been displaced by new contenders as these markets have evolved. In each case changing market requirements have resulted in a *closing* strategic window for incumbent competitors and an *opening window for new entrants*.

MARKET EVOLUTION

The evolution of a market usually embodies more far-reaching changes than the relatively systematic changes in customer behavior and marketing mix due to individual product life cycles. Four major categories of change stand out:

1. The development of new primary demand opportunities; whole marketing requirements differ radically from those of existing market segments.
2. The advent of new competing technologies which cannibalize the existing ones.
3. Market redefinition caused by changes in the definition of the product itself and/or changes in the product market strategies of competing firms.
4. Channel changes.

There may be other categories of change or variants in particular industries. That doesn't matter; understanding of how such changes may qualify or disqualify different types of competitors can still be derived from a closer look at examples within each of the four categories above.

New Primary Demand

In a primary demand growth phase, decisions have to be reached by existing competitors about whether to spend the majority of the resources fighting to protect and fortify market positions that have already been established, or whether to seek new development opportunities.

In some cases, it is an original entrant who ploughs new territory—adjusting his approach to the emergent needs of the marketplace; in other cases it is a new entrant who, maybe basing his entry on expertise developed elsewhere, sees a "strategic window" and leapfrogs over the original market leader to take advantage of the new growth opportunity. Paradoxically, pioneering competitors who narrowly focus their activities in the early stages of growth may have the most difficulty in making the transition to new primary demand growth opportunities later. Emery Air Freight provides an example of a company that did face up to a challenge in such a situation.

Emery Air Freight   This pioneer in the air freight forwarding business developed many of the early applications of air freight in the United States. In particular, Emery's efforts were focused on servicing the "emergency" segment of the market, which initially accounted for a substantial portion of all air freight business. Emery served this market via an extensive organization of regional and district offices. Among Emery's major assets in this market was a unique nationwide, and later worldwide, communications network; and the special competence of personnel located in the district offices in using scheduled carriers in the most efficient possible way to expedite deliveries.

As the market evolved, however, many new applications for air freight emerged. This included regular planned shipments of high value-low weight merchandise, shipments of perishables, "off-line" service to hard-to-reach locations, and what became known as the TCC (Total Cost Concept) market. Each of these new applications required a somewhat different approach than that demanded by the original emergency business.

TCC applications, for example, required detailed logistics planning to assess the savings and benefits to be obtained via lower inventories, quicker deliveries and fewer lost

sales through the use of air freight. Customer decisions about whether or not to use air freight required substantially more analysis than had been the case for "emergency" use; furthermore, decisions which had originally been made by traffic managers now involved marketing personnel and often top management.

A decision to seek this kind of business thus implied a radical change in Emery's organization—the addition of capability to analyze complex logistics systems and to deal with upper echelons of management.

New Competing Technologies

When a fundamental change takes place in the basic technology of an industry, it again raises questions of the adaptability to new circumstances of existing firms using obsolete technology.

In many cases established competitors in an industry are challenged, not by another member of the same industry, but by a company which bases its approach on a technology developed outside that industry. Sometimes this results from forward integration of a firm that is eager to develop applications for a new component or raw material. Texas Instruments' entry into a wide variety of consumer electronic products from a base of semi-conductor manufacture is a case in point. Sometimes it results from the application by firms of a technology developed in one market to opportunities in another. Or sometimes a breakthrough in either product or process technology may remove traditional barriers to entry in an industry and attract a completely new set of competitors. Consider the following examples:

> Watchmakers have recently found that a new class of competitor is challenging their industry leadership—namely electronic firms who are seeking end market applications for their semiconductors, as well as a new breed of assemblers manufacturing digital watches.

Manufacturers of mechanical adjustable speed drive equipment found their markets eroded by electrical speed drives in the early 1900's. Electrical drives were based on rotating motor-generator sets and electronic controls. In the late 1950's, the advent of solid state electronics, in turn, virtually obsoleted rotating equipment. New independent competitors, basing their approach on the assembly of electronic components, joined the large electrical equipment manufacturers in the speed drive market. Today, yet another change is taking place, namely the advent of large computer controlled drive systems. This is ushering yet another class of competitors into the market—namely, companies whose basic competence is in computers.

In each of these cases, recurrent waves of new technology fundamentally changed the nature of the market and usually ushered in an entirely new class of competitors. Many firms in most markets have a limited capability to master all the technologies which might ultimately cannibalize their business. The nature of technological innovation and diffusion is such that most *major* innovations will originate outside a particular industry and not within it.

In many cases, the upheaval is not only technological; indeed the nature of competition may also change dramatically as technology changes. The advent of solid state electronics in the speed drive industry, for example, ushered in a number of small, low overhead, independent assemblers who based their approach primarily on low price. Prior to that, the market had been dominated by the large electrical equipment manufacturers basing their approach largely on applications engineering coupled with high prices and high margins.

The "strategic window" concept does not preclude adaptation when it appears feasible, but rather suggests that certain firms may be better suited to compete in certain

technological waves than in others. Often the cost and the difficulty of acquiring the new technology, as well as the sunk-cost commitment to the old, argue against adaptation.

MARKET REDEFINITION

Frequently, as markets evolve, the fundamental definition of the market changes in ways which increasingly disqualify some competitors while providing opportunities for others. The trend towards marketing "systems" of products as opposed to individual pieces of equipment provides many examples of this phenomenon. The situation of Docutel illustrates this point.

Docutel   This manufacturer of automatic teller machines (ATM's) supplied virtually all the ATM's in use up to late 1974. In early 1975, Docutel found itself losing market share to large computer companies such as Burroughs, Honeywell, and IBM as these manufacturers began to took at the banks' total EFTS (Electronic Funds Transfer System) needs. They offered the bank a package of equipment representing a complete system of which the ATM was only one component. In essence their success may be attributed to the fact that they redefined the market in a way which increasingly appeared to disqualify Docutel as a potential supplier.

Market redefinition is not limited to the banking industry; similar trends are underway in scientific instrumentation, process control equipment, the machine tool industry, office equipment, and electric control gear, to name but a few. In each case, manufacturers basing their approach on the marketing of individual hardware items are seeing their "strategic window" closing as computer systems producers move in to take advantage of emerging opportunities.

CHANNEL CHANGES

Changes in the channels of distribution for both consumer and industrial goods can have far reaching consequences for existing competitors and would-be entrants.

Changes take place in part because of product life-cycle phenomena—the shift as the market matures to more intensive distribution, increasing convenience, and often lower levels of channel service. Changes also frequently take place as a result of new institutional development in the channels themselves. Few sectors of American industry have changes as fast as retail and wholesale distribution, with the result that completely new types of outlets may be employed by suppliers seeking to develop competitive advantage.

Whatever the origin of the change, the effect may be to provide an opportunity for a new entrant and to raise questions about the visibility of existing competitors. Gillette's contemplated entry into the blank cassette tape market is a case in point.

Gillette   As the market for cassettes evolved due to increased penetration and new uses of equipment for automotive, study, business, letter writing, and home entertainment, so did distribution channels broaden into an increasing number of drug chains, variety stores, and large discount stores.

Presumably it was recognition of a possible "strategic window" for Gillette that encouraged executives in the Safety Razor Division to look carefully at ways in which Gillette might exploit the cassette market at this particular stage of its evolution. The question was whether Gillette's skill in marketing low-priced, frequently purchased package goods, along with its distribution channel resources, could be applied to marketing blank cassettes. Was there a place for a competitor in this market to offer a quality, branded product, broadly distributed and supported by heavy media advertising in much the same way that Gillette marketed razor blades?

Actually, Gillette decided against entry, apparently not because a "strategic window" did not exist, but because profit prospects were not favorable. They did, however, enter the cigarette lighter business based on similar analysis and reportedly have had considerable success with their *Cricket* brand.

PROBLEMS AND OPPORTUNITIES

What do all these examples indicate? *First*, they suggest that the "resource requirements" for success in a business—whether these be financial requirements, marketing requirements, engineering requirements, or whatever—may change radically with market evolution. *Second*, they appear to suggest that, by contrast, the firm's resources and key competencies often cannot be so easily adjusted. The result is a *predictable* change in the fit of the firm to its market—leading to defined periods during which a "strategic window" exists and can be exploited.

The "strategic window" concept can be useful to incumbent competitors as well as to would-be entrants into a market. For the former, it provides a way of relating future strategic moves to market evolution and of assessing how resources should be allocated to existing activities. For the latter, it provides a framework for diversification and growth.

Existing Businesses

Confronted with changes in the marketplace which potentially disqualify the firm from continued successful participation, several strategic options are available:

1. An attempt can be made to assemble the resources needed to close the gap between

the new critical marketing requirements and the firm's competencies.

2. The firm may shift its efforts to selected segments, where the "fit" between requirements and resources is still acceptable.
3. The firm may shift to a "low profile" approach—cutting back severely on all further allocations of capital and deliberately "milking" the business for short-run profit.
4. A decision may be taken to exit from that particular market either through liquidation or through sale.

All too frequently, however, because the "strategic window" phenomenon is not clearly recognized, these strategic choices are not clearly articulated. Instead, "old" approaches are continued long after the market has changed with the result that market position is lost and financial losses pile up. Or, often only half-hearted attempts are made to assemble the new resources required to compete effectively; or management is simply deluded into believing that it can adapt itself to the new situation even where this is actually out of the question.

The four basic strategic choices outlined above may be viewed hierarchically in terms of *resource commitment,* with No. 1 representing the highest level of commitment. Only the company itself can decide which position on the hierarchy it should adopt in particular situations, but the following guideline questions may be helpful:

To what extent do the changes call for skills and resources completely outside the traditional competence of the firm? A careful analysis has to be made of the gap which may emerge between the evolving requirements of the market and the firm's profile.

To what extent can changes be anticipated? Often it is easier to adapt through a series of

minor adjustments—a stepping stone approach to change—than it is to be confronted with a major and unexpected discontinuity in approach.

How rapid are the changes which are taking place? Is there enough time to adjust without forfeiting a major share of the market which later may be difficult to regain?

How long will realignment of the functional activities of the firm take? Is the need limited to only some functions, or are all the basic resources of the firm affected—e.g., technology, engineering, manufacturing, marketing, sales, and organization policies?

What existing commitments—e.g., technical skills, distribution channels, manufacturing approaches, etc.—constrain adaptation?

Can the new resources and new approaches be developed internally or must they be acquired?

Will the changes completely obsolete existing ways of doing business or will there be a chance for coexistence? In the case of new technologies intruding from outside industry, the decision often has to be made to "join-em rather than fight-em." Not to do so is to risk complete obsolescence. In other cases, coexistence may be possible.

Are there segments of the market where the firm's existing resources can be effectively concentrated?

How large is the firm's stake in the business? To the extent that the business represents a major source of revenues and profit, a greater commitment will probably need to be made to adapt to the changing circumstances.

Will corporate management, in the event that this is a business unit within a multibusiness corporation, be willing to accept different goals for the business in the future than it has in the past? A decision not to adapt to changes may result in high short-run returns from that particular business. Looking at the problem from the position of corporate planners interested in the welfare of the total corporation, a periodic market-by-market analysis in the terms described above would appear to be imperative prior to setting goals, agreeing on strategies, and allocating resources.

New Entrants

The "strategic window" concept has been used implicitly by many new entrants to judge the direction, timing, and scale of new entry activities. Gillette's entry into cigarette lighters, major computer manufacturers' entry into ATM's, and Procter & Gamble's entry into many consumer markets *after* pioneers have laid the groundwork for a large scale, mass market approach to the specific product areas, all are familiar examples.

Such approaches to strategic market planning require two distinctly different types of analysis:

1. Careful assessment has to be made of the firm's strengths and weaknesses. This should include audits of all the key resources of the company as well as its various existing programs of activity.
2. Attention should be directed away from the narrow focus of familiar products and markets to a search for opportunities to put unique competencies to work. This requires a broader appreciation of overall environmental, technical and market forces and knowledge of many more markets, than is encountered in many firms today. It puts a particular burden on marketing managers, general managers, and business planners used to thinking in terms of existing activities.

Analysis of patterns of market evolution and diagnosis of critical market require-

ments in the future can also be of use to incumbent competitors as a forewarning of a potential new entry. In such cases, adjustments in strategy can sometimes be made in advance, which will ultimately deter would-be new competitors. Even where this is not the case, resource commitments may be adjusted to reflect the future changes in structure of industrial supply.

CONCLUSION

The "strategic window" concept suggests that fundamental changes arc needed in marketing management practice, and in particular in strategic market planning activities. At the heart of these changes is the need to base marketing planning around predictions of future patterns of market evolution and to make assessments of the firm's capabilities to deal with change. Such analyses require considerably greater strategic orientation than the sales forecasting activities which underpin much marketing planning today. Users of product portfolio chart analysis, in particular, should consider the dynamic as opposed to the static implications in designating a particular business.

Entry and exit from markets is likely to occur with greater rapidity than is often the case today, as firms search for opportunities where their resources can be deployed with maximum effectiveness. Short of entry and exit, the allocation of funds to markets should be timed to coincide with the period when the fit between the firm and the market is at its optimum. Entering a market in its early stages and evolving with it until maturity may, on closer analysis, turn out to be a serious management error.

It has been said that while the life of the product is limited, a market has greater longevity and as such can provide a business with a steady and growing stream of revenue and profit if management can avoid being myopic about change. This article suggests that as far as any one firm is concerned, a market also is a temporary vehicle for growth, a vehicle which should be used and abandoned as circumstances dictate—the reason being that the firm is often slower to evolve and change than is the market in which it competes.

How Competitive Forces Shape Strategy

Michael E. Porter

The essence of strategy formulation is coping with competition. Yet it is easy to view competition too narrowly and too pessimistically. While one sometimes hears executives complaining to the contrary, intense competition in an industry is neither coincidence nor bad luck.

Moreover, in the fight for market share, competition is not manifested only in the other players. Rather, competition in an industry is rooted in its underlying economics, and competitive forces exist that go well beyond the established combatants in a particular industry. Customers, suppliers, potential entrants, and substitute products are all competitors that may be more or less prominent or active depending on the industry.

The state of competition in an industry depends on five basic forces, which are diagrammed in Figure 20-1. The collective strength of these forces determines the ultimate profit potential of an industry. It ranges

Reprinted by permission of *Harvard Business Review*. "How Competitive Forces Shape Strategy" by Michael E. Porter (March–April 1979). Copyright © 1979 by the President and Fellows of Harvard College; all rights reserved.

from *intense* in industries like tires, metal cans, and steel, where no company earns spectacular returns on investment, to *mild* in industries like oil field services and equipment, soft drinks, and toiletries, where there is room for quite high returns.

In the economists' "perfectly competitive" industry, jockeying for position is unbridled and entry to the industry very easy. This kind of industry structure, of course, offers the worst prospect for long-run profitability. The weaker the forces collectively, however, the greater the opportunity for superior performance.

Whatever their collective strength, the corporate strategist's goal is to find a position in the industry where his or her company can best defend itself against these forces or can influence them in its favor. The collective strength of the forces may be painfully apparent to all the antagonists; but to cope with them, the strategist must delve below the surface and analyze the sources of each. For example, what makes the industry vulnerable to entry? What determines the bargaining power of suppliers?

Figure 20-1
Forces Governing Competition in an Industry

Knowledge of these underlying sources of competitive pressure provides the groundwork for a strategic agenda of action. They highlight the critical strengths and weaknesses of the company, animate the positioning of the company in its industry, clarify the areas where strategic changes may yield the greatest payoff, and highlight the places where industry trends promise to hold the greatest significance as either opportunities or threats. Understanding these sources also proves to be of help in considering areas for diversification.

CONTENDING FORCES

The strongest competitive force or forces determine the profitability of an industry and so are of greatest importance in strategy formulation. For example, even a company with a strong position in an industry unthreatened by potential entrants will earn low returns if it faces a superior or a lower-cost substitute product—as the leading manufacturers of vacuum tubes and coffee percolators have learned to their sorrow. In such a situation, coping with the substitute product becomes the number one strategic priority.

Different forces take on prominence, of course, in shaping competition in each industry. In the ocean-going tanker industry the key force is probably the buyers (the major oil companies), while in tires it is powerful OEM buyers coupled with tough competitors. In the steel industry the key forces are foreign competitors and substitute materials.

Every industry has an underlying structure, or a set of fundamental economic and technical characteristics, that gives rise to these competitive forces. The strategist, wanting to position his company to cope best with its industry environment or to influence that environment in the company's favor, must learn what makes the environment tick.

This view of competition pertains equally to industries dealing in services and to those selling products. To avoid monotony in this article, I refer to both products and services as "products." The same general principles apply to all types of business.

A few characteristics are critical to the strength of each competitive force. I shall discuss them in this section.

Threat of Entry

New entrants to an industry bring new capacity, the desire to gain market share, and often substantial resources. Companies diversifying through acquisition into the industry from other markets often leverage their resources to cause a shake-up, as Philip Morris did with Miller beer.

The seriousness of the threat of entry depends on the barriers present and on the reaction from existing competitors that the entrant can expect. If barriers to entry are high and a newcomer can expect sharp retaliation from the entrenched competitors, obviously he will not pose a serious threat of entering.

There are six major sources of barriers to entry:

1. *Economies of scale*—These economies deter entry by forcing the aspirant either to come in on a large scale or to accept a cost disadvantage. Scale economies in production, research, marketing, and service are probably the key barriers to entry in the mainframe computer industry, as Xerox and GE sadly discovered. Economies of scale can also act as hurdles in distribution, utilization of the sales force financing, and nearly any other part of a business.

2. *Product differentiation*—Brand identification creates a barrier by forcing entrants to spend heavily to overcome customer loyalty. Advertising, customer service, being first in the industry, and product differences are among the factors fostering brand identification. It is perhaps the most important entry barrier in soft drinks, over-the-counter drugs, cosmetics, investment banking, and public accounting. To create high fences around their businesses, brewers couple brand identification with economies of scale in production, distribution, and marketing.

3. *Capital requirements*—The need to invest large financial resources in order to compete creates a barrier to entry, particularly if the capital is required for unrecoverable expenditures in up-front advertising or R&D. Capital is necessary not only for fixed facilities but also for customer credit, inventories, and absorbing start-up losses. While major corporations have the financial resources to invade almost any industry, the huge capital requirements in certain fields, such as computer manufacturing and mineral extraction, limit the pool of likely entrants.

4. *Cost disadvantages independent of size*—Entrenched companies may have cost advantages not available to potential rivals, no matter what their size and attainable economies of scale. These advantages can stem from the effects of the learning curve (and of its first cousin, the experience curve), proprietary technology, access to the best raw materials sources, assets purchased at preinflation prices, government subsidies, or favorable locations. Sometimes cost advantages are legally enforceable, as they are through patents. (For an analysis of the much-discussed experience curve as a barrier to entry, see Exhibit 20-1, p. 290.)

5. *Access to distribution channels*—The new boy on the block must, of course, secure distribution of his product or service. A new food product, for example, must displace others from the supermarket shelf via price breaks, promotions, intense selling efforts, or some other means. The more limited the wholesale or retail channels are and the more that existing competitors

Exhibit 20-1
THE EXPERIENCE CURVE AS AN ENTRY BARRIER

In recent years, the experience curve has become widely discussed as a key element of industry structure. According to this concept, unit costs in many manufacturing industries (some dogmatic adherents say in *all* manufacturing industries) as well as in some service industries decline with "experience," or a particular company's cumulative volume of production. (The experience curve, which encompasses many factors, is a broader concept than the better-known learning curve, which refers to the efficiency achieved over a period of time by workers through much repetition.)

The causes of the decline in unit costs are a combination of elements, including economies of scale, the learning curve for labor, and capital-labor substitution. The cost decline creates a barrier to entry because new competitors with no "experience" face higher costs than established ones, particularly the producer with the largest market share, and have difficulty catching up with the entrenched competitors.

Adherents of the experience curve concept stress the importance of achieving market leadership to maximize aggressive action to achieve it, such as price cutting in anticipation of falling costs in order to build volume. For the combatant that cannot achieve a healthy market share, the prescription is usually, "Get out."

Is the experience curve an entry barrier on which strategies should be built? The answer is: not in every industry. In fact, in some industries, building a strategy on the experience curve can be potentially disastrous. That costs decline with experience in some industries is not news to corporate executives. The significance of the experience

curve for strategy depends on what factors are causing the decline.

If costs are falling because a growing company can reap economies of scale through more efficient, automated facilities and vertical integration, then the cumulative volume of production is unimportant to its relative cost position. Here the lowest-cost producer is the one with the largest, most efficient facilities.

A new entrant may well be more efficient than the more experienced competitors; if it has built the newest plant, it will face no disadvantage in having to catch up. The strategic prescription, "You must have the largest, most efficient plant," is a lot different from, "You must produce the greatest cumulative output of the item to get your costs down."

Whether a drop in costs with cumulative (not absolute) volume erects an entry barrier also depends on the sources of the decline. If costs go down because of technical advances known generally in the industry or because of the development of improved equipment that can be copied or purchased from equipment suppliers, the experience curve is no entry barrier at all—in fact, new or less experienced competitors may actually enjoy a *cost advantage* over the leaders. Free of the legacy of heavy past investments, the newcomer or less experienced competitor can purchase or copy the newest and lower-cost equipment and technology.

If, however, experience can be kept proprietary, the leaders will maintain a cost advantage. But new entrants may require less experience to reduce their costs than the leaders needed. All this suggests that the experience curve can be a shaky entry barrier on which to build a strategy.

While space does not permit a complete treatment here, I want to mention a few other crucial elements in determining the appropriateness of a strategy built on the entry barrier provided by the experience curve:

- The height of the barrier depends on how important costs are to competition compared with other areas like marketing, selling and innovation.
- The barrier can be nullified by product or process innovations leading to a substantially new technology and thereby creating an entirely new experience curve.* New entrants can leapfrog the industry leaders and alight on the new experience curve, to which those leaders may be poorly positioned to jump.
- If more than one strong company is building its strategy on the experience curve, the consequences can be nearly fatal. By the time only one rival is left pursuing such a strategy, industry growth may have stopped and the prospects of reaping the spoils of victory long since evaporated.

*For an example drawn from the history of the automobile industry, see William J. Abernathy and Kenneth Wayne, "The Limits of the Learning Curve," *Harvard Business Review,* September–October 1974, p. 109.

---

have these tied up, obviously the tougher that entry into the industry will be. Sometimes this barrier is so high that, to surmount it, a new contestant must create its own distribution channels, as Timex did in the watch industry in the 1950s.

6. *Government policy*—The government can limit or even foreclose entry to industries with such controls as license requirements and limits on access to raw materials. Regulated industries like trucking, liquor retailing, and freight forwarding are noticeable examples; more subtle government restrictions operate in fields like ski-area development and coal mining. The government can also play a major indirect role by affecting entry barriers through controls such as air and water pollution standards and safety regulations.

The potential rival's expectations about the reaction of existing competitors also will influence its decision on whether to enter. The company is likely to have second thoughts if incumbents have previously lashed out at new entrants or if:

- The incumbents possess substantial resources to fight back, including excess cash and unused borrowing power, productive capacity, or clout with distribution channels and customers.
- The incumbents seem likely to cut prices because of a desire to keep market shares or because of industrywide excess capacity.
- Industry growth is slow, affecting its ability to absorb the new arrival and probably causing the financial performance of all the parties involved to decline.

Changing Conditions   From a strategic standpoint there are two important additional points to note about the threat of entry.

First, it changes, of course, as these conditions change. The expiration of Polaroid's basic patents on instant photography, for instance, greatly reduced its absolute cost entry barrier built by proprietary technology. It is not surprising that Kodak plunged into the market. Product differentiation in printing has all but disappeared. Conversely, in the auto industry economies of scale increased enormously with post-World War II automation and vertical integration—virtually stopping successful new entry.

Second, strategic discussions involving a large segment of an industry can have a major impact on the conditions determining the threat of entry. For example, the actions of many U.S. wine producers in the 1960s to step up product introductions, raise advertising levels, and expand distribution nationally surely strengthened the entry roadblocks by raising economies of scale and making access to distribution channels more difficult. Similarly, decisions by members of the recreational vehicle industry to vertically integrate in order to lower costs have greatly increased the economies of scale and raised the capital cost barriers.

Powerful Suppliers and Buyers

Suppliers can exert bargaining power on participants in an industry by raising prices or reducing the quality of purchased goods and services. Powerful suppliers can thereby squeeze profitability out of an industry unable to recover cost increases in its own prices. By raising their prices, soft drink concentrate producers have contributed to the erosion of profitability of bottling companies because the bottlers, facing intense competition from powdered mixes, fruit drinks, and other beverages, have limited freedom to raise *their* prices accordingly. Customers likewise can force down prices, demand higher quality or more service, and play competitors off against each other—all at the expense of industry profits.

The power of each important supplier or buyer group depends on a number of characteristics of its market situation and on the relative importance of its sales or purchases to the industry compared with its overall business.

A *supplier* group is powerful if:

- It is dominated by a few companies and is more concentrated than the industry it sells to.
- Its product is unique or at least differentiated, or if it has built up switching costs. Switching costs are fixed costs buyers face in changing suppliers. These arise because, among other things, a buyer's product specifications tie it to particular suppliers, it has invested heavily in specialized ancillary equipment or in learning how to operate a supplier's equipment (as in computer software), or its production lines are connected to the supplier's manufacturing facilities (as in some manufacture of beverage containers).
- It is not obliged to contend with other products for sale to the industry. For instance, the competition between the steel companies and the aluminum companies to sell to the can industry checks the power of each supplier.
- It poses a credible threat of integrating forward into the industry's business. This provides a check against the industry's ability to improve the terms on which it purchases.
- The industry is not an important customer of the supplier group. If the industry *is* an important customer, suppliers' fortunes will be closely tied to the industry, and they will want to protect the industry through reasonable pricing and assistance in activities like R&D and lobbying.

A *buyer* group is powerful if:

- It is concentrated or purchases in large volumes. Large-volume buyers are particularly potent forces if heavy fixed costs characterize the industry—as they do in metal containers, corn refining, and bulk chemicals, for example—which raise the stakes to keep capacity filled.

- The products it purchases from the industry are standard or undifferentiated. The buyer, sure that they can always find alternative suppliers, may play one company against another, as they do in aluminum extrusion.
- The products it purchases from the industry form a component of its product and represent a significant fraction of its cost. The buyers are likely to shop for a favorable price and purchase selectively. Where the product sold by the industry in question is a small fraction of buyers' cost, buyers are usually much less sensitive.
- It earns low profits, which create great incentive to lower its purchasing costs. Highly profitable buyers, however, are generally less price sensitive (that is, of course, if the item does not represent a large fraction of their costs).
- The industry's product is unimportant to the quality of the buyers' products or services. Where the quality of the buyers' products is very much affected by the industry's product, buyers are generally less price sensitive. Industries in which this situation obtains include oil field equipment, where a malfunction can lead to large losses, and enclosures for electronic medical and test instruments, where the quality of the enclosure can influence the user's impression about the quality of the equipment inside.
- The industry's product does not save the buyer money. Where the industry's product or service can pay for itself many times over, the buyer is rarely price sensitive; rather, he is interested in quality. This is true in services like investment banking and public accounting, where errors in judgment can be costly and embarrassing,

and in businesses like the logging of oil wells, where an accurate survey can save thousands of dollars in drilling costs.
- The buyers pose a credible threat of integrating backward to make the industry's product. The Big Three auto producers and major buyers of cars have often used the threat of self-manufacture as a bargaining lever. But sometimes an industry engenders a threat to buyers that its members may integrate forward.

Most of these sources of buyer power can be attributed to consumers as a group as well as to industrial and commercial buyers; only a modification of the frame of reference is necessary. Consumers tend to be more price sensitive if they are purchasing products that are undifferentiated, expensive relative to their incomes, and of a sort where quality is not particularly important.

The buying power of retailers is determined by the same rules, with one important addition. Retailers can gain significant bargaining power over manufacturers when they can influence consumers' purchasing decisions as they do in audio components, jewelry, appliances, sporting goods, and other goods.

Strategic Action   A company's choice of suppliers to buy from or buyer groups to sell to should be viewed as a crucial strategic decision. A company can improve its strategic posture by finding suppliers or buyers who possess the least power to influence it adversely.

Most common is the situation of a company being able to choose whom it will sell to—in other words, buyer selection. Rarely do all the buyer groups a company sells to enjoy equal power. Even if a company sells to a single industry, segments usually exist within that industry that exercise less power (and that are therefore less price sensitive) than others. For example, the replacement market for most products is less price sensitive than the overall market.

As a rule, a company can sell to powerful buyers and still come away with above-average profitability only if it is a low-cost producer in its industry or if its product enjoys some unusual, if not unique, features. In supplying large customers with electric motors, Emerson Electric earns high returns because its low cost position permits the company to meet or undercut competitors' prices.

If the company lacks a low cost position or a unique product, selling to everyone is self-defeating because the more sales it achieves, the more vulnerable it becomes. The company may have to muster the courage to turn away business and sell only to less potent customers.

Buyer selection has been a key to the success of National Can and Crown Cork & Seal. They focus on the segments of the can industry where they can create product differentiation, minimize the threat of backward integration, and otherwise mitigate the awesome power of their customers. Of course, some industries do not enjoy the luxury of selecting "good" buyers.

As the factors creating supplier and buyer power change with time or as a result of a company's strategic decisions, naturally the power of these groups rises or declines. In the ready-to-wear clothing industry, as the buyers (department stores and clothing stores) have become more concentrated and control has passed to large chains, the industry has come under increasing pressure and suffered falling margins. The industry has been unable to differentiate its product or engender switching costs that lock in its buyers enough to neutralize these trends.

Substitute Products

By placing a ceiling on prices it can charge, substitute products or services limit the potential of an industry. Unless it can upgrade the quality of the product or differentiate it somehow (as via marketing), the industry will suffer in earnings and possibly in growth.

Manifestly, the more attractive the price-performance trade-off offered by substitute products, the firmer the lid placed on the industry's profit potential. Sugar producers confronted with the large-scale commercialization of high-fructose corn syrup, a sugar substitute, are learning this lesson today.

Substitutes not only limit profits in normal times; they also reduce the bonanza an industry can reap in boom times. In 1978 the producers of fiberglass insulation enjoyed unprecedented demand as a result of high energy costs and severe winter weather. But the industry's ability to raise prices was tempered by the plethora of insulation substitutes, including cellulose, rock wool, and styrofoam. These substitutes are bound to become an even stronger force once the current round of plant additions by fiberglass insulation producers has boosted capacity enough to meet demand (and then some).

Substitute products that deserve the most attention strategically are those that (a) are subject to trends improving their price-performance trade-off with the industry's product, or (b) are produced by industries earning high profits. Substitutes often come rapidly into play if some development increases competition in their industries and causes price reduction or performance improvement.

Jockeying for Position

Rivalry among existing competitors takes the familiar form of jockeying for position—using tactics like price competition, product introduction, and advertising slugfests. Intense rivalry is related to the presence of a number of factors:

- Competitors are numerous or are roughly equal in size and power. In many U.S. industries in recent years foreign contenders, of course, have become part of the competitive picture.
- Industry growth is slow, precipitating fights for market share that involve expansion-minded members.
- The product or service lacks differentiation or switching costs, which lock in buyers and protect one combatant from raids on its customers by another.
- Fixed costs are high or the product is perishable, creating strong temptation to cut prices. Many basic materials businesses, like paper and aluminum, suffer from this problem when demand slackens.
- Capacity is normally augmented in large increments. Such additions, as in the chlorine and vinyl chloride businesses, disrupt the industry's supply—demand balance and often lead to periods of overcapacity and price cutting.
- Exit barriers are high. Exit barriers, like very specialized assets or management's loyalty to a particular business, keep companies competing even though they may be earning low or even negative returns on investment. Excess capacity remains functioning, and the profitability of the healthy competitors suffers as the sick ones hang on.[1] If the entire industry suffers from overcapacity, it may seek government help—particularly if foreign competition is present.
- The rivals are diverse in strategies, origins, and "personalities." They have different ideas about how to compete and continually run head-on into each other in the process.

As an industry matures, its growth rate changes, resulting in declining profits and (often) a shakeout. In the booming recreational vehicle industry of the early 1970s, nearly every producer did well; but slow growth since then has eliminated the high returns, even for the strongest members, not to mention many of the weaker companies. The same profit story has been played out in industry after industry—snowmobiles, aerosol packaging, and sports equipment are just a few examples.

An acquisition can introduce a very different personality to an industry, as has been the case with Black & Decker's takeover of McCullough, the producer of chain saws. Technological innovation can boost the level of fixed costs in the production process, as it did in the shift from batch to continuous-line photo finishing in the 1960s.

While a company must live with many of these factors—because they are built into industry economics—it may have some latitude for improving matters through strategic shifts. For example, it may try to raise buyers' switching costs or increase product differentiation. A focus on selling efforts in the fastest-growing segments of the industry or on market areas with the lowest fixed costs can reduce the impact of industry rivalry. If it is feasible, a company can try to avoid confrontation with competitors having high exit barriers and can thus sidestep involvement in bitter price cutting.

FORMULATION OF STRATEGY

Once the corporate strategist has assessed the forces affecting competition in his industry and their underlying causes, he can identify his company's strengths and weaknesses. The crucial strengths and weaknesses from a strategic standpoint are the company's posture vis-à-vis the underlying causes of each force. Where does it stand against substitutes? Against the sources of entry barriers?

Then the strategist can devise a plan of action that may include (1) positioning the company so that its capabilities provide the best defense against the competitive force; and/or (2) influencing the balance of the forces through strategic moves, thereby improving the company's position; and/or (3) anticipating shifts in the factors underlying the forces and responding to them, with the hope of exploiting change by choosing a strategy appropriate for the new competitive balance before opponents recognize it. I shall consider each strategic approach in turn.

Positioning the Company

The first approach takes the structure of the industry as given and matches the company's strengths and weaknesses to it. Strategy can be viewed as building defenses against the competitive forces or as finding positions in the industry where the forces are weakest.

Knowledge of the company's capabilities and of the causes of the competitive forces will highlight the areas where the company should confront competition and where avoid it. If the company is a low-cost producer, it may choose to confront powerful buyers while it takes care to sell them only products not vulnerable to competition from substitutes.

The success of Dr Pepper in the soft drink industry illustrates the coupling of realistic knowledge of corporate strengths with sound industry analysis to yield a superior strategy. Coca-Cola and Pepsi-Cola dominate Dr Pepper's industry, where many small concentrate producers compete for a piece of the action. Dr Pepper chose a strategy of avoiding the largest-selling drink segment, maintaining a narrow flavor line, forgoing the development of a captive bottler network, and marketing heavily. The company positioned itself so as to be least vulnerable to its competitive forces while it exploited its small size.

In the $11.5 billion soft drink industry, barriers to entry in the form of brand identifi-cation, large-scale marketing, and access to a bottler network are enormous. Rather than accept the formidable costs and scale economies in having its own bottler network—that is, following the lead of the Big Two and of Seven-Up—Dr Pepper took advantage of the different flavor of its drink to "piggyback" on Coke and Pepsi bottlers who wanted a full line to sell to customers. Dr Pepper coped with the power of these buyers through extraordinary service and other efforts to distinguish its treatment of them from that of Coke and Pepsi.

Many small companies in the soft drink business offer cola drinks that thrust them into head-to-head competition against the majors. Dr Pepper, however, maximized product differentiation by maintaining a narrow line of beverages built around an unusual flavor.

Finally, Dr Pepper met Coke and Pepsi with an advertising onslaught emphasizing the alleged uniqueness of its single flavor. This campaign built strong brand identification and great customer loyalty. Helping its efforts was the fact that Dr Pepper's formula involved lower raw materials cost, which gave the company an absolute cost advantage over its major competitors.

There are no economies of scale in soft drink concentrate production, so Dr Pepper could prosper despite its small share of the business (6%). Thus Dr Pepper confronted competition in marketing but avoided it in product line and in distribution. This artful positioning combined with good implementation has led to an enviable record in earnings and in the stock market.

Influencing the Balance

When dealing with the forces that drive industry competition, a company can devise a strategy that takes the offensive. This posture is designed to do more than merely cope with the forces themselves; it is meant to alter their causes.

Innovations in marketing can raise brand identification or otherwise differentiate the product. Capital investments in large-scale facilities or vertical integration affect entry barriers. The balance of forces is partly a result of external factors and partly in the company's control.

Exploiting Industry Change

Industry evolution is important strategically because evolution, of course, brings with it changes in the sources of competition I have identified. In the familiar product life-cycle pattern, for example, growth rates change, product differentiation is said to decline as the business becomes more mature, and the companies tend to integrate vertically.

These trends are not so important in themselves; what is critical is whether they affect the sources of competition. Consider vertical integration. In the maturing minicomputer industry, extensive vertical integration, both in manufacturing and in software development, is taking place. This very significant trend is greatly raising economies of scale as well as the amount of capital necessary to compete in the industry. This in turn is raising barriers to entry and may drive some smaller competitors out of the industry once growth levels off.

Obviously, the trends carrying the highest priority from a strategic standpoint are those that affect the most important sources of competition in the industry and those that elevate new causes to the forefront. In contract aerosol packaging, for example, the trend toward less product differentiation is now dominant. It has increased buyers' power, lowered the barriers to entry, and intensified competition.

The framework for analyzing competition that I have described can also be used to predict the eventual profitability of an industry. In long-range planning the task is to examine each competitive force, forecast the magnitude of each underlying cause, and then construct a composite picture of the likely profit potential of the industry.

The outcome of such an exercise may differ a great deal from the existing industry structure. Today, for example, the solar heating business is populated by dozens and perhaps hundreds of companies, none with a major market position. Entry is easy, and competitors are battling to establish solar heating as a superior substitute for conventional methods.

The potential of this industry will depend largely on the shape of future barriers to entry, the improvement of the industry's position relative to substitutes, the ultimate intensity of competition, and the power captured by buyers and suppliers. These characteristics will in turn be influenced by such factors as the establishment of brand identities, significant economies of scale or experience curves in equipment manufacture wrought by technological change, the ultimate capital costs to compete, and the extent of overhead in production facilities.

The framework for analyzing industry competition has direct benefits in setting diversification strategy. It provides a road map for answering the extremely difficult question inherent in diversification decisions: "What is the potential of this business?" Combining the framework with judgment in its application, a company may be able to spot an industry with a good future before this good fortune is reflected in the prices of acquisition candidates.

MULTIFACETED RIVALRY

Corporate managers have directed a great deal of attention to defining their businesses as a crucial step in strategy formulation. Theodore Levitt, in his classic 1960 article in the *Harvard Business Review,* argued strongly for avoiding the myopia of narrow, product-oriented industry definition.[2] Numerous other authorities have also stressed the need to look beyond product to function in defining a business, beyond national boundaries to potential international competition, and beyond the ranks of one's competitors today to those that may become competitors tomorrow. As a result of these urgings, the proper definition of a company's industry or industries has become an endlessly debated subject.

One motive behind this debate is the desire to exploit new markets. Another, perhaps more important motive is the fear of overlooking latent sources of competition that someday may threaten the industry. Many managers concentrate so single-mindedly on their direct antagonists in the fight for market share that they fail to realize that they are also competing with their customers and their suppliers for bargaining power. Meanwhile, they also neglect to keep a wary eye out for new entrants to the contest or fail to recognize the subtle threat of substitute products.

The key to growth—even survival—is to stake out a position that is less vulnerable to attack from head-to-head opponents, whether established or new, and less vulnerable to erosion for the direction of buyers, suppliers, and substitute goods. Establishing such a position can take many forms—solidifying relationships with favorable customers, differentiating the product either substantively or psychologically through marketing, integrating forward or backward, establishing technological leadership.

NOTES

1. For a more complete discussion of exit barriers and their implications for strategy, see my article, "Please Note Location of Nearest Exit," *California Management Review,* Winter 1976, p. 21.
2. Theodore Levitt, "Marketing Myopia," reprinted as a *Harvard Business Review Classic,* September–October 1975, p. 26.

◆

Toward Strategic Intelligence Systems

David B. Montgomery and Charles B. Weinberg

In the past 10 years, there has been a dramatic increase in the use of strategic planning tools such as BCG's growth/share matrix, AD Little's life cycle strategy, Shell's Directional Policy Matrix, and GE's stoplight strategy matrix. This has resulted from the much-needed perception by management that projecting yesteryear's trends into the future and then concentrating on day-to-day operating decisions is not enough for success. Strategic planning is rapidly being included in the definition of essential managerial tasks, and a tremendous amount of managerial interest has been focused on the techniques outlined above.

While this focus has been and should continue to be of great value, a critical point is often overlooked. *A strategic plan can be no better than the information on which it is based.* There has been little focus on strategic intelligence systems, the selection, gathering, and analysis of information needed for strategic planning. Yet it is obvious that without good market share information, a growth/share matrix will be unreliable, or that knowledge of a competitor's intentions can be the key determinant of a strategy.

This paper is designed first to present an overview of strategic intelligence systems (SIS)—their purpose and the kinds of information they gather. The second section discusses the collection of strategic intelligence. The final section provides a brief discussion of the analysis and processing of strategic intelligence.

Examples are provided describing different companies' approaches to SIS, based on a research project in which, in addition to an extensive literature review, more than 100 executives in over 30 companies were interviewed. Although corporate names need to be disguised, the firms interviewed come from a broad range of industries and in most cases had sales in excess of $100 million. These examples are not intended to add up to "the" one complete, integrated approach to be copied, but rather are illustrations and stimuli for thought.

David B. Montgomery and Charles B. Weinberg, "Toward Strategic Intelligence Systems," Vol. 43 (Fall 1979). Reprinted from *Journal of Marketing,* published by the American Marketing Association.

STRATEGIC INTELLIGENCE SYSTEMS—AN OVERVIEW

Purposes

It is important that the design of a SIS consider the purposes for which it is intended. Some method is needed to avoid collecting vast quantities of meaningless data, while simultaneously preventing a focus so narrow that crucial information is missed. An understanding of the purposes of a SIS is helpful in achieving this aim.

Defensive intelligence is oriented towards avoiding surprises. A company plans and manages itself on the basis of certain implicit and explicit assumptions about the world. A properly designed SIS should monitor the world to make certain that these assumptions continue to hold and to send up a flag if a major change (usually a threat) occurs. In one company which desired to implement this mode of thinking, a policy was made that unanticipated "surprises" would not be accepted as a reason for not meeting a strategic business unit's (SBU) targets. The view taken was that if an event was potentially so important, the manager should have a SIS watching for it and would therefore be able to prepare contingency plans.

Passive intelligence is designed to provide benchmark data for objective evaluation. An example of this is Dayton-Hudson's gathering of competitive retailer performance in order to reward management performance on a basis relative to competition.

Offensive intelligence is designed to identify opportunities. Often opportunities that would not otherwise be discovered can be identified through a SIS. For example, one company's strategic intelligence indicated that a major competitor was laying off R&D people of a certain type during a recession. From this, the company knew that the competitor would be unable to respond on a timely basis to a certain class of research-generated

product improvements. The company used this knowledge to justify current R&D expenditures which enabled it to capture market position when the competitor was weakest. Another example was when a company's intelligence system indicated that a competitor had a serious service problem. From its own previous experience, the company recognized this as an inventory investment problem and knew that it would take the competitor about two years to straighten out its problems. Armed with this knowledge, the company substantially increased its market share.

Areas of Focus

In order to accomplish the three purposes of defensive, passive, and offensive intelligence, a SIS should focus on the following environments.

Competitive

The competitive environment is of critical importance. However, a firm should not simply monitor its current competitors, but should scan the environment for potential competitors. The price of ignoring potential competitors and neglecting to take proactive steps to avoid or blunt their effect can be extremely high. For example, Scott Paper's preoccupation with acquisitions apparently diverted its attention from the threat posed by Procter and Gamble's potential and actual emergence as a substantial force in Scott's major paper markets (Hyatt and Coonly 1971).

Customers may also be potential competitors. One company which was heavily dependent upon a large customer analyzed that customer's incentives for backward integration. This analysis, triggered by an explicit requirement for contingency plans, suggested that, from the customer's viewpoint, backward integration was not in the customer's best interest. The next year, when the company's intelligence agents—its salespeople—learned about the customer's plans to integrate backward, the previous analysis was used to dissuade the customer from that course of action.

Technological

The technological environment is crucial not only because of its evolutionary impact on existing products but also because many innovations are introduced from outside a traditional industry—e.g., ball point pens, xerography, instant photography. Cooper and Schendel's (1976) study of 22 companies in seven industries (locomotives, vacuum receiving tubes, fountain pens, safety razors, fossil fuel boilers, propellers, and leather) found the first commercial introduction of an innovation occurred from outside the industry in four out of seven industries. The study further found that the old technologies did not decline immediately, but continued to expand in four out of the seven cases. In fact, it took anywhere from five to 14 years for the dollar volume of the new technology to exceed that of the old technology. The mode of penetration of the new technology tended to be the capturing of a series of submarkets. This study suggests that replacement technologies may emerge and develop even while companies engaged in the old technology are lulled into complacency by near term prosperity. From a strategic perspective, long-run survival requires at least a monitoring of emerging technology. In one company interviewed in our study, the corporate planning staff provides a list of emerging technologies and division managers then are required in their strategic plans to indicate the likely impact of these technologies upon their division. The purpose is not only to sensitize division managers, but the corporation as a whole to coming opportunities and threats.

Customer

Thorough analysis of a firm's customers and noncustomers is possibly the most valuable and most neglected area of strategic intelli-

gence, Customer analysis means more than figuring out how to get Customer X to repeat or expand an order. Good customer and noncustomer analysis should reveal emerging technologies, competitive advantages and disadvantages and new product ideas. Von Hippel's (1977) study of technological innovation in two industries found that in 74% of the 137 innovations studied, the source of the innovation was the supplier's customers. In these two industries, customers provided about three times as many new ideas as the company research departments.

Economic

The economic environment is of overriding importance to a company's future. Issues such as GNP, inflation, the money market, and interest rates are of obvious importance. Changes in the price of raw materials (e.g., oil) significantly affect most companies. It is also important to try to determine the secondary implications of these benchmark indicators. For example, a move towards balancing the federal bridge may lower the amount of government-sponsored R&D forthcoming in a particular field. Government responses to continuing inflation, such as price and wage guidelines, should be anticipated and contingency plans prepared.

Examination of the effects of these issues on suppliers is also crucial. For example, many institutional food services on long-term, fixed price contracts have had profits severely hurt due to very sharp increases which their suppliers have imposed on certain products due to worldwide shortages.

Political and Regulatory

The political and regulatory environment is a difficult one as international companies are particularly aware. However, the increasing number of federal and state agencies which seek to impact on corporate policies, often with conflicting objectives, affects virtually all companies. In a recent survey of CEOs of the 1975 Fortune 500, government was cited as the number one area of concern (Burk 1976). Several companies such as Mobil and General Electric have adopted a proactive stance to try to improve the political climate within which private corporations must function (Ross 1976).

The fact that government agencies often do not correctly anticipate either the impact or the response to regulatory actions indicates the opportunity for a broadening of business/government contact. A recent example would be the FTC's de facto voiding (by unacceptable restrictions) the Bic purchase of American Safety Razor from Phillip Morris. The FTC rejected this acquisition on the grounds that it would be anticompetitive. This FTC action has been considered a remote possibility, and was apparently a surprise to the companies involved. Perhaps better intelligence would have identified the FTC as a potential major problem. Extensive advance briefing could have conceivably altered the outcome, or else the effort could have been abandoned before significant amounts of managerial time were expended.

Social

The final environment to be reviewed here relates to the rapidly changing social environment which has led to concerns with such issues as pollution control, conservation, and the rights of minorities. Again, appropriate intelligence may enable corporations to anticipate and react to such shifts in a more functional manner than has been typical of the past. As a case in point, GE claims that its environmental system led it to anticipate the emerging women's movement which enabled it to produce guidelines for women's employment one year ahead of the government (Wilson 1975). Anticipating social concerns generates a time advantage in which companies can provide positive, helpful input to government policy makers charged with establishing guidelines and regulations.

STRATEGIC INTELLIGENCE SYSTEMS IN THE STRATEGIC INTELLIGENCE CYCLE

Strategic intelligence systems can be seen as being part of the strategic intelligence cycle (see Figure 21-1). As mentioned above, most current work has been concerned with the latter stages of this cycle—processing and analysis, dissemination, and use. A SIS is essentially the feeder process to the analysis and use segments of the strategic intelligence cycle. The SIS performs two crucial functions, directing the intelligence function and collecting the information. This section will focus on these tasks.

Directing the Intelligence Function

This first stage of the intelligence cycle is concerned with establishing parameters for what information is needed, what priorities should be established, and what indicators should be monitored. Since a specific corporate application must account for idiosyncracies in the company's situation and its management style, the discussion in this section will not prescribe a formula, but rather will provide a broad outline of the issues and offer several specific illustrations.

Needs

There has been a substantial and praiseworthy increase in management's desires for environmental information. However, a word of caution is in order. The problem is not to generate data, but to determine what information is relevant and actionable. The emerging tools

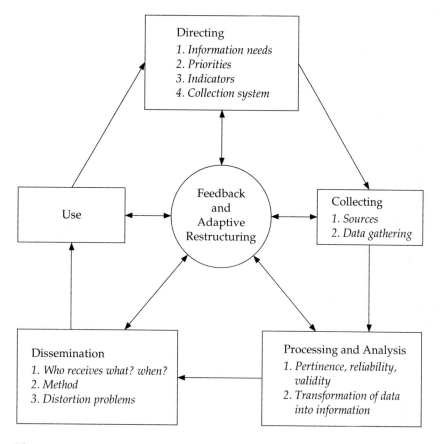

Figure 21-1
The Intelligence Circle

of strategic planning and analysis—product portfolios, competitive audits, etc.—provide a framework for ascertaining what information is needed and how it might be used if obtained. As the USE portion of the strategic intelligence cycle has become more sophisticated, the need for focused information also has increased.

A potentially useful framework for specifying information needs can be generated from the tripartite military paradigm of (1) areas of influence, (2) immediate zone, and (3) area of interest. The areas of influence would be the product/market segments in

which the company is currently engaged. The immediate zone represents areas of competitive activity which are close to, but not directly competitive with, the company's current operations. The area of interest represents areas of potential opportunities or threats in the longer term. Generally there is less need for detail and a longer time horizon as the focus shifts outward from areas of influence.

Many companies fail to utilize available opportunities due to their exclusive concentration on their areas of influence and consequent lack of attention to their immediate zone and areas of interest. As an example of this kind of opportunity, Gillette noted that Bic, which had been a formidable competitor in the disposable lighter market, had pioneered disposable razors in Europe in 1975 (*Business Week* Feb. 28, 1977). When Gillette learned that Bic had introduced the disposable razor in Canada in early 1976, it became clear that a major potential competitor was drawing near to the U.S. market. In response, Gillette rushed its "Good News" disposable razor into production and onto the national market in early 1976. Bic followed with U.S. test markets in mid-1976, but Gilette had apparently already paved the way for its dominance of this market. It is clear that by paying attention to its immediate zone and area of interest, Gillette was able to capitalize on an opportunity it would have lost had it only focused on its domestic markets.

Priorities

A useful conceptual approach to establishing priorities may be stated as follows:

Importance of becoming aware of an event of interest =
1. Importance of event to the organization.
2. Speed with which the event can impact the organization.
3. Speed with which the organization can react to the event.

Intelligence priorities should be established based upon (1) the importance of becoming aware of an event, (2) the likelihood the event will occur, and (3) the costs of anticipation and reaction. A SIS is justified if the costs of reacting to events exceed the costs of anticipating them and responding proactively. We believe that if companies were to carefully make such evaluations and tradeoffs, then far more companies would attend to the development and nurturing of strategic intelligence systems.

Indicators

While a company might like to have some direct measures of a competitor's intentions, such measures are usually lacking. Hence firms must resort to using indicators or surrogate measures. For example, content analysis of corporate annual reports might be used in order to assess the extent to which a competitor's management is proactive or reactive in its approach to the world.

An indicator need not be unambiguous in its potential impact on the company. For example, if a competitor should make an unexpectedly low bid on a contract, this could be an indicator of one or more conditions such as: (1) the competitor's backlog is running dangerously low and he is getting desperate for work, (2) the persons in charge of the bid erred, or (3) the competitor has leap frogged existing technology. The indicator—an unusually low bid—may therefore relate to a variety of true states, each of which has substantially different strategic implications for the company.

Collecting Intelligence

Intelligence collection entails the notion of scanning the environments of a company in search of data which individually or collectively will provide decision relevant inputs to the firm.

Scanning can be subdivided into two subcomponents: surveillance and search. Surveillance is a viewing and monitoring function which does not focus upon a single target or objective, but rather observes multiple aspects of the environment being scanned in an effort to detect relevant changes. In contrast, search implies deliberate investigation and research. The detection of significant events in the environment by surveillance will often trigger a search for further answers. To illustrate, one of the companies interviewed learned, through its conventional competitive surveillance activities (e.g., attending to articles and announcements concerning competitors in the business press), that a major competitor had sold a particular manufacturing operation. Since the company knew from its own operations that this manufacturing activity was the most profitable portion of its own vertically integrated chain of activities, the question arose as to why the competitor had sold this operation. Two potential reasons seemed apparent: (1) the competitor, a closely held company, was in a serious cash bind and was forced to sell this profitable operation in order to improve its financial position or (2) the competitor had made a breakthrough that would render the old technology either obsolete or at least substantially less valuable. Set against the background of data the company had, both answers seemed plausible. Learning the true answer had important strategic significance. If done for financial reasons, this could signal either competitor vulnerability or a reduction in his vulnerability depending upon the results of a further investigation. On the other hand, if the competitor had made some technological breakthroughs, then the company could no longer assume a stable environment. Clearly, early resolution of these uncertainties was required. This example illustrates how a signal detected by the surveillance function of scanning can lead to questions which require search to answer.

There is some empirical evidence indicating that scanning can be beneficial. In his analysis of a contingency theory of strategy formulation, Miller (1975) concludes that successful firms tend to use more scanning. Or, to view the situation conversely, Schendel, Patten, and Riggs's (1976) study of corporate turn-around strategies in some 54 companies concluded that the original downturn typically resulted from the failure of the firm's scanning or management control procedure to identify more than one or two of the major problems confronting the firm. Thus, there

can be both upscale reward and downside risk attached to environmental scanning. These results are consistent with Grinyer and Norburn's (1975) study which found that higher financial performance was positively associated with the use of more informal channels of communication and with the number of items of information used in reaching decisions.

Sources of Intelligence

Legitimate sources of intelligence are in abundant supply for the manager and company willing to apply imagination and effort in structuring a strategic intelligence system. Table 21-1 illustrates primary sources of intelligence along with selected examples of each. While it would be of doubtful value for any given company to pursue all sources on a continuing basis, a company should review a wide range of potential sources before choosing which one to use. The text will highlight some of the sources in Table 21-1 and examples of their use. Hopefully this will suggest the possibilities available to management.

Federal Government A significant recent development has been the emergence of the federal government as a source of strategic intelligence.[1] While the government has long been a source of commercially relevant information, recent amendments to the Freedom of Information Act (FOIA) have greatly expanded the potential role of the government as an intelligence source. The 1966 FOIA was amended in 1974 in order to give it greater force. The amended Act provides that any person has the right of access to and can obtain copies of any document, file, or other record in the possession of any federal agency or department. To limit noncompliance by delay, the amended FOIA provides that requests must either be granted or denied within 10 working days in most cases. Nine specific dis-

Table 21-1
Sources of Intelligence

Source	Examples	Comment
Government	Freedom of Information Act	1974 amendments have led to accelerating use.
	Government Contract Administration	Examination of competitor's bids and documentation may reveal competitor's technology and indicate his costs and bidding philosophy.
	Patent filings	Belgium and Italy publish patent applications shortly after they are filed. Some companies (e.g., pharmaceutical) patent their mistakes in order to confuse their competitors.
Competitors	Annual reports and 10Ks	FTC and SEC line of business reporting requirements will render this source more useful in the future.
	Speeches and public announcements of competitor's officers	Reveal management philosophy, priorities, and self-evaluation systems.
	Products	Systematic analysis of a competitor's products via back engineering may reveal the competitor's technology and enable the company to monitor changes in the competitor's engineering and assembly operations. Forecasts of a competitor's sales may often be made from observing his serial numbers over time.
	Employment ads	May suggest the technical and marketing directions in which a competitor is headed.
	Consultants	For example, if a competitor has retained Boston Consulting, then portfolio management strategies become more likely.
Suppliers	Banks, advertising agencies, public relations firms, and direct mailers and catalogers, as well as hard goods suppliers	Have a tendency to be more talkative than competitors since the information transmitted may enhance supplier's business. Can be effective sources of information on such items as competitor's equipment installations and on what retail competitors are already carrying certain product lines. Suppliers biases can usually be recognized.
Customers	Purchasing agents	Generally regarded as self serving. Low reliability as a source.

Table 21-1
Continued

Source	Examples	Comment
	Customer engineers and corporate officers	Valued sources of intelligence. One company taught its salespersons to perform elementary service for customers in order to get the salespersons past the purchasing agent and on to the more valued sources of intelligence.
Professional Associations and Meetings	Scientific and technical society meetings, management association meetings	Examine competitor's products, research and development, and management approach as revealed in displays, brochures, scientific papers, and speeches.
Company Personnel	Executives, sales force, engineers and scientists, purchasing agents	Sensitize them to the need for intelligence and train them to recognize and transmit to the proper organizational location relevant intelligence which comes to their attention.
Other Sources	Consultants, management service companies, and the media	Wide variety of special purpose and syndicated reports available.

cretionary exemptions are provided in the amended Act; exemption 4, which exempts "trade secrets and commercial or financial information obtained from a person and privileged or confidential," is of the greatest interest from the standpoint of corporate FOIA use.

It should be emphasized that the exemptions may be used at the discretion of the agency in question. Further, if the government is to use the exemptions to protect information, it must prove, if challenged, that the requested information is confidential and that its disclosure would result in substantial competitive injury to the company which originally supplied the information or would impair the agency's ability to obtain future information. Recent practice illustrates reluctance by some agencies to invoke the discretionary exemptions. For example, in response

to FOIA requests, the Securities and Exchange Commission plans to release illegal or dubious payments information which had been voluntarily supplied by companies after a promise of confidentiality. Another example of this tendency to release information is the FTC's decision to make material submitted by a defendant publicly available whenever hearings are held on proposed consent decrees in antitrust or consumer protection actions.

In the years since FOIA amendments have taken effect, business has made increasing use of the FOIA as an intelligence source. The experience of Air Cruisers Co. illustrates both the threats and opportunities provided by the amended FOIA. In August 1975, Air Cruisers received Federal Aviation Administration (FAA) approval of its design for a 42-person inflatable life raft for commercial aircraft. As the largest raft ever to gain FAA approval, it constituted a substantial competitive advantage to Air Cruisers. Six months later, Air Cruisers learned that the FAA was about to release an 18-inch high stack of confidential technical documents to a competitor, Switlik Parachute Company, which had made an FOIA request for the documents. The material included results of performance tests and construction designs, which would enable Switlik to shortcut costly design, testing, and certification procedures. While Air Cruisers was able to block the FAA from releasing all of the data, it had to accept the release of some documents. This information helped Switlik design its own large raft with which it defeated Air Cruisers in a contest for an important European contract.

Additional examples abound. Consider the following which provide some notion of the breadth and type of competitive information potentially available from government agencies and departments under FOIA requests:

- A Washington, D.C. lawyer, presumably on behalf of a rival drug company, obtained an FDA inspector's report on conditions in the Midwestern plant of a larger pharmaceutical company. It included such useful trade secrets as a description of proposed new products, manufacturing capabilities, and sterilization procedures at the inspected plant.
- Crown Zellerbach requested all FTC information on the Procter & Gamble announcement that "New White Cloud bathroom tissue is the softest bathroom tissue on earth. We have been called on to prove this claim by the United States Government and have."
- Westinghouse received from the Department of Commerce 10 reports which had been paid for and submitted by other corporations on how Japanese nontariff barriers hurt sales in Japan.

- Both Honeywell and Burroughs requested details of an $8 million Interior Department contract with Control Data Corporation.

Further evidence of substantial business use of FOIA may be found at the FTC and the FDA. In the nearly eight years between the July 1967 effective date of the original FOIA and the February 1975 effective date for the amendments, the FTC is estimated to have received less than 1,000 FOIA requests with 10% coming from business. Requests reached this same level, in the first 18 months after the amendments took effect, with almost 20% coming from business. To be sure, these figures understate total business use of FOIA because the original source of a request can often be masked by having attorneys and FOIA service companies make the direct request of a government agency. Nevertheless, the above usage data underscore the impact of the 1974 amendments on the functioning of the FOIA.

The agency with one of the largest volumes of FOIA requests and a substantial share from business is the FDA. In 1974, 2,000 FOIA requests were received by the FDA. The volume exploded to 13,052 in 1975, the year in which the amendments took effect, and doubled in 1976 to nearly 22,000. Over 70% of all requests were from industry or FOI service companies. One reason for this rapid growth has been this agency's liberal interpretation of the FOIA.

While a substantial amount of business use has been made of the FOIA, the potential has just begun to be realized. Although corporate attorneys often claim that their managers know about the operation of the Act (usually because the attorneys had circulated a memo about it), field research indicated that only a tiny minority of managers were at all well informed about the Act and its managerial significance. Managers must be made aware of both the opportunities and inherent threats in the FOIA. The opportunities for learning about competitors are amply illustrated in the above examples. On the other hand, it is imperative that managers become aware of just how vulnerable their own confidential data are when in the hands of the government. Companies should plan in advance, as part of any submission of confidential data to the government, for the defense of such data against a FOIA request from a competitor for these data. Not to do so will increasingly expose a company to the prospect of meeting a 10 working day deadline in which it must convince an agency not to release the company's data. So whether for offensive or defensive purposes, companies must learn to live with and utilize for FOIA as a source of strategic intelligence.

The amended FOIA along with the Sunshine Laws which took effect in March 1977 have broader strategic implications than competitive intelligence. Together they have the potential to reduce the uncertainty which plagues business and government relations by more fully opening government decision processes to outside scrutiny. As discussed earlier, this potential is particularly important because the CEOs of Fortune's 500 indicated that government is their most troublesome area.

Competitors   A second major source of strategic intelligence is competitors themselves. Use of strategic planning tools such as one of the variants of product portfolio analysis helps management focus on critical strategy issues. Some of the most important of these issues relate to the incentives and opportunities facing various competitors and their financial and managerial capacities for carrying out alternative strategies. In a very real sense, the introduction of these strategic planning tools has raised a host of questions relating to competitive response and reaction. A variety of intelligence sources are available for addressing such questions. Annual reports and 10Ks may provide considerable insight into the philosophy and management capability of

a competitor as well as his financial capabilities and technological and product plans. For example, GE was stimulated to take a careful look at solid state controls on washers and dryers as a result of having seen both Whirlpool and Hitachi mention these devices in their annual reports (Allen 1978). The FTC and SEC requirements for line of business reporting should greatly enrich annual reports and 10Ks as a source of intelligence. Further, a careful perusal of the footnote to a competitor's annual report may reveal, for example, pension obligations which will drastically impact the ability of a competitor to respond flexibly.

The priorities and self-evaluation systems of a competitor may also be revealed by public announcements and speeches as well as in 10Ks and annual reports. Presidents often cannot resist the opportunity to "brag," and in so doing may reveal much about the firm's growth objectives, investment strategy, tradeoffs between long-term and short-term results, and product/market policies. The advantage of knowing a competitor's personality was underlined in the field study at one company. This company knew that one of its major competitors tended to be extremely inconsistent in its marketing activities. This knowledge enabled the company to avoid overreaction to any one of the competitor's scattered moves.

Much valuable competitive intelligence may be gleaned from scanning a competitor's personnel activities. For example, if technical personnel of a given type are being laid off, this can be indicative of the competitor's intentions and capabilities in that technical area. A company who observes a competitor taking such action may have an excellent opportunity to gain a technical and marketing edge on that competitor, as was discussed earlier. On the other hand, analysis of a competitor's employment ads may tell a great deal about that competitor's future plans. There is some evidence that such an approach may be valuable. In one case, an outside team was assigned to monitor the personnel ads of a company for one month. At the end of the month, the team reported on what they thought was going on. Not only were they accurate in most cases, but they spotted three problems in production and quality control which the firm's own top management didn't even know existed.

Own Personnel   A company's own personnel can be invaluable sources of intelligence if they have been trained to be receptive to intelligence and if they are encouraged to transmit the intelligence to appropriate organizational locations. Sales call reports which explicitly encourage reporting of intelligence and debriefing reports submitted by scientists and engineers upon return from professional meetings are two of the more common methods used. In many instances, a firm's purchasing agents may play a key role in intelligence acquisition. The key issue in tapping this internal source is to sensitize personnel to the need for intelligence, train them to recognize it, and reward them for transmitting it. In this area, the firm should bear in mind Pasteur's statement that " . . . chance favors the prepared mind."

In summary, most firms have a large number of potential intelligence sources. Some of these are common and widely used, such as trade association data, but others, such as studies of competitor's want ads, may be less so. The proper choice of intelligence sources depends not only upon the data that it provides, but also how it interrelates with other aspects of the company's strategic intelligence system.

ANALYSIS AND PROCESSING OF STRATEGIC INTELLIGENCE

A firm and its managers use a variety of approaches to combine, sort, and process the environmental *data* in order to produce timely and relevant information for forming, monitoring, evaluating, and modifying strategy. The strategic data management problem is complicated by the considerable emphasis placed on personal communications by senior managers. For example, Rohlf and Wish (1974) found that managers spend an average of six hours a day in personal or telephone communications. Further, the unstructured nature of many strategic decisions, especially in the problem finding state, increases the difficulty of transforming data into strategic information.

Despite these difficulties, the process of intelligence derivation is a critical one in the formulation of strategies. After data are generated or enter the system, they should be evaluated. The formal evaluation of data, although frequently carried out in military intelligence systems, appears to be rarely done by business.

Evaluation of Data

Evaluation includes determining the pertinence, reliability, and validity (accuracy) of data obtained. Evaluation of pertinence can include pertinence to a number of people in the organization and specifically determines if the data are relevant to the company, if needed immediately, and, if so, by whom.

Reliability is an evaluation of the source or agency by which the data are gathered or transmitted. The principal basis for judging reliability is previous experience with a source. This is particularly relevant for businesses which use such recurrent sources as the sales force, security analysts, and suppliers. Although it would seem that a "track record" of these sources can be built up over time, for example, to identify the biases of salesmen in reporting only certain events or in being overly optimistic, such practices were rarely observed in the field interviews. It should be noted that suppliers recognize that they are being used as a source of data and try to draw a line between "providing something of value, but not too much."

Validity or accuracy means the probable truth of the data itself. Methods for assessing validity include comparison with other data which may be available from other sources, searching for associated indicators, and face validity. For example in a long-term policy study for the Environmental Protection Agency, 16 different futures studies were reviewed in a fixed format as one approach to convergent validity (Elgin, MacMichael, and Schwartz 1975).

Transformation of Data into Information

The six transformation functions—transmission, accumulation, aggregation, analysis, pattern recognition, and mixing—by which data can become information vary considerably in complexity (see Table 21-2). Although the six functions overlap, each has at its core a distinctive transformation. Obviously, the functions do not necessarily occur sequentially and can occur at several levels in an organization.

Transmission

Transmission, conceptually a very simple notion, is the movement of data from one point or person in the organization to another. Transmission can also occur simultaneously with some of the other processing functions. However, data which are received through many corporate entry points are often not communicated to those who can use them most effectively. In consequence, transmission should be at least conceptually considered as a separate function. Companies need to develop methods to facilitate ("force") the transmission of information by providing incentives for the reporting of certain types of information or by providing ways for a manager to know the information needs of others.

Accumulation

Accumulation is the storage of data in such a way that it can be retrieved by the managers in a company. A substantial data base provides a source from which the organization can learn about itself and its environment. This is particularly true when attempting to resolve unstructured strategic problems, for which information needs are difficult to define beforehand.

The field interviews revealed limited amounts of accumulation of strategic environmental data. Several reasons explain why this accumulation does not take place. First, because the data often originate from the personal sources of a manager, the effort required to record it and enter it into a more formal and permanent system may not seem worthwhile, especially for "soft data." The remedies would seem to be easing the transmission process and increasing the rewards. In one company, the central collector receives data varying from rumors to documented facts by telephone or in person. The central collector then alerts line managers on an individual basis of particularly significant events, publishes a weekly newsletter, prepares special reports, and maintains files on competitors. There are substantial behavioral advantages to this system. The managers do not fill out forms, they input data verbally and are rewarded, in turn, by receiving pertinent information.

Second, information accumulation may not take place because managers do not think the system works well. For instance, computer-based systems often concentrate on the easily quantified factors in formats which reflect the needs of accounting systems rather than those of operating or strategy managers.

Table 21-2
Six Transformation Functions

Name	Description	Brief Examples
1. Transmission	1. Moving data from one point to another	1a) Manager in one company who receives information personally or by telephone from line managers and distributes information personally or by weekly newsletter 1b) Highly mechanized interactive computer system to make data base reachable by numerous managers
2. Accumulation	2. Storing data in one place; implies some notion of retrievability	2a) Corporate libraries or computer systems 2b) Not frequently observed in practice, managers tend to keep data in their heads or in individualized data bases ("little black book")
3. Aggregation	3. Many data points brought together into a smaller set which is usually more easily accessed	3a) Use of computer program to reduce thick Nielsen reports to much shorter documents 3b) Page length limitation on planning documents
4. Analysis	4. The analysis, usually formal, of data in order to seek and measure relations	4a) Use of econometric consulting firms to provide forecasts of the economy 4b) Use of Shell's Directional Policy Matrix to locate businesses for a portfolio analysis
5. Mix	5. Passing of data around to a variety of managers looking for possible links. The data is often not well ordered	5a) CEO insists on plans which show multiple inputs at each phase 5b) Open planning meetings in which managers must give and defend plans before colleagues
6. Pattern Recognition	6. A more informal, less analytic process than analysis (4) in which patterns or relations are sought. Can be a result of the other five functions described	6a) Combining plant closing, financial and product change information to recognize a competitor is short of cash 6b) Special purpose competitor studies & role playing or the use of adversary teams

Third, managers may have incentives for not wanting others to have their full data set. In a corporate budgeting system, a manager may be able to present plans which maximize his or her capital allocation or limit his or her performance goals based on his or her unique knowledge of the data.

One consumer durables manufacturer has a particularly interesting central collection system based on a substantial disaggregated data base which includes such factors as factory shipments, survey data on consumer habits, and construction reports. The system is unique because rather than distribution of a large number of reports (as had been done in the past), the main way to use it is for managers to visit the central facility, which is located in the marketing department. The location was chosen to provide user access and the overall style is casual and user oriented to create an environment "painless and pleasant for the harried marketing executive" (from a company brochure).

Aggregation

Aggregation is the function in which many data points are collapsed into a smaller set of pertinent information. It is the first of the functions in which something is done to the data beyond making it available to managers. Summarization of environmental data occurs in virtually all companies, although with various degrees of care and attention. Given the massive amounts of data potentially available and a manager's limited time for reviewing information, aggregation is a vital function.

Corporate staff groups are often responsible for the summarization of economic trends. In a relatively smaller number of companies, social, political, and regulatory factors are summarized as well. Thus, on a macro or corporate level, summarization or aggregation of data takes place. However, only lim-

ited aggregation of environmental data, especially competitive data, was observed on a SBU or product-market basis except as part of the annual planning process or, in a few cases, when special purpose competitive assessment reports were made.

Analysis

The analysis of data is a formal process which attempts to find and measure relations among variables. Although at times it may draw heavily on mathematics and numeric procedures, it is a logical and not a mathematical process. A number of companies employ econometric consulting firms and others do similar work on their own. Many consumer goods companies employ analytical approaches to measure relationships between sales and marketing mix variables. In several companies, the main focus of analysis is on predicting industry capacity.

The level of analysis of environmental data varies extensively across companies. For example, in some companies, competitive balance sheets are used primarily as a benchmark or "scoreboard" to rate the company as compared to its competition. In others, it is used more aggressively to anticipate threats or provide opportunities. As an illustration, when one company noticed that a competitor was highly leveraged and consequently would be unable to finance new product development, it gained considerable market share by improving its own product.

Pattern Recognition

Pattern recognition, although not as structured or formal as the analysis process just discussed, also attempts to find patterns or relations among variables. Human abilities to perceive and determine patterns among disparate sets of information and data are the critical distinctive elements in the process of pattern recognition. Although computerized systems can be of great assistance, in strategic analysis the "lack of simple alpha-numeric indicators, combined with enormous textural complexity, suggests that [pattern recognition] . . . will not be trivial or automatic in the foreseeable future" (Webb 1969, p. 10). An example of pattern recognition occurred in one company when the information that a competitor was closing a plant and changing his product line was combined with balance sheet analysis to realize that the competitor was short of cash. This, of course, left the competitor vulnerable to a number of aggressive strategies. The generation and use of indepth competitive assessment reports, the preparation of strategy documents from the viewpoint of a major competitor, and the formation of inhouse competitor teams exemplify different organizational approaches to pattern recognition.

Mixing

The unstructured and often unstable nature of strategic problems requires that an additional transformation function be defined which brings together the apparently unrelated data spread throughout an organization in order to identify linkages. This function is termed "mixing."

A somewhat analogous notion is Cohen, March, and Olsen's (1972) garbage can model. In that conceptualization, an organization is conceived of as a collection of problems and solutions in which organizational members find ways either to enrich the collection of problems and solutions or to find links between the problems and solutions. The approach formulated here emphasizes two major factors. First, problems and solutions are viewed as being dynamic so that "windows" as to when linkages can be established are limited. Thus, problems and opportunities

should be viewed as moving through a container rather than residing in a collection. Second, an active approach can be taken to ensure that problems and solutions are actively interchanged or mixed within an organization.

Companies appear to use a variety of techniques to force mixing including participative planning meetings across divisions and organizational levels, weekly senior executive sessions with invited presentations, and rejection of plans which do not reflect mixing. For example, in one company, the CEO rejected divisional plans out of hand because they did not show any evidence of interaction across divisions. In another, marketing managers were asked to write the finance plan, financial managers were asked to write the production plan, etc. In large companies, facing a broad variety of strategic options, mixing can help the company to become aware of the range of opportunities and threats facing it and to develop synergistic responses.

SUMMARY AND PERSPECTIVES

As more organizations implement strategic planning and management activities, there will be an increasing need for strategic intelligence systems which can help managers to learn about the important environments with which their organization interrelates and to become aware of threats and opportunities that are posed.

The construction of viable strategic intelligence systems is exceedingly complex because of the unstructured nature of strategic decisions, the difficulty of separating out important and relevant information from the vast amounts of data accessible to the manager, and the reliance of managers on personal information sources. As would be expected, in most of the companies interviewed tactical information systems were better articulated than strategic ones. On the other hand, a number of companies have developed effective means of learning about their environments and, most importantly, have implemented strategic decision systems which allow them to capitalize on opportunities and to defend themselves against threats. This article has developed a framework for examining intelligence systems which is sensitive to the character of the strategic process.

For a strategic intelligence system to be useful, a company must have a real commitment to strategic planning. Otherwise, the planning process, if carried out at all, becomes only an exercise and managers appear to place limited effort towards gathering and communicating accurate, relevant intelligence. There are a number of different organizational policies which can be utilized to promote the transformation of data into information and the utilization of this information. Elaboration on this issue is beyond the scope of this article. However, only in rare circumstances do effective intelligence systems emerge without organizational incentives to encourage their operation.

There appear to be a number of asymmetries in managers' perceptions about information collection. Four, in particular, stand out. (1) Companies tend to believe that their competitors nearly always detect and rapidly decide how to respond to company actions such as a price change. This perception persists in spite of knowledge of substantial delays in their own detection and response decision time in reacting to the competitors. This can lead a company to rescind prematurely an effort to lead a price increase based upon a belief competitors won't follow, when in fact the lack of response by the competitor may merely be symptomatic of a poor and slow intelligence system. (2) The government is viewed as an extensive collector of information, but not as a source; the discussion of the FOIA indicated how companies could access

data held by the government. (3) Conversely, to the case of the government, suppliers are more often viewed as a source of information about competitors than as a source to the competitors. (4) Companies send engineers and managers to meetings with instructions to gather more information than they reveal; it would seem unlikely for this outcome to occur for all companies involved. These asymmetries, which obviously are not shared by all managers, suggest some of the potential available from a review of an organization's procedures to gather and process strategic data.

Information systems are a means to an end—decision making which leads to more profitable results. The concepts and structures for strategic intelligence systems discussed in this article are designed to help organizations make more profitable strategic decisions.

NOTE

1. The following discussion of the Freedom of Information Act is based on Montgomery, Peters, and Weinberg (1978).

REFERENCES

Allen, Michael G. (1978), "Strategic Planning with a Competitive Focus," *The McKinsey Quarterly* (Autumn), 2–13.

Burk, Charles G. (1976), "A Group Profile of the Fortune 500 Chief Executives," *Fortune*, 19 (May), 173.

Business Week (1977), "Gillette: after the Diversification that Failed," (February 28), 58.

Cohen, Michael D., James G. March, and Johan P. Olsen (1972), "A Garbage Can Model of Organizational Choice," *Administrative Science Quarterly* (March), 1.

Cooper, A. C. and D. Schendel (1976), "Strategic Responses to Technological Threats," *Business Horizons*, 19 (February), 61.

Elgin, D. S., D. C. MacMichael, and P. Schwartz (1975), "Alternative Futures for Environmental Policy Planning: 1975–2000," Environmental Protection Agency (October).

Grinyer, P. H. and D. Norburn (1975), "Planning for Existing Markets: Perceptions of Executives and Financial Performance," *Journal of the Royal Statistical Society A,* 138 (Part 1), 70.

Hyatt, J. and J. Coonly (1971), "How Procter & Gamble Put the Big Squeeze on Scott Paper Company," *The Wall Street Journal* (October 20), 1.

Miller, D. (1975), "Toward a Contingency Theory of Strategy Formulation," paper presented at 35th annual Academy of Management Meeting (August).

Montgomery, David B., Anne H. Peters, and Charles B. Weinberg (1978), "The Freedom of Information Act: Strategic Opportunities and Threats," *Sloan Management Review,* 19 (Winter), 1–13.

Rohlf, J. and M. Wish (1974), "Analysis of Demand for Video Communication," Telecommunication Policy Research Conference, Airlie, Virginia (April 18).

Ross, I. (1976), "Public Relations Isn't Kid Gloves Stuff at Mobil," *Fortune,* 93 (September), 106.

Schendel, D. E., G. R. Patten, and J. Riggs (1976), "Corporate Turnaround Strategies: A Study of Profit, Decline, and Recovery," *Journal of General Management,* 3 (Spring), 3.

von Hippel, E. (1977), "Has a Customer Already Developed Your Next Product?" *Sloan Management Review,* 18 (Winter), 63.

Webb, Eugene J. (1969), "Individual and Organizational Forces Influencing the Interpretation of Indicators," unpublished working paper, Stanford: Graduate School of Business, Stanford University (April), 10.

Wilson, I. (1975), "Does GE Really Plan Better," *MBA,* 9 (November), 42.

◆

Customer-Oriented Approaches to Identifying Product-Markets

George S. Day, Allan D. Shocker, and Rajendra K. Srivastava

The problems of identifying competitive product-markets pervade all levels of marketing decisions. Such strategic issues as the basic definition of the business, the assessment of opportunities presented by gaps in the market or threats posed by competitive actions, and major resource allocation decisions are strongly influenced by the breadth or narrowness of the competitive arena. Share of market is a crucial tactical tool for evaluating performance and guiding territorial advertising, sales force, and other budget allocations. The quickening pace of antitrust prosecution is a further source of demands for better definitions of relevant market boundaries that will yield a clearer understanding of the competitive consequences of acquisitions.

This paper is primarily concerned with the needs of marketing planners for strategic analyses of competitive product-markets.[1]

Their needs presently are served by approaches to defining product-markets which emphasize similarity of production processes, function, or raw materials used. Seldom do these approaches give a satisfactory picture of either the threats or the opportunities facing a business. In response, there has been considerable activity directed toward defining product-markets from the customers' perspective. Our objectives are first, to examine the merits of a customer perspective in the context of a defensible definition of a product-market, and second, to evaluate progress toward providing this perspective. The paper's structure corresponds to these objectives. The first two sections are concerned with the nature of the strategic problem, and the development of a customer-oriented definition of a product-market. This definition is used in the third section to help evaluate a variety of methods for identifying product-market boundaries. In this discussion, a sharp distinction is drawn between methods which rely on purchase or usage behavior and those which use customer judgments.

George S. Day, Allan D. Shocker, and Rajendra K. Srivastava, "Customer-Oriented Approaches to Identifying Product-Markets," Vol. 43 (Fall 1979), pp. 8–19. Reprinted from *Journal of Marketing*, published by the American Marketing Association.

SOURCES OF DEMAND FOR BETTER INSIGHTS

Ultimately all product-market boundaries are arbitrary. They exist because of recurring needs to comprehend market structures and impose some order on complex market environments. But this situation could not be otherwise. One reason is the wide variety of decision contexts which dictate different definitions of boundaries.

Market and product class definitions appropriate for tactical decisions tend to be narrow, reflecting the short-run concerns of sales and product managers who regard a market as "a chunk of demand to be filled with the resources at my command." These resources are usually constrained by products in the present product line. A longer-run view, reflecting strategic planning concerns, invariably will reveal a larger product-market to account for (1) presently unserved but potential markets; (2) changes in technology, price relationships, and supply which broaden the array of potential substitute products; and (3) the time required by present and prospective buyers to react to these changes.

Of necessity, a single market definition is a compromise between the long-run and the short-run views. All too often, the resulting compromise is not consistent with customers views of the competitive alternatives to be considered for a particular usage situation or application. One consequence of these problems is the development of different definitions for different purposes. Thus, for some strategic planning purposes, General Electric treats hair dryers, hair setters, and electric brushes as parts of distinct markets while for other purposes they are part of a "personal appliance" business since they tend to compete with one another in a "gift market." General Foods has taken an even broader approach in a reorganization of its strategic business units. Each SBU now concentrates on marketing families of products made by different processing technologies but consumed by the same market segments (Hanon 1974). Thus, all desserts are in the same division whether they are frozen, powdered, or ready-to-eat.

A further reason for the inevitable arbitrariness of product-market boundaries is the frequent absence of natural discontinuities which can be readily identified—and accepted—without argument. Moran (1973) states the problem bluntly:

> In our complex service society, there are no more product classes—not in any meaningful sense, only as a figment of file clerk imagination. . . . To some degree, in some circumstances, almost anything can be a partial substitute for almost anything else. A (fifteen-cent) stamp substitutes to some extent for an airline ticket.

When a high degree of ambiguity or compromise is present in the identification of the product-market, a number of problems are created. Some will stem from inadequate and delayed understanding of emerging threats in the competitive environment. These threats may come from foreign competition, product substitution trends, shifts in price sensitivity, or changed technological possibility. Thus fiberglass and aluminum parts have displaced steel in many automotive applications due in some measure to increasing willingness to pay higher prices to obtain lower weight and consequent gas economy. Conversely, opportunities may be overlooked when the definition is drawn too narrowly for tactical purposes and the nature and size of the potential market are understated. Finally, whenever market share is used to evaluate the performance of managers or to determine resource allocations (Day 1977), there is a tendency for managers to manipulate the market boundaries to show an increasing or at least static share.

A CUSTOMER-ORIENTED CONCEPT OF A COMPETITIVE PRODUCT-MARKET

Market definitions have, in the past, focused on either the *product* (as with the following definition, " . . . products may be closely related in the sense that they are regarded as substitutes by consumers" Needham 1969, which assumes homogeneity of consumer behavior), or on the *buyers* (" . . . individuals who in the past have purchased a given class of products." Sissors 1966). Neither approach is very helpful for clarifying the concept, or evaluating alternative approaches for identifying product-market boundaries.

A more productive approach can be derived from the following premises:

- People seek the benefits that products provide rather than the products per se. Specific products or brands represent the available combinations of benefits and costs.
- Consumers consider the available alternatives from the vantage point of the usage contexts with which they have experience or the specific applications they are considering (Belk 1975; Lutz and Kakkar 1976; Stout et al. 1977). It is the usage requirement which dictates the benefits being sought.[2]

From these two premises, we can define a product-market as the *set of products* judged to be substitutes, within those usage situations in which similar patterns of benefits are sought, and the *customers* for whom such usages are relevant.

This definition is *demand* or customer-oriented in that customer needs and requirements have primacy. The alternative is to take a *supply* perspective and define products by such operational criteria as similarity of manufacturing processes, raw materials, physical appearance, or function. These criteria are the basis of the Standard Industrial Classification (SIC) system—and have generally wide acceptance because they appear easy to implement. They lead to seemingly stable and clear-cut definitions, and importantly, involve factors largely controllable by the firm; implying that the definition is somehow controllable as well. They are also helpful in identifying potential competitors, because of similarities in manufacturing and distribution systems. Demand-oriented criteria, on the other hand, are less familiar and consequently appear more difficult to implement (as a consequence of the variety of methods available and the inevitable problems of empirical measurement, sampling errors, and aggregation over individual customer differences). Moreover, such definitions may be less stable over time because of changing needs and tastes. Finally, the organization must initiate a research program to collect and analyze relevant data and monitor change rather than relying on government or other external sources to make the information available. The consequence is most often a decision to use supply-oriented measures despite their questionable applicability in many circumstances (Needham 1969).

Hierarchies of Products The notion of a unique product category is an oversimplification in the face of the arbitrary nature of the boundaries. Substitutability is a measure of degree. Thus it is better to think in terms of the levels in a hierarchy of products within a generic product class representing all possible ways of satisfying a fundamental consumer need or want. Lunn (1972) makes the following useful distinctions between:

- Totally different *product types* or subclasses which exist to satisfy significantly different patterns of needs beyond the fundamental or generic. For example, both hot and cold cereals serve the same need for breakfast nutrition, but otherwise are different. Over the long run, product types may behave like substitutes.

- Different *product variants* are available within the same overall type, e.g., natural, nutritional, presweetened, and regular cereals. There is a high probability that some short-run substitution takes place among subsets of these variants (between natural and nutritional, for example). If there is too much substitution, then alternatives within the subset do not deserve to be distinguished.
- Different *brands* are produced within the same specific product variant. Although these brands may be subtly differentiated on many bases (color, package type, shape, texture, etc.), they are nonetheless usually direct and immediate substitutes.

There may be many or few levels in such a hierarchy, depending on the breadth and complexity of the genuine need and the variety of alternatives available to satisfy it. Thus, this typology is simply a starting point for thinking about the analytical issues.

Submarkets and Strategic Segments   The product-market definition proposed above implies submarkets composed of customers with common uses or applications of the product. These are segments according to the traditional definition of groups that have similar purchase or usage behavior or reactions to marketing efforts (Frank, Massy, and Wind 1973). For our purposes, it is more useful to consider these as submarkets within *strategic market segments*. While each of these submarkets may serve as the focus of a positioning decision, the differences between them may not present significant strategic barriers for competitors to overcome. Such barriers may be based on factors such as differences in geography, order quantities, requirements for technical assistance and service support, price

sensitivity, or perceived importance of quality and reliability. The test of strategic relevance is whether the segments defined by these or other characteristics must be served by substantially different marketing mixes. The boundaries could then be manifested by discontinuities in price structures, growth rates, share patterns, and distribution channels when going from one segment to another.

ANALYTICAL METHODS FOR CUSTOMER-ORIENTED PRODUCT-MARKET DEFINITIONS

Customer-oriented methods for identifying product-markets can be classified by whether they rely upon behavioral or judgmental data. Purchase behavior provides the best indication of what people actually do, or have done, but not necessarily what they might do under changed circumstances. As such, its value is greater as a guide to tactical planning. Judgmental data, in the form of perceptions or preferences, may give better insights into future patterns of competition and the reasons for present patterns. Consequently, it may better serve as the basis for strategic planning. In this section we will evaluate seven different analytical approaches within the two basic classes as follows:

Purchase or Usage Behavior	Customer Judgments
A1. Cross-elasticity of demand	B1. Decision sequence analysis
A2. Similarities in behavior	B2. Perceptual mapping
A3. Brand switching	B3. Technology substitution analysis
	B4. Customer judgments of substitutability

Within the broad category of customer judgments of substitutability (B4), five related approaches, using free associations, the "dollar metric," direct grouping of products, products-by-uses analysis and substitution-in-use analysis will be examined.

Analysis of Purchase or Usage Behavior

A1. *Cross elasticity of demand* is considered by most economists to be the standard against which other approaches should be compared (Scherer 1970). Despite the impressive logic of the cross-elasticity measure, it is widely criticized and infrequently used:

- The conceptual definition of this measure presumes that there is no response by one firm to the price change of another (Needham 1969). This condition is seldom satisfied in practice.
- It is a static measure, and "breaks down in the face of a market characterized by changing product composition" (Cocks and Virts 1975). This is so because a priori it is not known what all the potential substitutes or complements may be. Over time new entrants or departures from a market may affect the cross-elasticity between any two alternatives.
- Finally, "in markets where price changes have been infrequent, or all prices change together, or where factors other than prices have also changed, there is simply not enough information contained in the data to permit valid statistical estimation of the elasticities," (Vernon 1972).

These problems may be overcome with either an experimental study, which can introduce problems of measure validity, or extensive monitoring of the factors affecting demand and use of econometric methods to control, where possible, for the effects of such factors. Not surprisingly, such studies are expensive and rather infrequently undertaken.

Generally, empirical cross-elasticity studies have focused on only two goods (typically product-types as opposed to variants or brands). It is also worth noting that if simultaneous estimation of all cross-elasticities were to be attempted, some a priori determination of the limits to a product-market would be needed in order to include price change and other market data for all potential competitive brands. The estimation of any specific cross-elasticity should be sensitive to such product-market definition.

A2. *Similarities in customer usage behavior.* This approach was successfully used in a study of the ethical pharmaceutical market (Cocks and Virts 1975). The basic question was the extent to which products made up of different chemicals, but with similar therapeutic effects, could be significant substitutes. The key to answering this question was the availability of a unique set of data on physician behavior. Each of the 3,000 physicians in a panel recorded: (1) patient characteristics, (2) the diagnosis, (3) the therapeutic measures—drugs—used to treat the patient, (4) the desired action of the drugs being used, and (5) characteristics of the reporting physician.

The first step in the analysis was to estimate the percentage usage of each drug in the treatment of patients diagnosed as having the same ailment. When a drug was found to be the only one used for a certain disease, and seldom or never used in the treatment of any other diagnosis, it was assumed to represent a distinct class. Generally, it was found that several drugs were used in several diagnosis categories. The next step was to see if drugs which were used together had similar desired actions. Some drugs, such as analgesics, are frequently used along with other drugs, without being substitutes (strictly speaking, they also are not complements). Finally, drugs were classed as substitutes—and hence in the same product class—if 10% or more of the total usage of each drug was in the treatment of a specific diagnosis.

While it was not claimed that every drug in the resulting product-market competed for all uses of every other drug in that market, the data revealed a substantial amount of substitutability. The key to understanding the patterns of competition in this market was knowledge of the usage situation. As yet, few consumer panels have incorporated similar data with the usual measures of purchase behavior. The potential to conduct similar analyses suggests that usage data could be valuable when available for categories which are purchased for multiple uses.

A3. *Brand switching* measures are usually interpreted as conditional probabilities, i.e., the probability of purchasing brand A, given that brand B was purchased on the last occasion. Such measures are typically estimated from panel data where the purchases of any given respondent are represented by a sequence of indefinite length. The probabilities are computed from counts of the frequency with which each condition arises in the data (e.g., purchases of brand A are preceded by different brands in the sequence). The premise is that respondents are more likely to switch between close substitutes than distant ones and that brand switching proportions provide a measure of the probability of substitution.

As with cross-elasticity, the brand-switching measure is usable only after a set of competitive products has first been established. Since estimation of brand-switching rates is based upon a sequence of purchases, there must be some logical basis to determine which brands to include in such a sequence. Similarity of usage patterns, as discussed above, is one promising basis.

Brand switching rates as measures of degree of substitutability are flawed in several respects. (1) Applicability is typically limited to product categories having high repeat purchase rates to ensure that a sufficiently long sequence of purchases is available over a short time period for reliable estimates of switching probabilities. (2) The customer choice process, which determines switching, must be presumed stable throughout the sequence of purchases. If a long time series is used to provide reliable estimates, this assumption may be questionable. (3) Panel data, upon which switching probabilities are based, often obscure individual switching behavior since data are typically reported by only one member of a family who completes a diary of purchases. Apparent switching can result from different members of the family making consistent but different brand choices at differing points in time. A similar distortion is created by an individual who regularly purchases different brands for different usage occasions. (4) Analyses of panel data are further complicated by multiple brand purchases at the same time (does purchase of A precede B or vice versa in determining the sequence?), by lack of uniformity in package sizes across brands (since package size affects frequency of purchase), and by different sized packages of the same brand (is purchase of a large size equivalent to some sequence of purchases of smaller sizes?).

The Hendry model (Butler and Butler 1970, 1971) uses brand switching data directly to determine the market structure. Although details have been slow to appear in the literature (Kalwani and Morrison 1977; Rubison and Bass 1978) there has been a good deal of utilization of the empirical regularities uncovered by the model for marketing planning purposes.

This model does not rely solely on behavioral data, as it can also incorporate retrospective reports of switching or purchase intentions data from surveys. In essence, the model seeks an underlying structure of brand-switching maximally "consistent" with the input data. It posits a hierarchical ordering in consumer decision making: consumers are presumed to form categories within the product class (e.g., cold or hot, presweetened or regular, Kellogg's, General Mills, or Post cereals), select those classes in which they are interested, and then consider for purchase only the alternatives within the chosen class (e.g., brands within a particular type of product *or* product types within a brand name). Analysis is carried out at each submarket level. Customers may purchase brands within more than one submarket, but within any submarket all customers are considered potential purchasers of all brands. Each customer is assumed, at equilibrium, to have stable purchase probabilities.

To determine which ordering or structuring of the market best characterizes customer views, a heuristic procedure is employed. Initially, judgment is used to hypothesize a limited number of plausible partitionings of a market, i.e., *alternative* submarket definitions. For each hypothesized definition, the Hendry framework is used to predict various switching probabilities among the products/brands within each submarket and between submarkets (switching *between* submarkets should be much less than *within* any one submarket). The predictions can then be compared with the actual data. That hypothesized partitioning (market structure) yielding switching patterns in closest correspondence with actual data is selected as the appropriate definition for the structure of the market.

A procedure elaborating hierarchical partitioning concepts similar to those of Hendry, but with the ability to incorporate usage occasion has recently been discussed by Urban and Hauser (1979). As in the Hendry model, a hierarchical tree structure is specified. More switching should occur within than between branches. Individual probability estimates are derived by measuring preferences among products with a consumer interview and statistically matching these preferences to observed or reported purchase behavior using the conditional logic model (McFadden 1970). The derived trees are tested by comparing predicted with actual choices in a simulated buying situation which occurs at the end of the consumer interview.

The Hendry procedure has a substantial subjective component, depending upon the criterion used to generate the hypothetical market structure definitions to be evaluated. (The alternative to a good criterion is the testing of potentially large numbers of definitions.) It is also quite arbitrary, possessing elements of the chicken-egg controversy: the prior specification of "the market" is quite critical to the empirical determination of "market shares" for each brand but these in turn are necessary to calibrate the Hendry model (i.e., estimate its parameters). Thus the "correct" definition of the market will depend upon how well predictions of the model correspond to the actual data. The model ought to always do reasonably well in predicting switching patterns in the same market environment from which share data were taken. In other words, to use the model for purposes of selecting the superior market definition, one must presume the model valid. But to test its validity, one must already possess a valid definition of the market. Thus the Hendry model may provide a reasonable approach to market definition only if either the model itself can be independently validated or if independent criteria exist for validating the market definition it suggests.

The Hendry model presumes all customers have stable probabilities of purchasing every brand within a partition (submarket). This assumes preferences, market shares, attitudes, and all other factors of significance are stable and that learning is negligible. Such assumptions may suggest applicability of the Hendry framework only in mature product categories, where such conditions may reasonably hold. Moreover, confirmation of any a priori partitioning of a market rests solely upon analysis of the aggregate switching probabilities as these become the measures of substitutability. Since analysis is carried out on an aggregate level, individual or segment differences are largely ignored. The premise that any given brand may have a varying set of competitors depending upon intended usage and brand familiarity is assumed away by such aggregation.

Summary. Behavioral measures suffer from an endemic weakness because they are influenced by what "is" or "was" rather than what "might be." Actual switching is affected by current market factors such as the set of existing brands, their availability, current pricing structures, promotional message and expenditures, existing legislation and social mores, etc. An imported beer could be substitutable for a local brand insofar as usage is concerned, but price differences may discourage actual substitution. Similarly, a private label brand may be substitutable for a nationally distributed one, but unless the customer shops the stores in which the private label is sold, they cannot make the substitution. If data are developed over long periods of time or from a diverse set of people in differing circumstances, sufficient variability may have taken place in the determinants of demand to reveal such potential substitutability. Otherwise, if some kind of behavioral measure is desired, laboratory manipulation may be necessary.

Analyses Based upon Customer Judgments

Customers often have considerable knowledge of existing brands through personal or friends' experiences and exposure to promotion. Their perceptions may not always correspond to what manufacturers may believe about their own or competitive products. They may have purchase and consumption objectives which influence their consideration of alternatives and choices among them. They may create new uses for existing products. If

such perceptual and decision making processes prove relatively stable, they may be useful for predicting which products and brands will be regarded as potential or actual substitutes and why.

B.1 *Decision Sequence Analysis* utilizes protocols of consumer decision making, which indicate the sequence in which various criteria are employed to reach a final choice (Bettman 1971; Haines 1974). The usual procedure asks individuals to verbalize what is going through their mind as they make purchase decisions in the course of a shopping trip. This verbal record is called a protocol as distinguished from retrospective questioning of subjects about their decisions. With such data, a model of the way the subject makes decisions can be developed. These models specify the *attributes* of the choice objects or situations that are considered and the *sequence* and *method* of combination of these attributes or cues. Generally, the attributes or cues are arrayed in a hierarchical structure called a decision tree. The order in which they are examined is modeled by the path structure of the tree. The branches are based merely on whether or not the level of the attribute is satisfactory or a certain condition is present ("is the price too high?" "is the store out of my favorite brand?").

Analysis of protocols is at the individual level. This has the advantage of enabling individual differences in knowledge and beliefs about alternative products and choice criteria to be recognized. Individuals may, in principle, be grouped into segments on the basis of similar decision procedures. Measures of the extent of competition between brands can be obtained from protocols of different segments by noting which alternatives are even considered and when they are eliminated from further consideration by criteria used at each stage of the decision process (alternatives eliminated at later stages should be more competitive than those eliminated earlier).

Applications of decision sequence analysis have focused on choices at the brand level. Yet the real benefits of this approach would seem to be better insights into the hierarchy of product types and variants within a generic product class. Thus in understanding patterns of competition in the vegetable market, it is important to know whether buyers first decide on the type of vegetable (corn, beans, peas, etc.) or the form (fresh, frozen, or canned). Proposals for a similar kind of study have been made by economists in connection with the concept of a "utility tree" (Strotz 1957) and are similar in intent to the Hendry procedure.

There are numerous empirical problems to be considered in any effort to collect protocols of choice hierarchies. The typical representations of decision sequences appear quite complex and pose serious difficulties for aggregation of the individual models into any small number of segments. Aggregation requires some definition of "similarity" in order to group different decision structures. Further, since it is generally expensive to develop protocols, a representative sample of customers may be unrealizable. Customers are not used to reporting their decision processes so explicitly. A trained interviewer is needed to coax information which is specific enough to be meaningful (e.g., what is too high a price or a satisfactory level of preference?) and yet not unduly bias the process. Since customer decision making for some product categories may take place over prolonged periods of time, it may be necessary for the length of the interviewing to be similarly extended or to rely on respondent's recall of certain events. Finally, since protocol data are collected in the context of the purchase situation, factors associated with that situation may assume greater importance than factors of intended usage. This could place misleading emphasis on in-store factors as determinants of competition.

B.2. *Perceptual mapping* includes a large family of techniques used to create a geometric representation of customer's perceptions of the qualities possessed by products/brands comprising a previously defined product-market (Green 1975). Brands are represented by locations (points or, possibly, regions) in the space. The dimensions of this space distinguish the competitive alternatives and represent benefits or costs perceived important to the purchase. Thus any product/brand might be located in such a space according to a set of coordinates which represent the extent to which the product is believed to possess each benefit or cost attribute. Relative "distances" between product alternatives may be loosely interpreted as measures of perceived substitutability of each alternative for any other.

There are several different techniques which can be used to create perceptual configurations of product-markets (e.g., direct scaling, factor analysis, multiple discriminant analysis, multidimensional scaling). Analysis may be based upon measures of perceived overall similarity/dissimilarity, perceived appropriateness to common usage situations, and correlations between attribute levels for pairs of products. Unfortunately such diversity of criteria and method can lead to somewhat different perceptual maps and possibly different product-market definitions. Much empirical research is still needed to compare the alternatives and assess which produce definitions that are more valid for particular purposes (Shocker and Srinivasan 1979).

When perceptual maps can be represented in two or three dimensions without destroying the data, there is a great improvement in the understanding of the competitive structure. Further, to the extent that substitutability in such a representation corresponds in some straightforward way to interproduct distance, analytic techniques such as cluster analysis (or simply looking for "open spaces" in the map) could prove useful in identifying product-market boundaries. The eventual decision must necessarily be judgmental, with the geometric representation simply facilitating that judgment. Customers or segments may also be represented in such a space by the location of their "most preferred" combination of attribute levels—termed their ideal point.

The major advantage offered by perceptual mapping methods is versatility. Maps can be created for each major usage situation. When care is taken to control for customer knowledge of available product/brand alternatives, perceptual homogeneity may be sufficient to permit the modeling of preference and choice for different user segments within a common perceptual representation (Pessemier 1977). Moreover, perceptual maps can be created for different levels of product competition to explore competitive relations at the level of product types, variants, or brands. For example, Jain and Etgar (1975) have used multidimensional scaling to provide a geometric representation of the beverage market which incorporates all these different levels in the same configuration. These analyses become cumbersome when it is not possible to assume perceptual homogeneity (Day, Deutscher, and Ryans 1976). Then it is necessary to cluster the respondents into homogeneous "points-of-view" groups, based on the commonality in their perceptions, and conduct a separate analysis for each group. Alternatively, one can assume that respondents use the same perceptual dimensions, but differ with respect to the weights they attach to the various dimensions.

In principle, new product concepts can be positioned in the space, or existing brands repositioned or deleted, and the effects on the individual or segment choice behavior predicted. Unfortunately, the relation between interproduct distances in the perceptual space and substitutability is not rigorously established. Stefflre (1972) has argued that a per-

ceptual space contains only labeled regions and hence that gaps may simply represent discontinuities. The question is not whether such discontinuities in fact exist, but rather whether a preference model based upon distances from ideal-points to products remains a reasonable predictor of individual or segment behavior. If so, the decision framework of a common perceptual space coupled with models of individual/segment decision making can be used to assess the relative substitutability of different brands for each segment. These measures can then be aggregated over segments to estimate patterns of competition for the broader market.

B.3. *Technology substitution analysis* adapts the idea of preference related to distance in a multiattribute space to the problem of forecasting the substitution of one material, process, or product for another—aluminum for copper in electrical applications and polyvinyl for glass in liquor bottles, for example. Each successful substitution tends to follow an S-shaped or "logistic" curve representing a slow start as initial problems and resistance to change have to be overcome, followed by more rapid progress as acceptance is gained and applications can be publicized, and finally a slowing in the pace of substitution as saturation is reached.

A simple approach to forecasting the course and speed of the substitution process is to project a function having the appropriate logistics curve, using historical data to determine its parameters (Lenz and Lanford 1972). This curve-fitting method overlooks many potential influences on the process, such as: the age, condition, and rate of obsolescence of the capital equipment used in the old technology; the price elasticity of demand; and the "utility-in-use" or relative performance advantage. Recent efforts to model substitution rates have focused on relative "utility" as the basis for improvements in forecasting ability (Stern, Ayres, and Shapanko 1975). The procedure for assessing "utility-in-use" involves: first, identifying the relevant attributes and performance characteristics of each of the competing products or technologies, followed by ratings by experts of the extent to which each alternative possesses each attribute and the perceived importance of each attribute in each end-use market. Finally, an overall utility for each product in each usage situation is obtained by multiplying the attribute possession score by the importance ratings, summing the resulting products, and adjusting for differences in unit price. While criticism can be made of the model structure and the seeming reliance on measurable physical properties to specify the attributes, the value of the basic approach should not be discounted. The outcome is a highly useful quantitative measure of utility which can be used to estimate substitutability among competing products or technologies in specific usage situations.

B.4. *Customer judgments of substitutability* may be obtained in a variety of ways. The simplest is to ask a sample of customers to indicate the degree of substitutability between possible pairs of brands on a rating scale such as: none, low, some, or substantial substitutability. Beyond this familiar approach, several methods of utilizing customer judgments have recently been developed which provide far greater diagnostic insights into patterns of competition.

1. *The free response approach* (Green, Wind, and Jain 1973). Respondents are presented with various brands and asked to free-associate the names of similar or substitute brands. Two kinds of data are obtained. One is the *frequency* of mention of one brand as a substitute for another, which could be used as a measure of similarity of the two brands in order to establish a perceptual space. Secondly, the *order of mention* of substitute brands can be treated as rank-order data (Wind 1977). These data represent an aggregate judgment across situations, and leave it to the respon-

dent to decide how similar two brands must be before they become substitutes.

A useful variant of the free-response question asks respondents what they would do if they were unable to buy their preferred brand. One advantage of this question is that it can realistically be tailored to specific situations. For example, one study asked scotch drinkers what they would do if scotch were not available in a variety of situations, such as a large cocktail party in the early evening. Evidently, there were some situations where white wine was the preferred alternative.

2. *The dollar metric approach* (Pessemier et al. 1970/71). Respondents first are presented with all possible pairs of brands, each of the brands being marked with their regular prices. In each case, the respondent selects the brand he/she would buy in a forced choice purchase. They are then asked the price to which the preferred brand must rise before they would switch their original preference. Strength of preference is measured in terms of this price increment. Such data must be further "processed" to compute aggregated preference measures.

This procedure is somewhat analogous to a laboratory measurement of cross-elasticity of demand. The set of potentially competitive brands must be again identified in advance. The procedure is reasonably easy to administer and analyze; although the simplicity may be eroded if considerations of intended usage, brand familiarity, and market segmentation are incorporated. It appears that respondents are able to reveal their preferences for different alternatives in the forced-choice situation. Whether they can relate validly how they arrived at the preference—by estimating the minimum-price change that would cause a switch—remains an open question (Huber and James 1977).

3. *Direct grouping into product categories.* Bourgeois, Haines, and Sommers (1979) have taken broadly related sets of brands and

asked samples of customers to: (1) divide the set into as many groups as they consider meaningful, (2) explain the criteria used for each grouping, and (3) judge the similarity of the brands within each group. A measure of the similarity of brands is created by summing across customers to find the frequency with which pairs of brands are assigned to the same group. These data are analyzed by nonmetric, multidimensional scaling programs to obtain interval-scaled measures of brand similarity (according to their proximity in a reduced space). These are input to a cluster analysis routine to obtain groupings of brands regarded as "customer product types." Products are assigned to one type only. An application of this procedure to the generic "personal care" market yielded intuitively appealing groups of brands. However the data were reported to be quite "noisy," which is not surprising in view of the wide latitude given the respondents. Potentially, respondents could differ both in the frame of reference for the task (the intended application or usage) and the criterion for grouping. Some, for example, might emphasize physical similarity while others might elect appropriateness-in-use or similarity of price as the criterion.

4. *Products-by-uses analysis.* In the procedure developed by Stefflre (1979; Myers and Tauber 1977), a sample of customers is given a list of target products or brands and asked to conjecture as many uses for them as possible. They are then asked to suggest additional products or brands appropriate to these same uses and additional uses appropriate to these new products. This sequence of free response questions generates large lists of products/brands and potential uses. An independent sample is then asked to judge the appropriateness of each product for each use. In one study of proprietary medicines, for example, respondents were asked to judge the acceptability of each of 52 medicines for 52 conditions of use ranging from "when you

have a stuffy nose" to "when the children have a fever."

Two assumptions underlie analyses of the products-by-uses matrix: (1) the set of products constitutes a representative sample of the benefits sought by customers and (2) two usage situations are similar if similar benefits are desired in both situations. If these assumptions are valid, then grouping usage situations according to similarity of products judged appropriate should be equivalent to grouping them explicitly by the benefits desired. The net result is a somewhat circular procedure:

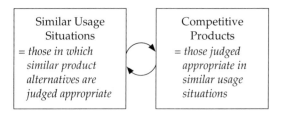

The merits of the Stefflre (1972, 1979) procedure are first, that the introduction of specific situations gives respondents frames of reference for their judgments of substitutability or appropriateness and second, that the criteria can be modified to reflect greater concern with *potential* competition (respondents are asked which existing products or descriptions of concepts would be appropriate to specified uses) or with *actual* competition (which products they would consider for purchase in the situation.) This ability to use descriptions of concepts greatly extends the flexibility of the approach to provide data relevant to actual or proposed changes in the product-market. A further advantage, shared with the direct grouping approach, is an ability to cope with large numbers of alternatives if necessary, without a requirement for large numbers of respondents because of a high degree of homogeneity in perceptual judgments.

These advantages are seemingly offset by the evident impracticability of the demands on respondents to complete a matrix with as many as 2,500 cells. For many purposes, however, it is not necessary that each respondent complete the entire matrix. A related problem is the lack of a sound basis for deciding how many situations and at what level of specificity, to include in the matrix.

5. *Substitution-in-use analysis.* This extends the Stefflre procedure in two directions (Srivastava, Shocker, and Day 1977). First, a separate analysis step is introduced to ensure that the set of usage situations is parsimonious and representative. If the latter condition is not met, it is likely there will be too many of one "type" of situation, with consequent distortion in the grouping of products. Secondly, the measure of appropriateness-in-use is modified to measure the degree of suitability. This is feasible as the number of situations the respondents are given is significantly smaller than in the Stefflre procedure. The result is a three-stage procedure:

1. The *exploratory* stage uses free response plus repertory grid and focused group methods to elicit usage situations associated with a generic need.
2. A *typology* of usage situations is then developed from a principal components analysis of the products-by-uses matrix (after a check for perceptual homogeneity). Both uses and products can be plotted in the reduced space described by the first two or three principal components. A typology of uses may be derived from factorial combinations of different levels of the independent dimensions of this space.
3. A new sample is employed to obtain a measure of the suitability or appropriateness of each brand or product for each of the usage situations in the typology. Each alternative can be rated separately, or all alternatives can be ranked, within each situation.

There are several ways to analyze the resulting matrix. Insights into a firm's competitive position within distinct situational submarkets can be obtained from a principal components analysis similar to stage 2 of the procedure described above. Experience with breath fresheners and banking services (Srivastava and Shocker 1979) indicates that ideas for new products or product positions can come from the identification of inadequately served usage situations. A useful test of the effectiveness of a company's positioning efforts is the extent of variability of customer perceptions of the appropriateness of a specific brand for a distinct usage submarket. The analysis can also help assess the possibility of cannibalization. If two or more products or brands of a single manufacturer are seen as appropriate for the same usage submarket, then efforts to promote one may be at the expense of a loss in sales of the other.

The data can also be analyzed with categorical conjoint or similar procedures, as long as the factorial combinations of usage situations are properly balanced. Here the focus would be on both the patterns of competition within a usage situation and the elements of the situation which have the greatest influence on these patterns. Wind (1977) used this approach to study the relative positions of finance companies. Automobile dealers were given 16 different financing situations and asked to assign each to one of five possible financing alternatives. The situations represented combinations of six different factors including customer's credit rating, familiarity with customer, amount to finance, and length of term. The estimated utility functions suggested the degree of appropriateness of each source of financing for each level of the six factors. It was found, for example, that the client (a finance company associated with an automobile dealer) faced quite different competition depending on the amount to be financed.

Many of the advantages of the substitution-in-use approach derive from the consistency of the approach with the conceptual definition of a product-market. Despite these potential advantages, the procedure produces only a relative measure of substitutability. Managerial judgment must still decide the level of judged appropriateness that permits each product/brand to be considered as part of a situational submarket.

SUMMARY AND CONCLUSIONS

The questions of how to identify product-market boundaries cannot be separated from the ways results are to be used. Strategic or long-run definitions of market structure inevitably hold more significance even though they are mainly obtainable from customer judgments rather than behavior. Very narrowly defined boundaries appear adequate for short-run, tactical decisions in most product categories. The value of a valid and strategically relevant product-market definition lies in "stretching" the company's perceptions appropriately far enough so that significant threats and opportunities are not missed, but not so far as to dissipate information gathering and analysis efforts on "long shots." This is a difficult balance to achieve given the myriad of present and potential competitors faced by most companies.

The principal conclusions from the analysis of the nature of boundaries and the various empirical methods for identifying competitive product-markets are:

- Boundaries are seldom clear-cut—ultimately, all boundaries are arbitrary,
- The suitability of different empirical methods is strongly influenced by the character of the market environment,
- On balance, those empirical methods which explicitly recognize the variety of usage situations have widest applicability and yield maximum insights. The concept of usage situation appears to be the most prevalent common denominator of market environments which can be used as the basis for empirical methods,
- Most methods, particularly those based upon behavioral measures are static and have difficulty coping with changes in preferences or additions and deletions of choice alternatives in the market,
- Regardless of method, the most persistent problem is the lack of defensible criteria for recognizing boundaries.

These conclusions add up to a situation where the state of knowledge has not kept abreast of either the present need to understand, or the changing technological, social, and economic factors which are constantly reshaping market environments. To redress this situation, there is a clear need for a strategically oriented program of research in a variety of market situations. Research in each market should be characterized by the use of multiple techniques to seek confirmation through cross validation and longitudinal approaches in which judgmental methods are followed by behavioral methods which can validate inferences. As we have noted, different methods have different strengths and weaknesses, and more needs to be learned about the sensitivity of results to the shortcomings of each method. Also there will inevitably be points of contradiction and consistency in the insights gained from boundaries established by different methods. The process of resolution should be most revealing, both in terms of understanding a firm's competitive position and suggesting strategy alternatives.

NOTES

1. Many of the same issues are encountered during efforts to define the relevant product-

market for antitrust purposes. Here the question is whether a company so dominates a market that effective competition is precluded, or that a past or prospective merger has lessened competition. The conceptual approach to this question is very similar to the one developed in this paper (Day, Massy, and Shocker 1978). However, because of the adversarial nature of the proceedings and the existence of prior hypotheses of separation to be tested, the treatment of "relevant market" issues is otherwise quite different.

2. This premise was directly tested, and supported, in a study of the variation of judged importance of various fast food restaurant attributes across eating occasions (Miller and Ginter 1979). This study and others also have found that some needs, and benefits sought, are reasonably stable across situations. Thus it is usually productive to segment a market on the basis of both people and occasions (Goldman and McDonald 1979).

REFERENCES

Belk, Russell (1975), "Situational Variables and Consumer Behavior," *Journal of Consumer Research*, 2 (December), 157–164.

Bettman, James R. (1971), "The Structure of Consumer Choice Processes," *Journal of Marketing Research*, 8 (November), 465–471.

Bourgeois, Jacques D., George H. Haines, and Montrose S. Sommers (1979), "Defining an Industry," paper presented to the TIM/ORSA Special Interest Conference on Market Measurement and Analysis, Stanford, CA, March 26.

Butler, Ben Jr. and David H. Butler (1970 and 1971), "Hendrodynamics: Fundamental Laws of Consumer Dynamics," Hendry Corp., Croton-on-Hudson, NY, Chapter 1 (1970) and Chapter 2 (1971).

Cocks, Douglas L. and John R. Virts (1975), "Market Definition and Concentration in the Ethical Pharmaceutical Industry," Internal publication of Eli Lilly and Co., Indianapolis.

Day, George S. (1977), "Diagnosing the Product Portfolio," *Journal of Marketing,* 41 (April), 29–38.

———, Terry Deutscher, and Adrian Ryans (1976), "Data Quality, Level of Aggregation and

Nonmetric Multidimensional Scaling Solutions," *Journal of Marketing Research*, 13 (February), 92–97.

———, William F. Massy, and Allan D. Shocker (1978), "The Public Policy Context of the Relevant Market Question," in *Public Policy Issues in Marketing*, John F. Cady, ed., Cambridge, MA: Marketing Science Institute, 51–67.

Frank, Ronald, William F. Massy, and Yoram Wind (1973), *Market Segmentation,* Englewood Cliffs, NJ: Prentice-Hall, Inc.

Goldman, Alfred and Susan S. McDonald (1979), "Occasion Segmentation," paper presented to American Marketing Association Attitude Research Conference, Hilton Head, S.C., February 25–28.

Green, Paul E. (1975), "Marketing Applications of MDS: Assessment and Outlook," *Journal of Marketing*, 39 (January), 24–31.

———, Yoram Wind, and Arun K. Jain (1973), "Analyzing Free Response Data in Marketing Research," *Journal of Marketing Research*, 10 (February), 45–52.

Haines, George H. (1974), "Process Models of Consumer Decision-Making," in *Buyer/Consumer Information Processing*, G. D. Hughes and M. L. Ray, eds., Chapel Hill, NC: University of North Carolina Press.

Hanon, Mack (1974), "Reorganize Your Company around Its Markets," *Harvard Business Review*, 79 (November–December), 63–74.

Huber, Joel and Bill James (1977), "The Monetary Worth of Physical Attributes: A Dollarmetric Approach," in *Moving Ahead with Attitude Research*, Yoram Wind and Marshall Greenberg, eds., Chicago: American Marketing Association.

Jain, Arun K. and Michael Etgar (1975), "How to Improve Antitrust Policies with Marketing Research Tools," in *1975 Combined Proceedings of the American Marketing Association,* Edward M. Mazze, ed., Chicago: American Marketing Association, 72–75.

Kalwani, Manohar U. and Donald G. Morrison (1977), "A Parsimonious Description of the Hendry System," *Management Science*, 23 (January), 476–477.

Lenz, Ralph C. Jr. and H. W. Lanford (1972), "The Substitution Phenomena," *Business Horizons*, 15 (February), 63–68.

Luhn, Tony (1972), "Segmenting and Constructing Markets," in *Consumer Market Research Handbook*, R. M. Worcester, ed. Maindenhead, Berkshire: McGraw-Hill.

Lutz, Richard J. and Pradeep Kakkar (1976), "Situational Influence in Interpersonal Persuasion," in *Advances in Consumer Research*, Vol. III, Beverlee B. Anderson, ed., Atlanta: Association for Consumer Research, 370–378.

McFadden, Daniel (1970), "Conditional Logit Analysis of Qualitative Choice Behavior" in *Frontiers in Econometrics*, P. Zarembka, ed., New York: Academic Press, 105–142.

Miller, Kenneth E. and James L. Ginter (1979), "An Investigation of Situational Variation in Brand Choice Behavior and Attitude," *Journal of Marketing Research*, 16 (February), 111–123.

Moran, William R. (1973), "Why New Products Fail," *Journal of Advertising Research*, 13 (April), 5–13.

Myers, James H. and Edward Tauber (1977), *Market Structure Analysis*, Chicago: American Marketing Association.

Needham, Douglas (1969), *Economic Analysis of Industrial Structure*, New York: Holt, Rinehart, and Winston, Chapter 2.

Pessemier, Edgar A. (1977), *Product Management: Strategy and Organization*, Santa Barbara, CA: Wiley/Hamilton, 203–254.

_____ , Philip Burger, Richard Teach, and Douglas Tigert (1970/71), "Using Laboratory Brand Preference Scales to Predict Consumer Brand Purchases," *Management Science*, 17 (February), 371–385.

Rubison, Joel R. and Frank M. Bass (1978), "A Note on 'A Parsimonious Description of the Hendry System,'" paper 658, West Lafayette, IN: Krannert School, Purdue, March.

Scherer, Frederic (1970), *Industrial Market Structure and Economic Performance*, Chicago: Rand McNally.

Shocker, Allan D. and V. Srinivasan (1979), "Multiattribute Applications for Product Concept Evaluation and Generation: A Critical Review," *Journal of Marketing Research*, 16 (May), 159–180.

Sissors, Jack Z. (1966), "What is a Market?" *Journal of Marketing*, 30 (July), 17–21.

Srivastava, Rajendra and Allan D. Shocker (1979), "The Validity/Reliability of a Method for Developing Product-Specific Usage Situational Taxonomies," working paper, Pittsburgh: University of Pittsburgh, Graduate School of Business (September).

_____ , _____ , and George S. Day (1978), "An Exploratory Study of Situational Effects on Product Market Definition," in *Advances in Consumer Research*, Vol. V., H. Keith Hunt, ed., Ann Arbor: Association for Consumer Research, 32–38.

Stefflre, Volney (1972), "Some Applications of Multidimensional Scaling to Social Science Problems," in *Multidimensional Scaling: Theory and Applications in the Behavioral Sciences*, Vol. III, A. K. Romney, R. N. Shepard, and S. B. Nerlove, eds., New York: Seminar Press.

_____ (1979), "New Products: Organizational and Technical Problems and Opportunities," in *Analytic Approaches to Product and Marketing Planning*, A. D. Shocker, ed., Cambridge, MA: Marketing Science Institute, April Report 79–104, 415–480.

Stern, M. O., R. V. Ayres, and A. Shapanko (1975), "A Model for Forecasting the Substitution of One Technology for Another," *Technological Forecasting and Social Change*, 7 (February), 57–79.

Stout, Roy G., Raymond H. S. Suh, Marshall G. Greenberg, and Joel S. Dubow (1977), "Usage Incidents as a Basis for Segmentation," in *Moving Ahead with Attitude Research*, Yoram Wind and Marshall Greenberg, eds., Chicago: American Marketing Association.

Strotz, Robert H. (1957), "The Empirical Implications of a Utility Tree," *Econometrica*, 25 (April), 269–280.

_____ , and John R. Hauser (1979), "Market Definition" in *Design and Marketing of New Products and Services*, Cambridge, MA: MIT, Sloan School of Management, Ch. 5.

Vernon, John (1972), *Market Structure and Industrial Performance*, Boston: Allyn and Bacon.

Wind, Yoram (1977), "The Perception of a Firm's Competitive Position," in *Behavioral Models for Market Analysis*, F. M. Nicosia and Y. Wind, eds., New York: The Dryden Press, 163–181.

◆

Market Share—A Key to Profitability

Robert D. Buzzell, Bradley T. Gale, and Ralph G. M. Sultan

It is now widely recognized that one of the main determinants of business profitability is market share. Under most circumstances, enterprises that have achieved a high share of the markets they serve are considerably more profitable than their smaller-share rivals. This connection between market share and profitability has been recognized by corporate executives and consultants, and it is clearly demonstrated in the results of a project undertaken by the Marketing Science Institute on the Profit Impact of Market Strategies (PIMS). The PIMS project, on which we have been working since late 1971,[1] is aimed at identifying and measuring the major determinants of return on investment (ROI) in individual

Authors' note: We wish to acknowledge the contributions of our associates in the PIMS project to the results reported in this paper. Sidney Schoeffler, Donald F. Heany, and James Conlin made valuable suggestions, and Paula Nichols carried out numerous analyses very efficiently and cheerfully. The authors are, of course, solely responsible for any errors or misrepresentations that remain.

businesses. Phase II of the PIMS project, completed in late 1973, reveals 37 key profit influences, of which one of the most important is market share.

There is no doubt that market share and return on investment are strongly related. Figure 23-1 shows average pretax ROI figures for groups of businesses in the PIMS project that have successively increasing shares of their markets. (For an explanation of how businesses, markets, and ROI results are defined and measured in the PIMS project, see the insert on p. 344.) On the average, a difference of 10 percentage points in market share is accompanied by a difference of about 5 points in pretax ROI.

While the PIMS data base is the most extensive and detailed source of information on the profit/market-share relationship, there is additional confirming evidence of its existence. For instance, companies enjoying strong competitive positions in their primary product markets tend to be highly profitable. Consider, for example, such major companies as IBM, Gillette, Eastman Kodak, and Xerox, as

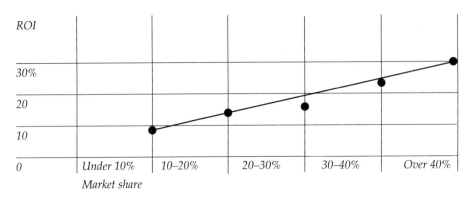

Figure 23-1
Relationship between Market Share and Pretax ROI

well as smaller, more specialized corporations like Dr. Scholl (foot care products) and Hartz Mountain (pet foods and accessories).

Granted that high rates of return usually accompany high market share, it is useful to explore the relationship further. Why is market share profitable? What are the observed differences between low- and high-share businesses? Does the notion vary from industry to industry? And, what does the profitability/market-share relationship imply for strategic planning? In this article we shall attempt to provide partial answers to these questions by presenting evidence on the nature, importance, and implications of the links between market share and profit performance.

WHY MARKET SHARE IS PROFITABLE

The data shown in Figure 23-1 demonstrate the differences in ROI between high- and low-market-share businesses. This convincing evidence of the relationship itself, however, does not tell us why there is a link between market share and profitability. There are at least three possible explanations:

Economies of Scale   The most obvious rationale for the high rate of return enjoyed by large-share businesses is that they have achieved economies of scale in procurement, manufacturing, marketing, and other cost components. A business with a 40% share of a given market is simply twice as big as one with 20% of the same market, and it will attain, to a much greater degree, more efficient methods of operation within a particular type of technology.

Closely related to this explanation is the so-called "experience curve" phenomenon widely publicized by the Boston Consulting Group.[2] According to BCG, total unit costs of producing and distributing a product tend to decline by a more or less constant percentage with each doubling of a company's cumulative output. Since, in a given time period, businesses with large market shares generally also have larger cumulative sales than their smaller competitors, they would be expected to have lower costs and correspondingly higher profits.

Market Power   Many economists, especially among those involved in antitrust work, believe that economies of scale are of relatively little importance in most industries. These economists argue that if large-scale businesses earn higher profits than their smaller competitors, it is a result of their greater market power: their size permits them to bargain more effectively, "administer" prices, and, in the end, realize significantly higher prices for a particular product.[3]

Quality of Management   The simplest of all explanations for the market-share/profitability relationship is that both share and ROI reflect a common underlying factor: the quality of management. Good managers (including, perhaps, lucky ones!) are successful in achieving high shares of their respective markets; they are also skillful in controlling costs, getting maximum productivity from employees, and so on. Moreover, once a business achieves a leadership position—possibly by developing a new field—it is much easier for it to retain its lead than for others to catch up.

These explanations of why the market-share/profitability relationship exists are not mutually exclusive. To some degree, a large-share business may benefit from all three kinds of relative advantages. It is important, however, to understand from the available information how much of the increased profitability that accompanies high market share comes from each of these or other sources.

HOW MARKET SHARE RELATES TO ROI

Analysis of the PIMS data base sheds some light on the reasons for the observed relationship between market share and ROI. Businesses with different market-share levels are compared as to financial and operating ratios and measures of relative prices and product quality in Table 23-1. In examining these figures, remember that the PIMS sample of businesses includes a wide variety of products and industries. Consequently, when we compare businesses with market shares under 10%, say, with those having shares over 40%, we are not observing differences in costs and profits within a single industry. Each subgroup contains a diversity of industries, types of products, kinds of customers, and so on.

Differences between High- and Low-Share Businesses

The data in Table 23-1 reveal four important differences between high-share businesses and those with smaller shares. The samples used are sufficiently large and balanced to ensure that the differences between them are associated primarily with variations in market share, and not with other factors. These differences are:

1. As market share rises, turnover on investment rises only somewhat, but profit margin on sales increases sharply. ROI is, of course, dependent on both the rate of net profit on sales and the amount of investment required to support a given volume of sales. Table 23-1 reveals that the ratio of investment to sales declines only slightly, and irregularly, with increased market share. The data show too that capacity utilization is not systematically related to market share.

On the surface then, higher investment turnover does not appear to be a major factor contributing to higher rates of return. However, this observation is subject to some qualification. Our analysis of the PIMS data base shows that investment intensity (investment relative to sales) tends to vary directly with a business's degree of vertical integration.

(The degree of vertical integration is measured as the ratio of the total value added by the business to its sales. Both the numerator and denominator of the ratio are adjusted

Table 23-1
Relationships of Market Share to Key Financial and Operating Ratios for
Overall PIMS Sample of Businesses

Financial and Operating Ratios	Market Share Under 10%	10%–20%	20%–30%	30%–40%	Over 40%
Capital structure:					
Investment/sales	68.66	67.74	61.08	64.66	63.98
Receivables/sales	15.52	14.08	13.96	15.18	14.48
Inventory/sales	9.30	8.97	8.68	8.68	8.16
Operating results:					
Pretax profit/sales	−0.16	3.42	4.84	7.60	13.16
Purchases/sales	45.40	39.90	39.40	32.60	33.00
Manufacturing/sales	29.64	32.61	32.11	32.95	31.76
Marketing/sales	10.60	9.88	9.06	10.45	8.57
R&D/sales	2.60	2.40	2.83	3.18	3.55
Capacity/utilization	74.70	77.10	78.10	75.40	78.00
Product quality:					
Average of percents superior minus inferior	14.50	20.40	20.40	20.10	43.00
Relative price*	2.72	2.73	2.65	2.66	2.39
Number of businesses	156	179	105	67	87

*Average value on 5-point scale:
5 = 10% or more lower than leading competitors' average;
3 = within 3% of competition;
1 = 10% or more higher than competition.

by subtracting the pretax income and adding the PIMS average ROI, multiplied by the investment.)

Vertical integration thus has a strong negative relation to the ratio of purchases to sales. Since high market-share businesses are on the average somewhat more vertically integrated than those with smaller shares, it is likely that investment turnover increases somewhat more with market share than the figures in Table 23-1 suggest. In other words, as shown in Table 23-2, for a given degree of vertical integration, the investment-to-sales ratio declines significantly, even though overall averages do not.

Nevertheless, Table 23-1 shows that the major reason for the ROI/market-share relationship is the dramatic difference in pretax profit margins on sales. Businesses with market shares under 10% had average pretax losses of 0.16%. The average ROI for businesses with under 10% market share was about 9%. Obviously, no individual business can have a negative profit-to-sales ratio and still earn a positive ROI. The apparent inconsistency between the averages reflects the fact

Table 23-2
Effect of Vertical Integration on Investment/Sales Ratio

Vertical Integration	Market Share Under 10%	10–20%	20%–30%	30%–40%	Over 40%
Low	65	61	46	58	55
High	77	76	75	70	69

that some businesses in the sample incurred losses that were very high in relation to sales but that were much smaller in relation to investment. In the PIMS sample, the average return on sales exhibits a strong, smooth, upward trend as market share increases.

Why do profit margins on sales increase so sharply with market share? To answer this, it is necessary to look in more detail at differences in prices and operating expenses.

2. The biggest single difference in costs, as related to market share, is in the purchase-to-sales ratio. As shown in Table 23-1, for large-share businesses—those with shares over 40%— purchases represent only 33% of sales, compared with 45% for businesses with shares under 10%.

How can we explain the decline in the ratio of purchases to sales as share goes up? One possibility, as mentioned earlier, is that high-share businesses tend to be more vertically integrated—they "make" rather than "buy," and often they own their own distribution facilities. The decline in the purchases-to-sales ratio is quite a bit less (see Table 23-3) if we control for the level of vertical integration. A low purchases-to-sales ratio goes hand in hand with a high level of vertical integration.

Other things being equal, a greater extent of vertical integration ought to result in a rising level of manufacturing costs. (For the nonmanufacturing businesses in the PIMS sample, "manufacturing" was defined as the primary value-creating activity of the business. For example, processing transactions is the equivalent of manufacturing in a bank.) But the data in Table 23-1 show little or no connection between manufacturing expense, as a percentage of sales, and market share. This could be because, despite the increase in vertical integration, costs are offset by increased efficiency.

This explanation is probably valid for some of the businesses in the sample, but we believe that, in the majority of cases, the decline in costs of purchased materials also reflects a combination of economies of scale in buying and, perhaps, bargaining power in dealing with suppliers. Economies of scale in procurement arise from lower costs of manufacturing, marketing, and distributing when suppliers sell in large quantities. For very large-scale buyers, custom-designed components and special formulations of materials that are purchased on long-term contracts may offer "order of magnitude" economies.

Still another possible explanation of the declining purchases-to-sales ratio for large-share businesses might be that they charge higher prices, thus increasing the base on which the percentage is figured. This does not, however, appear to be the case.

In Table 23-2 we give measures of price relative to competition for each group of businesses that indicate otherwise. Because of the great difficulty of computing meaningful relative price-index numbers, the measure we used here is rather crude. We asked the PIMS participants to indicate on a five-point scale

Table 23-3
Purchase-to-Sales Ratio Corrected for Vertical Integration

Vertical Integration	Market Share Under 10%	10–20%	20%–30%	30%–40%	Over 40%
Low	54	51	53	52	46
High	32	27	29	24	23

whether their prices were "about the same" as major competitors, "somewhat" higher or lower, or "substantially" higher or lower for each business. The average values for this scale measure are virtually identical for each market-share group, except for those with shares over 40%.

Despite the similarity of relative prices for the first four share groups, the purchases-to-sales ratios decline in a regular, substantial fashion as share increases. In light of this, we do not believe that the decline in purchase costs is a reflection of higher price levels imposed by "market power."

3. *As market share increases, there is some tendency for marketing costs, as a percentage of sales, to decline.* The difference in marketing costs between the smallest and largest market-share groups amounts on the average to about 2% of sales. We believe that this reflects true scale economies, including the spreading of fixed marketing costs and the ability of large-share businesses to utilize more efficient media and marketing methods. In the case of industrial products, large scale permits a manufacturer to use his own sales force rather than commissioned agents and, at some point, to utilize specialized sales forces for specific product lines or markets. For consumer goods, large-scale businesses may derive an important cost advantage from their ability to utilize the most efficient mass-advertising media.

In addition, leading brands of consumer products appear to benefit to some extent from a "bandwagon effect" that results

from the brand's greater visibility in retail stores or greater support from retail store sales personnel. For example, Anheuser-Busch has for some time enjoyed lower advertising costs per case of beer than its smaller rivals—just as the advertising expense per car of General Motors is significantly lower than that of other competing auto manufacturers.

4. *Market leaders develop unique competitive strategies and have higher prices for their higher-quality products than do smaller-share businesses.* The figures in Table 23-1 do not show smooth, continuous relationships between market share and the various components of price, cost, and investment. Indeed, it appears that one pattern operates as share increases up to 40%, but a somewhat different pattern above that figure.

Particularly, there are substantial differences in relative price and product quality between market leaders and the rest of the sample. Market leaders obtain higher prices than do businesses with smaller market shares. A principal reason for this may be that market leaders also tend to produce and sell significantly higher-quality products and services than those of their lower-share competitors.

We measured quality as follows: We asked the participating companies to judge for each business the proportions of total sales comprised of products and services that were "superior," "equivalent," and "inferior" to those of leading competitors. The figures shown in Table 23-1 are averages of the differences between the superior quality and the inferior quality percentages.

The measures we used for relative price and relative quality are not, of course, directly comparable. Thus it is impossible to determine which is greater—the price premiums earned by market leaders, or the differential in the quality of their products. But it is clear that the combination of significantly higher prices and quality represents a unique competitive position for market leaders.

Market leaders, in contrast to their smaller competitors, spend significantly higher amounts on research and development, relative to sales. As shown in Table 23-1, the average ratio of R&D to sales for the highest-share group of businesses was 3.55%—nearly 40% greater than the ratio for the under-10% share group. This, combined with the quality advantage enjoyed by market leaders, suggests that they typically pursue a strategy of product leadership. Certainly this is consistent with what is known about innovative leaders such as Eastman Kodak, IBM, and Procter & Gamble.

Given that market leaders have a high market share and thus the profitability that goes with it, it is natural to question whether the share and profitability ratio shifts from industry to industry. In other words, do businesses in some kinds of industries need a higher share than others to be profitable?

Variations among Industries

While our analyses of the PIMS data base clearly demonstrate a strong general relationship between ROI and market share, they also indicate that the importance of share varies considerably from one type of industry or market situation to another. Two of the more striking variations are summarized in Table 23-3. These figures show that:

1. Market share is more important for infrequently purchased products than for frequently purchased ones. For infrequently purchased products, the ROI of the average market leader is about 28 percentage points greater than the ROI of the average small-share business. For frequently purchased products (those typically bought at least once a month), the corresponding ROI differential is approximately 10 points.

Why? Infrequently purchased products tend to be durable, higher unit-cost items such as capital goods, equipment, and consumer durables, which are often complex and difficult for buyers to evaluate. Since there is a bigger risk inherent in a wrong choice, the purchaser is often willing to pay a premium for assured quality.

Frequently purchased products are generally low unit-value items such as foods or industrial supplies. The risk in buying from a lesser-known, small-share supplier is lower in most cases, so a purchaser can feel free to shop around.

2. Market share is more important to businesses when buyers are "fragmented" rather than concentrated. As Figure 23-2 shows, when buyers are fragmented (i.e., no small group of consumers accounts for a significant proportion of total sales), the ROI differential is 27 percentage points for the average market leader. However, when buyers are concentrated, the leaders' average advantage in ROI is reduced to only 19 percentage points greater than that of the average small-share business.

A likely explanation for this is that when buyers are fragmented, they cannot bargain for the unit cost advantage that concentrated buyers receive, thus allowing higher profits for the large-share business. Obviously, then, the ROI differential is smaller when buyers are somewhat concentrated. In this case, powerful buyers tend to bargain away some of the seller's cost differential by holding out for low prices.

Clearly, the strategic implications of the market-share/profitability relationship

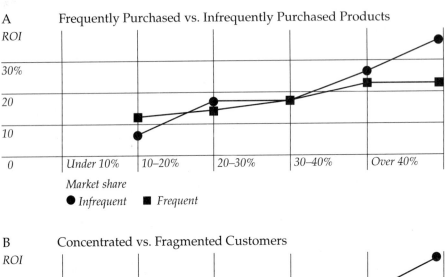

A   Frequently Purchased vs. Infrequently Purchased Products

B   Concentrated vs. Fragmented Customers

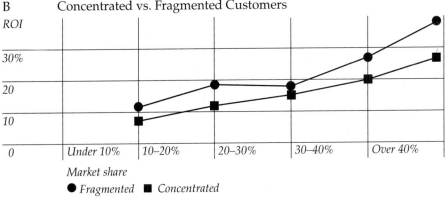

Figure 23-2
Industry Variations in the Share/ROI Relationship

vary according to the circumstances of the individual business. But there is no doubt that the relationship can be translated into dynamic strategies for all companies trying to set market goals.

WHAT THE ROI/MARKET SHARE LINK MEANS FOR STRATEGY

Because market share is so strongly related to profitability, a basic strategic issue for top management is to establish market-share ob-jectives. These objectives have much to do with the rate of return that can reasonably be budgeted in the short and long runs, as well as the capital requirements and cash flow of a business.

Setting Market-Share Goals

What market-share goals are feasible, or even desirable, obviously depends on many things, including the strength of competitors, the resources available to support a strategy, and the willingness of management to forgo present earnings for future results. At the risk of oversimplification, we can classify market-share strategies into three rather broad groups:

1. Building strategies are based on active efforts to increase market share by means of new product introductions, added marketing programs, and so on.
2. Holding strategies are aimed at maintaining the existing level of market share.
3. Harvesting strategies are designed to achieve high short-term earnings and cash flow by permitting market share to decline.

When does each of these market-share strategies seem most appropriate? How should each be implemented? The experiences documented in the PIMS data base provide some clues.

Building Strategies   The data presented in Figure 23-1 imply that, in many cases, even a marginally acceptable rate of return can be earned only by attaining some minimum level of market share. If the market share of a business falls below this minimum, its strategic choices usually boil down to two: increase share or withdraw. Of course there are exceptions to this rule.

But we are convinced that in most markets there is a minimum share that is required for viability. RCA and General Electric apparently concluded that they were below this minimum in the computer business, and they pulled out. Similarly, Motorola, with an estimated 6% to 7% share of U.S. TV-set sales, and a rumored loss of $20 million in the period from 1970 to 1973, announced its intention early in 1974 to sell the business to Matsushita.

On the other hand, when share is not so low as to dictate withdrawal, but is still not high enough to yield satisfactory returns, managers can consider aggressive share-building strategies. They should recognize, however, that (a) big increases in share are

seldom achieved quickly; and (b) expanding share is almost always expensive in the short run.

Among the 600 businesses in the PIMS sample, only about 20% enjoyed market share gains of 2 points or more from 1970 to 1972. As might be expected, successful building strategies were most common among relatively new businesses. Of those that have begun operations since 1965, over 40% achieved share increases of 2 points or more—compared with only 17% of the businesses established before 1950.

Generally speaking, businesses that are building share pay a short-run penalty for doing so. Table 23-4 compares ROI results for businesses with different beginning market shares and for businesses with decreasing, steady, and increasing shares over the period 1970 to 1972. Generally, the businesses that were "building" (i.e., had share increases of at least 2 points) had ROI results of 1 to 2 points lower than those that maintained more or less steady ("holding") positions. The short-term cost of building was greatest for small-share businesses, but even for market leaders, ROI was significantly lower when share was rising than it was when share was stable.

Schick's campaign to build sales of the "Flexamatic" electric shaver during 1972 and 1973 dramatically illustrates the cost of increasing market share. In late 1972 Schick introduced the Flexamatic by means of a controversial national advertising campaign in which direct performance comparisons were made with its leading competitors. Trade sources have estimated that Schick spent $4.5 million in 1972 and $5.2 million in 1973 on advertising, whereas the company's advertising expenditures in 1970 and 1971 had been under $1 million annually.

In one sense the effort was successful: by late 1972 Schick's market share had doubled from 8% to 16%. But the impact on company profits was drastic. Schick's operating

Table 23-4
How ROI Is Affected by Market-Share Changes

Market Share 1970	Market-Share Strategies		
	Building: Up 2 Points or More	Holding: Less Than 2 Points Up or Down	Harvesting: Down 2 Points or More
	Average ROI, 1970–1972		
Under 10%	7.5%	10.4%	10.0%
10%–20%	13.3	12.6	14.5
20%–30%	20.5	21.6	9.5
30%–40%	24.1	24.6	7.3
40% or over	29.6	31.9	32.6

losses for the fiscal year ending February 28, 1974 amounted to $14.5 million on sales of $93.8 million, and it appears that although it was not the only cause, the high promotional cost of the Flexamatic campaign was a major contributing factor. Only time can tell whether Schick's short-term losses will prove to be justified by increased future cash flows.

The Schick example is, no doubt, an extreme one. Nevertheless, a realistic assessment of any share-building strategy should take into account the strong likelihood that a significant price will have to be paid—at least in the short run. Depending on how great the gains are and how long it takes to achieve them, this cost may or may not be offset by the longer-term gains.

In a recent article, William Fruhan demonstrated that there was a positive relation between market share and rate of return for automobile manufacturers and for retail food chains.[4] Yet he also cited examples of disasters stemming from overambition in the market-share dimension from the computer industry, the retail food business, and the airline companies.

The main thrust of Fruhan's article was to encourage business strategists to consider

certain questions before launching an aggressive market-share expansion strategy: (1) Does the company have the necessary financial resources? (2) Will the company find itself in a viable position if its drive for expanded market share is thwarted before it reaches its market share target? (3) Will regulatory authorities permit the company to achieve its objective with the strategy it has chosen to follow? Negative responses to these questions would obviously indicate that a company should forgo market-share expansion until the right conditions are created.

It is fairly safe for us to say, therefore, that whenever the market position of a business is reasonably satisfactory, or when further building of share seems excessively costly, managers ought to follow holding strategies.

Holding Strategies   By definition, a holding strategy is designed to preserve the status quo. For established businesses in relatively mature markets—which is to say, for the majority of businesses in advanced economies—holding is undoubtedly the most common strategic goal with respect to market share.

A key question for businesses that are pursuing holding strategies is, "What is the most profitable way to maintain market position?" The answer to this question depends on many things, including the possibilities and costs of significant technological change and the strength and alertness of competitors. Because competitive conditions vary so much, few reliable generalizations can be made about profit-maximizing methods of maintaining market share.

Nevertheless, our analyses of the PIMS data base do suggest some broad relationships between ROI and competitive behavior. For example, our data indicate that large-scale businesses usually earn higher rates of return when they charge premium prices. (Recall that this pricing policy is usually accompanied by premium quality.) Also, ROI is usually greater for large-share businesses when they spend more than their major competitors, in relation to sales, on sales force effort, advertising and promotion, and research and development.

For small-share businesses, however, the most profitable holding strategy is just the opposite: on the average, ROI is highest for these businesses when their prices are somewhat below the average of leading competitors and when their rates of spending on marketing and R&D are relatively low.

Harvesting Strategies   Opposed to a share-building strategy is one of "harvesting"—deliberately permitting share to fall so that higher short-run earnings and cash flow may be secured. Harvesting is more often a matter of necessity than of strategic choice. Cash may be urgently needed to support another activity—dividends, for example, or management's earning record. Whatever the motivation, corporate management sometimes does elect to "sell off" part of a market-share position.

The experience of the businesses in the PIMS data pool, summarized in Table 23-4, indicates that only large-scale businesses are generally able to harvest successfully. Market leaders enjoyed rates of return about three quarters of a point higher when they allowed market share to decline than when they maintained it over the period 1970–1972. For the other groups of businesses shown in Table 23-4, differences in ROI between "holding" and "harvesting" are irregular. Of course, these comparisons also reflect the influence of factors other than strategic choice. Market share was lost by many businesses because of intensified competition, rising costs, or other changes which hurt both their profitability and their competitive positions. For this reason, it is impossible to derive a true measure of the profitability of harvesting. Nevertheless, the PIMS data support our contention that, under proper conditions, current profits can be increased by allowing share to slide.

When does harvesting make sense, assuming it is a matter of choice? A reduction in share typically affects profits in a way directly opposite to that of building: ROI is increased in the short run but reduced in the longer term. Here again, a trade-off must be made. The net balance will depend on management's assessment of the direction and timing of future developments such as technological changes, as well as on its preference for immediate rather than deferred profits.

Balancing Costs and Benefits

Evidence from the PIMS study strongly supports the proposition that market share is positively related to the rate of return on investment earned by a business. Recognition of this relationship will affect how managers decide whether to make or buy to decrease purchasing costs, whether to advertise in certain media, or whether to alter the price or quality of a product. Also, recognizing that emphasis on market share varies considerably among industries and types of market situations, decisions concerning product and customer are likely to be influenced. For instance, a small competitor selling frequently purchased, differentiated consumer products can achieve satisfactory results with a small share of the market. Under other conditions, it would be virtually impossible to earn satisfactory profits with a small share (e.g., infrequently purchased products sold to large, powerful buyers).

Finally, choices among the three basic market share strategies also involve a careful analysis of the importance of market share in a given situation. Beyond this, strategic choice requires a balancing of short-term and long-term costs and benefits. Neither the PIMS study nor any other empirical research can lead to a "formula" for these strategic choices. But we hope that the findings presented here will at least provide some useful insights into the probable consequences of managers' choices.

THE PIMS DATA BASE

The data on which this article is based come from the unique pool of operating experience assembled in the PIMS project, now in its third year of operations at the Marketing Science Institute. During 1973, 57 major North American corporations supplied financial and other information on 620 individual "businesses" for the three-year period 1970–1972.

Each business is a division, product line, or other profit center within its parent company, selling a distinct set of *products* or *services* to an identifiable group or groups of *customers*, in competition with a well-defined set of competitors. Examples of businesses include manufacturers of TV sets; man-made fibers; and nondestructive industrial testing apparatus.

Data were compiled for individual businesses by means of special allocations of existing company data and, for some items,

judgmental estimates supplied by operating managers of the companies.

For each business, the companies also provided estimates of the total sales in the market served by the business. Markets were defined, for purposes of the PIMS study, in much narrower terms than the "industries" for which sales and other figures are published by the Bureau of the Census. Thus the data used to measure market size and growth rates cover only the specific products or services, customer types, and geographic areas in which each business actually operates.

The *market share* of each business is simply its dollar sales in a given time period, expressed as a percentage of the total market sales volume. The figures shown are average market shares for the three-year period 1970–1972. (The average market share for the businesses in the PIMS sample was 22.1%.)

Return on investment was measured by relating *pretax operating profits* to the *sum of equity and long-term debt*. Operating income in a business is after deduction of allocated corporate overhead costs, but *prior* to any capital charges assigned by corporate offices. As in the case of market share data, the ROI figures shown in Figures 23-1 and 23-2 and Table 23-4 are averages for 1970–1972.

As explained in the earlier HBR article, the focus of the PIMS project has been primarily on ROI because this is the performance measure most often used in strategic planning. We recognize, however, that ROI results are often not entirely comparable between businesses. When the plant and equipment used in a business have been almost fully depreciated, for example, its ROI will be inflated. Also, ROI results are affected by patents, trade secrets, and other proprietary aspects of the products or methods of operation employed in a business. These and other differences among businesses should naturally be kept in mind in evaluating the reasons for variations in ROI performance.

NOTES

1. See the earlier article on Phases I and II of the project by Sidney Schoeffler, Robert D. Buzzell, and Donald F. Heany, "Impact of Strategic Planning on Profit Performance," HBR March–April 1974.

2. Boston Consulting Group, Inc., *Perspectives on Experience* (Boston, 1968 and 1970).

3. This general argument has been made in numerous books, articles, and speeches dealing with antitrust economics, see, for example, Joe S. Bain, *Industrial Organization*, 2nd edition (New York, John Wiley & Sons, 1968), especially Chapter 6.

4. "Pyrrhic Victories in Fights for Market Share," HBR September–October 1972.

◆

A Strategic Perspective on Product Planning

George S. Day

INTRODUCTION

The past decade has seen growing recognition that the product planning function within diversified companies of all sizes involves tradeoffs among competing opportunities and strategies. During this period the combination of more complex markets, shorter product life cycles and social, legal and governmental trends puts a premium on minimizing the degree of risk in the product mix. More recently, managers have had to cope with severe resource constraints, stemming partly from weaknesses in the capital markets and a general cash shortage, and the triple traumas of the energy crisis, materials shortages and inflation.

Some of the manifestations of the new climate for product planning are skepticism toward the value of full product lines, unwillingness to accept the risks of completely new products, an emphasis on profit growth rather than volume growth and active product elimination and divestment programs.[1] Yet man-

agements cannot afford to turn their backs on all opportunities for change and attempt to survive by doing a better job with the established products and services. Eventually all product categories become saturated or threatened by substitutes and diversification becomes essential to survival. Consumer goods companies are especially feeling this pressure as the productivity of line extensions or product adaptations directed at narrow market segments declines. Also the likelihood of regulatory actions directed at products, such as aerosols and cyclamates, points up the risks of having a closely grouped product line.[2] More than ever, long-run corporate health is going to depend on the ability of product planners to juggle those conflicting pressures of diversification and consolidation.

The pervasive nature of the resource allocation problem in product planning is the focus of this article. The emphasis is on the basic issues of the role of new and established products and markets and the choice of areas of new product development to pursue. The first issue is addressed in the context of the product portfolio, which describes the mix-

Reprinted with permission from *Journal of Contemporary Business*. Copyright © 1975, pp. 1–34 ture of products that generate cash and in which the company can invest cash. A detailed examination of the product portfolio begins with its component parts, the product life cycle and the notion of market dominance, and then turns to the implications for strategic planning and resource allocation.

Once the role of new products has been established, the issue of where to look is addressed with an explicit statement of a search strategy. This statement defines the characteristics of desirable opportunities in terms that are meaningful to product planners.

STRATEGIC PLANNING AND PRODUCT PLANNING

There are as many concepts of strategy as writers on the subject.[3] Several of the more useful definitions for our immediate purposes are:

- Decisions today which affect the future (not future decisions)
- Major questions of resource allocation that determine a company's long-run results
- The calculated means by which the firm deploys its resources—i.e., personnel, machines and money—to accomplish its purpose under the most advantageous circumstances
- A competitive edge that allows a company to serve the customers better than its competitors
- The broad principles by which a company hopes to secure an advantage over competitors, an attractiveness to buyers and a full exploitation of company resources

Following these definitions, the desired output of the strategic planning process is a long-run plan "that will produce an attractive growth rate and a high rate of return on investment by achieving a market position so advantageous that competitors can retaliate only over an extended time period at a prohibitive cost."[4]

Most strategic planning processes and the resulting plans show a distinct family resemblance, although the specifics obviously vary greatly. These specifics usually include[5]: (1) a statement of the mission of the strategic business unit (SBU),[6] (2) the desired future position the SBU and the corporation want to attain, comprising measurable profitability, sales, market share, efficiency and flexibility objectives, (3) the key environmental assumptions and the opportunities and threats, (4) a statement of the strengths, weaknesses and problems of the SBU and its major competitors, (5) the strategic gap between the desired and forecasted position of the SBU, (6) actions to be taken to close the gap—the strategy and (7) the required resources and where they can be obtained, including financial resources such as net cash flow, the equity base and debt capacity and management capabilities. These are the main elements of the planning process that are relevant to product planning, leaving aside the issues of detailed implementation plans, contingency plans, which state in advance what modifications will be made if key environmental or competitor assumptions turn out to be false, and the monitoring procedures.

What is lacking in the planning process just described is a systematic procedure for generating and choosing strategic alternatives. One of the greatest weaknesses of current strategic plans is the lack of viable strategy alternatives which present very different approaches and outcomes. Too frequently top management sees only one strategy which the SBU has decided is best in terms of its own and the managers' personal needs and objectives. This ignores the interdependency among products (the portfolio aspect)[7] and the possibility that what is best for each SBU is not necessarily best for the entire company.[8] In recognition of this problem, the planning process shown in Figure 24-1 incor-

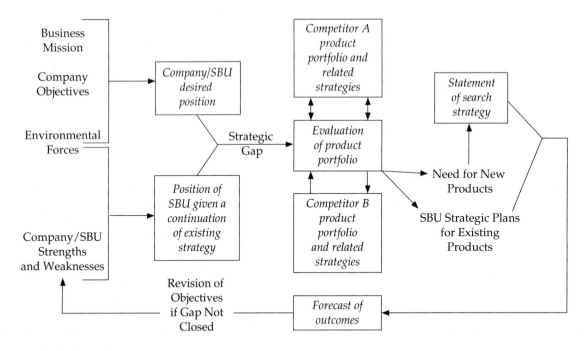

Figure 24-1
Highlighting Product Planning Activities in the Strategic Planning Process

porates an analysis of the product portfolio. The remainder of this paper is devoted to the uses and limitations of the product portfolio and the implications for developing strategy alternatives that optimize the long-run position of the firm.

THE COMPONENTS OF
THE PRODUCT PORTFOLIO

Market share and stage in the product life cycle have long been regarded as important determinants of profitability. The contribution of the product portfolio concept is that it permits the planner to consider these two measures simultaneously in evaluating the products of an entire company or a division or SBU.

The Value of Market Share Dominance

The belief in the benefits of a dominant market share is rooted deeply in the experience of executives. It is reinforced by the facts of life in most markets:

- The market leader is usually the most profitable.
- During economic downturns, customers are likely to concentrate their purchases in suppliers with large shares, and distributors and retailers will try to cut inventories by eliminating the marginal supplier.
- During periods of economic growth, there is often a bandwagon effect with a large share presenting a positive image to customers and retailers.[9]

Of course, market domination has its own pitfalls, beyond antitrust problems, " . . . monopolists flounder on their own complacency rather than on public opposition. Market domination produces tremendous internal resistance against any innovation and makes adaptation to change dangerously difficult. Also, it usually means that the enterprise has too many of its eggs in one basket and is too vulnerable to economic fluctuations."[10] The leader is also highly vulnerable to competitive actions, especially in the pricing area, since the leader establishes the basic industry price from which smaller competitors can discount.

The clearest evidence of the value of market share comes from a study of The Profit Impact of Market Strategies (PIMS) of 620 separate businesses by the Marketing Science Institute which, in turn, draws on earlier work by General Electric. Early results indicated that market share, investment intensity (ratio of total investment to sales) and product quality were the most important determinants of pretax return on investment, among a total of 37 distinct factors incorporated into a profit model.[11] On average it was found that a difference of 10 points in market share was accompanied by a difference of about 5 points in pretax ROI. As share declines from more than 40 percent to less than 10 percent, the average pretax ROI dropped from 30 percent to 9.1 percent.

The PIMS study also provided some interesting insights into the reasons for the link between market share and profitability.[12] The results point to economies of scale and, especially, the opportunities for vertical integration as the most important explanations. Thus high-share businesses (more than 40 percent) tend to have low ratios of purchases to sales because they make rather than buy and own their distribution facilities. The ratio of purchases to sales increases from 33 percent

for high-share businesses to 45 percent for low-share (less than 10 percent) businesses. But because of economies of scale in manufacturing and purchasing there is no significant relationship between manufacturing expenses or the ratio of sales to investment and the market share. To some degree these results also support the market power argument of economists; market leaders evidently are able to bargain more effectively (either through the exercise of reciprocity or greater technical marketing skills) and obtain higher prices than their competition (but largely because they produce and sell higher-quality goods and services). The fact that market leaders spend a significantly higher percentage of their sales on R and D suggests that they pursue a conscious strategy of product leadership.

Experience Curve Analysis The importance of economies of scale in the relationship of market share and profitability is verified by the experience curve concept. Research, largely reported by the Boston Consulting Group, has found that in a wide range of businesses (including plastics, semiconductors, gas ranges and life insurance policies), the total unit costs, in constant dollars, decline by a constant percentage (usually 20 to 30 percent) with each doubling of accumulated units of output or experience.[13] Since the experience effect applies to all value added, it subsumes economies of scale and specialization effects along with the well-known learning curve which applies only to direct labor costs.

An experience curve, when plotted on a log-log scale as in Figure 24-2, appears as a straight line. The locations of the competitors on this curve are determined approximately by their respective accumulated experience, for which relative market share is a good surrogate (this may not be true if some competitors recently have entered the market by buying experience through licenses or acqui-

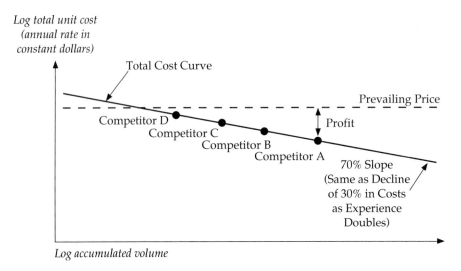

Log total unit cost
(annual rate in
constant dollars)

Total Cost Curve

Prevailing Price

Competitor D
Competitor C
Competitor B
Competitor A

Profit

70% Slope
(Same as Decline
of 30% in Costs
as Experience
Doubles)

Log accumulated volume

Figure 24-2
Cost Experience Curve Showing Relative Profit Levels of Competitors

sitions). Then it follows that the competitor with the greatest accumulated experience will have the lowest relative costs and, if prices are similar between competitors, also will have the greatest profits. Of course, companies that fail to reduce costs along the product category experience curve and who are not dominant will be at an even greater competitive disadvantage.

Figure 24-2 shows a price prevailing at one point in time. Over the long run, prices also will decline at roughly the same rate as costs decline. The major exception to this rule occurs during the introduction and growth rate of the life cycle, when the innovator and/or dominant competitor, is tempted to maintain prices at a high level to recoup the development costs. The high price umbrella usually achieves this immediate end because unit profits are high. The drawback is the incentive to higher cost competitors to enter the market and attempt to increase their market shares. In effect, the dominant competitor is trading future market share for current profits. This may be sensible if the early leader:

(1) has a number of attractive new product opportunities requiring cash, (2) there are potential competitors whose basic business position will enable them eventually to enter the product category regardless of the pricing strategy[14] or (3) significant barriers to entry can be erected.

Product Life Cycle

That products pass through various stages between life and death (introduction → growth → maturity → decline) is hard to deny. Equally accepted is the notion that a company should have a mix of products with representation in each of these stages.

Thus the concept of a product life cycle would appear to be an essential tool for understanding product strategies.[15] Indeed this is true, but only *if* the position of the product and the duration of the cycle can be determined. This caveat should be kept in mind when considering the following summary of the important aspects of the product life cycle:

- Volume and profit growth attract competition during the early *growth* (or takeoff) stage of the life cycle. The product market is even more attractive if the innovator lacks the capacity to satisfy demand. However, these competitors may contribute to the growth of sales by their market development expenditures and product improvements.

- Purchase patterns and distribution channels are still fluid during the rapid *growth* stage. For this reason, market shares can be increased at relatively low cost over short periods of time by capturing a disproportionate share of incremental sales (especially where these sales come from new users rather than heavier usage by existing users).

- As a product reaches *maturity* there is evidence of saturation, finer distinctions in benefits surrounding the product and appeals to special segments.

- There is often an industry shake-out to signal the *end* of the rapid growth stage. The trigger might be an excessive number of competitors who have to resort to price cutting to survive; a dominant producer who seeks to regain share; or a large competitor buying into the market (and all these effects will be accentuated by an economic slow down). The result is a period of consolidation during which marginal competitors either drop out, merge with other small competitors or sell out to larger competitors.

- During the *maturity* stage, market-share relationships tend to stabilize; distribution patterns have been established and are difficult to change. This, in turn, contributes to inertia in purchasing relationships and selling oriented toward maintaining relationships. Any substantial increase in share of market will require a reduction in a competitor's capacity utilization which will be resisted vigorously. As a result, gains in share are both time-consuming and costly. This is not necessarily the case if the attempt to gain shares is spearheaded by a significant improvement in product value or performance which the competitor cannot easily match. A case in point is the growth in private labels, or distributor-controlled labels, in both food and general merchandising categories.

- As substitutes appear and/or sales begin to decline, the core product behaves like a commodity and is subject to intense and continuing price pressure. The result is further competitors dropping out of the market since only those with extensive accumulated experience and cost-cutting capability are able to generate reasonable profits and ROI'S.

- The *decline* stage can be forestalled by vigorous promotion (plus, a new creative platform) and product improvement designed to generate more frequent usage or new users and applications.[16] Of course, if these extensions are sufficiently different, a new product life cycle is launched.

Measurement and Interpretation Problems

The concepts underlying the product portfolio are much easier to articulate than to implement.

What Is the Product-Market?   The crux of the problem is well stated by Moran:

> In our complex service society there are no more product classes—not in any meaningful sense, only as a figment of file clerk imagination. There are only use classes—users which are more central to some products and peripheral to others—on a vast overlapping continuum. To some degree, in some circumstances almost anything can be a partial substitute for almost anything else. An eight-cent stamp substitutes to some extent for an airline ticket.[17]

Where does this leave the manager who relies on share of some (possibly ill-defined) market as a guide to performance evaluation and resource allocation. First he or she must recognize that most markets do not have neat boundaries. For example, patterns of substitution in industrial markets often look like continua, i.e., zinc, brass, aluminum and engineered plastics such as nylon and polycarbonates can be arrayed rather uniformly along dimensions of price and performance. A related complication, more pertinent to consumer product markets, is the possibility of segment differences in perceptions of product substitutability. For example, there is a timid, risk-averse segment that uses a different product for each kind of surface cleaning (i.e., surface detergents, scouring powders, floor cleaners, bleaches, lavatory cleaners and general-purpose wall cleaners). At the other extreme is the segment that uses detergent for every cleaning problem. Thirdly, product/markets may have to be defined in terms of distribution patterns. Thus, tire companies treat the OEM and replacement tire markets as separate and distinct, even though the products going through these two channels are perfect substitutes so far as the end customer is concerned.

Perhaps the most important consideration is the time frame. A long-run view, reflecting strategic planning concerns, invariably will reveal a larger product-market to account for: (1) changes in technology, price relationships and availability which may remove or reduce cost and performance limitations, e.g., the boundaries between minicomputers, programmable computers and time-sharing systems in many use situations are becoming very fuzzy; (2) the time required by present and prospective buyers to react to these changes, which includes modifying behavior patterns, production systems, etc. and (3) considerable switching among products over long periods of time to satisfy desires for variety and change, as is encountered in consumer goods with snacks, for example.

Despite these complexities, the boundaries of product markets usually are established by four-digit Standard Industrial Classification (SIC) categories and/or expert judgment. The limitations of the SIC are well known[18] but often do not outweigh the benefits of data availability in a convenient form that can be broken down further to geographic markets. In short, the measure is attractive on tactical grounds (for sales force, promotional budget, etc., allocation) but potentially misleading for strategic planning purposes.

What Is Market Dominance?   A measure of market share, per se, is not a good indicator of the extent to which a firm dominates a market. The value of a 30 percent share is very different in a market where the next largest competitor has 40 percent than in one where the next largest has only 20 percent. Two alternative measures which incorporate information on the structure of the competition are:

- Company share ÷ share of largest competitor
- Company share ÷ share of three largest competitors

The former measure is more consistent with the implications of the experience curve, while the latter is perhaps better suited to highly concentrated markets (where the four-firm concentration ratio is greater than 80 percent, for example). Regardless of which measure is used it is often the case that the dominant firm has to be at least 1.5 times as large as the next biggest competitor in order to ensure profitability. When there are two large firms of roughly equal shares, especially in a growth business such as nuclear power generators, the competition is likely to be severe. In this instance, both General Electric and Westinghouse have about 40 percent shares and don't expect to be profitable on new installations until after 1977. Conversely, when the two largest firms have small shares, say less than 5 percent, neither measure of market dominance is meaningful.

Return on Investment

Share Market	Infrequently Purchased (<once/month)	Frequently Purchased (>once/month)
Under 10%	6.9%	12.4%
10–19	14.4	13.7
20–29	17.8	17.4
30–39	24.3	23.1
Over 40	34.6	22.9

Evidence of market share dominance, no matter how it is measured, will not be equally meaningful in all product markets. Results from the PIMS study[19] suggest that importance of market share is influenced most strongly by the frequency of purchases.

While the full reasons for this difference in profitability are obscure they probably relate to differences in unit costs and prior buyer experience with the available alternatives which, in turn, determine willingness to reduce risk by buying the market leader and/or paying a premium price. Also, the frequently purchased category is dominated by consumer goods where there is considerable proliferation of brand names through spin offs, flankers, fighting brands, etc. in highly segmented markets. Each of these brands, no matter how small, shares production facilities and will have low production and distribution costs, although they may be treated as separate businesses.[20] It is hardly surprising that the experience curve concept is difficult to apply to consumer goods. Most of the successful applications have been with infre-

quently purchased industrial products relatively undifferentiated, with high value added compared to raw material costs and fairly stable rates of capacity utilization.

A further caveat regarding the experience curve concerns the extent to which costs ultimately can be reduced. The experience curve clearly does not happen according to some immutable law; it requires careful management and some degree of long-run product stability (and ideally, standardization). These conditions cannot be taken for granted and will be threatened directly by the customer demand for product change and competitive efforts to segment the market. In effect, product innovation and cost efficiency are not compatible in the long-run.[21]

A related question concerns the relevance of the experience curve to a new competitor in an established market. It is doubtful that a new entrant with reasonable access to the relevant technology would incur the same level of initial costs as the developers of the market.

What Is the Stage in the Product Life Cycle?   It is not sufficient to simply know the current rate of growth of the product category. The strategic implications of the product life cycle often hinge on forecasting changes in the growth rate and, in particular, on establishing the end of the growth and maturity stages.

The first step in utilizing the life cycle is to ensure that the product class is identified properly. This may require a distinction between a broad product type (cigarettes) and a more specific product form (plain filter cigarettes). Secondly, the graph of product (type or form) sales needs to be adjusted for factors that might obscure the underlying life cycle, i.e., price changes, economic fluctuations and population changes. The third and most difficult step is to forecast when the product will move from one stage to another. The specific problems are beyond the scope of this article. However, the range of possibilities is illustrated by these various leading indicators of the "top-out" point.[22]

- Evidence of saturation; declining proportion of new trier versus replacement sales
- Declining prices and profits
- Increased product life
- Industry over capacity
- Appearance of new replacement product or technology
- Changes in export/import ratio
- Decline in elasticity of advertising and promotion, coupled with increasing price elasticity
- Changes in consumer preferences

These measures generally will indicate only the *timing* of the top-out point, and each is sufficiently imprecise that it is strongly advisable to use as many as possible in combination. Forecasts of the product sales level to be achieved at the top-out point may be obtained by astute incorporation of the leading indicators into: (1) technological forecasts, (2) similar product analysis (where sales patterns of products with analogous characteristics are used to estimate the sales pattern of the new product) or (3) epidemiological models whose parameters include initial sales rates and market saturation levels estimated with marketing research methods.[23]

ANALYZING THE PRODUCT PORTFOLIO

The product life cycle highlights the desirability of a variety of products/services with different present and prospective growth rates. However, this is not a sufficient condition for a well balanced portfolio of products that will ensure profitable long-run growth. Two other factors are market share position and the need to balance cash flows within the corporation.

Some products should *generate* cash (and provide acceptable reported profits) and others should *use* cash to support growth; otherwise, the company will build up unproductive cash reserves or go bankrupt.[24] These issues are clarified by jointly considering share position and market growth rate, as in the matrix of Figure 24-3. The conceptualization used here is largely attributable to the Boston Consulting Group.[25]

It must be stressed that the growth-share matrix discussed here is simply one way of conceptualizing the product portfolio. It has been useful as a device for synthesizing the analyses and judgments of the earlier steps in the planning process, especially in facilitating an approach to strategic decision making that considers the firm to be a whole that is more than the sum of its separate parts. For these purposes, the arbitrary classifications of products in the growth-share matrix are adequate to differentiate the strategy possibilities.[26]

Product Portfolio Strategies

Each of the four basic categories in the growth-share matrix implies a set of strategy alternatives that generally are applicable to the portfolio entries in that category.[27]

Stars   Products that are market leaders, but also growing fast, will have substantial reported profits but need a lot of cash to finance the rate of growth. The appropriate strategies are designed primarily to protect the existing share level by reinvesting earnings in the form of price reductions, product improvement, better market coverage, production efficiency increases, etc. Particular attention must be given to obtaining a large share of the new users or new applications that are the source of growth in the market. Management may elect, instead, to maximize short-run profits and cash flow at the expense

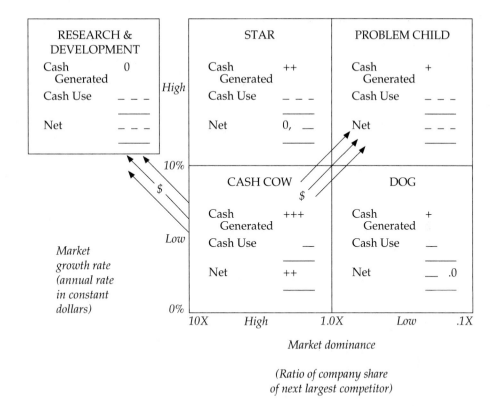

Figure 24-3
Describing the Product Portfolio in the Market Share Growth Matrix
(Arrows indicate principal cash flows.)

of long-run market share. This is highly risky because it usually is predicated on a continuing stream of product innovations and deprives the company of a cash cow which may be needed in the future.

Cash Cows   The combination of a slow market growth and market dominance usually spells substantial net cash flows. The amount of cash generated is far in excess of the amount required to maintain share. All strategies should be directed toward maintaining market dominance—including investments in technological leadership. Pricing decisions should be made cautiously with an

eye to maintaining price leadership. Pressure to overinvest through product proliferation and market expansion should be resisted unless prospects for expanding primary demand are unusually attractive. Instead, excess cash should be used to support research activities and growth areas elsewhere in the company.

Dogs   Since there usually can be only one market leader and because most markets are mature, the greatest number of products fall in this category.[28] Such products are usually at a cost disadvantage and have few opportunities for growth at a reasonable cost. Their markets are not growing, so there is little new business to compete for, and market share gains will be resisted strenuously by the dominant competition.

The product remains in the portfolio because it shows (or promises) a modest book profit. This accounting result is misleading because most of the cash flow must be reinvested to maintain competitive position and finance inflation.[29] Another characteristic of a dog is that individual investment projects (especially those designed to reduce production costs) show a high ROI. However, the competitive situation is such that these returns cannot be realized in surplus cash flow that can be used to fund more promising projects. In addition there are the potential hidden costs of unproductive demands on management time (and consequent missed opportunities) and low personnel morale because of a lack of achievement.

The pejorative label of dog becomes increasingly appropriate the closer the product is to the lower-right corner of the growth/share matrix.[30] The need for positive action becomes correspondingly urgent. The search for action alternatives should begin with attempts to alleviate the problem without divesting. If these possibilities are unproductive, attention then can shift to finding ways of making the product to be divested as attractive as possible; then to liquidation and, finally if need be, to abandonment.

- Corrective action. Naturally, all reasonable cost-cutting possibilities should be examined, but, as noted above, these are not likely to be productive in the long-run. A related alternative is to find a market segment that can be dominated. The attractiveness of this alternative will depend on the extent to which the segment can be protected from competition—perhaps because of technology or distribution requirements.[31] What must be avoided is the natural-tendency of operating managers to

arbitrarily redefine their markets in order to improve their share position and thus change the classification of the product when, in fact, the economics of the business are unchanged. This is highly probable when the product-market boundaries are ambiguous.

- Harvest. This is a conscious cutback of all support costs to the minimum level to maximize the product's profitability over a foreseeable lifetime, which is usually short. This cutback could include reducing advertising and sales effort, increasing delivery time, increasing the acceptable order size and eliminating all staff-support activities such as marketing research.

- Value added. Opportunities may exist for reparceling a product or business that is to be divested. This may involve dividing the assets into smaller units or participating in forming a "kennel of dogs" in which the weak products of several companies are combined into a healthy package. This latter alternative is especially attractive when the market is very fractionated.

- Liquidation. This is the most prevalent solution usually involving a sale as a going concern but, perhaps, including a licensing agreement. If the business/product is to be sold as a unit, the problem is to maximize the selling price—a function of the prospective buyers need for the acquisition (which will depend on search strategy) and their overhead rate. For example, a small company may find a product attractive and be able to make money because of low overhead.

- Abandonment. The possibilities here include giveaways and bankruptcy.

Problem Children   The combination of rapid growth rate and poor profit margins creates an enormous demand for cash. If the cash is not forthcoming, the product will become a dog as growth inevitably slows. The basic strategy options are fairly clearcut; either invest heavily to get a disproportionate share of the new sales or buy existing share by acquiring competitors and thus move the product toward the star category or get out of business using some of the methods just described.

Consideration also should be given to a market segmentation strategy, but only if a defensible niche can be identified and resources are available to gain dominance. This strategy is even more attractive if the segment can provide an entree and experience base from which to push for dominance of the whole market.

Further Strategic Implications

While the product portfolio is helpful in suggesting strategies for specific products, it is equally useful for portraying the overall health of a multiproduct company. The issue is the extent to which the portfolio departs from the balanced display of Figure 24-4, both for the present and in 3 to 5 years.

Among the indicators of overall health are size and vulnerability of the cash cows (and the prospects for the stars, if any) and the number of problem children and dogs. Particular attention must be paid to those products with large cash appetites. Unless the company has abundant cash flow, it cannot afford to sponsor many such products at one time. If resources (including debt capacity) are spread too thin, the company simply will wind up with too many marginal products and suffer a reduced capacity to finance promising new product entries or acquisitions in the future. Some indication of this type of resource misallocation can be obtained from a comparison of the growth rates of the product class and the company's entrant (as illustrated in Figure 24-5). Ideally, nothing should be in

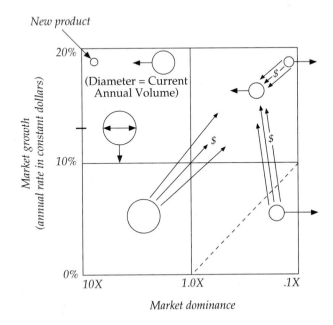

Figure 24-4
A Balanced Product Portfolio

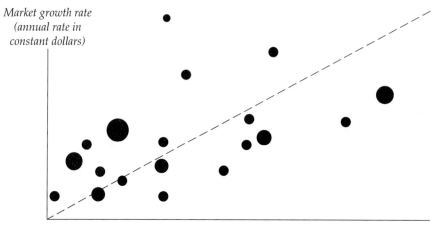

Market growth rate (annual rate in constant dollars)

Company growth rate (annual rate in constant dollars)

Figure 24-5
Market Industry versus Company Growth Rates (Illustrative diversified company—diameters are proportional to current annual sales volume.)

the upper sector where market growth exceeds company growth—unless the product is being harvested.

Competitive Analysis   Product portfolios should be constructed for each of the major competitors. Assuming competitive management follows the logic just described, they eventually will realize that they can't do everything. The key question is which problem children will be supported aggressively and which will be eliminated. The answer obviously will be difficult to obtain, but has an important bearing on the approach the company takes to its own problem children.

Of course, a competitive position analysis has many additional dimensions which must be explored in depth before specific competitive actions and reactions within each product category can be forecast.[32] This analysis, coupled with an understanding of competitive portfolios, becomes the basis for any fundamental strategy employing the military concept of concentration which essen-

tially means to concentrate strength against weakness.[33]

Dangers in the Pursuit of Market Share   Tilles has suggested a number of criteria for evaluating strategy alternatives.[34] The product portfolio is a useful concept for addressing the first three: (1) environmental consistency, (2) internal consistency and (3) adequacy of resources. A fourth criterion considers whether the degree of risk is acceptable, given the overall level of risk in the portfolio.

The experience of a number of companies, such as G.E. and RCA, in the mainframe computer business, points to the particular risks inherent in the pursuit of a market share. An analysis of these "pyrrhic victories"[35] suggests that greatest risks can be avoided if the following questions can be answered affirmatively: (1) Are company financial resources adequate? (2) If the fight is stopped short for some reason, will the corporation's position be competitively viable? and (3) Will government regulations permit the corporation to follow the strategy it has chosen? The last question includes antitrust policies which now virtually preclude acquisitions made by large companies in related fields[36] and regulatory policies designed to proliferate competition, as in the airline industry.

Organizational Implications Although this discussion has focused on the financial and market position aspects of the product portfolio, the implications encompass the deployment of all corporate resources—tangible assets as well as crucial intangibles of management skills and time.

One policy that clearly must be avoided is to apply uniform performance objectives to all products, or SBU's, as is frequently attempted in highly decentralized profit-center management approaches. The use of flexible standards, tailored to the realities of the business, logically should lead to the recognition that different kinds of businesses require very different management styles. For example, stars and problem children demand an entrepreneurial orientation, while cash cows emphasize skills in fine tuning marketing tactics and ensuring effective allocation of resources. The nature of specialist support also will differ; e.g., R and D support being important for growth products and financial personnel becoming increasingly important as growth slows.[37] Finally, since good managers, regardless of their styles are always in short supply, the portfolio notion suggests that they not be expended in potentially futile efforts to turn dogs into profitable performers. Instead they should be deployed into situations where the likelihood of achievement and, hence, of reinforcement, is high.

Other Methods of Portraying the Portfolio The growth-share matrix is far from a complete synthesis of the underlying analyses and judgments as to the position of the firm in each of its product-markets. The main prob-

lem of the matrix concerns the growth rate dimension. While this is an extremely useful measure in that it can have direct implications for cash flows, it is only one of many possible determinants of the attractiveness of the market. A list of other possible factors is summarized in Table 24-1. (Not all these factors will

Table 24-1
Factors Determining Market and Industry Attractiveness

Market	• Size (present and potential) • Growth/stage in life cycle • Diversity of user segments • Foreign opportunities • Cyclicality
Competition	• Concentration ratio • Capacity utilization • Structural changes (e.g., entries and exits) • Position changes • Vertical threats/opportunities • Sensitivity of shares and market size to price, service, etc. • Extent of "captive" business
Profitability	• Level and trend of leaders • Contribution rates • Changes/threats on key leverage factors (e.g., scale economies and pricing) • Barriers to entry
Technology	• Maturity/volatility • Complexity • Patent protection • Product/process opportunities
Other	• Social/environmental • Governmental/political • Unions • Human factors

be relevant to all markets.) The importance of each factor depends on the company's capabilities, but careful considerations will help to identify unusual threats, such as impending government regulations, that might significantly reduce future attractiveness. Similarly, market share may not provide a comprehensive indication of the company's position in each market as in the case of a leader in a market that is rapidly fragmenting.

The qualitative aspects of overall attractiveness and position also can be incorporated into a matrix which portrays the product portfolio (see Figure 24-6). This matrix does not have the immediate cash flow implication of the growth-share matrix, thus, it should be used as a complementary, rather than a replacement approach.

NEW PRODUCT PLANNING

A product portfolio analysis identifies the need for new products or new markets and the probable level of available resources but does not indicate where to look. This presents management with a number of difficult questions:

- What degree of relationship to the present business is necessary and desirable?
- What are the possibilities for internal development versus acquisition?
- When is an innovation preferred to an imitation and vice versa?
- What are the characteristics of desirable new products?

These and innumerable other questions have to be answered before personnel in the product planning, corporate development or other responsible functions can pursue their tasks efficiently. In short, top management must decide how much growth is desired and feasible, the contribution of new versus established products and the broad direction as to how the growth will be achieved.

What is needed is a strategy statement that specifies those areas where development is to proceed and identifies (perhaps by exclusion) those areas that are off-limits. As Crawford notes, "the idea of putting definitive

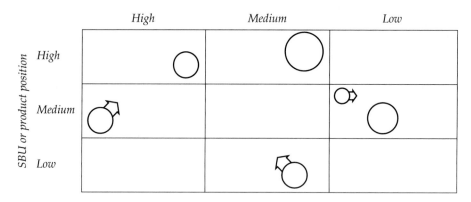

Figure 24-6
Industry or Market Attractiveness (Arrow represents forecast of change in position. Diameter [of circles] is proportional to share of company sales contributed by product.)

restrictions on new product activity is not novel, but use of it, especially sophisticated use, is still not widespread."[38] The major criticisms of a comprehensive statement of new product development strategy are that it will inhibit or restrict creativity and that ideas with great potential will be rejected. Experience suggests that clear guidance improves creativity by focusing energy on those areas where the payoff is likely to be greatest. Also, experience shows that significant breakthroughs outside the bounds of the product development strategy statement can be accommodated readily in an ongoing project evaluation and screening process.

The New Product Development Strategy Statement

The essential elements of this statement are the specification of the product-market scope, the basic strategies to be used for growing within that scope and the characteristics of desirable alternatives. These elements guide the search for new product ideas, acquisitions, licenses, etc., and form the basis for a formal screening procedure.

Product-Market Scope   This is an attempt to answer the basic question, "what business(es) do we want to be in" and is a specific manifestation of the mission of the SBU or company. There is no ready-made formula for developing the definition of the future business. One approach is to learn from definitions that have been useful in guiding successful strategies. For example, the General Electric Housewares SBU defines their present (circa 1973) business as "providing consumers with functional aids to increase the enjoyment or psychic fulfillment of selected lifestyles"—especially those dealing with preparation of food, care of the person, care of personal surroundings and planning assistance. In the future their business will expand to include recreation, en-

hancement of security and convenient care of the home.

This statement of the future business satisfied one important criteria [*sic*]: that it be linked to the present product-market scope by a clearly definable common thread. In the case of G.E. Housewares, the common thread is with generic needs being satisfied (or problems being solved, as the case may be). Ansoff argues that the linkage also can be with product characteristics, distribution capability or underlying technology—as long as the firm has distinctive competency in these areas.[39]

Other criteria for appraising the usefulness of a description of the future business opportunities are: (1) specificity—if the definition of product-market scope is too general, it won't have an impact on the organization (e.g., consider the vagueness of being in the business of supplying products with a plug on the end), (2) flexibility—the definition should be adapted constantly to recognize changing environmental conditions (e.g., Gerber no longer can say that babies are their only business), (3) attainability—can be undertaken within the firm's resources and competencies and (4) competitive advantage—it always is preferable to protect and build on these strengths and competencies that are not possessed as fully by the competition.[40]

Basic Strategies for Growth   At the broad level of a new product development strategy, the basic issues are the *growth* vector, or the direction the firm is moving within the chosen product-market scope, and the emphasis on *innovation* versus *imitation*.

There are almost an infinite number of possibilities for growth vectors. The basic alternatives are summarized in Figure 24-7.[41] There is no intention here to suggest that these strategies are mutually exclusive; indeed, various combinations can be pursued simultaneously in order to close the strategic gaps identified in the overall planning proc-

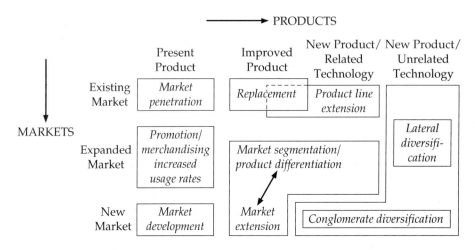

Figure 24-7
Growth Vector Alternatives

ess. Furthermore, most of the strategies can be pursued either by internal development or acquisition and coupled with vertical diversification (either forward toward a business that is a customer or backward toward a business that is a supplier).

The choice of growth vector will be influenced by all the factors discussed earlier as part of the overall corporate planning process. Underlying any choice is, by necessity, an appraisal of the risks compared with the payoffs. The essence of past experience is that growth vectors within the existing market (or, at least, closely related markets) are much more likely to be successful than ventures into new markets.[42] Therefore, diversification is the riskiest vector to follow—especially if it is attempted by means of internal development. The attractiveness of acquisitions for diversification is the chance to reduce the risks of failure by buying a known entity with (reasonably) predictable performance.

An equally crucial basic strategy choice is the degree of emphasis on innovation versus imitation. The risks of being an innovator are well known so few, if any, diversified corporations can afford to be innovators in each product-market. There are compelling advantages to being first in the market if barriers to entry (because of patent protections, capital requirements, control over distributions, etc.) can be erected, the product is difficult to copy or improve on and the introductory period is short. The imitator, by contrast, is always put at a cost disadvantage by a successful innovator and must be prepared to invest heavily to build a strong market position. While profits over the life of the product may be lower for an imitator, the risks are much lower because the innovator has provided a full-scale market test which can be monitored to determine the probable growth in future sales. Also, the innovator may provide significant opportunities by not serving all segments or, more likely, by not implementing the introduction properly.

The conscious decision to lead or follow pervades all aspects of the firm. Some of the important differences that result can be seen from the various strategic orientations to high technology markets discussed by Ansoff and Steward:

- First to market . . . based on strong R and D, technical leadership and risk taking
- Follow the leader . . . based on strong development resources and the ability to act quickly as the market starts its growth phase
- Applications engineering . . . based on product modifications to fit needs of particular customers in mature markets
- Me-too . . . based on superior manufacturing efficiency and cost control.[43]

Characteristics of Desirable Alternatives Three fundamental questions have to be asked of each new product or service being sought or considered: (1) How will a strong competitive advantage be obtained? The possibilities range from superiority in underlying technology or product quality, to patent protection, to marketing requirements. Another dimension of this question is the specification of markets or competitors to be avoided on the grounds that these situations would blunt the pursuit of a competitive advantage. (2) What is the potential for synergy? This asks about joint effects, or "the mutually reinforcing impact a product-market entry has on a firm's efficiency and effectiveness."[44] Synergy can be sought for defensive reasons, in order to supply a competence that the firm lacks or to spread the risks of a highly cyclical industry, as has motivated a number of mergers in the machine tool industry. Alternatively, synergy can utilize an existing competence such as a distribution system (notable examples here are Gillette and Coca Cola), a production capability, promotional skills, etc. In addition, "financial reinforcement may occur either because of the relative pattern of funds generation and demand . . . or because the combination is more attractive to the financial community than the pieces would be separately."[45] (3) What specific operating results are required? The possibilities here usually are expressed in terms of threshold or minimum desirable levels:

- Rate of market growth
- Payback period (despite its deficiencies it is a reflection of the risk level)
- Minimum sales level. (This is a function of fixed costs and scale of operations: the danger is that a product with good long-run potential will be rejected because of modest short-run sales possibilities.)
- Profit levels, cash flow and return on assets. (Each of these financial requirements must be developed in light of the firm's product portfolio.)

SUMMARY

Too often product planning is conducted as though each established product or service, and new product opportunity being sought or evaluated were independent of the other products of the firm. The implication is that corporate performance is the sum of the contributions of individual profit centers or product strategies.[46]

This article emphasizes the need to consider the interdependencies of products as parts of a portfolio described by market share dominance and market growth rate before overall corporate performance can be optimized. Only then can decisions as to resource allocation, growth and financial objectives and specific strategies be developed for established products and the need for new products identified.

There is little doubt that the future will see increasing acceptance of a broad systems approach to overall corporate strategy, in general, and to product planning, in particular. There are already a number of successful practitioners to emulate (who have gained a competitive edge that cannot be ignored).[47] More importantly, as the business environment becomes increasingly resource-constrained there may be no other choice for most firms.

NOTES

1. "The Squeeze on Product Mix," *Business Week* (5 January 1974), pp. 50–55; "Toward Higher Margins and Less Variety," *Business Week* (14 September 1974), pp. 98–99; E. B. Weiss, "We'll See Fewer New Products in 1975—Culprit Is Shortage of Capital, Resources," *Advertising Age* (2 December 1974); "Corrective Surgery," *Newsweek* (27 January 1975), p. 50; and Jack Springer, "1975: Bad Year for New Products; Good Year for Segmentation," *Advertising Age* (10 February 1975), pp. 30–39.

2. Barry R. Linsky, "Which Way to Move with New Products," *Advertising Age* (22 July 1974), pp. 45–56.

3. George A. Steiner, *Top Management Planning* (London: Macmillan, 1969); H. Igor Ansoff, *Corporate Strategy* (New York: McGraw-Hill, 1965).

4. David T. Kollat, Roger D. Blackwell and James F. Robeson, *Strategic Marketing* (New York: Holt, Rinehart and Winston, 1972), p. 12.

5. This description of the planning process has been adapted from Kollat, et al., *Strategic Marketing;* Louis V. Gerstner, "The Practice of Business: Can Strategic Planning Pay Off?" *Business Horizons* (December 1972): Herschner Cross, "New Directions in Corporate Planning," An address to Operations Research Society of America (Milwaukee, Wisconsin: 10 May 1973).

6. The identification of "strategic business units" is a critical first step in any analysis of corporate strategy. Various definitions have been used. Their flavor is captured by the following guidelines for defining a business: (1) no more than 60 percent of the expenses should represent arbitrary allocations of joint costs, (2) no more than 60 percent of the sales should be made to a vertically integrated (downstream) subsidiary and (3) the served market should be homogeneous; i.e., segments are treated as distinct if they represent markedly different shares, competitors and growth rates.

7. E. Eugene Carter and Kalman J. Cohen, "Portfolio Aspects of Strategic Planning," *Journal of Business Policy,* 2(1972), pp. 8–30.

8. C. H. Springer, "Strategic Management in General Electric," *Operations Research* (November–December 1973), pp. 1177–1182.

9. Bernard Catry and Michel Chevalier, "Market Share Strategy and the Product Life Cycle," *Journal of Marketing,* 38 (October 1974), pp. 29–34.

10. Peter F. Drucker, *Management: Tasks, Responsibilities, Practices* (New York: Harper and Row, 1973), p. 106.

11. Sidney Schoeffler, Robert D. Buzzell and Donald F. Heany, "Impact of Strategic Planning on Profit Performance," *Harvard Business Review* (March–April 1974), pp. 137–145.

12. Robert D. Buzzell, Bradley T. Gale and Ralph G. M. Sultan, "Market Share, Profitability and Business Strategy," unpublished working paper (Marketing Science Institute, August 1974).

13. For more extended treatments and a variety of examples, see Patrick Conley, "Experience Curves as a Planning Tool," *IEEE Transactions* (June 1970); *Perspectives on Experience* (Boston: Boston Consulting Group, 1970); and "Selling Business a Theory of Economics," *Business Week* (8 September 1974).

14. "An example of this situation was DuPont's production of cyclohexane. DuPont was the first producer of the product but the manufacture of cyclohexane is so integrated with the operations of an oil refinery that oil refiners have an inherent cost advantage over companies, such as DuPont, without an oil refinery." Robert B. Stobaugh and Philip L. Townsend, "Price Forecasting and Strategic Planning: The Case of Petrochemicals," *Journal of Marketing Research,* 12 (February 1975), pp. 24–29.

15. Theodore Levitt, "Exploit the Product Life Cycle," *Harvard Business Review* (November–December 1965), pp. 81–94.

16. Harry W, McMahan, "Like Sinatra, Old Products Can, Too, Get a New Lease on Life," *Advertising Age* (25 November 1974), p. 32.

17. Harry T. Moran, "Why New Products Fail," *Journal of Advertising Research* (April 1973).

18. See Douglas Needham, Economic Analysis and Industrial Structure (New York: Holt, Rinehart and Winston); Sanford Rose, "Bigness Is a Numbers Game," *Fortune* (November 1969).

19. Buzzell, Gale and Sultan, "Market Share, Profitability."
20. An extreme example is Unilever in the UK with 20 detergent brands all sharing joint costs to some degree.
21. William J. Abernathy and Kenneth Wayne, "Limit of the Learning Curve," *Harvard Business Review*, 52 (September–October 1974), pp. 109–119.
22. Aubrey Wilson, "Industrial Marketing Research in Britain," *Journal of Marketing Research*, 6 (February 1969), pp. 15–28.
23. John C. Chambers, Satinder K. Mullick and Donald D. Smith, *An Executives' Guide to Forecasting* (New York: John Wiley and Sons, 1974): Frank M. Bass, "A New Product Growth Model for Consumer Durables," *Management Science*, 15 (January 1969), pp. 215–227.
24. Of course the cash flow pattern also may be altered by changing debt and/or dividend policies. (For most companies, the likelihood of new equity funding is limited.) Limits on growth are imposed when the additional business ventures to be supported have too high a business risk for the potential reward and/or the increase in debt has too high a (financial) risk for the potential rewards.
25. Among the publications of the Boston Consulting Group that describe the portfolio are: Perspectives on Experience (1970) and the following pamphlets authored by Bruce D. Henderson in the general perspectives series; "The Product Portfolio" (1970); "The Experience Curve Reviewed: The Growth Share Matrix or the Product Portfolio" (1973); and "Cash Traps" (1972).
26. A similar matrix reportedly is used by the Mead Corporation; see John Thackray, "The Mod Matrix of Mead," *Management Today* (January 1972), pp. 50–53, 112. This application has been criticized on the grounds of oversimplification, narrow applicability and the unwarranted emphasis on investment versus new investment. Indeed the growth-share matrix is regarded by Thackray as primarily a device for achieving social control.
27. William E. Cox, Jr., "Product Portfolio Strategy: An Analysis of the Boston Consulting Group Approach to Marketing Strategies," *Proceedings of the American Marketing Association, 1974.*
28. It is also typical that the weighted ratio of average market share versus the largest competitor is greater than 1.0. This reflects the contribution of the cash cows to both sales and profits. It also accounts for the familiar pattern whereby 20 percent of the products account for 80 percent of the dollar margin (a phenomena generally described as Pareto's Law).
29. The Boston Consulting Group defines such products as cash traps when the required reinvestment, including increased working capital, exceeds reported profit plus increase in permanent debt capacity: Bruce D. Henderson, "Cash Traps," *Perspectives*, Number 102 (Boston Consulting Group, 1972).
30. The label may be meaningless if the product is part of a product line, an integral component of a system or where most of the sales are internal.
31. It should be noted that full line/full service competitors may be vulnerable to this strategy if there are customer segments which do not need all the services, etc. Thus, Digital Equipment Corp. has prospered in competition with IBM by simply selling basic hardware and depending on others to do the applications programming. By contrast, IBM provides, for a price, a great deal of service backup and software for customers who are not self-sufficient. "A Minicomputer Tempest," *Business Week* (27 January 1975), pp. 79–80.
32. Dimensions such as product and pricing policy, geographic and distributor strength, delivery patterns, penetration by account size and probable reaction to our company initiatives need to be considered. See C. Davis Fogg, "Planning Gains in Market Share," *Journal of Marketing*, 38 (July 1974), pp. 30–38.
33. This concept is developed by Harper Boyd, "Strategy Concepts" unpublished manuscript, 1974, and is based on B. H. Liddel Hart, *Strategy: the Indirect Approach* (London: Faber and Faber, 1951).
34. Seymour Tilles, "How to Evaluate Corporate Strategy," *Harvard Business Review*, 41 (July–August 1963).

35. William E. Fruhan, "Pyrrhic Victories in Fights for Market Share," *Harvard Business Review*, 50 (September–October 1972).

36. "Is John Sherman's Antitrust Obsolete?" *Business Week* (23 March 1974).

37. Stephen Dietz, "Get More Out of Your Brand Management," *Harvard Business Review*, (July–August 1973).

38. C. Merle Crawford, "Strategies for New Product Development: Guidelines for a Critical Company Problem," *Business Horizons* (December 1972), pp. 49–58.

39. H. Igor Ansoff, *Corporate Strategy*.

40. Kenneth Simmonds, "Removing the Chains from Product Policy," *Journal of Management Studies* (February 1968).

41. This strategy matrix was influenced strongly by the work of David T. Kollat, Roger D. Blackwell and James F. Robeson, *Strategic Marketing* (New York: Holt, Rinehart and Winston, 1972), pp. 21–23 which, in turn, was adapted from Samuel C. Johnson and Conrad Jones, "How to Organize for New Products," *Harvard Business Review*, 35 (May–June 1957), pp. 49–62.

42. According to the experience of A. T. Kearney, Inc., the chances of success are a direct function of how far from home the new venture is aimed. Specifically, the likelihood of success for an improved product into the present market is assessed as 0.75, declines to 0.50 for a new product with unrelated technology into the present market and to 0.25 for an existing product into a new market. The odds of success for external diversification are as low as 0.05. These numbers are mainly provocative because of the difficulties of defining what constitutes a failure (is it a product that failed in test or after national introduction, for example). See "Analyzing New Product Risk," *Marketing for Sales Executives* (The Research Institute of America, January 1974).

43. H. Igor Ansoff and John Steward, "Strategies for a Technology-Based Business," *Harvard Business Review*, 45 (November–December 1907), pp. 71–83.

44. Kollat, Blackwell and Robeson, *Strategic Marketing*, p. 24.

45. Seymour Tilles, "Making Strategy Explicit," in H. Igor Ansoff (ed.), *Business Strategy* (London: Penguin Books, 1969), p. 203.

46. Bruce D. Henderson, "Intuitive Strategy," *Perspectives*, No. 96 (The Boston Consulting Group, 1972).

47. See "Selling Business a Theory of Economics," *Business Week* (8 September 1973); "G.E.'s New Strategy for Faster Growth," *Business Week* (8 July 1972); "First Quarter And Stockholders Meeting Report" (Texas Instruments, Inc., 8 April 1973); "The Winning Strategy at Sperry Rand," *Business Week* (24 February 1973), "How American Standard Cured Its Conglomeritis," *Business Week* (28 September 1974): "G.E. Revamps Strategy: Growth through Efficiency," *Advertising Age* (3 June 1974).

◆

Evolution of Global Marketing Strategy: Scale, Scope and Synergy

Susan P. Douglas and C. Samuel Craig

In recent years, issues relating to international marketing strategy have stirred increasing interest. To date, however, much of the discussion has focused on specific decisions rather than broader strategic issues. The inherent complexity and dynamic aspects of strategy formulation in international markets have frequently been ignored. Yet, a firm's strategic thrust and key decisions will change as it expands its operations overseas. The process of internationalization thus involves a firm moving through successive phases, each characterized by new strategic challenges and decision priorities.

Previous discussion of international marketing strategy has, however, tended to focus on the initial stage of entry into international markets. Often the perspective of a novice in international markets is adopted. Consequently, attention has centered on decisions such as the choice of countries to enter, the mode of operation to adopt, or the extent to which products or positioning can be standardized or must be adapted for different country markets (Cavusgil and Nevin 1981; Keegan 1969; Still 1984). This latter issue in particular has attracted considerable attention and has been the source of much controversy in recent years (Levitt 1983; Douglas and Craig 1986; Douglas and Wind 1987; Walters 1986).

Emphasis on initial international market entry and issues of standardization were appropriate in the 1960s and early 1970s, when many companies, whether of US or other national origin, had only limited experience in international markets. Today, however, many companies already have operations in a number of countries. Consequently, the issues they face are infinitely more complex than those faced by companies contemplating initial foreign market entry. In determining the direction for future growth, the costs of expansion into new countries have to be weighed with those of expansion within the existing matrix of country operations. The extent to which operations are coordinated and integrated across countries and

Reprinted from *Columbia Journal of World Business*, Vol. 24 (Fall '89), pp. 47–59. Copyright 1989, *Columbia Journal of World Business*. Reprinted with permission.

product divisions must also be determined in order to optimize the transfer of knowledge and experience, and take advantage of potential synergies arising from the multinational character of operations.

The key issues and strategic imperatives facing the firm will vary depending on the degree of experience and the nature of operations in international markets. In the initial phase of entry into international markets, a key objective is the geographic expansion of operations to identify markets overseas for existing products and services and to leverage potential economies of scale in production and marketing. Once an initial beachhead has been established, emphasis shifts to developing local markets and exploiting potential economies of scope, building upon the existing geographic base. In the third phase, attention shifts to consolidation and integration of operations to take advantage of potential synergies in multinational operations.

The purpose of this article is to examine each of these phases, together with their underlying dynamics, and the forces which trigger movement from one phase to another. The key issues and levers which characterize each phase are highlighted, and the implications for the formulation of global marketing strategy are discussed.

STRATEGY FORMULATION IN INTERNATIONAL MARKETS

An evolutionary perspective of internationalization of the firm has been adopted by a number of authors in the areas of international economics and international management. The theory of the international product life-cycle, propounded by Vernon and others (Vernon 1966; Wells 1972), identifies a number of phases in the internationalization process based on the location of production. In the initial phase, a firm exports to overseas markets from a domestic production base. As

market potential builds up, overseas production facilities are established. Low cost local competition then enters the market, and ultimately exports to the home market of the initial entrant, thus challenging its international market position.

A number of empirical studies examining this theory have been conducted (Davidson 1983; Hirsh 1967). These suggest that the theory provides an adequate explanation of U.S. foreign direct investment in the 1960s and 1970s. More recent developments such as the emergence of global competition and integration of markets suggest, however, a considerably more complex pattern of internationalization.

In-depth studies of the internationalization process of several firms have also been conducted, focusing on their acquisition and use of knowledge about foreign markets and the growth of involvement overseas (Johanson and Vahlue 1977; Johanson and Wiedershein-Paul 1975; Wiedershein-Paul, Olson and Welch 1978; Cavusgil 1980). These studies suggest that the internationalization process is gradual, involving incremental commitments to overseas markets rather than major foreign production investments at a single point in time. These studies tend, however, to focus on the early stages of internationalization, and on the relation between information acquisition and market commitment, rather than issues related to strategy formulation.

The EPRG framework developed by Perlmutter (Perlmutter 1969) also identifies four stages in the evolution of the multinational corporation, each characterized by different management attitudes and orientations. In the first stage, ethnocentrism, overseas operations are viewed as subordinate to domestic operations, and domestic performance standards are applied to overseas subsidiaries. The polycentric or host country orientation emphasizes local cultural differences, and evaluation and control procedures are established locally, with little communication between headquarters and subsidiaries. A regiocentric orientation focuses on regional organization of authority and communication flows, while a geocentric or global orientation aims for collaboration between headquarters and subsidiaries to identify standards and procedures which meet both worldwide and local goals and objectives. While this approach has been linked to different organizational structures and policies, it provides few explicit guidelines for strategy formulation and implementation.

Formulating strategy explicitly with regard to international markets is crucial for a number of reasons. Initial forays into international markets are often unsystematic and somewhat haphazard, resulting from an unsolicited export order from a foreign buyer, an order from a domestic customer for his overseas operations, or interest expressed by an importer or potential business partner in a foreign market. Consequently, it is important

to establish objectives with regard to international market operations, especially in terms of the level of involvement and degree of risk as part of a systematic evaluation of opportunities worldwide. Otherwise, international activities will lack direction, resulting from creeping commitment and sporadic efforts, and will not necessarily be targeted to the most attractive opportunities for the firm in world markets.

Strategy formulation in international markets involves a number of key parameters whose nature and impact will depend on the phase in the internationalization process. These are shown diagramatically in Figure 25-1. At each phase a number of triggers will prompt movement into a new phase stimulating generation of a new strategic thrust. The direction of this is channeled by the key international levers associated with each phase. Together these will define investment and resource allocation priorities, thus establishing the key strategic decisions and expected outcomes.

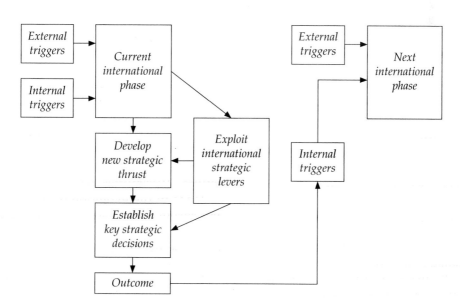

Figure 25-1
The Dynamics of Global Strategy Development

The Triggers

The triggers which prompt a firm to move from one phase to the next are both external and internal. External triggers, such as environmental factors, or industry trends, or competitive pressures, cause the firm to reassess its current strategy. Internal triggers, on the other hand, are caused by factors such as internal sales and profits or management initiatives. Certain internal triggers, for example, declining sales volume, may be the result of external factors, such as increased competition from foreign firms. Also, firms may respond differently to the same set of external factors. Internal and external triggers may thus combine to generate the development of a new strategic thrust.

The Strategic Thrust

The strategic thrust determines the direction the firm will pursue and defines the arena in which the firm will compete, as well as its strategic priorities.

In international markets, defining the geographic extent of operations and direction for expansion is of critical importance. As noted above, this varies with the phase of internationalization. In the initial phase, emphasis is placed on geographic expansion, and hence the specific countries to be targeted must be determined. The subsequent phase is one of geographic consolidation, and hence growth within each country centers around expansion of product lines. This leads to rationalization of product lines across country boundaries, and the transfer of product ideas and lines, so that the concept of a domestic market disappears, and planning is formulated on a global basis.

Key International Levers

The key strategic levers aid in further redefining the direction of the firm's efforts and determining the decision and investment priorities at each successive stage of internationalization. In the initial phase, lacking experience or familiarity with overseas markets, a firm will seek to leverage its domestic position internationally thus achieving economies of scale. This might, for example, be grounded in superior product quality or technological expertise, cost efficiency, mass-merchandising expertise, or a strong corporate or brand image. As familiarity with the local market environment increases, and a marketing and distribution infrastructure and contacts with local distributors and other organizations are developed, a firm will seek to leverage these across a broader range of products and services in order to achieve economies of scope. In the final phase, a firm will try to leverage both internal skills and environment-related experience, transferring learning across national boundaries, so as to take maximum advantage from potential synergies in multinational operations.

Strategic Decisions

The firm's strategic thrust and the levers to internationalization together determine key strategic decisions at each phase of internationalization. In the initial phase, the key decisions center on the choice of countries to enter, the mode of operation and the timing and sequencing of entry. Once initial entry has been successfully achieved, decisions at the next phase center around the development of local market potential through product modification, product line extension, and development of new products tailored to specific local market needs. This typically results in the creation of a patchwork of local operations, and hence leads to the need to improve efficiency, and to establish mechanisms to coordinate and integrate strategy across national markets, allowing for the transfer and exchange of learning and experience, and leading eventually to the establishment of strategy relative to regional and global rather than multi-domestic markets.

Thus, in international markets, the strategic thrust, the key decisions and levers evolve with the degree of experience and stage of involvement in overseas operations. This is analogous to the product life-cycle concept (Day 1981), where the key strategic imperatives vary with the stage of its evolution. While in practice this evolution is a continuous process, for the purposes of analytical simplicity, three phases may be identified, in addition to a preliminary phase of pre-internationalization: 1) initial foreign market entry; 2) local or national market expansion; and 3) globalization. (See Figure 25-2 which depicts the relation between the different stages.)

PHASES OF INTERNATIONAL MARKET DEVELOPMENT

Pre-Internationalization

Prior to entry into international markets, the domestic market is the focal point of strategy development and defines the boundaries of operations. Strategy is designed and developed based on information relating to customer needs and interests, industry trends, and economic, sociocultural and technological trends likely to influence demand for the firm's products and services in the domestic market. Similarly, attention is centered on the strategies of domestic competitors viewed as major threats to the firm.

Although in some cases a firm may deliberately decide *not* to enter international markets, and concentrate instead on serving its domestic market, a domestically-oriented firm is likely to be inwardly focused with limited interest or concern for events outside its immediate sphere of operation. Often such a firm will be characterized by a certain lethargy and lack of dynamism, content to supply its traditional customer base with existing technology through established marketing channels. Such an attitude may well be tinged with a certain complacency, satisfaction with

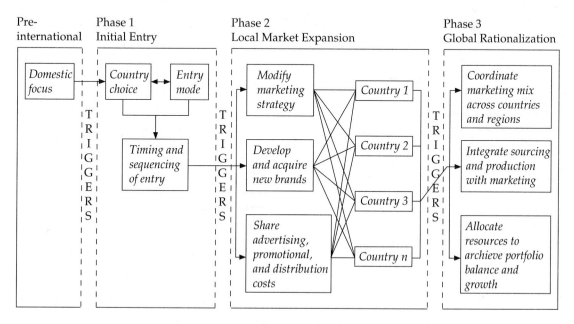

Figure 25-2
Marketing Evolution

present performance and few ambitions to tackle new frontiers.

A domestic orientation may lead to lack of attention to changes taking place in the global marketplace such as new life-styles or target segments, new customer needs, growth of new competition, and the restructuring of market forces worldwide. A firm may thus be vulnerable to the emergence of new technology or the advent of foreign competition armed with a superior product or an aggressive marketing strategy. Such competitors may be quicker to respond to new challenges and opportunities in the marketplace. The failure of the US TV manufacturers to monitor developments in the Japanese TV market in the 1960s and 1970s, and to respond to the entry of low-cost Japanese TV sets into the US market by moving to low-cost off-shore production locations led to their ultimate demise (Rapp 1973). As a result, Zenith is the sole US manufacturer with a significant share (12% of the US market) in the industry (*Business Week* May 15, 1989).

Triggers to Internationalization

A variety of factors may prompt the domestically-oriented firm to reexamine its position. (See Table 25-1 for a summary of typical events.) Trends within the industry or product market, in terms of demand and supply conditions, competitive developments or other discrete events may all open up new opportunities in markets abroad. Each of these factors, alone or in concert, may provide impetus for the firm to venture into overseas markets.

These include:

- *Saturation of the domestic market* resulting from slackening rates of growth or limited potential for expansion.
- *Movement of customers overseas,* stimulating interest in following suit in order to retain the account and supply customers more cost effectively.

- Desire to *diversify risk* across a range of countries and product markets.
- Identification of *advantageous sourcing opportunities,* i.e., lower labor or production costs in other countries.
- Retaliation to the *entry of foreign competition* into the firm's domestic market.
- Concern over keeping abreast of *technological change* in world markets.
- *Government incentives* such as information, credit insurance, tax exemptions.
- *Advances in transportation and communications technology,* such as the growth of international telephone linkages, fax systems, satellite networks, containerization, etc.

Any one or a combination of these factors may stimulate investigation of developments in markets overseas, and of opportunities for sourcing and/or marketing products and services in other countries and trigger initial entry into international markets.

Phase 1. Initial International Market Entry

The decision to move into international markets constitutes a bold step forward. It opens up new opportunities in a multitude of countries throughout the world and new horizons for expansion and growth. At the same time, lack of experience in and of familiarity with conditions in overseas markets creates a considerable strain on management to acquire the knowledge and skills necessary to operate effectively in these markets. Information relating to differences in environmental conditions, market demand and the degree of competition will therefore be needed in order to select the most attractive country markets, and to develop a strategy to guide the firm's thrust into international markets.

This step is especially crucial, since a false move at this stage may result in withdrawal or retreat from international markets. Mistakes made in initial entry can damage a

Table 25-1

Triggers to Each Stage of Internalization

Initial Market Entry	Local Market	Globalization
1. Saturation of domestic market duplication of efforts	1. Local market growth	1. Cost inefficiencies and duplication of efforts between countries
2. Movement overseas of domestic customers	2. Meeting local competition	2. Learning via transfer of ideas and experience
3. Diversification of risk	3. Local management initiative and motivation	3. Emergence of global customers
4. Sourcing opportunities in overseas markets	4. Desire to utilize local assets more effectively	4. Emergence of global competition
5. Entry of foreign competition in home market	5. Natural market boundaries	5. Development of global marketing infrastructure
6. Desire to keep abreast of technological changes		
7. Government incentives to export		
8. Advances in communications technology and marketing infrastructure		

firm's reputation, and be difficult to surmount. Renault's efforts to penetrate the US compact car market have, for example, been haunted by its early mistakes with the Renault Dauphine. Careful formulation of initial entry strategy is thus crucial in shaping the pattern of international market evolution.

Key Strategic Thrust

The firm's efforts are therefore directed toward identifying the most attractive market opportunities overseas for its existing (i.e., domestic) products and services. Attention is centered on pinpointing the closest match between the firm's current offerings and market conditions overseas so that the minimal adaptation of products or marketing strategies is required. The guiding principle is to extend

the geographic base of operations without incurring major incremental marketing or production costs, other than those required to obtain distribution.

International Levers

The firm therefore seeks to leverage its domestic competitive position and core competency internationally so as to extend economies of scale by establishing a presence in multiple markets (see Figure 25-3, a). Given the firm's lack of experience and knowledge in overseas markets, it will focus on product or skill-related assets which can be leveraged internationally. These might include innovative or high-quality products, a patented process, a brand name, or other proprietary assets (Caves 1982). In industries such as comput-

a. Scale Economies

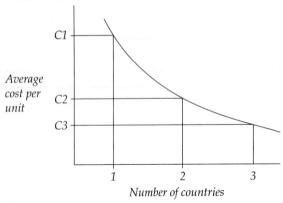

b. Scope Economies

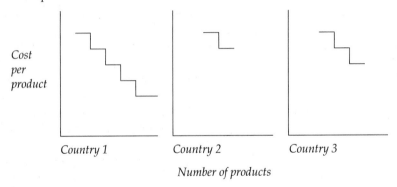

c. Synergies

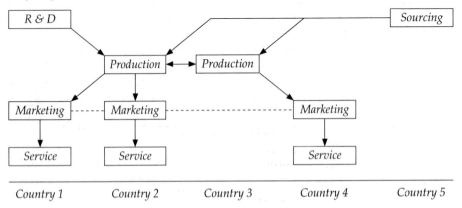

Figure 25-3
Levers Underlying Global Marketing Development

ers and medical equipment, the success of many firms has been contingent on the introduction of products new to these markets. High quality price ratios, the outgrowth of superior production skills, have also been a key element in the penetration of world markets for consumer electronics and compact cars by Japanese companies. Patented processes may also be leveraged internationally as in the expansion of Xerox and Polaroid into world markets in the 1960s. In consumer markets, well-known brand names, such as Coca-Cola, Levis or Kelloggs, are often an important proprietary asset which can be exploited in overseas markets. Process skills such as mastery of mass-merchandising techniques and expertise in managing distribution channels may also be exploited in foreign markets. Such skills have enabled companies such as P&G and Colgate to outpace competitors in markets throughout the world, but are typically more difficult to leverage directly, especially in the initial stages of entry. Furthermore, they may require some degree of adaptation to local market conditions, and hence are less likely to be susceptible to scale economies.

Benetton, the Italian manufacturer of casual clothing, has been highly successful in leveraging its brand image worldwide. In 1978, the company realized $78 million in sales, 98% in Italy. By 1987, the company grossed $830 million with profits of $86.9 million throughout its worldwide network of over 4,000 independently owned retail outlets, in sixty countries, of which 1,500 are in Italy, and 600 in the US. Not only is the Benetton image projected worldwide through the uniform design format of their clear open-shelved stores, and the use of the bright green Benetton logo, but also through uniform advertising campaigns such as the award-winning "United Colors of Benetton" campaign.

Key Decisions In the phase of initial entry, the key decisions relate to:

1. the choice of countries to enter,
2. the timing of entry, and
3. how operations are to be conducted in these countries.

While each of these decisions is discussed separately here, they are, nonetheless, highly interrelated. The mode of operation or entry, as well as the timing of entry will depend on perceived opportunities and risks in a given country. Similarly, the timing of entry may affect the choice of mode of entry.

Choice of Countries In choosing which countries to enter, risk and opportunities need to be evaluated relative to both the general business climate of a country and the specific product or service. The stability and rate of economic growth of a country have to be examined as well as the political, financial and legal risks of entry. Similarly, the size and growth of market potential have to be considered relative to the level of competition and costs of market entry. Often a trade-off has to be made between risk and return. Countries with high growth potential frequently also entail high competitive or country risks or entry costs.

For the novice in international markets, the degree of familiarity or knowledge about a foreign market and its perceived similarity are often key factors in influencing choice. Countries which are perceived as similar in terms of language, culture, education, business practices, or industrial development are viewed as lower in risk and likely to offer a more favorable climate for entry than those where the psychic distance is large (Davidson 1980). In examining foreign investment patterns of US firms, one study found that close to two-thirds chose to enter Canada first and then the UK, though such choices were clearly not warranted by country size and growth potential relative to other countries such as West Germany or France. Similarly, Australia ranked considerably higher in investment priorities than its size would suggest.

Knowledge and familiarity with a country is often an important factor influencing perceived risk and uncertainty of market entry. Both objective information and experiential knowledge affect this uncertainty. Thus, proximity and prior contact or experience in a country will influence market choice. Swedish companies have, for example, been found to enter neighboring countries such as Denmark, Norway and Finland first, and more distant countries such as Brazil, Argentina and Australia last (Johanson and Wiedershein-Paul 1975).

Timing of Entry   An important issue is whether to enter a number of country markets simultaneously, or alternatively, enter one country first, and then building on this experience, enter other country markets sequentially (Doyle and Gidengil 1976; Davidson 1980, 1982). A major consideration in this decision is the level of resource commitment required to enter a given market overseas. Given the lack of familiarity and experience in operating in overseas market environments, financial, managerial and other resource requirements may be significant, especially where an overseas sales organization and/or production facilities are to be established. On the other hand, simultaneous entry will enable the firm to preempt competition by establishing a beachhead in all potential markets, limiting opportunities for imitation. Potential scale economies arising from multiple market entry and interdependence of country markets may also be realized (Ayal and Zif 1979).

Mode of Entry   The decision concerning how to operate in a foreign market is closely interrelated with the evaluation of market potential and country risk (Goodnow and Hanz 1972). A wide variety of modes of operating in foreign markets may be adopted ranging from exporting, licensing and contract manufacturing, to joint ventures and wholly-owned subsidiaries (Root 1982). These vary in terms of the level of resource or equity commitment to overseas markets. Companies can thus limit their equity exposure by adopting low-commitment modes such as licensing, contract manufacturing or minority joint ventures in high-risk countries or those which are perceived as socio-culturally different, and, hence, unfamiliar operating environments (Anderson and Gatignon 1986; Gatignon and Anderson 1987; Root 1982).

In the latter case, a company may prefer to enter a country in a joint venture with a local partner, who can provide knowledge and contacts with the local market. This strategy has often been adopted by foreign companies entering the Japanese market. For example, Wella, the German manufacturer of hair care products, initially entered the Japanese market in a joint venture with a manufacturer of beauty salon chairs. Subsequently, as it acquired greater familiarity and understanding of the market, Wella bought out the Japanese company.

Another important element in the choice of modes of operation is the desired degree of control and perceived significance of international operations (Anderson and Gatignon 1986). Non-equity modes such as licensing or contract manufacturing entail minimal risk and commitment, but at the same time afford little control and limited returns (Contractor 1985). Joint ventures and wholly-owned subsidiaries provide greater control and potential returns. Thus, companies which desired to retain a high degree of control over operations in entering the Japanese markets, for example, P&G, Scott, Bristol-Meyers and Ore-Ida, have typically done so through establishing wholly-owned subsidiaries rather than joint ventures. Companies with limited experience and expectations with regard to overseas markets may also prefer low commitment modes (Bilkey 1978).

The decision of how to enter a foreign market will also depend on the size of the market and its growth potential, as well as the existence of potential economies of scale and other cost-related factors such as local production costs, shipping costs, and tariff and other barriers. Markets of limited size surrounded by tariff barriers may be supplied most cost effectively via licensing or contract manufacturing. Where there are potential economies of scale, exporting may, however, be preferred. Then, as local market potential builds up and the minimum economic size is reached, a local production and marketing subsidiary may be established.

A firm may also benefit from certain scale economies and other advantages by internalizing or controlling overseas operations rather than contracting them out. These may occur not only in centralization of production, but also in sourcing, R&D, finance and capital asset management, etc. A firm with operations in two or more countries may, for example, be better able to establish large-scale distribution networks and achieve economies in transportation as well as in balancing production scheduling thus diversifying risk (Aliber 1970).

The decision with regard to the mode of operation is thus often a key factor in determining the rate of international growth. It not only determines the commitment of resources and hence risk exposure in different countries and markets, but also the degree of control exercised over operations and strategy in overseas markets, the flexibility to adjust to changes in market conditions, and the evolution of operations in these markets.

Triggers to Overseas Market Expansion

Once the firm has investigated opportunities overseas and started to establish operations in a number of markets, various factors will trigger a shift in emphasis toward the development of local market potential. The need to develop effective strategies to combat competition in these markets will result in reliance on local market know-how and expertise in local market conditions. The focus thus

swings away from foreign opportunity assessment to local market development.

Some of the factors which may underlie this shift are:

- *Concern with increasing market penetration* and hence adapting or developing new products for the local market;
- *Need to meet local competition,* and to respond to local competitive initiatives in pricing and promotion;
- *Desire to foster local management initiative and motivation;*
- *Concern for more effective utilization of local assets,* i.e., the sales organization and distribution infrastructure, or contacts with local organizations;
- *Constraints imposed by natural market boundaries and barriers* such as transportation systems, media networks, distribution systems, and financial and other institutions.

Such pressures lead to adoption of a nationally-oriented focus in strategy development. Planning again becomes organized on a domestic or national market basis, though this time in the form of a series of multi-domestic markets of businesses.

Phase 2. Local Market Expansion

Once the firm has firmly established a beachhead in a number of foreign markets, it will begin to seek new directions for growth and expansion, thus moving into the second phase of internationalization. Here, attention is centered on fueling growth in each overseas market and identifying new opportunities within countries where a base of operations has already been established. The expansion effort is, therefore, often directed by local management overseas in each country rather than from corporate headquarters.

The focus shifts toward penetrating local markets more fully, and building on knowledge, experience and contacts established in the initial phase of entry into overseas markets. Often local management is recruited, and responsibility for strategy development as well as day-to-day operations is shifted to the local subsidiaries, on the grounds that local managers are best qualified to understand the local market environment and to run country operations (Perlmutter 1969).

Key Strategic Thrust

The driving force underlying this phase is thus market expansion within countries entered in the initial phase, rather than entering additional markets. Attention is directed to making product and strategy modifications in each country which will broaden the local market base and tap new segments. Product line extensions and new product variants may be considered as well as development of new products and services geared to specific local preferences. The emphasis shifts from "export" of strategy and its direction from the domestic market base, to development of strategy on a country-by-country basis.

Internationalization Lever

The major lever for effective expansion in this phase is to build strategy based on the organizational structure established in each country, in order to achieve economies of scope and to leverage assets and core competencies so as to foster local market growth. Attention centers on identifying opportunities for shared marketing expenditures, joint utilization of production and distribution facilities across product lines and product businesses (Teece 1980, 1983). Administrative overheads may thus be spread across a higher sales volume, reducing unit operating costs. (See Figure 25-3, b.) These may include not only sharing of physical assets such as production facilities, or a distribution network, but also intangible assets such as R&D knowledge or

market familiarity (Wind and Douglas 1981). The latter may be a particularly critical factor in this phase of operations. Often, the costs associated with initial entry into a country may be substantial, as, for example, in developing familiarity with market conditions and competition, and establishing relations with distributors, agents or regulatory bodies and officials. Consequently, it may be advantageous to amortize such costs across a broad range of products.

In addition to leveraging the organizational structure in each country, proprietary assets such as brand names, and specific skills such as technological expertise, may also be leveraged to expand the product line. The benefits accruing from a well-known brand name or company image may, for example, be further exploited by marketing new products or product variants under the same brand or company names. Swatch, the Swiss fashion watch manufacturer, has leveraged its "chic" image in marketing a range of other products such as sunglasses, casual sweaters and clothing under the Swatch name. Similarly, a well-known company name and its reputation for product quality, reliability and service, may be leveraged in the promotion of new products and product lines, either to end customers or to distributors.

Technological expertise and R&D skills may be applied to the development of new products geared to specific local market needs. P&G has leveraged its expertise in surfactant technology to develop liquid heavy-duty detergents such as Vizir and liquid Ariel adapted to hard-water conditions in Europe. Similarly, marketing and mass-merchandising skills may be spread over a broader range of product or product lines, or applied to the development of new product businesses. In some cases, brands or product businesses may be acquired from local companies. Thus, the firm may be able to capitalize on the "goodwill" or customer franchise associated with an established local brand or local company, while at the same time applying its management expertise and marketing skills to operations management.

Key Decisions

Concern with local market growth implies that the key decisions center around the development of products, product lines and product businesses which offer promise of market growth in each country, as well as strategies to market them effectively in each context. This will, therefore, include not only adaptation and modification of products, but also the development and acquisition of new products and brands. Following the strategic thrust and growth levers, the key criteria in making these decisions are the potential for local market development and the realization of economies of scope.

Product modification and adaptation in order to expand the potential market base, for example, may be examined. In developing countries, machine tool manufacturers may consider streamlining and simplifying their products as well as rendering their use and maintenance easier so as to tap less-sophisticated customer segments. Nabisco reduced the salt content of its snack products and increased the sugar content of its cookies to meet local tastes in Japan. Similarly, Kentucky Fried Chicken reduced the amount of sugar content in its coleslaw, and added fish to its menu in Japan.

Opportunities for developing product variants, extending the product line or developing new products specifically adapted to local market preferences may also be considered. Canada Dry has added a range of different flavors such as melon in the Far East, orange, pineapple and bitter orange in the UK, and strong ginger in Japan. Heinz developed a special line of rice-based baby foods for the Chinese market, and a fruit-based drink for children called Frutsi for Mexico, which was subsequently rolled out in a number of other Latin American markets. Coca-

Cola has also developed a number of products specifically for the Japanese market, including "Georgia," a highly successful canned cold coffee drink, and Real Gold, an isotonic drink. Nabisco has developed "Parfait," thumb-sized chocolate cupcakes for the Japanese markets, as well as Chipstar, a Pringles-type potato chip packaged in a tall can in two flavors, natural and seaweed.

Based on the economies of scope criterion, additions of new products or product variants within a country are especially attractive if they enable more effective utilization of the existing operational structure as, for example, administrative capabilities, the distribution network or the salesforce, or if they capitalize on experience acquired in operating in a specific market environment, or contacts and relations established with distributors, advertising agencies and other external organizations. As noted previously, such economies are likely to be particularly marked where there are substantial initial investment or set-up costs in establishing contact with distributors, or developing good-will among the trade in entering a country. In line with the strategic thrust, marketing strategies, including advertising, sales promotion to trade and end users, pricing and distribution channels are geared to local market development. Adaptation of advertising copy and development of new themes should thus be undertaken whenever the costs are outweighed by the potential increase in sales. Similarly, pricing decisions should be designed to stimulate local market penetration. This may, therefore, imply greater attention to pricing based on evaluation of price elasticities in local markets and prices of competing and substitute products rather than on a cost plus basis.

Triggers to Global Rationalization

The country-by-country orientation associated with this phase, while enabling the consolidation of operations within countries will, however, tend to result in market fragmentation worldwide. Overseas operations functioning as independent profit centers evolve into a patchwork of diverse national businesses. Each national business markets a range of different products and services targeted to different customer segments, utilizing different marketing strategies with little or no coordination of operations between countries. The inefficiencies generated by this system, as well as the external forces integrating markets worldwide, will thus create pressures toward improved coordination across countries.

Some of the factors which may trigger this trend include:

- *Cost inefficiencies and duplication of effort* between country organizations;
- *Opportunities for the transfer of products, brands and other ideas* and of learning from experience in one country to other countries;
- *Emergence of global customers* in both consumer and industrial markets;
- *Emergence of competition* on a global scale;
- *Improved linkages* between national marketing infrastructures leading to the development of a global marketing infrastructure.

Thus, once again both internal factors and changes in the external environment will trigger a shift in orientation and create pressures toward global nationalization. Attention will thus center on the elimination of inefficiencies generated by a multiplicity of domestic businesses, and improved coordination and integration of strategy across national boundaries, moving toward the development of strategy on a global rather than a country-by-country basis. (It should, however, be noted that this does not necessarily imply standardization of products, promotion, etc., worldwide, but rather adoption of a global rather than a multi-domestic perspective in designing strategy.)

Phase 3. Global Rationalization

In the final phase of internationalization, the firm moves toward the adoption of a global orientation in strategy development and implementation. Attention focuses on improving the efficiency of operations worldwide and developing mechanisms for improved transnational coordination of operations and for integrating strategy across countries. Direction shifts toward development of strategy and resource allocation on a global basis. The national orientation thus disappears, and markets are viewed as a set of interrelated, interdependent entities which are becoming increasingly integrated and interlinked worldwide.

Key Strategic Thrust

In this phase, the firm seeks to capitalize on potential synergies arising from operating on a global scale, and seeks to take maximum advantage of the multinational character of its operations. Attention, therefore, centers on optimal allocation of resources across countries, product markets, target segments and marketing strategies so as to maximize profits on a global basis rather than on a country-by-country basis.[24]

A dual thrust is thus adopted, combining a drive to improve the efficiency of operations worldwide with a search for opportunities for global expansion and growth. Greater efficiency may be sought through improved coordination and integration of operations across countries. This includes not only marketing activities such as product development, advertising, distribution and pricing, but also production, sourcing and management. Standardization of product lines across countries, for example, may facilitate improved coordination of production, global sourcing, and the establishment of a global production and logistical system, thus resulting in greater cost efficiencies.

At the same time, development on a global scale becomes a key principle guiding strategy formulation. Opportunities for transferring products, brand names, successful marketing ideas or specific skills and expertise acquired or developed in one country to operations in other countries are explored. Global and regional market segments or target customers are also identified, and products and services developed and marketed on a worldwide basis.

Internationalization Levers

In this phase, the key levers lie in exploitation of potential synergies arising from operating on a global scale. Skills or assets which are transferable across national boundaries such as production technology, management expertise, and brand or company image, for example, may be leveraged globally. (See Figure 25-3, c.) While a similar type of leverage occurs in the initial phase from the domestic market to an overseas market, leverage across multiple markets has a synergistic effect.

Improved coordination and integration of marketing strategy across countries may also facilitate realization of potential economies of scale in production and logistics as well as the employment of skills and expertise which would not otherwise be feasible. Leverage may also be achieved through the transfer of experiences, skills and resources from one country or product business to another. Products or promotional campaigns successful in one country may, for example, be transferred to another, just as cash or profits from one business or country may be used to grow a business or compete aggressively in another country (Hamel and Prahalad 1985).

Key Decisions

Following the dual strategic thrust, key decisions focus on a) improving the efficiency of operations worldwide and b) developing a global strategy.

Improving Efficiency   Efficiency may be increased by improved coordination and rationalization of operations across countries and between different functional areas. This may result in consolidation or centralization of R&D, production, sourcing, or other activities, thus eliminating duplication of effort as well as allowing for realization of potential economies of scale.

For example, in 1982 Black and Decker operated 25 plants in 13 countries on six continents. Overseas operations were organized into three operating groups, below which were individual companies which operated autonomously in more than 50 countries with little or no communication between them (Saporito 1984). This led to considerable duplication of effort. For example, its eight design centers produced 260 different motor sizes. A global restructuring of operations reduced this number to ten.

Similarly, in preparation for 1992, Suchard, the Swiss packaged goods manufacturer, is rationalizing production operations on a European-wide scale. Production of individual brands is being consolidated in specific factories to gain manufacturing economies of scale. A plant outside Stuttgart and one in Paris were recently closed, and production transferred to plants outside Basel and Strasbourg. Other factories have been modernized and equipped with state-of-the-art automation and flexible manufacturing systems to drive costs down further (Friberg 1989). Similarly, Electrolux has either closed or focused every factory it has acquired over the past ten years. It now manufactures all front-loading washing machines in Pordenone, Italy, all top-loaders in Revin, France, and all microwave ovens in Luton, England.

Scott Paper has also developed a pan-European approach for 1992, which encompasses not only production and logistics, but also marketing and financial operations. Plants in the UK, France, Spain, Italy and Belgium still supply predominantly local markets, since tissue and paper-towels are high volume/low price items where transportation costs outweigh gains from a high degree of production centralization. Brand names such as Scottex are, however, used throughout Europe (with the exception of the UK) and experience in product launches, brand positioning and advertising in one market are applied in others. Three new plants are being constructed in France, Italy and Spain, and will all use the same technology, thus allowing for the sharing and transfer of experience in plant management. Capital is now being borrowed globally, rather than being raised locally on a country-by-country basis.

In fact, opportunities for rationalization of production, sourcing and logistical systems are enhanced by product standardization across countries. Moves toward greater product standardization thus open up possibilities for increased rationalization upstream (Takeuchi and Porter 1986). The Stanley Works, for example, decided to effect a compromise between French preferences for handsaws with plastic handles and "soft" teeth with British preferences for handsaws with wooden handles and "hard" teeth, by producing a plastic-handled saw with "hard" teeth. The objective was thus to consolidate production for the two markets and realize substantial economies of scale.

Improved coordination of marketing strategies, such as brand names, advertising themes across countries and standardization of products and product lines, can be facilitated by the establishment of coordinating mechanisms between country management groups. These may take the form of coordinating committees which facilitate transfer of information and ideas across groups and are responsible for coordinating and integrating their activities, or the widely publicized Eurobrand teams developed by P&G, or regional marketing or sales organizations such as that established by Ford of Europe to direct activities within the region.

Global Strategy Development   In addition to improving the efficiency of existing operations, a global strategy should be established to guide the direction of the firm's efforts, and the allocation of resources across countries, product businesses, target segments and modes of operation worldwide. This should combine global vision and the integration of activities across national boundaries with responsiveness to local market conditions and demand.

A global strategy should determine the customers and segments to be targeted, as well as their specific needs and interest, and the geographic configuration of segments and their needs. As markets for both industrial and consumer products become increasingly international, opportunities for identifying segments which are regional or global rather than national in scope are on the increase. Thus, for example, Bodyshop targets its shampoos and body oils to those concerned with ecology and animal rights, desiring natural-based products not tested on animals, as is generally the case. In the advertising industry, Saatchi and Saatchi targets corporations with multinational operations, supplying services and meeting their needs worldwide.

Marketing programs to meet the specified need of these regional and global target segments also must be established. This will require putting into place the organization to implement the program. In some instances, this requires establishing an organizational infrastructure which matches that of potential customers. Companies servicing the needs of multinational corporations may establish a system of account executives, with an executive specifically responsible for ensuring that the needs of a given client are satisfied worldwide.

Citibank, for example, instituted a Global Account Management System to coordinate world relations with large multinational corporations and develop its international business. Prior to this reorganization, clients were serviced on a geographic basis, i.e., by the country office in which they were located. Each country branch had responsibility for operations within its area, including both local companies and subsidiaries of multinational corporations, and acted as a local profit center. This led to a number of problems, as local country management often preferred to lend to a local borrower rather than the subsidiary of a multinational corporation, as "spreads," and hence profitability, were perceived to be higher and more likely to generate additional business. In addition, internal communications were fraught with difficulties, as client account managers in the US were not in contact or often even aware of their counterparts handling the client's subsidiaries in a foreign country.

Another decision is the appropriate mix of product businesses worldwide. Here, their complementarity in meeting production, resource or cash-flow requirements on an international basis needs to be considered. Thus, for example, Thomson has retained a semi-conductor business in France in order to supply its consumer electronics businesses worldwide. Similarly, BiTicino uses profits from its protected domestic light switch business to finance R&D for the development of its global fiber-optics business.

Effective implementation of a global rationalization strategy thus necessitates establishment of mechanisms to coordinate and control activities and flows of information and resources, both across national boundaries and product businesses (Ghoshal 1987; Bartlett and Ghoshal 1986). In addition, coordination with other functional areas such as production, logistics, and finance, will need to be achieved. Thus, in some cases, a radical restructuring and management system, including lines of responsibility and communication, may be required to achieve globalization.

CONCLUSIONS

Strategy formulation in international markets is thus an evolutionary process, in which the dominant strategic thrust, the international levers and consequently, the key decisions vary at each successive phase of involvement in international operations. The major strategic challenges facing the firm: how to transfer strategies and skills developed in response to local market conditions to markets overseas; how to acquire and build on local market knowledge and experience; and how to take advantage of potential synergies of multinational operations, will thus differ in each phase.

The dynamic character of international operations thus implies that strategic priorities should be tailored to the stage of evolution in international markets. Thus, rather than assuming, as is commonly the case, that the basic parameters underlying strategy formulation and specifically the key decisions will be the same for all firms, recognition that these will depend on the nature and evolution of international operations is imperative. Strategy should thus be formulated in the light of the firm's current position overseas, and geared to its vision of growth and future position in markets worldwide. The pattern of strategy evolution in international markets suggests a number of prescriptions for the successful formulation of global strategy.

In the first place, strategy should be tailored to the degree of experience in overseas markets. Thus, in the initial phase of international market entry, the firm's key strength is likely to lie in its existing (domestic) product line and attention should be focused on acquiring experience in marketing that line overseas. As this experience builds up, emphasis should shift to new product development geared to overseas market needs. Only in the final stages, once experience in both marketing and new product development for international markets has been acquired, should the more complex issue of strategy integration and coordination across country markets be addressed.

Secondly, potential economies of scale and scope should be maximized. Economies of scale may be realized through attention to opportunities for marketing existing product lines on a broader geographic scale, while centralizing production and sourcing operations, and extending management and logistical systems. Economies of scope, on the other hand, will be achieved through identification of opportunities for shared production, marketing and distribution facilities, and utilization of the same management and logistical systems by different product lines or product businesses.

Thirdly, marketing strategy, especially relating to product line decisions and product standardization should be closely coordinated with production and sourcing operations. This establishes guidelines for the design of management, information and logistical systems to direct these operations. Effective coordination of key strategy components becomes especially crucial as the scope and complexity of international operations expand and improved global rationalization of strategy is achieved.

Finally, the ultimate goal of global strategy should be to achieve optimal integration and rationalization of operations and decision systems on a global scale. Potential synergies arising from coordination and integration of strategy and of decision systems across country and product markets will thus be captured, and maximal efficiency in the allocation of resources worldwide achieved. Focus on the unique advantages provided by the multinational character of operations is thus the key to the formulation of a successful strategy in a global marketplace.

REFERENCES

Abegglen, James G. and George Stalk, Jr., "The Japanese Corporation as Competition," *California Management Review,* 28, Spring, pp. 9–27, 1986.

"Alain Gomez, France's High Tech Warrior," *Business Week,* May 15, 1989, pp. 100–106.

Aliber, Robert Z., "A Theory of Direct Foreign Investment," in Charles P. Kindleberger (ed.), *The International Corporation: A Symposium,* Cambridge, Mass., 1970, pp. 17–34.

Anderson, Erin and Hubert Gatignon, "Modes of Foreign Entry: Transaction Cost Analysis and Propositions," *Journal of International Business Studies,* 11, Fall, 1986, pp. 1–26.

Ayal, Igal and Jehiel Zif, "Market Expansion Strategies in Multinational Marketing," *Journal of Marketing,* 43, Spring, 1979, pp. 84–94.

Bartlett, Christopher A. and Sumantra Ghoshal, "Tap Your Subsidiaries for Global Reach," *Harvard Business Review,* November–December, 1986, pp. 87–94.

Bilkey, Warren J., "An Attempted Integration of the Literature on the Export Behavior of Firms," *Journal of International Business Studies,* 9, Spring–Summer, 1978, pp. 33–46.

Caves, Richard E., *Multinational Enterprise and Economic Analysis,* Cambridge: Cambridge University Press, 1982.

Cavusgil, S. Tamer, "On the Internationalization Process of Firms," *European Research,* 8, November, 1980, pp. 273–281.

Cavusgil, S. Tamer and John R. Nevin, "State-of-the-Art in International Marketing: An Assessment," *Review of Marketing 1981,* Ben M. Enis and Kenneth J. Roering (eds.), Chicago: American Marketing Association, 1981, pp. 195–216.

Contractor, Farok, *Licensing in International Strategy: A Guide for Planning and Negotiation,* Quorum Books Greenwood Press, 1985.

Davidson, William H., "Marketing Similarity and Market Selection: Implications for International Market Strategy," *Journal of Business Research,* 11, December, 1983, pp. 439–456.

Davidson, William H., *Global Strategic Management,* New York: John Wiley and Sons, 1982.

Davidson, William H., "The Location of Foreign Direct Investment Activity: Country Characteristics and Experience Effects," *Journal of International Business Studies,* 3, Spring, 1980, pp. 33–50.

Day, George, "The Product Life Cycle: Analysis and Application Issues," *Journal of Marketing,* 45, Fall, 1981, pp. 60–67.

Douglas, Susan P. and C. Samuel Craig, "Global Marketing Myopia," *Journal of Marketing Management*, 2, Winter, 1986, pp. 155–169.

Douglas, Susan P. and Yoram Wind, "The Myth of Globalization," *Columbia Journal of World Business*, Winter, 1987, pp. 19–29.

Doyle, Peter and Zeki Gidengil, "A Strategic Approach for International Market Selection," *Proceedings European Academy for Advanced Research in Marketing*, Copenhagen, Denmark, 1976.

Friberg, Eric "1992: Moves Europeans Are Making," *Harvard Business Review*, May–June, 1989, pp. 85–89.

Gatignon, Hubert and Erin Anderson, "The Multinational Corporation's Degree of Control over Foreign Subsidiaries: An Empirical Test of a Transaction Cost Explanation," MSI Report No. 87–103, October, 1987, pp. 1–41.

Ghoshal, Sumantra, "Global Strategy: An Organizing Framework," *Strategic Management Journal*, 8, 1987, pp. 425–440.

Goodnow, James D. and James E. Hanz, "Environmental Determinants of Overseas Market Entry Strategies," *Journal of International Business Studies*, 3, Spring, 1972, pp. 33–50.

Hamel, Gary and C. K. Prahalad, "Do You Really Have a Global Strategy?" *Harvard Business Review*, July/August, 1985, pp. 139–144.

Hill, J. S. and R. R. Still, "Adapting Products to LDC Tastes," *Harvard Business Review*, 62, March/April, 1984, pp. 92–101.

Hirsh, Sev, *Location of Industry and International Competitiveness*, Oxford: Clarendon Press, 1967.

Johanson, Jan and Finn Wiedershein-Paul, "The Internationalization of the Firm—Four Swedish Cases," *Journal of Management Studies*, October, 1975, pp. 305–322.

Johanson, Jan and Jan-Erik Vahlue, "The Internationalization Process of the Firm—A Model of Knowledge Development and Increasing Foreign Market Commitments," *Journal of International Business Studies*, Spring/Summer, 1977, pp. 47–58.

Keegan, Warren J., "Multinational Product Planning: Strategic Alternatives," *Journal of Marketing*, January, 1969, pp. 58–62.

Levitt, T. "The Globalization of Markets," *Harvard Business Review*, May–June, 1983, pp. 92–102.

Perlmutter, Howard, "The Torturous Evolution of the Multinational Corporation," *Columbia Journal of World Business*, January–February, 1969.

Prahalad, C. K. and Yves Doz, *The Multinational Mission*, New York: The Free Press, 1987.

Rapp, W. V. "Strategy Formulation and International Competition," *Columbia Journal of World Business*, Summer, 1973, pp. 98–112.

Root, Franklin J., *Foreign Market Entry Strategies*, New York: AMACON, 1982.

Saporito, Bill, "Black and Decker's Gamble on Globalization," *Fortune*, May 14, 1984.

Takeuchi, H. and M. E. Porter, "The Strategic Role of International Marketing: Managing the Nature and Extent of Worldwide Coordination," in Michael E. Porter (ed.), *Competition in Global Industries*, Cambridge, Mass: Harvard Graduate School of Business Administration, 1986.

Teece, David J., "Economies of Scope and the Scope of the Enterprise," *Journal of Economic Behavior and Organization*, 1, 1980, pp. 233–247.

Teece, David J., "Technological and Organizational Factors in the Theory of the Multinational Enterprise," in Mark Casson, (ed.), *The Growth of International Business*, New York: George Allen and Irwin, 1983 pp. 51–62.

Vernon, Raymond, "International Investment and International Trade in the Product Cycle." *Quarterly Journal of Economics*, May, 1966, pp. 190–207.

Walters, Peter G. P., "International Marketing Policy: A Discussion of the Standardization Construct and Its Relevance for Corporate Policy," *Journal of International Business Studies*, Summer, 1986, pp. 55–69.

Wells, Louis T., *The Product Life-Cycle and International Trade*, Boston: Division of Research, Graduate School of Business Administration, Harvard University, 1972.

Wiedershein-Paul, Finn, Haus G. Olson and Lawrence S. Welch, "Pre-Export Activity: the First in Internationalization," *Journal of International Business Studies*, Spring/Summer, 1978, pp. 47–58.

Wind, Y. and S. Douglas, "International Portfolio Analysis and Strategy: The Challenge of the 1980s," *Journal of International Business Studies*, Special Issue, Fall, 1981.

◆

A Model of Strategy Mix Choice for Planned Social Change

Jagdish N. Sheth and Gary L. Frazier

PLANNED SOCIAL CHANGE

A significant hallmark of mid-century America is the greatly accelerated growth of institutions that choose to—or are mandated to—bring about what they define as "socially desirable attitudes and behaviors" (Andreasen 1981, p. 1). These social marketers include such organizations and/or groups as health maintenance organizations, Alcoholics Anonymous, the Office of Cancer Communications, and the United Way. Public sector agencies are often concerned with creating significant changes in consumption behavior and patterns in the marketplace (e.g., decrease alcohol and cigarette purchases, decrease food consumption among overweight people, increase the use of contraceptives). Fox and Kotler (1980) indicate that many of these organizations have recently discovered marketing as a potentially useful tool to help them achieve their objectives, which often deal with planned social change.

Zaltman (1974) defines social change as an alteration in the structure and functioning of a social unit or social system. Therefore, planned social change refers to active intervention by change agents (e.g., officials in public agencies) with a conscious policy objective to bring about a change in magnitude and/or direction of a particular social or consumption behavior by means of one or more strategies of change (Hornstein et al. 1971, Jones 1969, Lippitt, Watson, and Westley 1968, Niehoff 1966, Zaltman and Duncan 1977).[1] Planned social change consists of the following characteristics:

- The social behavior to be changed must be identified and well-defined.
- There should be a policy objective with respect to the magnitude and/or direction of social change.
- Some entity should be earmarked as the change agent and supplied with appropriate resources or powers.
- One or more strategies of change should be utilized.

"A Model of Strategy Mix Choice for Planned Social Change," Sheth, Jagdish N. and Gary L. Frazier, Vol. 46 (Winter '82), pp. 15–26. Reprinted from the *Journal of Marketing,* published by the American Marketing Association.

This definition of planned social change, therefore, excludes the following types of social changes:

- Changes that are evolutionary, accidental, or random phenomena (Arensberg and Niehoff 1971, Bennis 1966, Lippitt, Watson, and Westley 1968).
- Changes that arise by the process of contagion as is so typical in the diffusion of innovations (Rogers and Shoemaker 1971, Zaltman 1974, Zaltman and Stiff 1973). The contagion process is merely a behavioral phenomenon (Bass 1969, Mansfield 1961). Of course it can be harnessed and utilized as a strategy by a change agent to achieve a policy objective in a given social change arena, but by itself it does not constitute planned social change as often implied in the diffusion of innovation literature.

Planned social change is, therefore, a *managerial rather than a behavioral task* that requires making decisions as to which strategies to use, in what combination, and for which target groups in order to achieve policy objectives related to bringing about a prespecified magnitude and/or direction of change in a given social or consumption behavior (Chin and Benne 1969, Zaltman 1974). As such, it must possess elements of strategic planning and decision making. Only after these decisions are made does planned social change become an implementation task for managers. If the managerial task stage is skipped or performed poorly, the chances of widespread social change in the direction desired by the change agent will be relatively low.

PROBLEMS IN THE PRESENT SOCIAL CHANGE APPROACH

Two major problems now exist in the way change agents attempt to motivate planned

social change. First, very often only a single strategy is utilized in an attempt to bring about a planned social change at a given point in time and sometimes over a period of time. Different appeals for different population segments are typically not designed under this single strategy approach (Zaltman and Duncan 1977). In other words, change agents have practiced a universal approach as opposed to a segmentation approach toward planned social change.

Secondly, change agents have been primarily concerned with implementing specific strategies for specific programs. Little attention has been paid to developing a more global picture to predict when and where certain strategies may be relatively appropriate. At present, there is no theory of strategy mix but only an acknowledgement that efficient selection and application of varying strategies is highly complex. Zaltman (1974, p. 92) states, "Many factors affect the success of a particular strategy; not uncommonly factors favoring different strategies are simultaneously present and factors which contraindicate a particular strategy coexist with factors favoring its use." It seems that change agents believe in a particular strategy based on some ideological value system and utilize it universally without regard to allocating resources in an optimal manner among a mixture of strategies.

PURPOSES OF THIS STUDY

This study presents a model of strategy mix choice for planned social change that will provide the change agent with a more global picture of the planned social change process. Based on the concept of attitude-behavior consistency/discrepancy, a model is proposed that provides insights to the change agent about different processes and objectives of planned social change. Later, (1) influence strategies that can be utilized by a change agent in facilitating a given process and attaining a given objective are identified, and (2) a consumer based methodology (based on the use of discriminant analysis) to help change agents decide which of the behavior-attitude processes they must facilitate in given social change situations is explained. The basic value of this method is to provide change agents with a starting point in strategy negotiations and selections within their organizations. While additional trade-off factors such as money, personal agendas, agency politics, other stakeholder attitudes, and time constraints must be considered and incorporated in the final choice of a specific mix of strategies, they are treated as ceteris paribus in our model.

This paper also highlights the importance of a consumer orientation (especially in regard to varying population segments with different needs, wants, attitudes, and behavior) within public agencies. A consumer orientation is often missing in public sector decision making and programs designed to change consumption patterns in the marketplace (Deshpande and Krishnan 1981, Fox and Kotler 1980).

A MODEL OF STRATEGY MIX CHOICE

Attitudes and Behavior

A significant body of literature on the attitude-behavior relationship supports the general assumption that attitudes and behavior are, on the whole, positively related (cf Engel, Warshaw, and Kinnear 1979, McGuire 1978). People often manifest behaviors towards which they have positive attitudes (contributions to charity) and avoid those behaviors towards which they have negative attitudes (deviant behavior). As such, attitude-behavior consistency generally holds in an aggregate analysis.

However, in a case by case analysis, attitude-behavior discrepancy also certainly exists (Belk 1981, Sheth and Horowitz 1977, Sheth and Newman 1981, Sheth and Wong 1981). This construct implies that there are situations in which peoples' attitudes and behavior are at odds with each other. For example, many people possess positive attitudes toward wearing seat belts but they don't use them; conversely, some people may have negative attitudes toward going to church but still attend.[2]

Except in a very homogeneous society, it is not likely that everyone will manifest the same degree or direction of attitude-behavior consistency/discrepancy, especially toward socially relevant behaviors. For example, some couples practice birth control and have a positive attitude toward birth control (segment one), others avoid it because they have negative attitudes (segment two), still others practice birth control but more out of necessity (segment three), and finally some believe in birth control but do not practice it (segment four).[3]

Processes of Planned Social Change

The conceptual framework suggests that there are four major processes of planned social change, each one most appropriate for each of four combinations of attitude-behavior consistency/discrepancy, as summarized in Table 26-1. When attitudes and behavior are consistent as well as in the positive direction toward the relevant social behavior (cell one in Table 26-1), a *reinforcement process* seems most appropriate for sustaining the planned social change. It refers to rewarding people for engaging in a behavior they enjoy (like) and which the change agent wants to continue and sustain.

The general objective of the reinforcement process is to keep people in the positive attitude, engaged behavior cell. This can be

Table 26-1
A Typology of Strategy Mix for Planned Social Change

	Attitude	
	Positive	*Negative*
Engaged **Relevant Behavior** *Non-engaged*	Cell 1 Reinforcement Process 1. Behavioral Reinforcement 2. Psychological Reinforcement	Cell 2 Rationalization Process Attitude Change
	Cell 4 Inducement Process Behavioral Change	Cell 3 Confrontation Process 1. Behavioral Confrontation 2. Psychological Confrontation

accomplished through (1) reinforcing the behavior, (2) reinforcing the attitude, and/or (3) reinforcing both. Behavioral reinforcement involves providing economic rewards to the individual so as to strengthen the probability of future compliant behavior as suggested by operant conditioning (Nord and Peter 1980, Skinner 1953). On the other hand, psychological reinforcement centers on the attitude towards the behavior and is based on intrinsic rewards (e.g., encouragement, compliments) and logic (e.g., the "whys" behind the behavior) rather than on economic rewards. A carrot (rather than a stick) approach should be the basis for the reinforcement process for this segment, since people here are already performing the desired behavior and have a positive attitude toward it.

When people possess a positive attitude toward a desirable social behavior but do not or cannot presently engage in the concomitant behavior (cell four), an *inducement process* needs to be facilitated. It refers to minimizing or removing organizational, socioeconomic, time, and place constraints that intervene between the positive attitude and the consequent behavior (Howard and Sheth 1969, Sheth 1974). Behavioral change is the primary objective, given that a positive attitude already exists in this segment and, as such, movement of people from cell four to cell one (Table 26-1) is desired.

The *rationalization process* is most appropriate when people are currently engaged in a desirable social behavior but have a negative attitude toward it (cell two). Often, this may be due to lack of choice or due to a temporary situation. In each case, the behavior may only be temporary and may not lead to subsequent attitude change. Thus the primary objective of this process is to generate attitude change that will be consistent with the behavior and, therefore, may be more difficult to alter when the temporary situation is removed. Movement of people to cell one by the process of attitude change is desirable.

Finally, when both attitude and behavior are consistent but in the negative direction toward a desirable social behavior (cell three), a *confrontation process* may be necessary (Bennis et al. 1976). This is the most painful and difficult process of planned social change. The change agent must, therefore, decide whether it is worth the effort to change the social behavior in light of negative public opinion as well as the apparent high costs associated with this strategy.

Behavioral confrontation requires the change agent to utilize his/her power base to create blockades toward the existing, undesirable behavior and alter peoples' motivations toward performing the desirable social behavior. Psychological confrontation involves a direct attack on the existing attitudes that individuals have toward the planned social change. In each case, a stick approach appears to be necessary. Movement of people directly to cell one may be too radical a change in some situations. If so, the change agent can utilize a two-stage process in which he/she first moves people from cell three to either cell two or four and then eventually to cell one in Table 26-1.

STRATEGIES OF PLANNED SOCIAL CHANGE

Thus far only the processes of planned social change and their basic objectives have been discussed. To implement these processes and attain their objectives, influence or communication strategies must be selected and utilized by the change agent. The most basic implication of the model is that the change agent must use different types of influence strategies and/or change the orientation (tactics) of specific strategies across the different attitude-behavior consistency/discrepancy groups. While a particular strategy and tactic may be effective in facilitating one process or objective, it may not work well in facilitating each process or objective.

Given this viewpoint, it is vital that available influence strategies are linked to the processes of planned social change to aid the change agent in their implementation (cf Zaltman 1974). Table 26-2 briefly describes eight categories of influence strategies available for use by change agents. An attempt to link these strategies and the processes of planned social change is exhibited in Table 26-3. Here, an evaluation of each strategy is presented in terms of its apparent appropriateness in facilitating each social change process. Where a reasonably high level of confidence does not exist concerning whether a given strategy is appropriate or inappropriate in facilitating a

given process, a "maybe" prediction is included in the table.

The predictions within Table 26-3 are based on the character of each strategy, the nature of each process, and the logic that either attitude change, behavior change, or both must be attained within a given process. For example, to promote psychological reinforcement, the informing and educating strategy appears most effective (cf Zaltman and Duncan 1977). Objective information on the situation and the value and benefits of the relevant social behavior will tend to be processed (not selectively screened) by consumers in this group and serve to remind them, in a nonpressurized way, why their current attitudes and behavior are justified (Engel, Warshaw, and Kinnear 1979). A detailed description of the logic behind each of the predictions in Table 26-3 is beyond the scope of this paper. However, three additional points must be stressed at this time:

- Several strategies appear to be appropriate in more than one cell. However, the specific character and orientation of a strategy may change across conditions. For example, use of persuasion and propaganda in the rationalization process might include information packaged in a biased way in favor of the desired behavior. Often this entails partial disclosure of facts, exaggeration of positive aspects in the given social behavior, and minimization of negative consequences. On the other hand, use of this strategy in the confrontation process appears to require a more direct, pressurized approach centering on fear appeals. Similar examples can be made for variations in social controls and mandatory rules across the processes.
- The stick approach recommended in the confrontation process is very risky. When people have negative attitudes and are not performing the behavior, pressurized mea-

Table 26-2
Strategies of Planned Social Change

1. *Informing and Educating* (Chin and Benne 1969, Zaltman, Kotler, and Kaufman 1972). Objective information is disseminated to the population with no conclusions drawn within the communication; left to the recipient to process the objective information and make conclusions on his/her own.

2. *Persuasion and Propaganda* (Boyk 1973, Lee 1975, Rogers 1972). Conclusion drawing and dramatic statements of benefits or ill effects of performing or avoiding a certain behavior are stressed; may involve a biased presentation of facts and figures in an aggressive manner to impact and change attitude.

3. *Social Controls* (Hornstein et al. 1971, Smith 1973). Refer to group identification and norms, values, and pressures that peer groups bring to bear for both ensuring and sustaining social change; involve subtle or direct pressure and even implied punishments for nonconformity.

4. *Delivery Systems* (Spreke 1971, Zaltman 1974). The emphasis is to minimize the accessibility problems associated with the usage of many public services. This entails offering flexible time schedules, more delivery contact points, and, in general, making the public feel welcomed in making use of the public services associated with a specific planned social change.

5. *Economic Incentives* (Pohlman 1971, Rogers 1972, Zaltman 1974). Include not only cost reduction tactics (e.g., tax credits for home insulation) but also cash or other tangible incentives (e.g., cash payments for a vasectomy).

6. *Economic Disincentives* (Rogers 1973, Zaltman 1974). Involve tangible punishments for performing a certain behavior (e.g., adding extra duties, tariffs, surcharges, and taxes to the cost of a product or service).

7. *Clinical Counseling and Behavior Modification* (Hornstein et al. 1971). Involve the unlearning of socially undesirable behavior or learning of a socially desirable behavior among a hard core of individuals in a society; the psychiatric and psychoanalytic programs tailored for each deviant individual as well as small group therapy programs are examples of this strategy.

8. *Mandatory Rules and Regulations* (Jones 1969, Niehoff 1966, Zaltman, Duncan, and Holbek 1973). Legal restrictions on behavior are by definition involuntary and universal in nature; punitive measures can be utilized given noncompliance.

sures may merely serve to alienate them. Defense mechanisms may arise, causing such an approach to fail (cf Argyris 1970). However, use of other strategies or a more indirect approach appear even less effective here.

- The emphasis of certain strategies on either behavior or attitudes in the reinforcement and confrontation processes, from the viewpoint of the change agent, is to aid them in formulating specific social change plans for facilitating each process. Certainly, feedback effects from attitudes to behaviors and from behavior to attitudes may result. For example, providing economic incentives to people as rewards in the behavioral reinforcement process directly centers on behavior. Subsequently, because more positive connotations surround the performance of the behavior, in-

Table 26-3
Appropriateness of the Strategies in Facilitating the Processes of Planned Social Change

Strategies	Reinforcement		Inducement	Rationalization	Confrontation	
	Behavioral	Psychological	Behavioral	Psychological	Behavioral	Psychological
Informing and Educating	No	Yes	No	Maybe	No	No
Persuasion and Propaganda	No	Maybe	No	Yes	No	Yes
Social Controls	No	Maybe	Yes	Yes	Maybe	Yes
Delivery Systems	Maybe	No	Yes	No	No	No
Economic Incentives	Yes	No	Yes	No	No	No
Economic Disincentives	No	No	Yes	No	Yes	No
Clinical Counseling and Behavior Modification	No	No	No	No	Yes	No
Mandatory Rules	Yes	No	Maybe	No	Yes	No

dividuals' attitudes toward the behavior may become more positive.

The predictions within Table 26-3 must be considered tentative at this time. However, they should provide change agents with a greater understanding of the processes of planned social change and guidance in normatively evaluating the costs and benefits of the strategies identified in Table 26-2 and their applicability under varying attitude-behavior conditions.

ESTIMATING WHICH PROCESSES SHOULD BE FACILITATED

How to allocate resources among the alternative processes of planned social change and whether or not a single process will be sufficient or not depends, in large part, on the distribution of the general population in the four cells of the attitude behavior consistency/discrepancy matrix. The larger the percentage of people exhibiting attitude-behavior consistency, the greater the need to implement reinforcement and confrontation processes (cells one and three in Table 26-1). On the other hand, the larger the percentage of people who exhibit attitude-behavior discrepancy (the lower the aggregate positive correlation between attitudes and behavior), the greater the need to implement inducement and rationalization processes (cells two and four in Table 26-1). The more heterogeneous the cultural and economic backgrounds of people in a society, the less likely it is that all of them will be concentrated in any one cell (cf

Okediji 1972). Therefore, in highly diverse and complex societies it appears necessary to utilize a mix of processes and strategies for an optimal achievement of planned social change.

Knowledge of the population distribution is necessary but not sufficient for determining which social change processes should be implemented. As suggested previously, there will likely be differential (1) coefficients of effectiveness, depending on the percentage of a target group that a strategy moves in a desired direction, (2) constraints, and (3) costs associated with facilitating each process through use of an influence strategy or a combination of strategies. Such considerations must be taken into account by the change agent along with information about the population distribution.

Two methods of estimating the population distribution within the attitude-behavior consistency/discrepancy matrix are now described.

A Simple Estimation Method

The simple method rests on the proposition that attitude is a unidimensional phenomenon and can be reliably measured in terms of like-dislike, enjoy-hate, good-bad, favorable-unfavorable, and other semantic differential rating scales (Fishbein 1967, Howard and Sheth 1969, Triandis 1971). Through distribution analysis, the sample can be divided into positive and negative groups engaged or disengaged in that social behavior. This is a simple procedure but can be very useful as a first cut to understand whether there is a lopsided distribution in favor of a particular cell in the strategy mix matrix.

A More Complex Estimation Method

A more complex approach is to measure a person's evaluative beliefs (Sheth 1974) that underlie his/her attitudes toward a social behavior. It is a two-stage process. In the first stage, the cognitive structure underlying the attitudinal judgment is assessed by qualitative research on small groups of people who are engaged *and* disengaged in the behavior or by assessment of prior research findings. In the second stage, a multiattribute profile of evaluative beliefs is generated from a large sample study to measure the composition of people's attitudes toward the specified behavior.

Given a multiattribute vector of attitudinal beliefs, it is now possible to perform a two-group discriminant analysis between those who are engaged and those who are disengaged in a given social behavior. The multiattribute attitudinal profile represents the predictor set of variables, and the dichotomous behavioral manifestation represents the criterion variable in the two-group discriminant analysis.

Since the objective in discriminant analysis is to maximize the correlation between group membership and the predictor variable profile, it is possible to measure the degree and direction of consistency or discrepancy between attitudes and behavior by the use of the classification procedures in the discriminant analysis. In other words, the proportion of people whose attitudes and behavior are consistent as well as those whose attitudes and behavior are inconsistent or discrepant in each direction can be estimated. For example, some people in the sample may have a negative attitude profile even though they are engaged in a given behavior. The discriminant analysis model will clearly classify them as people who should not be engaged in that behavior. Similarly, there may be other people whose attitude profile is positive, but they are not engaged in that behavior. This discriminant analysis model will classify them as people who should be engaged in that behavior even though they are not. In short, the correct classifications in the discriminant analysis reflect the attitude-behavior discrepancy (Wind 1977).

CAR POOLING EXAMPLE

An operationalization of the simple and complex approaches just described is illustrated by a research study of van pooling or car pooling behavior (Sheth and Horowitz 1977). Despite powerful personal and societal advantages, car pooling has received very low acceptance in the U.S. It is estimated that less than 10% of commuters use car pooling as a mode of travel to work (Herman and Lam 1975, Zwanzig 1977). As such, it provides a useful scenario for estimating which processes of planned social change should be considered to promote this behavior better.

Collection of Data

A survey was conducted among residents of the Chicago metropolitan area contacted through their employers. Personnel departments of 43 firms, chosen randomly from a large list of companies employing at least 100 people, were first contacted and asked to contact roughly equal numbers of car poolers, solo drivers, and public transit users to answer a self-administered mail back questionnaire, which was hand delivered. Of 2,000 questionnaires distributed, 1,020 were returned. After eliminating those with relevant missing data, 822 questionnaires remained for analysis: 323 car poolers, 382 solo drivers, and 117 public transit users.

Because almost all car poolers in our sample owned at least one automobile while 75% of transit users did not, it was assumed that automobile ownership is a necessary condition for sharing a ride to work. For this reason, only data relating to car poolers and solo drivers were analyzed for this study.

Data and Analysis

The respondents indicated the degree to which they liked or disliked the idea of being a member of a car pool on a seven-point scale

ranging from extreme like to extreme dislike. This item was used to represent their overall attitude toward car pooling. Table 26-4 presents the cross-tabulation of respondents with positive or negative attitudes toward car pooling and their actual commuting behavior. It represents the simple estimation method discussed earlier. As evident, the table reflects a reasonably high attitude-behavior consistency. Still, of those people with a positive attitude, 27% were solo drivers and of those with negative attitudes toward car pooling, 19% actually were car pooling, which suggests that there may be significant market niches where policy planners can utilize inducement and/or rationalization processes.

Figure 26-1 shows the specific evaluative beliefs utilized in operationalizing the complex method. They were developed based on past literature, in-depth interviews with a small group of car poolers, and our own thinking. It also shows the profiles of car poolers and solo drivers with respect to their attitudes toward car pooling. As can be seen from the profile, the attitudes toward car pooling between solo drivers and car poolers are similar with respect to expense, energy, traffic, and

Table 26-4
Population Distribution on Overall Attitude Scale toward Car Pooling

	Car Pooling Attitude		
	Positive	*Negative*	*Behavior Totals*
Car Poolers	257 (73%)	66 (19%)	323
Behavior Solo Drivers	97 (27%)	285 (81%)	382
Attitude Totals	354	351	705

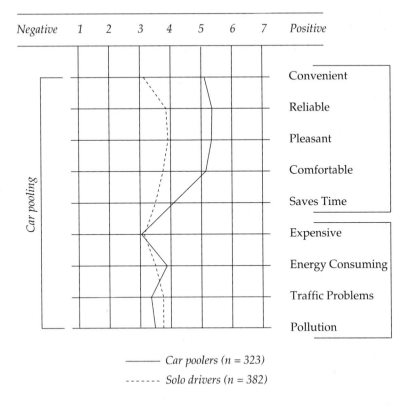

Negative   1   2   3   4   5   6   7   *Positive*

Convenient
Reliable
Pleasant
Comfortable
Saves Time
Expensive
Energy Consuming
Traffic Problems
Pollution

———— *Car poolers (n = 323)*

- - - - - *Solo drivers (n = 382)*

Figure 26-1
Evaluation of Car Pooling Profile

pollution problems. On the other hand, car poolers are far more positive than solo drivers toward car pooling with respect to convenience, reliability, comfort, pleasantness, and time saving. In other words, there are significant differences on personal experience attributed but virtually no differences on social and economic consequences of car pooling behavior between the two groups.

As suggested by the theory and its operationalization, a two-group discriminant analysis was performed utilizing the above evaluative beliefs as the predictor variables of car pooling behavior. The discriminant analysis results are summarized in Table 26-5, a.[4] As would be expected, those beliefs on which there were significant differences between car

poolers and solo drivers (convenient, reliable, pleasant, saves time) were retained in the discriminant function, and others were discarded as not relevant since they did not contribute toward maximizing the correlation between behavior and attitudes of two groups of commuters.

The classification matrix that results from the discriminant analysis is shown in Table 26-5, b. First of all, notice that the population distribution in Table 26-5, b is highly similar to the distribution in Table 26-4 that resulted from the simple method. This provides a predictive validity check on each of the methods. However, the multiattribute profile and the discriminant function go one step beyond and enable the policy planner not

Table 26-5

a. Discriminant Analysis between Solo Drivers and Car Poolers—Attitude toward Car Pooling

i	Variable	F Value	d.f.	SOLO α_1	CP $-\alpha_1$
1	Convenient	197.6**	1;703	0.12	0.52
2	Reliable	38.9**	1;702	0.33	0.68
3	Pleasant	10.8**	1;701	0.43	0.64
4	Saves Time	4.1*	1;700	−0.11	−0.04
0	(Constant)	—	—	−13.60	−17.50
	F between groups	66.6**	4;700	—	—

b. Classification Matrix Results—Car Pooling Attitude

	Positive	Negative	Behavior Totals
Car Poolers	239 (70%)	84 (23%)	323
Behavior Solo Drivers	102 (30%)	280 (77%)	382
Attitude Totals	341	364	705

*: $p \leq 0.05$
**: $p \leq 0.001$

only to estimate the relative sizes of each segment but what specific beliefs to use in carrying out various processes such as inducement, reinforcement, confrontation, and rationalization processes.[5]

As can be seen from Table 26-5, b, the vast majority of people with positive attitudes toward car pooling (70%) do actually engage in it. Similarly, a vast majority of people with negative attitudes toward car pooling actually engage in solo driving (77%). This suggests that primary approaches for increasing car pooling behavior should be a combination of the reinforcement and confrontation proc-

esses. Since our data with respect to car poolers versus solo drivers are not proportional to the population ratios, it will be necessary to estimate the population proportions of car poolers statistically. Since car pooling is practiced by less than 10% of the population, the dominant approach for increasing car pooling behavior appears to be the confrontation process.

However, as stated previously, the confrontation process is both very difficult and painful to implement since it requires fundamental changes in both the values and habits of people and may be accompanied by political risks and negative public opinion. As an alternative, perhaps the policy planner should lower his/her aspirations and attempt to make modest improvements in car pooling behavior by concentrating on those people with positive attitudes who do not presently car pool (30% of all those with positive attitudes), as well as on those who do car pool at present but have negative attitudes toward it (23%). The former group would require an emphasis on the inducement process involving such strategies as a change in work schedules, providing a vehicle exclusively for car pooling purposes, and facilitating the matching process of car pooler to minimize time and distance inconveniences. The latter group would require implementation of the rationalization process including the use of persuasive strategies involving propaganda leaflets, appeals to national pride, mass media campaigns to "hang in there," and special interpersonal support through pep talks and workshops.

If we presume that 75% of all commuters are solo drivers (the balance divided between car pooling and mass transit), then nearly 55% of all commuters would need more drastic measures underlying the confrontation process to motivate them to change to car pooling behavior. An additional 20% will need strategies involved with the inducement process, and the remaining 25% of all commuters will require a combination of strategies dealing with the reinforcement and rationalization processes. Looking at this from a different perspective, it suggests that with the adoption of strategies that foster the rationalization and inducement processes, the policy maker should be able to increase car pooling behavior to a level where combined with mass transit, it will have market share of approximately 45% of all commuters. In other words, solo driving and other modes of commuting to work can be brought to a more or less parity level without the utilization of

more painful and politically risky strategies associated with the confrontation process. Furthermore, based on increased acceptability of car pooling, it may generate sufficiently strong pressures on the current solo drivers to encourage them to switch to car pooling, resulting in a snowball effect as suggested in diffusion research.

DISCUSSION

Both the simple approach and the technique of discriminant analysis suggest something about the magnitude of attitude-behavior consistency/discrepancy and the consequent managerial decision as to which processes of planned social change should be facilitated. They involve a microlevel analysis which enables the change agent to identify people in each cell and target a specific mix of strategies to each of the four segments.

The primary use of discriminant analysis in the paper is to develop a predictive model to classify individuals as either car poolers or solo drivers. However, the multiattribute attitude profile also provides clues about the substantive elements to be included in each of the selected strategies. Let us illustrate this with an example. Suppose we find a group of people who engage in birth control and those who do not. We measure their attitudes on a multiattribute profile consisting of cost, convenience, accessibility, social taboo, and fear of side effects. Based on the two-group discriminant analysis, we find that the most significant discriminating attributes are fear of side effects and cost. We also find that there is a group of people who have fear of side effects and cost problems even though they are engaged in birth control. Implementation of the rationalization process might consist of a campaign stressing safety as well as lowering the cost of birth control targeted to this segment of the population.

On the other hand, there is another group of people who have a positive attitude with respect to side effects and cost of birth control, but they are not engaged in birth control practices. They need to be induced to manifest their positive attitudes into actual behavior. This can be achieved by strategies such as more efficient delivery systems (birth control devices practically available everywhere) as well as strong encouragement from social or organizational structures similar to the current physical fitness programs.

Finally, to reach those who do not practice birth control and have a fear of side effects as well as high cost perception, implementation of the confrontation process may be required. Clinical counseling, establishing mandatory product safety guidelines for the suppliers of birth control devices, and generating economic disincentives toward nonpractice of birth control are strategies that could be utilized.

It is relatively easy to identify the four segments of the total population on their socioeconomic and demographic profiles. In addition, it may be useful to collect data on their daily activities and interests (lifestyles) to pinpoint the role a particular social behavior plays in their daily life.

The change agent would now have sufficient information about the target segments to plan the process and strategy mix with respect to both resource allocation and substantive content for each strategy. He/she can now decide which processes and strategies to use based on the population distribution in the attitude-behavior consistency/discrepancy matrix and the normative evaluation of each strategy, what specific attributes should be emphasized in his/her strategy based on the discriminant coefficients of the attitude profile, whom to target a specific strategy mix element based on the demographic profile of each of the segments, and how to implement or communicate to each identified and tar-geted segment based on the lifestyle and value profile of each of the segments in the population.

AN EXTENDED MODEL

There are at least two improvements that can be made to the model presented herein. The first improvement relates to extending the model to a situation where people are distributed as positive, negative, or neutral in their attitudes. There are several examples in the area of planned social change where apathy is dominant and, therefore, people really don't care or they are truly indifferent toward alternative courses of behavior. For example, a large percentage of people are not concerned about nutrition in their diet. Secondly, the social behavior in question may not be a dichotomous phenomenon but a continuous phenomenon such as heavy vs. light usage. For example, we may want to reduce the per capita consumption of cigarettes among smokers as well as encourage people to quit smoking. The challenge in developing such an extended model would be to determine which process or combination of processes would be most appropriate for each cell.

An extended attitude-behavior consistency/discrepancy model is presented in Table 26-6 with underlying processes of planned social change and examples of specific strategies that can be used to implement them identified in each cell. Two important differences concerning processes of planned social change are evident in this model in comparison with the simpler model presented in Table 26-1. First, for the rationalization, inducement, and confrontation processes, a distinction is made between moderate and radical processes; that is, in a given cell a change agent may face moderate difficulty in successfully implementing a certain process, while in another cell stiffer resistance may be encountered. For example, for a segment of people who have negative attitudes toward the use of contraceptives and currently don't use them, a radical confrontation process may need to be implemented with rather direct influence strategies such as mandatory rules. A moderate confrontation process appears appropriate in situations where a negative attitude toward use of contraceptives exists but where people use them on an infrequent basis. Less drastic strategies such as those dealing with economic disincentives may be more appropriate here.

Secondly, attitude enhancement and behavioral enhancement processes are identified in Table 26-6. Their implementation involves a less drastic approach in comparison with the implementation of the radical rationalization and moderate inducement processes. Thus important distinctions in degree of directness and difficulty of implementing a process in achieving desired objectives are made within the extended model which change agents must carefully consider and

evaluate in attempts to motivate planned social change.

Operationalization of the extended model is straightforward if the simple method of measuring unidimensional attitudes is utilized. It will require generating a 3×3 matrix based on positive, neutral, or negative unidimensional attitudes and nonusers, light users, or heavy users of a particular social phenomenon. However, when we have multiattribute beliefs, it will be necessary to perform a three-group discriminant analysis. While the analysis is more complex in this case, the output in terms of the classification matrix is the same. The interpretation of multiple discriminant functions and individual variables is more complex but certainly manageable. A given belief is likely to be associated with a given discriminant function, especially after rotation. The sign of its weight will indicate how a change in that belief will change group membership as affected by the first discriminant axis. If a given belief is

Table 26-6
An Extended Model of Strategy Mix Choices for Planned Social Change

		Attitude		
		Positive	*Neutral*	*Negative*
	Regular Users	Reinforcement Process (information)	Attitude Enhancement Process (education)	Radical Rationalization Process (persuasion and propaganda)
Relevant Behavior	*Infrequent Users*	Behavior Enhancement Process (social controls)	Moderate Rationalization Process (social controls)	Moderate Confrontation Process (economic disincentives)
	Nonusers	Moderate Inducement Process (delivery systems)	Radical Inducement Process (economic incentives)	Radical Confrontation Process (mandatory rules, clinical counseling)

significantly loaded on two discriminant axes with opposite signs, this would mean that it will have opposite or differential impacts in various segments and, therefore, proper care must be undertaken in choosing and implementing specific strategies that will maintain "walls" around each group. In other words, a rifle versus shotgun approach will be needed.

A limitation of the extended model is that it is restricted to a binary choice of engaging or not engaging in social behavior. However, often the choice is not dichotomous but multichotomous in nature. For example, the choices of transportation modes for commuting purposes consist of driving, car pooling, trains, or the bus transit system in any metropolitan area. In other words, the change agent must pinpoint what the alternative options are and estimate the degree of cross-elasticity of a given planned social change with respect to the competing alternatives. Thus, if one wants to increase car pooling behavior, one must understand whether the change will come from people who now drive or from people who now take the train or bus. This is an important policy issue that needs to be addressed in future research.

One solution is to measure people's multiattribute attitude profiles toward the planned social behavior but sample them from each of the competing behavior domains. For example, we can ask people to express their attitudes toward car pooling although at present they are driving, taking the train, riding the bus, car pooling, or bicycling to work. It is now possible to extend the model by utilizing multiple group discriminant analysis. The classification table would be extended to all alternative options besides car pooling. An analysis of the classification matrix will then reveal those segments of the total population that are likely to be attracted toward car pooling behavior from each of the substitute modes of commuting.

SUMMARY

This article has attempted to offer a conceptual model of strategy mix choice for planned social change. The fundamental axiom on which the framework is developed is the attitude-behavior consistency/discrepancy with respect to a given social behavior. The model suggests that the change agent must not think in terms of a universal strategy approach but seriously consider segmenting the total population and utilize a mix of influence strategies on a selective basis from among those that facilitate reinforcement, inducement, rationalization, and confrontation processes.

It is evident that considerable work remains in investigating processes of planned social change and evaluating influence strategies that may be used in implementing these processes. This paper lays a basic foundation upon which others must build and provides change agents and researchers with insights into where future planning and research must proceed in analyzing the nature and effectiveness of planned social change.

NOTES

1. The social change process is also important within and between formal organizations, but such an emphasis is beyond the scope of this paper. Andreasen (1981) considers this topic as he discusses varying strategies that social marketers can use in attempting to gain influence on the behavior of other organizations.

2. See Zaltman and Duncan (1977) for reasons why a conflict between attitudes and behaviors might exist.

3. Of course this situation can be considerably more complex if a husband and wife within one family unit lack congruence or agreement in their attitudes and behavior concerning birth control.

4. In view of the fact that the variance-covariance matrices for the solo drivers and car poolers were not equal ($\Sigma_1 \neq \Sigma_2$) in our sample, it was necessary to utilize the likelihood

ratio criterion C (see Anderson 1958, p. 141–142) rather than the traditional discriminant function criterion to allow for the effects of unequal variance-covariances of the predictor variables between the two groups. This requires calculating separate linear combinations of each group (solo drivers and car poolers), utilizing each group's mean vector as deviation from the total sample, and dividing by its unique variance-covariance matrix estimated by the sample.

5. Multicolinearity among the variables did not appear to present serious problems. While multicolinearity could bias the impact that individual variables have on the discriminant function, given that the primary objective of this analysis is prediction (i.e., to attain a classification matrix of the sample), this would not present a serious problem in this study.

REFERENCES

Anderson, T. W. (1985). *An Introduction to Multivariate Statistical Analysis*, New York: Wiley.

Andreasen, Alan (1981), "Power Potential Channel Strategies in Social Marketing," working paper #743, Bureau of Economic and Business Research, University of Illinois.

Arensberg, Conrad M. and Arthur H. Niehoff (1971), *Introducing Social Change: A Manual for Community Development*, 2nd edition, Chicago: Aldine-Atherton.

Argyris, Chris (1970, *Intervention Theory and Method*, Reading, MA: Addison-Wesley.

Bass, Frank M. (1969), "A New Product Growth Model for Consumer Durables," *Management Science*, 15 (January), 215–17.

Belk, Russel (1981), "Theoretical Issues in the Intention-Behavior Discrepancy," paper presented at the American Psychological Association Convention (Division 23), Los Angeles.

Bennis, Warren (1966), *Changing Organization*, New York: McGraw-Hill.

————, Kenneth D. Benne, Robert Chin, and Kenneth E. Corey (1976), *The Planning of Change*, 3rd edition, New York: Holt, Rinehart, and Winston.

Boyk, J. (1973), "Research Report: Learning Performance in the Defensive Drive Course (DDC) and the DDC Self-Instruction Program," Washington, DC: National Safety Council Research Department, November.

Chin, Robert and Kenneth D. Benne (1969), "General Strategies for Effecting Changes in Human Systems," in *The Planning of Change*, W. G. Bennis, Kenneth D. Benne, and Robert Chin, eds., New York: Holt.

Deshpande, Rohit and S. Krishnan (1981), "A Consumer Based Approach for Establishing Priorities in Consumer Information Programs: Implications for Public Policy," in *Advances in Consumer Research*, Vol. VIII, K. B. Monroe, ed., 338–343.

Engel, James, Martin Warshaw, and Thomas Kinnear (1979), *Promotional Strategy*, Homewood, IL: Richard D. Irwin, Inc.

Fishbein, Martin, ed. (1969), *Readings in Attitude Theory and Measurement*, New York: John Wiley & Sons.

Fox, Karen and Philip Kotler (1980), "The Marketing of Social Causes: The First Ten Years," *Journal of Marketing*, 44 (Fall), 24–33.

Herman, R. and T. Lam (1975), "Carpools at Large Suburban Technical Center," *Transportation Engineering Journal*, 101 (May), 311–19.

Hornstein, Harvey A. et al. (1971), *Social Intervention: A Behavioral Approach*, New York: Free Press.

Howard, J. A. and J. N. Sheth (1969), *The Theory of Buyer Behavior*, New York: John Wiley & Sons.

Jones, Garth N. (1969), *Planned Organizational Change*. New York: Praeger.

Lee, Kam Han (1975), "Social Marketing Strategies and Nutrition Education," unpublished Ph.D. dissertation. Northwestern University.

Lippitt, R., Jeanne Watson, and Bruce Westley (1968), *The Dynamics of Planned Change*, New York: Harcourt.

Mansfield, Edwin (1961), "Technical Change and the Rate of Imitation," *Econometrica*, 29 (October), 741–66.

McGuire, William (1978), "Psychological Factors Influencing Consumer Choice," in *Selected Aspects of Consumer Behavior*, Robert Ferber, ed., Washington, DC: National Science Foundation.

Niehoff, Arthur (1966), *A Casebook of Social Change*, Chicago: Aldine-Atherton.

Nord, Walter and J. Paul Peter (1980), "A Behavior Modification Perspective on Marketing," *Journal of Marketing*, 44 (Spring), 36–47.

Okediji, Francis O. (1972), "Overcoming Social and Cultural Resistances," *International Journal of Health Education*, 15 (July–September), 3–10.

Pohlman, Edward (1971), "Incentives and Compensations in Birth Planning," Monograph 2, Durham: University of North Carolina. Carolina Population Center.

Rogers, E. M. (1972), "Field Experiments in Family Planning Incentives," Lansing: Michigan State University, Department of Communications.

—— (1973), "Effects of Incentives on the Diffusion of Innovations: The Case of Family Planning in Asia," in *Processes and Phenomena of Social Change*, Gerald Zaltman, ed., New York: Wiley Inter-Science.

—— and F. F. Shoemaker (1971), *The Communication of Innovations*. New York: Free Press.

Sheth, Jagdish N. (1974), "A Field Study of Attitude Structure and Attitude-Behavior Relationship," in *Models of Buyer Behavior*, J. N. Sheth, ed., New York: Harper and Row, 242–68.

—— and A. D. Horowitz (1977), "Strategies of Increasing Car Pooling Behavior among Urban Commuters," in *Social Research*, Amsterdam: ESOMAR, 183–198.

—— and Bruce Newman (1981), "Determinants of Intention-Behavior Discrepancy in the 1980 National Elections," paper presented at the American Psychological Association Convention (Division 23), Los Angeles.

—— and John Wong (1981), "Impact of Unexpected Events on Intention-Behavior Consistency: An Experimental Study," faculty working paper, Bureau of Economic and Business Research, University of Illinois.

Skinner, B. F. (1953), *Science and Human Behavior*, New York: Macmillan.

Smith, Anthony D. (1973), *The Concept of Social Change*, London: Routledge and Kegan Paul.

Spreke, J. T. (1971), "Incentives in Family Planning Programs: Time for a New Look," working paper, U.S. Agency for International Development, Office of Population.

Triandis, Harry C. (1971), *Attitude and Attitude Change*, New York: John Wiley & Sons.

Wind, Yoram (1977), "Brand Loyalty and Vulnerability," in *Consumer and Industrial Buying Behavior*, Arch Woodside, Jagdish N. Sheth, and Peter Bennett, eds., New York: North Holland.

Zaltman, Gerald (1974), "Strategies for Diffusing Innovations," in *Marketing Analysis for Societal Problems*, Jagdish N. Sheth and Peter Wright, eds., Urbana: University of Illinois Press.

—— and Robert Duncan (1977), *Strategies for Planned Social Change*, New York: Wiley-Inter-science.

——, ——, and Jonny Holbek (1973), *Innovations and Organizations*, New York: Wiley-Inter-science.

—— Philip Kotler, and Ira Kaufman, eds. (1972), *Creating Social Change*, New York: Holt.

—— and Ronald Stiff (1973), "Theories of Diffusion," in *Consumer Behavior: Theoretical Sources*, S. Ward and T. Robertson, eds., Englewood Cliffs, NJ: Prentice-Hall.

Zwanzig, Francis R., ed. (1977), *Forecasting Passenger and Freight Travel*, (Transportation Research Record 637), Washington DC: Transportation Research Board.

◆

A Conceptual Model of Service Quality and Its Implications for Future Research

A. Parasuraman, Valarie A. Zeithaml, and Leonard L. Berry

People want some wise and perceptive statement like, 'Quality is ballet, not hockey.'
—Philip Crosby (1979)

Quality is an elusive and indistinct construct. Often mistaken for imprecise adjectives like "goodness, or luxury, or shininess, or weight" (Crosby 1979), quality and its requirements are not easily articulated by consumers (Takeuchi and Quelch 1983). Explication and measurement of quality also present problems for researchers (Monroe and Krishnan 1983), who often bypass definitions and use unidimensional self-report measures to capture the concept (Jacoby, Olson, and Haddock 1973; McConnell 1968; Shapiro 1972).

While the substance and determinants of quality may be undefined, its importance to firms and consumers is unequivocal. Research has demonstrated the strategic benefits of

quality in contributing to market share and return on investment (e.g., Anderson and Zeithaml 1984; Phillips, Chang, and Buzzell 1983) as well as lowering manufacturing costs and improving productivity (Garvin 1983). The search for quality is arguably the most important consumer trend of the 1980s (Rabin 1983) as consumers are now demanding higher quality in products than ever before (Leonard and Sasser 1982, Takeuchi and Quelch 1983).

Few academic researchers have attempted to define and model quality because of the difficulties involved in delimiting and measuring the construct. Moreover, despite the phenomenal growth of the service sector, only a handful of these researchers have focused on service quality. We attempt to rectify this situation by (1) reviewing the small number of studies that have investigated service quality, (2) reporting the insights obtained in an extensive exploratory investigation of quality in four service businesses, (3) developing a model of service quality, and (4) offering propositions to stimulate future research about quality.

"A Conceptual Model of Service Quality and Its Implications for Future Research," Parasuraman, A., Valarie A. Zeithaml and Leonard L. Berry, Vol. 49 (Fall '85), pp. 41–50. Reprinted from the *Journal of Marketing*, published by the American Marketing Association.

EXISTING KNOWLEDGE ABOUT SERVICE QUALITY

Efforts in defining and measuring quality have come largely from the goods sector. According to the prevailing Japanese philosophy, quality is "zero defects—doing it right the first time." Crosby (1979) defines quality as "conformance to requirements." Garvin (1983) measures quality by counting the incidence of "internal" failures (those observed before a product leaves the factory) and "external" failures (those incurred in the field after a unit has been installed.)

Knowledge about goods quality, however, is insufficient to understand service quality. Three well-documented characteristics of services—*intangibility, heterogeneity,* and *inseparability*—must be acknowledged for a full understanding of service quality.

First, most services are intangible (Bateson 1977, Berry 1980, Lovelock 1981, Shostak 1977). Because they are performances rather than objects, precise manufacturing specifications concerning uniform quality can rarely be set. Most services cannot be counted, measured, inventoried, tested, and verified in advance of sale to assure quality. Because of intangibility, the firm may find it difficult to understand how consumers perceive their services and evaluate service quality (Zeithaml 1981).

Second, services, especially those with a high labor content, are heterogeneous: their performance often varies from producer to producer, from customer to customer, and from day to day. Consistency of behavior from service personnel (i.e., uniform quality) is difficult to assure (Booms and Bitner 1981) because what the firm intends to deliver may be entirely different from what the consumer receives.

Third, production and consumption of many services are inseparable (Carmen and Langeard 1980, Gronroos 1978, Regan 1963, Upah 1980). As a consequence, quality in services is not engineered at the manufacturing plant, then delivered intact to the consumer. In labor intensive services, for example, quality occurs during service delivery, usually in an interaction between the client and the contact person from the service firm (Lehtinen and Lehtinen 1982). The service firm may also have less managerial control over quality in services where consumer participation is intense (e.g., haircuts, doctor's visits) because the client affects the process. In these situations, the consumer's input (description of symptoms) becomes critical to the quality of service performance.

Service quality has been discussed in only a handful of writings (Gronroos 1982; Lehtinen and Lehtinen 1982; Lewis and Booms 1983; Sasser, Olsen, and Wyckoff 1978). Examination of these writings and other literature on services suggests three underlying themes:

- Service quality is more difficult for the consumer to evaluate than goods quality.
- Service quality perceptions result from a comparison of consumer expectations with actual service performance.
- Quality evaluations are not made solely on the outcome of a service; they also involve evaluations of the *process* of service delivery.

Service Quality More Difficult to Evaluate

When purchasing goods, the consumer employs many tangible cues to judge quality: style, hardness, color, label, feel, package, fit. When purchasing services, fewer tangible cues exist. In most cases, tangible evidence is limited to the service provider's physical facilities, equipment, and personnel.

In the absence of tangible evidence on which to evaluate quality, consumers must depend on other cues. The nature of these other cues has not been investigated by researchers, although some authors have suggested that the price becomes a pivotal quality indicator in situations where other information is not available (McConnell 1968, Olander 1970, Zeithaml 1981). Because of service intangibility, a firm may find it more difficult to understand how consumers perceive services and service quality. "When a service provider knows how [the service] will be evaluated by the consumer, we will be able to suggest how to influence these evaluations in a desired direction" (Gronroos 1982).

Quality Is a Comparison between Expectations and Performance

Researchers and managers of service firms concur that service quality involves a comparison of expectations with performance:

> Service quality is a measure of how well the service level delivered matches customer expectations. Delivering quality service means conforming to customer expectations on a consistent basis. (Lewis and Booms 1983)

In line with this thinking, Gronroos (1982) developed a model in which he contends that consumers compare the service they expect with perceptions of the service they receive in evaluating service quality.

Smith and Houston (1982) claimed that satisfaction with services is related to confirmation or disconfirmation of expectations. They based their research on the disconfirmation paradigm, which maintains that satisfaction is related to the size and direction of the disconfirmation experience where disconfirmation is related to the person's initial expectations (Churchill and Suprenaut 1982).

Quality Evaluations Involve Outcomes and Processes

Sasser, Olsen, and Wyckoff (1978) discussed three different dimensions of service performance: levels of material, facilities, and personnel. Implied in this trichotomy is the notion that service quality involves more than outcome; it also includes the manner in which the service is delivered. This notion surfaces in other research on service quality as well.

Gronroos, for example, postulated that two types of service quality exist: *technical quality*, which involves what the customer is actually receiving from the service, and *functional quality*, which involves the manner in which the service is delivered (Gronroos 1982).

Lehtinen and Lehtinen's (1982) basic premise is that service quality is produced in the interaction between a customer and elements in the service organization. They use three quality dimensions: *physical quality*, which includes the physical aspects of the service (e.g., equipment or building); *corporate quality*, which involves the company's image or profile; and *interactive quality*, which derives from the interaction between contact personnel and customers as well as between some customers and other customers. They further differentiate between the quality associated with the process of service delivery and the quality associated with the outcome of the service.

EXPLORATORY INVESTIGATION

Because the literature on service quality is not yet rich enough to provide a sound conceptual foundation for investigating service quality, an exploratory qualitative study was undertaken to investigate the concept of service quality. Specifically, focus group interviews with consumers and in-depth interviews with executives were conducted to develop a conceptual model of service quality. The approach used is consistent with procedures recommended for marketing theory development by several scholars (Deshpande 1983; Peter and Olson 1983; Zaltman, LeMasters, and Heffring 1982).

In-depth interviews of executives in four nationally recognized service firms and a set of focus group interviews of consumers were conducted to gain insights about the following questions:

- What do managers of service firms perceive to be the key attributes of service quality? What problems and tasks are involved in providing high quality service?
- What do consumers perceive to be the key attributes of quality in services?
- Do discrepancies exist between the perceptions of consumers and service marketers?
- Can consumer and marketer perceptions be combined in a general model that explains service quality from the consumer's standpoint?

Service Categories Investigated

Four service categories were chosen for investigation: retail banking, credit card, securities brokerage, and product repair and maintenance. While this set of service businesses is not exhaustive, it represents a cross-section of industries which vary along key dimensions used to categorize services (Lovelock 1980, 1983). For example, retail banking and securities brokerage services are more "high contact services" than the other two types. The nature and results of the service act are more tangible for product repair and maintenance services than for the other three types. In terms of service delivery, discrete transactions characterize credit card services and product repair and maintenance services to a greater extent than the other two types of services.

Executive Interviews

A nationally recognized company from each of the four service businesses participated in the study. In-depth personal interviews comprised of open-ended questions were conducted with three or four executives in each

firm. The executives were selected from marketing, operations, senior management, and customer relations because each of these areas could have an impact on quality in service firms. The respondents held titles such as president, senior vice president, director of customer relations, and manager of consumer market research. Fourteen executives were interviewed about a broad range of service quality issues (e.g., what they perceived to be service quality from the consumer's perspective, what steps they took to control or improve service quality, and what problems they faced in delivering high quality services).

Focus Group Interviews

A total of 12 focus group interviews was conducted, three of each for each of the four selected services. Eight of the focus groups were held in a metropolitan area in the southwest. The remaining four were conducted in the vicinity of the participating companies' headquarters and were therefore spread across the country: one on the West Coast, one in the Midwest, and two in the East.

The focus groups were formed in accordance with guidelines traditionally followed in the marketing research field (Bellenger, Berhardt, and Goldstucker 1976). Respondents were screened to ensure that they were current or recent users of the service in question. To maintain homogeneity and assure maximum participation, respondents were assigned to groups based on age and sex. Six of the twelve groups included only males and six included only females. At least one male group and one female group were interviewed for each of the four services. Consistency in age was maintained within groups; however, age diversity across groups for each service category was established to ascertain the viewpoints of a broad cross-section of consumers.

Identities of participating firms were not revealed to focus group participants. Discussion about quality of a given service centered on consumer experiences and perceptions relating to that service *in general,* as opposed to the specific service of the participating firm in that service category. Questions asked by the moderator covered topics such as instances of and reasons for satisfaction and dissatisfaction with the service; descriptions of an ideal service (e.g., ideal bank or ideal credit card); the meaning of service quality; factors important in evaluating service quality; performance expectations concerning the service; and the role of price in service quality.

INSIGHTS FROM EXPLORATORY INVESTIGATION

Executive Interviews

Remarkably consistent patterns emerged from the four sets of executive interviews. While some perceptions about service quality were specific to the industries selected, commonalities among the industries prevailed. The commonalities are encouraging for they suggest that a general model of service quality can be developed.

Perhaps the most important insight obtained from analyzing the executive responses is the following:

> A set of key discrepancies or gaps exists regarding executive perceptions of service quality and the tasks associated with service delivery to consumers. These gaps can be major hurdles in attempting to deliver a service which consumers would perceive as being of high quality.

The gaps revealed by the executive interviews are shown in the lower portion (i.e., the Marketer side) of Figure 27-1. This figure summarizes the key insights gained (through the focus group as well as executive interviews) about the concept of service quality and factors affecting it. The remainder of this section discusses the gaps on the service marketer's side (GAP1, GAP2, GAP3, and GAP4) and presents propositions implied by those gaps. The consumer's side of the service quality model in Figure 27-1 is discussed in the next section.

Consumer Expectation—Management Perception Gap (GAP1) Many of the executive perceptions about what consumers expect in a quality service were congruent with the consumer expectations revealed in the focus groups. However, discrepancies between executive perceptions and consumer expectations existed, as illustrated by the following examples:

- Privacy or confidentiality during transactions emerged as a pivotal quality attribute in every banking and securities brokerage focus group. Rarely was this consideration mentioned in the executive interviews.
- The physical and security features of credit cards (e.g., the likelihood that unauthorized people could use the cards) generated substantial discussion in the focus group interviews but did not emerge as critical in the executive interviews.
- The product repair and maintenance focus groups indicated that a large repair service firm was unlikely to be viewed as a high quality firm. Small independent repair firms were consistently associated with high quality. In contrast, most executive comments indicated a firm's size would signal strength in a quality context.

In essence, service firm executives may not always understand what features connote high quality to consumers in advance, what features a service must have in order to meet consumer needs, and what levels of performance on those features are needed to deliver high quality service. This insight is consistent with previous research in services, which sug-

CONSUMER

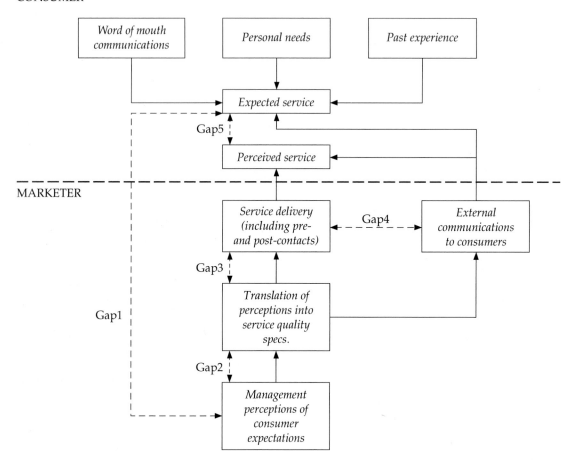

Figure 27-1
Conceptual Model of Service Quality

gests that service marketers may not always understand what consumers expect in a service (Langeard et al. 1981, Parasuraman and Zeithaml 1982). This lack of understanding may affect quality perceptions of consumers:

Proposition 1: The gap between consumer expectations and management perceptions of those expectations will have an impact on the consumer's evaluation of service quality.

Management Perception—Service Quality Specification Gap (GAP2) A recurring theme in the executive interviews in all four service firms was the difficulty experienced in attempting to match or exceed consumer expectations. Executives cited constraints which prevent them from delivering what the consumer expects. As an example, executives in the repair service firm were fully aware that consumers view quick response to appliance breakdowns as a vital ingredient of high quality service. However, they find it difficult to establish specifications to deliver quick response consistently because of a lack of trained service personnel and wide fluctuations in demand. As one executive observed, peak demand for repairing air conditioners and lawnmowers occurs during the summer months, precisely when most service personnel want to go on vacation. In this and numerous other situations, knowledge of consumer expectations exists but the perceived means to deliver to expectations apparently do not.

Apart from resource and market constraints, another reason for the gap between expectations and the actual set of specifications established for a service is the absence of total management commitment to service quality. Although the executive interviews indicated a genuine concern for quality on the part of managers interviewed, this concern may not be generalizable to all service firms. In discussing product quality, Garvin (1983) stated: " . . . the seriousness that management attached to quality problems [varies]. It's one thing to say you believe in defect-free products, but quite another to take time from a busy schedule to act on that belief and stay informed" (p. 68). Garvin's observations are likely to apply to service businesses as well.

In short, a variety of factors—resource constraints, market conditions, and/or management indifference—may result in a discrepancy between management perceptions of consumer expectations and the actual specifications established for a service. This discrepancy is predicted to affect quality perceptions of consumers:

Proposition 2: The gap between management perceptions of consumer expectations and the firm's service quality specifications will affect service quality from the consumer's viewpoint.

Service Quality Specifications, Service Delivery Gap (GAP3)   Even when guidelines exist for performing services well and treating consumers correctly, high quality service performance may not be a certainty. Executives recognize that a service firm's employees exert a strong influence on the service quality perceived by customers and that employee performance cannot always be standardized. When asked what causes service quality problems, executives consistently mentioned the pivotal role of contact personnel. In the repair and maintenance firm, for example, one executive's immediate response to the source of service quality problems was, "Everything involves a person—a repair person. It's so hard to maintain standardized quality."

Each of the four firms had formal standards or specifications for maintaining service quality (e.g., answer at least 90% of phone calls from consumers within 10 seconds; keep error rates in statements below 1%). However, each firm reported difficulty in adhering to these standards because of variability in employee performance. This problem leads to a third proposition:

Proposition 3: The gap between service quality specifications and actual service delivery will affect service quality from the consumer's standpoint.

Service Delivery–External Communications Gap (GAP4)   Media advertising and other communications by a firm can affect consumer expectations. If expectations play a major role in consumer perceptions of service quality (as the services literature contends), the firm must be certain not to promise more in communications than it can deliver in reality. Promising more than can be delivered will raise initial expectations but lower perceptions of quality when the promises are not fulfilled.

The executive interviews suggest another perhaps more intriguing way in which external communications could influence service quality perceptions by consumers. This occurs when companies neglect to inform consumers of special efforts to assure quality that are not visible to consumers. Comments of several executives implied that consumers are not always aware of everything done behind the scenes to serve them well.

For instance, a securities brokerage executive mentioned a "48-hour rule" prohibiting employees from buying or selling securities for their personal accounts for the first 48 hours after information is supplied by the firm. The firm did not communicate this information to its customers, perhaps contributing to a perception that "all the good deals are probably made by the brokers for themselves" (a perception which surfaced in the securities brokerage focus groups). One bank executive indicated that consumers were unaware of the bank's behind the counter, online teller terminals which would "translate into visible effects on customer service." Making consumers aware of not readily apparent service related standards such as these could improve service quality perceptions. Consumers who are aware that a firm is taking concrete steps to serve their best interests are likely *to perceive* a delivered service in a more favorable way.

In short, external communications can affect not only consumer expectations about a service but also consumer *perceptions* of the delivered service. Alternatively, discrepancies between service delivery and external communications—in the form of exaggerated promises and/or the absence of information about service delivery aspects intended to serve consumers well—can affect consumer perceptions of service quality.

Proposition 4: The gap between actual service delivery and external communications about the service will affect service quality from a consumer's standpoint.

Focus Group Interviews

As was true of the executive interviews, the responses of focus group participants about service quality were remarkably consistent across groups and across service businesses. While some service-specific differences were revealed, common themes emerged—themes which offer valuable insights about service quality perceptions of consumers.

Expected Service–Perceived Service Gap (GAP5)
The focus groups unambiguously supported the notion that the key to ensuring good service quality is meeting or exceeding what consumers expect from the service. One female participant described a situation when a repairman not only fixed her broken appliance but also explained what had gone wrong and how she could fix it herself if a similar problem occurred in the future. She rated the quality of this service as excellent because it exceeded her expectations. A male respondent in a banking services focus group described the frustration he felt when his bank would not cash his payroll check from a nationally known employer because it was postdated by one day. When someone else in the group pointed out legal constraints preventing the bank from cashing his check, he responded, "Well, nobody *in the bank* explained that to me!" Not receiving an explanation in the bank, this respondent perceived that the bank was *unwilling* rather than *unable* to cash the check. This in turn resulted in a perception of poor quality service.

Similar experiences, both positive and negative, were described by consumers in every focus group. It appears that judgments of high and low service quality depend on how consumers perceive the actual service performance in the context of what they expected.

Proposition 5: The quality that a consumer perceives in a service is a function of the magnitude and direction of the gap between expected service and perceived service.

A SERVICE QUALITY MODEL

Insights gained from the executive interviews and the focus groups form the basis of a model summarizing the nature and determinants of service quality as perceived by consumers. The foundation of this model is the set of gaps discussed earlier and shown in Figure 27-1. Service quality as perceived by a consumer depends on the size and direction of GAP5 which, in turn, depends on the nature of the gaps associated with the design, marketing, and delivery of services:

Proposition 6: GAP5 = f(GAP1, GAP2, GAP3, GAP4)

It is important to note that the gaps on the marketer side of the equation can be favorable or unfavorable from a service quality perspective. That is, the magnitude *and direction* of each gap will have an impact on service quality. For instance, GAP3 will be favorable when actual service delivery exceeds specifications; it will be unfavorable when service specifications are not met. While proposition 6 suggests a relationship between service quality as perceived by consumers and the gaps occurring on the marketer's side, the functional form of the relationship needs to be investigated. This point is discussed further in the last section dealing with future research directions.

The Perceived Service Quality Component

The focus groups revealed that, regardless of the type of service, consumers used basically similar criteria in evaluating service quality.

These criteria seem to fall into 10 key categories which are labeled "service quality determinants" and described in Table 27-1. For each determinant, Table 27-1 provides examples of service specific criteria that emerged in the focus groups. Table 27-1 is not meant to suggest that the 10 determinants are nonoverlapping. Because the research was exploratory, measurement of possible overlap across the 10 criteria (as well as determination of whether some can be combined) must await further empirical investigation.

The consumer's view of service quality is shown in the upper part of Figure 27-1 and further elaborated in Figure 27-2. Figure 27-2 indicates that perceived service quality is the result of the consumer's comparison of expected service with perceived service. It is quite possible that the relative importance of the 10 determinants in molding consumer expectations (prior to service delivery) may differ from their relative importance vis-à-vis consumer perceptions of the delivered service. However, the general comparison of expectations with perceptions was suggested in past research on service quality (Gronroos 1982, Lehtinen and Lehtinen 1982) and supported in the focus group interviews with consumers. The comparison of expected and perceived service is not unlike that performed by consumers when evaluating goods. What differs with services is the *nature* of the characteristics upon which they are evaluated.

One framework for isolating differences in evaluation of quality goods and services is the classification of properties of goods proposed by Nelson (1974) and Darby and Karni (1973). Nelson distinguished between two categories of properties of consumer goods: *search properties*, attributes which a consumer can determine prior to purchasing a product, and *experience properties*, attributes which can only be discerned after purchase or during consumption. Search properties include attributes such as color, style, price, fit,

Table 27-1
Determinants of Service Quality

RELIABILITY involves consistency of performance and dependability. It also means that the firm performs the service right the first time. It also means that the firm honors its promises. Specifically, it involves:
—accuracy in billing;
—keeping records correctly;
—performing the service at the designated time.

RESPONSIVENESS concerns the willingness or readiness of employees to provide service. It involves timeliness of service:
—mailing a transaction slip immediately;
—calling the customer back quickly;
—giving prompt service (e.g., setting up appointments quickly).

COMPETENCE means possession of the required skills and knowledge to perform the service. It involves:
—knowledge and skill of the contact personnel;
—knowledge and skill of operational support personnel;
—research capability of the organization, e.g., securities brokerage firm.

ACCESS involves approachability and ease of contact. It means:
—the service is easily accessible by telephone (lines are not busy and they don't put you on hold);
—waiting time to receive service (e.g., at a bank) is not extensive;
—convenient hours of operation;
—convenient location of service facility.

COURTESY involves politeness, respect, consideration, and friendliness of contact personnel (including receptionists, telephone operators, etc.). It includes:
—consideration for the consumer's property (e.g., no muddy shoes on the carpet);
—clean and neat appearance of public contact personnel.

COMMUNICATION means keeping customers informed in language they can understand and listening to them. It may mean that the company has to adjust its language for different consumers—increasing the level of sophistication with a well-educated customer and speaking simply and plainly with a novice. It involves:
—explaining the service itself;
—explaining how much the service will cost;
—explaining the trade-offs between service and cost;
—assuring the consumer that a problem will be handled.

CREDIBILITY involves trustworthiness, believability, honesty. It involves having the customer's best interests at heart. Contributing to credibility are:
—company name;
—company reputation;
—personal characteristics of the contact personnel;
—the degree of hard sell involved in interactions with the customer.

Table 27-1
Continued

SECURITY is the freedom from danger, risk, or doubt. It involves:
—physical safety (Will I get mugged at the automatic teller machine?);
—financial security (Does the company know where my stock certificate is?);
—confidentiality (Are my dealings with the company private?).

UNDERSTANDING/KNOWING THE CUSTOMER involves making the effort to understand the customer's needs. It involves:
—learning the customer's specific requirements;
—providing individualized attention;
—recognizing the regular customer.

TANGIBLES include the physical evidence of the service:
—physical facilities;
—appearance of personnel;
—tools or equipment used to provide the service;
—physical representation of the service, such as a plastic credit card or a bank statement;
—other customers in the service facility.

---

feel, hardness, and smell, while experience properties include characteristics such as taste, wearability, and dependability.

Darby and Karni (1973) added to Nelson's two-way classification system a third category, *credence properties*—characteristics which the consumer may find it impossible to evaluate even after purchase and consumption. Examples of offerings high in credence properties include appendectomies and brake relinings on automobiles. Few consumers possess medical or mechanical skills sufficient to evaluate whether these services are necessary or are performed properly, even after they have been prescribed and produced by the seller.

Consumers in the focus groups mentioned search, experience, and credence properties when asked to describe and define service quality. These aspects of service quality can be categorized into the 10 service quality determinants shown in Table 27-1 and can be arrayed along a continuum ranging from *easy to evaluate* to *difficult to evaluate*.

In general, offerings high in search properties are easiest to evaluate, those high in experience properties more difficult to evaluate, and those high in credence properties hardest to evaluate. Most services contain few search properties and are high in experience and credence properties, making their quality more difficult to evaluate than quality of goods (Zeithaml 1981).

Only two of the ten determinants—tangibles, and credibility—can be known in advance of purchase, thereby making the number of search properties few. Most of the dimensions of service quality mentioned by the focus group participants were experience properties: access, courtesy, reliability, responsiveness, understanding/knowing the customer, and communication. Each of these determinants can only be known as the customer is purchasing or consuming the service. While customers may possess some information based on their experience or on other customers' evaluations, they are likely to reevalu-

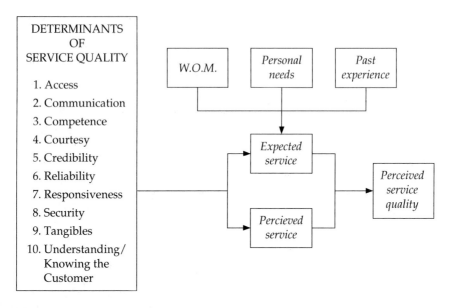

Figure 27-2
Determinants of Perceived Service Quality

ate these determinants each time a purchase is made because of the heterogeneity of services.

Two of the determinants that surfaced in the focus group interviews probably fall into the category of credence properties, those which consumers cannot evaluate even after purchase and consumption. These include competence (the possession of the required skills and knowledge to perform the service) and security (freedom from danger, risk, or doubt). Consumers are probably never certain of these attributes, even after consumption of the service.

Because few search properties exist with services and because credence properties are too difficult to evaluate, the following is proposed:

Proposition 7: Consumers typically rely on experience properties when evaluating service quality.

Based on insights from the present study, perceived service quality is further posited to exist along a continuum ranging from ideal quality to totally unacceptable quality, with some point along the continuum representing satisfactory quality. The position of a consumer's perception of service quality on the continuum depends on the nature of the discrepancy between the expected service (ES) and perceived service (PS):

Proposition 8: (a) When ES > PS, perceived quality is less than satisfactory and will tend toward totally unacceptable quality, with increased discrepancy between ES and PS; (b) when ES = PS, perceived quality is satisfactory; (c) when ES < PS, perceived quality is more than satisfactory and will tend toward ideal quality, with increased discrepancy between ES and PS.

DIRECTIONS FOR FUTURE RESEARCH

The proposed service quality model (Figure 27-1) provides a conceptual framework in an area where little prior research has been done.

It is based on an interpretation of qualitative data generated through a number of in-depth executive interviews and consumer focus groups—an approach consistent with procedures recommended for marketing theory development. The conceptual model and the propositions emerging from it imply a rich agenda for further research.

First, there is a need and an opportunity to develop a standard instrument to measure consumers' service quality perceptions. The authors' exploratory research revealed 10 evaluative dimensions or criteria which transcend a variety of services (Table 27-1). Research is now needed to generate items or statements to flesh out the 10 dimensions, to devise appropriate rating scales to measure consumers' perceptions with respect to each statement, and to condense the set of statements to produce a reliable and comprehensive but concise instrument. Further, the statements generated should be such that with appropriate changes in wording, the same instrument can be used to measure perceived quality for a variety of services.

Second, the main thesis of the service quality model is that consumers' quality perceptions are influenced by a series of distinct gaps occurring on the marketers' side. A key challenge for researchers is to devise methods to measure these gaps accurately. Reliable and valid measures of these gaps will be necessary for empirically testing the propositions implied by the model.

Third, research is needed to examine the *nature* of the association between service quality as perceived by consumers and its determinants (GAPS1–4). Specifically, are one or more of these gaps more critical than the others in affecting quality? Can creating one "favorable" gap—e.g., making GAP4 favorable by employing effective external communications to create realistic consumer expectations and to enhance consumer perceptions—offset service quality problems stemming from other gaps? Are there differences across service industries regarding the relative seriousness of service quality problems and their impact on quality as perceived by consumers? In addition to offering valuable managerial insights, answers to questions like these may suggest refinements to the proposed model.

Fourth, the usefulness of segmenting consumers on the basis of their service quality expectations is worth exploring. Although the focus groups consistently revealed similar criteria for judging service quality, the group participants differed on the *relative importance* of those criteria to them, and their *expectations* along the various quality dimensions. Empirical research aimed at determining whether distinct, identifiable service quality segments exist will be valuable from a service marketer's viewpoint. In this regard, it will be useful to build into the service quality measurement instrument certain statements for ascertaining whether, and in what ways, consumer expectations differ.

Fifth, as shown by Figure 27-1, expected service—a critical component of perceived service quality—in addition to being influenced by a marketer's communications, is shaped by word-of-mouth communications, personal needs, and past experience. Research focusing on the relative impact of these factors on consumers' service expectations, within as well as across service categories, will have useful managerial implications.

SUMMARY

The exploratory research (focus group and in-depth executive interviews) reported in this article offers several insights and propositions concerning consumers' perceptions of service quality. Specifically, the research revealed 10 dimensions that consumers use in forming expectations about and perceptions of services, dimensions that transcend different types of services. The research also pinpointed four key discrepancies or gaps on the service provider's side that are unlikely to affect service quality as perceived by consumers. The major insights gained through the research suggest a conceptual service quality model that will hopefully spawn both academic and practitioner interest in service quality and serve as a framework for further research in this important area.

REFERENCES

Anderson, Carl and Carl P. Zeithaml (1984), "Stage of the Product Life Cycle, Business Strategy, and Business Performance," *Academy of Management Journal*, 27 (March), 5–24.

Bateson, John E. G. (1977), "Do We Need Service Marketing?" in *Marketing Consumer Services: New Insights*, Cambridge, MA: Marketing Science Institute, Report #77–115.

Bellenger, Danny N., Kenneth L. Berhardt, and Jac L. Goldstucker (1976), *Qualitative Research in Marketing*, Chicago: American Marketing.

Berry, Leonard L. (1980), "Services Marketing Is Different," *Business*, 30 (May–June), 24–28.

Booms, Bernard H. and Mary J. Bitner (1981), "Marketing Strategies and Organization Structures for Services Firms," in *Marketing of Services*, J. Donnelly and W. George, eds., Chicago: American Marketing, 47–51.

Carmen, James M. and Eric Langeard (1980), "Growth Strategies of Service Firms," *Strategic Management Journal*, 1 (January–March), 7–22.

Churchill, G. A., Jr., and C. Suprenaut (1982), "An Investigation into the Determinants of Customer Satisfaction," *Journal of Marketing Research*, 19 (November), 491–504.

Crosby, Philip B. (1979), *Quality Is Free: The Art of Making Quality Certain*, New York: New American Library.

Darby, M. R. and E. Karni (1973), "Free Competition and the Optimal Amount of Fraud," *Journal of Law and Economics*, 16 (April), 67–86.

Deshpande, Rohit (1983), " 'Paradigms Lost': On Theory and Method in Research in Marketing," *Journal of Marketing*, 47 (Fall), 101–110.

Garvin, David A. (1983). "Quality on the Line," *Harvard Business Review*, 61 (September–October), 65–73.

Gronroos, Christian (1978), "A Service-Oriented Approach to Marketing of Services," *European Journal of Marketing*, 12 (no. 8), 588–601.

——— (1982), *Strategic Management and Marketing in the Service Sector*, Helsingfors: Swedish School of Economics and Business Administration.

Jacoby, Jacob, Jerry C. Olson, and Rafael A. Haddock (1973), "Price, Brand Name and Product Composition Characteristics as Determinants of Perceived Quality," *Journal of Applied Psychology*, 55 (no. 6), 570–579.

Langeard, Eric, John E. G. Bateson, Christopher H. Lovelock, and Pierre Eiglier (1981), *Service Marketing: New Insights from Consumers and Managers*, Cambridge, MA: Marketing Science Institute.

Lehtinen, Uolevi and Jarmo R. Lehtinen (1982), "Service Quality: A Study of Quality Dimensions," unpublished working paper, Helsinki: Service Management Institute, Finland OY.

Leonard, Frank S. and W. Earl Sasser (1982), "The Incline of Quality," *Harvard Business Review*, 60 (September–October), 163–171.

Lewis, Robert C. and Bernard H. Booms (1983), "The Marketing Aspects of Service Quality," in *Emerging Perspectives on Services Marketing*, L. Berry, G. Shostack, and G. Upah, eds., Chicago: American Marketing, 99–107.

Lovelock, Christopher H. (1980), "Towards a Classification of Services," in *Theoretical Developments in Marketing*, C. Lamb and P. Dunne, eds., Chicago: American Marketing, 72–76.

——— (1981), "Why Marketing Management Needs to Be Different for Services," in *Marketing of Services*, J. Donnelly and W. George, eds., Chicago: American Marketing, 5–9.

——— (1983), "Classifying Services to Gain Strategic Marketing Insights," *Journal of Marketing*, 47 (Summer), 9–20.

McConnell, J. D. (1968), "Effect of Pricing on Perception of Product Quality," *Journal of Applied Psychology*, 52 (August), 300–303.

Monroe, Kent B. and R. Krishnan (1983), "The Effect of Price on Subjective Product Evaluations," Blacksburg: Virginia Polytechnic Institute, working paper.

Nelson, P. (1974), "Advertising as Information," *Journal of Political Economy*, 81 (July/August), 729–754.

Olander, F. (1970), "The Influence of Price on the Consumer's Evaluation of Products," in *Pricing Strategy*, B. Taylor and G. Wills, eds., Princeton, NJ: Brandon/Systems Press.

Parasuraman, A. and Valerie A. Zeithaml (1982), "Differential Perceptions of Suppliers and Clients of Industrial Services," in *Emerging Perspectives on Services Marketing*, L. Berry, G. Shostack, and G. Upah, eds., Chicago: American Marketing, 35–39.

Peter, J. Paul and Jerry C. Olson (1983), "Is Science Marketing?" *Journal of Marketing*, 47 (Fall), 111–125.

Phillips, Lynn W., Dae R. Chang, and Robert D. Buzzell (1983), "Product Quality, Cost Position, and Business Performance: A Test of Some Key Hypotheses," *Journal of Marketing*, 47 (Spring), 26–43.

Rabin, Joseph H. (1983), "Accent Is on Quality in Consumer Services This Decade," *Marketing News*, 17 (March 4), 12.

Regan, William J. (1963), "The Service Revolution," *Journal of Marketing*, 27 (July), 57–62.

Sasser, W. Earl, Jr., R. Paul Olsen, and D. Daryl Wyckoff (1978), *Management of Service Operations: Text and Cases*, Boston: Allyn and Bacon.

Shapiro, Bensen (1972), "The Price of Consumer Goods: Theory and Practice," Cambridge, MA: Marketing Science Institute, working paper.

Shostack, G. Lynn (1977), "Breaking Free from Product Marketing," *Journal of Marketing*, 41 (April), 73–80.

Smith, Ruth A. and Michael J. Houston (1982), "Script-Based Evaluations of Satisfaction with Services," in *Emerging Perspectives on Services Marketing*, L. Berry, G. Shostack, and G. Upah, eds., Chicago: American Marketing, 59–62.

Takeuchi, Hirotaka and John A. Quelch (1983), "Quality Is More Than Making a Good Product," *Harvard Business Review*, 61 (July–August), 139–145.

Upah, Gregory D. (1980), "Mass Marketing in Service Retailing: A Review and Synthesis of Major Methods," *Journal of Retailing*, 56 (Fall), 59–76.

Zaltman, Gerald, Karen LeMasters, and Michael Heffring (1982), *Theory Construction in Marketing: Some Thought on Thinking*, New York: Wiley.

Zeithaml, Valarie A. (1981), "How Consumer Evaluation Processes Differ between Goods and Services," in *Marketing of Services*, J. Donnelly and W. George, eds., Chicago: American Marketing, 186–190.

PART FOUR

Competitive Marketing Programs

After buying and market behaviors have been analyzed and basic strategy formulated, marketing managers operationalize and implement strategy by combining many different decision elements into coherent competitive marketing programs. Part Four begins with Borden's seminal article describing the variable components of the marketing program and labeling them "the marketing mix." The remaining articles focus on classic expositions of the elements of the mix and their management.

Bucklin connects retail institutions to the types of goods that they market. He reviews the standard convenience/shopping/specialty goods taxonomy first introduced to the discipline in 1923 by Melvin Copeland. The product life cycle (PLC) is one of the discipline's most widely recognized managerial frameworks. Smallwood describes the conventional PLC concept and suggests how it relates to the marketing mix elements. Lambkin and Day critique the traditional product life-cycle framework and then offer a reconceptualization of it that incorporates both demand and supply factors.

Pricing is an area of concern and significance for marketing decision-makers. Most traditional pricing literature is derived from economic theories, which often make tenuous assumptions about consumer and market behaviors. Zeithaml draws on an exploratory consumer study and thorough review of past research to create an integrative framework for managing price, value, and quality. "Value oriented" marketing strategies for the 1990s can be based on principles described here. Next, Tellis presents a relatively comprehensive classification of pricing strategies and probes the many factors involved in pricing decisions.

The area of promotion in marketing is broad and diverse. Lavidge and Steiner address the purpose of advertising and present the classic "hierarchy of effects" model that describes the mental stages through which buyers pass as they respond to promotional information and make purchase decisions. Ryans and Weinberg synthesize knowledge in personal selling and sales force management, providing rich insights for implementing and directing selling efforts.

The "channel of distribution" is a distinctive concept developed in marketing thought. Stern and Reve relate political, economic, and marketing theories to create a framework for understanding and managing behaviors in distribution channels. Their work provides insights into the sociopolitical environment and interorganizational dynamics of marketing. Frazier, Spekman, and O'Neal use the exchange perspective of marketing to consider just-in-time relationships in industrial markets, a distinctive marketing context. They demonstrate the power of the exchange perspective and the importance of relationship management in marketing.

Marketing managers must evaluate and control their programs and continuously reshape strategies. Kotler, Gregor, and Rogers advocate the use of marketing audits to evaluate marketing practices and stimulate change in marketing strategies and programs. They define a marketing audit as a comprehensive, systematic, independent, and periodic performance evaluation and then highlight its structure and methods.

The Concept of the Marketing Mix

Neil H. Borden

I have always found it interesting to observe how an apt or colorful term may catch on, gain wide usage, and help to further understanding of a concept that has already been expressed in less appealing and communicative terms. Such has been true of the phrase "marketing mix," which I began to use in my teaching and writing some 15 years ago. In a relatively short time it has come to have wide usage. This note tells of the evolution of the marketing mix concept.

The phrase was suggested to me by a paragraph in a research bulletin on the management of marketing costs, written by my associate, Professor James Culliton.[1] In this study of manufacturers' marketing costs he described the business executive as a

> "decider," and "artist"—a "mixer of ingredients," who sometimes follows a recipe as he goes along, sometimes adapts a recipe to the ingredients immediately available, and sometimes experiments with or invents ingredients no one else has tried.

I liked his idea of calling a marketing executive a "mixer of ingredients," one who is constantly engaged in fashioning creatively a mix of marketing procedures and policies in his efforts to produce a profitable enterprise.

For many years previous to Culliton's cost study the wide variations in the procedures and policies employed by managements of manufacturing firms in their marketing programs and the correspondingly wide variation in the costs of these marketing functions, which Culliton aptly ascribed to the varied "mixing of ingredients," had become increasingly evident as we had gathered marketing cases at the Harvard Business School. The marked differences in the patterns or formulae of the marketing programs not only were evident through facts disclosed in case histories, but also were reflected clearly in the figures of a cost study of food manufacturers made by the Harvard Bureau of Business Research in 1929. The primary objective of this study was to determine common figures of expenses for various marketing functions among food manufacturing companies, similar to the common cost figures which had

Reprinted from *Journal of Advertising Research*, © Advertising Research Foundation, Inc. (June, 1964), pp. 2–7.

been determined in previous years for various kinds of retail and wholesale businesses. In this manufacturer's study we were unable, however, with the data gathered to determine common expense figures that had much significance as standards by which to guide management, such as had been possible in the studies of retail and wholesale trades, where the methods of operation tended toward uniformity. Instead, among food manufacturers the ratios of sales devoted to the various functions of marketing such as advertising, personal selling, packaging, and so on, were found to be widely divergent, no matter how we grouped our respondents. Each respondent gave data that tended to uniqueness.

Culliton's study of marketing costs in 1947–48 was a second effort to find out, among other objectives, whether a bigger sample and a more careful classification of companies would produce evidence of operating uniformities that would give helpful common expense figures. But the result was the same as in our early study: there was wide diversity in cost ratios among any classifications of firms which were set up, and no common figures were found that had much value. This was true whether companies were grouped according to similarity in product lines, amount of sales, territorial extent of operations, or other bases of classification.

Relatively early in my study of advertising, it had become evident that understanding of advertising usage by manufacturers in any case had to come from an analysis of advertising's place as one element in the total marketing program of the firm. I came to realize that it is essential always to ask: what overall marketing strategy has been or might be employed to bring about a profitable operation in light of the circumstances faced by the management? What combination of marketing procedures and policies has been or might be adopted to bring about desired behavior of trade and consumers at costs that will permit

a profit? Specifically, how can advertising, personal selling, pricing, packaging, channels, warehousing, and the other elements of a marketing program be manipulated and fitted together in a way that will give a profitable operation? In short, I saw that every advertising management case called for a consideration of the strategy to be adopted for the total marketing program, with advertising recognized as only one element whose form and extent depended on its careful adjustment to the other parts of the program.

The soundness of this viewpoint was supported by case histories throughout my volume, *The Economic Effects of Advertising.*[2] In the chapters devoted to the utilization of advertising by business, I had pointed out the innumerable combinations of marketing methods and policies that might be adopted by a manager in arriving at a marketing plan. For instance, in the area of branding, he might elect to adopt an individualized brand or a family brand. Or he might decide to sell his product unbranded or under private label. Any decision in the area of brand policy in turn has immediate implications that bear on his selection of channels of distribution, sales force methods, packaging, promotional procedure, and advertising. Throughout the volume the case materials cited show that the way in which any marketing function is designed and the burden placed upon the function are determined largely by the overall marketing strategy adopted by managements to meet the market conditions under which they operate. The forces met by different firms vary widely. Accordingly, the programs fashioned differ widely.

Regarding advertising, which was the function under forces in the economic effects volume, I said at one point:

In all the above illustrative situations it should be recognized that advertising is not an operating method to be considered as something apart, as something whose profit value is to be judged alone. An able management does not ask, "Shall we use or not use advertising," without consideration of the product and of other management procedures to be employed. Rather the question is always one of finding a management formula giving advertising its due place in the combination of manufacturing methods, product form, pricing, promotion and selling methods, and distribution methods. As previously pointed out different formulae, i.e., different combinations of methods, may be profitably employed by competing manufacturers.

From the above it can be seen why Culliton's description of a marketing manager as a "mixer of ingredients" immediately appealed to me as an apt and easily understandable phrase, far better than my previous references to the marketing man as an empiricist seeking in any situation to devise a profitable "pattern" or "formula" of marketing operations from among the many procedures and policies that were open to him. If he was a "mixer of ingredients," what he designed was a "marketing mix."

It was logical to proceed from a realization of the existence of a variety of "marketing mixes" to the development of a concept that would comprehend not only this variety, but also the market forces that cause management to produce a variety of mixes. It is the problems raised by these forces that lead marketing managers to exercise their wits in devising mixes or programs which they hope will give a profitable business operation.

To portray this broadened concept in a visual presentation requires merely:

1. A list of the important elements or ingredients that make up marketing programs.
2. A list of the forces that bear on the marketing operation of a firm and to which the marketing manager must adjust in his search for a mix or program that can be successful.

The list of elements of the marketing mix in such a visual presentation can be long or short, depending on how far one wishes to go in his classification and sub-classification of the marketing procedures and policies with which marketing managements deal when devising marketing programs. The list of elements which I have employed in my teaching and consulting work covers the principal areas of marketing activities which call for management decisions as revealed by case histories. I realize others might build a different list. Mine is as follows:

Elements of the Marketing Mix of Manufacturers

1. *Product Planning*—policies and procedures relating to:
   a. Product lines to be offered—qualities, design, etc.
   b. Markets to sell—whom, where, when, and in what quantity.
   c. New product policy—research and development program.
2. *Pricing*—policies and procedures relating to:
   a. Price level to adopt.
   b. Specific prices to adopt—odd-even, etc.
   c. Price policy—one price or varying price, price maintenance, use of list prices, etc.
   d. Margins to adopt—for company, for the trade.
3. *Branding*—policies and procedures relating to:
   a. Selection of trade marks.
   b. Brand policy—individualized or family brand.
   c. Sale under private label or unbranded.
4. *Channels of Distribution*—policies and procedures relating to:
   a. Channels to use between plant and consumer.

b. Degree of selectivity among wholesalers and retailers.

c. Efforts to gain cooperation of the trade.

5. *Personal Selling*—policies and procedures relating to:

a. Burden to be placed on personal selling and the methods to be employed in:
1. Manufacturer's organization.
2. Wholesale segment of the trade.
3. Retail segment of the trade.

6. *Advertising*—policies and procedures relating to:

a. Amount to spend—i.e., the burden to be placed on advertising.

b. Copy platform to adopt:
1. Product image desired.
2. Corporate image desired.

c. Mix of advertising—to the trade, through the trade, to consumers.

7. *Promotions*—policies and procedures relating to:

a. Burden to place on special selling plans or devices directed at or through the trade.

b. Form of these devices for consumer promotions, for trade promotions.

8. *Packaging*—policies and procedures relating to:

a. Formulation of package and label.

9. *Display*—policies and procedures relating to:

a. Burden to be put on display to help effect sale.

b. Methods to adopt to secure display.

10. *Servicing*—policies and procedures relating to:

a. Providing service needed.

11. *Physical Handling*—policies and procedures relating to:

a. Warehousing.

b. Transportation.

c. Inventories.

12. *Fact Finding and Analysis*—policies and procedures relating to:

a. Securing, analysis, and the use of facts in marketing operations.

Also, if one were to make a list of all the forces which managements weigh at one time or another when formulating their marketing mixes, it would be very long indeed, for the behavior of individuals and groups in all spheres of life has a bearing, first, on what goods and services are produced and consumed, and second, on the procedures that may be employed in bringing about exchange of these goods and services. However, the important forces which bear on marketers, all arising from the behavior of individuals or groups, may readily be listed under four heads, namely, the behavior of consumers, the trade, competitors, and government.

The next outline contains these four behavior forces with notations of some of the important behavioral determinants within each force. These must be studied and understood by the marketer, if his marketing mix is to be successful. The great quest of marketing management is to understand the behavior of humans in response to the stimuli to which they are subjected. The skillful marketer is one who is a perceptive and practical psychologist and sociologist, who has keen insight into individual and group behavior, who can foresee changes in behavior that develop in a dynamic world, who has creative ability for building well-knit programs because he has the capacity to visualize the probable response of consumers, trade, and competitors to his moves. His skill in forecasting response to his marketing moves should well be supplemented by a further skill in devising and using tests and measurements to check consumer or trade response to his program or parts thereof, for no marketer has so much prescience that he can proceed without empirical check.

Here, then, is the suggested outline of forces which govern the mixing of marketing elements. This list and that of the elements taken together provide a visual presentation of the concept of the marketing mix.

Market Forces Bearing on the Marketing Mix

1. *Consumers' Buying Behavior*—as determined by their:
   a. Motivation in purchasing.
   b. Buying habits.
   c. Living habits.
   d. Environment (present and future, as revealed by trends, for environment influences consumers' attitudes toward products and their use of them).
   e. Buying power.
   f. Number (i.e., how many).
2. *The Trade's Behavior*—wholesalers' and retailers' behavior, as influenced by:
   a. Their motivations.
   b. Their structure, practices, and attitudes.
   c. Trends in structure and procedures that portend change.
3. *Competitors' Position and Behavior*—as influenced by:
   a. Industry structure and the firm's relation thereto.
      1. Size and strength of competitors.
      2. Number of competitors and degree of industry concentration.
      3. Indirect competition—i.e., from other products.
   b. Relation of supply to demand—oversupply or undersupply.
   c. Product choices offered consumers by the industry—i.e., quality, price, service.
   d. Degree to which competitors compete on price vs. nonprice bases.
   e. Competitors' motivations and attitudes—their likely response to the actions of other firms.

   f. Trends technological and social, portending change in supply and demand.
4. *Government Behavior*—controls over marketing:
   a. Regulations over products.
   b. Regulations over pricing.
   c. Regulations over competitive practices.
   d. Regulations over advertising and promotion.

When building a marketing program to fit the needs of his firm, the marketing manager has to weigh the behavioral forces and then juggle marketing elements in his mix with a keen eye on the resources with which he has to work. His firm is but one small organism in a large universe of complex forces. His firm is only a part of an industry that is competing with many other industries. What does the firm have in terms of money, product line, organization, and reputation with which to work? The manager must devise a mix of procedures that fit these resources. If his firm is small, he must judge the response of consumers, trade, and competition in light of his position and resources and the influence that he can exert in the market. He must look for special opportunities in product or method of operation. The small firm cannot employ the procedures of the big firm. Though he may sell the same kind of product as the big firm, his marketing strategy is likely to be widely different in many respects. Innumerable instances of this fact might be cited. For example, in the industrial goods field, small firms often seek to build sales on a limited and highly specialized line, whereas industry leaders seek patronage for full lines. Small firms often elect to go in for regional sales rather than attempt the national distribution practiced by larger companies. Again, the company of limited resources often elects to limit its production and sales to products whose potential is too small to attract the big fellows. Still again, companies with small resources in the cosmetic field not infrequently have set up introductory marketing programs employing aggressive personal selling and a "push" strategy with distribution limited to leading department stores. Their initially small advertising funds have been directed through these selected retail outlets, with the offering of the products and their story told over the signatures of the stores. The strategy has been to borrow kudos for their products from the leading stores' reputations and to gain a gradual radiation of distribution to smaller stores in all types of channels, such as often comes from the trade's follow-the-leader behavior. Only after resources have grown from mounting sales has a dense retail distribution been aggressively sought and a shift made to place the selling burden more and more on company-signed advertising.

The above strategy was employed for Toni products and Stoppette deodorant in their early marketing stages when the resources of their producers were limited (cf. case of Jules Montenier, Inc. in Borden and Marshall).[3] In contrast, cosmetic manufacturers with large resources have generally followed a "pull" strategy for the introduction of new products, relying on heavy campaigns of advertising in a rapid succession of area introductions to induce a hoped-for, complete retail coverage from the start (cf. case of Bristol-Myers Company in Borden and Marshall).[4] These introductory campaigns have been undertaken only after careful programs of product development and test marketing have given assurance that product and selling plans had high promise of success.

Many additional instances of the varying strategy employed by small versus large enterprises might be cited. But those given serve to illustrate the point that managements must fashion their mixes to fit their resources. Their objectives must be realistic.

LONG VS. SHORT TERM ASPECTS OF MARKETING MIX

The marketing mix of a firm in a large part is the product of the evolution that comes from day-to-day marketing. At any time the mix represents the program that a management has evolved to meet the problems with which it is constantly faced in an ever-changing, ever-challenging market. There are continuous tactical maneuvers: a new product, aggressive promotion, or price-change initiated by a competitor must be considered and met; the failure of the trade to provide adequate market coverage or display must be remedied; a faltering sales force must be reorganized and stimulated; a decline in sales share must be diagnosed and remedied; an advertising approach that has lost effectiveness must be replaced; a general business decline must be countered. All such problems call for a management's maintaining effective channels of information relative to its own operations and to the day-to-day behavior of consumers, competitors, and the trade. Thus, we may observe that short-range forces play a large part in the fashioning of the mix to be used at any time and in determining the allocation of expenditures among the various functional accounts of the operating statement.

But the overall strategy employed in a marketing mix is the product of longer-range plans and procedures dictated in part by past empiricism and in part, if the management is a good one, by management foresight as to what needs to be done to keep the firm successful in a changing world. As the world has become more and more dynamic, blessed is that corporation which has managers who have foresight, who can study trends of all kinds—natural, economic, social, and technological—and, guided by these, devise long-range plans that give promise of keeping their corporations afloat and successful in the turbulent sea of market change. Accordingly, when we think of the marketing mix, we need to give particular heed today to devising a mix based on long-range planning that promises to fit the world of five or ten or more years hence. Provision for effective long-range planning in corporate organization and procedure has become more and more recognized as the earmark of good management in a world that has become increasingly subject to rapid change.

To cite an instance among American marketing organizations which have shown foresight in adjusting the marketing mix to meet social and economic change, I look upon Sears Roebuck and Company as an outstanding example. After building an unusually successful mail order business to meet the needs of a rural America, Sears management foresaw the need to depart from its marketing pattern as a mail order company catering primarily to farmers. The trend from a rural to an urban United States was going on apace. The automobile and good roads promised to make town and city stores increasingly available to those who continued to be farmers. Relatively early, Sears launched a chain of stores across the land, each easily accessible by highway to both farmer and city resident, and with adequate parking space for customers. In time there followed the remarkable telephone and mail order plan directed at urban residents to make buying easy for Americans when congested city streets and highways made shopping increasingly distasteful. Similarly, in the areas of planning products which would meet the desires of consumers in a fast-changing world, of shaping its servicing to meet the needs of a wide variety of mechanical products, of pricing procedures to meet the challenging competition that came with the advent of discount retailers, the Sears organization has shown a foresight, adaptability,

and creative ability worthy of emulation. The amazing growth and profitability of the company attest to the foresight and skill of its managements. Its history shows the wisdom of careful attention to market forces and their impending change in devising marketing mixes that may assure growth.

USE OF THE MARKETING MIX CONCEPT

Like many concepts, the marketing mix concept seems relatively simple, once it has been expressed. I know that before they were ever tagged with the nomenclature of "concept," the ideas involved were widely understood among marketers as a result of the growing knowledge about marketing and marketing procedures that came during the preceding half century. But I have found for myself that once the ideas were reduced to a formal statement with an accompanying visual presentation, the concept of the mix has proved a helpful advice in teaching, in business problem solving, and, generally, as an aid to thinking about marketing. First of all, it is helpful in giving an answer to the question often raised as to "what is marketing?" A chart which shows the elements of the mix and the forces that bear on the mix helps to bring understanding of what marketing is. It helps to explain why in our dynamic world the thinking of management in all functional areas must be oriented to the market.

In recent years I have kept an abbreviated chart showing the elements and the forces of the marketing mix in front of my classes at all times. In case discussion it has proved a handy device by which to raise queries as to whether the student has recognized the implications of any recommendation he might have made in the areas of the several elements of the mix. Or, referring to the forces, we can question whether all the pertinent market forces have been given due consideration. Continual reference to the mix chart leads me to feel that the students' understanding of "what marketing is" is strengthened. The constant presence and use of the chart leaves a deeper understanding that marketing is the devising of programs that successfully meet the forces of the market.

In problem solving the marketing mix chart is a constant reminder of:

1. The fact that a problem seemingly lying in one segment of the mix must be deliberated with constant thought regarding the effect of any change in that sector on the other areas of marketing operations. The necessity of integration in marketing thinking is ever present.
2. The need of careful study of the market forces as they might bear on problems in hand.

In short, the mix chart provides an ever-ready checklist as to areas into which to guide thinking when considering marketing questions or dealing with marketing problems.

MARKETING: SCIENCE OR ART?

The quest for a "science of marketing" is hard upon us. If science is in part a systematic formulation and arrangement of facts in a way to help understanding, then the concept of the marketing mix may possibly be considered a small contribution in the search for a science of marketing. If we think of a marketing science as involving the observation and classification of facts and the establishment of verifiable laws that can be used by the marketer as a guide to action with assurance that predicted results will ensue, then we cannot be said to have gotten far toward establishing

a science. The concept of the mix lays out the areas in which facts should be assembled, these to serve as a guide to management judgment in building marketing mixes. In the last few decades American marketers have made substantial progress in adopting the scientific method in assembling facts. They have sharpened the tools of fact finding—both those arising within the business and those external to it. Aided by these facts and by the skills developed through careful observation and experience, marketers are better fitted to practice the art of designing marketing mixes than would be the case had not the techniques of gathering facts been advanced as they have been in recent decades. Moreover, marketers have made progress in the use of the scientific method in designing tests whereby the results from mixes or parts of mixes can be measured. Thereby marketers have been learning how to subject the hypotheses of their mix artists to empirical check.

With continued improvement in the search for and the recording of facts pertinent to marketing, with further application of the controlled experiment, and with an extension and careful recording of case histories, we may hope for a gradual formulation of clearly defined and helpful marketing laws. Until then, and even then, marketing and the building of marketing mixes will largely lie in the realm of art.

NOTES

1. James W. Culliton, *The Management of Marketing Costs* (Boston: Division of Research, Graduate School of Business Administration, Harvard University, 1948).
2. Neil H. Borden, *The Economic Effects of Advertising* (Homewood, Illinois: Richard D. Irwin, 1942).
3. Neil H. Borden and M. V. Marshall, *Advertising Management: Text and Cases* (Homewood, Illinois: Richard D. Irwin, 1959), pp. 498–518.
4. *Ibid.*, pp. 518–33.

◆

Retail Strategy and the Classification of Consumer Goods

Louis P. Bucklin

When Melvin T. Copeland published his famous discussion of the classification of consumer goods, shopping, convenience, and specialty goods, his intent was clearly to create a guide for the development of marketing strategies by manufacturers.[1] Although his discussion involved retailers and retailing, his purpose was to show how consumer buying habits affected the type of channel of distribution and promotional strategy that a manufacturer should adopt. Despite the controversy which still surrounds his classification, his success in creating such a guide may be judged by the fact that through the years few marketing texts have failed to make use of his ideas.

The purpose of this article is to attempt to clarify some of the issues that exist with respect to the classification, and to extend the concept to include the retailer and the study of retail strategy.

Reprinted from *Journal of Marketing*, published by the American Marketing Association (January, 1963), pp. 51–56.

CONTROVERSY OVER THE CLASSIFICATION SYSTEM

The starting point for the discussion lies with the definitions adopted by the American Marketing Association's Committee on Definitions for the classification system in 1948.[2] These are:

Convenience Goods: Those consumers' goods which the customer purchases frequently, immediately, and with the minimum of effort.

Shopping Goods: Those consumers' goods which the customer in the process of selection and purchase characteristically compares on such bases as suitability, quality, price and style.

Specialty Goods: Those consumers' goods on which a significant group of buyers are habitually willing to make a special purchasing effort.

This set of definitions was retained in virtually the same form by the Committee on Definitions in its latest publication.[3]

429

Opposing these accepted definitions stands a critique by Richard H. Holton.[4] Finding the Committee's definitions too imprecise to be able to measure consumer buying behavior, he suggested that the following definitions not only would represent the essence of Copeland's original idea, but be operationally more useful as well.

Convenience Goods: Those goods for which the consumer regards the probable gain from making price and quality comparisons as small compared to the cost of making such comparisons.

Shopping Goods: Those goods for which the consumer regards the probable gain from making price and quality comparisons as large relative to the cost of making such comparisons.

Specialty Goods: Those convenience or shopping goods, which have such a limited market as to require the consumer to make a special effort to purchase them.

Holton's definitions have particular merit because they make explicit the underlying conditions that control the extent of a consumer's shopping activities. They show that a consumer's buying behavior will be determined not only by the strength of his desire to secure some good, but by his perception of the cost of shopping to obtain it. In other words, the consumer continues to shop for *all goods* so long as he feels that the additional satisfaction from further comparisons are at least equal to the cost of making the additional effort. The distinction between shopping and convenience goods lies principally in the degree of satisfaction to be secured from further comparisons.

The Specialty Good Issue

While Holton's conceptualization makes an important contribution, he has sacrificed some of the richness of Copeland's original ideas. This is essentially David J. Luck's complaint in a criticism of Holton's proposal.[5] Luck objected to the abandonment of the *willingness* of consumers to make a special effort to buy as the rationale for the concept of specialty goods. He regarded this type of consumer behavior as based upon unique consumer attitudes toward certain goods and not the density of distribution of those goods. Holten, in a reply, rejected Luck's point; he remained convinced that the real meaning of specialty goods could be derived from his convenience goods, shopping goods continuum, and market conditions.[6]

The root of the matter appears to be that insufficient attention has been paid to the fact that the consumer, once embarked upon some buying expedition, may have only one of two possible objectives in mind. A discussion of this aspect of consumer behavior will make possible a closer synthesis of Holton's contributions with the more traditional point of view.

A Forgotten Idea

The basis for this discussion is afforded by certain statements, which the marketing profession has largely ignored over the years, in Copeland's original presentation of his ideas. These have regard to the extent of the consumer's awareness of the precise nature of the item he wished to buy, *before* he starts his shopping trip. Copeland stated that the consumer, in both the case of convenience goods and specialty goods, has full knowledge of the particular good, or its acceptable substitutes, that he will buy before he commences his buying trip. The consumer, however, lacks this knowledge in the case of a shopping good.[7] This means that the buying trip must not only serve the objective of purchasing the good, but must enable the consumer to discover which item he wants to buy.

The behavior of the consumer during any shopping expedition may, as a result, be regarded as heavily dependent upon the state of his decision as to what he wants to buy. If the consumer knows precisely what he wants, he needs only to undertake communication activities sufficient to take title to the desired product. He may also undertake ancillary physical activities involving the handling of the product and delivery. If the consumer is uncertain as to what he wants to buy, then an additional activity will have to be performed. This involves the work of making comparisons between possible alternative purchases, or simply search.

There would be little point, with respect to the problem of classifying consumer goods, in distinguishing between the activity of search and that of making a commitment to buy, if a consumer always performed both before purchasing a good. The crucial point is that he does not. While most of the items that a consumer buys have probably been subjected to comparison at some point in his life, he does not make a search before each purchase. Instead, a past solution to the need is frequently remembered and, if satisfactory, is implemented.[8] Use of these past decisions for many products quickly moves the consumer past any perceived necessity of undertaking new comparisons and leaves only the task of exchange to be discharged.

REDEFINITION OF THE SYSTEM

Use of the concept of problem solving permits one to classify consumer buying efforts into two broad categories which may be called shopping and nonshopping goods.

Shopping Goods

Shopping goods are those for which the consumer *regularly* formulates a new solution to his need each time it is aroused. They are goods whose suitability is determined through search before the consumer commits himself to each purchase.

The motivation behind this behavior stems from circumstances which tend to perpetuate a lack of complete consumer knowledge about the nature of the product that he would like to buy.[9] Frequent changes in price, style, or product technology cause consumer information to become obsolete. The greater the time lapse between purchases, the more obsolete will his information be. The consumer's needs are also subject to change, or he may seek variety in his purchases as an actual goal. These forces will tend to make past information inappropriate. New search, due to forces internal and external to the consumer, is continuously required for products with purchase determinants which the consumer regards as both important and subject to change.[10]

The number of comparisons that the consumer will make in purchasing a shopping good may be determined by use of Holton's hypothesis on effort. The consumer, in other words, will undertake search for a product until the perceived value to be secured through additional comparisons is less than the estimated cost of making those comparisons. Thus, shopping effort will vary according to the intensity of the desire of the consumer to find the right product, the type of product and availability of retail facilities. Whether the consumer searches diligently, superficially, or even buys at the first opportunity, however, does not alter the shopping nature of the product.

Nonshopping Goods

Turning now to nonshopping goods, one may define these as products for which the consumer is both willing and able to use stored solutions to the problem of finding a product to answer a need. From the remarks on shopping goods it may be generalized that nonshopping goods have purchase determinants which do not change, or which are perceived as changing inconsequentially, between purchases.[11] The consumer, for example, may assume that price for some product never changes or that price is unimportant. It may be unimportant because either the price is low, or the consumer is very wealthy.

Nonshopping goods may be divided into convenience and specialty goods by means of the concept of a preference map. Bayton introduces this concept as the means to show how the consumer stores information about products.[12] It is a rough ranking of the relative desirability of the different kinds of products that the consumer sees as possible satisfiers for his needs. For present purposes, two basic types of preference maps may be envisaged. One type ranks all known product alternatives equally in terms of desirability. The other ranks one particular product as so superior to all others that the consumer, in effect, believes this product is the only answer to his need.

Distinguishing the Specialty Good

This distinction in preference maps creates the basis for discriminating between a convenience good and a specialty good. Clearly, where the consumer is indifferent to the precise item among a number of substitutes which he could buy, he will purchase the most accessible one and look no further. This is a convenience good. On the other hand, where the consumer recognizes only one brand of a product as capable of satisfying his needs, he will be willing to bypass more readily accessible substitutes in order to secure the wanted item. This is a specialty good.

However, most nonshopping goods will probably fall in between these two polar extremes. Preference maps will exist where

the differences between the relative desirability of substitutes may range from the slim to the well marked. In order to distinguish between convenience goods and specialty goods in these cases, Holton's hypothesis regarding consumer effort may be employed again. A convenience good, in these terms, becomes one for which the consumer has such little preference among his perceived choices that he buys the item which is most readily available. A specialty good is one for which consumer preference is so strong that he bypasses, or would be willing to bypass, the purchase of more accessible substitutes in order to secure his most wanted item.

It should be noted that this decision on the part of the consumer as to how much effort he should expend takes place under somewhat different conditions than the one for shopping goods. In the nonshopping good instance the consumer has a reasonably good estimate of the additional value to be achieved by purchasing his preferred item. The estimate of the additional cost required to make this purchase may also be made fairly accurately. Consequently, the consumer will be in a much better position to justify the expenditure of additional effort here than in the case of shopping goods where much uncertainty must exist with regard to both of these factors.

THE NEW CLASSIFICATION

The classification of consumer goods that results from the analysis is as follows:

Convenience Goods: Those goods for which the consumer, before his need arises, possesses a preference map that indicates a willingness to purchase any of a number of known substitutes rather than to make the additional effort required to buy a particular item.

Shopping Goods: Those goods for which the consumer has not developed a complete preference map before the need arises, requiring him to undertake search to construct such a map before purchase.

Specialty Goods: Those goods for which the consumer, before his need arises, possesses a preference map that indicates a willingness to expend the additional effort required to purchase the most preferred item rather than to buy a more readily accessible substitute.

EXTENSION TO RETAILING

The classification of the goods concept developed above may now be extended to retailing. As the concept now stands, it is derived from consumer attitudes or motives toward a *product*. These attitudes, or product motives, are based upon the consumer's interpretation of a product's styling, special features, quality, and social status of its brand name, if any. Occasionally the price may also be closely associated with the product by the consumer.

Classification of Patronage Motives

The extension of the concept to retailing may be made through the notion of patronage motives, a term long used in marketing. Patronage motives are derived from consumer attitudes concerning the retail establishment. They are related to factors which the consumer is likely to regard as controlled by the retailer. These will include assortment, credit, service, guarantee, shopping ease and enjoyment, and usually price. Patronage motives, however, have never been systematically categorized. It is proposed that the procedure developed above to discriminate among product motives be used to classify consumer buying motives with respect to retail stores as well.

This will provide the basis for the consideration of retail marketing strategy and will aid in clearing up certain ambiguities that would otherwise exist if consumer buying motives were solely classified by product factors. These ambiguities appear, for example, when the consumer has a strong affinity for some particular brand of a product, but little interest in where he buys it. The manufacturer of the product, as a result, would be correct in defining the product as a specialty item if the consumer's preferences were so strong as to cause him to eschew more readily available substitutes. The retailer may regard it as a convenience good, however, since the consumer will make no special effort to purchase the good from any particular store. This problem is clearly avoided by separately classifying product and patronage motives.

The categorization of patronage motives by the above procedure results in the following three definitions. These are:

Convenience Stores: Those stores for which the consumer, before his need for some product arises, possesses a preference map that indicates a willingness to buy from the most accessible store.

Shopping Stores: Those stores for which the consumer has not developed a complete preference map relative to the product he wishes to buy, requiring him to undertake a search to construct such a map before purchase.

Specialty Stores: Those stores for which the consumer, before his need for some product arises, possesses a preference map that indicates a willingness to buy the item from a particular establishment even though it may not be the most accessible.

The Product-Patronage Matrix

Although this basis will not afford the retailer a means to consider alternative strategies, a finer classification system may be obtained by relating consumer product motives to consumer patronage motives. By cross-classifying each product motive with each patronage motive, one creates a three-by-three matrix, representing nine possible types of consumer buying behavior. Each of the nine cells in the matrix may be described as follows:

1. *Convenience Store—Convenience Good:* The consumer, represented by this category, prefers to buy the most readily available brand of product at the most accessible store.
2. *Convenience Store—Shopping Good:* The consumer selects his purchase from among the assortment carried by the most accessible store.
3. *Convenience Store—Specialty Good:* The consumer purchases his favored brand from the most accessible store which has item in stock.
4. *Shopping Store—Convenience Good:* The consumer is indifferent to the brand of product he buys, but shops among different stores in order to secure better retail service and/or lower retail price.
5. *Shopping Store—Shopping Good:* The consumer makes comparisons among both retail controlled factors and factors associated with the product (brand).
6. *Shopping Store—Specialty Good:* The consumer has a strong preference with respect to the brand of the product, but shops among a number of stores in order to secure the best retail and/or price for this brand.
7. *Specialty Store—Convenience Good:* The consumer prefers to trade at a specific store, but is indifferent to the brand of product purchased.
8. *Specialty Store—Shopping Good:* The consumer prefers to trade at a certain store, but is uncertain as to which product he wishes to buy and examines the store's assortment for the best purchase.

9. *Specialty Store—Specialty Good:* The consumer has both a preference for a particular store and a specific brand.

Conceivably, each of these nine types of behavior might characterize the buying patterns of some consumers for a given product. It seems more likely, however, that the behavior of consumers toward a product could be represented by only three or four of the categories. The remaining cells would be empty, indicating that no consumers bought the product by these methods. Different cells, of course, would be empty for different products.

THE FORMATION OF RETAIL STRATEGY

The extended classification system developed above clearly provides additional information important to the manufacturer in the planning of his marketing strategy. Of principal interest here, however, is the means by which the retailer might use the classification system in planning his marketing strategy.

Three Basic Steps

The procedure involves three steps. The first is the classification of the retailer's potential customers for some product by market segment, using the nine categories in the consumer buying habit matrix to define the principal segments. The second requires the retailer to determine the nature of the marketing strategies necessary to appeal to each market segment. The final step is the retailer's selection of the market segment, and the strategy associated with it, to which he will sell. A simplified, hypothetical example may help to clarify this process.

A former buyer of dresses for a department store decided to open her own dress shop. She rented a small store in the downtown area of a city of 50,000, ten miles distant from a metropolitan center of several hundred thousand population. In contemplating her marketing strategy, she was certain that the different incomes, educational backgrounds, and tastes of the potential customers in her city meant that various groups of these women were using sharply different buying methods for dresses. Her initial problem was to determine, by use of the consumer buying habit matrix, what proportion of her potential market bought dresses in what manner.

By drawing on her own experience, discussions with other retailers in the area, census and other market data, the former buyer estimated that her potential market was divided, according to the matrix, in the proportions [shown in Table 29-1].

This analysis revealed four market segments that she believed were worth further consideration. (In an actual situation, each of these four should be further divided into sub-market segments according to other possible

Table 29-1
Proportion of Potential Dress Market in Each Matrix Cell

Buying Habit	% of Market
Convenience store—convenience good	0
Convenience store—shopping good	3
Convenience store—specialty good	20
Shopping store—convenience good	0
Shopping store—shopping good	35
Shopping store—specialty good	2
Specialty store—convenience good	0
Specialty store—shopping good	25
Specialty store—specialty good	15
	100

factors such as age, income, dress size required, location of residence, etc.) Her next task was to determine the type of marketing mix which would most effectively appeal to each of these segments. The information for these decisions was derived from the characteristics of consumer behavior associated with each of the defined segments. The following is a brief description of her assessment of how elements of the marketing mix ought to be weighted in order to formulate a strategy for each segment.

A Strategy for Each Segment

To appeal to the convenience store—specialty good segment she felt that the two most important elements in the mix should be a highly accessible location and selection of widely-accepted brand merchandise. Of somewhat lesser importance, she found, were depth of assortment, personal selling and price. Minimal emphasis should be given to store promotion and facilities.

She reasoned that the shopping store—shopping good requires a good central location, emphasis on price, and a broad assortment. She ranked store promotion, accepted brand names and personal selling as secondary. Store facilities would, once again, receive minor emphasis.

The specialty store—shopping good market would, she believed, have to be catered to with an exceptionally strong assortment, a high level of personal selling and more elaborate store facilities. Less emphasis would be needed upon prominent brand names, store promotions, and price. Location was of minor importance.

The specialty store—specialty good category, she thought, would require a marketing mix heavily emphasizing personal selling and highly elaborate store facilities and service. She also felt that prominent brand names would be required, but that these would probably have to include the top names in fashion, including labels from Paris. Depth of assortment would be secondary, while least emphasis would be placed upon store promotion, price, and location.

Evaluation of Alternatives

The final step in the analysis required the former dress buyer to assess her abilities to implement any one of these strategies, given the degree of competition existing in each segment. Her considerations were as follows. With regard to the specialty store—specialty good market, she was unprepared to make the investment in store facilities and services that she felt would be necessary. She also thought, since a considerable period of time would probably be required for her to build up the necessary reputation, that this strategy involved substantial risk. Lastly, she believed that her experience in buying high fashion was somewhat limited and that trips to European fashion centers would prove burdensome.

She also doubted her ability to cater to the specialty store—shopping good market, principally because she knew that her store would not be large enough to carry the necessary assortment depth. She felt that this same factor would limit her in attempting to sell to the shopping store—shopping good market as well. Despite the presence of the large market in this segment, she believed that she would not be able to create sufficient volume in her proposed quarters to enable her to compete effectively with the local department store and several large department stores in the neighboring city.

The former buyer believed her best opportunity was in selling to the convenience store—specialty good segment. While there were already two other stores in her city which were serving this segment, she believed that a number of important brands were still not represented. Her past contacts with resources led her to believe that she would stand an excellent chance of securing a number of these lines. By stocking these brands, she thought that she could capture a considerable number of local customers who currently were purchasing them in the large city. In this way, she believed, she would avoid the full force of local competition.

Decision

The conclusion of the former buyer to use her store to appeal to the convenience store—specialty good segment represents the culmination to the process of analysis suggested here. It shows how the use of the three-by-three matrix of consumer buying habits may aid the retailer in developing his marketing strategy. It is a device which can isolate the important market segments. It provides further help in enabling the retailer to associate the various types of consumer behavior with those elements of the marketing mix to which they are sensitive. Finally, the analysis forces the retailer to assess the probability of his success in attempting to use the necessary strategy in order to sell each possible market.

NOTES

1. Melvin T. Copeland, "Relation of Consumers' Buying Habits to Marketing Methods," *Harvard Business Review* (April, 1923), pp. 282–289.
2. Definitions Committee, American Marketing Association, "Report of the Definitions Committee," *Journal of Marketing* (October, 1948), pp. 202–217, at p. 206, p. 215.
3. Definitions Committee, American Marketing Association, *Marketing Definitions*, (Chicago: American Marketing Association, 1960), pp. 11, 21, 22.
4. Richard H. Holton, "The Distinction between Convenience Goods, Shopping Goods, and Specialty Goods," *Journal of Marketing* (July, 1958), pp. 53–56.

5. David J. Luck, "On the Nature of Specialty Goods," *Journal of Marketing* (July, 1959), pp. 61–64.

6. Richard H. Holton, "What Is Really Meant by 'Specialty Goods'?" *Journal of Marketing* (July, 1959), pp. 64–67.

7. Melvin T. Copeland, same reference as footnote 1, pp. 283–284.

8. George Katona, *Psychological Analysis of Economic Behavior* (New York: McGraw-Hill Book Co., Inc., 1951), p. 47

9. Same reference, pp. 67–68.

10. George Katona and Eva Mueller, "A Study of Purchase Decisions in Consumer Behavior," Lincoln Clark, editor, *Consumer Behavior* (New York: University Press, 1954), pp. 30–87.

11. Katona, same reference as footnote 8, p. 68.

12. James A. Bayton, "Motivation, Cognition, Learning—Basic Factors in Consumer Behavior," *Journal of Marketing* (January, 1958), pp. 282–289, at p. 287.

◆

The Product Life Cycle: A Key to Strategic Marketing Planning

John E. Smallwood

Modern marketing management today increasingly is being supported by marketing information services of growing sophistication and improving accuracy. Yet the task remains for the marketing manager to translate information into insights, insights into ideas, ideas into plans, and plans into reality and satisfactory programs and profits. Among marketing managers there is a growing realization of the need for concepts, perspectives, and for constructs that are useful in translating information into profits. While information flow can be mechanized and the screening of ideas routinized, no alternative to managerial creativity has yet been found to generate valuable marketing ideas upon which whole marketing programs can be based. The concept of the product life cycle has been extremely useful in focusing this creative process.

The product life cycle concept in many ways may be considered to be the marketing equivalent of the periodic table of the elements concept in the physical sciences; like

Reprinted from *MSU Business Topics* (Winter 1973), pp. 29–35.

the periodic table, it provides a framework for grouping products into families for easier predictions of reactions to various stimuli. With chemicals—it is a question of oxidation temperature and melting point; with products—it is marketing channel acceptance and advertising budgets. Just as like chemicals react in similar ways, so do like products. The product life cycle helps to group these products into homogeneous families.

The product life cycle can be the key to successful and profitable product management, from the introduction of new products to profitable disposal of obsolescent products. The fundamental concept of the product life cycle (PLC) is illustrated in Figure 30-1.

In application, the vertical scale often is measured in saturation of the product (percentage of customer units using), while the horizontal scale is calibrated to represent the passage of time. Months or years are usually the units of time used in calibration, although theoretically, an application along the same concept of much shorter or longer durations (milliseconds in physical sciences, millenia in archaeology) might be found. In Figure 30-1

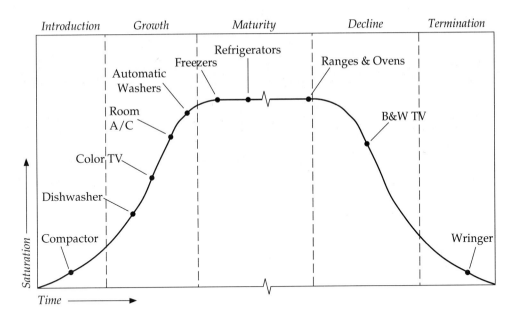

Figure 30-1
Life Cycle Stages of Various Products

the breakdown in the time scale is shown by stages in the maturity of product life. The saturation scale, however, is a guide only and must be used accordingly. When comparing one product with another, it is sometimes best treated by use of qualitative terms, not quantitative units. It is important to the user of the product life cycle concept that this limitation be recognized and conceptual provisions be made to handle it. For example, if the basic marketing unit chosen is "occupied U.S. households," one cannot expect a product such as room air conditioners to attain 100 percent saturation. This is because many households already have been fitted with central air conditioning; thus, the potential saturation attainment falls well short of 100 percent of the marketing measurement chosen.

To overcome this difficulty, marketing managers have two basic options. They can choose a more restrictive, specific marketing unit such as "all occupied U.S. households

that do not have forced air heating"; homes without forced air heating are unlikely candidates for central air conditioning. It can be anticipated that room air conditioners will saturate not only *that* market, but portions of other markets as well. On the other hand, on the basis of informed judgment, management can determine the *potential* saturation of total households and convert the PLC growth scale to a measurement representing the degree of attainment of potential saturation in U.S. households. The author has found the latter approach to be the more useful one. By this device, automatic washers are considered to be at 100 percent saturation when they are at their full potential of an arbitrarily chosen 80 percent.

Consider Figure 30-1, where various products are shown positioned by life cycle stages: the potential saturations permit the grouping of products into like stages of life cycle, even when their actual saturation attainments are dissimilar. One can note that in Figure 30-1 automatic washers (which are estimated at 58 percent saturation) and room air conditioners (30 percent) are positioned in the same growth stage in Figure 30-1; freezers (29 percent) and refrigerators (99 percent), on the other hand, are in the maturity stage. This occurs because, *in our judgment,* freezers have a potential of only about one-third of "occupied households" and thus have attained almost 90 percent of that market. Automatic clothes washers, however, have a potential of about four-fifths of the occupied households and at about 70 percent of their potential still show some of the characteristics of the growth stage of the PLC. General characteristics of the products and their markets are summarized in Table 30-1.

The product life cycle concept is illustrated as a convenient scheme of product classification. The PLC permits management to assign given products to the appropriate stages of acceptance by a given market: *introduction, growth, maturity, decline,* and *termination.* The actual classification of products by appropriate stages, however, is more art than science. The whole process is quite imprecise; but unsatisfactory as this may be, a useful classification can be achieved with management benefits that are clearly of value. This can be illustrated by examining the contribution of the PLC concept in the following marketing activities: sales forecasting, advertising, pricing, and marketing planning.

Table 30-1
Product Life Cycle

	Introduction	Growth	Maturity	Decline	Termination
		Marketing			
Customers	Innovative/ High income	High income/ Mass market	Mass market	Laggards/ Special	Few
Channels	Few	Many	Many	Few	Few
Approach	Product	Label	Label	Specialized	Availability
Advertising	Awareness	Label superiority	Lowest price	Psychographic	Sparse
Competitors	Few	Many	Many	Few	Few
		Pricing			
Price	High	Lower	Lowest	Rising	High
Gross margins	High	Lower	Lowest	Low	Rising
Cost Reductions	Few	Many	Slower	None	None
Incentives	Channel	Channel/ Consumer	Consumer/ Channel	Channel	Channel
		Product			
Configuration	Basic	Second generation	Segmented/ Sophisticated	Basic	Stripped
Quality	Poor	Good	Superior	Spotty	Minimal
Capacity	Over	Under	Optimum	Over	Over

APPLICATIONS OF THE PLC TO SALES FORECASTING

One of the most dramatic uses of the PLC in sales forecasting was its application in explaining the violent decline in sales of color TV during the credit crunch recession of 1969–70. This occurred after the experience of the 1966–67 mini-recession which had almost no effect on color TV sales that could be dis-

cerned through the usual "noise" of the available product flow data. A similar apparent insensitivity was demonstrated in 1958, in 1961, and again in 1966–67, with sales of portable dishwashers. However, it too was followed by a noticeable sales reduction in the 1969–71 period, with annual factory shipments as shown in Figure 30-2.

In early 1972 sales of both portable dishwashers and color TV sets showed a posi-

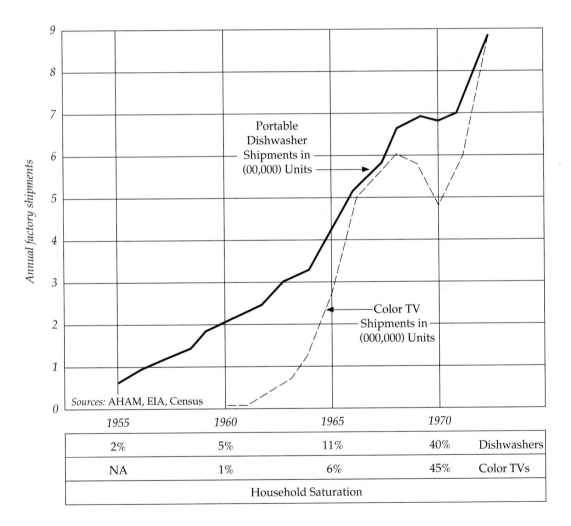

Figure 30-2
Effect of Recession on Product Sales

tive response to an improving economic climate, raising the question as to why both products had become vulnerable to economic contractions after having shown a great degree of independence of the business cycle during previous years. The answer to the question seems to lie in their stage in the product life cycle. In comparing the saturation of color TV and dishwashers, as shown in Figure 30-2, consider first the case of color TV sales.

We can ascertain that as late as 1966, saturation of color TV was approximately 8 percent. By late in 1969, however, saturation had swiftly increased to nearly 40 percent.

The same observation is true in the case of dishwashers—considered a mass market appliance only since 1965. This is the key to the explanation of both situations. At the early, introductory stages of their life cycles, both appliances were making large sales gains as the result of being adopted by consumers with high incomes. Later, when sales growth depended more upon adoption by the less affluent members of the mass market whose spending plans are modified by general economic conditions, the product sales began to correlate markedly to general economic circumstances.

It appears that big ticket consumer durables such as television sets and portable dishwashers tend to saturate as a function of customer income. This fact is illustrated by the data displayed in Figure 30-3, concerning refrigerators and compactors, where one can note the logical relationship between the two products as to the economic status of their most important customers and as to their position in the product life cycle. The refrigerator is a mature product while the compactor is the newest product in the major appliance family.

The refrigerator once was in the introduction stage and had marketing attributes similar to the compactor. The refrigerator's present marketing characteristics are a good guide to proper expectations for the compactor as it matures from the *introductory* stage through *growth* to *maturity*. One can anticipate that the compactor, the microwave oven, and even nondurables such as good quality wines will someday be included in the middle income consumption patterns, and we will find their sales to be much more coincident with general economic cycles.

PRODUCT LIFE STAGES AND ADVERTISING

The concept of a new product filtering through income classes, combined with long-respected precepts of advertising, can result in new perspectives for marketing managers. The resulting observations are both strategic and tactical. New advertising objectives and new insights for copy points and media selection may be realized. Consider the advertising tasks by the following phases:

Phase 1. Introduction

The first objective is to make the best customer prospects aware that the new product or service is now available; to tell him what it does, what are the benefits, why claims are to be believed, and what will be the conditions of consumption.

Phase 2. Growth

The next objective is to saturate the mass market with the same selling points as used in Phase 1. In addition, it is to recognize that a particular brand of the product is clearly superior to other "inferior" substitutes while, at the same time, to provide a rationalization that this purchase is not merely a wasteful, luxury indulging activity, but that it will make

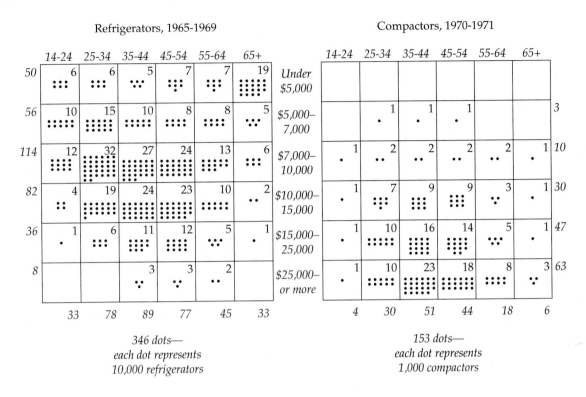

Figure 30-3
Purchase Patterns by Age and Income of Households

the consumer a better *something*, a better husband, mother, accountant, driver, and so forth.

Phase 3. Maturity

A new rationalization, respectability, is added, besides an intensification of brand superiority ("don't buy substitutes; get the real XYZ original, which incidentally, is *new* and *improved* . . . "). To a great extent, the *product* registration is dropped. Respectability is a strong requisite of the American lower class, which in this phase is the economic stratum containing the most important opportunities for sales gains. Companies do not abandon higher income customers, but they now match advertising to a variety of market segments instead

of concentrating on only one theme for the market. Several distinct advertising programs are used. All elements of the marketing mix— product, price, sales promotion, advertising, trading and physical distribution channels— are focused on specific market segments.

Phase 4. Decline

Superior substitutes for a product generally will be adopted first by the people who before were the first to adopt the product in consideration. These people usually are from the upper economic and social classes. Advertising themes reflect this situation when they concentrate on special market segments such as West Coast families or "consumption societies" such as beer drinkers or apartment dwellers.

PRODUCT LIFE STAGES AND PRICING

As a product progresses through all five stages of the life cycle shown in Figure 30-1, the price elasticity can be expected to undergo dramatic changes. Generally speaking, price elasticity of a relatively simple product will be low at first. Thus, when customers are drawn from the higher income classes, demand is relatively inelastic. Later, when most customers are in the lower income categories, greater price elasticity will exist.

Of course, increased price elasticity will not automatically lower prices during the growth stage of the PLC. It is in this growth stage, however, that per unit costs *are* most dramatically reduced because of the effect of the learning curve in engineering, production, and marketing. Rising volume and, more important, the *forecasts* of higher volumes, justifies increased capital investments and higher fixed costs, which when spread over a larger number of units thereby reduce unit costs markedly. New competitors surface with great rapidity in this stage as profits tend to increase dramatically.

Pricing in the mature phase of the PLC usually is found to be unsatisfactory, with no one's profit margins as satisfactory as before. Price competition is keener within the distribution channel in spite of the fact that relatively small price differences seldom translate into any change in aggregate consumer activity.

PRODUCT PLANNING AND THE PLC

Curiously enough, the very configuration of the product takes on a classical pattern of evolution as it advances through the PLC. At first, the new device is designed for function alone; the initial design is sometimes crude by standards that will be applied in the future. As the product maturation process continues, performance sophistication increases. Eventually the product develops to the point where competitors are hard-pressed to make meaningful differences which are perceptible to consumers.

As the product progresses through the product life cycle these modifications tend to describe a pattern of metamorphosis from "the ugly box" to a number of options. The adjustment cycle includes:

Part of house: the built-in look and function. Light fixtures, cooking stoves, wall safes, and furnaces are examples.

Furniture: a blending of the product into the home decor. This includes television, hi-fi consoles, radios, clocks, musical instruments, game tables, and so forth.

Portability: a provision for increased *presence* of the product through provisions for easier movement (rollers or compactness), or multiple unit ownership (wall clocks, radios, even refrigerators), or miniaturization for portability. Portability and *personalization,* such as the pocket knife and the wristwatch, can occur.

System: a combination of components into one unit with compatible uses and/or common parts for increased convenience, lower cost, or less space. Home entertainment centers including television, radio, hi-fi, refrigerator-freezers, combination clothes washers-dryers, clock radios, pocket knife-can-and-bottle openers are illustrative.

Similar changes can also be observed in the distribution channel. Products often progress from specialty outlets in the introductory stage to mass distribution outlets such as discount houses and contract buyers during the "maturity" and "decline" phases of the PLC. Interestingly enough, the process eventually is reversed. Buggy whips can still be found in some specialty stores and premium prices are paid for replicas of very old products.

CONCLUSION

The product life cycle is a useful concept. It is the equivalent of the periodic table of the elements in the physical sciences. The maturation of production technology and product configuration along with marketing programs proceeds in an orderly, somewhat predictable course over time with the merchandising nature and marketing environment noticeably similar between products that are in the same stage of their life cycle. Its use as a concept in forecasting, pricing, advertising, product planning, and other aspects of marketing management can make it a valuable concept, although considerable amounts of judgment must be used in its application.

◆

Evolutionary Processes in Competitive Markets: Beyond the Product Life Cycle

Mary Lambkin and George S. Day

Few management concepts have been so widely accepted or thoroughly criticized as the product life cycle. As criticisms of the conceptual deficiencies and strategic shortcomings mount, the basic notion of life cycles may be so eroded that little of value will remain. However, out of the criticism has come a clearer picture of the limitations of product life cycles and directions for needed improvement.

In addressing the shortcomings of the product life cycle (PLC), we first spell out the requirements for a comprehensive framework for understanding market evolution. This framework is used to identify the areas most in need of further development. Finally, we examine the potential of population ecology models of organizations for new insights into evolutionary processes in competitive product-markets.

"Evolutionary Processes in Competitive Markets: Beyond the Product Life Cycle," Lambkin, Mary and George S. Day, Vol. 53 (July '89), pp. 4–20. Reprinted from the *Journal of Marketing*, published by the American Marketing Association.

A FRAMEWORK FOR UNDERSTANDING PRODUCT-MARKET EVOLUTION

The first requirement in building a framework for understanding market evolution is to specify the unit of analysis. Several candidates have been suggested—industries (Porter 1980), product classes (Day 1981; Harrell and Taylor 1981), product forms and brands (Enis, La Garce, and Prell 1977; Rink and Swan 1979)—but each has its problems. Industries have been ruled out because they generally embrace several classes of noncompetitive products, each with its own pattern of evolution. For example, the major home appliance industry includes stoves, refrigerators, and dishwashers. At the other end of the spectrum, product forms or other brands are not appropriate because they tend to be close substitutes for one another—such as front-loading washing machines—reflecting competitive developments within life cycles rather than overall life cycle patterns.

To capture an overall life cycle pattern, the product class seems the most appropriate unit of analysis. This level reflects the aggregate effects of interbrand rivalry and of extensions brought about through the emergence of new or improved product forms. The product class also corresponds most closely to the business unit level where competition between firms occurs most directly.

The next requirement for understanding market evolution is to incorporate the factors that influence the pattern of product class sales over the life cycle. Consensus is emerging that the evolution of product-markets reflects the outcome of numerous market, technological, and competitive forces, each force acting in concert with others to facilitate or inhibit the rate of sales growth or decline (Day 1981; Porter 1980; Tellis and Crawford 1981; Weitz 1985). The particular "forces" referred to by the authors cited have not been spelled out systematically, but usually fit into three categories: the demand system, the supply system, and the supporting resource environment.

The Demand System: Market Environment and Pattern of Diffusion

The fundamental demand factor is the size of the pool of prospective buyers that is the *market potential*. This factor is dynamic to the extent it may be altered over time by exogenous factors such as demographic and economic trends and the evolution of complementary markets (Mahajan and Muller 1979).

In this system potential buyers pass through (or drop out of) an adoption process that culminates in observable trial and first-purchase adopter behavior. The determinants of the likelihood and rate of acceptance include:

- the perceived comparative advantage of the new product in relation to the best available alternative,

- the perceived risk, jointly determined by financial exposure in the event of failure and uncertainty about the outcome,
- barriers to adoption (such as commitment to present facilities or incompatibility with prevailing values) that slow acceptance even though other factors are supportive, and
- information and availability. Not only must the product be readily available (for purchase and servicing), but the prospective buyers must be aware of the product and informed of the benefits.

These determinants are dynamic, so the rate of acceptance is likely to increase as suppliers of the new product improve performance (and comparative advantage), overcome the barriers of risk and availability, and invest in communications that build awareness and change perceptions.

The Supply System: Competitive Environment and Supplier Behavior

The rate at which a new market develops is also influenced strongly by the *number* and *types* of suppliers that enter the market and by their particular *strategic choices*. The firms that enter and develop new markets typically differ in size and in the resources they have to invest. The extent and form of their investment vary according to their expectations about market potential and their aspirations for their own competitive position.

The product offering that initiates a new life cycle results from the resource commitments and strategic choices of the pioneering entrant, which may stimulate or impede the rate of sales growth in the new market. For example, the initial market appeal of the Apple microcomputer was limited significantly by the fact that it was sold in kit form requiring self-assembly. The decisions of pioneering firms about pricing strategy and level of marketing support also are significant in determining the speed with which the primary demand for the product is developed.

Once evidence of a substantial new market has been revealed by efforts of the pioneering firms, the subsequent pattern of development is likely to be influenced by the number of other firms that enter the market, the speed of their arrival, and the level of resources they invest in their entry moves. Generally, the more intense the competitive activity, the faster the sales growth will be, though this benefit may be offset by a downward pressure on profit margins for individual competitors.

An important and commonly neglected facet of the supply system is the presence and behavior of substitutes. Seldom do entrenched substitutes give up their market without a fight; their defensive efforts are directed to narrowing the perceived comparative advantage of the new product by price cutting, performance enhancements, and extensions. Substitution is also a symmetric phenomenon. The decline stage of a life cycle often is precipitated by an emerging substitute with a new basis of comparative advantage.

Resource Environment:
Exogenous and Industry Factors

The dynamic variables in the supply and demand systems are mediated constantly by trends and events in the surrounding resource environment. The primary resources include:

- the developments in *product and process technology* that enable the product to be commercialized and to be refined and improved thereafter,
- the availability and cost of input *materials and systems*, which determine the cost and market attractiveness of the finished products,

- the presence or absence of an industry *infrastructure*, which may hasten or delay the market penetration,
- and a favorable regulatory environment to legitimize the new industry.

The evolutionary framework suggested by these variables is illustrated in Figures 31-1 and 31-2. No one theory or model could reasonably be expected to include all of these elements and their potential interactions. What is more striking, however, is how little of the complete framework has been illuminated by any of the available theories and, in particular, by the PLC.

INSIGHTS FROM PRODUCT LIFE CYCLE ANALYSIS

In reviewing the PLC literature, both demand-side and supply-side perspectives can be identified. The demand-side stream has adhered closely to the tenets of diffusion theory in studying the rates at which new products penetrate their markets (Mahajan and Muller 1979; Mahajan and Wind 1985). The counterpart supply-side contributions have virtually ignored the details of the diffusion process while deriving normative strategy prescriptions from the pattern of competitive behavior said to characterize each stage of the PLC. Neither of these perspectives, however, addresses very many of the strategic issues confronted in dynamic markets.

Demand-Side Perspectives:
Diffusion Theory and Models

Diffusion theory attempts to explain the distribution of time of adoption across a population of prospective buyers, which in turn determines the rate and pattern of diffusion within the market. Though the theory considers several determinants of adoption time, in-

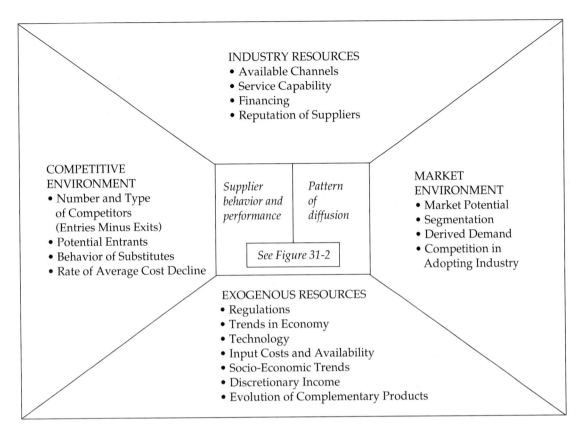

Figure 31-1
A Framework for Understanding Market Evolution

cluding attributes of the product and social system, the emphasis of the research is on the characteristics of individual adopters and their responsiveness to interpersonal communication (Gatignon and Robertson 1986; Rogers 1983).

Robertson and Gatignon (1986) have proposed several dynamic additions to the basic diffusion model to reflect supply-side influences on the size of market and speed of diffusion. They include *structural* factors, such as competitive intensity, credibility of suppliers, and standardization of designs, and *resource commitments,* such as expenditures on R&D and the amount and focus of marketing

support. Their interest however, is in broadening the set of determinants of the diffusion rate and only tangentially in the interplay among competitors. Nothing is said about such important variables as rates of entries and exits, the characteristics, resources, and strategies of competitors, or the implications of these issues for market share and financial performance.

Diffusion Models   The models used to forecast rates of diffusion have been quicker than the theory to recognize supply-side variables. The basic model, which centers on the part of the life cycle contributed by the first-purchase

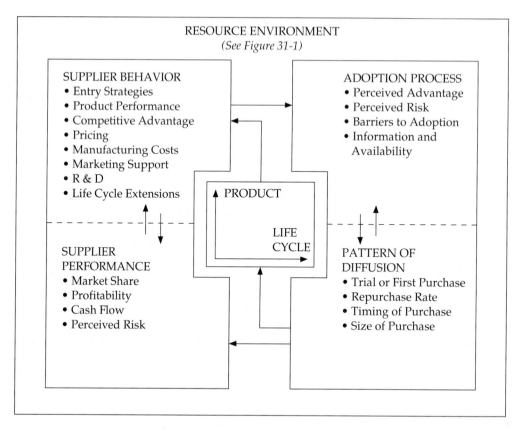

Figure 31-2
*The Interaction of the Supply and Demand Determinants of the Product
Life Cycle (see Figure 31-1)*

sales volume (Bass 1969), has been extended to include supply-side variables, including price (Bass 1980; Dolan and Jeuland 1981; Robinson and Lakhani 1975), advertising (Dodson and Muller 1978; Horsky and Simon 1983), and personal selling (Lilien, Rao, and Kalish 1981). Though these variables generally have been entered one at a time rather than in combination, the extensions offer persuasive evidence of the impact of supply-side factors on adoption rate.

These models have advanced understanding of the diffusion process, but have contributed little to the broader strategic questions. Like diffusion theory, the models ignore the structure and interplay of competition. The marketing mix variables that have been added would all be considered tactical decision variables in a broader competitive context. No consideration is given to strategic variables such as competitive advantage, investment intensity, or resource allocation patterns. Even for the variables that are included there is uncertainty about the precise form of their influence on the speed or pattern of diffusion of new products—for example, how advertising affects potential adopters and whether it has a direct influence or is filtered through the perceptions of opinion leaders (Mahajan and Muller 1979).

Supply-Side Perspectives: The PLC as a Managerial Framework

The product life cycle (PLC) concept has long afforded marketers a framework to guide the adaptation of strategies to changing market conditions and requirements (Kotler 1984). Consequently, some marketers judge the life cycle concept to rival the segmentation concept in value to strategy-making (Schendel 1986). Among its virtues are that it "enables marketers to think dynamically" (Biggadike 1981) and that it is "the most fundamental variable in determining an appropriate business strategy" (Hofer 1975).

These claims are seriously undermined by a notable absence of conceptual validity or rigorous empirical support (Gardner 1987). The life cycle pattern ostensibly is derived from the theory of diffusion of innovations. In reality, diffusion theory has only a slight relationship to the product life cycle concept. Diffusion theory is derived deductively from postulates about individual behavior, largely descriptive in both character and intent, and has been tested extensively. In contrast, the product life cycle concept is inductive, normative in its insistence on prescribing strategies, and infrequently and inadequately tested.

The *normative* bias of the product life cycle framework is evident in textbook enumerations of the appropriate strategies for each stage. These prescriptions usually are preceded by a brief description of the defining features of each stage and some underlying assumptions (e.g., that profit rises sharply in the growth stage and begins to decline in maturity because of competitive pressures even as volume continues to rise). This approach was pushed to its limit by Rink and Swan (1979), who catalogued 567 recommended strategies for each of five life cycle stages and seven functional areas of business.

These prescriptions are like most business policy frameworks or approaches that have been characterized as checklists, based on inductive, armchair generalizations from detailed case studies (Camerer 1985). Because they aspire to be exhaustive, all possibilities are mentioned indiscriminately. The impression is given that just about everything makes some contribution to performance. However, we want to know what strategic moves will make the most contribution in each situation.

Testing the Life Cycle Framework   Few conclusive answers can yet be gleaned from the research literature on the product life cycle, though the topic has been popular for many years. This lack of progress is due partly to a difference in focus between researchers and practitioners and partly to the inherent problems of studying this dynamic phenomenon.

The early work in this area was concerned with verifying the evidence of an S-shaped life cycle curve by measuring the sales patterns of various products (Buzzell 1966; Cox 1967; Polli and Cook 1969). Only when it became clear that this effort was misdirected—there appear to be as many different curves as there are products—was this approach abandoned in favor of an emphasis on the factors shaping the various life cycle patterns (Rink and Swan 1979).

The more recent work (Buzzell and Gale 1987, Ch. 10; Thietart and Vivas 1984; Thorelli and Burnett 1981) has contributed useful insights about the changes in market structures over the life cycle (variables such as entries and exits of competitors, degree of concentration, and extent of differentiation) and in the strategies and performance of the market participants. However, all of these studies are based on cross-sectional data—normally the PIMS database—with change being inferred by comparing profiles of firm characteristics at different stages, rates of growth, or age of the market.

With this design the actual pattern of adjustments of businesses to changing conditions cannot be revealed. A further flaw of cross-section designs is that they miss firms that did not survive the previous stages. For these reasons, as well as reliance on a sample that underrepresents businesses in the very early and very late stages of the life cycle (Day 1986), the research using the PIMS database has not shed much light on the adequacy of the strategy propositions or of the framework itself.

Conceptual Gaps in the Product Life Cycle Framework

Even with adequate research methods, the typically generalized descriptions and prescriptions in the product life cycle literature would be unlikely to find empirical support because key assumptions are flawed and important dimensions of evolutionary processes are overlooked.

1. Little account is taken of the different competitive positions or resources of the competing business units that might alter the applicability of the generalized courses of action. The normative life cycle literature has largely ignored differences between large and small firms, between established firms and new firms, between firms that develop their own entry and those that enter the market by acquisition, licensing, or joint venture, or between firms that choose to follow different strategies. The generalized treatment of the relationship between market growth and market share inherent in portfolio models is the only significant attempt so far to recognize the importance of differing competitive positions over the stages of market evolution. The Arthur D. Little Matrix of Industry Maturity and Competitive position offers specific propositions about appropriate strategic moves that account for life cycle and market position (Day 1986), but apparently has never been tested empirically.

2. Apart from studies of the experiences of market pioneers (Bond and Lean 1977; Robinson and Fornell 1985; Urban et al. 1986; Whitten 1981; Robinson 1988), there is no recognition that the "strategic window" for competitive entry opens at different times for different types of prospective entrants (Abell 1978) and the risks and rewards of entry depend on the choice of timing.

3. The framework has no capacity to reflect the conditions that trigger competitive "shakeouts," yet a recurring risk in high growth markets is that too many competitors will enter with unrealistic market share expectations (Aaker and Day 1986). Absence of a supply-side dimension to the product life cycle means little guidance on when and why shakeouts are triggered or which types of businesses are likely to be winners or losers in the event (Willard and Cooper 1985).

4. Feedback effects of the choice of strategy on the shape of the growth curve usually are ignored, despite evidence from diffusion models that supply-side factors can accelerate or slow the rate of growth. One possible consequence is a premature identification of maturity (Dhalla and Yuspeh 1976). The result is a self-fulfilling prophecy in which the established competitors collectively decide their best action is to reduce marketing and R&D investments to a sustaining level that will protect their market share position. The resulting slowdown in sales initially confirms the wisdom of the change in strategy, which leads to complacency that is an open invitation to competitors from adjacent markets or geographic areas. When they enter with

product innovations, segmented offerings, and heavy marketing expenditures, the market begins to grow again.

5. The apparent one-way determinism of the birth → life → death analogy from biology can prompt a fatalistic and unwarranted acceptance of eventual decline (Chakravarthy 1984). This analogy often has been repudiated by evidence of successful strategies to rejuvenate and extend life cycles. In the mid-1970s the product category called "radios" was presumed by most North American producers to be living out its natural life. The Japanese made no such assumption and rejuvenated the whole category with a flood of product improvements, putting the Sony Walkman in the vanguard.

6. The environmental context is either ignored or subordinated in most frameworks, though product life cycles are influenced by what is happening in the overall industry environment. The stage of industry life cycle reflects the sum of the life cycles of the products that make up the industry. In an embryonic industry the distribution, delivery, and service infrastructure is not in place and market penetration of the first product is low. As the industry structure develops, the introduction of new product classes becomes easier (Day 1986); customers are more knowledgeable, sales and promotion efforts are more effective, and service and distribution networks are already in place.

7. The most pervasive feature of emerging markets is uncertainty about customer acceptance and the eventual size of the market, which process and product technology will be dominant, whether cost declines will be realized, and the identity, structure, and actions of competitors. Life cycle strategy frameworks appear to assume there is no uncertainty, for no consideration is given to the tradeoffs involved in confronting uncertainty (Wernerfelt and Karnani 1987). Firms have the choice of acting early or waiting and can elect to focus their resources or spread them over several technology, marketing, and process options to lower the risk by maintaining flexibility.

The nature of the conceptual gaps suggests that greater progress can be made by attending to supply-side issues than by making incremental gains with diffusion models. Especially needed is a mechanism for modeling the dynamics of competitive behavior in evolving market structures. One such model that has attracted considerable attention in other management disciplines, and some interest in marketing, is the theory of natural selection applied within a broader ecological framework.

POPULATION ECOLOGY PERSPECTIVES ON MARKET EVOLUTION

The term "population ecology" originates in biology, where it was introduced to describe the study of how different populations of organisms (i.e., species) adapt to their environments (Hawley 1968). In essence, the bio-ecological model considers the evolution of different species inhabiting the same environment to be a dynamic process based on competition for scarce resources. The theory of natural selection (Darwin 1859) provides the mechanism for explaining the differential allocation of resources across competing species. In general, the theory predicts that the species best "fitted" to the contingencies of the environment will survive and prosper and their less fit rivals will fail and disappear because of their inability to secure adequate resources.

Marketers have long recognized the potential of the ecological paradigm for understanding competition in commercial product-markets. The basic ideas first were introduced by Alderson (1957), who borrowed ecological terminology such as "behavior systems" and "ecological niches." Other scholars have addressed this topic over the years (Gross 1968; Thorelli 1967), but only recently has significant progress been made in realizing the potential of the ecological paradigm for studying market evolution (Boxer and Wensley 1983; Tellis and Crawford 1981; Wind 1982). Tellis and Crawford in particular spell out in detail the recasting of the product life cycle in terms of the biological model of evolution.

All of the articles cited, however, are descriptive in content, focusing on finding marketing referents for each of the terms of the ecological model. No attempt is made to develop an explanatory model or to put forward testable propositions. Hence this work can be considered a first phase in the development of ecological models in marketing. The next phase is to extend the ecological ideas to explain the differential selection and adaptation of competitors as product-markets evolve.

Our purpose is to show that the ecology model can be used to provide a supply-side theory of market evolution including the following three elements:

- A *population growth process* that accounts for differences in the competitive environment over time, particularly in the intensity of competition.
- A *typology of strategies* for competing in new markets that recognizes the diversity of resources and skills among the business population, as well as differences in their order of entry.
- An *integrative model* that provides predictions about the likely success of different generic strategies as the product-market evolves through different stages.

The version of the ecology model used as the basis for this discussion is that of Hannan and Freeman (1977), which is an adaptation of the original bio-ecological model developed specifically for the study of organizations. This organization ecology model is widely accepted and obviates the need to work with complex and unfamiliar biological terms.

The Population Growth Process

A population can be defined as the aggregate of businesses serving a particular product-market. Because the emergence of a new population of businesses coincides with the commencement of a new product life cycle, the same criteria should be used for identification of both. A new PLC, and consequently a new population of businesses, commences only when a substantial change in technology, customer function, or customer group occurs that is outside the scope of all or most of the current suppliers (Day 1981). The exploitation of the opportunity created by such a change requires the setting up of new ventures by individuals or established corporations.

Given such an event, whether initiated by a new firm or by a new division of an established firm, the population ecology model specifies the process by which the population of suppliers grows to some ultimate equilibrium level. This process is depicted as a logistic or S-shaped curve that is identical to the PLC, modeled formally as (Hannan and Freeman 1977; 1988):

$$\frac{dN}{dt} = rN\left[\frac{k-N}{K}\right].$$

In this equation, the rate of change in a population of size N is a function of some natural rate of increase, r, and the upper limit or carrying capacity, K.

The r term in this process represents the difference between the rates of organizational births and deaths in the population.[1] This rate is assumed to be strongly positive in the early stages of development of a new population when the number of members is small in relation to the carrying capacity. In this situation, the effect of K is not significant and the population growth equation reduces to

$$\frac{dN}{dt} = rN ,$$

indicating that growth is exponential.

As the population size approaches its upper limit, K, the rate of growth slows until eventually it reaches zero or overshoots the carrying capacity of the resource environment. Thus, the K term becomes the determining factor in the later stages of population growth, indicating an increasing scarcity of resources and therefore the likelihood of more intense competition.

A Typology of Strategies

Because of the different competitive conditions characterizing the early and late stages of population growth, ecologists have adopted the convention of describing alternative time-based strategies in terms of the parameters of the growth equation, that is, as r-strategies and K-strategies (Brittain and Freeman 1980). According to this view, r-strategists are organizations that enter a new resource space at an early stage when the population contains few other members, whereas K-strategists enter later when the competitors are more numerous. This distinction between early and late entrants highlighted by the concept of r- and K-strategies is the first building block in a typology of competitive entry strategies. Further building blocks are provided by the concepts of density dependence, environmental niches, and niche width strategies.

The Concept of Density Dependence According to this concept, competitive conditions in any population are a function of the number of organizations competing for the finite level of resources available to that population. In a new population containing few members, competition is likely to be indirect and diffuse because the abundance of resources means that the growth of one competitor need not suppress the growth of another (Brittain and Wholey 1988).

As the density of the population increases, it becomes increasingly difficult to avoid direct competition wherein the gains of one competitor must result from losses to another. This situation leads to an intensification of competitive activity with an emphasis on the achievement of large scale and functional efficiency. Competition is likely to be particularly aggressive in a situation of oversupply, that is, when the size of a population exceeds the carrying capacity of its environment. This situation seems equivalent to the "shakeout" phase in PLC terms, which can be resolved only when the overcapacity disappears through business failures or mergers.

Given that the density of a developing population is constantly changing with the increasing number of new competitors, it follows that the level of resources facing prospective entrants and the nature of the prevailing competitive conditions are also continually in flux. Hence, each competitor entering a market at a given point in time faces a unique set of resources and competitive conditions.

The Concept of Niches In ecological terms, each unique combination of resources and competitive conditions that is sufficient to support any one type of organization is defined as a niche. However, because a single resource space (market) typically contains several overlapping niches, competition is likely to alter the extent to which individual organization forms can proliferate in their chosen niches. To capture this competitive process, ecologists distinguish between *fundamental* niches and *realized* niches (Hannan and Freeman 1977). The fundamental niche refers to the size of the potential niche (market segment) available to any new category of competitors and the realized niche describes the size of the segment that is actually available once competitors have secured a certain amount of that segment.

If follows from this distinction that the boundaries of fundamental niches cannot be identified readily. To overcome this difficulty, ecologists have directed their attention to realized niches identified by the characteristics of the organizations that occupy them, with each different type of organization considered to occupy a distinct niche (Freeman and Boeker 1984).

This convention is based on the premise that because organizations are fashioned from the resources available at their time of founding, those founded at the same time tend to have a similar structure or form and those founded at different times have different forms (Stinchcombe 1965). Hence, the development of a new population of competing firms can be thought of in terms of *waves of organizing*, with different types of organizations appearing in each stage.

A further corollary of this argument is that once a particular type of organization emerges, it tends to be preserved in its original form because of factors such as commitments to past technologies, the vesting of interests, and the development of common ideologies. This phenomenon, which ecologists describe as *structural inertia* (Hannan and Freeman 1977), produces a resistance to change that impedes the ability of established competitors to adapt their structure to meet changes in environmental conditions. The inertia of established organizations provides the opportunity for new organizations to emerge

and, given that the later entrants are unlikely to displace established organizations completely, the mature population seems likely to contain a variety of organization forms, each adapted to suit certain niche conditions.

The Concept of Niche Width Many dimensions might be used to describe the unique character of organizations occupying separate niches, but one particular dimension known as "niche width" has been emphasized in the ecology literature (Freeman and Hannan 1983; Hannan and Freeman 1977). This variable usually is represented as a continuum from *generalism* to *specialism*. The distinction between these strategies refers to whether an organization chooses to spread its resources across a broad spectrum of the environment in the hope of balancing its risks or concentrates its resources in a narrow segment of the environment in the hope of earning a high return. In a measurement context, the difference between these alternatives seems to be one of scale, though it includes other aspects of strategy that typically accompany variations in scale such as breadth of product line, size of customer base, and extent of geographic coverage (Carroll 1985).[2]

Specialists are depicted as small, often new organizations without access to substantial capital resources. They rely for their success on factors independent of scale, especially their ability to exploit first-mover advantages by either pioneering entirely new markets or being first to exploit new segments in mature markets. The r-specialists, which tend to be early entrants into entirely new markets, exemplify the first of these categories. A typical example of an r-specialist is Apple Computer when it first commenced operations; late entrants such as Compaq and Amstrad fit the definition of K-specialists.

Generalists, in contrast, tend to be large, established organizations with access to extensive skills and resources. Because of their size and commitment to current technologies through prior investments, these organizations have a structural inertia and may not be able to move as quickly as the specialists in exploiting new market niches. For this reason, they are more likely to be early followers of the pioneers. They compensate for their lateness by making a heavy investment in production and distribution scale to achieve market leadership on the basis of superior competitive efficiency (lower unit costs arising from economies of scale). The much-publicized entry of IBM into the microcomputer market seems a classic example of this category.

The objective of market dominance is achievable for generalist organizations whose skills and resources in related markets enable them to overcome barriers to entry such as technical knowledge, product differentiation, and access to distribution channels. However, large organizations whose activities are widely diversified do not have the same opportunities for achieving synergies across markets, except perhaps in the management of finance and in their accumulated experience in diverse startup situations. Diversified early followers of this type are referred to in the ecological literature as polymorphists, a variant of the generalist. Examples in the microcomputer industry are companies such as Xerox, Texas Instruments, AT&T, Sony, Zenith, and Ericsson.

In summary the typology of market entry provided by the ecology model enables us first to distinguish between early and late entries, with early entrants being described as r-strategists and late entrants as K-strategists. We then can divide these two categories into generalists and specialists, extending the typology to include market pioneers (r-specialists and r-generalists), early followers (K-generalists and polymorphists), and late entrants (K-specialists). The full typology of competitive strategies derived from the ecology model is give in Table 31-1.

The Process of Natural Selection

Given the descriptive typology, the next important question is which of these strategies has the best prospects of success or, in ecological terms, which is likely to achieve the best fit to its environment. Success in this sense can have several levels of meaning. At the extreme, it means literally the survival or failure

Table 31-1
Competition and Selection in Developing Markets: Strategies for Success*

Niche Configuration	Embryonic	Developing	Maturing
Population density	Low	Increasing	High
Size and rate of environmental change	High	Reducing	Low
Predominant organization form	r-specialists	K-generalists	K-generalists
Other forms	r-generalists	Polymorphists	K-specialists
Best performers	r-specialists	K-generalists	K-generalists

*r-specialists are small-scale pioneers and r-generalists are large-scale pioneers. K-generalists are early followers with established businesses in related markets. Polymorphists are early followers with widely diversified portfolios. K-specialists are small-scale late entrants occupying narrow market segments.

of entire organizations, failure being evidenced by withdrawal or dissolution. A less drastic outcome is what is referred to as *mobility*, in which the organization fails in the sense that it is substantially transformed so that it is no longer recognizable in its original form (Hannan and Freeman 1977). A large increase in scale, for example, when a specialist becomes a generalist, exemplifies this phenomenon, as does the occurrence of mergers and acquisitions. The least extreme measure of success is described as *viability*, which refers to the relative performance of surviving competitors. Variables such as market share and profitability may be considered as measures of viability (Aldrich 1979).

Predictions from Niche Theory   Niche theory provides a set of general predictions to indicate which strategies are most likely to be successful under various types of environmental conditions. The sets of conditions considered in this theory result from differences in the degree of variability (radical or minor) and the frequency or rate of change. An environment undergoing radical and frequent change is highly unstable and therefore a difficult one in which to operate; the opposite conditions imply a stable and benign competitive environment. The essential difference between the states of environmental variation is in the cost of suboptimal strategies in the face of the uncertainty.

1. When changes are extreme and rapidly paced, the population experiences widely varying conditions over time that make it extremely difficult to design an organization that can perform equally well under all of the conditions. The emergent phase of a radically new market in which both production and marketing methods must be developed from scratch typifies these conditions. A specialist strategy in which the organization is designed to perform

well under one set of conditions is optimal in this environment because the cost of maladaptation is far higher for an organization that makes a heavy investment in pursuing a generalist strategy.

2. Change that is frequent but minor in amplitude, as in the case of cyclical fluctuations, favors large-scale generalists with sufficient "slack" (Cyert and March 1963) to cope with the changing conditions. They have an advantage over specialists that may not have sufficient resources to absorb the frequent small shocks.

3. Change that is radical though infrequent, such as a major recession, requires a more flexible, combination strategy, known as polymorphism. This strategy involves a federation of several specialist organizations, each well suited to at least one state of the environment.

4. When change is minor and infrequent, generalists again tend to outcompete specialists over the full range of conditions to which they are adapted because of their relatively large scale and superior competitive efficiency. When the conditions approach certainty, however, some specialists may again outcompete the generalists, which are well adapted overall but which may not be so efficient in marginal areas of the niche (individual market segments).

The practical implications of these predictions are seen in the evolution of competitive product-markets.

THE STAGES OF MARKET EVOLUTION

As a market evolves, three processes are set in motion and become the driving forces for change in competitive structure and in performance. These processes seem directly analogous to the ecological patterns just described.

- New markets attract increasing numbers of competitors, leading to an increasing level of population density until eventually the resource space is filled and a shakeout occurs (the timing depends on whether resource supplies expand or efficiency in resource use rises).
- Each wave of entrants introduces new structures and strategies in response to shifts in the availability of resources (r-strategists and K-strategists).
- The nature of the competitive conditions alters over time with a tendency toward lower risk and uncertainty and higher competitive intensity.

The operation of these processes results in an unfolding series of distinct niche configurations (Brittain and Freeman 1980) that correspond to the traditional stages of the product life cycle. As resource conditions change and new niche configurations emerge, the resulting market structure and resource profile of each life cycle stage also change in predictable directions.

The onset of a new pattern of market and competitive conditions can be identified by inflexion points in the S-shaped population growth curve. To be consistent with this convention and for clarity of exposition, we discuss the implications of the ecological predictions according to the commonly identified stages of market evolution.

Embryonic Markets: Low Population Density

The introduction stage in the development of a radically new product-market has the highest level of uncertainty in the whole life cycle. The fact that a substantial level of market demand has not yet been proven creates a high level of risk for the pioneering business (Levitt 1965). Also, substantial diversity is likely among pioneering entrants in all facets of their operations, including product and process design and marketing methods. Initial development is a matter of trial and error, with rapid changes occurring as competitors try to match or exceed one another's performance (Porter 1980).

Niche theory predicts that r-specialists are likely to be the predominant form among the organizations pioneering the development of the new population. These r-specialists are typically small new organizations set up specifically to exploit first-mover advantages in the new resource space. They are frequently "spinoffs" from established organizations by individuals who have the skills and resources to exploit a perceived new opportunity but are impatient with the slowness of response of their employer organizations (Freeman 1982). These individuals typically do not have access to large resources, so they tend to concentrate on activities that require relatively low levels of investment and simple structures.

The opportunity for such small firms to gain a foothold in the new market arises from the fact that the population density is low and competition is not very intense. However, the apparent richness of the competitive environment is no guarantee of success. The uncertainty of resource availability coupled with the firms' own inexperience exposes these early entrants to a "liability of newness" (Stinchcombe 1965), which inevitably results in some failures. Future competition by fast followers presents a further threat to viability.

The theory indicates that these factors will lead to the demise of a majority of the pioneering firms. This prediction certainly seems to have been borne out in the microcomputer industry, where several of the early entrants filed for bankruptcy (e.g., Osborne, Computer Devices, and Vector Technologies) and many others had serious trading difficulties (e.g., Vector Graphic, Fortune, Intertec Data Systems, Altos Computer Systems, and Grid Systems).

The few pioneering firms that manage to survive are those able to exploit first-mover advantages such as (Brittain and Freeman 1980):

- The establishment of their first version of the product as the industry standard against which all later variants will be compared.
- The development of cost and pricing advantages from acquired production experience, and
- the accumulation of monopoly profit during the interval before competition increases, which can be reinvested to increase capacity and thereby to dominate the market as it develops.

Developing Markets: Increasing Population Density

As sales gain momentum in the growth stage, the ultimate potential of the market becomes more clearly understood and the initial uncertainties gradually are resolved. Customers with homogeneous needs begin to be identified, which allows marketing effort to be targeted more precisely, and experience with the product, process, and materials technologies leads to greater efficiency and increased standardization.

In ecological terms, the environment is changing from highly uncertain to moderately uncertain. Such conditions make it feasible to design a large-scale generalist organization that can achieve adequate performance in several environmental states by exploiting a wide range of environmental resources. Another significant feature is the increasing density of the population, which puts an emphasis on competitive efficiency as the criterion for survival.

These conditions favor K-strategists and, in particular, K-generalists, as the dominant form. In a few cases, K-generalists will have evolved from r-strategists that have exploited first-mover advantages successfully in the previous niche and have acquired sufficient resources to undertake the large expansion in scale that defines the K-generalist strategy. However, such transformations are very difficult to achieve because of the intrinsic inefficiencies of new organizations in comparison with their longer established peers (the liability of newness) and because once a firm is structured in a particular way, structural inertia begins to inhibit adaptation. K-generalists therefore are more likely to enter the resource space for the first time at this point; they tend to be organizations from closely related or overlapping niches. They inherit a strong brand identification from their parent and have the parent's resources to fund a large-scale entry with standardized high quality products.

If the niche is still subject to major and abrupt changes in market requirements, production processes, and technology—albeit at a reduced frequency—the variant of the K-generalist strategy known as polymorphism may be the dominant form. Because of the widely varying contingencies in this environment, committing all or most of an organization's resources to a narrow band of the environment is risky. In this case, an organization form with a loosely structured federation of activities, each specialized to different niches, is likely to be positively selected.

Overall, the model predicts that in this relatively uncertain market both K-generalists and polymorphists generally will outperform the r-strategists that initially appeared dominant because of their relative advantage in scale and experience. Some of these r-strategists may fail in the sense of withdrawing from the market, but many may continue as a result of mergers or acquisitions. A typical event is that widely diversified companies following a polymorphist strategy acquire r-specialists as a way of making a fast entry into an evidently growing market. The acquisition of Scientific Data systems by Xerox and of a 20% stake in Sun Microsystems by AT&T exemplifies this strategy.

Maturing Markets: High Population Density

As the size of the population approaches the ultimate carrying capacity, the pattern of environmental variation approaches certainty. In markets where economies of scale are present, a tendency toward concentration is probably evident by this time, with a small number of firms coming to dominate the market. These long-term market leaders are most likely to be K-generalists—large, long-established firms selling closely related products.

Even in highly concentrated markets, the market leaders do not usually control all of the resource space. Typically, a generalist strategy appeals to some common denominator across all areas of the markets in order to maximize economies of scale. The cost advantage of such a strategy, however, may be offset by an inability to cater to segments of the market that have heterogeneous requirements. Areas of the market that are not served or are poorly served by the market leaders are therefore available to specialist firms offering tailormade products. The result is a kind of resource partitioning in which generalist and specialist firms can coexist without engaging in direct competition (Carroll 1985).

The resource partitioning is most likely to occur as the market approaches a stable maturity because it is at this point that untapped market segments and weaknesses among current competitors can be most easily identified. By this time also, knowledge about the relevant technologies and marketing methods is likely to be widely available and is no longer a significant barrier to entry even for small, specialist firms.

These conditions tend to stimulate a third wave of entrants belonging to the general category of K-strategists because of the late point at which they join the population. These late entrants are more appropriately described as K-specialists, however, because of the types of competitive strategy they follow. Some variants are (Brittain and Freeman 1980):

1. *Independent producers*—small and possibly new organizations with lower overhead costs than the large generalists. Companies such as Compaq and Amstrad are in this category, as are the producers of microcomputer clones, which have proliferated in recent years (companies such as Access, Otrona, Athena, Gavilan, and Cromenco).
2. *Captive producers*—supply or support other units of the same firm, but sell nothing on the open market. They generally have been acquired by r-strategists to support vertical integration moves. The chip manufacturing and software divisions of companies such as IBM belong in this category.
3. *Subordinate producers*—stand-alone divestments of K-generalists and polymorphists that market products with temporary or permanent declines in demand. They have the advantages of low carrying costs of assets and lower coordination costs than the generalists. The revamped Osborne Computers represents this category, as do the personal computer divisions sold off by Xerox and Texas Instruments.

Winners and Losers during the Shakeout Two classes of competitors are especially vulnerable as the population density reaches and exceeds the carrying capacity of the market. The most likely failures or below-par performers are polymorphists—the small-scale specialized subunits of large diversified companies. They are trapped between two sets of competitors better suited to a more predictable, albeit competitive, environment. On one side are larger K-generalists with a relative scale and efficiency advantage in their niche. On the other side is a new threat from K-specialists, recently attracted to the increasing segmentation possibilities. These new players have an advantage over polymorphists because of lower coordination (overhead) costs.

This prediction certainly has been borne out in the microcomputer market in the very poor performance records of such companies as AT&T, Xerox, Texas Instruments, and Ericsson. In fact, all of these companies but AT&T have by now cut their losses and exited this market.

Additional dropouts are also likely among the earlier specialists, because they lack the ability to withstand the constriction in resources when too many competitors are chasing too little volume. Their strategy of early concentration on a narrow range of the environment means they have little slack to withstand any unexpected shocks in an overcrowded environment. As a result the weaker members of the population either fail or become subordinate or captive producers. The trading difficulties experienced by companies such as Vector Graphic, Fortune, Intertec, Altos Computer Systems, and Apollo Computers might reasonably be attributed to such a cause. Only time will tell whether these problems are temporary or permanent.

Shakeouts follow the same pattern in many markets, including discount audio-video retailers (Saporito 1987). The rapid growth of these retailers was fueled by videocassette recorders introduced in 1981, but in 1987 sales growth slowed abruptly to 10% while the top 10 discounters expanded store space by 25%. The overexpansion was dictated partly by the need for each chain to have a major presence in each local market it served. This concentration provided economies of scale, especially in advertising costs that might be as high as 8% of sales. However, most markets usually have room (resources)

for only two such "power" retailers. With overcapacity, margins dropped sharply and the original local entrepreneurs were compressed into a few well-run national chains. The "generalists" like Circuit City are expected to survive and prosper because they have the control, warehousing, and distribution systems needed to achieve very low costs.

TESTING THE ECOLOGY MODEL

The predictions from the ecology model can be summarized in the following propositions.

P_1 (pioneers): Firms pioneering the development of radically new markets are likely to be predominantly r-specialists. They are typically independent new ventures that enter the market with a low level of capital investment. Because of inherent difficulties in developing a new primary market, as well as the small size and inexperience of these firms, the attrition rate among them is likely to be high though a few may succeed in becoming major long-term players.

P_2 (early followers): Early followers into rapidly growing markets are likely to be the most numerous category. The predominant form will be subsidiaries or divisions of large, integrated firms that have a high degree of synergy with the new product-market (K-generalists). These businesses are likely to enter on a relatively large scale (in terms of both production and distribution) in comparison with the pioneers and to market their product more intensively. This strategy, when backed by extensive resources, enables these businesses to become the long-term market leaders and achieve strong financial performance.

Other early followers will be subsidiaries or divisions of large, diversified firms that have extensive resources but few market-specific skills (polymorphists). This disadvantage restricts them to a relatively small market share and correspondingly weak level of financial performance. In fact, the combination of heavy capital investment and low market share is likely to result in the poorest performance of all entrant categories.

P_3 (late entrants): Late entrants into mature markets are likely to be the least numerous category. They are typically small new ventures set up to exploit a competitive advantage in meeting the needs of one particular market segment (usually centered either on quality or price) Even the most successful of these K-specialists is unlikely to achieve a large market share, but this disadvantage may be offset by a disproportionately strong financial performance.

Empirical Testing

Because the ecological model is relatively new to the marketing discipline, it has not been adequately tested. Preliminary testing has yielded promising results and evidence from other sources supports individual propositions from the model.

Industry Case Studies   The first attempt to test the overall model was an analysis of the semiconductor industry by Brittain and Freeman (1980). They clearly demonstrated that competitive conditions did change over time as the density of the supplier population increased and that there was a definite pattern of succession as new entrants with superior products or more appropriate competitive strategies usurped the positions of earlier entrants. However, this study was purely qualitative with no attempt to quantify such issues as the number and size of entrants, the precise timing of their entry, their attrition rate, or the relative performance of survivors.

These deficiencies were largely overcome in a recent study of the evolution of the minicomputer industry (Romanelli 1988). The qualitative analysis was bolstered with the collection of detailed product, market, competitive, and financial data on the population of 108 entrants into the market. The basic data on entry strategies and probability of surviving at least six years are summarized in Table 31-2. Firms were classified as specialists or generalists on the basis of a median split on the number of market segments they served by year three.

The results confirmed expectations that early entrants tend to be specialists (75%) and that early followers during the rapid growth stage are the most numerous category. An unexpected finding was the very high proportion of early followers that were specialists. Nonetheless, the most successful early followers were generalists like Data General—subject to the qualification that their entry was aggressive. This group had a 100% survival rate. Interestingly, fast followers that were conservative generalists had only a 20% survival rate. They appear to share the debilitating characteristics of polymorphists.

Also as expected, the late entrants were the least numerous, with the lowest survival rate. Most were small specialists, though Tandem succeeded in a big way by entering in

Table 31-2
*Early Strategies and Survival in the Microcomputer Industry (percentage of firms surviving 6 years)**

Entry Strategy	Pioneers (1957–1966)	Early Followers (1967–1971)	Later Entrants (1972–1981)
Generalist	66 (n = 3)	63 (n = 11)	20 (n = 5)
Specialist	77 (n = 9)	75 (n = 47)	64 (n = 33)

*Adapted from Romanelli (1988).

1976 with a specialist strategy based on dominance of the severe operating environment segment. Overall, this study provides encouraging support for the propositions derived from the ecology model and demonstrates the insights to be gained from longitudinal industry studies. What is now needed is a diverse array of studies to test for consistency of the findings in different environments.

Cross-Sectional Analysis of New Ventures   One recent study used the database of new ventures launched by firms represented in the PIMS database (Lambkin 1988) to corroborate further the propositions about the different strategic profiles of successive waves of market entrants. The results of this study showed that pioneers, early followers, and late entrants were systematically different on several dimensions of their structure and strategy, including production and distribution scale and their choice of marketing mix. Furthermore, these differences were found to translate into differences in market shares and profit performance. However, this study was limited by the fact that it focused only on survivors and, in particular, on new businesses launched by large, successful corporations (predominantly members of the *Fortune Top 500*). It provided no additional information on either the survival/failure rates of successive market entrants or the experiences of small, independent ventures in comparison with their larger corporate rivals.

Similar problems apply to most of the studies that have a bearing on constituent elements of the ecological model. Studies of market pioneers, which are relevant in testing the first proposition, generally concentrate on firms that survived their entry attempts, thereby excluding any failures from the calculations (Bond and Lean 1977; Whitten 1981). The usual approach is to define pioneers as firms that first promoted the product on a national basis. This definition excludes small local firms that may have sold the product at an earlier time or firms that failed to achieve national distribution. For example, in the semiconductor industry, Intel would be regarded as the *de facto* pioneer though a company called Advanced Memory Systems was actually the first to sell microprocessors (Brittain and Freeman 1980).

This selectivity bias means the general finding that pioneers tend to outperform all later entrants is likely to be overstated. Furthermore, the propensity to concentrate on average values means that little information is provided on the range of performance by pioneering businesses apart from their survival or failure. The only thing that is clear from the evidence is that all pioneers, regardless of their degree of success, tend to lose share over time as additional competitors enter the market.

A more stringent test of the ecological proposition on pioneers would require that the definition of this category of entrants be broadened to include all firms attempting to market a new product and that the sample studied track failures as well as successes. It seems reasonable to speculate that such an approach would produce a result different from that of the previous studies.

Related Research on Diversification   For the second ecological proposition on early followers, the research stream concerned with the relationship between diversification strategies and performance seems of most relevance (Montgomery 1982; Rumelt 1974). These studies are all consistent in the finding that related diversifiers, which seem to correspond to K-generalists, significantly outperform unrelated and conglomerate diversifiers, which seem to match closely the concept of polymorphism. A recent study has found that the performance of the highly diversified firms is related to the rate of market growth, with higher growth enhancing profitability

(Wernerfelt and Montgomery 1986). This finding may imply that degree of diversification interacts with timing of entry in influencing performance so that early entry improves the performance prospects of widely diversified firms more than those of closely related firms. Clearly, such possibilities provide interesting questions for future research.

In the case of the third proposition on late entrants, some evidence suggests that even small, new competitors entering mature markets—the profile of K-specialists—can earn attractive returns by concentrating on narrow market segments not served by the market leaders (Hamermesh, Anderson and Harris 1978; Woo and Cooper 1982). Again, however, these studies examine only successful late entrants. They give no indication of the incidence of failure among late entrants or, indeed, of whether the successful businesses studied were the exception rather than the rule in their respective markets. Future research should explore whether the survival chances are any higher for late entrants than for market pioneers, given the risk of strong competitive reaction in place of the uncertainties involved in developing new markets.

In sum, though research has provided several insights on the ecological propositions, clearly some major questions have not been addressed. The first question, which might be termed demographic, concerns the pattern of entries and exits at different stages of market evolution, the numbers and types of firms that enter and leave at different points. The second question concerns the competitive behavior of the various firms in the market, specifically differences in strategies between new entrants and incumbent firms and the nature and extent of competitive reaction. Finally, work is needed to establish the full range of performance outcomes of different types of competitors at different stages of evolution, with equal emphasis given to the failures and the successes.

Questions such as these represent a novel perspective in terms of research on market evolution, and the capacity to raise interesting new questions is one of the important contributions of the ecological approach.

AN ASSESSMENT OF THE ECOLOGY MODEL

Advantages of the Model

The first and most basic advantage of the model is the focus on the supply side of market transactions and on the process of competition, which is a fundamental feature of most populations of suppliers in a free-market economy. This focus parallels the normative, managerial stream of the PLC literature and affords an opportunity to develop and refine that branch by recasting it in a stricter theoretical framework.

Second, population ecology is a dynamic model concerned explicitly with the pattern of entries and exits among the organizations competing within particular populations. It implies a longitudinal research design that provides a direct contrast to the cross-sectional designs prevalent in marketing research. The availability of data places a significant constraint on longitudinal designs, but more insight may be gained by sacrificing large sample size in favor of analysis of single industries.

Third, the ecological model treats the performance of individual competitors as a function of its complex underlying causes. It recognizes that performance is a consequence of the effects of the prevailing competitive conditions in combination with the structures and strategies of different firms. In a research context, this approach treats the product life cycle as a causal model that overcomes the risks of tautological reasoning, which has been a frequent criticism of research attempting to model the product sales curve (Tellis and Crawford 1981). Furthermore, this ecological approach is suitable for testing by causal modeling methods using multiple measures and latent variables.

In a management context, this causal model also has the benefit of avoiding self-fulfilling prophecies by focusing on factors that can be manipulated to enhance the firm's position or at least to minimize damage.

Limitations of the Model

The first and perhaps most fundamental criticism of the population ecology model—which also applies to the PLC—pertains to the appropriateness of biological analogies for the analysis of social organizations. Detractors argue that the life cycles of social organizations do not have the same uniformity and predictability as the life cycles of biological organisms and therefore that organizational theories derived from biology cannot have much predictive validity (Perrow 1979). The fact that many large organizations seem to persist indefinitely without any evidence of decline is considered a particularly cogent example of this problem (Aldrich 1979).

Supporters of the ecological paradigm accept these limitations but argue that it can still offer many novel and valuable insights into organizational life (Aldrich 1979; Kimberley et al. 1980; McKelvey 1979). Though ecological models do not have perfect predictive validity (nor do other organizational theories), they provide a useful contingency approach that allows "what if" questions to be asked about the relationships between variations in the environment and changes in populations of organizations. Furthermore, the introduction of new models, even those with limited theoretical status, always opens the possibility for new research questions to be identified or for current questions to be recast in new ways, which may stimulate productive new research directions.

The particular issue of population decline and of the decline of constituent organizations is less easy to resolve. The conceptual literature in ecology has a major imbalance in its emphasis on the development phase with almost no consideration of the other end of the life cycle curve (Wholey and Brittain 1986). A few empirical studies within the ecological tradition have begun to focus on describing and explaining differential levels of mortality within and between populations of organizations (Carroll and Delacroix 1982; Freeman and Hannan 1983), but they have examined mature and fragmented industries (newspapers and restaurants) and therefore have not contributed significantly to our understanding of evolutionary phenomena.

A second problem with the ecological model is its reliance on "natural selection" as the mechanism that determines the success or failure of competing organizations. This approach is considered by some people to be antithetical to the management disciplines because a strict interpretation suggests performance is determined fully by the environment and is indifferent to management behavior (Perrow 1979; Van de Ven 1979). Ecological scholars have responded to this criticism by specifically acknowledging that organizational performance results from the joint effects of management actions and environmental conditions (Aldrich 1979; Hannan and Freeman 1977; Singh, Tucker, and House 1986). However, the basic model takes no account of management behavior.

A final problem with the ecological model, which may be attributable to the recency of its introduction into an organizational context, is that many of the variables lack clear, unambiguous definitions and directions for how they should be applied (Carroll 1985; Freeman 1982; Wholey and Brittain 1986). Central concepts such as resource spaces, niches, organizational form, natural selection, and performance typically are discussed at a very abstract level without much consideration of measurement issues. Researchers who want to apply this model are merely recommended to develop definitions and operational referents that are relevant to the context of their own research (Freeman 1982; Hannan and Freeman 1977), as we have done, with the attendant risks of misinterpretation and lack of standardization. However, organization theorists are now well aware of these problems. Undoubtedly the current high interest in this area will result in many of these problems being resolved.

NOTES

1. The classic logistic model of population growth assumes that the rate of growth, n, is equal to $a_0 - b_0$ which is the difference between the rates of births and deaths of organizations (Hannan and Freeman 1988). It further assumes that birth and death rates vary with the size or density of the population. In particular, the birth rate, a, is believed to fall approximately linearly with the population size and the death rate is believed to increase approximately linearly with the population size.

    The net effect of these tendencies is that when the size of the population is small in relation to its carrying capacity, the rate of births far exceeds the rate of deaths, resulting in an exponential growth in the total number of organizations; the reverse applies when the size of the population equals or exceeds the carrying capacity, resulting in a zero or negative growth rate.

2. Carroll (1985) argues that generalist organizations are usually larger than specialists but that the relationship between niche width and size is not exact. By definition, the fundamental niche for generalists is wider than that for specialists. Therefore generalist organizations that achieve maximum size within their fundamental niches would be expected to show a direct relationship between the degree of generalization and size as long as resources are distributed fairly evenly across environmental conditions.

If resources are distributed unevenly, however, certain specialists may find their preferred resources in abundance and grow very large. Conversely, such conditions provide few advantages to generalists, which therefore may be small.

REFERENCES

Aaker, David A. and George S. Day (1986), "The Perils of High Growth Markets," *Strategic Management Journal*, 7 (September–October), 409–21.

Abell, Derek F. (1978), "Strategic Windows," *Journal of Marketing*, 42 (July), 21–16.

Alderson, Wroe E. (1957), *Marketing Behavior and Executive Action*. Homewood, IL: Richard D. Irwin, Inc.

Aldrich, Howard E. (1979), *Organizations and Environments*. Englewood Cliffs, NJ: Prentice-Hall, Inc.

Bass, Frank M. (1969), "A New Product Growth Model for Consumer Durables," *Management Science*, 15 (January), 215–27.

_____ (1980), "The Relationship between Diffusion Curves, Experience Curves and Demand Elasticities, for Consumer Durable Technological Innovations," *Journal of Business*, 53 (July), 551–7.

_____ (1986), "The Adoption of a Marketing Model: Comments and Observations," in *Innovation Diffusion Models of New Product Acceptance*, Vijay Mahajan and Yoram Wind, eds. Cambridge, MA: Ballinger Publishing Company, 27–36.

Biggadike, Ralph (1981), "The Contributions of Marketing to Strategic Management," *Academy of Management Review*, 4 (October), 621–33.

Bond, R. S. and D. F. Lean (1977), *Sales Promotion and Product Differentiation in Two Prescription Drug Markets*. Washington, DC: Federal Trade Commission, Bureau of Economics.

Boxer, Phillip J. and Robin Wensley (1983), "Niches and competition: The Ecology of Market Organization," Working Paper 83/8, London Business School.

Brittain, J. W. and J. H. Freeman (1980), "Organizational Proliferation and Density Dependent Selection," in *The Organizational Life Cycle: Issues in the Creation, Transformation and Decline of Organizations*, J. R. Kimberly, R. H. Wiley and Associates. San Francisco: Jossey-Bass Inc., Publishers.

_____ and Douglas R. Wholey (1988), "Competition Coexistence in Organizational Communities: Population Dynamics in Electronics Components Manufacturing," in *Ecological Models of Organizations*, Glenn R. Carroll, ed. Cambridge, MA: Ballinger.

Buzzell, Robert D. (1966), "Competitive Behavior and Product Life Cycles," in *New Ideas for Successful Marketing*, John Wright and Jac Goldstucker, eds. Chicago: American Marketing Association.

_____ (1981), "Are There Natural Market Structures?" *Journal of Marketing*, 45 (Winter), 42–51.

_____ and Bradley Gale (1987), *The PIMS Principles*. New York: The Free Press.

Camerer, Colin (1985), "Redirecting Research in Business Policy and Strategy," *Strategic Management Journal*, 6 (January–March), 1–16.

Carroll, Glenn R. (1981), "Organizational Ecology," *Annual Review of Sociology*, 10, 71–93.

_____ (1985), "Concentration and Specialization: Dynamics of Niche Width in Populations of Organizations," *American Journal of Sociology*, 90 (6), 1262–83.

_____ and Jacques Delacroix (1982), "Organizational Mortality in the Newspaper Industries of Argentina and Ireland: An Ecological Approach," *Administrative Science Quarterly*, 27, 167–98.

Chakravarthy, Balaj (1984), "Strategic Self-Renewal: A Planning Framework for Today," *Academy of Management Review*, 3, 536–47.

Cox, William, Jr. (1967), "Product Life Cycles as Marketing Models," *Journal of Business*, 40 (October), 375–84.

Cyert, Richard M. and James G. March (1963), *A Behavioural Theory of the Firm*. Englewood Cliffs, NJ: Prentice-Hall, Inc.

Darwin, C. (1859), *On the Origin of Species* (reprint). Cambridge, MA: Harvard University Press (1964).

Day, George S. (1981), "The Product Life Cycle: Analysis and Applications Issues," *Journal of Marketing*, 45 (Fall), 60–7.

_____ (1986), *Analysis for Strategic Market Decisions*. St. Paul, MN: West Publishing.

Dhalla, N. K. and S. Yuspeh (1976), "Forget the Product Life Cycle Concept," *Harvard Business Review*, 54 (January–February), 102–12.

Dodson, Joseph A. and E. Muller (1978), "Models of New Product Diffusion through Advertising and Word of Mouth," *Management Science*, 15 (November), 1568–78.

Dolan, Robert J. and Abel P. Jeuland (1981), "Experience Curves and Dynamic Demand Models: Implications for Optimal Pricing Strategies," *Journal of Marketing*, 45 (Winter), 52–62.

Enis, Ben M., Raymond LaGarce, and Arthur E. Prell (1977), "Extending the Product Life Cycle," *Business Horizons*, 20 (June), 46–56.

Freeman, John (1982) "Organizational Life Cycles and Natural Selection Process," *Research in Organizational Behavior*, B. M. Staw and L. L. Cummings, eds., 4, 1–32.

_____ and Warren Bocker (1984), "The Ecological Analysis of Business Strategy," *California Management Review*, 26 (Spring), 73–86.

_____ and Michael T. Hannan (1983), "Niche Width and the Dynamics of Organizational Populations," *American Journal of Sociology*, 88 (6), 1116–45.

Gardner, David M. (1987), "Product Life Cycle: A Critical Look at the Literature," in *Review of Marketing 1987*, Michael Houston, ed. Chicago: American Marketing Association, 162–94.

Gatignon, Hubert A. and Thomas S. Robertson, (1986), "Integration of Consumer Diffusion Theory and Diffusion Models: New Research Directions," in *Innovation Diffusion Models of New Product Acceptance*, Vijay Mahajan and Yoram Wind, eds. Cambridge, MA: Ballinger.

Gross, Irwin (1968), "Toward a General Theory of Product Evolution: A Rejection of the 'Product Life Cycle' Concept," Working Paper 43–10, Marketing Science Institute.

Hamermesh, R. G., M. J. Anderson, Jr., and G. E. Harris (1978), "Strategies for Low Market Share Businesses," *Harvard Business Review*, 56 (May–June), 95–102.

Hannan, Michael T. and John Freeman (19770, "The Population Ecology of Organizations," *American Journal of Sociology*, 82 (5), 929–64.

_____ and _____ (1988), "Density Dependence in the Growth of Organizational Populations," in *Ecological Models of Organizations*, Glenn R. Carroll, ed. Cambridge, MA: Ballinger.

Harrell, Stephen G. and Elmer D. Taylor (1981), "Modeling the Product Life Cycle for Consumer Durables," *Journal of Marketing*, 45 (Fall), 68–75.

Hawley, A. H. (1968), "Human Ecology," in *International Encyclopedia of the Social Sciences*, D. L. Sills, ed. New York: Macmillan Publishing Company, 328–37.

Hofer, Charles W. (1975), "Toward a Contingency Theory of Business Strategy," *Academy of Management Journal*, 18 (December), 784–809.

Horsky, Dan and L. S. Simon (1983), "Advertising and the Diffusion of New Products," *Marketing Science*, 2 (Winter), 1–17.

Kimberly, J. R., R. H. Miles and Associates (1980), *The Organizational Life Cycle: Issues in the Creation, Transformation and Decline of Organizations*. San Francisco: Jossey-Bass, Inc., Publishers.

Kotler, Philip (1984), *Marketing Management Analysis, Planning and Control*, 5th ed. Englewood Cliffs, NJ: Prentice-Hall, Inc.

Lambkin, Mary (1988), "Competition in Developing Markets: The Impact of Order of Entry," *Strategic Management Journal*, 9, 127–40.

Levitt, Theodore (1965), "Exploit the Product Life Cycle," *Harvard Business Review*, 43 (November–December), 81–94.

Lilien, Gary L., A. G. Rao, and S. Kalish (1981), "Bayesian Estimation and Control of Detailing Effort in a Repeat Purchase Diffusion Environment," *Management Science*, 27 (May), 493–506.

Mahajan, Vijay and Eitan Muller (1979), "Innovation, Diffusion and New Product Growth Models in Marketing," *Journal of Marketing*, 43 (Fall), 55–68.

_____ and Yoram Wind (1985), *Innovation Diffusion Models of New Product Acceptance*. Cambridge, MA: Ballinger.

McKelvey, B. (1979), "Comment of the Biological Analogy in Organizational Science," *Administrative Science Quarterly*, 24, 488–93.

Midgley, David F. (1981), "Toward a Theory of the Product Life Cycle: Explaining Diversity," *Journal of Marketing*, 45 (Fall, 109–15.

Montgomery, Cynthia A. (1982), "The Measurement of Firm Diversification: Some New Empirical Evidence," *Academy of Management Journal*, 25, 299–308.

Perrow, Charles (1979), *Complex Organizations*, 2nd ed. Palo Alto, CA: Scott, Foresman and Company.

Polli, Rolando and Victor Cook (1969), "Validity of the Product Life Cycle," *Journal of Business*, 42 (October), 385–400.

Porter, Michael E. (1980), *Competitive Strategy: Techniques for Analyzing Industries and Competitors*. New York: The Free Press.

Rink, David R. and John E. Swan (1979), "Product Life Cycle Research: A Literature Review," *Journal of Business Research*, 78 (September), 219–42.

_____ and _____ (1987), "Fitting Business Strategic and Tactical Planning to the Product Life Cycle," in *Planning and Management Handbook*, William R. King and David I. Cleland, eds. New York: Nostrand Reinhold Company.

Robertson, Thomas S. and Hubert Gatignon (1986), "Competitive Effects on Technology Diffusion," *Journal of Marketing*, 50 (July), 1–12.

Robinson, V. and C. Lakham (1975), "Dynamic Price Models for New Product Planning," *Management Science*, 21 (June), 1113–32.

Robinson, William T. (1988), "Sources of Market Pioneer Advantages: The Case of Industrial Goods Industries," *Journal of Marketing Research*, 25 (February), 87–94.

_____ and C. Fornell (1985), "The Sources of Market Pioneer Advantages in Consumer Goods Industries," *Journal of Marketing Research*, 22 (August), 305–17.

Rogers, Everett M. (1983). *Diffusion of Innovations*. New York: The Free Press.

Romanelli, Elaine (1988), "New Venture Strategies in the Microcomputer Industry," *California Management Review*.

Rumelt, Richard P. (1974), *Strategy, Structure and Economic Performance*. Boston, MA: Division of Research, Harvard Business School.

Saporito, Bill (1987), "Discounters in the Dumps," *Fortune* (August 3), 103–10.

Schendel, Dan E. (1986), "Strategic Management and Strategic Marketing: What's Strategic about Either One?" in *Strategic Marketing and Management*, Howard Thomas and David Gardner, eds. New York: John Wiley & Sons, Inc.

Simon, Herbert A. and Charles P. Bonini (1958), "The Size and Distribution of Business Firms," *American Economic Review*, 48 (September), 607–17.

Singh, Jitendra V., David J. Tucker, and Robert J. House (1986), "Organizational Legitimacy and the Liability of Newness," *Administrative Science Quarterly*, 31, 171–93.

Stinchcombe, A. L. (1965), "Social Structure and Organizations," in *Handbook of Organizations*,

James G. March, ed. Chicago: Rand-McNally, 153–93.

Tellis, Gerard J. and C. Merle Crawford (1981), "An Evolutionary Approach to Product Growth Theory," *Journal of Marketing*, 45 (Fall), 125–32.

Thietart, R. A. and R. Vivas (1984), "An Empirical Investigation of Success Strategies for Businesses along the Product Life Cycle," *Management Science*, 30 (December), 1405–22.

Thorelli, Hans B. (1967), "Ecology in Marketing," *Southern Journal of Business*, 2 (October), 19–25.

——— and Stephen C. Burnett (1981), "The Nature of Product Life Cycles for Industrial Goods Businesses," *Journal of Marketing*, 45 (Fall), 97–108.

Urban, Glen L., T. Carter, S. Gaskin, and Z. Mucha (1986), "Market Share Rewards to Pioneering Brands: An Empirical Analysis and Strategic Implications," *Management Science*, 32 (June), 645–59.

Van de Ven, Andrew H. (1979), "Review of H. E. Aldrich, Organizations and Environments," *Administrative Science Quarterly*, 24, 320–6.

Weitz, Barton (1985), "Introduction to Special Issue on Competition in Marketing," *Journal of Marketing Research*, 22 (August), 229–36.

Wernerfelt, Birger and Aneel Karani (1987), "Competitive Strategy under Uncertainty," *Strategic Management Journal*, 8 (March–April), 187–94.

——— and Cynthia Montgomery (1986), "What Is an Attractive Industry?" *Management Science*, 32 (October), 1223–30.

Whitten, R. (1981), "Brand Performance in the Cigarette Industry and the Advantage of Early Entry, 1913–74," Washington, DC: Federal Trade Commission.

Wholey, D. R. and J. W. Brittain (1986), "Organizational Ecology: Findings and Implications," *Academy of Management Review*, 11 (3), 513–33.

Willard, Gary E. and Arnold C. Cooper (1985), "Survivors of Industry Shake-Outs: The Case of the U.S. Color Television Set Industry," *Strategic Management Journal*, 6 (October–December), 299–318.

Wind, Yoram (1982), *Product Policy: Concepts, Methods and Strategy*. Reading, MA: Addison-Wesley Publishing Company.

Woo, Carolyn Y. and Arnold C. Cooper (1982), "The Surprising Case for Low Market Share," *Harvard Business Review*, 60 (November–December), 106–13.

◆

Consumer Perceptions of Price, Quality, and Value: A Means-End Model and Synthesis of Evidence

Valarie A. Zeithaml

Though consumer perceptions of price, quality, and value are considered pivotal determinants of shopping behavior and product choice (Bishop 1984; Doyle 1984; Jacoby and Olson 1985; Sawyer and Dickson 1984; Schlechter 1984), research on these concepts and their linkages has provided few conclusive findings. Research efforts have been criticized for inadequate definition and conceptualization (Monroe and Krishnan 1985; Zeithaml 1983), inconsistent measurement procedures (Monroe and Krishnan 1985), and methodological problems (Bowbrick 1982; Olson 1977; Peterson and Wilson 1985). One fundamental problem limiting work in the area involves the meaning of the concepts: quality and value are indistinct and elusive constructs that often are mistaken for imprecise adjectives like "goodness, or luxury, or shininess, or weight" (Crosby 1979). Quality and value are not well differentiated from each other and from similar constructs such as perceived

worth and utility. Because definition is difficult, researchers often depend on unidimensional self-report measures to capture the concepts (Jacoby, Olson, and Haddock 1973; McConnell 1968; Shapiro 1973) and thus must assume shared meanings among consumers.

What do consumers mean by quality and value? How are perceptions of quality and value formed? Are they similar across consumers and products? How do consumers relate quality, price, and value in their deliberations about products and services? This article is an attempt to provide answers to these questions by:

- defining the concepts of price, quality, and value from the consumer's perspective,
- relating the concepts in a model, and
- developing propositions about the concepts, examining the available evidence in support of the proportions, and suggesting areas where research is needed.

To accomplish these objectives, a review of previous research was augmented by an exploratory investigation of quality and value in

"Consumer Perceptions of Price, Quality, and Value: A Means-End Model and Synthesis of Evidence," Zeithaml, Valarie A. Vol. 52 (July '88), pp. 2–22. Reprinted from the *Journal of Marketing*, published by the American Marketing Association.

the product category of beverages. Company interviews, a focus group interview, and 30 in-depth consumer interviews conducted by free-elicitation approaches generated qualitative data that supplemented previous research and served as the basis for 14 proportions.

THE EXPLORATORY STUDY

In the exploratory phase of the research, company, focus group, and in-depth consumer interviews were conducted to gain insight into consumer perceptions of quality and value. Cooperation was obtained from a national company that markets three distinct product lines of beverages: a line of 100% fruit-flavored children's drinks, a line of 100% fruit juices, and a line of tomato-based juices. In-depth interviews were held with the marketing research director, the senior product manager for juices, two company strategic planners, and the president of the company's advertising agency. Open-ended questions pertained to issues such as company knowledge about quality and value perceptions of consumers, ways the company determined those perceptions, and how quality and value were communicated to consumers.

A focus group interview on the topics of quality and value in beverages was held in a metropolitan area in the Southeast. The focus group was formed in accordance with guidelines traditionally followed in the marketing research field (Bellenger, Bernhardt, and Goldstucker 1976). Participants were recruited to fit the demographic profile of purchasers of fruit- and tomato-based beverages. All participants were women between the ages of 25 and 49 and all had at least one child younger than 10 years of age. Participants were screened to ensure current or recent usage of fruit- and tomato-based beverages. The identity of the participating firm was not re-

vealed in the interview; discussion about price, quality, and value centered on consumer experiences and perceptions relating to beverages in general rather than to the specific brands of the sponsoring company. The moderator's questions covered such topics as the meaning of quality and value, the attributes used to evaluate quality and value, and the role of price in quality and value judgments.

A total of 30 in-depth interviews with female consumers were held in three metropolitan areas (one in the Southwest, one on the East Coast, and one in the Midwest). Free-elicitation approaches recommended by Olson and Reynolds (1983) were used to obtain information about the cognitive structures of consumers. These techniques included triad sorts and laddering. In the triad sorts, similar brands in the beverage category were divided into sets of three and subjects were probed for distinctions among them. This initial process uncovered the important distinctions that respondents used to discriminate among products. The laddering process, which followed the triad sorts, involved a sequence of in-depth probes designed to force the consumer up the ladder of abstraction. As these procedures had successfully elicited the more important higher levels of abstraction in previous studies (Gutman and Alden 1985; Reynolds, Gutman, and Fiedler 1984; Reynolds and Jamieson 1985), they were used to reveal the links among product attributes, quality, and value. After these indirect methods, subjects responded to open-ended questions covering such topics as information needed to make judgments about quality and value, impact of related factors (e.g., advertising and packaging) on perceptions, and definitions of the concepts. Before debriefing, demographic and beverage usage data were collected from respondents.

As is typical in exploratory studies using means-end chains (e.g., Olson and Reynolds 1983), the data generated were not numerical.

Instead, the data were in the form of protocols and means-end maps for individual consumers. Patterns of responses and observed similarities across individuals form the "results" of this type of exploratory study. When combined with the descriptive data from the executive and focus group interviews, the observations and insights provide a framework for speculating about the concepts and their relationships (Figure 32-1).

THE MODEL

Figure 32-1, an adaptation of a model first proposed by Dodds and Monroe (1985), affords an overview of the relationships among the concepts of price, perceived quality, and perceived value. In the following sections,

relevant literature and evidence from the exploratory investigation are used to define and describe each concept in the model. To differentiate between proposed relationships and empirically supported relationships, discussion of each proposition is divided into two parts. First, propositions are developed on the basis of the qualitative data from the exploratory study and other conceptual work from the literature. Second, for each proposition, empirical evidence that supports and refutes the proposition is reviewed.

THE CONCEPT OF PERCEIVED QUALITY

Quality can be defined broadly as superiority or excellence. By extension, perceived quality can be defined as the consumer's judgment

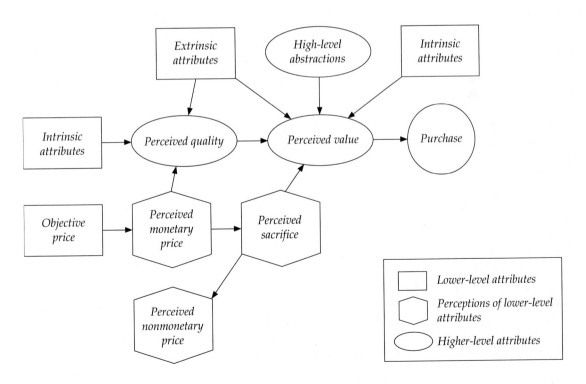

Figure 32-1
A Means-End Model Relating Price, Quality, and Value

about a product's overall excellence or superiority.[1] Perceived quality is (1) different from objective or actual quality, (2) a higher level abstraction rather than a specific attribute of a product, (3) a global assessment that in some cases resembles attitude, and (4) a judgment usually made within a consumer's evoked set.

Objective Quality versus Perceived Quality
Several researchers (Dodds and Monroe 1984; Garvin 1983; Holbrook and Corfman 1985; Jacoby and Olson 1985; Parasuraman, Zeithaml, and Berry 1986) have emphasized the difference between objective and perceived quality. Holbrook and Corfman (1985), for example, distinguish between mechanistic and humanistic quality: " . . . mechanistic [quality] involves an objective aspect or feature of a thing or event; humanistic [quality] involves the subjective response of people to objects and is therefore a highly relativistic phenomenon that differs between judges" (p. 33). "Objective quality" is the term used in the literature (e.g, Hjorth-Anderson 1984; Monroe and Krishnan 1985) to describe the actual technical superiority or excellence of the products.

As it has been used in the literature, the term "objective quality" refers to measurable and verifiable superiority on some predetermined ideal standard or standards. Published quality ratings from sources such as *Consumer Reports* are used to operationalize the construct of objective quality in research studies (see Curry and Faulds 1986). In recent years, researchers have debated the use of these measures of quality on methodological grounds (Curry and Faulds 1986; Hjorth-Anderson 1984, 1986; Maynes 1976; Sproles 1986). Concern centers on the selection of attributes and weights to measure objective quality; researchers and experts (e.g., *Consumer Reports*) do not agree on what the ideal standard or standards should be. Others (such as Maynes 1976) claim that objective quality does not exist, that all quality evaluations are subjective.

The term "objective quality" is related closely to—but not the same as—other concepts used to describe technical superiority of a product. For example, Garvin (1983) discusses product-based quality and manufacturing-based quality. Product-based quality refers to amounts of specific attributes or ingredients of a product. Manufacturing-based quality involves conformance to manufacturing specifications or service standards. In the prevailing Japanese philosophy, quality means "zero defects—doing it right the first time." Conformance to requirements (Crosby 1979) and incidence of internal and external failures (Garvin 1983) are other definitions that illustrate manufacturing-oriented notions of quality.

These concepts are not identical to objective quality because they, too, are based on perceptions. Though measures of specifications may be actual (rather than perceptual), the specifications themselves are set on the basis of what managers perceive to be important. Managers' views may differ considerably from consumers' or users' views. *Consumer Reports* ratings may not agree with managers' assessments in terms of either salient attributes or weights assigned to the attributes. In a research study for General Electric, Morgan (1985) points out striking differences between consumer, dealer, and manager perceptions of appliance quality. When asked how consumers perceive quality, managers listed workmanship, performance, and form as critical components. Consumers actually keyed in on different components: appearance, cleanability, and durability. Similarly, company researchers in the exploratory study measured beverage quality in terms of "flavor roundedness" and "astringency" whereas consumers focused on purity (100% fruit juice) and sweetness.

To reiterate, perceived quality is defined in the model as the consumer's judgment about the superiority or excellence of a product. This perspective is similar to the user-based approach of Garvin (1983) and differs from product-based and manufacturing-based approaches. Perceived quality is also different from objective quality, which arguably may not exist because all quality is perceived by someone, be it consumers or managers or researchers at *Consumer Reports*.

Higher Level Abstraction Rather Than an Attribute   The means-end chain approach to understanding the cognitive structure of consumers holds that product information is retained in memory at several levels of

abstraction (Cohen 1979; Myers and Shocker 1981; Olson and Reynolds 1983; Young and Feigen 1975). The simplest level is a product attribute; the most complex level is the value or payoff of the product to the consumer. Young and Feigen (1975) depicted this view in the "Grey benefit chain," which illustrates how a product is linked through a chain of benefits to a concept called the "emotional payoff."

Product → Functional → Practical → Emotional
           Benefit   Benefit   Payoff

Related conceptualizations (Table 32-1) pose the same essential idea: consumers organize information at various levels of abstraction rang-

Table 32-1
Selected Means-End Chain Models and Their Proposed Relationships with Quality and Value

Scheme	Attribute Level	Quality Level	Value Level	Personal Value Level
Young and Feigin (1975)	Functional benefits	Practical benefit	Emotional payoff	
Rokeach (1973) Howard (1977)	Product attributes	Choice criteria	Instrumental values	Terminal values
Myers and Shocker (1981)	Physical characteristics	Pseudophysical characteristics	Task or outcome referent	User referent
Geistfeld, Sproles, and Badenhop (1977)	Concrete, unidimensional, and measurable attributes (C)	Somewhat abstract, multidimensional but measurable (B)	Abstract, multidimensional, and difficult to measure attributes (A)	
Cohen (1979)	Defining attributes	Instrumental attributes		Highly valued states
Gutman and Reynolds (1979)	Attributes	Consequences	Values	
Olson and Reynolds (1983)	Concrete attributes	Abstract attributes	Functional consequences Psychosocial consequences Instrumental values	Terminal values

ing from simple product attributes (e.g., physical characteristics of Myers and Shocker 1981, defining attributes of Cohen 1979, concrete attributes of Olson and Reynolds 1983) to complex personal values. Quality has been included in multiattribute models as though it were a lower level attribute (criticisms of this practice have been leveled by Ahtola 1984, Myers and Shocker 1981, and others), but perceived quality is instead a second-order phenomenon: an abstract attribute in Olson and Reynold's (1983) terms, a "B" attribute (somewhat abstract, multidimensional but measurable) in Myers and Shockers' (1981) formulation.

Global Assessment Similar to Attitude

Olshavsky (1985) views quality as a form of overall evaluation of a product, similar in some ways to attitude. Holbrook and Corfman (1985) concur, suggesting that quality is a relatively global value judgment. Lutz (1986) proposes two forms of quality, "affective quality" and "cognitive quality." Affective quality parallels Olshavsky's and Holbrook and Corfman's views of perceived quality as overall attitude. Cognitive quality is the case of a superordinate inferential assessment of quality intervening between lower order cues and an eventual overall product evaluation (Lutz 1986). In Lutz's view, the higher the proportion of attributes that can be assessed before purchase (search attributes) to those that can be assessed only during consumption (experience attributes), the more likely it is that quality is a higher level cognitive judgment. Conversely, as the proportion of experience attributes increases, quality tends to be an affective judgment. Lutz extends this line of reasoning to propose that affective quality is relatively more likely for services and consumer nondurable goods (where experience attributes dominate) whereas cognitive quality is more likely for industrial products and consumer durable goods (where search attributes dominate).

Judgment Made within Consumer's Evoked Set

Evaluations of quality usually take place in a comparison context. Maynes (1976) claimed that quality evaluations are made within "the set of goods which . . . would in the consumer's judgment serve the same general purpose for some maximum outlay." On the basis of the qualitative study, and consistent with Maynes' contention, the set of products used in comparing quality appears to be the consumer's evoked set. A product's quality is evaluated as high or low depending on its relative excellence or superiority among products or services that are viewed as substitutes by the consumer. It is critical to note that the specific set of products used for comparison depends on the consumer's, not the firm's, assessment of competing products. For example, consumers in the exploratory study compared the quality of different brands of orange juice (which would be the comparison context of the firm), the quality of different forms (refrigerated vs. canned), and the quality of purchased versus homemade orange juice.

Figure 32-2 depicts the perceived quality component of the conceptual model in Figure 32-1.

P_{Q1}: Consumers use lower level attribute cues to infer quality.

Holbrook and Corfman (1985) note that early philosophers used the word "quality" to refer to explicit features (i.e., properties or characteristics) of an object as perceived by a subject (e.g., Austin 1964, p. 44; Russell 1912). Olshavsky (1985) terms this tendency to infer quality from specific attributes "surrogate-based preference forming behavior" and cites examples of product categories in which a given surrogate is highly associated with quality (e.g., size signals quality in stereo speakers, style signals quality in cars and clothes). In the exploratory study, consumers

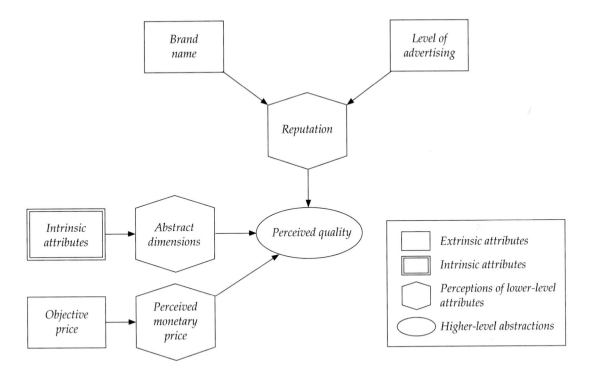

Figure 32-2
The Perceived Quality Component

repeatedly associated quality in fruit juices with purity (e.g., 100% fruit juice with no sugar added) or freshness. In these and other product categories, one or a few attributes from the total set of attributes appear to serve as reliable signals of product quality.

Attributes that signal quality have been dichotomized into intrinsic and extrinsic cues (Olson 1977; Olson and Jacoby 1972). Intrinsic cues involve the physical composition of the product. In a beverage, intrinsic cues would include such attributes as flavor, color, texture, and degree of sweetness. Intrinsic attributes cannot be changed without altering the nature of the product itself and are consumed as the product is consumed (Olson 1977; Olson and Jacoby 1972). Extrinsic cues are product-related but not part of the physical product itself. They are, by definition, out-

side the product. Price, brand name, and level of advertising are examples of extrinsic cues to quality.

The intrinsic-extrinsic dichotomy of quality cues is useful for discussing quality but is not without conceptual difficulties.[2] A small number of cues, most notably those involving the product's package, are difficult to classify as either intrinsic or extrinsic. Package could be considered an intrinsic or an extrinsic cue depending on whether the package is part of the physical composition of the product (e.g., a dripless spout in detergent or a squeezable ketchup container), in which case it would be an intrinsic cue, or protection and promotion for the product (e.g., a cardboard container for a computer), in which case it would be an extrinsic cue. For purposes of the model, package is considered an intrinsic cue but the information that appears on the package (e.g., brand name, price, logo) is considered an extrinsic cue.

Evidence   Researchers have identified key lower level attributes used by consumers to infer quality in only a few product categories. These lower level cues include price (Olson 1977; Olson and Jacoby 1972), suds level for detergents, size for stereo speakers (Olshavsky 1985), odor for bleach and stockings (Laird 1932), and produce freshness for supermarkets (Bonner and Nelson 1985).

P$_{Q2}$: The intrinsic product attributes that signal quality are product-specific, but dimensions of quality can be generalized to product classes or categories.

Generalizing about quality across products has been difficult for managers and researchers. Specific or concrete intrinsic attributes differ widely across products, as do the attributes consumers use to infer quality. Obviously, attributes that signal quality in fruit juice are not the same as those indicating quality in washing machines or automobiles. Even within a product category, specific attributes may provide different signals about quality. For example, thickness is related to high quality in tomato-based juices but not in fruit-flavored children's drinks. The presence of pulp suggests high quality in orange juice but low quality in apple juice.

Though the concrete attributes that signal quality differ across products, higher level abstract dimensions of quality can be generalized to categories of products. As attributes become more abstract (i.e., are higher in the means-end chains), they become common to more alternatives. Garvin (1987), for example, proposes that product quality can be captured in eight dimensions: performance, features, reliability, conformance, durability, serviceability, aesthetics, and perceived quality (i.e.,

image). Abstract dimensions that capture diverse specific attributes have been discussed by Johnson (1983) and Achrol, Reve, and Stern (1983). In describing the way consumers compare noncomparable alternatives (e.g., how they choose between such diverse alternatives as a stereo and a Hawaiian vacation), Johnson posited that consumers represent the attributes in memory at abstract levels (e.g., using entertainment value as the dimension on which to compare stereos and Hawaiian vacations). Similarly, Achrol, Reve, and Stern proposed that the multitude of specific variables affecting a firm in the environment can be captured in abstract dimensions. Rather than itemizing specific variables that affect particular firms in different industries under varying circumstances, they proposed conceptualizing the environment in terms of its abstract qualities or dimensions (e.g., homogeneity-heterogeneity, stability-instability, concentration-dispersion, and turbulence).

Olson (1978) pointed out that consumers may use informational cues to develop beliefs about products and that task response (i.e., choice or evaluation) may be a direct function of these mediating beliefs. According to Olson, these beliefs may be of two types: descriptive, which involve a restatement of the original information in more abstract terms (e.g., "accelerates from 0 to 60 in 5 seconds" generates the belief "high performance") and inferential, which involve an inference to information missing in the environment (e.g., "accelerates from 0 to 60 in 5 seconds" generates the belief "probably corners well, too"). This distinction roughly parallels Alba and Hutchinson's (1987) distinction between interpretive and embellishment inferences and both dichotomies illustrate the level at which dimensions of quality can be conceptualized.

Interviews with subjects in the exploratory study suggested that specific intrinsic attributes used to infer quality could not be generalized across beverages, but that higher level abstract dimensions could capture the meaning of perceived quality in whole categories or classes of beverages. Purity, freshness, flavor, and appearance were the higher level abstract dimensions subjects discussed in defining quality in the beverage category.

Evidence   In a study of quality in long distance telephone, banking, repair and maintenance, and brokerage services, Parasuraman, Zeithaml, and Berry (1985) found consistent dimensions of perceived quality across four consumer service industries. These abstract dimensions included reliability, empathy, assurance, responsiveness, and tangibles. Similarly, Bonner and Nelson (1985) found that sensory signals such as rich/full flavor, natural taste, fresh taste, good aroma, and appetizing looks—all higher level abstract dimensions of perceived quality—were relevant across 33 food product categories. Brucks and Zeithaml (1987) contend on the basis of exploratory work that six abstract dimensions (ease of use, functionality, performance, durability, serviceability, and prestige) can be generalized across categories of durable goods. Though empirical research has not verified the generalizability of dimensions for categories of packaged goods other than food products, for durable goods, or for industrial goods, abstract dimensions spanning these categories could be conceptualized, verified, and then used to develop general measures of quality in product categories.

P_{Q3}:   Extrinsic cues serve as generalized quality indicators across brands, products, and categories.

Extrinsic attributes (e.g., price, brand name) are not product-specific and can serve as general indicators of quality across all types of products. Price, brand name, and level of advertising are three extrinsic cues frequently associated with quality in research,

yet many other extrinsic cues are useful to consumers. Of special note are extrinsic cues such as product warranties and seals of approval (e.g., Good Housekeeping). Price, the extrinsic cue receiving the most research attention (see Olson 1977 for a complete review of this literature), appears to function as a surrogate for quality when the consumer has inadequate information about intrinsic attributes. Similarly, brand name serves as a "shorthand" for quality by providing consumers with a bundle of information about the product (Jacoby et al. 1978; Jacoby, Szybillo, and Busato-Schach 1977). Level of advertising has been related to product quality by economists Nelson (1970, 1974), Milgrom and Roberts (1986), and Schmalensee (1978). The basic argument holds that for goods whose attributes are determined largely during use (experience goods), higher levels of advertising signal higher quality. Schmalensee argues that level of advertising, rather than actual claims made, informs consumers that the company believes the goods are worth advertising (i.e., of high quality). Supporting this argument is the finding that many subjects in the exploratory study perceived heavily advertised brands to be generally higher in quality than brands with less advertising.

The exploratory investigation of beverages provided evidence that form of the product (e.g., frozen vs. canned vs. refrigerated) is an additional important extrinsic cue in beverages. Consumers held consistent perceptions of the relative quality of different forms of fruit juice: quality perceptions were highest for fresh products, next highest for refrigerated products, then bottled, then frozen, then canned, and lowest for dry product forms.

Evidence   The literature on hedonic quality measurement (Court 1939; Griliches 1971) maintains that price is the best measure of product quality. Considerable empirical research has investigated the relationship between price and quality (see Olson 1977 for a review of this literature in marketing) and has shown that consumers use price to infer quality when it is the only available cue. When price is combined with other (usually intrinsic) cues, the evidence is less convincing.

In forming impressions about quality of merchandise, respondents in a study by Mazursky and Jacoby (1985) selected brand name more frequently than any other information. Gardner (1970, 1971) found significant main effects on quality perceptions due to brand name.

Kirmani and Wright (1987a,b) found empirical support for the relationship between level of spending on advertising and quality inferences. Manipulating expenditures on media budgets and on production elements in advertisements, they found significant effects of both on consumers' quality perceptions.

Bonner and Nelson (1985) confirm that product form relates to quality perceptions. An empirical study revealed the same hierarchy of quality in package form (fresh, refrigerated, frozen, bottled, canned, dried) as was found in the exploratory study. Bonner and Nelson conclude: "The sensory maintenance ability of packaging differs by type and those packaging forms that can best deliver a rich/full flavor, natural and fresh taste, good aroma, and an appetizing appearance, are likely to gain market share" (p. 75).

P$_{Q4}$: Consumers depend on intrinsic attributes more than extrinsic attributes
  (a) at the point of consumption,
  (b) in prepurchase situations when intrinsic attributes are search attributes (rather than experience attributes), and
  (c) when the intrinsic attributes have high predictive value.

Which type of cue—intrinsic or extrinsic—is more important in signaling quality to the consumer? An answer to this question would help firms decide whether to invest resources in product improvements (intrinsic

cues) or in marketing (extrinsic cues) to improve perceptions of quality. Finding a simple and definitive answer to this question is unlikely, but the exploratory study suggests the type of attribute that dominates depends on several key contingencies.

The first contingency relates to the point in the purchase decision and consumption process at which quality evaluation occurs. Consumers may evaluate quality at the point of purchase (buying a beverage) or at the point of consumption (drinking a beverage). The salience of intrinsic attributes at the point of purchase depends on whether they can be sensed and evaluated at that time, that is, whether they contain search attributes (Nelson 1970). Where search attributes are present (e.g., sugar content of a fruit juice or color or cloudiness of a drink in a glass jar), they may be important quality indicators. In their absence, consumers depend on extrinsic cues.

At the point of consumption, most intrinsic attributes can be evaluated and therefore become accessible as quality indicators. Many consumers in the exploratory study on beverages used taste as the signal of quality at consumption. If a beverage did not taste fresh or tasted "tinny" or too thin, the evaluation was that quality was low.

Consumers depend on intrinsic attributes when the cues have high predictive value (Cox 1962). Many respondents in the exploratory study, especially those expressing concern for their children's health and teeth, unequivocally stated that purity (100% juice, no sugar) was the criterion they used to judge quality across the broad fruit juice category. The link between quality and this intrinsic attribute was clear and strong: all fruit beverages with 100% juice were high quality beverages and all others were not.

Evidence   Researchers addressing this question (Darden and Schwinghammer 1985; Etgar and Malhotra 1978; Olson and Jacoby

1972; Rigaux-Briemont 1982; Szybillo and Jacoby 1974) have concluded that intrinsic cues were in general more important to consumers in judging quality because they had higher predictive value than extrinsic cues. This conclusion does not account for the fact that many assessments about quality are made with insufficient information about intrinsic cues. Selected individual studies (e.g., Sawyer, Worthing, and Sendak 1979) have shown that extrinsic cues can be more important to consumers than intrinsic cues. Conflicting evidence about the importance of intrinsic and extrinsic cues become clearer if the conditions under which each type of cue becomes important are investigated.

P_{Q5}: Consumers depend on extrinsic attributes more than intrinsic attributes
  (a) in initial purchase situations when intrinsic cues are not available (e.g., for services),
  (b) when evaluation of intrinsic cues requires more effort and time than the consumer perceives is worthwhile, and
  (c) when quality is difficult to evaluate (experience and credence goods).

Extrinsic cues are posited to be used as quality indicators when the consumer is operating without adequate information about intrinsic product attributes. This situation may occur when the consumer (1) has little or no experience with the product, (2) has insufficient time or interest to evaluate the intrinsic attributes, and (3) cannot readily evaluate the intrinsic attributes.

At point of purchase, consumers cannot always evaluate relevant intrinsic attributes of a product. Unless free samples are being provided, consumers cannot taste new food products before buying them. Consumers do not know for certain how long a washing machine or automobile will last until they purchase and consume it. In these and similar situations, the consumer relies on extrinsic attributes such as warranty, brand name, and package as surrogates for intrinsic product attributes.

At other times, intrinsic attributes on which to evaluate quality are available but the consumer is unwilling or unable to expend the time and effort to evaluate them. Working women, men, and single shoppers, for example, have been reported to use supermarket product information significantly less than other demographic segments (Zeithaml 1985), in part because these segments are more time-conscious than other segments (Zeithaml 1985; Zeithaml and Berry 1987). Working women interviewed in the exploratory study reported that they shopped quickly and could not study nutritional information carefully on beverage containers. They selected beverages on the basis of the freshness or quality conveyed by packages or brand names.

In other situations, intrinsic product attributes indicating quality are simply too difficult for the consumer to evaluate. Evaluation may be difficult prior to purchase, as with haircuts, restaurant meals, and other experience goods. Complex stereo equipment, insurance policies, and major auto repairs are examples of products that for many consumers are difficult to evaluate even after purchase and consumption. For these "credence goods" (Darby and Karni 1973), consumers may rely on extrinsic cues because they are simpler to access and evaluate.

Evidence   Research has shown that price is used as a quality cue to a greater degree when brands are unfamiliar than when brands are familiar (Smith and Broome 1966; Stokes 1985). Research also has shown that when perceived risk of making an unsatisfactory choice is high, consumers select higher priced products (Lambert 1972; Peterson and Wilson 1985; Shapiro 1968, 1973).

P_{Q6}: The cues that signal quality change over time because of
(a) competition,
(b) promotional efforts of companies,
(c) changing consumer tastes, and
(d) information.

As improved technology and increasing competition lead to the development of technically better products, the features that signal superiority change. The exploratory study suggested that the attribute cues signaling quality in beverages are not static, but instead change over time. The shift from canned orange juice to frozen orange juice to refrigerated orange juice is one example of the evolving standards of quality in beverages. The replacement of saccharin with Nutrasweet in beverages is another.

Harness (1978, p. 17) illustrates the forces of change and the responses made by Procter & Gamble to keep Tide detergent the highest quality brand in the packaged soap category:

> Since Tide was first introduced in 1947, consumers have changed, washing machines have changed, fabrics have changed, laundry habits have changed, and competition has changed.... These are just a few of the more significant changes in the household laundry market, and every one of these changes has a meaning for the performance and the marketing plans for Tide. The product which we are selling today is importantly different from the Tide product which we introduced in 1947. It is different in its cleaning performance, in sudsing characteristics, aesthetics, physical properties, packaging. In total, there have been 55 significant modifications in this one brand during its 30-year lifetime.

THE CONCEPT OF PERCEIVED PRICE

From the consumer's perspective, price is what is given up or sacrificed to obtain a product. This definition is congruent with Ahtola's (1984) argument against including monetary price as a lower level attribute in multiattribute models because price is a "give" component of the model, rather than a "get" component. Defining price as a sacrifice is consistent with conceptualizations by other pricing researchers (Chapman 1986; Mazumdar 1986; Monroe and Krishnan 1985).

Figure 32-1 delineates the components of price: objective price, perceived nonmonetary price, and sacrifice. Jacoby and Olson (1977) distinguished between objective price (the actual price of a product) and perceived price (the price as encoded by the consumer). Figure 32-1 emphasizes this distinction: objective monetary price is frequently not the price encoded by consumers. Some consumers may notice that the exact price of Hi-C fruit juice is $1.69 for a 6-pack, but others may encode and remember the price only as "expensive" or "cheap." Still others may not encode price at all.

A growing body of research supports this distinction between objective and perceived price (Allen, Harrell, and Hutt 1976; Gabor and Granger 1961; *Progressive Grocer* 1964). Studies reveal that consumers do not always know or remember actual prices of products. Instead, they encode prices in ways that are meaningful to them (Dickson and Sawyer 1985; Zeithaml 1982, 1983). Levels of consumer attention, awareness, and knowledge of prices appear to be considerably lower than necessary for consumers to have accurate internal reference prices for many products (Dickson and Sawyer 1985; Zeithaml 1982). Dickson and Sawyer reported that the proportions of consumers checking prices of four types of products (margarine, cold cereal, toothpaste, and coffee) at point of purchase ranged from 54.2 to 60.6%. Among the groups of consumers not checking prices in these studies, a large proportion (from 58.5 to 76.6% in the four product categories) stated that price was just not important. Another recent study indicates that price awareness differs among demographic groups, the greatest levels of awareness being in consumers who are female, married, older, and do not work outside the home (Zeithaml and Berry 1987). Attention to prices is likely to be greater for higher priced packaged goods, durable goods, and services than for low priced beverages, but other factors in these categories—complexity, lack of price information, and processing time required—may interfere with accurate knowledge of prices. An additional factor contributing to the gap between actual and perceived price is price dispersion, the tendency for the same brands to be priced differently across stores or for products of the same type and quality to have wide price variance (Maynes and Assum 1982).

P_{P1}: Monetary price is not the only sacrifice perceived by consumers.

Full price models in economics (e.g., Becker 1964) acknowledge that monetary price is not the only sacrifice consumers make to obtain products. Time costs, search costs, and psychic costs all enter either explicitly or implicitly into the consumer's perception of sacrifice. If consumers cannot find products on the shelf, or if they must travel distances to buy them, a sacrifice has been made. If consumers must expend effort to assemble durable products or time to prepare packaged goods, and if this time and effort does not provide satisfaction to the consumer in the form of recreation or a hobby, a sacrifice has been made.

Evidence   Research in economics, home economics, and marketing supports the proposition that other costs—time, effort, search, psychic—are salient to consumers (Down 1961; Gronau 1973; Leibowitz 1974; Leuthold 1981; Linder 1970; Mabry 1970; Mincer 1963; Nichols, Smolensky, and Tideman 1971; Zeithaml and Berry 1987).

THE PRICE-QUALITY RELATIONSHIP

Nearly 90 research studies in the past 30 years have been designed to test the general wisdom that price and quality are positively related. Despite the expectation of a positive relationship, results of these studies have provided mixed evidence.

P_{PQ1}: A general price–perceived quality relationship does not exist.

Price reliance is a general tendency in some consumers to depend on price as a cue to quality (Lambert 1972; Shapiro 1968, 1973). The body of literature summarized by Olson (1977) is based on the assumption that a general price–perceived quality relationship exists. Despite a multitude of experimental studies on the topic, however, the relationship has not surfaced clearly except in situations where methodological concerns such as demand artifacts (Sawyer 1975) could offer alternative explanations for the results (Monroe and Krishnan 1985; Olson 1977). Bowbrick (1982) questioned the universality of the price–perceived quality relationship, called the stream of studies on the topic "pseudoresearch," and claimed that the price–perceived quality hypothesis is too general and untestable to produce anything other than trivial results. Peterson and Wilson (1985) argue that the relationship between price and perceived quality is not universal and that the direction of the relationship may not always be positive.

Evidence   Monroe and Krishnan (1985) concluded that a positive price–perceived quality relationship does appear to exist despite the inconsistency of the statistical significance of the research findings. They also noted, however, that multiple conceptual problems and methodological limitations compromised previous research. Monroe and

Dodds (1988) describe these limitations in greater detail and delineate a research program for establishing the validity of the price-quality relationship.

Many empirical studies have produced results that conflict with Monroe and Krishnan's assessment of a positive relationship. In several studies (Friedman 1967; Swan 1974), overall association between price and perceived quality is low. Other studies show the relationship to be nonlinear (Peterson 1970; Peterson and Jolibert 1976), highly variable across individuals (Shapiro 1973), and variable across products being judged (Gardner 1971). Other research, summarized by Olson (1977), shows that price becomes less important as a quality indicator when other product quality cues, such as brand name (Gardner 1971) or store image (Stafford and Enis 1969), are present. Exploratory and survey research (Bonner and Nelson 1985; Parasuraman, Zeithaml, and Berry 1985) indicates that price is among the least important attributes that consumers associate with quality.

Related studies (summarized by Hjorth-Anderson 1984) have consistently shown price to be correlated only weakly with objective (rather than perceived) quality. Typical of these studies is work by Sproles (1977), who correlated the prices of products with quality ratings obtained through *Consumer Reports* and *Consumers' Research Magazine*. Though a positive price–objective quality relationship was found in 51% of the 135 product categories, no relationship was found in 35% and a negative relationship was found in 14%. Similarly, Riesz found the mean rank correlation between price and objective quality to be .26 for 685 product categories reported in *Consumer Reports* between 1961 and 1975 and .09 for 679 brands of packaged foods (Riesz 1978). Geistfeld (1982) found variability among markets and across stores in the price–objective quality relationship. Most recently, Gerstner (1985) assessed the correlation between quality and price for 145 products and concluded that the

relationship appeared to be product-specific and generally weak.

Both Peterson and Wilson (1985) and Olshavsky (1985) argue that the emphasis in price-quality studies should not be on documenting the general price–perceived quality relationship, but on the conditions under which price information is likely to lead to an inference about product quality. One possibility is that some individuals rely heavily on price as a quality signal whereas others do not. Peterson and Wilson sorted respondents into groups on the basis of their having a price-reliance schema and confirmed in an experiment that "schematics" perceive a stronger relationship between price and quality than "aschematics." This general tendency on the part of some consumers to associate price and quality has been examined in the context of covariation assessment by Roedder-John, Scott, and Bettman (1986), who confirmed that consumers differ in their beliefs about the association between the price and quality variables. These studies provide evidence that some consumers have a schema of price reliance, rather than indicating a generalized tendency in consumers to associate price and quality.

P_{PQ2}: The use of price as an indicator of quality depends on
(a) availability of other cues to quality,
(b) price variation within a class of products,
(c) Product quality variation within a category of products,
(d) level of price awareness of consumers, and
(e) consumers' ability to detect quality variation in a group of products.

Monroe and Krishnan (1985) contend that most past price–perceived quality research has been exploratory and has not succeeded in resolving the question of when price is used to infer quality. Contingencies affecting the use of price as a quality indicator fit into three groups: informational factors, individual factors, and product category factors.

The first category of factors believed to affect the price–perceived quality relationship consists of other information available to the consumer. When intrinsic cues to quality are readily accessible, when brand names provide evidence of a company's reputation, or when level of advertising communicates the company's belief in the brand, the consumer may prefer to use those cues instead of price.

Several individual difference factors may account for the variation in the use of price as a quality signal. One explanatory variable is price awareness of the consumer: consumers unaware of product prices obviously cannot use price to infer quality. Another individual difference is consumers' ability to detect quality variation among products (Lambert 1972). If the consumer does not have sufficient product knowledge (or perhaps even interest) to understand the variation in quality (e.g., French, Williams, and Chance 1973), price and other extrinsic cues may be used to a greater degree.

Consumers appear to depend more on price as a quality signal in some product categories than in others. One explanation for this variation may be differences in price–objective quality relationships by category (e.g., the low price of Japanese automobiles does not diminish the well-established perception of quality in the category). Another explanation may be price variation in a category. In packaged goods categories (such as beverages) where products differ little in price, the consumer may not attribute higher quality to products that cost only a few cents more than those of competitors. Respondents in the exploratory study, for example, did not associate beverage price with quality. Still another category-specific contingency is quality variation: in categories where little variation is expected among brands (such as salt or paper sandwich bags), price may function only as an indication of sacrifice whereas in categories where

quality variation is expected (such as canned seafood or washing machines), price may function also as an indication of quality.

Evidence   Olson (1977) showed that availability of intrinsic and extrinsic cues other than price typically results in weighting those factors (e.g., brand name) as more important than price. He concluded that brand name is a stronger cue than price for evaluating overall quality (Gardner 1971; Jacoby, Olson, and Haddock 1973; Smith and Broome 1966; Stokes 1985).

Studies have indicated that use of price as a quality indicator differs by product category. Except for wine and perfume, most positive links have been found in durable rather than in nondurable or consumable products (Gardner 1970; Lambert 1972; Peterson and Wilson 1985). In an experimental setting, Peterson and Wilson documented the relationship between price variation and price–perceived quality association: the greater the price variation, the greater the tendency for consumers to use price as a quality indicator.

In a recent meta-analysis of 41 studies investigating the association between price and perceived quality, Rao and Monroe (1987) found that the type of experimental design and the magnitude of the price manipulation significantly influenced the size of the price–perceived quality effects obtained. The number of cues manipulated and the price level were not found to have a significant effect. Because of constraints imposed by the meta-analysis, the reviewers included only consumer products and eliminated several studies as outliers, so the full range of prices and types of products was not investigated.

Considerable empirical research supports individual differences in consumer knowledge of prices. Consumers are not uniformly aware of prices and certain consumer segments (such as working women and men) are less aware of prices than other segments (Zeithaml 1985; Zeithaml and Berry 1987;

Zeithaml and Fuerst 1983). Price awareness level has not been studied as it relates to quality perceptions, though Rao (1987) documented the impact of prior knowledge of products on the use of price as a quality cue.

THE CONCEPT OF PERCEIVED VALUE

When respondents in the exploratory study discussed value, they used the term in many different ways, describing a wide variety of attributes and higher level abstractions that provided value to them. What constitutes value—even in a single product category— appears to be highly personal and idiosyncratic. Though many respondents in the exploratory study agreed on cues that signaled quality, they differed considerably in expressions of value. Patterns of responses from the exploratory study can be grouped into four consumer definitions of value: (1) value is low price, (2) value is whatever I want in a product, (3) value is the quality I get for the price I pay, and (4) value is what I get for what I give. Each definition involves a different set of linkages among the elements in the model and each consumer definition has its counterpart in the academic or trade literature on the subject. The diversity in meanings of value is illustrated in the following four definitions and provides a partial explanation for the difficulty in conceptualizing and measuring the value construct in research.

Value Is Low Price   Some respondents equated value with low price, indicating that what they had to give up was most salient in their perceptions of value. In their own words:

- Value is price—which one is on sale.
- When I can use coupons, I feel that the juice is a value.
- Value means low price.
- Value is whatever is on special this week.

In industry studies, Schechter (1984) and Bishop 1984) identified subsets of consumers that equate value with price. Other industry studies, including Hoffman's (1984), reveal the salience of price in the value equations of consumers.

Value Is Whatever I Want in a Product   Other respondents emphasized the benefits they received from the product as the most important components of value:

- Value is what is good for you.
- Value is what my kids will drink.
- Little containers because then there is no waste.
- Value to me is what is convenient. When I can take it out of the refrigerator and not have to mix it up, then it has value.

This second definition is essentially the same as the economist's definition of utility, that is, a subjective measure of the usefulness or want satisfaction that results from consumption. This definition also has been expressed in the trade literature. Value has been defined as "whatever it is that the customer seeks in making decisions as to which store to shop or which product to buy" (*Chain Store Age* 1985). Schechter (1984) defines value as all factors, both qualitative and quantitative, subjective and objective, that make up the complete shopping experience. In these definitions, value encompasses all relevant choice criteria.

Value Is the Quality I Get for the Price I Pay   Other respondents conceptualized value as a tradeoff between one "give" component, price, and one "get" component, quality:

- Value is price first and quality second.
- Value is the lowest price for a quality brand.
- Value is the same as quality. No—value is affordable quality.

This definition is consistent with several others that appear in the literature (Bishop 1984; Dodds and Monroe 1984; Shapiro and Associates 1985).

Value Is What I Get for What I Give   Finally, some respondents considered all relevant "get" components as well as all relevant "give" components when describing value:

- Value is how many drinks you can get out of a certain package. Frozen juices have more because you can water them down and get more out of them.
- How many gallons you get out of it for what the price is.
- Whatever makes the most for the least money.
- Which juice is more economical.
- Value is what you are paying for what you are getting.
- Value is price and having single portions so that there is no waste.

This fourth definition is consistent with Sawyer and Dickson's (1984) conceptualization of value as a ratio of attributes weighted by their evaluations divided by price weighted by its evaluation. This meaning is also similar to the utility per dollar measure of value used by Hauser and Urban (1986), Hauser and Simmie (1981), Hauser and Shugan (1983), and others.

These four consumer expressions of value can be captured in one overall definition: perceived value is the consumer's overall assessment of the utility of a product based on perceptions of what is received and what is given. Though what is received varies across consumers (i.e., some may want volume, others high quality, still others convenience) and what is given varies (i.e., some are concerned only with money expended, others with time and effort), value represents a tradeoff of the salient give and get components.

Value and Quality   In the means-end chains, value (like quality) is proposed to be a higher level abstraction. It differs from quality in two ways. First, value is more individualistic and personal than quality and is therefore a higher level concept than quality. As shown in Table 32-1, value may be similar to the "emotional payoff" of Young and Feigen (1975), to "abstract, multi-dimensional, difficult-to-measure attributes" of Geistfeld, Sproles, and Badenhop (1977), and to "instrumental values" of Olson and Reynolds (1983). Second, value (unlike quality) involves a tradeoff of give and get components. Though many conceptualizations of value have specified quality as the only "get" component in the value equation, the consumer may implicitly include other factors, several that are in themselves higher level abstractions, such as prestige and convenience (see Holbrook and Corfman 1985 for a discussion of the difficulty involved in separating these abstractions in the value construct).

P_{V1}: The benefit components of value include salient intrinsic attributes, extrinsic attributes, perceived quality, and other relevant high level abstractions.

Differences among the benefit or get components shown in the model and listed in P_{V1} can be illustrated by findings from the exploratory study of fruit juices. As discussed before, perceived quality in fruit juices was signaled by the attribute "100% fruit juice" plus sensory attributes such as taste and texture.

Some intrinsic attributes of fruit juices—other than those signaling quality—were cited as providing value to respondents. Color was one important intrinsic attribute. Most mothers knew which colors or flavors of juice their children would drink; only those flavors were considered to be acceptable to the child and therefore to have value for the mother. Other intrinsic attributes (e.g., absence of pulp and visible consistency of the drinks) also affected value perceptions.

In addition to perceived quality and these intrinsic attributes, other higher level abstractions contributed to perceptions of value. A frequently mentioned higher level abstraction for fruit juice was convenience. Some consumers did not want to reconstitute the juice. Others wanted self-serve containers so that children could get juice from the refrigerator by themselves. For this reason, small cans with difficult-to-open tops were not as convenient as little boxes with insertable straws. Fully reconstituted, ready-to-serve, and easy-to-open containers were keys to adding value in the category. These intrinsic and extrinsic lower level attributes added value through the higher level abstraction of convenience.

Another higher level abstraction important in providing value in children's fruit juices was appreciation. When children drank beverages the mothers selected, when they mentioned them to mother or evidenced thanks, the mothers obtained value. This particular psychological benefit was not evoked directly in any of the consumer interviews, but came through strongly in the laddering process. The value perceptions filtered through the higher level abstraction of appreciation and did not come directly through intrinsic or extrinsic attributes. This indirect inferencing process illustrates a major difficult in using traditional multiattribute or utility models in measuring perceived value. The intrinsic attributes themselves are not always directly linked to value, but instead filter through other personal benefits that are themselves abstract.

Evidence   Though no empirical research has been reported on the pivotal higher level abstractions related to value, several dimensions have been proposed in selected catego-

ries. Bishop (1984), for example, claimed that value in supermarket shopping is a composite of the higher level abstractions of variety, service, and facilities in addition to quality and price. Doyle (1984) identified convenience, freshness, and time as major higher level abstractions that combine with price and quality to produce value perceptions in supermarket consumers.

P_{V2}: The sacrifice components of perceived value include monetary prices and nonmonetary prices.

Consumers sacrifice both money and other resources (e.g., time, energy, effort) to obtain products and services. To some consumers, the monetary sacrifice is pivotal: some supermarket shoppers will invest hours clipping coupons, reading food advertising in the newspaper, and traveling to different stores to obtain the best bargains. To these consumers, anything that reduces the monetary sacrifice will increase the perceived value of the product. Less price-conscious consumers will find value in store proximity, ready-to-serve food products, and home delivery—even at the expense of higher costs—because time and effort are perceived as more costly.

Evidence   Recent research reveals that saving time has become a pivotal concern of consumers in supermarket shopping and cooking. Supermarket shoppers have cited fast checkout as more important than low prices in selecting grocery stores (Food Marketing Institute 1985, 1986). Studies also show that consumers are willing to spend money to get more convenient packaging in food products (Morris 1985).

P_{V3}: Extrinsic attributes serve as "value signals" and can substitute for active weighing of benefits and costs.

How carefully do consumers evaluate these components of products in making assessments of value? To judge from the product category of beverages, cognitive assessment is limited. Rather than carefully considering prices and benefits, most respondents depended on cues—often extrinsic cues—in forming impressions of value. A few respondents carefully calculated the cheapest brand in their set on a regular basis, but most seemed to follow Langer's (1978) notion of mindlessness: most respondents bought beverages with only minimal processing of available information. They repeatedly bought a brand they trusted or used extrinsic value cues to simplify their choice process.

These value triggers were present regardless of the way consumers defined value. Many consumers who defined value as low price reported using a coupon as a signal to low price without actually comparing the reduced price of the couponed brand with the prices of other brands, or they reported that "cents-off" or "everyday low price" signs or a private label brand triggered the value perception. Respondents who defined value in terms of what they wanted in products cited small containers, single-serving portions, and ready-to-serve containers. Consumers who defined value as the quality they get for the price they pay used signals such as 100% fruit juice on special or brand name on special. Finally, consumers who defined value as what they get for what they pay depended on form (frozen vs. canned juice) and economy-sized packages as signals.

Not all consumers responded in this mindless way—many saw their role as economical shopper to be important enough to spend time and effort to weigh carefully the give and get components in their own equations of value. Moreover, not all products are as simple or inexpensive as beverages. One would expect to find more rational evaluation in situations of high information availability, processing ability, time availability, and involvement in purchase.

Evidence   To date, no reported empirical studies have investigated the potential of triggers that lead to perceptions of value.

P_{V4}: The perception of value depends on the frame of reference in which the consumer is making an evaluation.

Holbrook and Corfman (1985) maintain that value perceptions are situational and hinge on the context within which an evaluative judgment occurs. This view may help explain the diversity of meanings of value. In the beverage category, for example, the frame of reference used by the consumer in providing meanings included point of purchase, preparation, and consumption. Value meant different things at each of these points. At the point of purchase, value often meant low price, sale, or coupons. At the point of preparation, value often involved some calculation about whether the product was easy to prepare and how much the consumer could obtain for what she paid. At consumption, value was judged in terms of whether the children would drink the beverage, whether some of the beverage was wasted, or whether the children appreciated the mother for buying the drinks.

Evidence   No empirical studies have been conducted to investigate the variation in value perceptions across evaluation contexts.

P_{V5}: Perceived value affects the relationship between quality and purchase.

As Olshavsky (1985) suggested, not all consumers want to buy the highest quality item in every category. Instead, quality appears to be factored into the implicit or explicit valuation of a product by many consumers (Dodds and Monroe 1985; Sawyer and Dickson 1984). A given product may be high quality, but if the consumer does not have enough money to buy it (or does not want to spend the amount required), its value will not be perceived as being as high as that of a product with lower quality but a more affordable price. In other words, when $get_a - give_a > get_b - give_b$ but the shopper has a budget constraint, then $give_a$ > budget constraints > $give_b$ and hence b is chosen. The same logic may apply to products that need more preparation time than the consumer's time constraint allows.

The respondents in the beverage study illustrated this point as they discussed their typical purchasing behavior. For respondents with several children, beverages accounted for a large portion of their weekly food bill. Though most believed that pure fruit juice was of higher quality than fruit drinks, many of these respondents did not buy only pure fruit juice because it was too expensive. They tended to buy some proportion of pure fruit juice, then round out these more expensive purchases with fruit drinks. In their evaluation, high quality was not worth its expense, so lower levels of quality were tolerated in a portion of the weekly beverages. These consumers obtained more value from the lower quality juices because the low costs compensated for the reduction in quality.

Evidence   Several empirical studies have investigated the relationship between quality and purchase, but no empirical studies have investigated explicitly the role of value as an intervening factor between quality and purchase. However, studies on the use of unit price information (e.g., Aaker and Ford 1983; Dickson and Sawyer 1985; Zeithaml 1982) suggest that many consumers use unit price information (i.e., a measure of value) in making product choices in supermarkets.

RESEARCH IMPLICATIONS

The preceding propositions raise questions about ways in which quality and value have been studied in the past and suggest avenues for future research.

Current Practices in Measuring Quality

Academic research measuring quality has depended heavily on unidimensional rating scales, allowing quality to be interpreted in any way the respondent chooses. This practice does not ensure that respondents are interpreting quality similarly or in the way the researcher intends. Hjorth-Anderson (1984) claims that unidimensional scales are methodologically invalid by showing that the concept of overall quality has many dimensions. Holbrook and Corfman (1985) call for ambiguous quality measures to be replaced with scales based on conceptual definitions of quality. An example of the approach they recommend is illustrated by Parasuraman, Zeithaml, and Berry (1985), who investigated service quality in an extensive exploratory study, conceptualized it in dimensions based on that investigation, and operationalized it using the conceptual domain specified in the first phase (Parasuraman, Zeithaml, and Berry 1986). In that stream of research, quality was defined as a comparison between consumer expectations and perceptions of performance based on those dimensions, an approach that allows for individual differences across subjects in the attributes that signal quality.

The research approach used by Parasuraman, Zeithaml, and Berry (1985) could be used in different categories of products (e.g., packaged goods, industrial products, durable goods) to find the abstract dimensions that capture quality in those categories. Such an attempt is currently underway by Brucks and Zeithml (1987) for durable goods. Studies also are needed to determine which attributes signal these dimensions, when and why they are selected instead of other cues, and how they are perceived and combined (see also Gutman and Alden 1985, Olson 1977, and Olson and Jacoby 1972 for similar expressions of needed research). Finally, the relationship between the constructs of attitude and quality should be examined. The instrumentality of a product feature (Lewin 1936) and the quality rating of such a feature in separately determining choice may be an interesting research issue. The convergent and discriminant validity of the constructs of attitude and quality also warrant investigation. Quality measurement scales remain to be developed and validated.

Current Practices in Modeling Consumer Decision Making

Three aspects of modeling consumer decision making can be questioned if the propositions prove to be accurate representations: the tendency to use actual attributes of products rather than consumer perceptions of those attributes, the practice of duplicating and comingling physical attributes with higher order attributes (Myers and Shocker 1981), and the failure to distinguish between the give and get (Ahtola 1984) components of the model. Howard (1977, p. 28) clearly states the first problem.

> It is essential to distinguish between the attributes per se and consumers' perceptions of the attributes, because consumers differ in their perceptions. It is the perception that affects behavior, not the attribute itself. "Attribute" is often used to mean choice criteria, but this leads to confusion. To use "attribute" when you mean not the attribute itself but the consumer's mental image of it, is to reify what is in the consumer's mind.

Jacoby and Olson (1985) concur, claiming that the focus of marketers should not be objective reality but instead consumer perceptions, which may be altered either by changing objective reality or by reinterpreting objective reality for consumers.

Myers and Olson (1981) point out that comingling quality, a higher level abstraction, with lower level physical attributes in models limits the validity and confounds the interpretation of many studies, especially when this practice duplicates lower level attributes. Therefore, it is necessary to use attributes from the same general classification or level in the hierarchy in modeling consumer decision making. Ahtola (1984) confirms that when the hierarchical nature of attributes is not recognized in consumer decision models, double and triple counting of the impact of some attributes results. Techniques to elicit and organize attributes, in his opinion, should precede modeling of the attributes. Myers and Shocker (1981) discuss different consumer decision models appropriate for the levels and ways attributes should be presented in research instruments and analyzed later. Huber and McCann (1982) reveal the impact of inferential beliefs on product evaluations and acknowledge that understanding consumer inferences is essential both in getting information from consumers and in giving information to consumers. Finally, Ahtola (1984) calls for expanding and revising models to incorporate the sacrifice aspects of price. Sacrifice should not be limited to monetary price alone, especially in situations where time costs, search costs, and convenience costs are salient to the consumer.

Methods Appropriate for Studying Quality and Value

The approach used in the exploratory investigation is appropriate for investigating quality in other product categories. Olson and Reynolds (1983) developed methods to aggregate the qualitative data from individual consumers. Aggregate cognitive mapping, structural analysis, cognitive differentiation analysis, and value structure mapping are all techniques designed especially to analyze and represent higher order abstractions such as quality. These techniques are more appropriate than preference mapping or multiattribute modeling for investigating concepts like quality and value (for a complete discussion and explication of these techniques, see Gutman and Alden 1985 or Reynolds and Jamieson 1985).

Several researchers have developed approaches to link product attributes to perceptions of higher level abstractions. Mehrotra and Palmer (1985) suggest a methodological approach to relating product features to perceptions of quality based on the work of Olson and Reynolds (1983). In their procedure, lists of cues and benefits are developed from focus groups or in-depth interviews with consumers, semantic differential scales are constructed to capture the benefits, a tradeoff procedure is used to determine the importance of the cues, and respondents match cues to product concepts. Through this type of analysis, degree of linkage (between cues and benefits), value of a cue, and competitive brand information are provided.

Mazursky and Jacoby (1985) also recognized the need for procedures to track the inference process from consideration of objective cues to the higher level image of quality. Instead of free-elicitation procedures, they used a behavioral processing simulation whereby they presented attribute information to respondents and asked them to form an impression of quality by choosing any information they wished. Though this method can be criticized as unrealistic, it provides insights into the types of information that consumers believe signal quality. Modifications of the method to make the environment more realistic (such as by Brucks 1985) are also possible.

Other researchers have described analytic procedures to link attributes with perceptions. Holbrook (1981) provides a theoretical framework and analytic procedure for representing the intervening role of perceptions in evaluative judgments. Neslin (1981) describes the superiority of statistically revealed importance weights over self-stated importance weights in linking product features to perceptions.

Researching Value

A major difficulty in researching value is the variety of meanings of value held by consumers. Building a model of value requires that the researcher understand which of many (at least of four) meanings are implicit in consumers' expressions of value. Utility models are rich in terms of methodological refinements (see Schmalensee and Thisse 1985 for a discussion of different utility measures and equations), but do not address the distinction between attributes and higher level abstractions. They also presume that consumers carefully calculate the give and get components of value, an assumption that did not hold true for most consumers in the exploratory study.

Price as a Quality Indicator

Most experimental studies related to quality have focused on price as the key extrinsic quality signal. As suggested in the propositions, price is but one of several potentially useful extrinsic cues; brand name or package may be equally or more important, especially in packaged goods. Further, evidence of a generalized price–perceived quality relationship is inconclusive. Quality research may benefit from a de-emphasis on price as the main extrinsic quality indicator. Inclusion of other important indicators, as well as identification of situations in which each of those indicators is important, may provide more interesting and useful answers about the extrinsic signals consumers use.

MANAGEMENT IMPLICATIONS

An understanding of what quality and value mean to consumers offers the promise of improving brand positions through more precise market analysis and segmentation, product planning, promotion, and pricing strategy. The model presented here suggests the following strategies that can be implemented to understand and capitalize on brand quality and value.

Close the Quality Perception Gap

Though managers increasingly acknowledge the importance of quality, many continue to define and measure it from the company's perspective. Closing the gap between objective and perceived quality requires that the company view quality the way the consumer does. Research that investigates which cues are important and how consumers form impressions of quality based on those technical, objective cues is necessary. Companies also may benefit from research that identifies the abstract dimensions of quality desired by consumers in a product class.

Identify Key Intrinsic and Extrinsic Attribute Signals

A top priority for marketers is finding which of the many extrinsic and intrinsic cues consumers use to signal quality. This process involves a careful look at situational factors surrounding the purchase and use of the product. Does quality vary greatly among products in the category? Is quality difficult to evaluate? Do consumers have enough information about intrinsic attributes before purchase, or do they depend on simpler extrinsic cues until after their first purchase? What cues are provided by competitors? Identifying the important quality signals from the consumer's viewpoint, then communicating those signals rather than generalities, is likely

to lead to more vivid perceptions of quality. Linking lower level attributes with their higher level abstractions locates the "driving force" and "leverage point" for advertising strategy (Olson and Reynolds 1983).

Acknowledge the Dynamic Nature of Quality Perceptions

Consumers' perceptions of quality change over time as a result of added information, increased competition in a product category, and changing expectations. The dynamic nature of quality suggests that marketers must track perceptions over time and align product and promotion strategies with these changing views. Because products and perceptions change, marketers may be able to educate consumers on ways to evaluate quality. Advertising, the information provided in packaging, and visible cues associated with products can be managed to evoke desired quality perceptions.

Understand How Consumers Encode Monetary and Nonmonetary Prices

The model proposes a gap between actual and perceived price, making it important to understand how consumers encode prices of products. Nonmonetary costs—such as time and effort—must be acknowledged. Many consumers, especially the 50 million working women in the U.S. today, consider time an important commodity. Anything that can be built into products to reduce time, effort, and search costs can reduce perceived sacrifice and thereby increase perceptions of value.

Recognize Multiple Ways to Add Value

Finally, the model delineates several strategies for adding value in products and services. Each of the boxes feeding into perceived value provides an avenue for increasing value perceptions. Reducing monetary and nonmonetary costs, decreasing perceptions of sacrifice, adding salient intrinsic attributes, evoking perceptions of relevant high level abstractions, and using extrinsic cues to signal value are all possible strategies that companies can use to affect value perceptions. The selection of a strategy for a particular product or market segment depends on its customers' definition of value. Strategies based on customer value standards and perceptions will channel resources more effectively and will meet customer expectations better than those based only on company standards.

NOTES

1. Lewin's (1936) field theoretic approach to evaluating the instrumentality of actions and objects in achieving ends could be viewed as a foundation for this definition. In his view, instrumentality is the extent to which an object or action will achieve an end. In this case, quality could be viewed as instrumentality.

2. Other methods of classification could have been used for these cues. Possible alternative classification schemes include (1) tangible/intangible, (2) distal/proximal (Brunswick 1956), and (3) direct/inferential. However, each of these dichotomies has the same "fuzzy set" problems that are inherent in the intrinsic/extrinsic dichotomy. Notably, with each scheme, some cues (particularly package) would be difficult to classify. Because the intrinsic/extrinsic dichotomy has a literature underpinning it, because it is widely used and recognized, and because it has clear managerial implications, it was retained in this review.

REFERENCES

Aaker, David A. and Gary T. Ford (1983), "Unit Pricing Ten Years Later: A Replication," *Journal of Marketing*, 47 (Winter), 118–22.

Achrol, Ravi Singh, Torger Reve, and Louis Stern (1983), "The Environment of Marketing Channel Dyads: A Framework for Comparative Analysis," *Journal of Marketing*, 47 (Fall), 55–67.

Ahtola, Olli T. (1984), "Price as a 'Give' Component in an Exchange Theoretic Multicomponent Model," in *Advances in Consumer Research*, Vol. 11, Thomas C. Kinnear, ed. Ann Arbor, MI: Association for Consumer Research, 623–6.

Alba, Joseph W. and J. Wesley Hutchinson (1987), "Dimensions of Consumer Expertise," *Journal of Consumer Research*, 14 (March), 411–54.

Allen, John W., Gilbert D. Harrell, and Michael D. Hutt (1976), *Price Awareness Study*. Washington, DC: Food Marketing Institute.

Archibald, Robert B., Clyde Haulman, and Carlisle Moody, Jr. (1983), "Quality, Price, Advertising, and Published Quality Ratings," *Journal of Consumer Research*, 9 (4), 347–56.

Austin, J. L. (1964), "A Plea for Excuses," in *Ordinary Language*, V. C. Chappell, ed. New York: Dover Publications, 41–63.

Becker, Gary S. (1965), "Theory of the Allocation of Time," *Economic Journal*, 75 (September), 493–517.

Bellenger, Danny, Kenneth Bernhardt, and Jac Goldstucker (1976), *Qualitative Research in Marketing*. Chicago: American Marketing Association.

Bishop, Willard R., Jr. (1984), "Competitive Intelligence," *Progressive Grocer* (March), 19–20.

Bonner, P. Greg and Richard Nelson (1985), "Product Attributes and Perceived Quality: Foods," in *Perceived Quality*, J. Jacoby and J. Olson, eds. Lexington, MA: Lexington Books, 64–79.

Bowbrick, P. (1982), "Pseudoresearch in Marketing: The Case of the Price-Perceived-Quality Relationship," *European Journal of Marketing*, 14 (8), 466–70.

Brucks, Merrie (1985), "The Effects of Product Class Knowledge on Information Search Behavior," *Journal of Consumer Research*, 12 (1), 1–16.

―――― and Valarie A. Zeithaml (1987), "Price as an Indicator of Quality Dimensions," paper presented at Association for Consumer Research Annual Meeting, Boston, MA.

Brunswick, Egon (1956), *Perception and the Representative Design of Psychological Experiments*. Berkeley, CA: University of California Press.

Chain Store Age (1985), "Consumers Say Value Is More Than Quality Divided by Price" (May), 13.

Chapman, Joseph (1986), "The Impact of Discounts on Subjective Product Evaluations," working paper, Virginia Polytechnic Institute and State University.

Cohen, Joel B. (1979), "The Structure of Product Attributes: Defining Attribute Dimensions for

Planning and Evaluation," in *Analytic Approaches to Product and Marketing Planning*, A. Shocker, ed. Cambridge, MA: Marketing Science Institute.

Court, Andrew T. (1939), "Hedonic Price Indexes and Automotive Examples," in *The Dynamics of Automobile Demand*. New York: General Motors Corporation, 99–117.

Cox, Donald F. (1962), "The Measurement of Information Value: A Study in Consumer Decision Making," in *Proceedings*, Winter Conference. Chicago: American Marketing Association, 413–21.

Crosby, Philip B. (1979), *Quality Is Free*. New York: New American Library.

Curry, David J. and David J. Faulds (1986), "Indexing Product Quality: Issues, Theory, and Results," *Journal of Marketing*, 13 (June), 134–45.

Darby, M. R. and E. Karni (1973), "Free Competition and the Optimal Amount of Fraud," *Journal of Law and Economics*, 16 (April), 67–86.

Darden, William R. and JoAnn K. L. Schwinghammer (1985), "The Influence of Social Characteristics on Perceived Quality in Patronage Choice Behavior," in *Perceived Quality*, J. Jacoby and J. Olson, eds. Lexington, MA: Lexington Books, 161–72.

Dickson, Peter and Alan Sawyer (1985), "Point of Purchase Behavior and Price Perceptions of Supermarket Shoppers," Marketing Science Institute Working Paper Series.

Dodds, William B. and Kent B. Monroe (1985), "The Effect of Brand and Price Information on Subjective Product Evaluations," in *Advances in Consumer Research*, Vol. 12, Elizabeth C. Hirschman and Morris B. Holbrook, eds. Provo, UT: Association for Consumer Research, 85–90.

Down, S. A. (1961), "A Theory of Consumer Efficiency," *Journal of Retailing*, 37 (Winter), 6–12.

Doyle, Mona (1984), "New Ways of Measuring Value," *Progressive Grocer–Value*, Executive Report, 15–19.

Etgar, Michael and Naresh K. Malhotra (1978), "Consumers' Reliance on Different Product Quality Cues: A Basis for Market Segmentation," in *Research Frontiers in Marketing: Dialogues and Directions, 1978 Educators' Proceedings*, Subhash C. Jain, ed. Chicago: American Marketing Association, 143–7.

Food Marketing Institute (1985), *Trends—Consumer Attitudes and the Supermarket, 1985 Update*. Washington, DC: Food Marketing Institute.

——— (1986), *Trends—Consumer Attitudes and the Supermarket: 1986 Update*. Washington, DC: Food Marketing Institute.

French, N. D., J. J. Williams, and W. A. Chance (1973), "A Shopping Experiment on Price-Quality Relationships," *Journal of Retailing*, 48 (Spring), 3–16.

Friedman, L. (1967), "Psychological Pricing in the Food Industry," in *Prices: Issues in Theory, Practice, and Public Policy*, A. Phillips and O. Williamson, eds. Philadelphia: University of Pennsylvania Press.

Gabor, Andre and C. W. J. Granger (1961), "On the Price Consciousness of Consumers," *Applied Statistics*, 10 (2), 170–88.

Gardner, D. M. (1970), "An Experimental Investigation of the Price-Quality Relationship," *Journal of Retailing*, 46 (Fall), 25–41.

——— (1971), "Is There a Generalized Price-Quality Relationship?" *Journal of Marketing Research*, 8 (May), 241–3.

Garvin, David A. (1983), "Quality on the Line," *Harvard Business Review*, 61 (September–October), 65–73.

——— (1987), "Competing on the Eight Dimensions of Quality," *Harvard Business Review*, 65 (November–December), 101–9.

Geistfeld, Loren V. (1982), "The Price-Quality Relationship–Revisited," *Journal of Consumer Affairs*, 14 (Winter), 334–46.

———, G. B. Sproles, and S. B. Badenhop (1977), "The Concept and Measurement of a Hierarchy of Product Characteristics," in *Advances in Consumer Research*, Vol. 4, W. D. Perreault, Jr., ed. Ann Arbor, MI: Association for Consumer Research, 302–7.

Gerstner, Eitan (1985), "Do Higher Prices Signal Higher Quality?" *Journal of Marketing Research*, 22 (May), 209–15.

Griliches, Zvi (1971), "Introduction: Hedonic Price Indexes Revisited," in *Price Indexes and Quality Change*, Zvi Griliches, ed. Cambridge, MA: Harvard University Press, 3–15.

Gronau, R. (1973), "The Intrafamily Allocation of Time: The Value of the Housewife's Time," *American Economic Review*, 63 (4), 634–51.

Gutman, Jonathan and Scott D. Alden (1985), "Adolescents' Cognitive Structures of Retail Stores and Fashion Consumption: A Means-End Chain Analysis of Quality," in *Perceived Quality,* J. Jacoby and J. Olson, eds. Lexington, MA: Lexington Books, 99–114.

―――― and Thomas J. Reynolds (1979), "An Investigation of the Levels of Cognitive Abstraction Utilized by Consumers in Product Differentiation," in *Attitude Research Under the Sun,* J. Eighmey, ed. Chicago: American Marketing Association.

Harness, Edward (1978), "Some Basic Beliefs about Marketing," speech to the Annual Marketing Meeting of the Conference Board, New York City.

Hauser, J. R. and S. M. Shugan (1983), "Defensive Marketing Strategies," *Marketing Science,* 2 (Fall), 319–60.

―――― and P. Simmie (1981), "Profit-Maximizing Perceptual Positions: An Integrated Theory for the Selection of Product Features and Price," *Management Science,* 27 (January), 33–56.

―――― and Glen Urban (1986), "The Value Priority Hypotheses for Consumer Budget Plans," *Journal of Consumer Research,* 12 (March), 446–62.

Hjorth-Anderson, Chr. (1984), "The Concept of Quality and the Efficiency of Markets for Consumer Products," *Journal of Consumer Research,* 11 (2), 708–18.

―――― (1986), "More on Multidimensional Quality: A Reply," *Journal of Consumer Research,* 13 (June), 149–54.

Hoffman, Gene D. (1984), "Our Competitor Is Our Environment," *Progressive Grocer–Value.* Executive Report, 28–30.

Holbrook, Morris B. (1981), "Integrating Compositional and Decompositional Analyses to Represent the Intervening Role of Perceptions in Evaluative Judgments," *Journal of Marketing Research,* 18 (February), 13–28.

―――― and Kim P. Corfman (1985), "Quality and Value in the Consumption Experience: Phaedrus Rides Again," in *Perceived Quality,* J. Jacoby and J. Olson, eds. Lexington, MA: Lexington Books, 31–57.

Howard, J. A. (1977), *Consumer Behavior: Application of Theory.* New York: McGraw-Hill Book Company.

Huber, Joel and John McCann (1982), "The Impact of Inferential Beliefs on Product Evaluations," *Journal of Marketing Research,* 19 (August), 324–33.

Jacoby, J., R. W. Chestnut, W. D. Hoyer, D. W. Sheluga, and M. J. Donahue (1978), "Psychometric Characteristics of Behavioral Process Data: Preliminary Findings on Validity and Generalizability," in *Advances in Consumer Research,* Vol. 5, H. Keith Hunt, ed. Ann Arbor, MI: Association of Consumer Research, 546–54.

―――― and Jerry C. Olson (1977), "Consumer Response to Price: An Attitudinal, Information Processing Perspective," in *Moving Ahead with Attitude Research,* Y. Wind and P. Greenberg, eds. Chicago: American Marketing Association, 73–86.

―――― and ――――, eds. (1985), *Perceived Quality.* Lexington, MA: Lexington Books.

――――, ――――, and Rafael A. Haddock (1973), "Price, Brand Name and Product Composition Characteristics as Determinants of Perceived Quality," *Journal of Applied Psychology,* 55 (6), 570–9.

――――, G. J. Szybillo, and J. Busato-Schach (1977), "Information Acquisition Behavior in Brand Choice Situations," *Journal of Consumer Research,* 3 (March), 209–15.

Johnson, Michael D. (1983), "Decision Processing and Product Comparability: A Theory of Strategy Selection," unpublished doctoral dissertation, University of Chicago.

Kirmani, Amna and Peter Wright (1987a), "Money Talks: Advertising Extravagance and Perceived Product Quality," working paper, Stanford University.

―――― and ―――― (1987b), "Schemer Schema: Consumers' Beliefs About Advertising and Marketing Strategies," working paper, Stanford University.

Laird, Donald A. (1932), "How the Consumer Estimates Quality by Subconscious Sensory Impression," *Journal of Applied Psychology,* 16 (2), 241–6.

Lambert, Zarryl (1972), "Price and Choice Behavior," *Journal of Marketing Research,* 9 (February), 35–40.

Langer, Ellen (1978), "Rethinking the Role of Thought in Social Interactions," in *New Directions in Attribution Research,* John Harvey, William Ickes, and Robert Kidd, eds. Hillsdale, NJ: Lawrence Erlbaum Associates, 35–58.

Leibowitz, Arlene (1974), "Education and Home Production," *American Economic Review*, 64 (May), 243–50.

Leuthold, Jane (1981), "Taxation and the Consumption of Household Time," *Journal of Consumer Research*, 7 (March), 388–94.

Lewin, Kurt (1936), *Principles of Topological Psychology*. New York: McGraw-Hill Book Company.

Linder, S. B. (1970), *The Harried Leisure Class*. New York: Columbia University Press.

Lutz, Richard (1986), "Quality Is as Quality Does: An Attitudinal Perspective on Consumer Quality Judgments," presentation to the Marketing Science Institute Trustees' Meeting, Cambridge, MA.

Mabry, B. D. (1970), "An Analysis of Work and Other Constraints on Choices of Activities," *Western Economic Journal*, 8 (3), 213–25.

Maynes, E. Scott (1976), "The Concept and Measurement of Product Quality," *Household Production and Consumption*, 40 (5), 529–59.

—————— and Terje Assum (1982), "Informationally Imperfect Consumer Markets: Empirical Findings and Policy Implications," *Journal of Consumer Affairs*, 16 (Summer), 62–87.

Mazumdar, Tridik (1986), "Experimental Investigation of the Psychological Determinants of Buyers' Price Awareness and a Comparative Assessment of Methodologies for Retrieving Price Information from Memory," working paper, Virginia Polytechnic Institute and State University.

Mazursky, David and Jacob Jacoby (1985), "Forming Impressions of Merchandise and Service Quality," in *Perceived Quality*, J. Jacoby and J. Olson, eds. Lexington, MA: Lexington Books, 139–54.

McConnell, J. D. (1968), "Effect of Pricing on Perception of Product Quality," *Journal of Applied Psychology*, 52 (August), 300–3.

Mehrotra, Sunil and John Palmer (1985), "Relating Product Features to Perceptions of Quality: Appliances," in *Perceived Quality*, J. Jacoby and J. Olson, eds. Lexington, MA: Lexington Books, 81–96.

Milgrom, Paul and John Roberts (1986), "Price and Advertising Signals of Product Quality," *Journal of Political Economy*, 94 (4), 796–821.

Mincer, J. (1963), "Market Prices, Opportunity Costs, and Income Effects," in *Measurement in Economics: Studies in Mathematical Economics and Econometrics in Memory of Yehuds Grunfeld*. Stanford, CA: Stanford University Press, 67–82.

Monroe, Kent B. and R. Krishnan (1985), "The Effect of Price on Subjective Product Evaluations," in *Perceived Quality*, J. Jacoby and J. Olson, eds. Lexington, MA: Lexington Books, 209–32.

—————— and William B. Dodds (1988), "A Research Program for Establishing the Validity of the Price-Quality Relationship," *Journal of the Academy of Marketing Science*, forthcoming.

Morgan, Leonard A. (1985), "The Importance of Quality," in *Perceived Quality*, J. Jacoby and J. Olson, eds. Lexington, MA: Lexington Books, 61–4.

Morris, Betsy (1985), "How Much Will People Pay to Save a Few Minutes of Cooking? Plenty," *Wall Street Journal* (July 25), 23.

Myers, James H. and Allan D. Schocker (1981), "The Nature of Product-Related Attributes," *Research in Marketing*, Vol. 5. Greenwich, CT: JAI Press, Inc., 211–36.

Nelson, Philip (1970), "Information and Consumer Behavior," *Journal of Political Economy*, 78 (20), 311–29.

—————— (1974), "Advertising as Information," *Journal of Political Economy*, 81 (4), 729–54.

Neslin, Scott (1981), "Linking Product Features to Perceptions: Self-Stated Versus Statistically Revealed Importance Weights," *Journal of Marketing Research*, 18 (February), 80–93.

Nichols, D., E. Smolensky, and T. N. Tideman (1971), "Discrimination by Waiting Time in Merit Goods," *American Economic Review*, 61 (June), 312–23.

Olshavsky, Richard W. (1985), "Perceived Quality in Consumer Decision Making: An Integrated Theoretical Perspective," in *Perceived Quality*, J. Jacoby and J. Olson, eds. Lexington, MA: Lexington Books, 3–29.

Olson, Jerry C. (1977), "Price as an Informational Cue: Effects in Product Evaluation," in *Consumer and Industrial Buying Behavior*, Arch G. Woodside, Jagdish N. Sheth, and Peter D. Bennet, eds. New York: North Holland Publishing Company, 267–86.

_____ (1978), "Inferential Belief Formation in the Cue Utilization Process," Ann Arbor, MI: Association for Consumer Research, 706–13.

_____ and Jacob Jacoby (1972), "Cue Utilization in the Quality Perception Process," in *Proceedings of the Third Annual Conference of the Association for Consumer Research,* M. Venkatesan, ed. Iowa City: Association for Consumer Research, 167–79.

_____ and Thomas J. Reynolds (1983), "Understanding Consumers' Cognitive Structures: Implications for Advertising Strategy," *Advertising and Consumer Psychology,* L. Percy and A. Woodside, eds. Lexington, MA: Lexington Books.

Parasurman, A., Valarie A. Zeithaml, and Leonard Berry (1985), "A Conceptual Model of Service Quality and Its Implications for Future Research," *Journal of Marketing,* 49 (Fall), 41–50.

_____ , _____ , and _____ (1986), "SERVQUAL: A Scale for Measuring Service Quality," working paper, Marketing Science Institute.

Peterson, Robert A. (1970), "The Price-Perceived Quality Relationship: Experimental Evidence," *Journal of Marketing Research,* 7 (November), 525–8.

_____ and A. Jolibert (1976), "A Cross-National Investigation of Price Brand Determinants of Perceived Product Quality," *Journal of Applied Psychology,* 61 (July), 522–6.

_____ and William R. Wilson (1985), "Perceived Risk and Price-Reliance Schema and Price-Perceived-Quality Mediators," in *Perceived Quality,* J. Jacoby and J. Olson, eds. Lexington, MA: Lexington Books, 247–68.

Progressive Grocer (1964), "How Much Do Customers Know about Retail Prices?" (February), 103–6.

Rao, Akshay R. (1987), "The Moderating Effect of Prior Knowledge on Cue Utilization in Product Evaluations," working paper, Department of Marketing and Business Law, University of Minnesota, Minneapolis.

_____ and Kent B. Monroe (1987), "The Effects of Price, Brand Name and Store Name on Buyers' Subjective Product Assessments: An Integrative Review," working paper, Department of Marketing and Business Law, University of Minnesota, Minneapolis.

Reynolds, T. J., J. Gutman, and J. Fiedler (1984), "Translating Knowledge of Consumers' Cognitive Structures into the Development of Advertising Strategic Operations: A Case History," in *Proceedings: Second Annual Advertising and Consumer Psychology Conference.* Toronto: American Psychological Association.

_____ and Linda F. Jamieson (1985), "Image Representations: An Analytic Framework," in *Perceived Quality,* J. Jacoby and J. Olson, eds. Lexington, MA: Lexington Books, 115–38.

Riesz, P. (1978), "Price Versus Quality in the Marketplace, 1961–1975," *Journal of Retailing,* 54 (4), 15–28.

Rigaux-Briemont, Benny (1982), "Influences of Brand Name and Packaging on Perceived Quality," in *Advances in Consumers Research,* Vol. 9, Andrew A. Mitchell, ed. Ann Arbor, MI: Association for Consumer Research, 472–7.

Roedder-John, Deborah, Carol Scott, and James Bettman (1986), "Sampling Data for Covariation Assessment: The Effect of Prior Beliefs on Search Patterns," *Journal of Consumer Research,* 13 (1), 38–47.

Rokeach, M. J. (1973), *The Nature of Human Values.* New York: The Free Press.

Russell, Bertrand (1912), *The Problems of Philosophy.* New York: The Free Press.

Sawyer, Alan G. (1975), "Demand Artifacts in Laboratory Experiments in Consumer Research," *Journal of Consumer Research,* 1 (March), 20–30.

_____ and Peter Dickson (1984), "Psychological Perspectives on Consumer Response to Sales Promotion," in *Research on Sales Promotion: Collected Papers,* Katherine Jocz, ed. Cambridge, MA: Marketing Science Institute.

_____ , Parker M. Worthing, and Paul E. Sendak (1979), "The Role of Laboratory Experiments to Test Marketing Strategies," *Journal of Marketing,* 43 (Summer), 60–7.

Schechter, Len (1984), "A Normative Conception of Value," *Progressive Grocer,* Executive Report, 12–14.

Schmalensee, Richard (1978), "A Model of Advertising and Product Quality," *Journal of Political Economy,* 86 (3), 485–503.

_____ and J. Thisse (1985), "Perceptual Maps and the Optimal Location of New Products," working paper, Massachusetts Institute of Technology.

Shapiro and Associates (1985), "Value Is a Complex Equation," *Chain Store Age* (May), 14–59.

Shapiro, B. P. (1968), "The Psychology of Pricing," *Harvard Business Review,* 46 (July–August), 14–25, 160.

———— (1973), "Price Reliance: Existence and Sources," *Journal of Marketing Research*, 10 (August), 286–94.

Smith, E. M. and C. Broome (1966), "Experimental Determination of the Effect of Price and Market-Standing Information on Consumers' Brand Preferences," in *Proceedings*. Chicago: American Marketing Association.

Sproles, George B. (1977), "New Evidence on Price and Quality," *Journal of Consumer Affairs*, 11 (Summer), 63–77.

———— (1986), "The Concept of Quality and the Efficiency of Markets: Issues and Comments," *Journal of Marketing*, 13 (June), 146–7.

Stafford, J. E. and B. M. Enis (1969), "The Price-Quality Relationship: An Extension," *Journal of Marketing Research*, 7 (November), 456–8.

Stevenson, Jim (1984), "An Indifference toward Value," *Progressive Grocer–Value*, Executive Report, 22–3.

Stokes, Raymond C. (1985), "The Effect of Price, Package Design, and Brand Familiarity on Perceived Quality," in *Perceived Quality*, J. Jacoby and J. Olson, eds. Lexington, MA: Lexington Books, 233–46.

Swan, John (1974), "Price-Product Performance Competition between Retailer and Manufacturer Brands," *Journal of Marketing*, 38 (July), 52–9.

Szybillo, G. J. and J. Jacoby (1974), "Intrinsic Versus Extrinsic Cues as Determinants of Perceived Product Quality," *Journal of Applied Psychology*, 59 (February), 74–8.

Young, Shirley and Barbara Feigin (1975), "Using the Benefit Chain for Improved Strategy Formulation," *Journal of Marketing*, 39 (July), 72–4.

Zeithaml, Valarie A. (1982) "Consumer Response to In-Store Price Information Environments," *Journal of Consumer Research*, 8 (March), 357–69.

———— (1983), "Conceptualizing and Measuring Consumer Response to Price," in *Advances in Consumer Research*, Vol. 10, R. P. Bagozzi and A. M. Tybout, eds. Ann Arbor, MI: Association for Consumer Research, 612–16.

———— (1985), "The New Demographics and Market Fragmentation," *Journal of Marketing*, 49 (Summer), 64–75.

———— and Leonard Berry (1987), "The Time Consciousness of Supermarket Shoppers," working paper, Texas A&M University.

———— and William L. Fuerst (1983), "Age Differences in Response to Grocery Store Price Information," *Journal of Consumer Affairs*, 17 (2), 403–20.

◆

Beyond the Many Faces of Price: An Integration of Pricing Strategies

Gerald J. Tellis

In the last two decades the field of pricing strategy has made great progress in the form of better theoretical explanations, more precise models, and innovative pricing strategies (see Nagle 1984 for one review). However, the rich variety of pricing models and strategies developed in different time periods and contexts has resulted in a multiplicity of labels, several overlapping descriptions of strategies, and partially obsolete typologies. Some pricing strategies are not yet presented adequately in the marketing literature (e.g., price bundling, Stigler 1968; random discounting, Varian 1980; or price signaling, Cooper and Ross 1984) and others have not been developed formally (e.g., price skimming and penetration pricing, Dean 1951). A more pressing issue, however, is that because the principles underlying each strategy have not been presented together, it has not been possible to develop a unifying taxonomy of strategies that shows their relatedness or dif-

ferences and immediately suggests the circumstances under which each can be adopted. Thus there is a need to compare, rationalize, and reclassify the various pricing strategies in the literature.

The first objective of this article is to present a number of pricing strategies, some of which are simplifications and others elaborations of strategies described in the literature. A second objective is to state their underlying principles in comparable terms and thus demonstrate their relationship to each other and their practical applications. A third objective is to propose a classification of these strategies that is parsimonious, logically derived, and enlightening to the user. Such a taxonomy could stimulate alternate schemes or general theoretical models or new applications of empirical models or new strategies (Hunt 1983, pp. 348–60).

These objectives are carried out in the following order. First the classification is presented (though it can be fully appreciated only at the end of the article). Then each strategy is discussed in terms of a pricing problem presented in simple numerical form. A par-

"Beyond the Many Faces of Price: An Integration of Pricing Strategies," Gerald J. Tellis, Vol. 50 (October 1986), pp. 146–160. Reprinted from *Journal of Marketing*, published by the American Marketing Association.

ticular pricing strategy is shown to be the only one that can resolve the problem, given the demand, cost, competitive, and legal environment. The theoretical and welfare aspects of the strategy are summarized and applications discussed. Finally, the relationship among strategies is explained.

This article describes a set of normative pricing strategies. A pricing strategy is a reasoned choice from a set of alternative prices (or price schedules) that aim at profit maximization within a planning period in response to a given scenario. Thus, the article describes a set of ideal options one may choose and outcomes that result from such choices, assuming profit maximization by the strategist. Several important pricing topics are necessarily excluded from this discussion: managerial pricing approaches, price implementation, and price, cost, and demand estimation (see Monroe 1979 or Rao 1984 for excellent reviews).

In the case of consumer behavior, however, allowances are made for non-optimal behavior. Its most important cause is incomplete information, which leads to three types of behavior: consumers may purchase randomly, consumers may use a surrogate for an unknown attribute (e.g., price as a surrogate for quality), or consumers may evaluate choices incorrectly with resultant intransitivity in preferences. On the basis of this hypothesis, Kahneman and Tversky (1979) developed prospect theory as an alternative to traditional utility theory and Thaler (1980, 1985) extended that work. Their work has important implications for pricing strategy. This article shows the impact of all three types of information deficiencies on pricing strategies.

A CLASSIFICATION OF PRICING STRATEGIES

The underlying principle in all the strategies discussed here is that the best strategy in certain circumstances is not apparent until certain shared economies or cross-subsidies are taken into account. In a shared economy, one consumer segment or product bears more of the average costs than another, but the average price still reflects cost plus acceptable profit. The use of such economies may be triggered by heterogeneity among consumers, firms, or elements of the product mix. The pricing strategies can be broadly classified into three groups based on which of these three factors affects a firm's use of shared economies: differential pricing, whereby the same brand is sold at different prices to consumers; competitive pricing, whereby prices are set to exploit competitive position; and product line pricing, whereby related brands are sold at prices that exploit mutual dependencies. The pricing objective of the firm thus constitutes the first dimension on which this classification scheme is constructed.

The second dimension is the characteristics of consumers. Again there are three categories of interest. First, at least some consumers are assumed to have search costs. That is, consumers do not know exactly which firm sells the product they want and they have to search for it. Further, for some of them the opportunity cost of time exceeds the benefit of search, so that they are willing to purchase without full information. Second, at least some consumers have a low reservation price for the product. That is, some consumers are price sensitive or do not need the product urgently enough to pay the high price other consumers pay. Third, all consumers have certain transaction costs other than search costs—for example, traveling costs, the risk of investment, the cost of money, or switching costs.

The two dimensions—firm objectives and consumer characteristics—each with three categories yield nine cells into which the strategies discussed here are classified (see Table 33-1). Table 33-2 further compares and contrasts these strategies on several dimen-

Table 33-1
Taxonomy of Pricing Strategies

Characteristics of Consumers	**Objective of Firm**		
	Vary Prices among Consumer Segments	*Exploit Competitive Position*	*Balance Pricing over Product Line*
Some have high search costs	Random discounting	Price signaling	Image pricing
Some have low reservation price	Periodic discounting	Penetration pricing Experience curve pricing	Price bundling Premium pricing
All have special transaction costs	Second market discounting	Geographic pricing	Complementary pricing

sions and is discussed in the concluding section. The real world, however, is more complex and several of the conditions listed (search costs, transaction costs, or demand heterogeneity) may occur jointly. Accordingly, in reality a firm may adopt a combination of these strategies. What is demonstrated in the proposed classification is the necessary conditions for each strategy, conditions that are jointly sufficient to classify them conveniently. Similarly, in the following discussion the problems define fairly simple scenarios where "other things are assumed constant" and only factors affecting the choice of a strategy are allowed to vary.

The list of available strategies also is affected by the legal environment. Because of the potential for pricing abuses, especially against weak competitors or weak or uninformed buyers, Congress and the states have passed laws that regulate the pricing strategies firms can adopt. These laws generally ensure that there is no collusion among competitors, no deception of consumers, no explicit discrimination among industrial buyers, or no attempt to manipulate the competitive structure. Some of these laws rule out certain pricing options whereas others include new possibilities, and these effects are

discussed in the appropriate place. The laws are not always fully explicit, but the general motivation of the laws and the spirit in which they have been interpreted by the courts indicate that no strategy should reduce the impact of competitive forces unless it is to the benefit of consumers (Areeda 1974; Scherer 1980).

DIFFERENTIAL PRICING STRATEGIES

The price strategies discussed here all arise primarily because of consumer heterogeneity, so that the same product can be sold to consumers under a variety of prices. The three strategies discussed refer to consumer heterogeneity along three dimensions: transaction costs that motivate second market discounting, demand that motivates periodic discounting, and search costs that motivate random discounting.[1] These conditions enable a firm to discriminate implicitly in the prices it charges its consumers. In industrial and wholesale markets, explicit price discrimination whereby a firm charges different prices to two competing buyers under identical circumstances is illegal under the Robinson-Patman Act's (1936) amendment of the Clayton Act (1914), unless the price-cutting firm can meet specific defenses (Scherer 1980, p. 572; Werner 1982). In the consumer market, explicit price discrimination would lead to the ill-will of consumers. Aside from the special motivations for each type of discounting to be discussed hereafter, discounting in general has a sales enhancing effect, probably because consumers overweight the saving on a deal ("the silver lining," Thaler 1985) in relation to the cost still incurred in buying the product at the discounted price. If the product were regularly at the discounted price, many of these consumers may not buy it at all!

Second Market Discounting

Consider a competitive firm that sells 100,000 units of a product at $10 each, when variable costs are $1 and fixed costs are $500,000 for a capacity of 200,000 units. The firm gets a request to sell in a new market such that there will be a negligible loss of sales in the first market and a negligible increase in fixed or variable costs. What is the minimum selling price the firm should accept?

This is a classic problem in incremental costing and the solution is well known. The minimum acceptable price would be anything over $1, because any price over variable costs would make a contribution to this ongoing business. Generics, secondary demographic segments, and some foreign markets provide opportunities for profitable use of this strategy. Often pioneering drugs are faced with competition from identical but much lower priced generics after the expiry of the patent. The pioneering firm has the options of either maintaining its price and losing share or dropping price and losing margin. The relevant strategy would be to enter the generic market segment with an unbranded product and arrest loss of sales to that segment without foregoing either margin or position in the branded segment. The same principle also holds for a firm changing to a mixed

brand strategy after selling under a manufacturer brand only or a private label brand only. A second illustration of this strategy is the discounts to secondary demographic markets such as students, children, or new members.

Similarly, for some countries the foreign market represents an opportunity rather than a threat if the same theory is applied. Often a firm's selling price or even current average cost in the home market may be higher than the selling price in the foreign market. However, if its variable costs are sufficiently below the selling price in the foreign market, the firm can export profitably at a price somewhere between the selling price in the foreign market and its variable costs. The term "dumping" is sometimes used to describe the latter strategy if the firm's selling price in the foreign market is below its average costs.

The essential requirements for this strategy are that the firm have unused capacity and consumers have transaction costs so there is no perfect arbitrage between the two markets. In terms of profitability, additional revenues from the second market should exceed all increases in variable and fixed costs and loss of profits from the first market. Note here that the first market provides an external economy to the second, because the latter market gets goods at a lower price than it would otherwise. (For this reason some economists are not critical of dumping. Others, however, stress that there may be long-term damage to the foreign economy from lost wages and production facilities.) The second market provides neither an economy nor a diseconomy to the first in the short run.

Periodic Discounting

Consider a firm faced with the following pricing problem. Average economic costs[2] are $55 at 20 units and $40 at 40 units. There are 40 consum-

Table 32-2
Comparison of Pricing Strategies

Criteria	Differential Pricing			Competitive
	Second Market Discounting	*Periodic Discounts*	*Random Discounts*	*Penetration and Experience Curve Pricing*
Characteristic of price strategy varies systematically over:				
Consumer segments	Yes	Yes	Yes	No
Competitors in market	No	No	No	Yes
Product mix	No	No	No	No
Characteristics of consumers	High transaction costs: physically separated segments	Only some with low reserva-tion price: sensitive segment	High search costs: some uninformed about price	Some with low reservation price: price sensitive segment
Product and cost characteristics	Unused capacity	Economies of scale or unused capacity	Economies of scale or unused capacity	Economies of scale or experience, or unused capacity
Variants	Generic pricing, dumping	Price skimming, peak-load pricing, price discrimination, priority pricing	Variable price merchandising, cents-off, coupons	Limit pricing
Relevant legal constraints	Explicit price discrimination illegal	Explicit price discrimination illegal	Explicit price discrimination illegal	Predatory pricing illegal

Pricing		Product Line Pricing		
Price Signaling	Geographic Pricing	Price Bundling	Premium Pricing	Complementary Pricing
No	No	No	No	No
Yes	Yes	No	No	No
No	No	Yes	Yes	Yes
High search costs: some uninformed on quality; uninformed prefer high quality	High transportation costs: geographically distinct markets	Some prefer one product, others, another: asymmetric demand	Only some prefer basic products at low prices	High transaction costs: risk aversiveness or store or brand loyalty
Signaling firm has higher costs or sub-optimizes or cheats on quality	Higher production costs in adjacent market; economies of scale or unused capacity	Perishable product or purchase occasion	Joint economies of scale across products; features with low cost increase relative to price increase	Patents, superior technology
Reference pricing	FOB, base point, uniform, zone, and freight pricing	Mixed bundling, pure components, pure bundling	—	Captive pricing, two-part pricing, loss leadership
—	Price collusion, explicit price discrimination, predatory pricing illegal	Explicit price discrimination, pure bundling illegal	—	(Minimum) retail price maintenance illegal, tie-ins illegal

ers per period that are interested in its product. Half of them are fussy and want the product only at the beginning of each period even if they have to pay $50 per unit. The other half are price sensitive and would take the product at any time but will pay no more than $30 per unit. At what price should the firm sell its product?

Initially it may seem that the firm cannot bring the product to market profitably because costs exceed acceptable prices for each segment. However, in effect, the firm can produce and sell profitably if it exploits the consumers' heterogeneity of demand by a strategy of periodic discounting. It should produce at the level of 40 units per period at a cost of $40 per unit, price at $50 at the beginning of each period, and systematically discount the product at the end of the period to $30. In this way it would sell to the fussy consumers at the beginning and to the rest at the end of each period. Note that its average selling price is $40, which equals its average economic cost.

This is the principle often involved in the temporal markdowns and periodic discounting of off-season fashion goods, off-season travel fares, matinee tickets, and happy hour drinks, as well as peak-load-pricing for utilities (Hirshleifer 1958; Houthakker 1951; Steiner 1957; Williamson 1966). Similarly, this is the principle involved in the discounting of older models (Stokey 1981), the priority pricing of scarce products (Harris and Raviv 1981), and the strategy of price skimming, first suggested as one alternative for new products by Dean (1950a). Because of the circumstances in which this discounting strategy has been used, it often is referred to by different names. However, a more general label would be "periodic discounting," because of the essential principle underlying this strategy: the manner of discounting is predictable over time and not necessarily unknown to consumers (unlike random discounting dis-

cussed next) and the discount can be used by all consumers (unlike second market discounting).

An interesting issue in periodic discounting is that both segments of the market provide an external economy to each other.[3] The first segment that pays the higher price can be viewed as providing a sort of "venture" price to the firm to produce the product, whereas the second segment can be viewed as providing a "salvage" price to the firm for unsold items at the period's end. This intuition suggests that, even if the demand for the product is not exactly known, a strategy of pricing high and systematically discounting with time is likely to ensure that the firm covers its costs and makes a reasonable profit. However, the first segment provides a greater external economy than the second, because it bears more of the production costs.

Random Discounting

Consider a firm that has a minimum average economic cost of production of $30. Assume a distribution of prices for the same product between $30 and $50 because there are several other firms with other cost structures and $50 is the maximum consumers will pay for it. It takes one hour to search for the lowest price, $30. If a consumer does not search but buys from the first seller, he/she may if lucky get a $30 seller but if unlucky may get a $50 seller. Further, assume consumers' opportunity cost of time ranges from $0 to well over $20 per hour. What is the best shopping strategy for consumers and the best pricing strategy for firms? For consumers, the problem is fairly simple. Let us assume that the distribution of prices is such that on average a consumer who does not search and is uninformed about prices pays $40 for the product. Then on average a consumer who searches and is informed saves $10 (40 − 30). Hence consumers whose opportunity cost of time is more than $10 should not shop and the rest should. Let us assume that at least some consumers search and others buy randomly. What strategy should the firm with an average economic cost of $30 adopt?

The answer is a strategy of random discounts, which involves maintaining a high price of $50 regularly and discounting to $30. However, the manner of discounting is crucial. It should be undiscernible or "random" to the uninformed consumers and infrequent, so that these consumers do not get lucky too often. The uninformed consumers will not be able to second guess the price; they will buy randomly, usually at the high price. In contrast, the informed will look around or wait until they can buy at the low price. In this way the firm tries to maximize the number of informed at its low price instead of at a competitor's low price, while maximizing the number of uninformed at its high rather than its low price. Research on the intransitivity of preferences indicates some interesting twists to the appeal of discounts and coupons. First, searchers are likely to oversearch. They spend more time shopping than is justified by their gains, the result of what Thaler (1980) calls the "endowment effect." The real saving from the discounts is overweighted in relation to the opportunity cost of time. In contrast, nonsearchers are likely to undersearch for high cost products. This behavior can be explained by the psychophysics of pricing (Thaler 1980). Consumers relate the benefits of search to the cost of the good rather than to the cost of the time it takes to search.

Most discounting today by specialty stores, department stores, services, and especially supermarkets is of this type (referred to as "variable price merchandising" by Nelson and Preston 1966; Preston 1970). Out-of-store coupons or features are of this type unless motivated by periodic discounting, inventory buildup, or damaged goods.

The vast volume of business in this category has increased the importance of understanding the issues involved. A static model of interim price variation due to consumer search costs first was developed by Salop and Stiglitz (1977) in their well-known piece, "Bargains and Ripoffs." Varian (1980) developed a dynamic model of random price variation by each firm, similar to the mechanism described in the last example. Since then a whole body of literature has developed pursuing various ramifications of this strategy. The basic condition for this strategy is heterogeneity of perceived search costs, which enables firms to attract informed consumers by discounting. All consumers know there is a distribution of prices and have the same reservation price. However, for high income individuals hunting for the lowest price may not be worth their time. For others the opposite holds.

The individual firm should adopt a strategy of random discounts if the increased profit from new informed consumers at the discounted price exceeds the cost arising from the uninformed buying at the discounted price plus the cost of administering the discount (see McAlister 1983 and Neslin and Shoemaker 1983 for profitability models).

It is interesting to examine the implications of this strategy. First, note that the uninformed consumers provide a diseconomy to other uninformed consumers and to informed consumers. Inefficient firms that produce above $30 or efficient firms that price above $30 can exist because some consumers do not search. As a result, prices vary, so that the informed must search for the lowest price. Similarly, the average price paid by the uninformed increases. In contrast, the informed provide an external economy to the uninformed by encouraging the existence of low price firms, thus lowering the average price the uninformed pay. From a public policy perspective, all consumers as well as the efficient firms would benefit if some mechanism could be provided to disseminate price information in the market at relatively low cost.

COMPETITIVE PRICING

This category covers a group of pricing strategies based primarily on a firm's competitive position. Penetration pricing and experience curve pricing attempt to exploit scale[4] or experience[5] economics, respectively, by currently pricing below competitors in the same market and thus driving them out. Predatory pricing is a strategy of pricing low to hold out competition with the sole objective of establishing monopolistic conditions and subsequently raising price; this practice is illegal under Section 2 of the Sherman Act and the Robinson-Patman Act of 1936. Many states also have laws that forbid a firm from pricing below cost for extended periods of time. A third strategy is price signaling,[6] whereby a firm exploits consumer trust in the price mechanism developed by other firms. A fourth strategy, geographic pricing, involves competitive pricing for adjacent market segments.

Penetration Pricing

Consider the periodic discounting example with the following two modifications: the economic cost price at 40 units is $30 and other competitors can freely enter the market with the same cost structure. How should the firm price now?

The firm could still adopt a strategy of periodic discounting, producing 40 units a period at $30 each and selling to the first set of consumers at $50 and to the second at $30. Now, however, because its average cost price is $30, it would make an excess profit of $10 per unit. Given this scenario, any other firm would be willing to come in and sell the same product for an average price that is less than $40 but more than $30. To preempt competition and stay in business, the firm would have to sell at $30 to all consumers.

The same logic underlies penetration pricing, a strategy first proposed for new products by Dean (1950a,b, 1951) as an alternative to periodic discounting (or price skimming in Dean's terminology). Periodic discounting is obviously preferable for a firm, even if its costs are lower than demand prices (as in the modified example here), as long as there is no immediate threat of competitive entry. Besides being used for new products, penetration pricing can be observed in the growth of discount stores and in the consolidation of manufacturers during the "shake out" phase of the life cycle. A variation of penetration pricing that has been closely studied in the economics literature is limit pricing (Scherer 1980), whereby a firm prices above costs but just low enough to keep out new entrants.

Penetration pricing is relevant only when the average selling price can or does exceed the minimum average cost. Other essentials for penetration pricing strategy are price sensitivity on the part of some consumers and the threat of competitive entry. In penetration pricing, unlike periodic discounting, the presence of the price sensitive consumers and of competition provides a benefit to the price insensitive segment, who can now buy the product at a price lower than they were willing to pay.

Experience Curve Pricing

Assume a competitive market with experience effects as shown in Figure 33-1. There are four firms (A, B, C, and D), each with per period volume of 2000 units but the first having the most experience and average costs of $3.75 per unit. Current prices are $5 per unit. Consumers are price sensitive and react immediately to price changes. What would be a good pricing strategy for firm A?

Note that currently firm A makes more profit than the others and that, given the projections, cost declines will be less prominent after year 6. A good strategy for firm A would

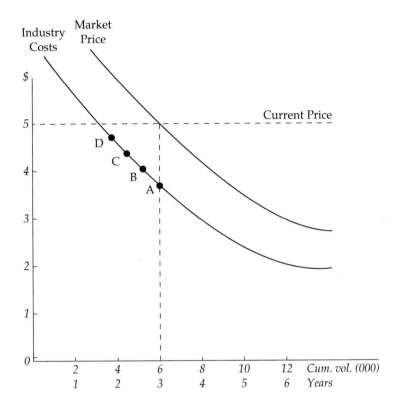

Figure 33-1
Effect of Experience Economies on Pricing Strategy

be to price aggressively, even below current costs, at $3.75. This strategy has two advantages. First, it will be uneconomical for firms B, C, and D, which may have to leave the market. Firm A is then faced with less rivalry. Second, firm A can benefit from the share of the others and gain experience more rapidly. Indeed, it would sell a cumulative volume of 12,000 units as early as year 6 and its costs would have dropped by then to $2 per unit. In addition, the low price is likely to encourage more consumers to enter the market, giving firm A an opportunity to exploit economies of scale. As a result the firm will soon be profitable again and total revenue and profits could be much higher in the future. The strategy for

the other firms is less clear. In general, unless there are other competitive advantages, it is inadvisable for the others to start a price war as they have a cost disadvantage to firm A.

Experience curve pricing, like penetration pricing, is an alternative strategy to periodic discounting. In this strategy the consumers who buy the product early in the life cycle gain an external economy from late buyers, as they buy the product at a lower price than they were willing to pay. They get this discount, however, because of economies of experience and active or potential competition that forces prices down.

The essential requirements for adopting an experience curve pricing strategy are that experience effects are strong, the firm has more experience than competitors, and that consumers are price sensitive. Typically, these conditions occur for nonessential durable goods in the early or growth stage, when a relatively large number of competitors are striving for a strong long-run position. The different sources of economies for penetration pricing and experience curve pricing must be clearly understood, because the circumstances in which they are applicable are often very similar but the mechanisms for tracking costs and pricing products are very different.

Price Signaling

Consider a market in which firms can produce products at two different quality levels, under the constraint that the minimum average economic cost is $30 for the low quality product and $50 for the high quality product. Assume that, to avoid image conflicts, each firm chooses to produce only one quality but may sell at either price, $30 or $50. Let us assume for convenience that there are at least a few firms selling the high quality product for $50 and the low quality product for $30. Consumers can easily find the lowest price (in negligible time), say by a phone call or consulting a price list. They generally prefer high quality, but it takes them 1 hour of study and consulting manuals to tell quality differences. Let these consumers have a distribution of opportunity costs of time as in the random discounting example. What are consumers' shopping strategies and firms' pricing strategies?

Firms can choose among three pricing strategies (no firm would sell the high quality product at less than $50). First, they could produce the low quality product and sell it at $30. Second, they could produce the high quality product and sell it at $50. Third, they could sell the low quality product at $50, with the intention that some consumers who cannot tell high quality but want it will be fooled. The latter strategy is called "price signaling." Consumers also have three strategies. Those with

low costs of time could study quality and buy the high quality product at $50. Those with high costs of time could adopt a risk aversive strategy and always buy the low priced product, or could buy the high priced product with the hope of getting a high quality product.

Extensive research in marketing has indicated that consumers may use price to infer quality (Monroe and Petroshius 1981; Olson 1977), but the equilibrium properties of such behavior in real markets have only recently been worked out (Cooper and Ross 1984; Tellis 1985). Three underlying conditions are necessary for price signaling to be an equilibrium strategy. First, consumers must be able to get information about price more easily than information about quality. Second, they must want the high quality enough to risk buying the high priced product even without a certainty of high quality. This motive is especially necessary because consumers underweight the value of uncertain events (the "certainty effect," Kahneman and Tversky 1979). Third, there must be a sufficiently large number of informed consumers who can understand quality and will pay the high price only for the high quality product. This third condition ensures a sufficiently positive correlation between price and quality so that those uninformed consumers who infer quality from price find it worthwhile to do so on average.

The issue of pricing in the presence of quality variation and asymmetric consumer information is typical of durable goods, though not uncommon for services and nondurable goods where it may involve less risk. For durables, quality is an important attribute yet consumer information on quality is low because of the difficulty of determining quality by inspection, the large number of brands, and the high innovation rate relative to repurchase time (Thorelli and Thorelli 1977). One result is the possibility of consumers using price to infer quality. However, another result is that the correlation between price and quality is low (Tellis and Werneifelt 1985) and consumers may often be mistaken. Price signaling is probably most common for new or amateur consumers in a market, who do not know the quality of competitive brands but find quality important. The purchase of a high priced wine by the casual buyer is a good example. The success of several high priced, inferior quality brands, as reported by *Consumer Reports,* is another illustration of consumers either buying randomly or using price to infer quality.

There are some other variations of price signaling that firms can adopt to exploit consumer behavior in other circumstances. Image pricing, discussed subsequently, and reference pricing are two common examples. In reference pricing, a firm places a high priced model next to a much higher priced version of the same product, so that the former may seem more attractive to risk aversive uninformed consumers. The latter model serves primarily as a reference point, though consumers who infer quality may buy it. Monroe and Petroshius (1981) document empirical support for consumers' use of reference prices. Kahneman and Tversky (1979) provide the rationale for this behavior in what they call the "isolation effect": a choice looks more attractive next to a costly alternative than it does in isolation. The strategy is sometimes adopted by retailers of durable goods. A more common variation is for firms to state that a product is on sale, with the "regular" sticker price adjacent, when actually the regular price is on for less than half the time. To minimize deception on the part of firms, several states now define minimum time periods for the regular price.

In this context it is worthwhile to consider the welfare aspects of such strategy. The most important point is that all consumers would be better off if a mechanism could be devised to provide information on quality to the market at low cost. Second, those firms

that sell the low quality product for the low price and those that sell the high quality product for the high price would also be better off if information on quality were disseminated, because they would not lose customers to firms that sell the low quality product at the high price. The last category of firms would vanish. Therefore, heterogeneous search costs on quality create benefits for some firms at the expense of others. Third, there could be many reasons for firms to sell the low quality product at the high price. Some could adopt such a strategy accidentally, others because they are inefficient producers, and still others because they intentionally cheat. Fourth, consumers who use price to infer quality may not necessarily be worse off. To the extent that obtaining information on quality is difficult for them, the correlation between price and quality is positive, and they prefer the high quality product, they may profitably use the high price to infer quality. In such a situation there is an external economy from the informed to the uninformed who gather information via the price mechanism.

Note that price signaling is independent of the strategy of random discounting. Both are used in situations in which consumers have heterogeneous search costs, but differ on other dimensions. For price signaling, there must be quality differences among products, information on quality must be more scarce than that on price, and quality must be important to consumers; further, each firm need adopt only one price level always and at least some efficient firms are necessary to establish consumer trust in the price mechanism.

Geographic Pricing

Consider two adjacent markets X and Y, of 20 consumers each, where all consumers have a reservation price of $50 for the product and incur a cost of more than $10 for purchasing the product in the adjacent market. A firm operating in market X is faced with free competitive entry and the following cost structure: the economic cost price for the product is $40 at 20 units and $30 at 40 units, with an added cost of $10 per unit to ship the product to the adjacent market. The cost of production is higher in market Y. What pricing strategy should the firm adopt?

The firm should produce 40 units and sell to both markets at an average economic cost price of $35 ($30 + $10 × 20 ÷ 40). To avoid competitive entry, the firm must set the average selling price over both markets at $35. However, the firm has several options for pricing the product to the two markets, called "geographic pricing strategies," depending on the competitive condition in market Y.

If the competitive price in market Y is above $40, the firm can sell the product at $30 in market X and $40 in market Y to reflect the transportation costs of $10 per unit to the latter market. Because price equals average costs, the price would be profitable yet ward off entry. This strategy is called "FOB." If the competitive price in market Y is a little over $35, the firm could sell at $35 in both markets and still achieve the same competitive effect. This strategy is called "uniform delivered price." Zone pricing is a strategy between the two when more markets are involved. When using zone pricing, the firm would charge different prices for different zones depending on the transportation costs to each, but within each zone it would charge one price, the average of all costs to all points in that zone. Basing point is still another variation of uniform delivered price; the firm chooses a base point for transportation costs to points other than the point of production.

If the competitive price is a little over $30 in market Y, the firm could sell profitably to both markets by pricing at $30 in market Y and $40 in market X. This strategy is called "freight absorption cost," because market Y bears none of the transportation cost it incurs for the product. In a monopolistic situation,

the firm may absorb the transportation cost or pass it on to consumers in market X. However, in a competitive market such as this one, all the transportation costs are borne by market X.

Geographic pricing strategies can be thought of as being between price penetration and second market discounting (see Table 33-1). As in price penetration, in geographic pricing the firm seeks to exploit economies of scale by pricing below competitors in a second market segment. As a result, the second market generally provides a benefit to the first. However, in geographic pricing the two segments are separated by transportation costs rather than by reservation prices. In this respect, geographic pricing is similar to the strategy of second market discounting, where two markets are also separated by transaction costs. In second market discounting, however, the firm explicitly attempts to exploit the differences between the two segments, providing considerable savings to the second market. By contrast, in geographic pricing the firm attempts to minimize differences between the two markets by sharing or "absorbing" the transportation costs between them. In spite of these transportation costs and because of economies of scale, the second market does not provide a diseconomy and generally provides an economy to the first.

Some of the geographic pricing strategies discussed may be illegal in certain circumstances. Three general principles can be used to guide policy in this respect. First, a firm should not discriminate between competing buyers in the same region (especially in zone pricing for buyers on either side of a zonal boundary) because such action may violate the Robinson-Patman Act of 1936. Second, the firm's strategy should not appear to be predatory, especially in freight absorption pricing, because such a strategy would violate Section 2 of the Sherman Act of 1890. Third, in choosing the basing point of zone pricing the firm should not attempt to fix prices among competitors because such action would violate Section I of the Sherman Act.

PRODUCT LINE PRICING STRATEGIES

Product line pricing strategies are relevant when a firm has a set of related products. In all of the cases considered, the firm seeks to maximize profit by pricing its products to match consumer demand. However, in each of these strategies, the nature of either the demand or the cross-subsidies varies among the firm's products. A firm uses price bundling when it faces heterogeneity of demand for nonsubstitute, perishable products. A firm uses premium pricing when it faces heterogeneity of demand for substitute products with joint economies of scale. Image pricing is used when consumers infer quality from prices of substitute models. Complementary pricing (including captive pricing, two-part pricing, and loss leadership) is used when a firm faces consumers with higher transaction costs for one or more of its products.

Price Bundling

Assume a distributor of two films, "Romancing the Stone" and "Places in the Heart," is faced by the following demand for theme films from two movie houses, Astro and Classic Theatres, that serve the same market.

For:	Maximum Prices ($'000) Paid by:	
	Classic Theatres	Astro
"Romancing the Stone"	12	18
"Places in the Heart"	25	10

What is the best pricing strategy for the distributor to adopt if we assume it cannot explicitly discriminate in price or use tying contracts (force a theatre to buy both movies)?

An explicit price discriminating strategy, charging each distributor the most it will pay for each movie, would yield a total revenue of $65K, but this practice is illegal. Assume the buyers are sufficiently informed and the products perishable so that differential pricing by periodic or random discounting is not possible. A penetration strategy is to price the first movie at $12K and the second at $10K, but in that case total revenue is only $44K from both theatres (2 × (12 + 10)). A "pure components" strategy is to price the first at $18K and the second at $25K, for a total revenue of $43K.

The best solution is to price the first movie at $18K, the second at $25K, and offer both at $28K for a total revenue of $56K. Note that Classic Theatres will take both movies at no more than $37K and Astro at no more than $28K. Thus both theatres will accept the package for $28K, which is the profit maximizing strategy. This strategy is called "mixed bundling" to contrast it with a pure bundling alternative in which case only the package is available for $28K. Pure bundling may be illegal as a tying contract (Scherer 1980; Werner 1982). The mixed bundling strategy has the added advantage of creating the reference price effect: the package is offered at a much lower price than the sum of the parts.

The economics of price bundling was first analyzed by Stigler (1968) and further developed by Adams and Yellen (1976), Telser 1979, Spence (1980), Paroush and Peles (1981), Phillips (1981), and Schmalensee (1984). Examples of such a strategy are the lower prices for season tickets, buffet dinners, packages of stereo equipment, and packages of options on automobiles. The basic requirement for mixed bundling is nonsubstitute (i.e., complementary or independent), perishable products with an asymmetric demand structure. Because the products are not perfect substitutes, it is possible to get consumers to buy both (or all). Because the products are perishable, the differential pricing strategies of periodic or random discounting are not feasible. The perishability of food items or seats for shows is apparent. The perishability in the purchase of durable goods is the purchase occasion, at which time it is in the interest of sellers to maximize revenues within consumers' demand schedule by price bundling. For example, consumers may buy automobiles once in 3 or 5 years. Each of those times is an opportunity for a firm to sell a maximum number of options by appropriate pricing.

The strategy of price bundling must not be confused with that of "trading up," in which consumers are persuaded to buy more or higher priced models than they originally intended. As the numerical example shows, a passive strategy of correctly bundling the prices of related items is all that is needed to maximize profit. It is also in the interest of consumers to buy at the price bundle. Thus, all consumers and sellers are better off with the mixed bundling strategy than with the pure components strategy.[7]

Premium Pricing

Consider a firm faced with the following pricing problem. There is free entry and average economic costs (for production and marketing) are $50 at 20 units and $35 at 40 units. At any volume, it costs the firm an additional $10 per unit to produce and market a superior version of the product. Assume that any fixed costs of marketing two products instead of one are negligible. Forty consumers per period are interested in its product. Half of them are price insensitive and want the superior version of the product even if they have to pay $50 per unit. The other half are price sensitive and want the basic version of the product but will pay no more than $30 per unit. In what version and at what price should the firm sell the product?

As in the periodic discounting example, costs seem to exceed prices if the firm chooses to sell to only one segment or at only one price. However, it can solve its problem by a premium pricing strategy that exploits consumer heterogeneity in demand. It should produce at 40 units, half of which will be of the superior version, for an average economic cost of $40. It should sell the basic product for $30 and the premium for $40, for an average selling price of $40, at which price it is profitable and wards off entry. Relative to its costs, the firm takes a premium on its higher priced version and a loss on its lower priced version. However, by exploiting joint economies of scale and the heterogeneity of demand, it can profitably produce and sell the product.

Premium pricing applies in a large number of circumstances in markets today. It is used in the pricing of durable goods, typically appliances, for which multiple versions differing in price and features cater to different consumer segments. It also could apply for the pricing of some nondurable goods such as basic and specialty breads or common and exclusive perfumes. A similar strategy is used for the pricing of alternate service plans such as term and preferred insurance policies, front and rear auditorium seating, and deluxe and basic hotel rooms. As is well known in the case of autos, firms do not find their lower priced models "very profitable," but typically make their profits on the premium versions. Often these premium versions differ from the basic only by features and options, whose production costs generally are not high enough to justify the higher markup. Why does the firm produce the lower priced version and why do other firms not enter the market with only the higher priced version? The preceding explanation is based on heterogeneity in demand and joint economies of scale. Notice that the firm, by using a premium strategy, sells at exactly its economic cost price, which is compatible with a competitive market with free entry.[8] No firm could enter and profitably produce only for the price insensitive segment.

Premium pricing also is used in retail, where it enables retailers to carry some otherwise unprofitable products desired only by select segments. The pricing of byproducts, though generally considered different from premium pricing, involves the same principle. A byproduct may carry a cost of disposal to the firm, and this may add to the price of the main product. In some cases a byproduct may be worth much more than it costs the firm to produce, and this advantage can be used to subsidize the price of the main product.

The essential difference between premium pricing and price bundling is that the former applies to substitutes and the latter to complementary products. Both require heterogeneity in demand, but in using premium pricing the firm tries to emphasize segment differences by pricing substitutes differently, whereas in using price bundling the firm seeks to bridge segment differences by selling at the lowest common package price. The difference between premium pricing and price signaling is that in the latter each firm produces only one type of product, which is sold at different prices to differently informed consumers. In the former, a firm produces two types of products to exploit joint economies of scale and markets them to heterogeneous but fully informed consumers.

The welfare aspects of premium pricing parallel those of periodic discounting. The main difference is in the fact that in periodic discounting the strategy is carried out for any one brand and the price variation is over time; in premium pricing, the strategy holds for any one time and the price variation is over related models. As in the periodic discounting example, each segment here provides an external economy to the other; however, the advantage to the price sensitive segment is greater because they buy a product below its average cost.

Image Pricing

By image pricing, a firm brings out an identical version of its current product with a different name (or model number) and a higher price. The intention is to signal quality. This strategy is between price signaling and premium pricing in that the demand characteristics are similar to those of price signaling and the cost aspects are similar to those of premium pricing (see Table 33-1). Thus the firm uses the higher priced version to signal quality to uninformed consumers and uses the profit it makes on the higher priced version to subsidize the price on the lower priced version. Image pricing differs from price signaling in that the prices are varied over different brands of the same firm's product line. It differs from premium pricing in that differences between brands are not real but only in the images or positions adopted. This strategy may account for some of the variation in prices of alternative brands of cosmetics, soaps, wines, and dresses that differ only in brand names.

Complementary Pricing

Complementary pricing includes three related strategies—captive pricing, two-part pricing, and loss leadership.

Captive pricing: Consider a firm that produces a durable good whose economic cost price is $100 and life span is 3 years. During that time the product needs supplies that have an economic cost price of $.50 a month. All consumers are willing to pay at most $50 for the product and $2 per month for supplies. Assuming all buyers will keep on purchasing supplies regularly and the discount rate for future earnings is zero, what pricing strategy should the firm adopt?

Under the given assumptions, the firm would do well to price the basic product at $50 and the supplies at $2. The accumulated premium over the life of the product would equal $54 (3 × 12 × $1.5) and would more than compensate for the loss at the time of selling the basic product. In actually computing the minimum price of the product, the firm would have to include as costs a discount for future earnings and the risk that consumers would not purchase supplies. The firm also needs to consider the potential gains from this strategy. For example, consumers may not view the basic product they purchased as a sunk cost, and may try to "recover" their investment by buying the accessories and using it (the "sunk cost effect," Thaler 1980). Alternatively, they may get involved in the product and use it more than expected. This possibility has led some authors to label this strategy "captive pricing" (e.g., Kotler 1984, p. 529).

An interesting question is whether consumers would buy the package with the product at $100 and the accessories at $.50 if they were informed they were incurring the same cost the other way around. Probably they would not. A consumer may be reluctant to incur a big immediate investment (a certain loss) for an uncertain future satisfaction ("the certainty effect," Kahneman and Tversky 1979), or may not have the funds for the purchase. In either case, the consumer has a "transaction cost," which the firm apparently absorbs.

The chief restraint on the use of captive pricing for durable goods and accessories is that there are often no major shared economies in the manufacture of the basic product and its accessories. Thus, if the premium on the accessories is too high, marginal producers of the accessories may enter the market and drive down prices. In some circumstances, as in the automobile industry, the accessories are themselves produced by smaller firms. Consequently this strategy has limited importance unless consumers are source loyal and would like to buy supplies from the original source even at a higher price. In other circumstances, manufacturers hold patents or are the only source of the technology for the production of the supplies. In this case captive pricing is crucial for the success of the product. Bain (1956) refers to the superior position of these firms as "absolute cost advantages." In no circumstances may the firm bind the buyer to purchase the supplies from it. Such a strategy of tying contracts may be illegal under the Sherman Act of 1890 or the Clayton Act of 1914 (Burstein 1960; Scherer 1980; Werner 1982).

The well-known examples of captive pricing are razors and blades, cameras and films, autos and spare parts, and videos or computers and software packages. In the case of services, this strategy is referred to as "two-part pricing" because the service price is broken into a fixed fee plus variable usage fees (e.g., the pricing by telephone companies, libraries, health or entertainment clubs, amusement parks, and various rental agencies). The economics of two-part pricing has been studied by several researchers, more recently by Schmalensee (1982).

In retailing, the corresponding strategy is called "loss leadership," and involves dropping the price on a well-known brand to generate store traffic. The drop in price should be large enough to compensate consumers for the transaction cost involved in making the extra trip, switching from their normal place of purchase, or foregoing the cheaper basket of prices they pay at the alternative store. However, in many cases the drop in price may not be exactly that high, primarily because consumers may see the price drop as a real gain while underestimating the transaction costs (Thaler 1985). Nevertheless, to ensure a success in this strategy, retailers normally feature several "super buys," nationally branded products sold below cost.

Manufacturers of nationally branded products have always disapproved of loss leadership for two reasons. First, a product that is often available on discount may give consumers the impression that the quality is inferior. Second, specialty stores that depend on the branded products for their source of income may lose sales to discount stores and therefore cease to distribute the product. Manufacturers have sought to restrain loss leadership by a strategy of retail price maintenance. However, (minimum) retail price maintenance is now illegal under a federal statute, the Consumer Goods Pricing Act of 1975 (Scammon 1985; Scherer 1980; Werner 1982).

The reverse case, maintaining maximum retail prices, is not illegal (Scammon 1985). This situation occurs when a retailer charges too high a price for a branded product over which it has exclusive or selective distributorship. In such a case the retailer may suboptimize the manufacturer's profits (Machlup and Taber 1960). The manufacturer can control this practice by advertising the "suggested (maximum) retail price" and then enforcing such a price during the advertising period. High priced durable goods such as appliances and automobiles are examples of products for which this strategy is used.

Complementary pricing is similar to premium pricing in that the loss in the sale of a product is covered by the profit from the sale of a related product. However, there are two important distinctions. First, premium pricing applies to substitutes and complementary pricing to complements. Second, complementary pricing requires variation in transaction costs over the products whereas premium pricing requires variation in preferences over consumer groups. As a result there is no sharing of economies among customer groups in complementary pricing.

AN INTEGRATION AND COMPARISON OF STRATEGIES

The preceding discussion demonstrates the variety of pricing strategies available to a firm. The theory underlying some of them has only recently been analyzed in the economics literature, though they all have been discussed in some form in the marketing discipline. A major contribution of this article is that all these strategies are discussed on the same basis and are compared in a manner that is theoretically rich yet typologically simple. The most important contribution is that the strategies are shown to have a common denominator—shared economies. This proposition makes possible an enlightening classification of the strategies and a summarization of their underlying principles. The classification is based on two dimensions: the objective of the firm in exploiting these shared economies and the consumer characteristics necessary for each strategy (see Table 33-1).

The relevance of the central idea of shared economies is summarized here with respect to Table 33-1. A more detailed explanation is given in the description of the welfare aspects of each strategy. In the class of differential pricing strategies, one product is sold to two segments at different prices. By this means the firm exploits economies of scale and each segment provides an economy to the other. In addition, in second market discounting and periodic discounting, one segment buys the product at a higher price and in so doing incurs more of the production costs so that the product can be made available to the other segment at its lower acceptable price. In random discounting, the searchers ensure that the product is available at a lower price at random periods, thus providing a lower average price to the nonsearchers.

In the class of competitive pricing strategies, firms sell one product to one or more market segments at the same price, but the pattern of shared economies is more complex. In price signaling, the searchers provide an economy to nonsearchers, who can get the quality they desire (either high or low) at an acceptable risk of an error just by observing prices. In penetration, experience curve, and geographic pricing, the two segments provide a simple cost economy to each other, enabling the firm to exploit economies of scale or experience. In addition, in penetration and experience curve pricing the common price is that of the more price sensitive segment, which therefore confers a great economy to the price insensitive segment. In geographic pricing, the lower the competitive price in the adjacent market, the higher the price and hence the greater the diseconomy borne by the home market.

In the class of product line pricing strategies, the shared economies are primarily over the production or marketing of the products in the line. In image pricing, premium pricing, and complementary pricing, one product is sold at a "loss" which is then recovered from the higher price of a complementary product sold to the same segment or of a substitute product sold to a less price sensitive segment. In price bundling, there is an asymmetric demand by two consumer segments over two nonsubstitute products. A firm using the optimum price sells both products at the lower of the joint reservation prices. In this way the firm sells one product below the acceptable price of one segment, but compensates by selling both products to both segments. In all of these cases the creative dimension of pricing is to identify the source and pattern of shared economies that can be exploited for the benefit of the individual firm and its consumers.

Besides delineating the classification scheme, this article compares and contrasts the various strategies with closely related alternatives. In addition, a summary comparison based on five criteria is presented in Table 33-2. These criteria are the characteristics of the strategy; the necessary consumer, product, and cost characteristics; the relevant legal constraints; and the variants of this strategy. The table demonstrates that the multiplicity of names distracts from the essential similarity among the strategies and the common principles that unify them. A small, theoretically based set of labels, like the one suggested here, enhances understanding and communication of the issues.

Besides the pedagogical and managerial benefits from this presentation of pricing strategies, the theoretical presentation suggests certain research avenues. One would be to review and further develop pricing models based on this classification scheme. Different models then could be usefully compared, new uses for older models identified, and newer models developed. Another avenue would be to determine to what extent these different strategies are carried out in practice, the types of firms that use particular strategies, and the factors that determine empirical success. A third avenue is to determine whether the principle of shared economies is in fact the main explanation for these strategies, as is proposed here.

NOTES

1. There are also other motivations for discounting, the most common being damaged goods, overstocking, or quantity purchases. These discounts are not considered pricing strategies because they are merely adjustments for costs, often of an *ad hoc* nature. The term "price discrimination" has been used in the literature very broadly to mean charging different customer groups prices not proportionate to costs for the same or related products. It would cover almost all the strategies discussed here (Cassady 1946a,b; Monroe 1979; Scherer 1980).

2. The term "average economic cost" is used to mean all costs, production and marketing,

fixed and variable, plus acceptable profit divided by number of units.

3. The discussion of welfare applies only to the competitive case as in the example described. Some of the applications of this strategy cited above have been to the monopolistic case, in which situation the price sensitive buyers are the primary beneficiaries. However, as the example illustrates, *monopoly is not a necessary condition for periodic discounting*, though some authors mistakenly say so.

4. "Economies of scale" refers to the decline in average total costs with scale. This effect is generally attributed to superior technology or more efficient organization or cheaper purchases (Mansfield 1983; Palda 1969). Average total costs also are believed to increase beyond a certain point because of the difficulty of managing very large operations.

5. "Experience curve" or "experience economies" refers to the decline in average total costs in constant dollars with *cumulative* volume (see Figure 1). Define C_1 as average costs at volume V_1, let V_1 hold for n_1 periods; define C_2 as average costs at volume V_2, let V_2 hold for n_2 periods. Then economies of scale are captured by the elasticity ε_s defined by

$$\frac{C_2}{C_1} = \left(\frac{V_2}{V_1}\right)^{\varepsilon_2}, V_2 \neq V_1, \tag{1}$$

and economies of experience by the elasticity ε_e defined by

$$\frac{C_2}{C_1} = \left[\frac{\displaystyle\sum_{j=1}^{n_2} V_{2j} + \sum_{i=1}^{n_1} V_{1i}}{\displaystyle\sum_{i=1}^{n_1} V_{1i}}\right]^{e_s} \tag{2}$$

$$= \left(\frac{n_2 V_2 + n_1 V_1}{n_1 V_1}\right)^{\varepsilon_s} = \left(1 + \frac{n_2 V_2}{n_1 V_1}\right)^{\varepsilon_s}$$

Note that change in the scale of operation, measured by V_2/V_1, affects the value of ε_s and ε_e, which are therefore related. However, ε_s does not *cause* ε_e or vice versa. Moreover,

unlike ε_s, ε_e is defined even if $V_2 = V_1$, and when $V_2 = V_1$ may still be dependent primarily on n_2/n_1, the time parameters. The strategic implications of the experience curve were best documented and popularized by the Boston Consulting Group (1972), though the issue was addressed in the literature earlier (e.g., Alchian 1959; Arrow 1962; Hirsch 1952; Preston and Keachie 1964). More recent theoretical contributions were made by Robinson and Lakhani (1975), Dolan and Jeuland (1981), and Kalish (1983). The decline in costs due to experience could be caused by a number of factors, most importantly labor efficiency and newer process technology (see Abell and Hammond 1979 and Porter 1980 for a complete list). Two important issues to be kept in mind when pricing are that economies of experience *can occur independently of scale* (as shown above) and that their decline generally takes place fairly constantly with cumulative volume. Because cumulative volume increases at a faster rate in the first few years of a product's production history, experience effects are most noticeable at that time period. Because of competitive pressures, prices also decline with costs.

6. The term is used here to mean firms signaling quality to consumers by price. It must be distinguished from various interfirm signaling strategies that firms may use to "implicitly collude" (Scherer 1980).

7. In this example all cost issues are ignored, which could lead to at least three scenarios. One is a monopolistic situation in which the costs are sufficiently low that any of the pricing options would be profitable. The second is a cost situation in which only the mixed bundling option would be profitable. This then would hold either for monopoly or pure competition. The third is a situation in which costs are sufficiently low that any option would be profitable, but there is free entry so firms would use only the penetration pricing strategy ($10 for the first and $12 for the second movie) which is always the preferable option for consumers.

8. In some markets oligopolistic or monopolistic situations exist, in which case a firm can mar-

ket profitably only to the premium segment. However, there are several reasons for marketing to both segments. First, dealers, especially of high priced durables, are more likely to accept an exclusive dealing strategy if the manufacturer has a complete line of products. Second, with a complete line it is easier to develop brand loyalty, especially as consumers tend to buy better versions of durables with each subsequent purchase. Third, a low priced basic version may be used to attract consumers into stores and then motivate them to buy the higher priced versions. Since an early note by Dean (1950b), there is an extensive literature on alternative theoretical models for premium pricing. However, without formal empirical analysis it is not possible to determine which model is relevant or what alternatives need to be developed (Katz 1984).

REFERENCES

Abell, Derek F. and John S. Hammond (1979), *Strategic Market Planning: Problems and Analytical Approaches*. Englewood Cliffs, NJ: Prentice-Hall, Inc.

Adams, W. J. and J. L. Yellen (1976), "Commodity Bundling and the Burden of Monopoly," *Quarterly Journal of Economics*, 90 (August), 475–98.

Alchian, A. (1959), "Costs and Outputs," in *The Allocation of Economic Resources*, M. Abramovitz et al., eds. Stanford, CA: Stanford University Press, 23–40.

Areeda, Phillip (1974), *Antitrust Analysis*. Boston: Little, Brown & Company.

Arrow, K. J. (1962), "The Economic Implications of Learning by Doing," *Review of Economic Studies*, 29 (June), 155–73.

Bain, Joe S. (1956), *Barriers to New Competition*. Cambridge, MA: Harvard University Press.

Boston Consulting Group (1972), *Perspectives on Experience*. Boston, MA: Boston Consulting Group, Inc.

Burstein, M. L. (1960), "The Economics of Tie-In Sales," *Review of Economics and Statistics*, 27 (February), 68–73.

Cassady, Ralph, Jr. (1946a), "Some Economic Aspects of Price Discrimination Under Nonperfect Market Conditions," *Journal of Marketing*, 11 (July), 7–20.

———— (1946b), "Techniques and Purposes of Price Discrimination," *Journal of Marketing*, 11 (October), 135–58.

Cooper, R. and T. W. Ross (1984), "Prices, Product Qualities and Asymmetric Information: The Competitive Case," *Review of Economic Studies*, 51, 197–207.

Dean, Joel (1950a), "Pricing Policies for New Products," *Harvard Business Review*, 28 (November–December), 45–53.

———— (1950b), "Problems of Product-Line Pricing," *Journal of Marketing*, 14 (4), 518–28.

———— (1951), *Managerial Economics*. Englewood Cliffs, NJ: Prentice-Hall, Inc.

Dolan, Robert, and Abel Jeuland (1981), "Experience Curves and Dynamic Demand Models: Implications for Optimal Pricing Strategies," *Journal of Marketing*, 45 (Winter), 52–62,

Harris, Milton and Arthur Raviv (1981), "A Theory of Monopoly Pricing Schemes with Demand Uncertainty," *American Economic Review*, 71 (June), 347–65.

Hirsch, W. (1952), "Manufacturing Progress Functions," *Review of Economics and Statistics*, 34 (May), 143–55.

Hirshleifer, Jack (1958), "Peak Loads and Efficient Pricing: Comment," *Quarterly Journal of Economics*, 72 (August), 451–62.

Houthakker, Hendrik (1951), "Electricity Tariffs in Theory and Practice," *Economic Journal*, 61 (March), 1–25.

Hunt, Shelby D. (1983), *Marketing Theory, The Philosophy of Marketing Science*. Homewood, IL: Richard D. Irwin, Inc.

Kahneman, Daniel and Amos Tversky (1979), "Prospect Theory: An Analysis of Decision Under Risk," *Econometrica*, 47 (March), 263–91.

Kalish, Shlomo (1983), "Monopolist Pricing with Dynamic Demand and Production Cost," *Marketing Science*, 2 (Spring), 135–60.

Katz, Michael L. (1984), "Firm-Specific Differentiation and Competition among Multiproduct Firms," *Journal of Business*, 57, 1, 2, S149–S166.

Kotler, P. (1984), *Marketing Management*. Englewood Cliffs, NJ: Prentice-Hall, Inc.

Machlup, Fritz and Martha Taber (1960), "Bilateral Monopoly, Successive Monopoly, and Vertical Integration," *Economica*, 27 (May), 101–19.

Mansfield, Edwin (1983), *Principles of Microeconomics,* 4th ed. New York: W. W. Norton & Company.

McAlister, Leigh (1983), "A Theory of Consumer Promotions: The Model," Sloan School Working Paper #1457–83, Massachusetts Institute of Technology.

Monroe, Kent B. (1979), *Pricing: Making Profitable Decisions.* New York: McGraw-Hill Book Company.

_____ and S. M. Petroshius (1981), "Buyers' Perceptions of Price: An Update of the Evidence," in *Perspectives in Consumer Behavior,* H. H. Kassarjian and T. S. Robertson, eds. Glenview, IL: Scott, Foresman and Company, 43–5.

Nagle, Thomas (1984), "Economic Foundations for Pricing," *Journal of Business,* 57, 1, 2, S3–S26.

Nelson, Paul E. and Lee E. Preston (1966), *Price Merchandising in Food Retailing: A Case Study.* Berkeley, CA: The Special Publications.

Neslin, Scott A. and Robert W. Shoemaker (1983), "A Model for Evaluating the Profitability of Coupon Promotions," *Marketing Science,* 2 (Fall), 361–88.

Olson, J. C. (1977), "Price as an Informational Cue: Effects on Product Evaluations," in *Consumer and Industrial Buying Behavior,* A. G. Woodside et al., eds. New York: North-Holland Publishing Company, 267–86.

Oren, Shmuel S. (1984), "Comments on Pricing Research in Marketing: The State of the Art," *Journal of Business,* 57, 1, 2, 561–4.

Palda, Kristian S. (1969), *Economic Analysis for Marketing Decisions.* Englewood Cliffs, NJ: Prentice-Hall, Inc.

Paroush, J. and Y. C. Peles (1981), "A Combined Monopoly and Optimal Packaging Model," *European Economic Review,* 15 (March), 373–83.

Phillips, O. R. (1981), "Product Bundles, Price Discrimination and the Two Product Firm," working paper, Texas A&M University.

Porter, M. E. (1980), *Competitive Strategy, Techniques for Analyzing Industries and Competitions.* New York: The Free Press.

Preston, Lee E. (1970), *Markets and Marketing.* Glenview, IL: Scott, Foresman and Company.

_____ and E. C. Keachie (1964), "Cost Functions and Progress Functions: An Integration," *American Economic Review,* 54 (March), 100–7.

Rao, Vithala R. (1984), "Pricing Research in Marketing: The State of the Art," *Journal of Business,* 57, 1, 2, S39–S60.

Robinson, Bruce and Chet Lakhani (1975), "Dynamic Price Models for New Product Planning," *Management Science,* 21 (June), 1113–22.

Salop, Steven and Joseph Stiglitz (1977), "Bargains and Ripoffs: A Model of Monopolistically Competitive Price Dispersion," *Review of Economic Studies,* 493–510.

Scammon, Debra (1985), "Price Control (Minimum and Maximum)," *Journal of Marketing,* 49 (Spring), 147.

Scherer, F. M. (1980), *Industrial Market Structure and Economic Performance.* Chicago: Rand-McNally College Publishing Company.

Schmalensee, Richard (1982), "Commodity Bundling by Single-Product Monopolies," *Journal of Law and Economics,* 25 (April), 67–72.

_____ (1984), "Gaussian Demand and Commodity Bundling," *Journal of Business,* 57, 1, 2, S211–S230.

Spence, A. M. (1980), "Multi-Product Quantity-Dependent Prices and Profitability Constraints," *Review of Economic Studies,* 47 (October), 821–42.

Steiner, Peter O. (1957), "Peak Loads and Efficient Pricing," *Quarterly Journal of Economics,* 71 (November), 585–610.

Stigler, G. J. (I 968), "A Note on Block Booking," reprinted in *The Organization of Industry,* G. J. Stigler, ed. Homewood, IL: Richard D. Irwin, Inc.

Stokey, Nancy L. (1981), "Rational Expectations and Durable Goods Pricing," *Bell Journal of Economics,* 12 (Spring), 112–28.

Tellis, Gerard J. (1985), "Do Prices Signal Quality: Theory, Measurement and Evidence," Working Paper #85–53, College of Business Administration, The University of Iowa.

_____ and Birger Wernerfelt (1985), "The Price of Quality," Working Paper #85–52, College of Business Administration, The University of Iowa.

Telser, L. G. (1979), "A Theory of Monopoly of Complementary Goods," *Journal of Business,* 52 (April), 211–30.

Thaler, Richard (1990), "Toward a Positive Theory of Consumer Choice," *Journal of Economic Behavior and Organization,* 1 (March), 39–60.

_____ (1985), "Mental Accounting and Consumer Choice," *Marketing Science,* 4 (Summer), 199–214.

Thorelli, Hans B. and Sarah V. Thorelli (1977), *Consumer Information Systems and Consumer Policy.* Cambridge, MA: Ballinger Publishing Company.

Tversky, Amos (1969), "Intransitivity of Preferences," *Psychological Bulletin,* 76, 31–48.

Varian, Hal (1980), "A Model of Sales," *The American Economic Review* (September), 651–9.

Werner, Ray O. (1982), "Marketing and the United States Supreme Court, 1975–1981," *Journal of Marketing,* 46 (Spring), 73–81.

Williamson, Oliver E. (1966), "Peak-Load Pricing and Optimal Capacity Under Indivisibility Constraints," *American Economic Review,* 56 (September), 810–27.

◆

A Model for Predictive Measurements of Advertising Effectiveness

Robert J. Lavidge and Gary A. Steiner

What are the functions of advertising? Obviously the ultimate function is to help product sales. But all advertising is not, should not, and cannot be designed to produce immediate purchases on the part of all who are exposed to it. Immediate sales results (even if measurable) are, at best, an incomplete criterion of advertising effectiveness.

In other words, the effects of much advertising are "long-term." This is sometimes taken to imply that all one can really do is wait and see—ultimately the campaign will or will not produce.

However, if something is to happen in the long run, something must be happening in the short run, something that will ultimately lead to eventual sales results. And this process must be measured in order to provide anything approaching a comprehensive evaluation of the effectiveness of the advertising.

Ultimate consumers normally do not switch from disinterested individuals to convinced purchasers in one instantaneous step. Rather, they approach the ultimate purchase through a process or series of steps in which the actual purchase is but the final threshold.

SEVEN STEPS

Advertising may be thought of as a force, which must move people up a series of steps:

1. Near the bottom of the steps stand potential purchasers who are completely *unaware of the existence* of the product or service in question.
2. Closer to purchasing, but still a long way from the cash register, are those who are merely *aware of its existence*.
3. Up a step are prospects who *know what the product has to offer*.
4. Still closer to purchasing are those who have favorable attitudes toward the product—those who *like the product*.
5. Those whose favorable attitudes have developed to the point of *preference over all other possibilities* are up still another step.

Reprinted from *Journal of Marketing*, published by the American Marketing Association (October 1961), pp. 59–62.

523

6. Even closer to purchasing are consumers who couple preference with a desire to buy and the *conviction* that the purchase would be wise.

7. Finally, of course, is the step which translates this attitude into actual *purchase.*

Research to evaluate the effectiveness of advertisements can be designed to provide measures of movement on such a flight of steps.

The various steps are not necessarily equidistant. In some instances the "distance" from awareness to preference may be very slight, while the distance to purchase is extremely large. In other cases, the reverse may be true. Furthermore, a potential purchaser sometimes may move up several steps simultaneously.

Consider the following hypotheses. The greater the psychological and/or economic commitment involved in the purchase of a particular product, the longer it will take to bring consumers up these steps, and the more important the individual steps will be. Contrariwise, the less serious the commitment, the more likely it is that some consumers will go almost "immediately" to the top of the steps.

An impulse purchase might be consummated with no previous awareness, knowledge, liking, or conviction with respect to the product. On the other hand, an industrial good or an important consumer product ordinarily will not be purchased in such a manner.

DIFFERENT OBJECTIVES

Products differ markedly in terms of the role of advertising as related to the various positions on the steps. A great deal of advertising is designed to move people up the final steps toward purchase. At an extreme is the "Buy Now" ad, designed to stimulate immediate overt action. Contrast this with industrial advertising, much of which is not intended to stimulate immediate purchase in and of itself. Instead, it is designed to help pave the way for the salesman by making the prospects aware of his company and products, thus giving them knowledge and favorable attitudes about the ways in which those products or services might be of value. This, of course, involves movement up the lower and intermediate steps.

Even within a particular product category, or with a specific product, different advertisements or campaigns may be aimed primarily at different steps in the purchase process—and rightly so. For example, advertising for new automobiles is likely to place considerable emphasis on the lower steps when new models are first brought out. The advertiser recognizes that his first job is to make the potential customer aware of the new product, and to give him knowledge and favorable attitudes about the product. As the year progresses, advertising emphasis tends to move up the steps. Finally, at the end of the "model year" much emphasis is placed on the final step—the attempt to stimulate immediate purchase among prospects who are assumed, by then, to have information about the car.

The simple model assumes that potential purchasers all "start from scratch." However, some may have developed negative attitudes about the product, which place them even further from purchasing the product than those completely unaware of it. The first job, then, is to get them off the negative steps—before they can move up the additional steps which lead to purchase.

THREE FUNCTIONS OF ADVERTISING

The six steps outlined, beginning with "aware," indicate three major functions of advertising. The first two, awareness and knowledge, relate to *information or ideas*. The second two steps, liking and preference, have to do with favorable *attitudes or feelings* toward the product. The final two steps, conviction and purchase, are to produce *action*—the acquisition of the product.

These three advertising functions are directly related to a classic psychological model which divides behavior into three components or dimensions:

1. The *cognitive* component—the intellectual, mental, or "rational" states.
2. The *affective* component—the "emotional" or "feeling" states.
3. The *conative* or *motivational* component—the "striving" states, relating to the tendency to treat objects as positive or negative goals.

This is more than a semantic issue, because the actions that need to be taken to stimulate or channel motivation may be quite different from those that produce knowledge. And these, in turn, may differ from actions designed to produce favorable attitudes toward something.

FUNCTIONS OF ADVERTISING RESEARCH

Among the first problems in any advertising evaluation program are to:

1. Determine what steps are most critical in a particular case, that is, what the steps leading to purchase are for most consumers.
2. Determine how many people are, at the moment, on which steps.
3. Determine which people on which steps it is most important to reach.

Advertising research can then be designed to evaluate the extent to which the advertising succeeds in moving the specified "target" audiences up the critical purchase steps.

Table 34-1 summarizes the stair-step model, and illustrates how several common advertising and research approaches may be organized according to their various "functions."

Over-All and Component Measurements

With regard to almost any product there are an infinite number of additional "subflights" which can be helpful in moving a prospect up the main steps. For example, awareness, knowledge and development of favorable attitudes toward a specific product feature may be helpful in building a preference for the line of products. This leads to the concept of other steps, subdividing or "feeding" into the purchase steps, but concerned solely with more specific product features or attitudes.

Advertising effectiveness measurements may, then, be categorized into:

1. Over-all or "global" measurements, concerned with measuring the results—the consumers' positions and movement on the purchase steps.
2. Segment or component measurements, concerned with measuring the relative effectiveness of various means of moving people up the purchase steps—the consumers' positions on ancillary flights of steps, and the relative importance of these flights.

Measuring Movement on the Steps

Many common measurements of advertising effectiveness have been concerned with movement up either the first steps or the final step on the primary purchase flight. Examples include surveys to determine the extent of brand awareness and information and measures of purchase and repeat purchase among "exposed" versus "unexposed" groups.

Table 34-1
Advertising and Advertising Research Related to the Model

Related Behavioral Dimensions	Movement toward Purchase	Examples of Types of Promotion or Advertising Relevant to Various Steps	Examples of Research Approaches Related to Steps of Greatest Applicability
Conative —the realm of motives. Ads stimulate or direct desires	PURCHASE ↑ CONVICTION	Point-of-purchase Retail store ads Deals "Last-chance" offers Price appeals Testimonials	Market or sales test Split-run tests Intention to purchase Projective techniques
Affective —the realm of emotions. Ads change attitudes and feelings	↑ PREFERENCE ↑ LIKING	Competitive ads Argumentative copy "Image" ads Status, glamour appeals	Rank order of preference for brands Rating scales Image measurements including check lists and semantic differentials Projective techniques
Cognitive —the realm of thoughts. Ads provide information and facts	↑ KNOWLEDGE ↑ AWARENESS	Announcements Descriptive copy Classified ads Slogans Jingles Sky writing Teaser campaigns	Information questions Play-back analyses Brand awareness surveys Aided recall

Self-administered instruments, such as adaptations of the "semantic differential" and adjective check lists, are particularly helpful in providing the desired measurements of movement up or down the middle steps. The semantic differential provides a means of scaling attitudes with regard to a number of different issues in a manner which facili-tates gathering the information on an efficient quantitative basis. Adjective lists, used in various ways, serve the same general purpose.

Such devices can provide relatively spontaneous, rather than "considered," responses. They are also quickly administered and can contain enough elements to make recall of specific responses by the test participant difficult, especially if the order of items is changed. This helps in minimizing "consistency" biases in various comparative uses of such measurement tools.

Efficiency of these self-administered devices makes it practical to obtain responses to large numbers of items. This facilitates measurement of elements or components differing only slightly, though importantly, from each other.

Carefully constructed adjective check lists, for example, have shown remarkable discrimination between terms differing only in subtle shades of meaning. One product may be seen as "rich," "plush," and "expensive," while another one is "plush," "gaudy," and "cheap."

Such instruments make it possible to secure simultaneous measurements of both *global* attitudes and *specific* image components. These can be correlated with each other and directly related to the content of the advertising messages tested.

Does the advertising change the thinking of the respondents with regard to specific product attributes, characteristics or features, including not only physical characteristics but also various image elements such as "status"? Are these changes commercially significant?

The measuring instruments mentioned are helpful in answering these questions. They provide a means for correlating changes in specific attitudes concerning image components with changes in global attitudes or position on the primary purchase steps.

Testing the Model

When groups of consumers are studied over time, do those who show more movement on the measured steps eventually purchase the product in greater proportions or quantities? Accumulation of data utilizing the stair-step model provides an opportunity to test the assumptions underlying the model by measuring this question.

THREE CONCEPTS

This approach to the measurement of advertising has evolved from these concepts:

1. Realistic measurements of advertising effectiveness must be related to an understanding of the functions of advertising. It is helpful to think in terms of a model where advertising is likened to a force which, if successful, moves people up a series of steps toward purchase.
2. Measurements of the effectiveness of the advertising should provide measurements of changes at all levels on these steps—not just at the levels of the development of product or feature awareness and the stimulation of actual purchase.
3. Changes in attitudes as to specific image components can be evaluated together with changes in over-all images, to determine the extent to which changes in the image components are related to movement on the primary purchase steps.

◆

Sales Force Management: Integrating Research Advances

Adrian B. Ryans and Charles B. Weinberg

Nearly half of the marketing expenses of industrial marketing companies are direct selling expenses. For most of these firms, selling expenditures exceed 5 percent of sales revenues.[1] In spite of this heavy commitment of marketing resources to personal selling, researchers have only recently given this area the attention it warrants. The surge of research in this area has been accompanied by the development of a number of models to provide conceptual frameworks for the research. As might be expected, the variety of research approaches and perspectives has resulted in a plethora of specialized models, each being well suited to the needs of the particular researchers, but integrating poorly with the models and conceptual frameworks developed by others. Even the most general of these conceptual models, the one proposed by Orville Walker, Gilbert Churchill, and Neil Ford, appears to emphasize psychological elements at the expense of organizational and situational factors.[2]

This fragmentation makes it difficult to determine the state of knowledge in the personal selling area, to integrate different research efforts, and, perhaps most importantly, to identify where the major gaps in knowledge lie. The specialized nature of the models used in much sales force research, and the lack of managerial perspective in many of the models, calls into question, at least for managers, the relevance of many of the research results achieved. In addition, when a model provides low explanatory power because of the omission of some intuitively important variables, managers may be skeptical about the reasonableness of the results. A major objective of this article is to help managers understand and interrelate different research directions in sales force management.

A three-stage conceptual model of personal selling and the management of the personal selling function is proposed. This multilevel framework incorporates factors ranging from the specification of the role of personal selling in the marketing mix to individual salesperson factors such as role perceptions and motivation. The three stages of the framework reflect the major decision-making levels—strategic, tactical, and operational (or implementation)—in the management of the personal selling function.

Other decision-oriented models of personal selling are available (David Montgomery and Glen Urban's and Kenneth Davis and Frederick Webster's are two early examples).[3] However, we believe that the proposed model goes further than these by providing a means to integrate current empirical results, behavioral science theories, and marketing models into a decision-oriented framework.

Much of the empirical research to date has focused on the operational level and has not fully considered the impact of decisions at the strategic and tactical levels on the situation at the operational level. We will review carefully the types of decisions that are made at the two prior levels and the factors that are important in making these strategic and tactical decisions. As limited empirical evidence is available about these two levels, this review will be largely expository; relevant empirical research will be cited at all three levels.

THE THREE-LEVEL MODEL

Conceptually, a model of personal selling and the management of the personal selling function can be viewed as being comprised of the three stages shown in Figure 35-1: a strategic, a tactical, and an operational or implementation level. A multilevel model is appropriate because sales force and personal selling decisions are made at several different levels in the marketing organization. The decisions at each level are made within guidelines set by the levels above it in the organization. The results and feedback obtained from the lower levels in the organization provide one basis for modifying the policies and plans at higher levels. From a research strategy perspective, it is usually necessary to focus on one part of the

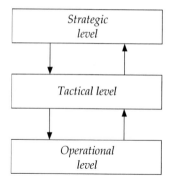

Figure 35-1
Structure of Conceptual Model

sales management system at a time, otherwise the problems encouraged in conducting research can become unmanageable.

Three stages are specified because this number seems to best capture the levels of sales force decision making, and the decisions at each stage tend to be the responsibility of, or to involve, different persons. At the strategic level, decisions are made by the top management of the company or business unit. At the tactical level, decisions are typically made by senior sales management but are frequently implemented by managers lower in the sales organization. At the operational or implementation level, the focus is on the salesperson, although many of the decisions are made or influenced by field sales management.

Strategic Level

The name of a firm's personal selling program and the contribution it makes to the achievement of the firm's objectives are ultimately determined by the firm's or business unit's marketing strategy and the plans developed to implement this strategy. In the briefest possible terms, as Figure 35-2 indicates, a well-formulated marketing strategy is based

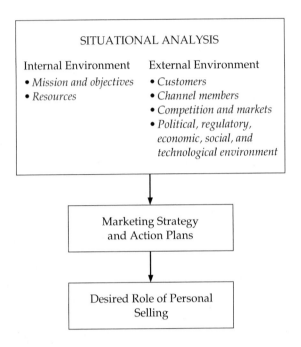

Figure 35-2
The Strategy Level

on a thorough analysis and understanding of the company's internal and external environment. The analysis of the internal environment involves a careful review of the company's mission and objectives and a critical assessment of its resources and capabilities. The analysis of the external environment includes analyses of the company's customers, channel members, competitors and markets, and the likely impact of political, regulatory, economic, social, and technological trends on these groups and on the company. From the possible marketing strategies that might be adopted to achieve the company's objectives, top management selects the strategy that appears most likely to capitalize on the opportunities and solve the problems uncovered by these analyses. The marketing strategy selected can imply very different roles for personal selling. The role assigned to

personal selling has two major dimensions: the emphasis on personal selling relative to the other elements of the marketing communication mix (advertising, sales promotion, and publicity); and the particular set of objectives that the personal selling function is expected to accomplish. This role of personal selling in the marketing strategy (the desired role) is the major influence on the tactical decisions made by senior managers in the sales force.

Researchers have recently begun to examine empirically the relationship of expenditures on personal selling activities to product-market characteristics and factors related to the firm's strategy. The ADVISOR project includes an analysis of the marketing budgeting practices of a number of major U.S. industrial marketers for a large number of products.[4] Two of the models estimated in the project provide some guidance on the norms for marketing expenditures and the advertising/ marketing expenditure ratio (and conversely some indication of the sales force/marketing expenditure ratio) given the characteristics of the product-market. Robert Buzzell and Paul Farris have also looked directly at the variables associated with the sales force/sales revenue ratio for three types of businesses using the PIMS data base.[5] While it is obviously difficult to infer a causal relationship for many of the independent variables, these models may be useful to managers charged with setting general levels for budgets for new or existing products given a particular strategy and particular market conditions.

Tactical Level

Typically, the top sales executive in the company and his or her staff are responsible for developing an organization and a set of policies and procedures (the tactical decisions) so that the sales force can achieve its desired role in the company's marketing strategy. Figure 35-3 indicates the main decision areas that must be considered.

Organization   The major organizational decision is whether the sales force should be organized on a geographic, product, or market basis, or some combination of these. Many companies find it more effective to deal with their major or national accounts with a special sales force. Other organizational decisions include the number of levels of sales management, the number of people who will report to each type of manager (the span of each manager's control in the organization), and whether staff specialists, such as sales trainers, are needed.

Deployment of Personal Selling Resources
Once the basic sales organization is determined, decisions must next be made about how the sales resources of the company should be

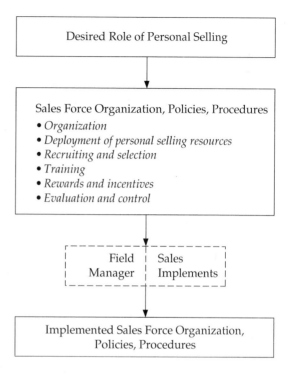

Figure 35-3
The Tactical Level

deployed. The issues include the assignment of accounts to salespersons—the territory design problem—and allocation of sales force time to accounts, product lines, and activities, such as opening new accounts versus servicing existing accounts. While a company's sales management usually develops general policy guidelines on deployment issues, the implementation of deployment policies are generally made by the field sales manager and the salesperson. Deployment is one aspect of the management of the personal selling function that lends itself quite well to quantitative modeling. A number of models have been proposed and several have been used to deal with deployment problems. Thomas Glaze and Charles Weinberg, Sidney Hess and Stuart Samuels, Leonard Lodish, and Roy Shanker, Ronald Turner, and Andrig

Zoltners have all proposed models to help with the territory design problem.[6] Zoltners and Kathy Gardner have recently reviewed the available sales force decision models.[7]

Recruiting and Selection The desired role of personal selling and the tasks the salesperson is expected to carry out help suggest the types of salespersons needed in the sales force, likely sources of these salespersons, and the criteria that should be used in the selection process. For example, corporate resources, the size of the sales force, and job requirements often determine whether the company should try to hire experienced or inexperienced people.

Training Almost all companies must do some training. For newly hired salespersons, training might provide selling skills, detailed understanding of the customers and their needs, extensive knowledge of products and services, and company policies and procedures. Besides this initial training, additional training for experienced salespersons is often needed in order to improve selling skills, to inform them about new products and policies, or to prepare them for new or more responsible positions within the sales organization.

Rewards and Incentives Rewards and incentives include both financial and nonfinancial elements. Rewards can be subdivided into two main categories, intrinsic and extrinsic rewards. Intrinsic rewards, which are linked to the coding out of the job, include such intangibles as feelings of competence, completion, and self-actualization. Managers and researchers are paying increasing attention to intrinsic rewards as part of the overall incentive system, but the relative importance and interrelationship of these rewards as compared to extrinsic ones are still controversial.[8]

Extrinsic rewards, tangible, external factors that are controlled by the organization, include financial and other benefits. The compensation systems should be designed to encourage the types of behavior desired by the company. The relative importance of salary, commissions, and bonuses can have a significant effect on the behavior and performance of the salesperson. A heavy emphasis on commissions often focuses the salesperson on the short term, sometimes causing him or her to pay insufficient attention to building long-term account relationships. Because a heavy emphasis on commissions lessens the roles of salary and bonuses, it also reduces the control the field sales manager has over the salespersons. The field sales manager usually has a good deal of influence over these latter forms of compensation and can use them to help guide the salesperson's efforts in directions that are important to the company's long-term needs. The compensation system also serves to attract and retain qualified people for the sales force.

Evaluation and Control The evaluation and control procedures in a sales force allow the sales executives to monitor the performance of the individual salespersons and units in the sales force against certain standards. This information can then be fed back to the involved parties so that corrective action can be taken if it is necessary. The standards can be in the form of measures of input—such as the number of sales calls to be made, number of new accounts to be contacted, and level of salesperson's knowledge—or output—such as sales quotas, perhaps by product line. Performance against some of these standards can be measured quite objectively, while performance against others must often rely on the subjective judgment of the field sales manager. Clearly, a good evaluation and control system can be an important management tool providing the field sales manager and the salesperson with an opportunity to identify areas of strength and weakness and to develop programs to correct any deficiencies that are identified.

Field Sales Manager   Limited empirical research, along with much folklore, suggests that the first-level field sales manager is a major factor in the success of a sales force.[9] Figure 35-3 positions the field sales manager as the critically important implementer of the policies and procedures developed by the senior sales executive. The field sales manager's responsibilities can include the deployment of sales resources, the final selection of salespersons, salesperson training, the setting of salaries and bonuses, the setting of quotas, and the evaluation and motivation of the salespersons. He or she must also be skilled in dealing with problem salespersons, including dismissing them when necessary. In addition, the field sales manager is responsible for tailoring the personal selling program in response to the particular environmental factors that obtain in his or her territories. The role of the field sales manager as an implementer requires that in empirical studies of a sales force, measurement should be based on the value of variables as implemented by the manager, which are not necessarily the same as those suggested by senior sales management.

Implementation or Operational Level

The model's third level, the implementation or operational level, focuses on the individual salesperson as the unit of analysis. As illustrated in Figure 35-4, this level consists of three types of constructs: situational characteristics and exogenous factors; the sales predisposition of the salesperson—motivation, knowledge and skills, and selling strategy; and salesperson-customer interactions and outcomes, including the salesperson's job performance and job satisfaction.

In developing the model at the salesperson level, we are using the term *implementation* in two senses. First, it represents the fact that we are examining the effect of exogenous variables as implemented by the field sales manager in particular and the company in general for that particular salesperson. To choose an obvious example, when examining the impact of span of control, the value to use is the one that the particular salesperson is supervised under, not the average for the organization as a whole. Second, the term is used to refer to whether (and how) the assigned selling tasks (the desired selling job) are carried out. In advertising, implementation concerns essentially cease once the advertisement is designed and placed in the media; however, a salesperson may not consistently carry out the assigned tasks and role. Does the salesperson allocate time across accounts, products, and selling activities in a manner consistent with the policies and procedures developed at the tactical level? The actions of the salespersons are influenced by the actual and anticipated reactions of customers. Most prior conceptualizations of the sales response model have been postulated at the individual salesperson level.[10]

Exogenous Factors and Situational Constructs

The four groups of exogenous factors and situational constructs are: sales force organization, policies, and procedures, as implemented for the salesperson; personal, enduring characteristics of the salesperson; competitive situation in the salesperson's territory; and characteristics of the customers in the salesperson's territory. The first group of variables is situational and is comprised of variables under the control of the company, whereas the last three groups are best regarded as exogenous, since the company has only very limited control over them in the short run. Thus, while the four groups are treated as exogenous with regard to analysis at the individual salesperson level, these variables are not necessarily exogenous at pre-

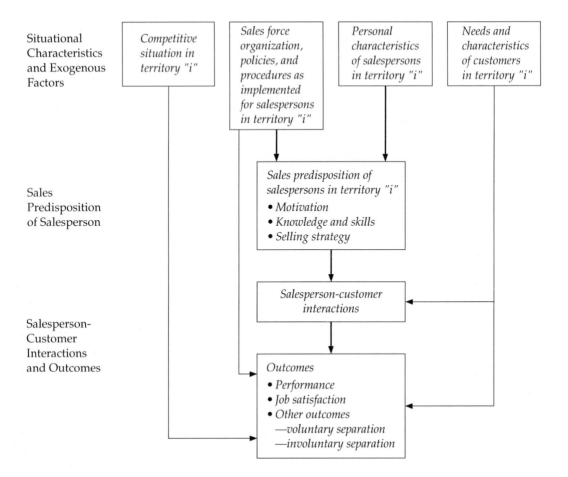

Figure 35-4
The Implementation or Operational Level

vious levels of the model.[11] For example, at the sales management level, the sales executive decides what the span of control will be. Furthermore, in the long run, the company's recruitment and selection programs will partially determine the personal characteristics of the salespersons, or at least the range of personal characteristics that are present in the sales force. The competitive situation in the territory can be most clearly classified as exogenous, but even here the company's actions with regard to territory de-

sign may influence the level of competitive activity encountered in any given territory. Similarly, the company's actions can influence which customers are actually served.

Personal Characteristics This set of constructs includes all characteristics which are defined as being part of the individual and are not contingent on organization and other factors. We would include such variables as verbal intelligence and age as personal characteristics, but we would not include the salesperson's perceived role ambiguity because it is a consequence of organizational as well as personal factors. We would also exclude measures of the salesperson's motivation, since it can be modified as a result of such things as the firm's compensation plan. We think it is important to identify constructs that are both individual-specific and not contingent on organizational factors. As Walker, Churchill, and Ford point out, one of the major failings in models of salesperson performance is the failure to recognize that some "determinants are *not* independent; there are substantial interaction effects among them."[12] Our approach attempts to identify exogenous and contingent variables a priori and classify them separately.

Personal characteristics include:

- physical factors, such as physical appearance, posture, sex, and age;
- historical factors, such as educational background, previous occupations, and previous sales experience;
- personality factors, such as interpersonal style, social sensitivity, locus of control, and risk taking;
- mental factors, such as general intelligence, verbal ability, quantitative ability, and cognitive style.

In the past few years there has been a growing realization among personality researchers that situational factors are at least as important as personality traits in understanding why individuals behave the way they do.[13] Thus, relationships found in personal selling contexts may have only limited generalizability. Similarly, findings from other settings must be used with careful attention to the situational contingencies present in a personal selling situation. An individual who exhibits a certain style of risk-taking behavior in his or her personal life may exhibit a different pattern at work.

Organization, Policies, and Procedures   This set of constructs includes those variables which are set for the sales force as a whole at the sales management (or tactical) level, but which are implemented at the level of the individual salesperson. Some of these variables may be set uniformly for the sales force, while others may vary. A company may rigidly adhere to a certain span of control in the field sales organization while allowing wide variations in the market potential of the individual sales territories. Special focus needs to be placed on the implementation of the organizational, policy, and procedures variables for the individual salesperson, particularly, as transmitted by the field sales manager. The salesperson's understanding of the specific selling tasks to be performed is dependent on how well the field sales manager interprets and explains those tasks. This clearly raises some difficult measurement issues with regard to what the assigned tasks are and what the field sales manager communicates to the salesperson.

Among the constructs we would include here are span of control (the number of salespersons that report to the first-level sales manager); territory characteristics, including potential, concentration of potential among accounts, and geographic dispersion of customers; type and level of marketing support provided to the territory, including direct mail effort, marketing support personnel, and seminars and advertising; salesperson training programs; salesperson's assigned tasks; and the compensation program as implemented for the individual salespersons. Although many organizations have undoubtedly made formal or informal assessments of the impact of these factors on performance, only limited published, empirical research exists. The most well-developed literature concerns territory characteristics, where several studies have indicated the relationships between territory potential and sales performance.[14]

Competitive Situation   Depending on the nature of the market the company is in, the competitive variables of concern may vary. These variables can include product and service attributes, the competitive equivalent of any type of marketing support that the company can provide for its own sales force, and finally, the nature and intensity of the competitor's personal selling efforts.

Characteristics of Customer   This is again largely an exogenous set of variables. As will be discussed later, there is evidence in the personal selling literature that indicates that the performance outcomes from the salesperson-customer interaction depend on the characteristics of both members of the dyad.

Sales Predisposition of the Salesperson

The performance of an individual salesperson can be viewed as being a function of three classes of factors: motivation, knowledge and skills, and selling strategy.[15] This classification, while consistent with the one proposed by Walker, Churchill, and Ford in which motivation, aptitude, and role perceptions are used, is more general and can be used to incorporate and categorize more of the research that has been conducted on sales performance and its antecedents.[16]

As Figure 35-4 indicates, the sales predisposition of the salesperson is viewed as being largely a function of the enduring personal characteristics of the salesperson (which are in part a result of the organization's recruiting and selection policies), and the sales force organization, policies, and procedures. In contrast to the enduring personal characteristics, sales predisposition is mediated by the tactical levers under the control of sales management.

Motivation   Motivation in the personal selling context has been defined as "the amount of effort the salesman desires to expend on

each of the activities and tasks associated with his job, such as calling on potential new accounts, planning sales presentations and filling out reports."[17] As Terence Mitchell has noted, theoretical research in motivation can be viewed as being focused on three problem areas: individual needs and motives, classification systems of needs and motives, and the motivational process itself.[18] Theories dealing with the first two of these areas are termed *content theories of motivation* since they are concerned with the factors that lead to motivational arousal. The third area involving process theories focuses directly on the mental processes underlying the behavioral choice—in the personal selling area, on the decision to devote effort to certain tasks.

Richard Bagozzi, in his study on sales force performance, approaches the motivational question largely from the first orientation using the theory of need for achievement.[19] Examples of the second orientation—the use of classification schemes in motivation research —includes Maslow's hierarchy of needs and the controversial dual factor theory of Frederick Herzberg, Bernard Mausner, and Barbara Snyderman, where potential organizational rewards are broken into two groups —the hygienes and the motivators.[20] Basically, Herzberg and his colleagues view the hygienes (monetary rewards and working conditions) as merely maintaining employees in a neutral state of satisfaction, whereas the motivators (advancement and recognition) can be used to generate high job satisfaction. While there appears to have been no formal research in the sales area on this theory, the approach has undoubtedly influenced the design of motivational policies in some sales organizations.

Process theories of motivation, as suggested above, are concerned with the process by which people decide to work hard and to allocate their efforts over the possible activities open to them. Expectancy theory has been the most widely used theoretical approach to motivation in personal selling research.[21] However, expectancy theory has been difficult to test in the personal selling area due to methodological problems. The results obtained to date, which are not particularly strong, have been summarized by Walker, Churchill, and Ford.[22]

Most managers would support the hypothesis that a salesperson's motivation is a function of both enduring personal characteristics and the full range of organizational, policy, and procedures factors. Span of control (an organizational factor), deployment policies, recruiting and selection policies, training, the evaluation and control system, and the incentive system all can clearly affect the motivation of a salesperson. The particular theoretical orientation to motivation adopted by the researcher would probably suggest a somewhat different emphasis on these factors if the motivational level of the salespersons is to be improved. For example, a need-for-achievement orientation might result in attention being paid to recruiting and selection policies and, to a lesser extent, training,[23] whereas other orientations might place greater emphasis on the incentive system. In spite of the obvious importance of motivation in sales performance, almost no empirical research has been conducted on how various organizational practices and sales force policies and procedures affect the motivation of salespersons.

Knowledge and Skills   The performance of a salesperson can be viewed as being a function of the following types of knowledge and skills:

- Product knowledge: this includes not only knowledge of the product line and its features, but knowledge of the benefits associated with each feature, the ability to handle common product-related objections, and a detailed understanding of the product line strengths and weaknesses relative to competitive products or services.
- Customer knowledge: this includes knowledge of the customer's business, how the product or service fits into the customer's operations, and a thorough understanding of the customer's decision-making process.
- Knowledge of company policy and procedures: this can be particularly critical in some industrial selling situations, where the salesperson's role is largely one of marshalling his or her company's resources and specialist talents to solve the customer's problems. It is essential to have a good in-depth knowledge of the company's organization and the location of specialist talent.
- Interpersonal and communication skills: this includes skills in establishing rapport with members of a customer decision-making unit, probing and questioning skills to uncover needs, communication and persuasion techniques, and skills in reading a customer's reactions to ideas and proposals. One persuasion technique that has received considerable attention is "foot-in-the-door": start with a small request (asking a retailer to place a manufacturer's sign in his store window) before going on to the large request (asking the retailer to attend a sales presentation at the manufacturer's office).[24] A considerable amount of empirical research (largely in nonmarketing contexts) has been conducted on foot-in-the-door and other compliance-gaining techniques.[25] However, as Richard Yalch points out in his excellent review, "There has been no published research adequately evaluating what happens when an individual is involved in a series of compliance-gaining strategies."[26] Recent research is also beginning to clarify other situational contingencies under which these techniques are likely to be effective.[27]

The knowledge and skills of the salespersons are largely the result of the recruiting and selection policies of the sales organization and the types of training programs it offers to the salespersons. The span of control in the organization and the level of sales manager-salesperson interaction it encourages undoubtedly also indirectly influence the knowledge and skills of the salespersons.

Selling Strategy   Selling strategy subsumes the role perceptions component that plays a central role in the Walker, Churchill, and Ford model.[28] It involves: allocation of effort across the salesperson's accounts and products; a perception of the role the salesperson is to play; and a strategy for dealing with each individual account. The first and third elements of the selling strategy are expected to change over time as a result of the feedback the salesperson receives from his or her interactions with the individual customers.

Little is known about how salespersons decide to allocate effort (particularly time) across their accounts, yet this appears to be a very important decision and is closely related to the salesperson's performance. Lodish, who developed the CALLPLAN model to help allocate salespersons' time across customers and prospects,[29] has reported that a salesperson using the model had, on average, sales 8 percent higher than a matched colleague who did not have access to the model.[30] Some companies influence the time and effort allocations for their salespersons by establishing rigid call policies—a certain number of calls per day, or a required number of calls per effort period for each type or size of account.

Walker, Churchill, and Ford have developed the role perceptions component most fully in the personal selling area, and we follow their discussion of this component.[31] The role attached to the position of salesperson in any firm represents the set of activities or behaviors to be performed by any person occu-

pying that position. This role is defined largely through the expectations, demands, and pressures communicated to the salesperson by his or her role partners—persons inside and outside the firm who have a vested interest in how the salesperson's job is performed, such as top management, the sales manager, customers, and family members. The salesperson's perceptions of these role partners' expectations and demands strongly influence his or her understanding of the job and the kinds of behavior necessary to perform it well.

It is clear from the above discussion that the elements of the role perceptions component are partly a function of the sales force organization, policies, and procedures. Training, in particular, can do a great deal to resolve issues of role accuracy and perceived role ambiguity. Recruiting and selection policies can also help seek out persons capable of handling the inevitable role conflict and who are less likely to experience serious perceived role ambiguity. While some research has been conducted on the relationship between aspects of role perceptions and such outcomes as job performance and job satisfaction,[32] only a very limited amount of research has been conducted on the antecedents of aspects of role perceptions. Walker, Churchill, and Ford found a significant negative relationship between salesperson experience and both role conflict and role ambiguity, and between both span of control and the salesperson's influence over supervisory standards and role ambiguity.[33]

The development of a strategy for dealing with the decision-making unit at each individual account is an important area that has received little research attention. Barton Weitz has done perhaps the most interesting and innovative research in this area.[34] He proposes a five-stage model of the sales process: developing an impression of the customer; formulating a strategy; transmitting the selected communication; evaluating the effect of the communication; and making appropriate adjustments in the strategy. While this five-step model clearly involves and requires the various types of knowledge and skills discussed in the earlier section, it requires more than them. It involves taking the information gathered, synthesizing and organizing it, developing alternative selling strategies for given situations, and selecting one, which must then be implemented. In many respects, effective interpersonal and communication skills of the type alluded to earlier are necessary, but not sufficient, skills in developing an effective strategy. In the empirical part of his study, Weitz demonstrated that there was a significant positive relationship between a salesperson's performance and understanding of the customer's choice decision process. Since Weitz only studies the first two stages of the model in a relatively simple selling environment (well-known product, single decision maker in the customer organization), much remains to be done in this area.

A salesperson's ability to develop effective strategies is likely to be largely the result of the salesperson's experience, the knowledge and skills he or she possesses to develop the necessary base of information about the customer, and the training the salesperson has received. A particularly important aspect of the training in more complicated selling situations where experiential learning may be very important is the coaching provided by the field sales manager. The degree to which this interaction can occur will be influenced by the span of control.

The Salesperson and the Customer

The ultimate success of the strategic and tactical decision made with respect to a company's personal selling program depends on the individual interactions of salespersons and customers. The inputs to this interaction process

can, to a large extent, be controlled, but the interaction process itself contains a significant set of uncontrollable elements as well. Researchers have attempted to probe aspects of this interaction process to gain a better understanding of what influences the productivity of a given salesperson-customer dyad. Early research by Franklin Evans and M. S. Gadel relates sales performance in a life insurance company to the similarity of the buyer-seller dyad.[35] However, a reanalysis of Evans's data by Noel Capon, Morris Holbrook, and James Hulbert suggests that given the number of variables studied, a significant correlation would be expected on a chance basis.[36] More recent research attempts to establish what types of similarity, or in more formal terms, bases of power in social exchanges, are the major sources of the relationship between similarity and performance.[37] The results to date have been inconclusive, and this research approach may not be as productive in the long term as research of the type conducted by Weitz.

The interrelationships between the various outcomes at the implementation level are only now beginning to receive attention from marketing scholars. It has been generally assumed that high job satisfaction leads to improved performance, but the relationship between the two constructs is proving to be a surprisingly weak one. Mitchell, in summarizing the industrial psychology literature on this point, reports that the average correlation between job satisfaction and performance is about .15. Bagozzi, in a further analysis of the data in his 1978 paper (he omits the territory potential variable) concludes that performance is an antecedent of satisfaction.[38] Other research in industrial psychology, such as Edwin Locke's, tends to support this finding.[39] As might be expected, this relationship appears to be contingent on individual difference factors and other situational factors. Finally, the relationship between job satisfaction and other outcomes, such as turnover and absenteeism, while an intuitively appealing one which has received support in other occupational groups, has not yet received much empirical support in marketing. Again, any relationship is likely to be a highly contingent one.

Unanswered Questions

The conceptual model proposed in this article is not intended to be a general theory, but a framework sufficiently comprehensive so that the major research streams in personal selling can be interrelated. It also suggests areas which might be productively explored in future research. Particularly from the manager's perspective, the model links the research and researchable issues in personal selling with the levels of decision making in the sales force and the types of decisions that must be made at each level. We now turn to some of the unanswered questions that the three-level model suggests are important areas warranting further research.

At the strategic level, the ADVISOR and PIMS data bases are being used to address a critical sales management issue—the budgeting decision. Both data bases are not adequate for the task. The ADVISOR project is focused on advertising issues and only tangentially touches on the personal selling expenditure issue, and the PIMS project has a much broader strategic marketing focus. Both lack the specific sales force data necessary for a more complete examination of the strategic sales issues. In particular, major tactical variables, such as the type of sales organization, the span of control, and the compensation system, need to be investigated in models designed to explain the sales force expenditures/sales ratio, the profitability of a product, and the like. This would begin to give some insight into the effectiveness of different tactical approaches in various product-market environments. A strategic issue that has received no attention in the literature to date is the decision to use

manufacturers' representatives versus a direct sales force. The markets and hierarchies approach espoused by Oliver Williamson might suggest some useful hypotheses about when the use of sales representatives would be the most productive approach.[40]

Only limited empirical research has focused on the tactical levers available to sales management, probably because of the difficulties involved in conducting such research. Few of the relevant variables show any variation within a given sales force—compensation systems are usually uniform throughout the sales force.[41] This area does not lend itself well to laboratory experimentation and field experimentation will likely meet a great deal of managerial resistance given the risks involved and the difficulty of developing research designs with strong internal and external validity. Empirical research must usually follow one of two directions: cross-sectional studies involving a number of different sales forces; or longitudinal studies within one or more companies covering a period when a significant change in policies and procedures occurs. Even in the latter case, variables may be confounded since a change in one variable, such as the organization, frequently occurs simultaneously with a change in other variables, such as the compensation system. Despite the difficulties involved, quasi-experimental research may be the best hope for establishing the direction of causality which is so frequently ambiguous in observational studies in the personal selling area.[42] Rene Darmon's investigation of a change in sales compensation system in a company is one of the few examples of longitudinal research on these types of sales force policies.[43]

The operational level has received the most attention from marketing researchers. Much of the research has focused on the "selling knowledge and skills" and "salesperson-customer interactions" constructs included in Figure 35-4. As Capon, Holbrook, and Hulbert point out, a number of studies have implicitly or explicitly used the source-message-receiver model from mass communications to study the effects of the personal characteristics of the salesperson, the needs and characteristics of the customer, and the content of the message on some output measure of interest. As was pointed out earlier, few of these studies have viewed the salesperson and customer as an interacting dyad. Most of these studies do not explicitly recognize situational characteristics and exogenous factors on which the findings may be contingent. Furthermore, researchers have just begun to grapple with the fact that from a sales force perspective many customer decision-making units are multiperson and that many salesperson-customer interactions are part of an ongoing process, not a one-shot meeting. These raise important, but complex, research questions.

Other researchers have approached the study of the operational level differently. These researchers have shown less interest in the results of the individual interactions between salespersons and customers and have focused on long-run, aggregate outcome measures of sales performance and job satisfaction. This research has generally involved a more comprehensive set of the constructs from Figure 35-4 than do models that emphasize the interaction level. It is useful to distinguish two approaches that have been followed in this type of research.

Walker, Churchill, and Ford's work, which exemplifies such research, is an attempt to develop a theory of motivation and performance in the industrial sales force.[44] Much of their empirical research to date has involved the testing of hypotheses from their theory in a number of sales forces. As a result of this systematic program of research, an improved understanding of many of the links of their model is emerging. Because a great deal of their attention is devoted to psychological variables and the relationships between these

variables, and because, to this point, their research has focused on dependent variables not closely related to sales performance (usually the variable of most direct managerial interest), the payoff in terms of results of high managerial relevance is likely to occur in the long run. Furthermore, as this research program proceeds and the contingent nature of many of the relationships in the model becomes apparent, their model will probably become more complex in order to incorporate these contingencies. In fact, this may already be occurring, as can be seen by comparing the model as originally conceived by Walker, Churchill, and Ford in 1977 with the 1978 version.[45]

The territory sales response models of Henry Lucas, Charles Weinberg, and Kenneth Clowes, Charles Beswick and David Cravens, Bagozzi, and Adrian Ryans and Charles Weinberg represent a second type of comprehensive model at the operational level.[46] Here, the focus has been on the relationship between an objective measure of sales performance and observable, readily measured factors that are believed to influence sales performance. These models, when set in the context of clear conceptual frameworks, can lead to greater understanding of the personal selling process through identification of important factors and measurement of their relationships. Moreover, such models can be tailored to the needs of, and readily estimated for, the individual sales force. In the four studies cited, the dependent variable is sales, which is the variable generally of most direct interest to sales management. This choice of dependent variable, combined with the operational nature of the independent variables, can have direct managerial impact.[47]

Using the Results

Although substantial gaps in knowledge exist, substantive findings of interest are available at all three levels of the model. However, a manager must be cautious in attempting to apply these findings to a specific setting for several reasons.

First, the research findings may have been developed in selling environments quite different than his or her own environment. As was pointed out above, much of the research on compliance-gaining strategies has been conducted in one-time selling situations. Even findings that seem quite robust, such as the foot-in-the-door strategy (demonstrated in field studies by Jacob Varella and Alice Tybout)[48] may not be effective if used on a continuing basis by a particular salesperson with a particular customer, or if the requested behavior is viewed as being very costly by the customer. As these findings are verified in richer, more externally valid settings (from the point of view of the individual manager), then the manager can have more confidence in applying the results.

Most importantly, as the three-stage model highlights, many relationships are likely to be contingent ones. The manager must try to determine if variables that were not considered in a particular study might not mediate the results. A general conceptual model such as the one proposed here provides the manager with a structure for reviewing these contingencies. If a manager finds it necessary to verify the relationships and findings for his or her own sales force, then the three-stage model will help to indicate which variables need to be studied. For example, the three-stage model can be used in conjunction with the emerging literature in the territory sales response area to provide a framework for developing such a function and to offer some guidelines on how particular variables might be put into operation.

Studies which rely heavily on attitudinal and other psychological variables will be difficult to verify in individual company settings. With increasing attention to invasion-of-privacy issues among the management of many companies, there may be serious concern about gathering much of this information.[49] Furthermore, for some variables, employees might be reluctant to give honest responses. Respondents who are asked for the valence of various rewards might attempt to "game" the researcher rather than provide honest responses. One potential tactical area where many of the findings from this stream of research might be valuable is the selection area, but it is in this area where it is difficult and expensive to demonstrate that psychological tests or other types of information do not unfairly discriminate against members of minority groups.[50]

One value of the three-stage model proposed here is that it provides a way for the manager to structure the different aspects of sales force decision making. The model emphasizes that the sales manager has a mix of tactical levers to implement a desired strategic sales force role and that these levers should not be treated in isolation.

Conclusions

The three-stage sales force model developed in this article emphasizes the relationship between sales force management decision making and the empirical research being conducted in the personal selling area should not be underestimated. Moreover, the situational contingencies upon which research findings depend need to be specified clearly. Current research has provided a base of knowledge for researchers who wish to work in the field, but no area of personal selling is so well understood that further research is foreclosed. In conclusion, we believe that the conceptual model provided in this article provides a useful way to summarize present knowledge, to approach personal selling decisions, and to identify areas for further study.

NOTES

1. Sales and Marketing Management, "Survey of Selling Costs" (26 February 1979), p. 57.
2. Orville C. Walker, Jr., Gilbert A. Churchill, Jr., and Neil M. Ford, "Motivation and Performance in Industrial Selling: Present Knowledge and Needed Research," *Journal of Marketing Research*, Vol. 14 (May 1977), pp.156–168.
3. David B. Montgomery and Glen L. Urban, *Management Science in Marketing* (Englewood Cliffs, New Jersey: Prentice-Hall, Inc., 1969); Kenneth R. Davis and Frederick E. Webster, Jr., *Sales Force Management* (New York: Ronald Press Company, 1968).
4. Gary L. Lilien, "ADVISOR 2: Modeling the Marketing Mix Decision for Industrial Products," *Management Science*, Vol. 25 (February 1979), pp. 191–204.
5. Robert D. Buzzell and Paul W. Farris, "Industrial Marketing Costs: An Analysis of Variations in Manufacturers' Marketing Expenditures," Report Number 76–118 (Cambridge, Massachusetts: Marketing Science Institute, 1976).
6. Thomas A. Glaze and Charles B. Weinberg, "A Sales Territory Alignment Program and Account Planning System," in Richard Bagozzi (ed.), *Sales Management: New Developments from Behavioral and Decision Model Research* (Cambridge, Massachusetts: Marketing Science Institute, 1979); Sidney W. Hess and Stuart A. Samuels, "Experiences with a Sales Districting Model: Criteria and Implementation," *Management Science*, Part II, Vol. 18 (December 1971), pp. 41–54; Leonard Lodish, " 'Vaguely Right' Approach to Sales Force Allocation," *Harvard Business Review*, Vol. 52 (January–February 1974), pp. 119–124; Roy J. Shanker, Ronald E. Turner, and Andris A. Zoltners, "Sales Territory Design: An Integrated Approach," *Management Science*, Vol. 22 (November 1975), pp. 309–320.
7. Andris A. Zoltners and Kathy S. Gardner, "A Review of Salesforce Decision Models," unpublished working paper (Evanston, Illinois: Northwestern University, 1980).
8. Terence R. Mitchell, *People in Organizations: Understanding Their Behavior* (New York: McGraw-Hill, 1978).
9. Robert T. Davis, "Sales Management in the Field," *Harvard Business Review*, Vol. 36 (January–February 1958), pp. 91–98; idem, "A Sales Manager in Action," in H. W. Boyd, Jr., and R. T. Davis (eds), *Readings in Sales Management* (Homewood, Illinois: Richard D. Irwin, 1970); J. S. Livingston, "Pygmalion in Management," *Harvard Business Review*, Vol. 47 (July–August 1969), pp. 81–89.
10. Richard P. Bagozzi, "Towards a General Theory for the Explanation of the Performance of Salespeople," unpublished doctoral dissertation (Northwestern University, 1976); Adrian B. Ryans and Charles B. Weinberg, "Sales Territory Response," *Journal of Marketing Research*, Vol. 16 (November 1979), pp. 453–465; Walker, Churchill, and Ford, op. cit.
11. Researchers attempting to estimate the effect of exogenous and situational factors on outcomes such as performance or job satisfaction must be concerned about whether the implemented sales force organization, policies, and procedures have suppressed the effects of interest. If the sales force's management has a policy of assigning territories of equal potential, then it would make little sense to include this variable in a research study designed to relate territory sales performance to territory characteristics. However, it would be incorrect to assume that territory potential has no effect on sales performance.
12. Orville C. Walker, Jr., Gilbert A. Churchill, Jr., and Neil M. Ford, "Where Do We Go From Here?—Selected Conceptual and Empirical Issues Concerning the Motivation and Performance of the Industrial Sales Force," paper presented at the American Institute for Decision Sciences, St. Louis (1978), p. 4.
13. Mitchell, op. cit.
14. Adrian B. Ryans and Charles B. Weinberg, "Managerial Implications of Models of Territory Sales Response," in Neil Beckwith et al. (eds.), *1979 Educators' Conference Proceedings* (Chicago, Illinois: American Marketing Asso-

ciation, 1979), pp. 426–430; Ryans and Weinberg, op. cit.

15. This is similar to the conceptualization used by J. Richard Hackman and Charles G. Morris in their discussion of the performance of task groups. See J. Richard Hackman and Charles G. Morris, "Group Tasks, Group Interaction Process, and Group Performance Effectiveness," in L. Berkowitz (ed.), *Advances in Experimental Social Psychology*, Vol. 7 (New York: Academic Press, 1975).

16. Walker, Churchill, and Ford, "Motivation and Performance."

17. Ibid., p. 162.

18. Mitchell, op. cit.

19. Bagozzi, op. cit.

20. Frederick Herzberg, Bernard Mausner, and Barbara B. Snyderman, *The Motivation to Work* (New York: John Wiley and Sons, 1975).

21. Walker, Churchill, and Ford, "Motivation and Performance."

22. Walker, Churchill, and Ford, "Where Do We Go?"

23. David McClelland, the originator of the need-for-achievement theory, has reported some success in increasing the level of need for achievement in adults through training. See David C. McClelland, *The Achieving Society* (Princeton, New Jersey: Van Nostrand, 1961).

24. Alice M. Tybout, "The Relative Effectiveness of Three Behavioral Influence Strategies as Supplements to Persuasion in a Marketing Context," *Journal of Marketing Research*, Vol. 15 (May 1978), pp. 229–242; Jacob A. Varella, *Psychological Solutions to Social Problems* (New York: Academic Press, 1971).

25. William DeJong, "An Examination of Self-Perception Mediation of the Foot-in-the-Door Effect," *Journal of Personality and Social Psychology*, Vol. 37 (December 1979), pp. 2221–2239; Richard F. Yalch, "Closing Sales: Compliance-Gaining Strategies for Personal Selling," in Bagozzi (ed.), op. cit. (Cambridge, Massachusetts: Marketing Science Institute, 1979).

26. Yalch, op. cit., p. 197.

27. Robert D. Foss and Carolyn B. Dempsey, "Blood Donation and the Foot-in-the-Door Technique: A Limiting Case," *Journal of Per-

sonality and Social Psychology*, Vol. 37 (1979), pp. 580–590; Yalch, op. cit.

28. Walker, Churchill, and Ford, "Motivation and Performance."

29. Leonard Lodish, "CALLPLAN: An Interactive Salesman's Call Planning System," *Management Science*, Part II, Vol. 18 (December 1971), pp. 25–40.

30. William K. Fudge and Leonard M. Lodish, "Evaluation of the Effectiveness of a Model Based Salesman's Call Planning System by Field Experimentation," *Interfaces*, Part II, Vol. 8 (November 1977), pp. 97–106.

31. Walker, Churchill, and Ford, "Motivation and Performance," and "Where Do We Go?"

32. Gilbert A. Churchill, Jr., Neil M. Ford, and Orville C. Walker, Jr., "Organizational Climate and Job Satisfaction in the Salesforce," *Journal of Marketing Research*, Vol. 13 (November 1976), pp. 323–332; and Bagozzi, op. cit.

33. Orville C. Walker, Jr., Gilbert A. Churchill, and Neil M. Ford, "Organizational Determinants of the Industrial Salesman's Role Conflict and Ambiguity," *Journal of Marketing*, Vol. 39 (January 1975), pp. 32–39.

34. Barton A. Weitz, "Relationship Between Salesperson Performance and Understanding of Customer Decision-Making," *Journal of Marketing Research*, Vol. 15 (November 1978), pp. 501–516.

35. Franklin Evans, "Selling as a Dyadic Relationship—A New Approach," *American Behavioral Scientist*, Vol. 6 (May 1963), pp. 76–79; M. S. Gadel, "Concentration by Salesmen on Congenial Prospects," *Journal of Marketing*, Vol. 28 (January 1964), pp. 64–66.

36. Noel Capon, Morris B. Holbrook, and James M. Hubert, "Selling Processes and Buying Behavior: Theoretical Implications of Recent Research," in Arch G. Woodside, Jagdish N. Sheth, and Peter D. Bennett (eds.), *Consumer and Industrial Buying Behavior* (New York: Elsevier North-Holland, 1977), pp. 323–332.

37. Timothy C. Brock, "Communicator-Recipient Similarity and Decision Change," *Journal of Personality and Social Psychology*, Vol. 1 (June 1965), pp. 650–654; Paul Busch and David T. Wilson, "An Experimental Analysis of a Sales-

man's Expert and Referent Bases of Social Power in the Buyer-Seller Dyad," *Journal of Marketing Research,* Vol. 13 (February 1976), pp. 3–11.

38. Richard P. Bagozzi, "Salesperson Performance and Satisfaction as a Function of Individual Difference, Interpersonal, and Situational Factors," *Journal of Marketing Research,* Vol. 15 (November 1978), pp. 517–531; idem, "Performance and Satisfaction in an Industrial Sales Force: An Examination of Their Antecedents and Simultaneity," *Journal of Marketing,* Vol. 44 (Spring 1980), pp. 65–77. The omission of territory potential from the Bagozzi 1980 model is surprising given the highly significant correlation between it and both performance and job satisfaction in his earlier paper. The framework proposed here emphasizes the need to include relevant precursors.

39. Edwin A. Locke, "The Nature and Causes of Job Satisfaction," in M. D. Dunnette (ed.), *Handbook of Industrial and Organizational Psychology* (Chicago, Illinois: Rand McNally, 1976), pp. 1297–1349.

40. Oliver E. Williamson, *Markets and Hierarchies: Analysis and Antitrust Implications* (New York: The Free Press, 1975).

41. However, considerable theoretical attention has been devoted to the design of optimal compensation systems under assumptions about the salesperson's objective function and constraints under which the salesperson operates. See John U. Farley, "Optimal Plan for Salesmen's Compensation," *Journal of Marketing Research,* Vol. 1 (May 1964), pp. 39–43; Venkataraman Srinivasan, "The Non-optimality of Equal Commission Rates in Multi-Product Sales Force Compensation Schemes," Working Paper No. 529 (Stanford, California:

Graduate School of Business, 1979); and Charles B. Weinberg, "Jointly Optimal Sales Commissions for Non-Income Maximizing Sales Force," *Management Science,* Vol. 24 (August 1978), pp. 1252–1258.

42. Territory sales response models could be used in some situations to increase the statistical precision of the experiment.

43. Rene Y. Darmon, "Salesmen's Response to Financial Incentives: An Empirical Study," *Journal of Marketing Research,* Vol. 11 (November 1974), pp. 418–426.

44. Walker, Churchill, and Ford, "Motivation and Performance," and "Where Do We Go?"

45. Ibid.

46. Bagozzi's research can be viewed as straddling both types of models, as it, for example, also examines some motivational components. See Bagozzi, "Salesperson Performance"; Charles A. Beswick and David W. Cravens, "A Multistage Decision Model for Sales Force Management," *Journal of Marketing Research,* Vol. 14 (May 1977); Henry C. Lucas, Jr., Charles B. Weinberg, and Kenneth Clowes, "Sales Response as a Function of Territorial Potential and Sales Representative Workload," *Journal of Marketing Research,* Vol. 12 (August 1975), pp. 298–305; and Ryans and Weinberg, "Sales Territory."

47. Ryans and Weinberg, "Managerial Implications."

48. Varella, op. cit.; Tybout, op. cit.

49. Frank T. Cary, "IBM's Guidelines to Employee Privacy," *Harvard Business Review,* Vol. 54 (September–October, 1976), pp. 82–90.

50. William C. Byham and Morton E. Spitzer, "Personal Testing: The Law and Its Implications," *Personnel,* Vol. 48 (September–October 1971), pp. 8–19.

◆

Distribution Channels as Political Economies: A Framework for Comparative Analysis

Louis W. Stern and Torger Reve

Published studies related to distribution channels present, collectively, a rather disjointed collage. This is due, in part, to the absence of a framework which can accommodate the various paradigms and orientations employed in performing research on distribution channel phenomena. What is needed is a comprehensive mapping of the field which depicts the various paths one could follow, the likely places where one might end up, and the boundaries of the various places within the entire conceptual space. If this mapping were successfully accomplished, then those individuals already within the field would have a better understanding of where their work stood relative to others' and would, hopefully, be encouraged to seek out complementary paradigms to those which they have adopted. The mapping would also indicate to many of those who perceive themselves as standing outside the field that much of what they are doing could easily have relevance to the sub-

stance of the field. They might even be motivated to advance the field themselves. And, most importantly, the mapping would be helpful to prospective scholars who, to a large extent, do not have a very solid understanding of the research opportunities available within the field. While no single article is ever likely to accomplish such a comprehensive mapping, there is clearly a strong need to make a beginning. If a meaningful start at ordering the field can be undertaken, then this will likely encourage others to pursue the completion and refinement of the ordering process.

Despite the centrality of distribution channels in marketing, there exist three major deficiencies in the current status of distribution channel theory and research. *First*, analyses of distribution channels have largely focused on the technologies (e.g., sales force incentive systems, pricing procedures, and the like) employed by individual organizations in their efforts to structure and control channel activities (cf., Gattorna 1978; McCammon and Little 1965; McCammen, Bates and Guiltinan 1971). These analyses have adopted

Louis W. Stern and Torger Reve, "Distribution Channels as Political Economies: A Framework for Comparative Analysis," Vol. 44 (Summer 1980). Reprinted from *Journal of Marketing,* published by the American Marketing Association.

a *micro* orientation in keeping with traditional problem-solving approaches in marketing management. Little attention has been given to questions of the maintenance, adaptation, and evolution of marketing channels as competitive entities.

Second, channel theory is fragmented into two seemingly disparate disciplinary orientations: an *economic* approach and a *behavioral* approach. The former attempts to apply macroeconomic theory and industrial organization analysis to the study of distribution systems and has been essentially "efficiency" oriented, focusing on costs, functional differentiation, and channel design (cf., Baligh and Richartz 1967; Bucklin 1966; Bucklin and Carman 1974; Cox, Goodman, and Fichandler 1965). The latter borrows heavily from social psychology and organization theory and has been essentially "socially" oriented, focusing on power and conflict phenomena (cf., Alderson 1957; Stern 1969). Rarely have there been attempts to integrate these two perspectives. Indeed, they should be viewed as complementary, because the former deals mainly with economic "outputs" while the latter is concerned with behavioral "processes."

Third, empirical studies of distribution networks have been extremely limited in their scope and methodological sophistication. The vast majority of empirical work in the channels area has been purely descriptive in nature, with little or no testing of formal hypotheses derived from theory (cf., McCammon and Little 1965). Although more recent studies evidence a trend toward more systematic testing of theoretical relationships, these investigations have typically been confined to an analysis of a single distribution channel within a particular industry (exceptions include Etgar 1976a, 1978; Hunt and Nevin 1974; Porter 1974; Weik 1972).[1] Future channel research must focus on making systematic *comparisons* of different distribution networks within and between various environmental conditions, irrespective of whether the different networks are found in the same industry or across industries.

A promising framework for addressing these issues is provided by the *political economy* approach to the study of social systems (Benson 1975; Wamsley and Zald 1973, 1976; Zald 1970a, 1970b). Basically, the *political economy approach views a social system as comprising interacting sets of major economic and sociopolitical forces which affect collective behavior and performance.* The purpose of this article, therefore, is to present a political economy framework which can be applied to gain deeper understanding of the *internal* functioning of a distribution channel. Such a framework also permits comprehension of the processes where distribution channels are influenced by and adapt to environmental conditions. It is, however, recognized that this framework is only one of many that might be suggested. It has been selected because of its strong potential for comprehensively mapping this area of marketing inquiry.

The political economy framework outlined here should be viewed as the first step in the direction of identifying and dimensionalizing the major variables influencing and ordering channel structure and behavior. A premise of the framework as initially formulated is that complex socioeconomic interrelations involve multilateral interactions as opposed to "simple" cause-effect mechanisms, such as those between power use and conflict or between channel design and costs. Given the present state of channel theory development, the initial task to be performed in accomplishing methodological and interpretive rigor is to lay out the relevant channel dimensions in terms of "fields," e.g., external-internal, economic-sociopolitical; structural-process. Otherwise, theoretical research in the area will continue to suffer from ad hoc operationalizations, where researchers select independent measures and globally hypothesize some dependent outcome without indicating or even being aware of which other interacting variables are being held or assumed constant. Hence, the political economy framework should be seen as an attempt to *chart out* or classify the total field of channel interaction. The political economy perspective as an organizing framework impels the generation of significant research questions and, therefore, has the potential for producing new theoretical insights.

As an aid to exploring the promise of the framework, a number of *illustrative* propositions have been generated throughout this article. They should be helpful in stimulating future research because they provide some insights into the kinds of meaningful relationships among core concepts which are motivated by employing the framework. However, it should be noted that there has been no attempt to specify research designs to "test" the propositions. This is because the propositions can be operationalized in a variety of ways. Given the existing state of knowledge in the channels area, it might be misleading for us to suggest specific operationalizations and would, almost certainly, deflect attention from the main purpose of the article due to the

controversy they might evoke. As an aid to the reader, we have provided an appendix which conceptually defines a few of the key constructs used. This "glossary" only serves to suggest the conceptual boundaries of the constructs; it is not intended to provide operation allegations.

In the following section, the full political economy framework is broadly outlined. Then, the remainder of the paper explores, in considerable detail, the *intra*-channel variables included in the framework.

THE POLITICAL ECONOMY FRAMEWORK

The political economy framework is capsulized in Figure 36-1. As indicated, there are two major systems: (I) the *internal political economy*, i.e., the internal structuring and functioning of the distribution channel, and (II) the *external political economy*, i.e., the channel's task environment. Both systems are divided into two component parts: an *economy* and a *polity*. The major relationships which need to be explored are indicated by arrows with capital letter notations (see Figure 36-1).

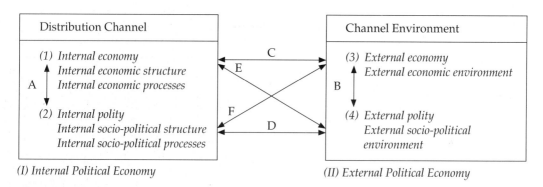

(I) Internal Political Economy

(II) External Political Economy

Figure 36-1
A Political Economy Framework for Distribution Channel Analysis

The Internal Political Economy

Distribution channels are interorganizational "collectives" of institutions and actors simultaneously pursuing self-interest and collective goals (Reve and Stern 1979; Van de Ven, Emmett, and Koenig 1974). As such, the actors interact in a socioeconomic setting of their own, called an internal political economy. To comprehend fully the relevant internal dimensions and interactions, the framework suggests that a channel be analyzed in relation to its (1) *internal economy,* i.e., the internal economic structure and processes and its (2) *internal polity,* i.e., the internal sociopolitical structure and processes.

The internal economic structure is described by the type of transactional form linking channel members, i.e., the vertical economic arrangement within the marketing channel, while the internal economic processes refer to the nature of the decision mechanisms employed to determine the terms of trade among the members. On the other hand, the internal sociopolitical structure is defined by the pattern of power-dependence relations which exist among channel members, while the internal sociopolitical processes are described in terms of the dominant sentiments (i.e., cooperation and/or conflict) within the channel.

Identifying that marketing channels consist of an internal economy and an internal polity is not a major departure from prior approaches to channel research. The contribution of the political economy framework is the explicit insistence that economic and sociopolitical forces not be analyzed in isolation. By considering the interactions between the economy and the polity, it is possible to understand and explain the internal structuring and functioning of distribution systems and to derive a number of illustrative propositions for channel research.

The 'External' Political Economy

Organizations always operate within an environment. The environment of a distribution channel is a complex of economic, physical, cultural, demographic, psychological, political, and technological forces. In the political economy framework, such forces are, as shown in Figure 36-1, incorporated in (3) *the external economy,* i.e., the prevailing and prospective economic environment and (4) *the external polity,* i.e., the external sociopolitical system in which the channel operates. The external economy of a distribution channel can be described by the nature of its vertical (input and output) and horizontal markets. The external polity can be described by the distribution and use of power resources among external actors (e.g., competitors, regulatory agencies, and trade associations) (cf., Palamountain 1955; Pfeffer and Salancik 1978; Thompson 1967; Yuchtman and Seashore 1967). An analysis of the external sociopolitical environment entails specification of the type of actors exercising power in the environment (Evan 1965), the power relations and means of control used between the external actors and the focal channel (Thompson 1967), the power relations between external actors (Terreberry 1968), and the extent to which the activities of channel members are actually controlled by environmental forces (Benson 1975).

The external economic and sociopolitical forces interact and define environmental conditions for the channel. The external political economy thus influences the internal political economy through adaptation and interaction processes (Aldrich 1979). Furthermore, channels not only adapt to their environments, but also influence and shape them (Pfeffer and Salancik 1978). The arrows in Figure 36-1 which indicate interactions between the component systems therefore point in both directions.

Attention is now turned to an elaboration of the internal political economy of distribution channels. The focus on intrachannel variables is a natural starting point, given that virtually all existing channel research has dealt with internal channel phenomena. Knowledge of environmental variables and their impact is fragmentary at best (Etgar 1977). Future examinations of the political economy framework must, however, focus on environmental variables and on the interactions between the internal and external economies.

THE INTERNAL POLITICAL ECONOMY OF DISTRIBUTION CHANNELS: AN ELABORATION OF THE FRAMEWORK

In this section the major internal economic and sociopolitical forces at work in distribution channels are described. These forces interact in shaping channel arrangements and in affecting marketing channel behavior and performance.

Internal Economy of Distribution Channels

Distribution channels are primarily set up to perform a set of essential *economic* functions in society, bridging the gap between production and consumption. Thus, it is no surprise that a substantial proportion of channel research, especially the earlier studies, has focused on an analysis of the *internal economy* of distribution channels (see Gattorna 1978; McCammon and Little 1965 for reviews).

As already indicated, the internal economy of a distribution channel may be divided into two components. The *internal economic structure* refers to the vertical economic arrangements or the transactional form in the channel. These arrangements range from a series of independently owned and managed specialized units which transact exchanges across markets to complete vertical integration where exchanges between wholly-owned units are conducted within a hierarchy (Williamson 1975). Whereas market transactions rely primarily on the use of the price mechanism, hierarchial transactions rely on administrative mechanisms. Between the two extreme economic arrangements lies a wide variety of structures in which the market mechanism is modified through some kind of formal or informal contractual arrangements between the parties involved (Blois 1972; Liebeler 1976).

Operating within each internal economic structure of a channel are certain *internal economic processes* or decision mechanisms. Thus, agreement on the terms of trade and the division of marketing functions among channel members may be reached in impersonal, routine, or habitual ways; through bargaining; or via centralized planning processes. The type of processes used to allocate resources in any given channel is likely to conform to or, at least, be constrained by the transactional form of the channel. Typically, competitive, price-mediated mechanisms are dominant in those market transactions where information is relatively complete and products are undifferentiated, as in soybean trading, while centralized planning is dominant in most hierarchical transactions. But competitive, price-mediated mechanisms have also been simulated in hierarchical structures through mathematical programming models using computed shadow prices as terms of transfer (Jennergren 1979). For other transactions which fall in between the two structural extremes, the allocation of many marketing activities is largely determined through bargaining among the parties.

Of critical importance for channel analysis is the need to compare the efficiency and effectiveness of various transactional forms of structures across each of the three decision making mechanisms. It is also important to consider cases where a specific economic process is employed across economic structures. For example, an illustrative proposition dealing with centralized planning processes might be:

P1. The more centralized planning processes predominate, irrespective of the transactional form, the more efficient and effective the marketing channel for a product or service is likely to be.

In this sense, efficiency could be defined in terms of output to input ratios (e.g., sales per square foot) and effectiveness could be some external market referent (e.g., market share). A number of theoretical rationales underlie P1: (1) the likely constraints on suboptimization within the channel derived from joint decision making, (2) the exploitation of potential scale economics, (3) the possible cost advantages gained via increased programming of distributive functions, and (4) the reduction of transaction costs due to reduced uncertainties and lessened opportunism (cf., Etgar 1976a, Grønhaug and Reve 1979).

There are, however, a number of rationales working against P1's central premise: (1) the sacrificing modes which operate when centralized planning processes predominate, (2) the danger of bureaucratization and loss of cost consciousness, and (3) the curbing of initiative at "lower" levels. Therefore, P1 demands investigation in concert with a second, counter proposition.

P2. The more centralized planning processes predominate, irrespective of the transactional form, the less likely is the marketing channel to be able to react quickly to external threats.

This proposition has its roots in the criticism which has often been directed at vertically integrated systems (cf., Arndt and Reve 1979; Sturdivant 1966). However, it may also apply to market transactions, because the more that the exchange process among channel members is organized, the more severe become trade-offs between efficiency and adaptiveness. On the other hand, while fast and specific adaptation to localized threats will likely be slow when centralized planning processes are prevalent, the adoption of such processes may permit better environmental scanning, more opportunities to influence external actors, and more ability to absorb shocks over the long run than those channels which are typified by bargaining or by routine or habitual decision making.

Analysis is also required within transactional forms across the various decision making mechanisms. Especially significant are the issues which Williamson (1975) raises in his markets and hierarchies framework. He shows how market transactions may become very costly due to human factors, such as bounded rationality and opportunism, coupled with environmental factors, such as uncertainty and economically concentrated input or output markets (i.e., small number bargaining). When information is unequally possessed, opportunistic behavior is likely to prevail, and exchange may be commercially hazardous. An illustrative proposition drawn from this line of reasoning is:

P3. Market transactions in oligopsonistic situations are likely to lead to information imbalances, opportunistic behavior, and high transaction costs. Impersonal, routine, or habitual decision making mechanisms in such situations will not suffice to overcome opportunistic behavior within the channel.

For example, when the members of atomistic industries, such as those found in the manufacture of maintenance, operating, and repair items, rely on open market forces to determine the terms of trade between themselves and the members of oligopolies, such as in the aerospace or automotive industries, the latter may withhold relevant information regarding demand projections and manipulate the exchange process by distorting any information passed along in order to achieve inequitable advantages from their fragmented suppliers. Extensive theoretical rationales underlying P3 are provided by Williamson (1975), Arrow (1974), and Lindblom (1977). Empirical research, using this internal economy perspective, is required to test the large number of Williamsonian hypotheses dealing with why channel structuring based on market transactions may tend to fail.

Internal Polity of Distribution Channels

As has been noted by several channel analysts (e.g., Alderson, Palamountain), distribution channels are not only economic systems but also social systems.[2] This observation has led to research on the behavioral aspects of distribution channels and the intrachannel sociopolitical factors (Stern 1969; Stern and El-Ansary 1977). In a political economy framework, these forces are referred to as the *internal polity* of distribution channels. The economy and the polity of channels are basically allocation systems, allocating scarce economic resources and power or authority, respectively. Both the economy and polity of channels can also be viewed as coordination systems (Hernes 1978) or ways of managing the economics and politics of interorganizational systems.

The polity of a marketing channel might be seen as oriented to the allocation and use of authority and power within the system. Similar to the internal economy, there are also structured and process variables which describe the working of the internal polity. Adopting Emerson's (1962, 1972) notion of power relationships as the inverse of the existing dependency relationships between the

system's actors, the *internal sociopolitical structure* is given by the initial pattern of power-dependence relations within the channel. The limiting cases of dependence are minimal power and completely centralized power. Power is a relational concept inherent in exchange between social actors (Emerson 1962, 1972). There will always be *some* power existing within channels due to mutual dependencies which exist among channel members, even though that power may be very low (El-Ansary and Stern 1972). However, power can also be fully concentrated in a single organization which then appears as the undisputed channel administrator (e.g., Lusch 1976). Such a power constellation can be referred to as a unilateral power system (Bonoma 1976). Because of the numerous marketing flows which tie the channel members together, the more common case is a mixed power situation where different firms exercise control over different flows, functions, or marketing activities (e.g., Etgar 1976b). The latter can be referred to as a mixed power system (Bonoma 1976).[3] Careful analysis is required to assess correctly the power-dependency patterns in a marketing channel (cf., El-Ansary and Stern 1972; Etgar 1976b; Frazier and Brown 1973; Hunt and Nevin 1974; Wilkinson 1973), because sociopolitical structures alter over time. Changing bases of power, coalition formations, and evolving linkages with external actors are among the factors causing such dynamism and creating measurement problems.

The various patterns of power-dependency relationships in a distribution channel are thought to be associated with various *sociopolitical processes*. The sociopolitical processes primarily refer to the dominant sentiments and behaviors which characterize the interactions between channel members. Although channel sentiments and behaviors are multidimensional constructs, two major dimensions in channel analysis are cooperation and conflict. Cooperation can be represented as joint striving towards an object (Stern 1971)—the process of coalescing with others for a good, goal, or value of mutual benefit. Cooperation involves a combination of object- and collaborator-centered activity which is based on a compatibility of goals, aims, or values. It is an activity in which the potential collaborator is viewed as providing the means by which a divisible goal or object desired by the parties may be obtained and shared. Conflict, on the other hand, is opponent-centered behavior (Stern 1971) because in a conflict situation, the object is controlled by the opponent while incompatibility of goals, aims, or values exists. The major concern in such situations is to overcome the opponent or counterpart as a means of securing the object. Conflict is characterized by mutual interference or blocking behavior.[4]

While they are highly interrelated, cooperation and conflict are separate, distinguishable processes. Exchange between social actors generally contains a certain dialect varying between conflictual and cooperative behavior (Guetzkow 1966). A common example is found in customer-supplier relationships ordered by long-term contracts. They reflect basically cooperative sentiments, but conflicts regularly take place regarding the interpretation of contractual details and problem-solving approaches.

At one extreme, dysfunctional conflict processes—those aimed at injuring or destroying another party—will severely impede any existing or potential cooperative behaviors among the parties. However, the absence of confrontation will not necessarily produce maximal joint-striving, because the complacency and passivity which may be present in the relationship may cause the parties to overlook salient opportunities for coalescing (cf., Coser 1956; Thomas 1976). Indeed, because of the mutual dependencies which exist in channels, it is likely that conflict, in some form, will always be present (Schmidt and Kochan

1972; Stern and El-Ansary 1977; Stern and Gorman 1969). In addition, channels cannot exist without a minimum level of cooperation among the parties. Thus, conflictual and cooperative processes will exist simultaneously in all channels.

Having specified major structure and process variables in the internal polity, it now is possible to examine their interactions for illustrative propositions. For instance, there exists a relatively large number of situations in distribution where power is somewhat balanced, e.g., when department store chains deal with well-known cosmetic manufacturers, when large plumbing and heating wholesalers deal with major manufacturers of air conditioning equipment, and when supermarket chains deal with large grocery manufacturers. Drawing from political science theory, it can be proposed that:

P4. In marketing channels typified by balanced power relationships, interactions will be predominantly cooperative as long as the balance of strength is preserved (e.g., Kaplan 1957). However, the potential for dysfunctional conflict is higher than it would be if power were imbalanced (Gurr 1970).

The first part of P4 is primarily drawn from balance of power theories of international politics which predict peaceful coexistence as long as balance of strength remains. This position is congruent with the insights offered by bilateral oligopoly and duopoly theories in economics (Scherer 1970) which forecast the development of informal or formal interfirm agreements regarding pricing and competitive actions. The second part of P4 draws on relative deprivation theories of collective conflict (Gurr 1970) which predict that conflict potential and the magnitude of manifest dysfunctional conflict will be highest in balanced power situations.

Even though P4 is intuitively appealing, counter propositions can be offered which indicate that empirical verification is required. For example, Korpi (1974), a political scientist, argues that conflict potential is higher in slightly imbalanced than in balanced power constellations while Williamson (1975), an economist, posits that a centralized power pattern—the extreme form of imbalanced power—will tend to exhibit predominantly cooperative modes of exchange when compared to a more balanced pattern. Furthermore, in an imbalanced situation, ideology is often used as a unifying and cooperation-inducing force by the more powerful party. The seeming cooperation in a balanced power constellation may be of a deterrent nature. Thus, there is a need to distinguish between detente-type cooperation and ideologically induced cooperation.

As with the variables specified for the internal economy, there is clearly a need to compare structural sociopolitical conditions across processes and vice versa in order to generate propositions which can permit predictions for channel management. At the same time, it is important to understand that conflict and cooperation processes are activities conducive to some economic end; they are not ends in themselves. Furthermore, the way in which power is used within a channel will clearly affect the sociopolitical processes. For example, it may be proposed that:

P5. In marketing channels characterized by imbalanced power, the use of coercive power will produce a dysfunctional level of conflict.

Additionally,

P6. Marketing channels characterized by imbalanced power and dominated by coercive influence strategies will be inherently unstable, resulting in decreased competitive viability.

To some extent, the works of Raven and Kruglanski (1970); Stern, Schulz, and Grabner (1973); and Lusch (1976) examining the relation between bases of power and resulting conflict point in the direction of these propositions.

Alternatively, in line with findings generated by Wittreich (1962), Kriesberg (1952), and Weik (1972), it is possible to propose that:

P7. Marketing channels characterized by minimal power will exhibit low levels of cooperation.

This is supported by McCammon (1970) who has argued that conventional marketing channels, comprised of isolated and autonomous decision making units, are unable to program distribution activities successfully. If power is low, so is dependence. Thus, two or more relatively independent entities may not be motivated to cooperate.

The above propositions indicate a few of the expected relations within the internal polity of distribution channels. As mentioned, they are merely illustrative of the meaningful insights for channel theory and management available in this kind of analysis.

Interaction between Internal Economy and Internal Polity of Distribution Channels

The essence of the political economy framework for the analysis of marketing systems is that economic and sociopolitical forces are not analyzed in isolation. Therefore, it is imperative to examine the interactions between the economy and the polity. To illustrate the potency of the combination, it is again possible to generate a series of propositions. Each of these propositions draws upon the variables enumerated previously.

The constellation of a given economic structure with a certain sociopolitical structure within a marketing channel will influence the economic and sociopolitical processes which take place. Considered first is the intersection between various power structures and economic structures typified by market transactions.

P8. In marketing channels in which market transactions are the predominant mode of exchange and in which power is centralized, centralized planning processes will emerge.

A relative power advantage within a channel is often used to program channel activities, and in such situations, decision making with respect to at least certain functions (e.g., promotion, physical distribution) tends to be centralized. Indicative of these types of channel arrangements are those found in the food industry where manufacturers, such as Nabisco and Kraft, develop shelf or dairy case management plans for supermarket chains; in the automotive aftermarket where warehouse distributors, such as Genuine Parts Company, evoke inventory management programs for jobbers (e.g., NAPA); in lawn care products where manufacturers, such as O. M. Scott, engage in detailed merchandise programming with the various retailers of their products; and in general merchandise retailing where retailers, such as Sears, Wards, and Penneys, preprogram the activities of their private label suppliers.

In addition to economic efficiency considerations, several behavioral considerations underlie P8. Thus, following Williamson (1975), some form of organizing process (in this case, centralized planning or programming) is required in order to overcome the tendencies toward opportunistic behavior present in market transactions and to cope with the bounded rationality of each channel member. The means to achieve centralized planning may be centralized power, although this is not always likely to be the case. For

example, even in cases where there are balanced power structures in channels, centralized planning processes have emerged. This was the case when the Universal Product Code was developed jointly by retailers and manufacturers operating through their food industry trade associations.

P8 can be elaborated by considering the sociopolitical processes which are likely to prevail in market transactions with centralized planning.

P9. Under the conditions specified by P8, marketing channels will exhibit a relatively high level of conflict, but they will also exhibit highly cooperative processes. Such channels will tend to be more competitively effective than others where market transactions are also the predominant mode of exchange.

Following Korpi's (1974) reasoning, P9 predicts that conflict potential will be high due to the imbalanced power situation. The expectation with respect to cooperation is based on the ability of the channel administrator to mitigate the opportunistic tendencies among the units in the channel and to establish superordinate goals. The overall effect of the combination of interacting variables in P9 will be to produce effective channel systems in which programmed merchandising is likely to be the rule rather than the exception. Such channels are likely to be more successful in improving their market shares relative to other channels typified by market transactions.

Anecdotal evidence supporting P8 and P9 can be found in the construction and farm equipment industries. In these industries, market transactions are the predominant means of exchange between the various manufacturers and their dealers. However, Caterpillar and Deere have gained sizable leads over their rivals by developing highly efficient and effective systems of distribution through the use of their considerable power in their channels. They have achieved an unusual amount of success by programming their networks and by managing conflict within them.

Another proposition in line with the discussion above is that:

P10. In marketing channels in which hierarchical transactions are the predominant mode of exchange and in which power is centralized, conflict processes are more likely to be effectively managed, superordinate goals are more likely to be established, and efficiency is more likely to be achieved relative to any other marketing channel.

The underlying rationale for this proposition is supplied by Williamson (1975):

> Unlike autonomous contractors, internal divisions that trade with one another in a vertical integration relationship do not ordinarily have pre-emptive claims on their respective profit streams. Even though the divisions in question may have profit center standing, this is apt to be exercised in a restrained way. For one thing, the terms under which internal trading occurs are likely to be circumscribed. Cost-plus pricing rules, and variants thereof, preclude supplier divisions from seeking the monopolistic prices to which their sole supply position might otherwise entitle them. In addition, the managements of the trading divisions are more susceptible to appeals for cooperation. Since the aggressive pursuit of individual interests redounds to the disadvantage of the system and as present and prospective compensation (including promotions) can be easily varied by the general office to reflect noncooperation, simple requests to adopt a cooperative mode are more apt to be heeded. Altogether, a more nearly joint profit maximizing attitude and result is to be expected. (p. 29)

However, it should be noted that, even within a vertically integrated channel, opportunism and bounded rationality may still be found. In addition, the large size of many vertically integrated organizations often creates problems of bureaucratization and inflexibility. Thus, P10 isolates centralized, as opposed to decentralized, power. For example, the power which Sears' field operations held with regard to inventory levels within its stores was one of the major reasons for the disastrous inventory situation the company faced in 1974. In order to reduce the opportunistic behavior which existed among Sears' various divisions (e.g., the retail stores refused to hold their rightful share of the inventories which were building to abnormal levels in Sears' distribution centers), the entire company was reorganized and power was centralized more firmly in its Chicago headquarters. Now it remains to be seen whether Sears' management is equal to the task of successfully controlling the organization. Clearly, the advantages of such an internal political economy can dissipate as increasing degrees of vertical integration lead to more complex organization, more impersonal relationships, less perception of the relationships between actions and results, less moral involvement, generally more self-serving behavior, and greater toleration for substandard performance.

It should be noted that the political economy framework also encourages the examination of more narrowly focused propositions than those already stated. Given the difficulties associated with researching channel issues (due primarily to the lack of accessibility to and the sensitivity of the data involved), it is likely that research using the political economy framework should start with relatively manageable tasks. Illustrative of such propositions are:

P11. The more that relationships between channel members are characterized by cooperative behavior, the greater the level of profits attainable to the channel as a whole.

P12. The greater the proportion of relative power possessed by any channel member, the greater the proportion of the channel's profits that member will receive.

Central issues in political economies are (1) how surpluses are generated and (2) how they are distributed among the members. These "processes" provide critical links between the "political" and "economic" aspects of the system. P11 suggests a positive relationship between the level of cooperation within the channel and the joint profits obtained by it. The rationale is that cooperative behavior facilitates coordination and programming of activities within the channel which, in turn, provides potential cost advantages and improved competitive strength. In some cases, cooperation is likely to be informal, requiring a minimum of interaction. In these cases, environmental factors such as professional or trade norms, the role of trade associations, and the impact of government regulations may play significant roles in encouraging joint striving behavior. In other cases, cooperation may take the form of ad hoc consultations, the formation of committees, the establishment of federative coordination bodies, or the construction of bilateral contracts, joint ventures, or other types of formal long-term agreements (Pfeffer and Salancik 1978).

P12 addresses the critical issue of the allocation of joint profits within the marketing channel. The division of returns clearly is a matter of relative power and bargaining skill. Thus, the benefits obtained in the economic arena are divided in the political arena, a situation which is analogous to the income reallocation problem in welfare economics. Porter (1974) has found some empirical support for P12 using mainly secondary data.

Focusing on the interaction between the economy and polity of marketing channels may also produce insights into the evolution and adaptation of channel institutions. Innovative distributive institutions, such as limited line-limited service grocery stores (e.g., Aldi) and catalogue showrooms (e.g., McDade), may emerge due to differential cost advantages achieved by improved logistical systems or sharper positioning relative to specific consumer segments. The initiative for such innovations often comes from "outsiders" who are at odds with traditional channel norms and practices (Kriesberg 1955; McCammon and Bates 1965). Thus, the innovations result, at least in part, because of functional conflicts within existing channels. As the new institutions mature, they tend to hire personnel from competitors, thereby gradually changing their professional orientation. At the same time, they become preoccupied with quality, add services, and begin to cater to broader market segments, thus moving towards the same practices as their competitors. The functional conflicts with other channel members tend to disappear, and opportunities for new outsiders to innovate emerge. Such scenarios as the "wheel of retailing" simply illustrate how sociopolitical circumstances often influence economic activities within a marketing channel. In turn, the economic form influences the sociopolitical sentiments surrounding the emerging transactions which lead, in turn, to further changes in economic activities.

CONCLUSION

Analysis of distribution channels as political economies provides a framework in which to incorporate and integrate the variety of approaches and findings found in the existing channel literature. More importantly, the emergent framework provides a basis for future research by isolating the critical dimension determining transactional effectiveness and efficiency in distribution. It also provides a conceptual mapping which may be useful to anyone with an interest in channel relationships.

The framework, including the illustrative propositions developed from it, presents a preliminary, general look at distribution channel structuring and functioning. In particular, the propositions advanced above serve to underscore the caveat that the economy and the polity of such systems are inseparably linked and cannot be studied in isolation (Frey 1978; Lindblom 1977; Thorelli 1965; Tivey 1978). Choosing an internal economic structure for a channel seems to have clear implications for the internal sociopolitical structure involved. The constellations formed by the intersection of the various economic and sociopolitical structures also have implications for the type of sociopolitical processes to be expected within channels. An internal economic structure may have certain benefits in terms of economic performance and the competitive effectiveness of the channel. On the other hand, the sociopolitical processes associated with a given internal economy may vary both in transaction costs and in the rationality of decision making for the channel as a whole. All of these factors directly influence channel performance. Another implication which may be drawn from this type of analysis is that the various political economies of channels require different interorganizational management strategies for maintaining and expanding channel operations and for dealing with channel conflicts.

Clearly, factors in the external political economy will have a profound influence on a channel's internal political economy. Any propositions generated by adopting the political economy framework, including those outlined here, need to be modified by circumstances in the external economy and polity. A description of the impact of external forces and internal-external interactions then emerges as a topic for future work. However,

this directive must be kept in proper perspective. In the only published empirical research focusing directly on the latter topic, Etgar (1977) has indicated that certain aspects of the internal political economy of channels can be expected to explain more of the variance in channel behavior than environmental factors. Following his findings, the strongest emphasis in future research should probably remain focused on achieving a deeper understanding of the internal political economy. The framework provided in this article should, hopefully, be of some assistance in this respect.

APPENDIX

Definitions of Key Concepts in the Political Framework

(See Fig. 36-A-1)

Political economy = collectively comprised of an economic system (economy) and a sociopolitical system (polity) which jointly influence collective behavior and performance.

I. *Internal political economy* = the internal structuring and functioning of an organized collectivity (e.g., marketing channel) analyzed in terms of an internal economy and an internal polity and their interactions.

II. *External political economy* = the task environment of an organized collectivity (e.g., marketing channel) analyzed in terms of an external economy and an external polity and their interactions.

I.1. *Internal economy* = the internal economic allocation system analyzed in terms of the internal economic structure and processes.

I.2. *Internal polity* = the internal sociopolitical allocation system analyzed in terms of the internal sociopolitical structure and processes.

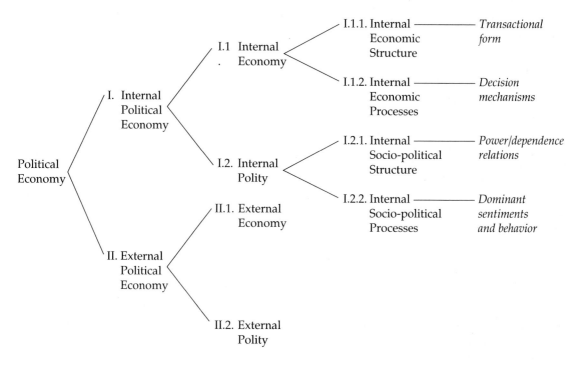

Figure 36-A-1
Key Concepts in the Political Economy Framework

II.1. *External economy* = the economic task environment of an organized collectivity (e.g., marketing channel) described by the nature of its vertical (input and output) and horizontal markets.

II.2. *External polity* = the sociopolitical task environment of an organized collectivity (e.g., marketing channel) described by the distribution and use of power resources among external actors and their prevailing sentiments.

I.1.1. *Internal economic structure* = the economic arrangements or transactional form within an organized collectivity (e.g., marketing channel) set up to complete internal exchanges.

I.1.2. *Internal economic processes* = the decision making processes within an organized collectivity (e.g., marketing channel)

which determine the terms of trade and the division of labor, functions, and activities among the internal actors.

I.2.1. *Internal sociopolitical structure* = the pattern of power/dependence relations within an organized collectivity (e.g., marketing channel).

I.2.2. *Internal sociopolitical processes* = the dominant sentiments and behaviors which characterize the interactions between actors within an organized collectivity (e.g., marketing channel).

I.1.1. *Transactional form* = internal economic arrangements ranging from markets to hierarchies (e.g., vertical integration).

I.1.2. *Decision making processes* = internal collective choice processes ranging from impersonal determination of terms of trade through the price mechanism, through bargaining processes, to centralized planning processes.

I.2.1. *Power/dependence relations* = internal power/dependence pattern ranging from minimal power (low dependence), through mixed power constellations of balanced and imbalanced power (mutual dependence), to centralized power (unilateral dependence).

I.2.2. *Dominant sentiments and behaviors* = internal sentiments and behaviors of cooperation and functional or dysfunctional conflict characterizing internal exchange, ranging from minimal cooperation, high dysfunctional conflict to maximal cooperation, functional conflict.

NOTES

1. Methodologically, many of the studies fall short due to the incorrect use of informant methodologies as well as insufficient and often single-item operationalizations of constructs, thus not allowing for reliability checks and construct validation. For an excellent critique, see Phillips (1980). Thus, more emphasis needs to be given to careful research designs and improved measurement.

2. Simply observing that many marketing channels are loosely aligned (e.g., McVey 1960) does not invalidate their systemic nature. For argumentation supporting the perspective that channels are social action systems, see Reve and Stern (1979).

3. Bonoma (1976) also proposes a third power constellation—the bilateral power system—in which the interactants are in a unit relation jointly determining unit policy for individual and group action. Such systems, which are held together by social altruism, have not yet been examined in distribution channel settings.

4. In the social sciences in general and the conflict literature in particular, there has been a considerable amount of controversy surrounding the distinction between conflict and competition. We believe that competition is distinguishable from conflict. Competition can be viewed as a form of opposition which is object-centered; conflict is opponent-centered behavior. Competition is indirect and impersonal; conflict is very direct and highly personal. In competition, a third party controls the goal or object; in conflict, the goal or object is controlled by the opponent. A swim meet is competition; a football game is conflict. For a discussion of the distinction between the two terms in a distribution channel context, see Stern (1971). For an excellent comprehensive review of the controversy, see Fink (1968).

REFERENCES

Alderson, W. (1957), *Marketing Behavior and Executive Action*, Homewood, IL: Irwin.

Aldrich, H. A. (1979), *Organizations and Environments*, Englewood Cliffs, NJ: Prentice-Hall, Inc.

Arndt, J. and T. Reve (1979), "Innovations in Vertical Marketing Systems," in *Proceedings of Fourth Macro Marketing Conference*, P. White & G. Fisk, eds., Boulder, CO: University of Colorado Press.

Arrow, K. J. (1974), *Limits of Organizations*, New York: John Wiley and Sons.

Baligh, H. H. and L. E. Richartz (1967), *Vertical Market Structures*, Boston: Allyn and Bacon.

Benson, J. K. (1975), "The Interorganizational Network as a Political Economy," *Administrative Science Quarterly*, 20 (June), 229–249.

Blois K. (1972), "Vertical Quasi-Integration," *Journal of Industrial Economics*, 20 (July), 253–260.

Bonoma, T. V. (1976), "Conflict, Cooperation and Trust in Three Power Systems," *Behavioral Science*, 21 (November), 499–514.

Bucklin, L. P. (1966), *A Theory of Distribution Channel Structure*, Berkeley, CA: Institute of Business and Economic Research, University of California.

_____, and J. M. Carman (1974), "Vertical Market Structure Theory and the Health Care Delivery System," in *Marketing Analysis of Societal Problems*, J. N. Sheth and P. L. Wright, eds., Urbana-Champaign, IL: Bureau of Economic and Business Research, 7–41.

Coser, L. A. (1956), *The Functions of Social Conflict*, Glencoe, IL: Free Press.

Cox, R., C. Goodman and T. Fichandler (1965), *Distribution in a High Level Economy*, Englewood Cliffs, NJ: Prentice-Hall, Inc.

El-Ansary, A. and L. W. Stern (1972), "Power Measurement in the Distribution Channel," *Journal of Marketing Research*, 9 (February), 47–52.

Emerson, R. M. (1962), "Power-Dependence Relations," *American Sociological Review*, 27 (February), 31–41.

———, (1972), "Exchange Theory, Part II: Exchange Relations and Network Structures," in *Sociological Theories in Progress*, J. Berger, M. Zelditch Jr., and A. Anderson, eds., Boston: Houghton Mifflin.

Etgar, M. (1976a), "The Effect of Administrative Control on Efficiency of Vertical Marketing Systems," *Journal of Market Research*, 13 (February), 12–24.

———, (1976b), "Channel Domination and Countervailing Power in Distribution Channels," *Journal of Marketing Research*, 13 (August), 254–262.

——— (1977), "Channel Environment and Channel Leadership," *Journal of Marketing Research*, 14 (February), 69–76.

——— (1978), "Differences in the Use of Manufacturer Power in Conventional and Contractual Channels," *Journal of Retailing*, 54 (Winter), 49–62.

Evan, W. M. (1965), "Toward a Theory of InterOrganizational Relations," *Management Science*, 11 (August), B-217–230.

Fink, C. F. (1968), "Some Conceptual Difficulties in the Theory of Social Conflict," *Journal of Conflict Resolution*, 12 (December), 412–460.

Frazier, G. L. and J. R. Brown (1978), "Use of Power in the Interfirm Influence Process," in *Proceedings, Eighth Annual Albert Haring Symposium*, Indiana University, 6–30.

Frey, B. S. (1978), *Modern Political Economy*, Oxford, England: Martin Robertson.

Gattorna, J. (1978), "Channels of Distribution," *European Journal of Marketing*, 12, 7, 471–512.

Grønhaug, K. and T. Reve (1979), "Economic Performance in Vertical Marketing Systems," *Proceedings of Fourth Macro Meeting Conference*, P. White and G. Fisk, eds., Boulder, University of Colorado Press.

Guetzkow, H. (1966). "Relations among Organizations," in *Studies in Organizations*, R. V. Bowers, ed., Athens, GA: University of Georgia Press, 13–44.

Gurr, T. R. (1970), *Why Men Rebel*, Princeton, NJ: Princeton University Press.

Hernes, G., editor (1978), *Forhandlingsøkonomi og Blandingsadministrasjon*, Bergen, Norway: Universitetsforlaget.

Hunt, S. D. and J. R. Nevin (1974), "Power in a Channel of Distribution: Sources and Consequences," *Journal of Marketing Research*, 11 (May), 186–193.

Jennergren, L. P. (1979), "Decentralization in Organizations," to appear in *Handbook of Organizational Design*, P. G. Nystrom and W. H. Starbuck, eds., Amsterdam: Elsevier.

Kaplan, M. A. (1957), "Balance of Power, Bipolar and Other Models of International Systems," *American Political Science Review*, 51 (September), 684–695.

Korpi, W. (1974), "Conflict and the Balance of Power," *Acta Sociologica*, 17, 2, 99–114.

Kriesberg, L. (1952), "The Retail Furrier: Concepts of Security and Success," *American Journal of Sociology*, 58 (March), 478–485.

——— (1955), "Occupational Control among Steel Distributors," *American Journal of Sociology*, 61 (November), 203–212.

Liebeler, W. J. (1976), "Integration and Competition," in *Vertical Integration in the U.S. Oil Industry*, E. Mitchell, ed., Washington DC: American Enterprise Institute for Public Policy Research, 5–34.

Lindblom, C. E. (1977), *Politics and Markets*, New York: Basic Books.

Lusch, R. F. (1976), "Sources of Power: Their Impact on Intrachannel Conflict," *Journal of Marketing Research*, 13 (November), 382–390.

McCammon, B. C. Jr. (1970), "Perspectives for Distribution Programming," in *Vertical Market Systems*, L. P. Bucklin, ed., Glenview, IL: Scott, Foresman, 32–51.

———, and A. D. Bates (1965), "The Emergence and Growth of Contractually Integrated Channels in the American Economy," in *Economic Growth, Competition, and World Markets*, P. D. Bennett, ed., Chicago: American Marketing Association, 496–515.

———, and R. W. Little (1965), "Marketing Channels: Analytical Systems and Approaches," in *Science in Marketing*, G. Schwartz, ed., New York: John Wiley and Sons, 321–384.

———, A. D. Bates and J. D. Guiltinan (1971), "Alternative Model for Programming Vertical Marketing Networks," in *New Essays in Marketing Theory*, G. Fisk, ed., Boston: Allyn and Bacon, 333–358.

McVey, P. (1960), "Are Channels of Distribution What the Textbooks Say?" *Journal of Marketing*, 24 (January), 61–65.

Palamountain, J. C. Jr. (1955), *The Politics of Distribution*, Cambridge, MA: Harvard University Press.

Pfeffer, J. and G. R. Salancik (1978), *The External Control of Organizations*, New York: Harper & Row.

Phillips, L. (1980), *The Study of Collection Behavior in Marketing: Methodological Issues in the Use of Key Informants*, unpublished doctoral dissertation, Evanston, IL: Northwestern University.

Porter, M. (1974), "Consumer Behavior, Retailer Power, and Market Performance in Consumer Goods Industries," *Review of Economics and Statistics*, 56 (November), 419–436.

Raven, B. H. and A. W. Kruglanski (1970), "Conflict and Power," in *The Structure of Conflict*, P. Swingle, ed., New York: Academic Press, 69–109.

Reve, T. and L. W. Stern (1979), "Interorganizational Relations in Marketing Channels," *Academy of Management Review*, 4 (July), 405–416.

Scherer, F. M. (1970), *Industrial Market Structure and Economic Performance*, Skokie, IL: Rand McNally.

Schmidt, S. M. and T. A. Kochan (1972), "Conflict: Toward Conceptual Clarity," *Administrative Science Quarterly* 17 (September), 359–370.

Stern, L. W., editor (1969), *Distribution Channels: Behavioral Dimensions*, Boston: Houghton Mifflin.

_____ (1971), "Antitrust Implications of a Sociological Interpretation of Competition, Conflict, and Cooperation in the Marketplace," *The Antitrust Bulletin*, 16 (Fall), 509–530.

_____, and A. I. El-Ansary (1977), *Marketing Channels*, Englewood Cliffs, NJ: Prentice-Hall, Inc.

_____ and R. H. Gorman (1969), "Conflict in Distribution Channels: An Exploration," in *Distribution Channels: Behavioral Dimensions*, L. W. Stern, ed., Boston, Houghton Mifflin, 156–175.

_____, R. A. Schulz and J. R. Grabner (1973), "The Power Base-Conflict Relationship: Preliminary Findings," *Social Science Quarterly*, 54 (September), 412–419.

Sturdivant, F. D. (1966), "Determinants of Vertical Integration in Channel Systems," in *Science, Technology and Marketing*, R. H. Haas, ed., Chicago: American Marketing Association, 472–479.

Terreberry, S. (1968), "The Evolution of Organizational Environments," *Administrative Science Quarterly*, (March), 590–613.

Thomas, K. (1976), "Conflict and Conflict Management," in *Handbook of Industrial and Organizational Psychology*, M. D. Dunnette, ed., Chicago: Rand McNally, 889–935.

Thompson, J. D. (1967), *Organizations in Action*, New York: McGraw Hill.

Thorelli, H. B. (1965), "The Political Economy of the Firm: Basis for a New Theory of Competition?" *Schweizerische Zeitschrift fur Volkwirtschaft und Statistik*, 101, 3, 248–262.

Tivey, L. (1978), *The Politics of the Firm*, Oxford: Martin Robertson.

Van de Ven, A., D. Emmett and R. Koenig, Jr. (1974), "Framework for Interorganizational Analysis," *Organization and Administrative Sciences*, 5 (Spring), 113–129.

Wamsley, G. and M. Zald (1973), "The Political Economy of Public Organizations," *Public Administration Review*, 33 (January–February), 62–73.

_____, and _____ (1976), *The Political Economy of Public Organizations*, Bloomington, IN: Indiana University Press.

Weik, J. (1972), "Discrepant Perceptions in Vertical Marketing Systems," in *1971 Combined Proceedings*, F. Aldine, ed., Chicago: American Marketing Association, 181–188.

Wilkinson, I. (1973), "Power in Distribution Channels," *Cranfield Research Papers in Marketing and Logistics*, Cranfield, England: Cranfield School of Management.

Williamson, O. E. (1975), *Markets and Hierarchies: Analysis and Antitrust Implications*, New York: Free Press.

Wittreich, W. (1962), "Misunderstanding the Retailer," *Harvard Business Review*, 40 (May–June), 147–155.

Yuchtman, E. and S. Seashore (1967), "A System Resources Approach to Organizational Effectiveness," *American Sociological Review*, 33 (December), 891–903.

Zald, M. (1970a), "Political Economy: A Framework for Comparative Analysis," in *Power in Organizations*, M. Zald, ed., Nashville: Vanderbilt University Press, 221–261.

_____ (1970b), *Organizational Change: The Political Economy of the YMCA*, Chicago; University of Chicago Press.

◆

Just-in-Time Exchange
Relationships in
Industrial Markets

Gary L. Frazier, Robert E. Spekman, and Charles R. O'Neal

Most marketing scholars seem to agree that the "exchange relationship" is the core phenomenon for study in the marketing discipline (cf. Alderson 1965; Bagozzi 1975; Dwyer, Schurr, and Oh 1987; Hunt 1983; Kotler 1972). Bagozzi (1975) goes so far as to argue that marketing theory is concerned primarily with two main questions, both relating to exchange relationships: (1) Why do people and organizations engage in exchange relationships? and (2) How are exchanges created, resolved, or avoided? However, relatively few studies in the marketing literature have directly addressed these critical questions. As Bagozzi (1979, p. 434) states, "We know very little about exchange behavior and lack a formal conceptualization of its parts."

One key "part" or area of exchange behavior of importance to the marketing discipline is the exchange of component parts-materials between suppliers and origi-

nal equipment manufacturers (OEMs) in industrial markets. This area of exchange has received little attention in the past. As Kotler (1984) points out, conceptual and empirical research in marketing has focused mainly on finished products rather than on goods that go into finished products.

Two forms of interfirm exchange relationship have been traditional between suppliers of component parts-materials and OEMs, "market exchanges" and "relational exchanges." Market exchanges occur when the OEM primarily buys on price, uses multiple sources of supply, and tends to switch suppliers frequently over time. Relational exchanges, well described by Dwyer, Schurr, and Oh (1987), occur when the OEM and supplier develop a relationship with more of a long-term orientation (also see Jackson 1985; Shapiro 1985; Spekman and Johnston 1986). The OEM still may use multiple sources of supply, but a relational exchange is less price driven and is based on a greater recognition of mutual commitment between trading partners than is found in a market exchange. One other traditional option for the OEM is to make

"Just-In-Time Exchange Relationships in Industrial Markets," Gary L. Frazier, Robert E. Spekman, and Charles R. O'Neal, Vol. 52 (Oct. '88) pp. 52–67. Reprinted from the *Journal of Marketing*, published by the American Marketing Association.

the component part-material rather than purchase it (i.e., a "hierarchical exchange").

During the past several years, a new form of relational exchange has developed between suppliers of component parts-materials and OEMs, commonly referred to as the "just-in-time" (JIT) exchange relationship. Such an exchange requires the supplier to produce and deliver to the OEM precisely the necessary units in the necessary quantities at the necessary time, with the objective that products produced by the supplier conform to performance specifications every time (cf. Hayes 1981; Wantuck 1982). The JIT exchange relationship requires the integration of the engineering-purchasing-production-materials management-marketing systems of the supplier and OEM to promote the efficient flow of parts-materials (cf. Hahn, Pinto, and Bragg 1983). JIT exchanges initially gained prominence in this country in the automobile industry. Today, a number of major firms across a variety of industries (e.g., Boeing, Ford, Harley Davidson, Hewlett Packard, IBM, Xerox) have assigned top priority to the establishment and maintenance of JIT exchanges (cf. Bertrand 1986).

The JIT exchange concept has received considerable attention in the purchasing, operations, and materials management literatures (cf. Bartholomew 1984; Hahn, Pinto, and Bragg 1983; Hall 1983; Manoocheri 1984; Schonberger 1982a; Schonberger and Ansari 1984). It has been conspicuously absent from the marketing literature. This lack of attention appears due to misconceptions in the marketing field about what the adoption and implementation of JIT exchange relationships entail (cf. Schonberger 1982a, p. 16). Obviously, the marketing function is influenced greatly by any change in interfirm exchange relationships, whether logistics-production centered or not.

The general purpose of this article is to expand our understanding of the exchange relationships between suppliers of compo-nent parts-materials and OEMs in industrial markets. Toward this end, the article has three specific objectives. One is to clarify the differences between market exchanges, relational exchanges as they have been conducted traditionally between suppliers of parts-materials and OEMs, and JIT exchanges.

The second objective is to develop a conceptual framework focusing on constructs and processes that help to explain levels of interest in and preference for JIT exchanges by OEMs. We examine the question of why organizations engage in a specific form of exchange relationship, which has received scant attention in the marketing literature. Bagozzi (1979) argues that explaining variation in forms or types of exchange behavior is among the more important issues for marketing researchers to address.

The third objective of the article is to develop a framework centering on factors posited to influence the success-failure of initiated JIT exchange relationships. We examine the question of how exchanges are maintained, resolved, or avoided (Bagozzi 1979). Elements of the political economies framework (Achrol, Reve, and Stern 1983; Stern and Reve 1980), the resource-dependence framework (Pfeffer and Salancik 1978), the transaction cost analysis framework (Williamson 1975, 1985), the interorganizational exchange framework (Frazier 1983), and the relational exchange framework (Dwyer, Schurr, and Oh 1987) are instrumental in the development of the conceptual frameworks.

THE JIT EXCHANGE RELATIONSHIP

The fundamental objective of the JIT exchange relationship is to eliminate waste of all kinds from the production and delivery systems of the supplier and OEM organizations. Waste is defined as anything other than the minimum amount of equipment, materials, parts, and workers that is absolutely essential to production (Shingo 1985). Exactness is a critical consideration because the JIT exchange, in its extreme form, does not tolerate variances.

Shipping the exact quantities of the part or material ordered and scheduling shipments on a precise timetable as parts or materials are needed in the OEM's production process are two fundamental elements of a JIT system.[1] Waste is minimized further by shipping parts or materials of perfect quality (i.e., that conform to performance specifications). Perfect quality helps to (1) ensure that the OEM's production process runs uninterrupted and (2) alleviate the need for incoming inspection by the OEM.

Another key element of a JIT exchange is that the part-material is intended to be designed in a creative, joint effort between the supplier and OEM. Continuous quality improvements over the duration of the relationship are sought. Joint design efforts can lead to greater simplicity and standardization of parts or materials, thus helping the firms to achieve shorter machine setup times, smaller production lot sizes, and smaller inventories at all stages of the purchasing-production-delivery sequence (Hay 1984; Shingo 1985). Waste is reduced further as a result.[2]

Finally, the emphasis on per-unit price from the supplier is supplanted in a JIT exchange by the notion of "total cost of ownership" and the array of value-added services provided by the supplier. The OEM begins to recognize that per-unit price is less important than the costs associated with inspection and re-inspection, handling, warehousing, inventory, scrap, and rework. If total costs are lowered because of waste reduction, the OEM can be more price competitive with its end-product. However, reducing the per-unit price of the supplier's part-material over time is still a prominent goal of a JIT exchange; cost information is intended to be shared openly between the firms.

The adoption and implementation of an "ideal" JIT relationship are impossible to achieve in a short period of time, if ever. There is no exact standard to meet in implementing a JIT exchange relationship, other than continuous progress toward the ultimate objectives of one-at-a-time delivery (i.e., the amount of the part-material required for one production run), perfectly synchronized and continuous product flows, perfect quality of incoming parts-materials that are simple and standardized in their design, and short production runs.[3]

COMPARISONS OF INTERFIRM EXCHANGE RELATIONSHIPS

In this section we highlight major differences between market exchanges, traditional relational exchanges, and JIT exchanges (see Table 37-1). This discussion lays the foundation for the conceptual frameworks focusing on (1) the conditions that appear to be conducive to the establishment of JIT exchanges and (2) the factors that are likely to influence the success or failure of initiated JIT exchanges.

As suggested in Table 37-1, market exchanges tend to be viewed as "discrete transactions" with the parties having little commitment to the relationship. Price drives the negotiation process and the OEM treats qualified suppliers, as well as their parts-materials, as homogeneous (Ames and Hlavacek 1984; Kotler 1984). The OEM uses several sources of supply for the part-material and the functional interdependence between the OEM and any given supplier is very low. Therefore, from the OEM's point of view, few risks or costs are associated with switching from one supplier to another. The supplier knows all too well that no future business is guaranteed and that its share of present business can be used by the OEM as a bargaining point for any follow-on sales (cf. Jackson 1985).

Table 37-1

Comparisons of Market, Relational, and JIT Relationships on Characteristics of Exchange

Characteristics of Exchange	Form of Exchange Relationship		
	Market	*Relational*	*JIT*
Time horizon of exchange	Short-term	Moderate to long-term	Long-term
Focus of exchange	Price of core product	Emphasis on core product, with some attention to value-added services	Joint emphasis on core product and value-added services
Number of interorganizational linkages	Few	Moderate	A tangled web of relations across functional areas
Frequency of communications	Low; tends to be formal only	Moderate; both formal and informal	High; both formal and informal
Nature of information exchanged	Limited to transaction	Transaction and some long-term planning	Joint product-, production-, and logistics-related; much long-term planning
Frequency of shipments	Low and irregular	Moderate and regular	High, and subject to revision
Number of suppliers	Many	Moderate number	Sole-sourcing in its ideal form
Transaction costs	Low	Moderate	High
Specialized investments	Low, if at all	Moderately low	Moderate to high
Functional interdependence	Low and limited to delivery system	Moderate and involves only a few functional areas	Very high and extends to many functional areas
Level of risk	Low	Moderate	High
Problem-solving orientation	After the fact and reactive	Largely reactive	Proactive and oriented toward prevention

The information exchanged in market exchanges normally is limited to issues directly germane to the purchase agreement. In addition, communication between the supplier and the OEM tends to be relatively formal and infrequent. Any communications, cross-functional ties, and evaluation processes are limited to areas directly related to the delivery system and the terms and conditions of the agreement. Such exchange characteristics encourage every party to approach the other in a self-serving way. There is little sense of joint gains and mutual benefits in the typical market exchange relationship (Stern and El-Ansary 1988).

As shown in Table 37-1, relational exchanges are somewhere between market exchanges and JIT exchanges in terms of characteristics of exchange. Suppliers with whom OEMs are interested in establishing relational exchanges have somehow differentiated themselves from competitors (Dwyer, Schurr, and Oh 1987). For example, Salmond (1987) argues that relational exchanges tend to develop when the supplier offers customized-differentiated component parts-materials to the OEM. This differentiation provides the incentives for an exchange relationship that has a moderate to long-term time horizon and a focus on the core product and some associated value-added services rather than on just price. Shared values and compatibility of goals are more important because of the higher level of functional interdependence in relational exchanges than in market exchanges. Strategic alliances between OEMs and suppliers begin to make sense under these conditions.

The OEM and the supplier tend to communicate more frequently with each other in a relational exchange than in a market exchange, even when the OEM uses multiple sources of supply for the part-material. Some efforts toward cost containment, value analysis, and joint designs are apparent in many relational exchanges (Dwyer, Schurr, and Oh 1987). Within many relational exchanges, OEMs work closely with suppliers to implement statistical process control procedures in an attempt to ensure consistent quality of the suppliers' parts-materials. Because of the level of interdependence between the OEM and supplier in a relational exchange, self-motivated behavior on the part of either trading partner diminishes to some degree.

In comparison with market and traditional relational exchanges, JIT exchanges have a longer term orientation. The focus of the JIT exchange is the core product (which may or may not be differentiated) and the value-added services made possible through close coordination between the OEM and the supplier organizations. Indeed, the need for close interfirm coordination in product development, quality assurance, and logistics is the key feature distinguishing JIT exchanges from the other forms of interfirm exchange for component parts-materials. Hence, JIT exchanges necessitate frequent communication between the firms, involving a large number of participants across many functional areas. Transaction costs (i.e., the costs of running a relationship; Williamson 1975) are likely to be moderate to moderately high throughout a JIT relationship, especially in the beginning as the supplier and OEM adapt to a new way of conducting business.[4]

JIT exchanges involve at least moderate levels of specialized investments (Williamson 1975) in human assets on the part of both the supplier and the OEM, as specialized design, production, and delivery policies and procedures are needed to implement them. For example, the OEM's production plans, schedules, and releases must be communicated clearly and completely to the supplier and at frequent intervals, as they are essential for the supplier's own production and delivery plans. Specialized investments in durable assets also are common, especially for the supplier (e.g., new plant next to the OEM plant, new warehouses, more delivery vehicles). These specialized investments and the high level of functional interdependence between the firms lead to a relatively "high risk" exchange from both the OEM's and supplier's point of view, especially if the OEM uses sole-sourcing for the part-material. Usually the OEM makes a transition from multiple sourcing to dual sourcing to single sourcing as the

JIT exchange is implemented (cf. Manoocheri 1984).[5]

Given the transaction costs, investments, and risks involved, OEMs and suppliers are likely to engage in a relatively extensive selection process before agreeing to establish a JIT exchange. Once the JIT exchange is implemented, the monitoring-review process is critical in a relative sense as the OEM and supplier must understand the impact that the JIT exchange is having on their performance levels. The problem-solving orientation between the OEM and supplier in a JIT exchange ideally is based on prevention rather than reaction to problems as they occur.

Dedication to mutually beneficial gains and a collaborative atmosphere are necessary if the JIT exchange is to prosper. Should "bounded rationality" and "opportunism" (John 1984; Williamson 1975) prevail, the costs of the JIT exchange are likely to outweigh its benefits. If collaborative behavior predominates, JIT partners can forge a strategic alliance whereby both look to the ultimate customer and join forces to compete in the marketplace. Such alliances normally are associated with joint ventures and other equity-based partnerships (see Harrigan 1983), but many of the stated advantages can be achieved through close, collaborative ties in a JIT exchange relationship. Indeed, JIT exchanges appear more similar to hierarchical exchanges than to traditional relational exchanges because of the resources committed to them and the way in which they are conducted.

JIT exchanges often facilitate the transfer of technological and managerial skills between the firms, thus serving to exploit synergies and leverage each partner's distinct competencies. These benefits translate to competitive advantage for the OEM through its ability to offer its customers higher quality products, more innovative products, and lower prices (Schonberger 1982b). The supplier gains a competitive advantage through product quality and increased sales over time to a stable buyer.

APPROPRIATE FORM OF EXCHANGE RELATIONSHIP

Figure 37-1 is a conceptual framework addressing the issue of when JIT exchanges are most likely to be initiated between suppliers of component parts-materials and OEMs. The framework consists of two stages. In the "interest stage" are constructs that are expected to influence whether or not an OEM will consider establishing a JIT exchange for a part or material. Once a moderately high level of interest is reached, the "initiation-rejection stage" is triggered. This stage comprises constructs posited to influence whether or not the OEM's interest is translated into a desire to initiate a JIT exchange for the part-material.

Levels of the perception-oriented constructs in Figure 37-1 (e.g., decision-making uncertainty) are based on the views of the dominant coalition in the firm (cf. Bacharach and Lawler 1980). Conceptual definitions of the constructs in Figure 37-1 are given in Appendix A.

Interest Stage

Levels of interest in JIT exchanges differ among OEMs within and across industries (cf. *Purchasing* 1985). In Figure 37-1, an OEM's level of interest in a JIT exchange (reflected by C5) is expected to be influenced by (1) decision-making uncertainty, (2) the firm's market position and aspirations, (3) part-material characteristics, and (4) end-product characteristics. Decision-making uncertainty (C4) in the OEM firm is driven by such environmental factors as the number and pattern of linkages among suppliers, OEMs, and cus-

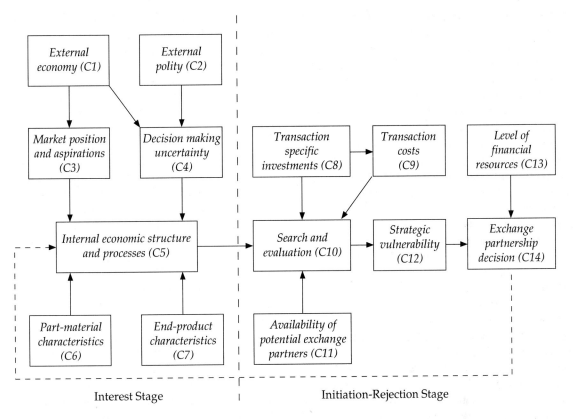

Figure 37-1
*The Appropriate Form of Exchange Relationships for Component Parts and
Materials in Industrial Markets*

tomers, the power of competitors and other outside actors, the favorableness-unfavorableness of economic conditions, and the level of environmental change (C1 and C2) (Achrol, Reve, and Stern 1983; Aldrich 1979; Child 1972; Duncan 1972; Pfeffer and Salancik 1978). If the level of uncertainty faced by the OEM is low, JIT exchanges are not likely to be considered to any degree; current means of conducting business are likely to be seen as acceptable under conditions of low uncertainty (cf. Achrol, Reve, and Stern 1983; Pfeffer and Salancik 1978; Rogers 1983). In contrast, if moderate to high levels of uncertainty are encountered,

the OEM is likely to be open to and interested in new ways of conducting business.

A dominant OEM firm whose market position is eroding is likely to have a keen interest in JIT exchanges, especially if it has high aspirations for regaining its lost market position (C3). The interest of such an OEM in JIT exchanges should be spurred also if a key competitor recently has adopted JIT exchanges for some parts-materials. Competitive pressures often force firms to find new ways to cut costs, gain technical superiority, and improve product quality (Schonberger and Ansari 1984). Similarly, an OEM might show keen interest in a JIT exchange if it views it as a way to gain a first-mover advantage over competitors.

If the part-material (C6) and end-product (C7) are moderately important to highly important to the firm, the OEM is expected to be open to new ways of acquiring/producing them. Therefore, interest in JIT exchanges is expected to be higher for such goods than for goods of lower importance. Interest levels in JIT exchanges also should be related to the need to improve the price and quality levels of the part-material and/or end-product; joint design efforts, technology transfers, and waste reduction can contribute to improved price and quality levels.

Initiation-Rejection Stage

When interest in a JIT exchange is at least moderately high because of the factors just discussed, the OEM is likely to undertake a search and evaluation process (C10) to assess in greater depth the costs and benefits of such an exchange relationship. Transaction-specific investments (C8), transaction costs (C9), and the availability of potential JIT exchange partners (C11) are considered in the process (Williamson 1975, 1985). On the basis of this evaluation, the OEM can develop an understanding of its strategic vulnerability (C12) in forming a JIT exchange. Moreover, the financial resources available to the OEM (C13) influence its range of options in acquiring the part-material. Combined with the constructs in the interest stage of Figure 37-1, the constructs in this second stage are expected to affect the OEM's decision of whether or not to attempt to form a JIT exchange (C14).

Aside from motivating interest in the JIT exchange initially, high uncertainty is expected to contribute to a desire to establish JIT exchanges, at least when market or relational exchanges are currently in use. Firms normally attempt to achieve greater stability-cer-

tainty when faced with an uncertain future (Vyas and Woodside 1984; Webster and Wind 1972). One way for a firm to ensure greater stability in a threatening-uncertain environment is to achieve higher levels of interfirm coordination (Pfeffer and Salancik 1978), as empirical results reported by Etgar (1977) suggest. Therefore, for OEMs currently using a market exchange or a traditional relational exchange for a part-material, establishment of a JIT exchange promises higher levels of interfirm coordination and greater stability.

When a market or relational exchange is currently in place, the OEM is likely to resist establishing a hierarchical exchange if faced with a highly uncertain environment. Such internal exchanges are very expensive to set up (e.g., acquisition of necessary plant and equipment) and raise the level of fixed costs incurred by the OEM. As Buzzell (1983) and Harrigan (1983) suggest, highly volatile environments may not be conducive to vertical integration because of the risks involved. JIT exchanges offer the OEM the possibility of a closely coordinated relationship without the risks and burden of ownership. JIT exchanges are more flexible than hierarchical exchanges, and flexibility and "looser organizational structures" are very desirable in uncertain environments (Archol, Reve, and Stern 1983; Dwyer and Welsh 1985; Stern and Reve 1980).

When a hierarchical exchange currently is used for the part-material, the risks associated with making the item in-house in an uncertain market, especially one in which long-term economic conditions appear unfavorable, may encourage a switch to a JIT exchange. However, the OEM may prefer to maintain use of a hierarchical exchange when faced with high uncertainty because it affords the firm more control in decision making.

OEMs are likely to resist establishing JIT exchanges if high levels of transaction-specific investments are required. Heavy investment in specialized assets by a supplier would expose the OEM to the possibility of "holdup" costs based on the supplier's opportunistic behavior (Williamson 1975, 1985), especially under conditions of high uncertainty. In other words, the costs of switching to another supplier would be so great that the OEM might feel compelled to relent to the supplier's demands, even if they were unfair. Furthermore, a high level of specialized investments implies a complex exchange in which the customer service requirements are high. Hierarchical exchanges might be preferred because the OEM could retain greater control. As a consequence, the OEM is likely to initiate JIT exchanges when levels of specialized investments are moderate for both trading partners.

However, the OEM is likely to want the supplier to make more specialized investments in a JIT relationship than the OEM does, especially in terms of durable assets. In a sense, investment in specialized durable assets by the supplier gives the OEM a "hostage" to which it can refer in future dealings with the supplier (Williamson 1985). This investment would increase the supplier's dependence in the relationship and give the OEM a power advantage (Emerson 1962); a firm's power reflects its potential for influence on the decision making and behavior of another firm (Frazier 1984). Firms generally strive to achieve a power advantage in their dealings with other firms, thereby avoiding, to the extent possible, situations that demand high levels of outside control and compliance (Emerson 1962; Pfeffer and Salancik 1978).

The OEM's desire for a power advantage also is expected to lead to a greater likelihood of JIT exchanges when the OEM is faced with a moderately concentrated supplier market for the part-material. In such markets, the group of potential exchange partners is larger than it is in concentrated markets and supplier power levels are relatively low.[6]

Though a power advantage is likely to be preferred by the OEM, it is expected to be less critical than the general competency of the supplier. That is, being an eligible JIT exchange partner means that the supplier has the capability and technological expertise to make the JIT exchange work. Many OEMs that have wanted to enter JIT exchanges with certain suppliers have been delayed by the suppliers' inability to provide parts-materials of consistent quality. Further, finding suppliers that are trustworthy appears extremely important. As Pruitt (1981) indicates, trust (i.e., the belief that a party's word or promise is reliable and a party will fulfill its obligations in an exchange) is likely to be related strongly to firms' desires to coordinate activities closely with one another (also see Dwyer, Schurr, and Oh 1987; Schurr and Ozanne 1985). Finally, the JIT exchange is much stronger if the fit between the organizations' cultures is as great as the complementary skills and competencies within each organization. As Ouchi (1980) points out, high levels of commitment over time presume a shared value system between trading partners. Obviously, a JIT exchange cannot be initiated if the OEM fails to identify any eligible exchange partners.

Moderate transaction costs should facilitate the initiation of JIT exchanges. As Williamson (1975) suggests, a moderate level of transaction-specific investments reduces transaction costs to a degree. Transaction costs also would be moderate if customer service requirements and the complexity of the exchange were not extreme. Further, reasonably high levels of trust between the OEM and the supplier should serve to reduce the costs of running a JIT exchange. However, the high uncertainty that is expected to be present when JIT exchanges are formed is likely to cause an upward pressure on transaction costs.

JIT exchanges appear to be more likely if the part-material and the end-product in which it is incorporated are only moderately important to the OEM. Parts-materials that are highly essential to the market acceptance of an extremely important end-product are more likely to be made in-house for two main reasons. First, hierarchical exchanges give the OEM more control over the production/delivery of essential parts-materials than do JIT exchanges. Second, the dependence of the OEM on a JIT supplier would be very high if the supplier provided an essential part-material for an extremely important end-product. As Pfeffer and Salancik (1978) indicate, firms attempt to maintain direct control over the most essential resources needed for survival. Empirical results of Lilien (1979), Anderson (1985), and Anderson and Coughlan (1987) suggest that hierarchical exchanges tend to be used for products that are relatively complex and highly differentiated.

High "strategic vulnerability" can preclude the establishment of particular forms of exchange relationships (Emerson 1962; Harrigan 1983; Pfeffer and Salancik 1978; Porter 1985). Several of the conditions discussed before appear to provide for a JIT exchange that is manageable in terms of the OEM's vulnerability, namely moderate levels of specialized investments and transaction costs, a high level of trust in the supplier, and an OEM power advantage in the exchange.

Dominant but declining OEMs with aspirations to regain their lost market position should desire to initiate JIT exchanges, which offer a way to regain market position through improvements in end-product prices and quality. JIT exchanges appear especially attractive to OEMs in this situation that are somewhat constrained in the available financial resources and hence less able to establish hierarchical exchanges, at least for parts-materials of moderate importance. When a hierarchical exchange is not possible or is deemed too costly, a JIT exchange is a logical and close alternative.

Finally, one *caveat* must be stressed. Just because an OEM desires to initiate a JIT exchange does not mean that it will be able to do so, as the terms and conditions of the JIT exchange must also be acceptable to the supplier. For example, the production group of an OEM may want to establish a JIT exchange. However, the traditional price-driven purchasing practices used in market exchanges may still persist in the firm, impeding the establishment of a JIT exchange with a preferred supplier.[7]

Table 37-2 is an overview of the research propositions suggested from the development of the interest stage and the initiation-rejection stage of Figure 37-1.

IMPLEMENTATION-REVIEW CHALLENGES FOR JIT EXCHANGES

Even when JIT exchanges are initiated under appropriate conditions, their success is not guaranteed because of the way in which they are carried out. Figure 37-2 is a framework of processes and constructs that influence the success or failure of initiated JIT exchanges. The framework is composed of two stages. The implementation stage represents the way in which the supplier and OEM work together to achieve desired outcomes from the JIT exchange. The review stage centers on how the firms evaluate and react to the outcomes achieved from the JIT exchange. Conceptual definitions of the constructs in Figure 37-2 are given in Appendix B.

Implementation Stage

Three constructs are expected to influence directly the exchange and interaction between the supplier and OEM from the very beginning of the JIT exchange: (1) the JIT exchange agreement, (2) expectations, and (3) internal sociopolitical structure. If the JIT exchange

Table 37-2
Propositions Relating to Interest in and the Initiation of JIT Exchanges

Interest Stage

Interest in JIT exchanges is present when:

P_1:   OEMs are faced with moderate to high levels of decision-making uncertainty.

P_2:   The OEM is a dominant but declining firm with high aspirations for regaining lost market position.

P_3:   Competitive pressures are high and the OEM must either respond to competitor moves or gain a first-mover advantage.

P_4:   The part-material and end-product are of at least moderate importance to the OEM and in need of price-quality improvements.

Initiation-Rejection Stage

JIT exchanges are initiated when:

P_1:   Market or relational exchanges currently are used, the OEM's decision-making uncertainty is high, and economic conditions are somewhat constrained but still favorable.

P_2:   Specialized investments by the OEM and the supplier are moderate; the supplier will make larger specialized investments in durable assets than the OEM.

P_3:   Several suppliers are viewed as eligible JIT partners for the part-material, largely on the basis of their capability and the fact that they are smaller and less powerful than the OEM.

P_4:   Transaction costs are moderate.

P_5:   The part-material and end-product are moderately important to the OEM.

P_6:   The OEM's strategic vulnerability is perceived as being moderately low.

P_7:   The OEM is a dominant but declining firm with high aspirations and is somewhat constrained in terms of available financial resources.

---

agreement is reasonably formalized, the supplier and OEM are likely to have a better idea of their respective roles and obligations. Formalization is especially important when interfirm interdependencies are high and the exchange is long-term and complex (cf. Dwyer, Schurr, and Oh 1987). However, formalization cannot be taken to an extreme, as it could hamper the potential benefits-innovations gained from the JIT relationship. For example, by allowing the supplier greater latitude and responsibility in the product de-

velopment process, the OEM may receive better and more innovative product designs.

Contractual solidarity refers to the nature of the regulation used to ensure performance of obligations in the exchange relationship, whether legal regulation or self-regulation (Macneil 1980). If the OEM and supplier are most interested in the process of their subsequent exchange (rather than legal recourses) and in self-regulation of disputes (rather than legal regulation) in designing the exchange agreement, the JIT exchange is

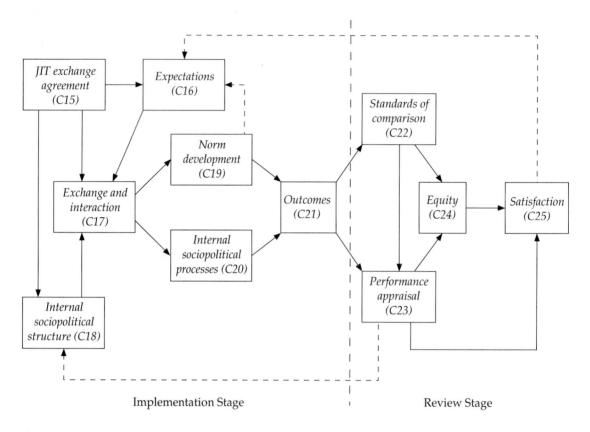

Figure 37-2
The Success-Failure of JIT Exchanges

likely to have the proper collaborative orientation from the start. Finally, the fairness of an agreement relates to the division of benefits and burdens between the supplier and the OEM (Macneil 1980). To the degree that the exchange agreement is perceived as being fair to both the OEM and the supplier, the JIT exchange will be on a stronger foundation.

The expectations (C16) of the supplier and OEM about their respective levels of performance on inherent responsibilities and the outcomes (e.g., profits) that the JIT exchange will produce undoubtedly affect their communications and behavior in the JIT ex-

change. Unrealistic expectations can hamper the success of the JIT exchange, as performance and outcomes are not likely to meet such expectation levels (Howard and Sheth 1969). A reasonably formalized exchange agreement should help to enhance the realism of the expectations held by the supplier and the OEM. JIT exchange partners must have patience in implementing their relationship because of the complexity and newness of this form of exchange (Schonberger 1982a).[8]

As the OEM is anticipated to prefer establishing JIT exchanges with smaller and less powerful suppliers to avoid external control and maintain autonomy (Pfeffer and Salancik

1978), an imbalance of power may be present in JIT exchanges (C18). This power imbalance will be heightened to the degree that the supplier makes more specialized investments in durable assets than the OEM. A firm with a power advantage in a relationship has the opportunity to exploit the other firm at times through the use of coercion (Dwyer and Walker 1981; Roering 1977; Stern and Reve 1980). Several empirical studies have shown that coercive use of power in interfirm relationships seriously weakens their collaborative nature (cf. Frazier and Summers 1984; Gaski and Nevin 1985; Hunt and Nevin 1974; Lusch 1976). Dwyer, Schurr, and Oh (1987) suggest that the noncoercive exercise of power is the key factor in determining the ultimate success of a relational exchange; high interdependence between firms in an exchange relationship increases the importance of the judicious application of power.

If the power asymmetry is extreme and the firm with the power advantage consistently abuses the other firm over time, the JIT exchange is unlikely to survive (cf. Stern and Reve 1980). For example, if sales of the OEM's end-product drop markedly, extreme pressure could be placed on the JIT exchange. The OEM could respond to such pressure by demanding concessions from the supplier. The supplier is likely to view such behavior as highly opportunistic and feel abused, especially when the sales of its part-material to the OEM are already below expectations and adjustment costs have been incurred (Walker and Weber 1987). If the supplier has made considerable investment in specialized assets, the JIT exchange may not dissolve as a result of this one instance. However, if such a situation is repeated over time, even specialized investments are not likely to hold the JIT exchange together. Both the OEM and supplier must recognize that the JIT exchange benefits both parties and each is dependent, to varying degrees, on the other.[9]

Two other aspects of the exchange and interaction (C17) component of Figure 37-2 warrant explicit attention. First, the more people and functional areas in each firm that become heavily involved in the JIT exchange, the more likely it is that the foundation of the exchange is stable. As Pfeffer and Salancik (1978, p. 146) state in discussing interfirm relationships, "The more each becomes enmeshed in the social networks of the other, such that there are overlaps in friendship networks and other business acquaintances, the more binding their friendship becomes, and the more stable and predictable it is likely to be."

Second, how well each firm carries out its role in the exchange may be the most critical aspect of the JIT exchange (Frazier 1983). A JIT exchange demands that the supplier deliver a perfect quality part-material on a timely basis. The OEM must set up its organization to be responsive to the actions of the supplier; every action of each firm must be synchronized carefully. Should either or both firms perform poorly on any responsibility, the "just-in-time" nature of the exchange can be severely disrupted. Several JIT exchanges have failed because of the inability of suppliers to deliver perfect quality parts-materials on a consistent and timely basis (cf. Schonberger 1982a).

Norms tend to develop (C19) in an exchange relationship when uncertainty must be stabilized (Lipset 1975). Moreover, norms are more likely to be adhered to when organizations expect to interact in the future (Kiesler and Kiesler 1969; Kiesler, Kiesler, and Pollak 1967). Given the high uncertainty levels when the JIT exchange is implemented and its long-term orientation, considerable opportunity is present in a JIT relationship for strong norm development. By adopting norms and establishing standards of conduct (C19), exchange partners set the general ground rules for future exchange (Dwyer, Schurr, and Oh 1987;

Pfeffer and Salancik 1978). The chances of success for the exchange are enhanced as a result. Positive norm development in a JIT exchange should be facilitated if (1) the exchange agreement is oriented toward self-regulation and is fair, (2) a relatively large number of committed personnel are involved in the operation of the JIT exchange, (3) the JIT exchange is seen as extremely important to the welfare of each organization, (4) expectations are realistic, (5) the role performance of each firm reaches high levels in a reasonably short time, and (6) each firm uses its power in a noncoercive, problem-solving way. If strong, positive norms fail to develop, the JIT exchange may not withstand the pressures placed on it over time.

In terms of internal sociopolitical processes (C20), Reingan and Woodside (1981, p. 2) indicate that each firm in an exchange " . . . has a motive for cooperation in order to reach a mutually agreeable solution and, simultaneously, a motive for competition in order to gain at the other's expense." Where strong, positive norms start to develop in the exchange, cooperation or the degree of joint striving toward common goals should be high (see John 1984). The frequency of interfirm conflicts characterized by mutual interference or blocking behaviors (Stern and Reve 1980) should be low; when conflicts do develop, they are handled in a joint, problem-solving way. In JIT exchanges where expectations are unrealistic, role performance is poor, power is used coercively, and positive norms do not develop, cooperation levels are likely to deteriorate and conflict levels are likely to rise—a situation that would seriously hamper the success of the JIT exchange.

Upon implementation of the JIT exchange, certain outcomes (C21) are achieved by each firm. Some outcomes are related to changes in costs (e.g., lower inventory carrying costs), technology, and product quality. The most important outcomes are changes in

sales and profits for each firm due to the implementation of the JIT exchange relationship.

Another key outcome contributes to the future success of the JIT exchange—the level of trust that develops between the supplier and OEM. Trust is extremely important in any exchange, but especially in a JIT exchange because of the investments and commitments by each side. As Williamson (1985, pp. 62–3) states, "Other things being equal, idiosyncratic exchange relations that feature personal trust will survive greater stress and will display greater adaptability" (also see Dwyer, Schurr, and Oh 1987; Pfeffer and Salancik 1978). A reasonably high level of trust is likely to be present between the supplier and OEM before the JIT exchange is initiated. However, a "wait-and-see" attitude may prevail in the JIT exchange as the firms determine how the change in the form of their exchange relationship influences their behavior. As the JIT exchange agreement is perceived as being fair, some evidence of trust is present. Trust is enhanced as tangible evidence of personal integrity accumulates, promises are upheld, and opportunistic behaviors are forgone.

Review Stage

Two standards of comparison (C22) are likely to be used by the supplier and OEM in judging the outcomes of the JIT exchange (Anderson and Narus 1984; Thibaut and Kelley 1959). The comparison level pertains to the quality of outcomes a firm has come to expect from a given kind of relationship, based on present and past experience with similar relationships and knowledge of other firms' similar relationships. The comparison level–alternatives, in contrast, pertains to the average quality of outcomes available from the best alternative exchange relationship.

Even if personnel in both firms have little, if any, experience with JIT exchanges, they still are likely to form perceptions about acceptable levels of performance on both standards of comparison. Such perceptions may be based on incomplete and ambiguous information and hence prone to error. If the comparison level is set too high, outcomes from the JIT exchange will be perceived to be marginal when in fact they may be good. If the comparison level alternatives standard is set too high, other suppliers (OEMs) will be seen as better JIT exchange partners when in fact they are not. Though high switching costs may keep the firms in the JIT exchange even if the outcomes from the JIT exchange are judged to be poor, the subsequent exchange relationship can be hurt by that tendency. It is extremely important, therefore, that these standards be given considerable thought by each firm and set at realistic levels.

The performance appraisal (C23) process used by each firm is influenced greatly by these standards, as well as by the firms' expectations (C16) about outcomes from the JIT exchange (which are likely to be different from either standard). However, other aspects of the appraisal system also influence the success or failure of the JIT exchange. A performance appraisal system that is well specified in terms of the criteria on which each firm's performance is judged is of great importance. It serves to make the appraisal process more accurate. Furthermore, many studies have shown that what is measured or appraised focuses activity and behavior (cf. Kerr 1975). Joint appraisals are also critical, as they reinforce the collaborative, problem-solving nature of the JIT exchange. Frequent appraisals provide the feedback necessary to make continual improvements in the JIT system. Conclusions from the performance appraisal are likely to influence the internal sociopolitical structure (C18) of the exchange because of their impact on the dependence of each firm on the exchange (note the feedback effect in Figure 37-2). If purchasing managers in OEMs have used very sophisticated vendor analysis

systems in the past to evaluate several dimensions of supplier performance in market and traditional relational exchanges, the chances are greater that an adequate appraisal system will be established in JIT exchanges.

After performance is appraised, each firm is in a better position to judge the equity (C24) of the JIT exchange (Frazier 1983). Equity is judged by comparing each firm's rewards or outputs with its investments-costs or inputs. When the ratios of outputs to inputs are seen as similar for each firm, the exchange is perceived to be equitable (Adams and Freedman 1976; Blumstein and Weinstein 1969). If equity is high in the exchange, satisfaction levels (C25) are likely to be relatively high (Foa and Foa 1974). Furthermore, if outcomes (e.g., sales, profits) gained from the exchange surpass expectations and standards of comparison for the exchange, satisfaction levels are enhanced. Because expectancy levels tend to change in the direction of the reinforcement received in the past (Blau 1964), a high level of satisfaction should reinforce if not heighten levels of expectations (C16) in the exchange (Frazier 1983). High levels of equity and satisfaction obviously are needed for the JIT exchange to be successful.

Table 37-3 is an overview of the research propositions developed herein on the factors likely to influence the success of JIT exchanges.

SUMMARY AND DISCUSSION

An understanding of exchange relationships lies at the core of the marketing discipline. We attempt to extend understanding of the exchange relationships between OEMs and suppliers of component parts-materials by bringing together several important streams of research, including the transaction cost analysis, resource-dependence, political economies, and relational exchange perspectives.

Table 37-3
Propositions Relating to the Success of Initiated JIT Exchanges

Implementation Stage

The success of the JIT exchange is enhanced when:

P_1:   The JIT exchange agreement is reasonably formalized, oriented toward self-regulation, and fair to each firm.

P_2:   The supplier and OEM have realistic expectations of their respective responsibilities, role performance, and the outcomes of the exchange.

P_3:   The firms use their levels of power in a noncoercive, problem-solving way and do not abuse the other firm.

P_4:   A large number of committed personnel in both firms are involved in the operation of the JIT exchange and develop strong personal bonds in the process.

P_5:   The role performance of each firm is high or at least improving.

P_6:   Positive norms or rules of conduct develop in the relationship.

P_7:   High levels of cooperation are present in the exchange.

P_8:   Conflicts are infrequent and those that do develop are brought into the open and effectively resolved.

P_9:   High levels of trust develop between the personnel of the two firms.

Review Stage

The success of the JIT exchange is enhanced when:

P_1:   Standards of comparison are realistic.

P_2:   The performance appraisal process is well specified and done frequently in a joint way.

P_3:   The exchange is perceived to be equitable in terms of the inputs and outputs of each firm.

P_4:   Satisfaction levels are high in each firm.

We begin by clarifying what a JIT exchange entails and how exchanges compare with market exchanges and traditional relational exchange in terms of their characteristics. This discussion is the foundation for the development of conceptual frameworks focusing on (1) the conditions conducive to the initiation of JIT exchanges and (2) the factors likely to influence the success or failure of initiated JIT exchanges.

The question of why organizations engage in specific forms of exchange relationships is a crucial one, as underscored by Bagozzi (1979). Williamson's (1975, 1985) transaction cost analysis (TCA) addresses this question and makes predictions of when market exchanges or hierarchical exchanges will occur. Though transaction cost analysis is an excellent framework that helps contribute to our understanding of organizational issues, some researchers have noted that it is limited in both depth and scope. For example, Harrigan (1983) argues that TCA ignores the strategic planning of the firm and the firm's drive to achieve a competitive advantage. Further, Heide and John (1988) suggest that TCA is incomplete in its ability to explain interdependencies among firms within an interorganizational system (also see Robins 1987). Of crucial importance is the fact that the relational form of exchange is not addressed to any degree by the TCA approach.

The framework in Figure 37-1 includes the main constructs of transaction cost analysis, as well as important constructs suggested from the political economies (Achrol, Reve, and Stern 1983; Stern and Reve 1980) and resource-dependence frameworks (Pfeffer and Salancik 1978). The end result of this integration of different perspectives appears to be a deepening of our understanding of when JIT exchanges, a form of relational exchange, are most appropriate.

Also important is our effort to develop a framework (Figure 37-2) that examines factors influencing the success or failure of initiated JIT exchanges. Even when the underlying conditions are right for a JIT exchange (Figure 37-1), it is not guaranteed to succeed, especially if the OEM and supplier lack the level of commitment necessary to execute a JIT exchange, have unrealistic expectations about what a JIT exchange can accomplish in a short period of time, and take an adversarial approach in the relationship. Again, elements from several research perspectives are integrated in Figure 37-2.

We hope our article will stimulate a variety of research efforts in the industrial marketing field. Empirical studies are needed to examine thoroughly the propositions developed here. None of the propositions can be accepted at this time because of the lack of empirical testing. Moreover, comparative studies contrasting traditional suppliers of component parts-materials with JIT suppliers of the same goods have the potential to make a major contribution. It would also be very useful to examine the "coping behaviors" of firms that are displaced by the trend to JIT, both suppliers not selected in the screening process and nonadopter OEMs. Theoretical research is needed to deepen and extend the frameworks we propose. The framework in Figure 37-1 can be extended to indicate when market exchanges, traditional relational ex-

changes, and hierarchical exchanges are most appropriate for firms to use. Future research also must address such questions as: How should the supplier's marketing function be organized to serve JIT customers? Which strategies are effective in breaking up JIT relationships established by competitors? How do the benefits and costs of a JIT relationship change over the course of its life cycle? Such research has the potential to contribute significantly to our understanding of exchanges of component parts-materials between suppliers and OEMs in industrial markets.

As many U.S. industrial firms strive to improve profitability by reducing the total costs of material acquisition and improving productivity, greater attention is being paid to JIT exchanges as one possible solution to the problem of gaining competitive advantage. Unfortunately, practitioners have many misconceptions about what constitutes JIT exchanges and the actions required on the part of OEMs and suppliers to implement them. More specifically and as pointed out by Schonberger (1982a), many practitioners have been slow to grasp fully the marketing implications of JIT exchange relationships and have viewed JIT only as an alternative production-delivery system. Our detailed description of JIT exchanges may prove useful to marketing managers in clarifying what JIT exchanges entail. Moreover, the frameworks developed here will raise issues that should be considered by managers in (1) deciding which form of exchange to use for given parts-materials and (2) attempting to implement JIT exchanges successfully. (Again, we emphasize that none of the propositions we offer can be accepted straightforwardly because of their preliminary nature.) Given the costs (both concrete and psychological), the potential loss of decision autonomy, and the increased interdependence between the OEM and the supplier in JIT exchanges, one must weigh very carefully the need for a JIT exchange and whether it does, in fact, make sense.

At the present time, the major stumbling block to the success of the JIT exchange appears to be the ability (or inability) of OEMs and suppliers to work together as full partners. For a JIT exchange to prosper, a strong, collaborative interfirm relationship is needed. In the past, many OEMs have seen JIT exchanges primarily as a way to get their suppliers to assume some of their inventory burden and to get lower prices (cf. Cunningham 1986; Hutchins 1986). Many suppliers see JIT exchanges as a "quick fix" and as a way to ensure high levels of sales volume over time (cf. *Purchasing* 1986b). Such viewpoints and behaviors invariably cause the JIT exchange to fail. Both the OEM and the supplier must be prepared to devote resources not only to meet the tangible requirements of the JIT system, but also to build the commitment and trust necessary for a strong JIT exchange to be established. JIT exchanges appear to be the ideal setting for implementation of the marketing concept (from both sides) because of each firm's desire to familiarize the other firm with its needs and business operations.

Finally, we note again that exchanges of component parts-materials have received relatively little attention in the marketing literature (Kotler 1984). Most conceptual frameworks and theories in marketing treat such goods as a relatively simple and uninteresting product category. As a case in point, component parts-materials commonly are classified as convenience items requiring low effort in the purchase decision and low risk (cf. Murphy and Enis 1986). Moreover, these products generally are talked about as fitting into the straight rebuy part of the buyclass framework (cf. Ames and Hlavacek 1984). The concepts of buying centers and selling centers typically are seen as being much more applicable to and important in other product categories, such as capital equipment or minor equipment (cf. Hutt and Speh 1984; Johnston and Bonoma 1981; Spekman and Johnston 1986). The personal selling and salesforce manage-

ment literatures have concentrated more on products and services requiring significant "creative selling" efforts, so to speak. These views appear generally correct if applied to market exchanges of component parts-materials. They do not apply to JIT exchanges of such goods. The JIT system is revolutionizing the ways in which component parts-materials are being exchanged between OEMs and suppliers in industrial markets. Consequently, our marketing frameworks and theories must be adjusted to take into account such changes.

CONCLUSION

The general purpose of this article is to extend our understanding of the exchange relationships between OEMs and suppliers of component parts-materials. Because of the formative stage of research in this area, we contrast JIT exchanges with other forms of interfirm exchange and develop frameworks focusing on the conditions under which JIT exchange relationships are likely to be initiated and successfully implemented. Propositions are developed that warrant empirical inquiry. Practically, we try to provide useful insights into how and why JIT exchanges emerge, evolve, grow, or fail. Our hope is that the article will stimulate thought, debate, and empirical research that will contribute to a greater understanding of OEM-supplier exchange relationships in the future.

APPENDIX A
DEFINITIONS OF CONSTRUCTS
IN FIGURE 37-1

Interest Stage

- *External economy (C1):* The prevailing and prospective economic environment faced by the firm (Stern and Reve 1980).
- *External polity (C2):* The external sociopolitical system in which the OEM operates; it

is primarily described by the distribution and use of power by competitors, suppliers, customers, government agencies, etc. (Stern and Reve 1980).

- *Market position and aspirations of the OEM (C3):* The OEM's current market standing in its industry, the trend in its market standing, and the magnitude of the goals it has set for the future.
- *Decision-making uncertainty (C4):* The degree to which future states of the world cannot be anticipated and accurately predicted (Pfeffer and Salancik 1978).
- *Internal economic structure and processes (C5):* The form of exchange relationship currently used by the OEM to satisfy its need for the part-material, as well as its level of interest in other forms of exchange not currently used (Stern and Reve 1980).
- *Part-material (C6) and end-product characteristics (C7):* Characteristics of the part-material and end-product on which the OEM is focusing attention.

Initiation-Rejection Stage

- *Transaction-specific investments (C8):* Investments that are highly specialized to the buyer-seller exchange and not easily redeployed, if at all, should the exchange fail (Williamson 1975, 1985).
- *Transaction costs (C9):* The costs associated with running a relationship (Williamson 1975, 1985); that is, they encompass the costs associated with negotiating, implementing, coordinating, monitoring, adjusting, enforcing, and terminating exchange agreements (also see Macneil 1980; Walker and Weber 1987).
- *Search and evaluation (C10):* The way in which the OEM gathers and analyzes information relating to the JIT exchange.
- *Availability of potential exchange partners (C11):* The number of eligible suppliers available for establishing a JIT exchange.

- *Strategic vulnerability (C12):* The degree to which the OEM perceives it will be at risk and will severely limit its strategic options if it enters a particular form of exchange relationship (Porter 1985).
- *Level of financial resources (C13):* The working capital and borrowing capacity of the OEM.
- *Exchange relationship decision (C14):* The OEM's decision whether or not to establish a JIT exchange.

APPENDIX B
DEFINITIONS OF CONSTRUCTS IN FIGURE 37-2

Implementation Stage

- *JIT exchange agreement (C15):* The nature of the JIT agreement between the supplier and OEM in terms of its formalization, contractual solidarity, and fairness.
- *Expectations (C16):* What the firms consider reasonable to anticipate in terms of behaviors and outcomes from the JIT exchange relationship.
- *Exchange and interaction (C17):* The way in which the firms communicate with one another and perform their respective roles (Frazier 1983).
- *Internal sociopolitical structure (C18):* The pattern of power-dependence relations in the exchange relationship (Stern and Reve 1980).
- *Norm development (C19):* The way in which rules of conduct and expected patterns of behavior become part of the culture of the OEM-supplier relationship (Lipset 1975).
- *Internal sociopolitical processes (C20):* The dominant sentiments and behaviors in the form of cooperation and conflict that characterize the interactions between the supplier and OEM in the JIT relationship (Stern and Reve 1980).
- *Outcomes (C21):* The results or consequences of conducting the JIT exchange.

Review Stage

- *Standards of comparison (C22):* The base measures by which the firms judge the outcomes of the JIT exchange (Anderson and Narus 1984).
- *Performance appraisal (C23):* The system-process used in judging the outcomes of the JIT exchange.
- *Equity (C24):* The degree to which the JIT exchange is perceived to be just, impartial, and fair.
- *Satisfaction (C25):* A party's affective state of feeling adequately or inadequately rewarded for the sacrifice undergone in facilitating an exchange relationship (Howard and Sheth 1969).

NOTES

1. Because the shipment quantity and delivery scheduling must be exactly coordinated if the JIT exchange is to work, the supplier's physical proximity to the OEM is a major issue. Many OEMs establish a "boundary" within which potential suppliers or their plants-warehouses must be located. In some instances, proximity can be gained through computer networks and related information technologies (cf. Cash and Konsynski 1985).

2. Keeping lot sizes as small as possible also helps to level demand rates for parts and materials, smooth capacity requirements, and shorten lead times. As a result, it becomes feasible for the OEM to fill individual customer orders for several different models from the production line rather than from inventories. The potential impact on customer service levels is obvious.

3. A true JIT exchange relationship is adopted and implemented only when all of the above features are a part of it. Many firms mislabel the systems they establish as JIT systems when only a few aspects of JIT (e.g. blanket contracts, improved delivery schedules, direct order entry) are actually being adopted and implemented (cf. *Purchasing* 1986a, b).

4. Marketing-sales personnel in the supplier organization often are involved in coordinating communications and behaviors with the OEM in a JIT relationship (cf. O'Neal 1986). Moreover, members of the marketing-sales group of the OEM also are frequently involved because of their experience in interfirm dealings and the implications that JIT exchanges have for marketing the OEM's end-products.

5. The drive to sole sourcing is perhaps the most dramatic change in interfirm relationships in industrial markets brought about by the adoption and implementation of JIT exchanges for component parts-materials. It will most certainly influence industry structure over time. Whether or not it leads to further industry concentration and a reduced supplier base is unclear, given that OEMs frequently look for small local suppliers with which to establish JIT exchanges (cf. Hahn, Pinto, and Bragg 1983).

6. A possible exception to this argument can be cited. In certain cases, an OEM may align with a supplier that is larger and more powerful than it is. The OEM's motivation to do so appears to be based on two interrelated factors. First, the potential benefits of a "strategic alliance" with a large and powerful supplier may be worth the inherent risks in certain instances (Porter 1985). Certain large suppliers may offer both a part-material and value-added services that will make the OEM's end-product extremely attractive to end-users. Second, a very high level of trust between the OEM and the large supplier may mitigate the risks of a power imbalance from the OEM's point of view. Extremely high levels of trust may offset potential weaknesses of any exchange relationship (Dwyer, Schurr, and Oh 1987). The degree to which more OEMs establish JIT exchanges with smaller (larger) and less (more) powerful suppliers is an important issue for future research.

7. One factor not addressed in Figure 37-1 is the consideration by the OEM of other concurrent JIT exchange relationships. Because of synergy and certain production linkages, for instance, an OEM might consider initiating JIT exchanges across a number of component parts-materials involving several different suppliers. Clearly, the decision to initiate a JIT exchange for one component part-material

with one supplier will be influenced by the presence or possibility of other JIT exchanges. As the OEM grows in its ability to manage multiple JIT exchanges, this factor is likely to decrease in importance.

8. Realistic expectations appear to be more critical in JIT exchanges than in other forms of interfirm exchange because the exploration phase of a JIT exchange is somewhat constrained. Dwyer, Schurr, and Oh (1987) point out that the exploration phase involves a "feeling out" period in the relationship during which minimal investment and interdependence make termination simple. The nature of the JIT exchange requires a relatively high level of investment and interdependence from the start. Therefore, the luxury of slowing forming expectations is lacking in a JIT exchange.

9. Empirical results of Frazier and Summers (1986), based on a study conducted in a franchise channel of distribution, suggest that if long-term cooperation is an important element of the exchange relationship, firms with a high power advantage will tend to use relatively non-coercive strategies in their interfirm influence attempts. Whether or not this tendency applies to OEM-supplier relationships in JIT exchanges is an important issue for future research.

REFERENCES

Achrol, Ravi, Torger Reve, and Louis Stern, "The Environment of Marketing Channel Dyads: A Framework for Comparative Analysis," *Journal of Marketing*, 47 (Fall), 55–67.

Adams, J. Stacey and Sara Freedman (1976), "Equity Theory Revisited: Comments and Annotated Bibliography," in *Advances in Experimental Social Psychology*, Vol. 9, L. Berkowitz and E. Walster, eds. New York: Academic Press, Inc., 43–90.

Alderson, Wroe (1965), *Marketing Behavior and Executive Action*. Homewood, IL: Richard D. Irwin, Inc.

Aldrich, Howard (1979), *Organizations and Environments*. Englewood Cliffs, NJ: Prentice-Hall, Inc.

Ames, B. Charles and James Hlavacek (1984), *Managerial Marketing for Industrial Firms*. New York: Random House.

Anderson, Erin (1985), "The Salesperson as Outside Agent or Employee: A Transaction Cost Analysis," *Marketing Science*, 4 (Summer), 234–54.

_____ and Anne Coughlin (1987), "International Expansion via Independent or Integrated Channels of Distribution," *Journal of Marketing*, 51 (January), 71–82.

Anderson, James and James Narus (1984), "A Model of the Distributor's Perspective of Distributor-Manufacturer Working Relationships," *Journal of Marketing*, 48 (Fall), 62–74.

Bacharach, Samuel and Edward Lawler (1980), *Power and Politics in Organizations*. San Francisco: Jossey-Bass Publishers.

Bagozzi, Richard (1975), "Marketing as Exchange," *Journal of Marketing*, 39 (October), 32–9.

_____ (1979), "Toward a Formal Theory of Marketing Exchanges," in *Conceptual and Theoretical Developments in Marketing*, O. C. Ferrell, Stephen Brown, and Charles Lamb, eds. Chicago: American Marketing Association, 431–7.

Bartholomew, Dean (1984), "The Vendor-Customer Relationship Today," *Production and Inventory Management* (2nd Quarter), 106–21.

Bertrand, Kate (1986), "The Just-in-Time Mandate," *Business Marketing* (November), 44–56.

Blau, Peter (1964), *Exchange and Power in Social Life*. New York: John Wiley & Sons, Inc.

Blumstein, Philip and Eugene Weinstein (1969), "The Redress of Distributive Injustice," *American Journal of Sociology*, 74 (January), 408–18.

Buzzell, Robert (1983), "Is Vertical Integration Profitable," *Harvard Business Review*, 61 (January–February), 92–102.

Cash, James and B. Konsynski (1985), "IS Redraws Competitive Boundaries," *Harvard Business Review*, 63 (March–April), 134–42.

Child, J. (1972), "Organizational Structure, Environment and Performance: The Role of Strategic Choice," *Sociology*, 6 (January), 2–22.

Cunningham, William (1986), "Some Potential Problems in Just-in-Time Inventory Systems: An Initial Investigation," *Business Insights*, 2 (Fall), 20–2.

Duncan, R. (1972), "Characteristics of Organizational Environments and Perceived Environmental Uncertainty," *Administrative Science Quarterly*, 17 (September), 313–27.

Dwyer, F. Robert, Paul Schurr, and Sejo Oh (1987), "Developing Buyer-Seller Relationships," *Journal of Marketing*, 51 (April), 11–27.

———— and Orville C. Walker, Jr. (1981), "Bargaining in an Asymmetrical Power Structure," *Journal of Marketing*, 45 (Winter), 104–15.

———— and M. Ann Welsh (1985), "Environmental Relationships of the Internal Political Economy of Marketing Channels," *Journal of Marketing Research*, 22 (November), 397–414.

Emerson, Richard (1962), "Power-Dependence Relations," *American Sociological Review*, 27 (February), 31–41.

Etgar, Michael (1977), "Channel Environment and Channel Leadership," *Journal of Marketing Research*, 15 (February), 69–76.

Foa, Uriel and Edna Foa (1974), *Societal Structures of the Mind.* Springfield, IL: Charles C Thomas.

Frazier, Gary (1983), "Interorganizational Exchange Behavior in Marketing Channels: A Broadened Perspective," *Journal of Marketing*, 47 (Fall), 68–78.

———— (1984), "The Interfirm Power-Influence Process Within a Marketing Channel," in *Research in Marketing*, Vol. 7, Jagdish Sheth, ed. Greenwich, CT: JAI Press, Inc., 63–91.

———— and John Summers (1984), "Interfirm Influence Strategies and Their Application within Distribution Channels," *Journal of Marketing*, 48 (Summer), 38–48.

———— and ———— (1986), "Perceptions of Interfirm Power and Its Use within a Franchise Channel of Distribution," *Journal of Marketing Research*, 23 (May), 169–76.

Gaski, John and John Nevin (1985), "The Differential Effects of Exercised and Unexercised Power Sources in a Marketing Channel," *Journal of Marketing Research*, 22 (May), 130–42.

Hahn, Chan, Peter Pinto, and Daniel Bragg (1983), "Just-in-Time Production and Purchasing," *Journal of Purchasing and Materials Management*, 19 (Fall), 2–10.

Hall, Robert (1983), *Zero Inventories.* Homewood, IL: Dow Jones–Irwin.

Harrigan, Katherine (1983). *Strategies for Vertical Integration.* Lexington, MA: Lexington Books.

Hay, Edward (1984), "Reduce Any Set-Up by 75%," in *APICS Zero Inventory Philosophy and Practices Seminar Proceedings* (October). St. Louis: American Production and Inventory Control Society, 173–8.

Hayes, Robert (1981), "Why Japanese Factories Work," *Harvard Business Review*, 59 (July–August), 57–66.

Heide, Jan and George John (1988), "The Role of Dependence Balancing in Safeguarding Transaction-Specific Assets in Conventional Channels," *Journal of Marketing*, 52 (January), 20–35.

Howard, John and Jagdish Sheth (1969), *The Theory of Buyer Behavior.* New York: John Wiley & Sons, Inc.

Hunt, Shelby (1983), "General Theories and the Fundamental Explananda of Marketing," *Journal of Marketing*, 47 (Fall), 9–17.

———— and John Nevin (1974), "Power in a Channel of Distribution: Sources and Consequences," *Journal of Marketing Research*, 11 (May) 186–93.

Hutchins, Dexter (1986), "Having a Hard Time with Just-in-Time," *Fortune* (June 9), 64–6.

Hutt, Michael and Thomas Speh (1984), "The Marketing Strategy Center: Diagnosing the Industrial Marketer's Interdisciplinary Role," *Journal of Marketing*, 48 (Fall), 53–61.

Jackson, Barbara (1985), *Winning and Keeping Industrial Customers.* Lexington, MA: Lexington Books.

John, George (1984), "An Empirical Investigation of Some Antecedents of Opportunism in a Marketing Channel," *Journal of Marketing*, 45 (Summer), 143–56.

Johnston, Wesley and Thomas Bonoma (1981), "The Buying Center: Structure and Interaction Patterns," *Journal of Marketing*, 45 (Summer), 143–56.

Kerr, Steve (1975), "On the Folly of Rewarding A While Hoping for B," *Academy of Management Journal*, 18 (December), 769–83.

Kiesler, C. and S. Kiesler (1969), *Conformity.* Reading, MA: Addison-Wesley Publishing Company.

————, S. Kiesler, and M. Pollak (1967), "The Effect of Commitment to Future Interaction on Reactions to Norm Violations," *Journal of Personality*, 35 (December), 585–99.

Kotler, Philip (1972), "A Generic Concept of Marketing," *Journal of Marketing*, 36 (April), 46–54.

———— (1984), *Marketing Management*, 5th ed. Englewood Cliffs, NJ: Prentice-Hall, Inc.

Lilien, Gary (1979), "Advisor 2: Modeling the Marketing Mix Decisions for Industrial Products," *Management Science*, 25 (February), 191–204.

Lipset, S. (1975), "Social Structure and Social Change," in *Approaches to the Study of Social Structure*, P. Blau, ed. New York: The Free Press.

Lusch, Robert (1976), "Sources of Power: Their Impact on Intrachannel Conflict," *Journal of Marketing Research*, 13 (November), 382–90.

Macneil, Ian (1980), *The New Social Contract: An Inquiry into Modern Contractual Relations*. New Haven, CT: Yale University Press.

Manoocheri, G. (1984), "Suppliers and the Just-in-Time Concept," *Journal of Purchasing and Materials Management*, 20 (Winter), 16–21.

Murphy, Patrick and Ben Enis (1986), "Classifying Products Strategically," *Journal of Marketing*, 50 (July), 24–42.

O'Neal, Charles (1986), "Customer-Supplier Relationships for Just-in-Time," *Journal of Computer Integrated Manufacturing Management*, 2 (Spring), 33–40.

Ouchi, William (1980) "Markets, Bureaucracies, and Clans," *Administrative Science Quarterly*, 25 (March), 129–42.

Pfeffer, Jeffrey and Gerald Salancik (1978), *The External Control of Organizations: A Resource-Dependence Perspective*. New York: Harper & Row Publishers, Inc.

Porter, Michael (1985), *Competitive Advantage*. New York: The Free Press.

Pruitt, Dean (1981), *Negotiation Behavior*. New York: Academic Press, Inc.

Purchasing (1985), "American Industry Goes Ape over Just-in-Time Strategy" (September 12), 21–3.

_____ (1986a), "MRO and JIT: How the Pros Pull Them Together" (May 22), 62–8.

_____ (1986b), "Are Distributors Selling JIT or Just-the-Sizzle" (May 22), 73–80.

Reingan, Peter and Arch Woodside (1981), *Buyer-Seller Interactions: Empirical Research and Normative Issues*. Chicago: American Marketing Association.

Robins, James (1987), "Organizational Economics: Notes on the Use of Transaction-Cost Theory in the Study of Organizations," *Administrative Science Quarterly*, 32 (March), 68–87.

Roering, Kenneth (1977), "Bargaining in Distribution Channels," *Journal of Business Research*, 5 (March), 15–26.

Rogers, Everett (1983). *Diffusion of Innovations*, 3rd ed. New York: The Free Press.

Salmond, Deborah (1987), "When and Why Buyers and Suppliers Collaborate: A Resource-Dependence and Efficiency View," unpublished Ph.D. dissertation, College of Business, University of Maryland.

Schonberger, Richard (1982a), *Japanese Manufacturing Techniques*. New York: The Free Press.

_____ (1982b), "Some Observations on the Advantages and Implementations of Issues of Just-in-Time Production Systems," *Journal of Operations Management*, 3 (November), 1–11.

_____ and Abdolhassian Ansari (1984), "Just-in-Time Purchasing Can Improve Quality," *Journal of Purchasing and Materials Management*, 20 (Spring), 2–7.

Schurr, Paul and Julie Ozanne (1985), "Influences on Exchange Processes: Buyers' Preconceptions of a Seller's Trustworthiness and Bargaining Toughness," *Journal of Consumer Research*, 11 (March), 939–53.

Shapiro, Benson (1985), "Towards Effective Supplier Management: International Comparisons," Harvard University Working Paper Series.

Shingo, Shigeo (1985), *Revolution in Manufacturing: SMED*. Cambridge, MA: Productivity Press.

Spekman, Robert and Wesley Johnston (1986), "Relationship Management: Managing the Selling and Buying Interface," *Journal of Business Research*, 14 (December), 519–33.

Stern, Louis and Torger Reve (1980), "Distribution Channels as Political Economies: A Framework for Comparative Analysis," *Journal of Marketing*, 44 (Summer), 52–64.

_____ and Adel El-Ansary (1988), *Marketing Channels*, 3rd ed. Englewood Cliffs, NJ: Prentice-Hall, Inc.

Thibaut, John and Harold Kelley (1959), *The Social Psychology of Groups*. New York: John Wiley & Sons, Inc.

Vyas, Niren and Arch Woodside (1984), "An Inductive Model of Industrial Supplier Choice Processes," *Journal of Marketing*, 48 (Winter), 30–45.

Walker, Gordon and David Weber (1987), "Supplier Competition, Uncertainty, and Make-or-Buy Decisions," *Academy of Management Journal*, 30 (September), 589–96.

Webster, Frederick and Yoram Wind (1972), "A General Model of Organizational Buying Behavior," *Journal of Marketing*, 36 (April), 12–19.

Williamson, Oliver (1975), *Markets and Hierarchies: Analysis and Antitrust Implications*. New York: The Free Press.

_____ (1985), *The Economic Institutions of Capitalism*. New York: The Free Press.

◆

The Marketing Audit Comes of Age

Philip Kotler, William Gregor, and William Rogers

Comparing the marketing strategies and tactics of business units today versus ten years ago, the most striking impression is one of marketing strategy obsolescence. Ten years ago U.S. automobile companies were gearing up for their second postwar race to produce the largest car with the highest horsepower. Today companies are selling increasing numbers of small and medium-size cars and fuel economy is a major selling point. Ten years ago computer companies were introducing ever-more powerful hardware for more sophisticated uses. Today they emphasize mini- and micro-computers and software.

It is not even necessary to take a ten-year-period to show the rapid obsolescence of marketing strategies. The growth economy of 1950–1970 has been superseded by a volatile economy which produces new strategic surprises almost monthly. Competitors launch new products, customers switch their business, distributors lose their effectiveness, advertising costs skyrocket, government regulations are announced, and consumer groups attack. These changes represent both opportunities and problems and may demand periodic reorientations of the company's marketing operations.

Many companies feel that their marketing operations need regular reviews and overhauls but do not know how to proceed. Some companies simply make many small changes that are economically and politically feasible, but fail to got to the heart of the matter. True, the company develops an annual marketing plan but management normally does not take a deep and objective look at the marketing strategies, policies, organizations, and operations on a recurrent basis. At the other extreme, companies install aggressive new top marketing management hoping to shake down the marketing cobwebs. In between there must be more orderly ways to reorient marketing operations to changed environments and opportunities.

Reprinted from "The Marketing Audit Comes of Age," by Philip Kotler, William Gregor, and William Rogers, *Sloan Management Review*, Vol. 18, No. 2, pp. 25–43, by permission of the publisher. Copyright © 1977 by the Sloan Management Review Association. All rights reserved.

ENTER THE MARKETING AUDIT

One hears more talk today about the *marketing audit* as being the answer to evaluating marketing practice just as the public accounting audit is the tool for evaluating company accounting practice. This might lead one to conclude that the marketing audit is a new idea and also a very distinct methodology. Neither of these conclusions is true.

The marketing audit as an idea dates back to the early fifties. Rudolph Dallmeyer, a former executive in Booz-Allen-Hamilton, remembers conducting marketing audits as early as 1952. Robert J. Lavidge, President of Elrick and Lavidge, dates his firm's performance of marketing audits to over two decades ago. In 1959, the American Management Association published an excellent set of papers on the marketing audit under the title *Analyzing and Improving Marketing Performance*, Report No. 32, 1959. During the 1960s, the marketing audit received increasing mention in the lists of marketing services of management consultant firms. It was not until the turbulent seventies, however, that it began to penetrate management awareness as a possible answer to its needs.

As for whether the marketing audit has reached a high degree of methodological sophistication, the answer is generally no. Whereas two certified public accountants will handle an audit assignment using approximately the same methodology, two marketing auditors are likely to bring different conceptions of the auditing process to their task. However, a growing consensus on the major characteristics of a marketing audit is emerging and we can expect considerable progress to occur in the next few years.

In its fullest form and concept, a marketing audit has four basic characteristics. The first and most important is that it is *broad* rather than narrow in focus. The term "marketing audit" should be reserved for a *horizontal (or comprehensive) audit* covering the company's marketing environment, objectives, strategies, organization, and systems. In contrast a *vertical (or indepth) audit* occurs when management decides to take a deep look into some key marketing function, such as sales force management. A vertical audit should properly be called by the function that is being audited, such as a sales force audit, an advertising audit, or a pricing audit.

A second characteristic feature of a marketing audit is that it is conducted by someone who is *independent* of the operation that is being evaluated. There is some loose talk about self-audits, where a manager follows a checklist of questions concerning his own operation to make sure that he is touching all the bases.[1] Most experts would agree, however, that the self-audit, while it is always a useful step that a manager should take, does not constitute a *bona fide* audit because it lacks objectivity and independence. Independence can be achieved in two ways. The audit could be an *inside audit* conducted by a person or group inside the company but outside of the operation being evaluated. Or it could be an *outside audit* conducted by a management consulting firm or practitioner.

The third characteristic of a marketing audit is that it is *systematic*. The marketing auditor who decides to interview people inside and outside the firm at random, asking questions as they occur to him, is a "visceral" auditor without a method. This does not mean that he will not come up with very useful findings and recommendations; he may be very insightful. However, the effectiveness of the marketing audit will normally increase to the extent that it incorporates an orderly sequence of diagnostic steps, such as there are in the conduct of a public accounting audit.

A final characteristic that is less intrinsic to a marketing audit but nevertheless desirable is that it be conducted *periodically*. Typically, evaluations of company marketing efforts are commissioned when sales have turned down sharply, sales force morale has fallen, or other problems have occurred at the company. The fact is, however, that companies are thrown into a crisis partly because they have failed to review their assumptions and to change them during good times. A marketing audit conducted when things are going well can often help make a good situation even better and also indicate changes needed to prevent things from turning sour.

The above ideas on a marketing audit can be brought together into a single definition:

> A marketing audit is a *comprehensive, systematic, independent,* and *periodic* examination of a company's—or business unit's—marketing environment, objectives, strategies, and activities with a view of determining problem areas and opportunities and recommending a plan of action to improve the company's marketing performance.

WHAT IS THE MARKETING AUDIT PROCESS?

How is a marketing audit performed? Marketing auditing follows the simple three-step procedure shown in Figure 38-1.

Setting the Objectives and Scope

The first step calls for a meeting between the company officer(s) and a potential auditor to explore the nature of the marketing operations and the potential value of a marketing audit. If the company officer is convinced of the potential benefits of a marketing audit, he and the auditor have to work out an agreement on the objectives, coverage, depth, data sources, report format, and the time period for the audit.

Consider the following actual case. A plumbing and heating supplies wholesaler with three branches invited a marketing consultant to prepare an audit of its overall marketing policies and operations. Four major objectives were set for the audit:

- determine how the market views the company and its competitors,
- recommend a pricing policy,
- develop a product evaluation system,
- determine how to improve the sales activity in terms of the deployment of the sales force, the level and type of compensation, the measurement of performance, and the addition of new salesmen.

Furthermore, the audit would cover the marketing operations of the company as a whole and the operations of each of the three branches, with particular attention to one of the branches. The audit would focus on the marketing operations but also include a review of the purchasing and inventory systems since they intimately affect marketing performance.

The company would furnish the auditor with published and private data on the industry. In addition, the auditor would con-

Figure 38-1
Steps in a Marketing Audit

tact suppliers of manufactured plumbing supplies for additional market data and contact wholesalers outside the company's market area to gain further information on wholesale plumbing and heating operations. The auditor would interview all the key corporate and branch management, sales and purchasing personnel, and would ride with several of those salesmen on their calls. Finally, the auditor would interview a sample of the major plumbing and heating contractor customers in the market areas of the two largest branches.

It was decided that the report format would consist of a draft report of conclusions and recommendations to be reviewed by the president and vice-president of marketing, and then delivered to the executive committee which included the three branch managers. Finally, it was decided that the audit findings would be ready to present within six to eight weeks.

Gathering the Data

The bulk of an auditor's time is spent in gathering data. Although we talk of a single auditor, an audit team is usually involved when the project is large. A detailed plan as to who is to be interviewed by whom, the questions to be asked, the time and place of contact, and so on, has to be carefully prepared so that auditing time and cost are kept to a minimum. Daily reports of the interviews are to be written up and reviewed so that the individual or team can spot new areas requiring exploration, while data are still being gathered.

The cardinal rule in data collection is not to rely solely for data and opinion on those being audited. Customers often turn out to be the key group to interview. Many companies do not really understand how their customers see them and their competitors, nor do they fully understand customer needs. This is vividly demonstrated in Table 38-1, which shows the results of asking end users,

Table 38-1
Factors in the Selection of a Manufacturer

Factor	All Users Rank	Company Salesmen Rank	Company Nonsales Personnel Rank
Reputation	5	①	4
Extension of Credit	9	11	9
Sales Representatives	8	5	7
Technical Support Services	①	△3	6
Literature and Manuals	11	10	11
Prompt Delivery	☐2	4	5
Quick Response to Customer Needs	△3	☐2	△3
Product Price	6	6	①
Personal Relationships	10	7	8
Complete Product Line	7	9	10
Product Quality	4	8	☐2

Source: Marketing and Distribution Audit, A Service of Decision Sciences Corporation, p. 32. Used with permission of the Decision Sciences Corporation.

company salesmen, and company marketing personnel for their views of the importance of different factors affecting the user's selection of a manufacturer. According to the table, customers look first and foremost at the quality of technical support services, followed by prompt delivery, followed by quick response to customer needs. Company salesmen think that company reputation, however, is the most important factor in customer choice, followed by quick response to customer needs and technical support services. Those who plan marketing strategy have a different opinion. They see company price and product quality as the two major factors in buyer choice, followed by quick response to customer needs. Clearly, there is lack of consonance between what buyers say they want, what company salesmen are responding to, and what company marketing planners are emphasizing. One of the major contributions of marketing auditors is to expose those discrepancies and suggest ways to improve marketing consensus.

Preparing and Presenting the Report

The marketing auditor will be developing tentative conclusions as the data come in. It is a sound procedure for him to meet once or twice with the company officer before the data collection ends to outline some initial findings to see what reactions and suggestions they produce.

When the data gathering phase is over, the marketing auditor prepares notes for a visual and verbal presentation to the company officer or small group who hired him. The presentation consists of restating the objectives, showing the main findings, and presenting the major recommendations. Then, the auditor is ready to write the final report, which is largely a matter of putting the visual and verbal material into a good written communication. The company officer(s) will usually ask the auditor to present the report to other groups in the company. If the report calls for deep debate and action, the various groups hearing the report should organize into subcommittees to do follow-up work with another meeting to take place some weeks later. The most valuable part of the marketing audit often lies not so much in the auditor's specific recommendations but in the process that the managers of the company be-

gin to go through to assimilate, debate, and develop their own concept of the needed marketing action.

MARKETING AUDIT PROCEDURES FOR AN INSIDE AUDIT

Companies that conduct internal marketing audits show interesting variations from the procedures just outlined. International Telephone and Telegraph, for example, has a history of forming corporate teams and sending them into weak divisions to do a complete business audit, with a heavy emphasis on the marketing component. Some teams stay on the job, often taking over the management.

General Electric's corporate consulting division offers help to various divisions on their marketing problems. One of its services is a marketing audit in the sense of a broad, independent, systematic look at the marketing picture in a division. However, the corporate consulting division gets few requests for a marketing audit as such. Most of the requests are for specific marketing studies or problem-solving assistance.

The 3M Company uses a very interesting and unusual internal marketing plan audit procedure. A marketing plan audit office with a small staff is located at corporate headquarters. The main purpose of the 3M marketing plan audit is to help the divisional marketing manager improve the marketing planning function, as well as come up with better strategies and tactics. A divisional marketing manager phones the marketing plan audit office and invites an audit. There is an agreement that only he will see the results and it is up to him whether he wants wider distribution.

The audit centers around a marketing plan for a product or product line that the marketing manager is preparing for the coming year. This plan is reviewed at a personal presentation by a special team of six company marketing executives invited by the marketing plan audit office. A new team is formed for each new audit. An effort is made to seek out those persons within 3M (but not in the audited division) who can bring the best experience to bear on the particular plans' problems and opportunities. A team typically consists of a marketing manager from another division, a national salesmanager, a marketing executive with a technical background, a few others close to the type of problems found in the audited plan, and another person who is totally unfamiliar with the market, the product, or the major marketing techniques being used in the plan. This person usually raises some important points others forget to raise, or do not ask because "everyone probably knows about that anyway."

The six auditors are supplied with a summary of the marketing manager's plan about ten days before an official meeting is held to review the plan. On the audit day, the six auditors, the head of the audit office, and the divisional marketing manager gather at 8:30 A.M. The marketing manager makes a presentation for about an hour describing the division's competitive situation, the long-run strategy, and the planned tactics. The auditors proceed to ask hard questions and debate certain points with the marketing manager and each other. Before the meeting ends that day, the auditors are each asked to fill out a marketing plan evaluation form consisting of questions that are accompanied by numerical rating scales and room for comments.

These evaluations are analyzed and summarized after the meeting. Then the head of the audit office arranges a meeting with the divisional marketing manager and presents the highlights of the auditor's findings and recommendations. It is then up to the marketing manager to take the next steps.

COMPONENTS OF THE MARKETING AUDIT

A major principle in marketing audits is to start with the marketplace first and explore the changes that are taking place and what they imply in the way of problems and opportunities. Then the auditor moves to examine the company's marketing objectives and strategies, organization, and systems. Finally he may move to examine one or two key functions in more detail that are central to the marketing performance of that company. However, some companies ask for less than the full range of auditing steps in order to obtain initial results before commissioning further work. The company may ask for a marketing environment audit, and if satisfied, then ask for a marketing strategy audit. Or it might ask for a marketing organization audit first, and later ask for a marketing environment audit.

We view a full marketing audit as having six major components, each having a semiautonomous status if a company wants less than a full marketing audit. The six components and their logical diagnostic sequence are discussed below. The major auditing questions connected with these components are gathered together in Appendix A at the end of this article.

Marketing Environment Audit

By marketing environment, we mean both the *macro-environment* surrounding the industry and the *task environment* in which the organization intimately operates. The macro-environment consists of the large-scale forces and factors influencing the company's future over which the company has very little control. These forces are normally divided into economic-demographic factors, technological factors, political-legal factors, and social-cultural factors. The marketing auditor's task is to assess the key trends and their implications for company marketing action. However, if the company has a good long-range forecasting department, then there is less of a need for a macro-environment audit.

The marketing auditor may play a more critical role in auditing the company's task environment. The task environment consists of markets, customers, competitors, distributors and dealers, suppliers, and marketing facilitators. The marketing auditor can make a contribution by going out into the field and interviewing various parties to assess their current thinking and attitudes and bringing them to the attention of management.

Marketing Strategy Audit

The marketing auditor then proceeds to consider whether the company's marketing strategy is well-postured in the light of the opportunities and problems facing the company. The starting point for the marketing strategy audit is the corporate goals and objectives followed by the marketing objectives. The auditor may find the objectives to be poorly stated, or he may find them to be well-stated but inappropriate given the company's resources and opportunities. For example, a chemical company had set a sales growth objective for a particular product line at 15 percent. However, the total market showed no growth and competition was fierce. Here the author questioned the basic sales growth objective for that product line. He proposed that the product line be reconsidered for a maintenance or harvest objective at best and that the company should look for growth elsewhere.

Even when a growth objective is warranted, the auditor will want to consider whether management has chosen the best strategy to achieve that growth.

Marketing Organization Audit

A complete marketing audit would have to cover the question of the effectiveness of the marketing and sales organization, as well as the quality of interaction between marketing and other key management functions such as manufacturing, finance, purchasing, and research and development.

At critical times, a company's marketing organization must be reviewed to achieve greater effectiveness within the company and in the marketplace. Companies without product management systems will want to consider introducing them, companies with these systems may want to consider dropping them, or trying product teams instead. Companies may want to redefine the role concept of a product manager from being a promotional manager (concerned primarily with volume) to a business manager (concerned primarily with profit). There is the issue of whether decision-making responsibility should be moved up from the brand level to the product level. There is the perennial question of how to make the organization more market-responsive including the possibility of replacing product divisions with market-centered divisions. Finally, sales organizations often do not fully understand marketing. In the words of one vice-president of marketing: "It takes about five years for us to train sales managers to think marketing."

Marketing Systems Audit

A full marketing audit then turns to examine the various systems being used by marketing management to gather information, plan, and control the marketing operation. The issue is not the company's marketing strategy or organization per se but rather the procedures used in some or all of the following systems: sales forecasting, sales goal and quota setting, marketing planning, marketing control, inventory control, order processing, physical distribution, new products development, and product pruning.

The marketing audit may reveal that marketing is being carried on without adequate systems of planning, implementation, and control. An audit of a consumer products division of a large company revealed that decisions about which products to carry and which to eliminate were made by the head of the division on the basis of his intuitive feeling with little information or analysis to guide the decisions. The auditor recommended the introduction of a new product screening system for new products and an improved sales control system for existing products. He also observed that the division prepared budgets but did not carry out formal marketing planning and hardly any research into the market. He recommended that the division establish a formal marketing planning system as soon as possible.

Marketing Productivity Audit

A full marketing audit also includes an effort to examine key accounting data to determine where the company is making its real profits and what, if any, marketing costs could be trimmed. Decision Sciences Corporation, for example, starts its marketing audit by looking at the accounting figures on sales and associated costs of sales. Using marketing cost accounting principles,[2] it seeks to measure the marginal profit contribution of different products, end user segments, marketing channels, and sales territories.

We might argue that the firm's own controller or accountant should do the job of providing management with the results of marketing cost analysis. A handful of firms have created the job position of marketing controllers who report to financial controllers and spend their time looking at the productivity and validity of various marketing costs. Where an organization is doing a good job of marketing cost analysis, it does not need a marketing auditor to study the same. But most companies do not do careful marketing cost analysis. Here a marketing auditor can pay his way by simply exposing certain economic and cost relations which indicate waste or conceal unexploited marketing opportunities.

Zero-based budgeting[3] is another tool for investigating and improving marketing productivity. In normal budgeting, top management allots to each business unit a percentage increase (or decrease) of what it got last time. The question is not raised whether that basic budget level still makes sense. The manager of an operation should be asked what he would basically need if he started his operation from scratch and what it would cost. What would he need next and what would it cost? In this way, a budget is built from the ground up reflecting the true needs of the operation. When this was applied to a technical sales group within a large industrial goods company, it became clear that the company had three or four extra technical salesmen on its payroll. The manager admitted to the redundancy but argued if a business upturn came, these men would be needed to tap the potential. In the meantime, they were carried on the payroll for two years in the expectation of a business upturn.

Marketing Function Audit

The work done to this point might begin to point to certain key marketing functions which are performing poorly. The auditor might spot, for example, sales force problems that go very deep. Or he might observe that advertising budgets are prepared in an arbitrary fashion and such things as advertising themes, media, and timing are not evaluated for their effectiveness. In these and other cases, the issue becomes one of notifying management of the desirability of one or more marketing function audits if management agrees.

WHICH COMPANIES CAN BENEFIT MOST FROM A MARKETING AUDIT?

All companies can benefit from a competent audit of their marketing operations. However, a marketing audit is likely to yield the highest payoff in the following companies and situations:

Production-Oriented and Technical-Oriented Companies. Many manufacturing companies have their start in a love affair with a certain product. Further products are added that appeal to the technical interests of management, usually with insufficient attention paid to their market potential. The feeling in these companies is that marketing is paid to sell what the company decides to make. After some failures with its "better mousetraps," management starts getting interested in shifting to a market orientation. But this calls for more than a simple declaration by top management to study and serve the customer's needs. It calls for a great number of organizational and attitudinal changes that must be introduced carefully and convincingly. An auditor can perform an important service in recognizing that a company's problem lies in its production orientation, and in guiding management toward a market orientation.

Troubled Divisions. Multidivision companies usually have some troubled divisions. Top management may decide to use an auditor to assess the situation in a troubled division rather than rely solely on the division management's interpretation of the problem.

High Performing Divisions. Multidivision companies might want an audit of their top dollar divisions to make sure that they are reaching their highest potential, and are not on the verge of a sudden reversal. Such an audit may also yield insights into how to improve marketing in other divisions.

Young Companies. Marketing audits of emerging small companies or young divisions of large companies can help to lay down a solid marketing approach at a time when management faces a great degree of market inexperience.

Nonprofit Organizations. Administrators of colleges, museums, hospitals, social agencies, and churches are beginning to think in marketing terms, and the marketing audit can serve a useful educational as well as diagnostic purpose.

WHAT ARE THE PROBLEMS AND PITFALLS OF MARKETING AUDITS?

While the foregoing has stressed the positive aspects of marketing audits and their utility in a variety of situations, it is important to note some of the problems and pitfalls of the marketing audit process. Problems can occur in the objective-setting step, the data collection step, or the report presentation step.

Setting Objectives

When the marketing audit effort is being designed by the auditor and the company officer who commissioned the audit, several problems will be encountered. For one thing, the objectives set for the audit are based upon the company officer's and auditor's best *a priori* notions of what the key problem areas are for the audit to highlight. However, new problem areas may emerge once the auditor begins to learn more about the company. The original set of objectives should not constrain the auditor from shifting his priorities of investigation.

Similarly, it may be necessary for the auditor to use different sources of information than envisioned at the start of the audit. In some cases this may be because some information sources he had counted on became unavailable. In one marketing audit, the auditor had planned to speak to a sample of customers for the company's electro-mechanical devices, but the company officer who hired him would not permit him to do so. In other cases, a valuable new source of information may arise that was not recognized at the start of the audit. For example, the auditor for an air brake system manufacturer found as a valuable source of market intelligence a long-established manufacturers' representatives firm that approached the company after the audit had begun.

Another consideration at the objective-setting stage of the audit is that the management most affected by the audit must have full knowledge of the purposes and scope of the audit. Audits go much more smoothly when the executive who calls in the auditor either brings the affected management into the design stage, or at least has a general introductory meeting where the auditor explains his procedures and answers questions from the people in the affected business.

Data Collection

Despite reassurances by the auditor and the executive who brought him in, there will still be some managers in the affected business who will feel threatened by the auditor. The auditor must expect this, and realize that an individual's fears and biases may color his statements in an interview.

From the onset of the audit, the auditor must guarantee and maintain confidentiality of each individual's comments. In many audits, personnel in the company will see the audit as a vehicle for unloading their negative feelings about the company or other individuals. The auditor can learn a lot from these comments, but he must protect the individuals who make them. The auditor must question interviewees in a highly professional manner to build their confidence in him, or else they will not be entirely honest in their statements.

Another area of concern during the information collection step is the degree to which the company executive who brought in the auditor will try to guide the audit. It will be necessary for this officer and the auditor to strike a balance in which the executive provides some direction, but not too much. While overcontrol is the more likely excess of the executive, it is possible to undercontrol. When the auditor and the company executive do not have open and frequent lines of communication during the audit, it is possible that the auditor may place more emphasis on some areas and less on others than the executive might have desired. Therefore, it is the responsibility of both the auditor and the executive who brought him in to communicate frequently during the audit.

Report Presentation

One of the biggest problems in marketing auditing is that the executive who brings in the auditor, or the people in the business being audited, may have higher expectations about what the audit will do for the company than the actual report seems to offer. In only the most extreme circumstances will the auditor develop surprising panaceas or propose startling new opportunities for the company. More likely, the main value of his report will be that it places priorities on ideas and directions for the company, many of which have already been considered by some people within the audited organization. In most successful audits, the auditor, in his recommendations, makes a skillful combination of his general and technical marketing background (e.g., designs of salesman's compensation systems, his ability to measure the size and potential of markets) with some opportunistic ideas that people in the audited organization have already considered, but do not know how much importance to place upon them. However, it is only in the company's implementation of the recommendations that the payoff to the company will come.

Another problem at the conclusion of the audit stems from the fact that most audits seem to result in organizational changes. Organizational changes are a common outcome because the audit usually identifies new tasks to be accomplished and new tasks demand people to do them. One thing the auditor and the executive who brought him in must recognize, however, is that organizational promotions and demotions are exclusively the executive's decision. It is the executive who has to live with the changes once the auditor has gone, not the auditor. Therefore, the executive should not be lulled into thinking that organizational moves are any easier because the auditor may have recommended them.

The final problem, and this is one facing the auditor, is that important parts of an audit may be implemented incorrectly, or not implemented at all, by the executive who commissioned the audit. Non-implementation of key parts of the audit undermines the whole effectiveness of the audit.

SUMMARY

The marketing audit is one important answer to the problem of evaluating the marketing performance of a company or one of its business units. Marketing audits are distinguished from other marketing exercises in being *comprehensive, independent, systematic,* and *periodic.* A full marketing audit would cover the company's (or division's) external environment objectives, strategies, organization, systems, and functions. If the audit covers only one function, such as sales management or advertising, it is best described as a marketing function audit rather than a marketing audit. If the exercise is to solve a current problem, such as entering a market, setting a price, or developing a package, then it is not an audit at all.

The marketing audit is carried out in three steps: developing an agreement as to objectives and scope; collecting the data; and presenting the report. The audit can be performed by a competent outside consultant or by a company auditing office at headquarters.

The possible findings of an audit include detecting unclear or inappropriate marketing objectives, inappropriate strategies, inappropriate levels of marketing expenditures, needed improvements in organization, and needed improvements in systems for marketing information, planning, and control. Companies that are most likely to benefit from a marketing audit include production-oriented companies, companies with troubled or highly vulnerable divisions, young companies, and nonprofit organizations.

Many companies today are finding that their premises for marketing strategy are growing obsolete in the face of a rapidly changing environment. This is happening to company giants such as General Motors and Sears as well as smaller firms that have not provided a mechanism for recycling their marketing strategy. The marketing audit is not the full answer to marketing strategy recycling but does offer one major mechanism for pursuing this desirable and necessary task.

APPENDIX A—COMPONENTS OF A MARKETING AUDIT

The Marketing Environment Audit

I. *Macro-Environment*

Economic-Demographic
1. What does the company expect in the way of inflation, material shortages, unemployment, and credit availability in the short run, intermediate run, and long run?
2. What effect will forecasted trends in the size, age distribution, and regional distribution of population have on the business?

Technology
1. What major changes are occurring in product technology? In process technology?
2. What are the major generic substitutes that might replace this product?

Political-Legal
1. What laws are being proposed that may affect marketing strategy and tactics?
2. What federal, state, and local agency actions should be watched? What is happening in the areas of pollution control, equal employment opportunity, product safety, advertising, price control, etc., that is relevant to marketing planning?

Social-Cultural
1. What attitudes is the public taking toward business and toward products such as those produced by the company?
2. What changes are occurring in consumer life-styles and values that have a bearing on the company's target markets and marketing methods?

II. *Task Environment*

Markets
1. What is happening to market size, growth, geographical distribution, and profits?
2. What are the major market segments? What are their expected rates of growth? Which are high opportunity and low opportunity segments?

Customers
1. How do current customers and prospects rate the company and its competitors, particularly with respect to reputation, product quality, service, sales force, and price?
2. How do different classes of customers make their buying decisions?
3. What are the evolving needs and satisfactions being sought by the buyers in this market?

Competitors
1. Who are the major competitors? What are the objectives and strategies of each major competitor? What are their strengths and weaknesses? What are the sizes and trends in market shares?
2. What trends can be foreseen in future competition and substitutes for this product?

Distribution and Dealers
1. What are the main trade channels bringing products to customers?
2. What are the efficiency levels and growth potentials of the different trade channels?

Suppliers
1. What is the outlook for the availability of different key resources used in production?

2. What trends are occurring among suppliers in their pattern of selling?

Facilitators
1. What is the outlook for the cost and availability of transportation services?
2. What is the outlook for the cost and availability of warehousing facilities?
3. What is the outlook for the cost and availability of financial resources?
4. How effectively is the advertising agency performing? What trends are occurring in advertising agency services?

Marketing Strategy Audit

Marketing Objectives
1. Are the corporate objectives clearly stated and do they lead logically to the marketing objectives?
2. Are the marketing objectives stated in a clear form to guide marketing planning and subsequent performance measurement?
3. Are the marketing objectives appropriate, given the company's competitive position, resources, and opportunities? Is the appropriate strategic objective to build, hold, harvest, or terminate this business?

Strategy
1. What is the core marketing strategy for achieving the objectives? Is it a sound marketing strategy?
2. Are enough resources (or too much resources) budgeted to accomplish the marketing objectives?
3. Are the marketing resources allocated optimally to prime market segments, territories, and products of the organization?
4. Are the marketing resources allocated optimally to the major elements of the marketing mix, i.e., product quality, service, sales force, advertising, promotion, and distribution?

Marketing Organization Audit

Formal Structure
1. Is there a high-level marketing officer with adequate authority and responsibility over those company activities that affect the customer's satisfaction?
2. Are the marketing responsibilities optimally structured along functional product, end user, and territorial lines?

Functional Efficiency
1. Are there good communication and working relations between marketing and sales?
2. Is the product management system working effectively? Are the product managers able to plan profits or only sales volume?
3. Are there any groups in marketing that need more training, motivation, supervision, or evaluation?

Interface Efficiency
1. Are there any problems between marketing and manufacturing that need attention?
2. What about marketing and R&D?
3. What about marketing and financial management?
4. What about marketing and purchasing?

Marketing Systems Audit

Marketing Information System
1. Is the marketing intelligence system producing accurate, sufficient, and timely information about developments in the marketplace?
2. Is marketing research being adequately used by company decision makers?

Marketing Planning System

1. Is the marketing planning system well-conceived and effective?
2. Is sales forecasting and market potential measurement soundly carried out?
3. Are sales quotas set on a proper basis?

Marketing Control System

1. Are the control procedures (monthly, quarterly, etc.) adequate to insure that the annual plan objectives are being achieved?
2. Is provision made to analyze periodically the profitability of different products, markets, territories, and channels of distribution?
3. Is provision made to examine and validate periodically various marketing costs?

New Product Development System

1. Is the company well-organized to gather, generate, and screen new product ideas?
2. Does the company do adequate concept research and business analysis before investing heavily in a new idea?
3. Does the company carry out adequate product and market testing before launching a new product?

Marketing Productivity Audit

Profitability Analysis

1. What is the profitability of the company's different products, served markets, territories, and channels of distribution?
2. Should the company enter, expand, contract, or withdraw from any business segments and what would be the short- and long-run profit consequences?

Cost-Effectiveness Analysis

1. Do any marketing activities seem to have excessive costs? Are these costs valid? Can cost-reducing steps be taken?

Marketing Function Audit

Products

1. What are the product line objectives? Are these objectives sound? Is the current product line meeting these objectives?
2. Are there particular products that should be phased out?
3. Are there new products that are worth adding?
4. Are any products able to benefit from quality, feature, or style improvements?

Price

1. What are the pricing objectives, policies, strategies, and procedures? To what extent are prices set on sound cost, demand, and competitive criteria?
2. Do the customers see the company's prices as being in line or out of line with the perceived value of its offer?
3. Does the company use price promotions effectively?

Distribution

1. What are the distribution objectives and strategies?
2. Is there adequate market coverage and service?
3. Should the company consider changing its degree of reliance on distributors, sales reps, and direct selling?

Sales Force

1. What are the organization's sales force objectives?
2. Is the sales force large enough to accomplish the company's objectives?
3. Is the sales force organized along the proper principle(s) of specialization (territory, market, product)?

4. Does the sales force show high morale, ability, and effort? Are they sufficiently trained and incentivized?
5. Are the procedures adequate for setting quotas and evaluating performances?
6. How is the company's sales force perceived in relation to competitors' sales forces?

Advertising, Promotion, and Publicity
1. What are the organization's advertising objectives? Are they sound?
2. Is the right amount being spent on advertising? How is the budget determined?
3. Are the ad themes and copy effective? What do customers and the public think about the advertising?

4. Are the advertising media well chosen?
5. Is sales promotion used effectively?
6. Is there a well-conceived publicity program?

NOTES

1. Many useful checklist questions for marketers are found in C. Eldridge, *The Management of the Marketing Function* (New York: Association of National Advertisers, 1967).
2. See P. Kotler, *Marketing Management Analysis Planning and Control* (Englewood Cliffs, N.J.: Prentice-Hall, Inc., 1976), pp. 457–462.
3. See P. J. Stonich, "Zero-Base Planning—A Management Tool," *Managerial Planning*, July–August 1976, pp. 1–4.

INDEX